Power

CAT POWER

A Good Woman

Elizabeth Goodman

THREE RIVERS PRESS
NEW YORK

For Benjamin Chappel

Library of Congress Cataloging-in-Publication Data

Goodman, Elizabeth, 1980–
Cat Power / Elizabeth Goodman.—1st ed.
    p.   cm.
1. Cat Power, 1972–   2. Rock musicians—United States—
Biography. I. Title.
ML420.C35G66   2009
782.42166092—dc22
[B]   2008039002

ISBN 978-0-307-39636-5

Printed in the United States of America

Design by Maria Elias

10 9 8 7 6 5 4 3 2 1

First Edition

Contents

Introduction
Chan Marshall does not want you to read this book.

On August 5, 2008, one year and seven months after I started re-searching *A Good Woman*, Chan Marshall's mother, who is in her six-ties and lives in a tobacco shack in rural North Carolina, called me on my private cell-phone number. I was at work at *Blender* magazine in Midtown Manhattan, where I am Editor at Large. An issue had just closed, so I was passing time drinking a latte and reading a blog post about Tyra Banks. I didn't recognize the number that appeared on the caller ID. "Someone wants money," I thought, anticipating the fake friendly tone of an Environmental Defense Fund solicitor or credit-card-company rep. I give a lot to environmental defense and I owe a lot to American Express. "Hello?" I said in my most professional voice, ready to pretend to be my own secretary if it was someone really threatening. "Hi, this is Myra Lee," the voice on the other end of the line said.

"Holy shit, Chan's mom is on the phone," I thought. "The woman she named her debut album for. The mythical, troubled Southern gothic creature who I'd only ever fantasized about actually getting an inter-view with—despite my many attempts."

I got up quickly and went into the makeshift office/conference room where people go to gossip, interview prospective interns, or cry after a bad edit or mid-workday breakup. I closed the door. The reviews editor walked by and gave me a sympathetic look.

"You called my son, Lenny?" Myra continued, her silky South Georgian drawl doing little to conceal her hostility.

"Yes, we spoke this weekend," I said.

"He's very upset," she continued. "Who exactly are you? We don't know anything about this."

"Who is 'we,' " I thought, envisioning an enraged clan of Chan's relatives armed with rifles and assembling outside on Sixth Avenue.

I explained that I was a journalist based in New York working on a book about Cat Power, and that I had spoken with Chan's younger brother, Lenny, the previous weekend. While he came across as a very frank and willing interviewee, I knew that getting Lenny on the record for the book would be a button pusher. Chan tells journalists exactly what she wants fans to know about her past, and she rarely mentions her twenty-nine-year-old brother, who has cerebral palsy, works three jobs, and lives in Atlanta.

While I understood Myra's protectiveness of her son, I became confused when she suggested that I was the latest in what was apparently a series of Chan stalkers. Myra asked if there was someone at the magazine she could call to confirm that I was who I said I was. I told her that the book was not related to my job at *Blender*, but that I would be happy to have my editor at Random House call her. "That could be anyone on the phone! I don't want someone to call me, I want to call!" she seethed.

Apparently the warmth, good humor, and eager-to-talk attitude projected by the men in Chan's family (including her father, Charlie, stepfather, Leamon, and her hidden half brother) doesn't extend to the women. "We have talons," Myra later admitted to me.

It turns out that Chan's mother reads *Blender*. ("I read everything Chan is in," she said with pride.) Myra had me hold the line while she located a recent issue. I felt like I'd been caught shoplifting and was waiting for the cops to arrive. Her tone softened, though, as she flipped through the pages to the masthead, where, lo and behold, she found my name. "Elizabeth Goodman, Editor at Large," she said, surprised.

I knew, of course, that I was who I said I was. But Myra somehow had me feeling like an impostor or, worse, some kind of degenerate.

Once Myra accepted that she was speaking with Elizabeth Goodman, she really started talking. Like a skilled raconteur, Myra shared information about her family's roots in southern Georgia, about her days as an idealistic hippie in the late sixties on Atlanta's politicized Fourteenth Street scene, and about Chan frankly and openly. She said that though she loves her daughter, many of the details Chan told reporters about her childhood over the years were false. Especially the ones that paint Myra as a bad mother and a drunk.

She promised a full interview. "I have to speak with Chan first," she warned, "but I'll talk to you. I'll tell it like it is. I'll tell you where I went wrong with her as a teenager and I'll tell you where she went wrong."

We never got that far.

Two hours later, Myra called back to tell me, person to person, that we wouldn't be speaking again. Then she kept dialing. She called the main switchboard at *Blender* and demanded to speak to "my superiors." The receptionist that day was a temp, and Myra scared the shit out of her much in the way she scared the shit out of me—only I had some context. Unsure of what to do, the girl patched the call through to a friend in the mailroom. Myra again demanded to speak with my bosses and accused me of harassing her family and preying upon her sick son. After assurances were made that I would be told about her concerns, she calmed down and hung up.

Two years had passed since Chan Marshall began her campaign to have this book stopped, and she'd finally gotten around to telling her mother about it.

After Chan declined to be interviewed for *A Good Woman* in early 2007, it took her less than a month to tell everyone at her label, Matador Records, not to talk to me. She told a painter friend of hers and an obscure French musician who she once toured with. She called a photographer with whom she once shared a loft in New York City. She told the flamboyant, internationally famous Chanel designer Karl Lagerfeld. But in a year and seven months, Chan never got around to telling even one member of her immediate family about this book. She never told her mother, whom Chan has repeatedly vilified in print as a negligent boozer. She never told her biological father, whom Chan has accused in national publications of abandonment and emotional abuse. She never told her half brother, Lenny, whom she has gone out of her way to hide from the press. She never told her sister or her stepfather or her grandmother, the person she's closest to in her family. She never told any of them. She left that to me, like a weird, passive-aggressive statement of tacit approval—or so I imagined in my more tortured moments during this writing process.

Chan may have assumed that I was a shoddy reporter who wouldn't be able to track down her family, but if that was the case, why the paranoia and terror directed at people who work for her like Matador Records staff and her lawyer, as well as random acquaintances who were unlikely to say anything but good things about her? It seemed like part of Chan wanted me, or any faceless reporter, to be the one to take her parents to task.

I don't really know why Chan didn't warn her family about the book. What I believe to be certain is that the contrast between Chan's professed virulent objection to this book and the fact that she never told those with the juiciest stories about her not to participate in it represents the irreconcilable conflict at the core of her identity. We are all studies in contrasts, but Chan is the very embodiment of diametric opposition. She is both an exhibitionist and a prude, transparent and private, friendly and cold, arrogant and insecure, generous and possessive, humble and entitled, frugal and extravagant, responsible and unaccountable, tomboy and glamour girl, homebody and transient, trusting and paranoid, sober and alcoholic, crazy and sane, light and dark, she is all of these things at once.

This core contrast, this hide-and-seek quality in Chan, is exactly what makes her personality so compelling, her music so mesmerizing, and the prospect of telling her story so challenging. It's also what makes dealing with her—directly or even indirectly—so utterly maddening.

When I started this project, I wanted to write about Chan in part because she made music that made me feel less alone. I felt close to her but I didn't really know her. Chan's surprisingly aggressive attempts to stop the book, juxtaposed with her leaving obvious opportunities for me to keep it going, made me realize that it was more important to really figure out this woman than it was to adore her. At launch point I knew Chan only as Gatsby, the finished product of an elaborate self-invention. I didn't yet know her as Jay Gatz: the real, flawed person behind the myth.

When I interviewed Chan over the telephone in 2005 for a small piece in *Spin* magazine (where I was freelancing), we talked about the blues (better to sing about them than to have them), moonshine (gets you through the long nights), and peanut-butter ice cream (gets you through the long days). It felt as if we were at a slumber party and had stayed up all night watching Christian Slater movies and eating Lucky Charms and sour straws. I hung up the phone feeling exhausted but sugar-high.

Chan, like Morrissey, Kurt Cobain, and Conor Oberst, comes across as so inclusive that it's easy to believe she is actually your friend. No one knows you the way she knows you. That feeling stuck with me throughout the first few weeks of this project in which I listened to all the music and dreamed of what would lie ahead. The idea of spending the next year of my life over at Chan's house made me giddy. I didn't seriously consider that this woman, who documented her most private thoughts on record for public consumption, who told every journalist with a pen and paper—credentialed or not—about her deranged parents and her wild Southern-gothic childhood, would have a problem with me picking up the narrative where she left off. After all, I was a fan.

So I wrote her a letter to reassure her. In early March 2007 Nils Bernstein, Chan's publicist at Matador and a friend of mine, forwarded it to her.

> Hi Chan,
> My name is Elizabeth Goodman, and I am working on a book about your work.
> . . . In addition to being a longtime fan of your music, I also think that you are increasingly becoming a true cultural icon. I know that might sound goofy—and it's the sort of thing that feels weird to read about oneself—but I believe that it's true, and that it's important. You have a real influence now on music, of course, but also on fashion, on literature, on art in general, and I think that you deserve a really serious, thoughtful, respectful book dedicated to your work, and to your story.

... I know that it's YOUR story, and that the idea that someone like me might sift through your past and handpick the parts that best illustrate a certain perception of you is really gross. That's not the book I've proposed, it's not one I would want to write, and it's not the one I've sold. This is not a tabloid-ish project. I want to write something that you would approve of, that, in an ideal world, you might even be proud of. ...

I understand why you might be hesitant to give the book your blessing, at the same time I hope that you will consider not opposing it . . . I want to honor you with this book, not exploit you.

I really thought this letter would take care of any potential static. Through various conversations I'd had with Matador representatives, I knew that the label wasn't opposed to this book. They figured that someone would eventually write a biography of Cat Power, and since I was as much a fan as a journalist, I was as good a candidate as they were likely to get. There are many who consider Cat Power's career to be one long marathon of unsubstantiated hype. Chan's next prospective biographer might agree. Matador knew that I did not. I would be professional but also affectionate.

I also felt confident in my reputation as a writer, even though this is my first book. When I began it, I was on staff at *Rolling Stone*. I'd written for England's esteemed weekly *NME* in the early 2000s, when the Strokes, the White Stripes, the Yeah Yeah Yeahs, and the Hives made rock suddenly exciting again. I'd worked at *Spin* during the same era and I wrote for magazines like *Nylon* and *Interview*, which glorified the intersection between fashion and music and pop culture that Chan so perfectly represents.

Mostly, though, I just had faith that any threat of antagonism would disappear because it was unwarranted. Then, on Tuesday, May 8, as I was preparing to travel to Atlanta to spend some time in Chan's hometown, I received an e-mail from her lawyer.

Elizabeth:

We represent Chan Marshall p/k/a "Cat Power." Chan has told us that she's heard that you are working on a bio of her—not sure if this is for a magazine piece and/or a book. At Chan's request, we're dropping you a line to see what the deal is.

Please don't interpret this as an attempt to intimidate, etc. Chan just asked us to find out if anything's going on.

I'd appreciate it if you could let me know when you have a moment.

Thanks,

Joe Penachio

Joseph D. Penachio, Esq.

Grubman Indursky & Shire, P.C.

Initially after reading this I felt ashamed, like I was five and wore muddy snow boots inside the house. That lasted for about three minutes. Then I felt angry. By the time this letter was sent, Chan had known for several months that the book was happening. She knew very well that it was not related to a magazine article. And her lawyers must have told her that as a public figure, she could be written about by any journalist, even without her approval. I realize now that this letter represented a combination of Chan's desperation and panic about this book as well as an attempt, in spite of Mr. Penachio's assurance to the contrary, to intimidate me into giving up the project. But at the time I was still mystified by Chan's reaction, and I committed myself to proving that it was unwarranted.

This weird game of mental warfare carried over into my first and second drafts of the book, which were seriously dull. My initial writing impulse, one I now realize Chan's resistance implanted in me, was to steer clear of anything that might upset her. Even the boatload of disturbing things she's routinely said about herself felt gauche in this new world where Chan was mad at me and I had to make amends. Chan has a nervous tic where she constantly inquires, "Are you mad at me?" She has asked this of dozens of journalists during what must now be hundreds of interviews. Ironically, I found myself wanting to ask her that question.

Chan has gone into elaborate detail about the steady stream of rock boys, drugs, and instability that defined her early childhood, the sanctuary she found in music, the mental illness that runs in her family, the psychosis she has personally battled over the years, the story behind how her pubic hair landed in the pages of *The New Yorker*, the play-by-play of what she saw and heard when she spent a week in a Miami hospital psych ward. Why would Chan tell these detailed, provocative stories, then act appalled and revolted when people listen intently?

For all of the singer's seemingly unfettered disclosures to journalists, she is actually very controlled in her interviews. She lobs confessions like deceptively well-guided grenades aimed to distract. No matter how cunning a reporter might be, if an interviewee tells you about her abortion, you don't ask if it was a boy or a girl. You ask if you can refresh her drink or light her cigarette.

This started to bother me. I now wanted to be the one, the only one, to ask the follow-up question. I wanted to ask her if it was a boy or a girl.

And I wanted her to know that even if she lit my cigarette and poured me a cup of green tea and let me pet her puppy, I would still ask and I would still wait for an answer. I wanted to call Chan on her bullshit.

The more intensely Chan protested the book, the deeper I was compelled to dig. And the more I learned about this woman's childhood, about the roots of her mental instability, about the cunning concealed beneath those shaggy bangs, the more I realized how naïve I'd been to imagine that she wouldn't object to someone writing a biography about her. No longer my idealized confidante, Chan became my subject. And as such I started to look at her without the filter of adoration.

I saw her addiction to fame, the natural flip side of an equally genuine repulsion to it that she often discusses. I saw the absurd hypocrisy in her deliberate self-mythologizing—her willingness to play up her tragic childhood and emotional instability in order to make us look closer, then her scandalized disgust when we do. I saw her as someone who will direct an assistant to secure impossible dinner reservations one minute, then pick her nose in front of strangers the next. I saw *her*.

In resisting the publication of this book so virulently, Chan showed me exactly why it was worth writing. I could have given the advance money back and gone on my way, and if Chan were one of her merely pleasant contemporaries—Feist, or Norah Jones—I probably would have. But like her idols Bob Dylan, Billie Holiday, and Madonna, Chan is a Gatsby, and while that means very little to the fangirl who started this book, it means everything to the journalist who finished it.

Chan Marshall didn't want me to write *A Good Woman* and she doesn't want you to read it. But given her protestations, I can only assume that for reasons that are still becoming clear to me, she needs us too.

1.

Redemption

June 9, Town Hall in New York City. Cat Power's sold-out engagement at the prestigious, eighty-six-year-old venue where Leonard Bernstein and Miles Davis once performed featured the Memphis Rhythm Band, a full Southern soul orchestra. They were all onstage. Chan Marshall was not, and people were starting to worry. This show was originally scheduled for February, but had been canceled for what were then referred to as "health reasons." By now everybody in the venue knew what that really meant. Chan had suffered one of the most highly publicized mental and physical flameouts in the modern rock era, with the *New York Times* reporting on the details of her institutionalization and one million fans all over the world wondering if her return to the stage would bring the same vulnerable beguiling presence they'd come to cherish and rely on. Chan Marshall had been long gone all winter, and almost for good. Would she be back with the spring? And if so, how damaged would she be?

After nearly an hour, the singer finally took the stage barefoot, wearing a strapless beaded Chanel couture dress carrying a hot-pink commuter mug filled with what she kept triumphantly insisting was chamomile tea, not single malt scotch, or wine, or beer, the preferred onstage beverages for most of her career. So invested in Chan's well-being were many of the fans in the audience that this revelation itself drew applause. The gown's pale, creamy tone showed off her deep tan and lithe frame, achieved during winter months spent trading booze and dark hotel rooms for the Miami sunshine, novels read by the pool, and Pilates. She looked happy, which, for anyone who knew her personally or had followed the evolution of her career, was stunning to witness: the mental-hygiene equivalent of onstage pyro.

She was tentative as she led the band, who were clearly pulling for her as well, through the first few songs, relying on weirdly equine galloping dance steps to neutralize the tension.

During the minimalist ballad "Where Is My Love" she left the stage for a while, prompting the background singer to add a wry tone to the lyric. It seemed like Chan was gone too long and a sense of here-she-goes-again nervous energy permeated the crowd. Her eventual return drew another wave of relieved whoops and applause. She flashed a huge grin, cantered over to her piano, and proceeded to sing with such smoky, lived-in authority that it was as if she finally knew her lines after fifteen years of tense rehearsal. It was the best Cat Power show I've ever seen.

Delayed gratification has always been Chan's signature stage move. During her earliest shows she would often stand feet away from the mike so that the audience could hear exactly enough to know what they were missing in not being able to hear more. This sort of vocal titillation was defiant, as if she resented being onstage and wanted to taunt her listeners. When Chan reappeared at Town Hall that night, beckoned by the increasingly insistent "Where is my love?" refrain sung by her backup vocalist, that sense of performance as being punitive was gone. In its place was unadulterated joy.

Onstage at Town Hall that night, the contrasting sides of Chan Marshall, which had been struggling vigorously against each other for most of her then thirty-four years, united for a brief two hours of fragile perfection. She was both shy and confident, glamorous in her gown and tomboyish in her ponytail and bare feet, nervous but happy when she played the piano alone, and forceful like a blues diva when she led her band through songs off her recently released album, *The Greatest*. Former Talking Heads frontman David Byrne, who was in attendance, wrote on his blog that the show was one of the best he'd ever seen. "This combination of Memphis rhythm section and her hesitant . . . phrasing was . . . a very strange idea," Byrne wrote. "The result is somewhere in the middle of two worlds. Some new thing came into being that had elements of both worlds but that was neither."

Those who are familiar with Chan know two main things about her:

She has the voice of a damaged angel, and she's probably crazy. Beginning very early in her career but reaching an apex during 1998 and 1999 when Chan toured in support of her fourth album, *Moon Pix*, Cat Power played a series of shows during which Chan would regularly self-destruct onstage. These displays were so gory—a combination of genuinely alarming psychosis and weirdly compelling performance art—that the singer soon became as famous for her eccentricity and mental instability as she was for her music. In the following years Cat Power released three more albums (2000's *The Covers Record*, 2003's *You Are Free*, and 2006's *The Greatest*), each of which earned her increasing amounts of mainstream media coverage. She used her access to the press to speak with disturbing candor about the history of mental illness in her family, the scary household she grew up in, and the paralyzing sense of worthlessness she felt every time she stepped onstage, walked outside, or took a breath.

When Chan opened her mouth to sing, fans and critics heard generations of poor Southerners crippled by a sense of inescapable illegitimacy. We longed to hear that voice really open up, to surpass the limitations imposed on it by Chan's evident self-loathing and insecurity. Every implosive Cat Power performance carried a sense of rooting for the underdog. We the fans knew what she had, what she was, what she was worth, and we longed to make her know, to make her see. If she saw and heard what we saw and heard perhaps she could get onstage and sing with strength, confidence, and freedom the way she did when she was just a little girl, singing hymns in church.

Chan has been struggling since birth. She was raised in a wild and unstable home, exposed to drugs and alcohol as a kid, endured her parents' divorce, attended countless different schools before dropping out of high school at seventeen to work in a pizza parlor, and by the age of twenty she was pregnant. If Chan Marshall had amounted to nothing, it would have surprised no one, especially not herself. And yet just as consistently as she has been underestimated, she has also defied expectations. Chan learned from her parents' mistakes and stayed clean while many of her friends became casualties of the nineties heroin scene. When she got pregnant at a young age by the wrong guy, she had an abortion, collected the money she'd wisely saved, and moved to New York City, becoming the first person in her family to leave the South for good.

When Chan first started playing her unusual breed of dour blues rock, she was marginalized by many as a cute girl with a dark past and an indie record deal. But Chan propelled Cat Power to international fame and her artistic potency went well past the sell-by date of most of her contemporaries. When success didn't exorcize the demons she'd been running from since childhood, Chan experienced a psychological breakdown and public tour cancellation that could have signaled the end of Cat Power. Instead, her return marked the most triumphant moment in her career and heralded the most spectacular critical and commercial success Cat Power has ever had.

"God shined on her," *Spin* editor Charles Aaron says of the *Greatest* shows with the Memphis Rhythm Band, a collection of extremely venerable bluesmen with decades of experience. "It made her realize she's not existing in this whole indie-rock world where whether you can or cannot sing is viewed as an interpretive thing. It's like, 'Okay, either perform to the very best of my ability, or I will be humiliated onstage.' They'll be nice. They're perfect gentlemen, but in their hearts of hearts they'll be like, 'Who is this child? Who is this white girl that we have to do this with? Whatever. Pay me.' But she stepped it up."

Before Chan was hospitalized in the winter of 2006, her shows were fearful. In the fall of 2006, after the *Greatest* tour ended and Chan stopped playing with the Memphis Rhythm Band she performed with sterile professionalism. But for a short, precious time between the spring of 2006 and the fall of that same year, Chan reached her potential. She got there. Onstage she was wounded and healed and sane and insane and young and old and feminine and masculine all at once, and it was magic. Then, like her best songs, the moment passed, disintegrated into the ether, and we were left, as was she, to wait for its return.

2

Southern Soul

Even though Atlanta is now an urban center, congested with labyrinthine freeways and tract housing, much of the city still embodies the feeling of traditional Southern life. Downtown, locals leisurely stroll the streets and chat naturally with each other at the grocery store or gas station, and at dusk it's not uncommon to see Atlantans gathering for a predinner cocktail out on the porch or stoop or backyard. Even where signs of a more sterile suburban life exist, the old ways persist. In the middle of a Thursday in July, at the Starbucks in Peachtree Center, you can find an Emory prelaw student passionately arguing politics for hours with a dreadlocked African American Vietnam veteran he met that day. Two hours and several cups of coffee later, they exchange e-mails, then part ways, the student off to his campus apartment, the veteran off to the shelter where he sleeps. This Atlanta—the one defined by a happy contradiction between traditional values and progressive liberal thought—is Chan's Atlanta.

The singer hasn't lived in the South full-time since she was twenty, but no matter what's going on in her life—whether she's caught up in one of Cat Power's epic European tours or enjoying a minibreak at Chanel designer Karl Lagerfeld's country home—Chan always finds time to come home for hush puppies and barbecue. And even though she'll help bake the sweet-potato pie at Christmas in North Carolina or gallivant around her old Atlanta stomping grounds with friends from high school, compared to the rest of her family, Chan is practically a Yankee. She's the first person in her family to move north of the Mason-Dixon Line. Chan's mother and father still live down South (her mom in Greensboro, North Carolina, her dad in Atlanta), as does every other living blood relative from her sister, Miranda; stepfather, Leamon; half brother, Lenny; niece, Audrey; nephew, Ian; brother-in-law, Mike; grandmother, Lillian; grandfather, Richard; and half sister, Ivy, to innumerable best friends whom this genteel but feisty Southern girl considers family.

Chan Marshall has friends everywhere from Barcelona to Montreal to Melbourne, but in her parents' sixty-some years on earth, neither of them has spent much time outside of the southern United States. Her father graduated from high school and briefly experimented with the idea of college, but found the pull of a rock 'n' roll life to be too strong and soon dropped out. Chan has indicated that Myra never finished high school. And yet these two young people, roots deeply planted in red clay soil, started out with dreams of living a kind of life that is not so different from the one Chan now leads. The identities of both Chan's parents were forged at a time when the rebel spirit of the sixties was alive and thriving. The young couple was musically inclined and naturally drawn to the artists lifestyle, which during the time was directly aligned with social and political revolution.

Charles Marshall was born Charles Fowler in 1947 in Talladega, then a small mill town in central Alabama. Today Talladega is known for being home to the longest and fastest superspeedway in stock-car racing, but the track wasn't built until the 1960s. In the 1950s, when Charlie and his younger brother, Jerry, were growing up, the place was a one-stoplight town in which you had to make your own fun. From a very early age, Charlie learned the three pillars of amusement: girls, liquor, and rock 'n' roll.

As a young boy, Charlie lived with his aunt and uncle. Then, when he was about ten years old, his mother, Lena Faye, remarried and Charlie went to live with her and her new husband. William Herman Marshall, who went by the name Benny, adopted Charlie when he was a teenager and Charlie changed his name from Charles Fowler to Charlie Marshall.

"We didn't have a lot of money," Charlie remembers. "At Christmastime, when I was a tiny boy, my mom would come visit. We'd sit around the fire and we'd sing Christmas songs. 'The Old Rugged Cross' was my aunt Ruby's favorite song. We would just sing."

As a child, Charlie quickly learned that he could use his natural charm to command the attention of whichever adults happened to be around, a skill he would pass on to Chan. Charlie's early knack for performance is something both he and Chan are proud of.

"My first professional gig—I always tell people this," Charlie begins, excited to relay one of his many favorite personal narratives. "In Talladega, music was everywhere. I remember there was one old couple, and if I'd walk by 'em just right they'd say, 'Sing for us, Charlie.' So I would do 'Hey Good Lookin'.' They'd give me a quarter." Chan often proudly tells this story as well.

Just as it would be in Chan's life, music was the one consistent presence in her father's world. Mom and Dad were inconsistent, but the music would always be there. Soon Charlie was playing in the most popular local band, the Turks, and enjoying the spoils of small-town fame. "All of the sudden, to all of the girls who didn't pay any attention to me—I was like top cat!" he remembers, laughing. "I said, 'I like this!' I was bit immediately." Between the electrifying feel of playing before a crowd and the collection of snug-bell-bottom-wearing female admirers who lined up to bat their eyes at him after the show, Charlie quickly realized the rock 'n' roll life was for him—and just as quickly concluded that the Turks were not the band to get him out of Talladega. He decided to go to technical college down in Childersburg, Alabama, where he joined a new band and started traveling on the local college-to-college circuit, playing frat parties for gas money and free beer. "All of the sudden I wasn't just small-town Charlie Marshall in Talladega, Alabama," he remembers. "I realized that you could actually travel and make money doing this."

Several bands later, Charlie and his friend Mike Lewis headed to Tuscaloosa, where Chan's father enrolled as a part-time student and the pair formed a new band called the Brick Wall. Mike Lewis went on to have an impressive career in the music business. He played with the Standells (of "Dirty Water" fame), was on two Quicksilver Messenger Service albums, and later became a disco producer. The Brick Wall was a long way from that kind of success, but they were aiming high. Relentless ambition brought tough times. Charlie remembers living on a single peanut-butter-and-banana sandwich a day during most of that fall before the band started to get some attention. They made it through the winter, and in early 1968 they recorded their first real single, the bluesy "Poor Mary Has Drowned," which Capitol Records released. Nearly thirty years before Matador Records signed Cat Power, a member of the Marshall family already had a record deal.

3.

The Age of Aquarius

Traditional blues and R&B music is the foundation of contemporary rock 'n' roll, yet during the genre's first golden era, Southern rock didn't really exist. During the 1950s, artists like Carl Perkins, Johnny Cash, and, of course,

Elvis left a sonic trail of bread crumbs from the spare, unadorned sound of the Delta blues to the explosive bravado that would define rock music in the 1960s. But as rock 'n' roll rose in prominence with artists like Roy Orbison and Chubby Checker in the early sixties, Southern music veered from the potent rock sound it had given birth to and toward a country-music twang. During the early 1960s, the South's contribution to contemporary music came mainly out of Nashville, where producers like Owen Bradley and Chet Atkins put a pop sheen on singles by distinctly country artists like Patsy Cline and Jim Reeves.

By the late 1960s, the two poles of Southern music—country and blues—began to merge. Bands like Creedence Clearwater Revival, the Byrds, and the Band popularized a rock sound that included a heavy country influence and revitalized interest in the South as a breeding ground for great rock 'n' roll. It was during this era that the Brick Wall was trying to break into the music business. By November 1969, when the Allman Brothers, from Macon, Georgia, released their first album—an eponymous debut that channeled both the riotous and forlorn sides of the South—Southern rock was considered highly commercial. During the 1970s, the Marshall Tucker Band, the Charlie Daniels Band, and eventually Lynyrd Skynyrd would make some of the most outrageous, raucous, and distinctly American music in history. The Brick Wall was poised to be a part of this movement, but first they had to find a home base, record some music, and hit the road on tour. In 1968 Capitol Records encouraged them to relocate to one of a handful of so-called major markets in America, where they would be best positioned to capitalize on any attention that came their way.

Arriving in Atlanta in the beatific summer of 1968 felt like coming home. "We pulled around Fourteenth Street, and there was about one hundred longhairs there," Charlie remembers. "In Tuscaloosa we had maybe one hundred longhairs in the whole county going to school, so when I saw all these people all congregated in one area I said, 'This is where I want to be.' "

It was also exactly where Chan's mom and Charlie's future bride, eighteen-year-old Myra Lee Russell, wanted to be. Though she was still living with her parents in Forest Park, a quiet and leafy middle-class suburb of the big city, Myra was already a revolutionary, activist, and artist in spirit, and spent as much time as she could down on Fourteenth Street and Peachtree Street, the main arteries of Atlanta's counterculture.

Myra grew up in a traditional Southern household. Along with her two brothers, Wayne and Dickie, and one sister, Kathy, Myra attended church on Sundays with her parents Lillian (Granny Lil to Chan and the other grandkids) and Richard Russell (who went by Pop). They lived in a modest but well-appointed brick house south of Atlanta.

Myra's family has deep roots in southern Georgia. Around the turn of the century, her grandparents migrated from the rural southern part of the state to Atlanta, where they worked in a cotton mill. Granny Lil, Myra's mom, would also occasionally pick cotton, though Myra says her daughter's description of her grandmother as a cotton picker is one of the many family mischaracterizations Chan made in print: "She would go out and pick cotton for fun, not because she had to," Myra explains.

Myra grew up wild. She spent hours outside in the verdant, sticky Georgia summers, wreaking havoc with her three siblings. "I was shooting a twenty-two when I was twelve," Myra recalls with a raspy laugh earned through decades of heavy smoking. "We'd collect bottles in Poulan, Georgia, and go down to the store and get an RC Cola and a Moon Pie for a nickel. We'd put 'em up on the fence posts and shoot 'em down."

For all the rowdy backwoods fun in the Russell household, there was also a lot of sorrow. When he was just sixteen, Myra's younger brother,

Wayne, was killed in a motorcycle accident. Wayne was the golden child of the family, a handsome and charismatic boy whose vastly contrasting light and dark sides remind Charlie a lot of Chan. When Wayne was just a teenager and Charlie and Myra were still married, the Russells sent their youngest son down to Atlanta to visit his sister, her husband, and their new baby, Miranda. "This is when we were living down with the hippies," Charlie remembers. "Everyone wanted to come see the hippies! Wayne couldn't have been more than fourteen or fifteen, and one of my friends had been giving him beer behind my back. He threw up all over."

Wayne's death rocked the Russell family, in particular Myra and Lillian. "That's a sore subject for both of them," Lenny Land, Chan's half brother, says. "I think they feel like they could have prevented it somehow. Like they could have talked him off the motorcycle that night. Guilt is the overwhelming theme with us."

Chan often talks about how deeply mental illness and alcoholism run in her family, and on Myra's side both are extremely prominent. According to Charlie, Myra's older brother, who served in the military, was eventually diagnosed as schizophrenic. Leamon puts it more succinctly: "Myra's brother is the crazy one. He went to spend some time in the service, said he had Agent Orange. He goes in and out." Myra's older sister, Kathy, now Kathy Brady, is another wild child. "Myra's sister, that's a whole other story," Leamon says with a soft laugh. "Kathy is like seventy now, the oldest bartender in Atlanta. There's been a lot of bars gone out of business over that girl. When Myra and her get together, they just roar."

As Myra got older, she became a beautiful young woman with the refined features of a big-city fashion model, but the wildness of spirit forged shooting guns and running barefoot through the Georgia woods stayed with her. In spite of her unusually light green eyes, fine, straight brown hair, and curtain-making mother back at home, Myra was no docile society girl. Even at eighteen, while still living in her father's house, Myra had a self-assuredness that was as compelling as her good looks.

For both Myra and Charlie, the political and social revolution of the late 1960s provided the perfect backdrop for postadolescent rebellion. "I used to sell *The Great Speckled Bird* on the streets," Myra says, referring to Atlanta's radical underground paper. "Oh, man, we were some rude hippies. We were antiestablishment, we were anti all war. Still am." The couple also shared a deep adoration of music. Myra spent a lot of her time as a teenager record shopping downtown and devising ways to get out of her parents' house at night so she could see rock shows.

"On Fourteenth Street, everybody hung out at a restaurant called the Pennant," Leamon Land, Myra's second husband and Chan's eventual stepfather, remembers. "And there was a hippie movement on Peachtree—it was kind of the Haight Ashbury of Atlanta. We used to hang out in the park. We'd see bands, the Allman Brothers, the Grateful Dead. I knew Charlie. We were all part of the same group. Everybody met down in that area."

In the fall of 1969, the Brick Wall played a gig at a local rock club in downtown Atlanta called the Spot. Myra Russell and a group of girlfriends were in the audience and stuck around after the show, eager to prolong the precious minutes spent out in the city and away from the oppressive peace of their parents' suburban homes. "She was very beautiful," Charlie says quietly. "I still say Myra had the most beautiful face I've ever seen on anyone." A few minutes into his first conversation with Myra, Charlie knew he'd met someone who would become more than just another pretty face. Armed with an understated wit, Myra was able to cut Charlie's expansive ego down to size. And the more she teased him about his outrageous stage moves, his hair, and his bombastic singing style, the harder he fell for her. (For her part, Chan has told the story of her parents' meeting slightly differently. "The story goes that he took this girl Nancy home that night, and that he asked Nancy for Mom's number," she has said.)

Within a few short years the utopian ideals of the sixties would recede as the doom, fear, and paranoia of the 1970s rode on the back of endless war, a broken, crooked government, and recession. But the Marshalls had no idea such dark times were on the horizon. It was still 1969! Free love was still alive! Without fear, the couple made the leap from madly-in-love rock kids to young married couple.

"Myra looked like a model," Leamon remembers. "And she was always smiling, just a really outgoing person. Charlie and Myra met and hit it off and got married."

In May of 1970, mere months after they met, Myra Russell married Charlie Marshall in a modest ceremony in Atlanta. He was twenty-three, she was nineteen. "On the day of the dawning of Aquarius, we got married," Charlie remembers, laughing. "It was a full hippie regalia. Flowers in the hair and everything." Local rockers, artists, and hipsters gathered near the couple's home and made the eight-block walk en masse to the ceremony. "There were a few people with actual tambourines," the former groom recalls. "We had a judge who was a wino who lived in the area, and the hippies just sort of adopted him. He'd given up on life, but he helped us perform the ceremony."

Charlyn (pronounced *Shar-Lin*) Marie Marshall was born at Crawford Long Hospital in Atlanta, Georgia, on January 21, 1972. Her birth was a very happy day, but within a few weeks the seriousness of Chan's parents' situation started to press upon them. They already had a young daughter at home, Miranda Lee Marshall, born in the first year of their marriage. Three short years before, Myra and Charlie had been carefree, impassioned kids, in love and confident that their ideals were powerful enough to support a marriage and a family. But three years after they first flirted at a rock show, Myra and Charlie Marshall had two baby daughters, serious financial problems, few professional prospects, and an increasingly troubled marriage.

The Brick Wall failed to ride the coattails of the Southern rock movement and broke up shortly before the wedding. For the first time in his adult life, Charlie Marshall considered giving up music and pursuing a more conventional livelihood. He traded band practice for a series of retail jobs and tried to prioritize being a good husband, father, and provider for his family above his musical aspirations. Selling shoes was steady work but it hardly paid more than playing in a rock band, and it must have bred resentment in Charlie against his new family for making him cash in his dream for a cheap suit and a straight job.

"I came to a realization years later, after Myra and I got a divorce," Chan's father explains, "that I can do whatever I want to do, but to really be happy and successful you need to do what you love."

Not that Charlie was particularly committed to doing anything but exactly what he wanted when he was still living with Myra and the girls. Professionally, both Myra and Charlie made sacrifices for their young family, working square jobs just to pay the rent, but at home there was little discernible difference between how they lived before they had children and how they lived after Miranda and Chan were born. As the disillusionment of the early 1970s gave way to the soullessness and hedonism that defined the later part of that decade, the South's dispirited bohemians congregated by default in a stagnant Atlanta.

Myra, meanwhile, was dealing with much more sinister troubles than the breakup of a band or a few unpaid bills. Her mind was starting to play tricks on her. It's unconfirmed whether or not she was ever clinically diagnosed as schizophrenic by a psychiatrist. What is clear is that her closest family members, including Lenny, Charlie, and Chan, speak about her as if she has been. The onset of schizophrenia typically occurs in late adolescence or the early twenties, and, according to Charlie and Chan, Myra was smack-dab in the middle of that range when she started displaying symptoms of the disease, including delusions, hallucinations, and erratic behavior.

Shortly after Chan's birth, Myra—who had intuitively good taste in music and art—discovered David Bowie, who was, at that point, barely known outside of London. At first Myra was just an impassioned fan, but soon her attraction transformed from enthusiastic interest to full-blown obsession. (Coincidentally, schizophrenia runs in Bowie's family as well. His infatuation with transformation and multiple identities may have appealed to Myra, who was battling contrasting versions of her own personality.) Myra became so infatuated with Bowie that in 1972, the year *Ziggy Stardust* came out, she dyed her hair rooster red like his and began referring to herself as Ziggy. "I grew up having to introduce my mom as Ziggy Stardust," Chan has said.

With her new identity intact, Myra became even more restless, Charlie says. "When Chan was two years old, Myra freaked out," Chan's dad remembers. "She just ran away." Charlie says he had no idea where Myra had gone, no means of getting in touch with her, and no idea of when she would be back. Left alone with his two young daughters, he panicked. He called Myra's parents, who came down from the family home in Forest Park and helped take care of Chan and Miranda.

Myra's disappearance sent her fledgling family into a state of total disarray, Charlie claims, but it also resulted in the beginning of a reconciliation between her parents and their son-in-law. With his long hair and bell-bottoms, inconsistent employment history, lust for rock stardom, and lack of education, Charlie was not the guy the Russells wanted their daughter to marry. But with Myra in the wind and their grandchildren left in Charlie's care, they were forced to deal with him.

Chan suffered from a lot of health problems as a child, including severe food allergies, so caring for her required the attention of both her father and her grandparents. "She couldn't drink milk, she couldn't have chocolate, she loved pets but was allergic to all of them," Charlie remembers. "We were always afraid for her." While Myra was gone, two-year-old Chan developed an ear infection so severe she had to be taken to the emergency room. "Chan's grandpop was there at the hospital," Charlie remembers. "He never really liked my hair, but there he was, and he was hugging both of us. Her mom is gone and he's hugging me and I'm hugging Chan. I got a little teary."

Charlie gives the impression that, at least for the first few years of his marriage to Myra, he was around, dutifully putting his nose to the grindstone at a series of jobs he vaguely hated while Myra combated increasingly debilitating mental problems. But according to Chan, Lenny, and Leamon, Charlie's presence in the girls' lives, even in those early years, was much more erratic than he lets on.

"Charlie left her for some reason," Leamon recalls. "Another girl? That's real foggy. . . . He wasn't around. Gone for whatever reason. I don't know if he decided it wasn't the right thing, or got cold feet 'cause she was having kids or they didn't get along or money. I don't know. I wasn't here." Chan has put it more bluntly: "My dad left when my mom was pregnant [with me]. My mother took off when I was two. They were young, drank too much, did drugs. They didn't really want kids." Chan has even gone so far as to suggest that Charlie Marshall might not be her biological dad, that instead she might be the daughter of pianist, songwriter, and fellow sixties Southern-rock scenester Spooner Oldham.

"My mom had my sister, then when she was pregnant with me, my dad left," Chan has explained. "When I met Spooner, his wife was like, 'Man, you really remind me of my husband.' I never understood why my dad wasn't around . . . so I started putting two and two together. I asked him and he says he doesn't remem— I haven't asked my mom yet. I don't wanna—but I don't think it's true. I think I am my father's kid. I don't know."

After being gone for a little over a month, Charlie says, Myra eventually reappeared in Atlanta, eager to reclaim her girls. According to Charlie, this was easier said than done. "They weren't going to give her the children back," Charlie says. "I sat down with Myra. I said, 'Why don't you get your life in order right now, and we'll get you the kids back, but you've got to get a job.' She got the babies back, but Myra had a lot of demons she was working with at that time."

Myra had always been precocious—her wit was one of the qualities that attracted Charlie to her on that first night at the Spot—but Myra's sass mutated into nastiness. "It was tough living with Myra because of mean things that she would do," Charlie recalls. "I'd have friends that would come over, and we'd be talking about music or me getting a job doing this or doing that, and she would just belittle me in front of everybody." Leamon isn't quite as blunt, but he confirms that Myra's outspoken nature continues to get her into trouble. "She's tempestuous," he says. "She can't hold a job for some reason. Gets a job and somebody makes her mad after a while. She's a pretty hard worker, but she doesn't know how to stay out of the way of everybody." At first, Charlie didn't realize that his wife may be unwell, and by the time he did, he didn't know what to do about it. And her increasingly erratic behavior put a serious strain on the couple's already tenuous marriage.

Decades later, Charlie regrets not getting his wife some help. "I wish we had gotten her diagnosed, maybe they could have given her medication," he says. At the time, the girls were living with Myra's parents and the young couple barely had money to buy food and pay rent. Doctor's-office visits for the adults in the family weren't on their list of priority expenditures. "We didn't even have money to do other things, much less go to doctors," Charlie remembers. "There were problems with Myra and there were problems with me, too."

With Myra back at home, the Marshall family settled into a state of relative stability, but not dealing with her problems almost ensured that in time they would eventually worsen. "It's bad for brains to be crazy," Dr. David Ewing, a psychiatrist and an expert on the subject, observes succinctly. "The longer they're crazy, the less likely they are to get better." Two years later, Myra and Charlie would split up for good, but in the interim the young parents tried to keep their own issues under control while they focused on providing for Chan and Miranda. Myra worked mostly during the day and Charlie worked mostly at night, so with Miranda's help, he made sure the girls got up, out of the house, and on their way to school.

"Miranda is very motherly," Lenny says of his and Chan's older sister. "They're sisters so they're the same in some instances, but they're different. Chan is more of a free spirit and Mandy is more of a motherly type." Miranda's evident maternal instincts meant that she took to responsible-older-sister tasks like packing lunches and organizing schoolbooks for the morning. Chan, on the other hand, was tough to get out of bed and moved at a slower pace, always singing to herself or trying to finish a picture she'd been coloring instead of focusing on getting out the door.

When the girls were very young and their parents were still together, Chan and Miranda attended elementary school in Buckhead, a sprawling, moneyed community in northern Atlanta. "It was a very simple time,"

Charlie remembers of the most stable years his daughters would ever have as children. "They would have lunch at school, then I'd pick them up or Myra would pick them up. We'd bring them home and they would both have to do their homework. Chan was not a good student, but she was interested in learning."

Chan agrees that she was an unwieldy child, easily distracted and shy but drawn to the spotlight. "I was pretty daydreamy and spazzy," the singer has recalled. "I was energetic. Never could sleep. Always running all over the place. I wanted to be a comedian. I liked making people laugh." She also agrees that conventional do-your-homework-get-an-A type scholastic behavior wasn't her strength, saying that of all the teachers she had as a kid, every one of them except her art teacher would be surprised to discover she's become successful. Art was Chan's favorite subject and the only one she was really good at. Both Miranda and Chan were extremely creative children who spent more time painting with their mother, or making collages and singing, than doing homework. "They were always drawing," Charlie remembers. "We'd buy them coloring books and Chan would say, 'See, Daddy, I stayed between the lines!' "

Even with some of the traditional comforts of childhood in place, the first seven years of Chan's life mostly resembled one long Molly Hatchet after-party. Three years before her birth, her parents had been drinking, drugging, rocking revolutionaries, and it would take more than two young girls and a stack of bills to turn them into a settled suburban couple. "It was like those movies where the stereo is playing Lynyrd Skynyrd, and people are on motorcycles and smoking mad dope, and little kids are running around," Chan has said. "It was a hippie drugged-out Southern kind of thing." At the Marshalls' house there was always a collection of stoned, aimless, broke rock boys and girls crashing on her family's floor. Everybody smoked, everybody drank, and everybody played guitar.

"During the Vietnam War, if you had money you went to San Francisco, if you went to college you went to New York, and if you were poor you stayed in the South," Chan has said of her parents' generation. "You get a lot of uneducated people jumping onto a Greyhound bus and going to Atlanta. I grew up with these people who had long hair, no money, and no jobs." As babies, Chan claims, the girls slept in drawers, not cribs. She has also said that her mother used to fill up her baby bottle with Budweiser and that she spent time at bars in Atlanta. The kitchen cabinets were stocked with cartons of cigarettes, records, guitar strings, and bottles of booze, not Kraft Macaroni & Cheese and Cheerios. Some days Chan would come home from school to the illusion of a stable home. The house would be neat, Myra would have prepared something simple for dinner, and the family would eat together before Charlie headed out to play one of his cocktail-lounge gigs. On other days, however, she would come home to a floor full of vagrant musicians sleeping off a wild night on the family's carpet, nothing but a fridgeful of condiments for dinner.

"I started when I was in second grade," Chan has said of her very first cigarette. "My mom would come home from work, before we'd go out with her, and she'd light a cigarette—Kool kings. We'd sit on her lap and play around for a minute, then she'd go take a shower. She'd always leave her Kool king lit in the ashtray, so that's how I started smoking. I remember first grade and kindergarten, I would beg her, 'Please, please don't smoke. You're going to die.' Then, when I was in second grade—I'll never forget it—I thought, Fuck. I'm hungry. All we had was bread, which was kind of old, and the toaster had caught on fire so many times I was scared of it. I used to put mustard on my bread and we didn't have any mustard. That cigarette was sitting there, so I started smoking it."

Both of Chan's parents have sugar-coated the extent to which their daughters were exposed to the drinking and the drugs that permeated the Marshall household. One of the first things Myra said, unprompted, when she contacted me with concerns about this book was that many of the details she reads about Chan's childhood are untrue—and not because Chan is misquoted, but because she exaggerates. "We drank, don't get me wrong, everybody drank," Myra says. "But she magnifies things." Charlie was initially similarly defensive. "I did have my cup of tea then," he admits. "We would do some drinking. We smoked and so forth around the kids, but never any heavy drugs. I would never allow drugs around my house with my daughters." When pushed a bit about his ability to shield his kids from what was happening in the next room, Charlie relents a little. "There was a lot of experimentation with myself with LSD and all these other things," he says quietly. "It was the early seventies. The drugs were mostly kept separate from the kids, but you can't really—you put up a wall, but kids hear and see everything."

As completely as Charlie and Myra both loved their daughters, they were not able to take care of them because they were not able to take care of themselves. Myra battled her untreated mental issues with booze, Charlie used drugs to ease the anguish of his failed attempt at rock stardom, and they took their pain out on each other. Whenever Charlie showed up at the house for one more try at committing to marriage and fatherhood, Charlie remembers Myra mocked him for his pathetic attempts to be a good man, almost daring him to fail her and the girls. Meanwhile, ever since Chan was a baby, Charlie knew that Myra was mentally unwell and that her increasingly troubling behavior wasn't necessarily her fault if it was related to her untreated disease. But instead of getting her the help she needed, he walked right out the door, leaving his two young daughters at her mercy.

Chan was almost four years old when her parents finally split up. The breakup had been building since a few months after the couple's bacchanal of a wedding, and when it finally came, it was not pretty. "About the third time we tried to get back together, we got into an argument," Charlie says. "She wanted to take the kids to school and I said, 'No you're not.' I took the kids and I pushed them in the closet and I closed the closet door. I wouldn't let her take them." In his fury, Charlie was deaf to the screams of his terrified daughters banging on the closet door. "I realized they were both hysterically crying in the closet," Charlie recalls, his voice quiet and his words labored. "Myra was just freaking out, so I went and sat down in the living room. She came to get the kids and she left. That was our last time together."

Today Charlie is appropriately candid and regretful when he talks about the emotional scars moments like this left on his daughters. "Those type of things for the kids are probably things they still remember now," he says. "It probably still touches them. I know they probably had nightmares about that. We had good times. There were happy times; the bad times—they were more memorable."

4.

A New Family

Charlie and Myra Marshall officially divorced on December 16, 1975. Charlie was twenty-seven, Myra was twenty-five. Free from the burden of trying to make life as a father and husband work, Charlie refocused on music and even considered moving out to Los Angeles. Ultimately, though, he decided that he didn't want to be that far from Myra and the girls.

Charlie remembers Myra remarrying shortly after the divorce, but Myra's second husband, Leamon Land, says they didn't marry until 1979, two years and a few months after Myra and Charlie legally split. "Myra and Charlie were not together long," Leamon says. "They had Mandy and they had Charlyn and for some reason they didn't get along. Charlie was off doing his thing and Myra raised the girls alone." The time that Myra spent as a single parent was difficult. She had a hard time holding down a job. "This is such a classic story," Dr. Ewing says. "One consequence of mental illness is there's going to be social chaos. Daddy is going to split because he's not going to be able to put up with the craziness. There's going to be a little of that. There's gonna be poverty. Mental illness will make you poor."

When things got too hard, Myra would send her girls to spend a few weeks with their grandmother. No stranger to struggle, Grandma Lil was dealing with the dissolution of her marriage to Myra's father, Richard. "He's kind of a short guy with a real hot temper," Leamon says of Myra's dad, who moved out around this time and now lives in Nashville. Grandma Lil turned to God to get her through. She attended church regularly, and as long as her granddaughter was living with her, so did Chan. It was in church and at home with her grandmother that Chan first learned to sing. "When I was very little, a baby girl, my grand-mother would always put a tape in a tape recorder and ask me to sing," Chan remembers. "I have one of them, from when I was seven. I re-member her doing it all the time. She had these religious tapes and she would record over them."

From the time Chan was less than a year old, Granny Lil was the clos-est thing Chan had to a trustworthy parental figure. An almost comically archetypal maternal presence, Granny Lil is protective of her family and resolute in her beliefs. To this day, she and Chan are still incredibly close. Chan wrote the *Greatest* track "Willie" while taking a cab from the airport in Tallahassee, Florida, to visit Lillian in Pensacola, a trip she makes several times a year.

Chan isn't a conventionally religious person, but through attending church with Granny Lil as a kid, she developed a deep sense of spirituality and respect for the idea of God. "I lived with my grandmother a lot growing up," Chan has said. "When she lost her son, Uncle Wayne, in a motorcycle accident, she found God. She brought God into my life as a little kid." Religion showed Granny Lil how to find redemption in pain, and it provided Chan with a safe haven from the madness she faced at home. "Church was a way to get out of my home, which was kinda a mess," the singer has explained.

Chan's relationship with religion is complex. In most obvious ways, she seems the furthest thing from a dutiful Christian. She swears like a sailor, has displayed her pubic hair in a national magazine, has had an abortion, drinks, and has experimented with drugs. As Lenny puts it, "If you know Charlyn for two seconds, you know she's not gonna be beating the Bible." On the other hand, Chan has a deep respect for the idea of faith. "I have a Bible by my bed," the singer has said. "If something gets weird, it distracts me. It's very philosophical or metaphysical that there's no real— nothing is permanent."

Chan's favorite Bible stories are the ones that convey this sense of faith as a way to make peace with the unknown. "[My favorites are] the mystical ones [where Jesus] goes into the desert. Or when the fishermen just drop their whole lives and follow him because they believe this person is so good," Chan has said. "They just believe him without even thinking about it. They realize, this is Him. Just things like that make the belief exist from somewhere. And Revelation, the end, like it's the end of a prayer. All children of God go out with the grace of God. It's final. You can either have the grace, or not."

Lenny describes the connection between his sister and grandmother as fueled in part by ongoing religious discourse. "Chan and Lillian are very close," Lenny confirms. "She's very sweet. Very Southern. Very religious. If there were something that would cause a little friction in their relationship, it is that my grandmother is super-religious. Talking-in-tongues kind of religious. I'm not judging her. Whatever gets you there. She has a strong, strong faith in Jesus. Strongest faith of anyone in my family. Charlyn may not agree with it completely. It's kind of a fifty-fifty deal: fifty percent being strongly rooted in the idea that religion is stabilizing, it's a comfort, and the other fifty is, 'Wow, you're fanatical.' But they don't have arguments about it. They talk about it like philosophy."

Between the ages of four and seven—when Myra was on her own— Chan spent a lot of time with her grandmother. But in 1979 things began to look up when Myra reconnected with her ex-husband Charlie's old friend Leamon Land. "She lived in Buckhead in an apartment with the girls," Leamon remembers. "I was working at an automotive company, and Myra got a job there. We ran into each other at the place we worked and decided to get married. Got pregnant with Lenny and got married in 1979."

Land, Chan's "second dad," as Charlie calls him, was a golden-haired Greg Allman look-alike from Atlanta. He was born in 1950 at the same hospital as Chan, Crawford Long, and became a fixture on the Peachtree Street scene in the late 1960s, where he met Chan's biological father. "My own father and Charlie Marshall knew each other before my father and my mother did," Lenny explains. "They were actually pretty close."

Leamon's hippie pedigree is as impressive as Chan's biological parents'. "I went to the original Woodstock," he remembers. "I worked there. I helped build the stage that went from the food tent to the back of the stage. I had to go to the little town the day before the show to get my pass. My paycheck. Had a backstage pass, was back there with Hendrix."

They were good friends as young men, but by their late twenties Leamon and Charlie had grown into very different people. Unlike Charlie, who tried on marriage and fatherhood but was pathologically distracted by lingering dreams of fame, Leamon was a solid guy with an unflappable personality and a good job. Land worked as a salesman with a magwheel company and was quickly climbing the ranks, which meant he made good money and was able to provide for the young family he inherited when he married Myra. He also absolutely adored the girls. "My father loved the girls very much," Lenny says. "He's a kind-hearted person. He's very laid back, very cool. He loves everybody."

Soon after the wedding and the birth of Chan's half brother, Lenny Wilder Lane, in late 1979, Leamon's job required him to move his new family to the suburbs of Memphis. The sixties may have been over, but between Charlie, Myra, and Leamon, there was still a thriving sense of free love: There was no animosity over Leamon supplanting Charlie as the father figure in the Marshall family. To this day, Charlie and Leamon are still good friends. "He's a great, great pianist," Leamon says. "I go see him play every couple of months. I have a cocktail and sit with him on his seat."

Charlie agrees. "They just didn't up and move," Charlie explains. "It was business. They had to leave. It was just a twist of fate. I understood." Seven-year-old Chan didn't have the same reasoned perspective on what was happening to her family. She had always been a daddy's girl. She's even admitted to having a crush on her father as a little girl.

Chan was distressed enough that her father hadn't been living with the family for several years, but now they were moving to another state, far away from her dad. It turned out to be only the first of a series of jarring moves Chan would make over the course of the next few years.

"We lived in Bartlett, Tennessee, in a little house," remembers Leamon, who now lives in Atlanta and runs his own wheel and tire business. "Chan and Mandy [Miranda] went to school in Bartlett. We stayed there about one year, then the company I was with had an opening in North Carolina. It was a better opportunity for me, so we moved to Greensboro. And we moved to McLeansville [North Carolina] after that. Our house was in the back of a tobacco mill in a little neighborhood. We were close to all the neighbors. We stayed there a couple of years before an opportunity to be a manager in Atlanta came up. Moved back there . . . then a different company wanted me to move to North Carolina again, so we moved again."

Though Myra would eventually settle in the Greensboro area for good, during her children's elementary and middle-school years the family lived like vagabonds, packing up their stuff every six months or so and hopping from one suburban home to another. Sometimes they wouldn't even get around to unpacking all the boxes before they were off again. Chan has said she attended ten different schools from second to eleventh grades, and the constant uprooting aversely affected her sense of peace with herself and with the world around her.

Each time Chan's family moved, she and her sister would register, once again, at a new school. The singer often found herself dropped midyear into a classroom filled with kids who'd known each other since kindergarten. Chan had to quickly catch up academically, adjust to a new house and city, and make new friends. With ample natural charm and good looks on her side, school could have served as a respite from the

instability at home, but the relentless displacement Leamon's job created made sure that she never had enough time to get comfortable at any
of her schools. Her vivacious, comedic side retreated, and in its place
emerged a self-conscious, shy girl, petrified of being conspicuous in any
way. "You were supposed to work your way around a new set of people
every time, but I was the most submissive child, didn't talk or anything," Chan has said.

In class, Chan was terrified of being called on. She was convinced she
wouldn't know how to answer whatever question was asked, and she
was also afraid of having to explain to yet another new teacher, another
new classful of kids, how to pronounce her unusual name. When Chan
was in sixth grade, both she and Miranda decided to stop going by their
birth names and instead adopt shorter, punchier, and distinctly less
Southern versions. Miranda, who was named after Myra (*MY-randa*),
decided to adopt her middle name, Lee, as her new first name. Chan
shortened hers from Charlyn (named after her father: *CHAR-lyn*, but
pronounced with a soft "ch") to Chan (pronounced *Shawn*). "I'd go to a
new school and they're like [adopts a thick Southern accent], 'What's
your name again?' " Chan remembers. "They never got it right, so I
changed it to Chan. My mom was like, 'How about Cher?' " Myra remembers suggesting Chan pronounce her name to rhyme with *fan* rather
than *dawn*. "I wanted to call her Chan, but she hated it," Myra recalls.
"She said, 'No, Mom! I hate Chan. It sounds like a dog.' I said, 'What
about your middle name, Marie?' She said, 'That's even worse!' "

It wasn't just the transience that got to Chan, it was the fact that
for all the moving around she was doing, she wasn't seeing much that interested her. The family never moved north or west; they always stayed
in the heart of the South, and with the exception of Atlanta, they never
lived anywhere urban, always staying in identical, blank suburbs. Each

house had grass out front and a swing set out back, each had a fresh coat of paint and a clean room for Chan to share with her sister, but none of these places, none of these prefab houses, was ever Chan's home.

Chan didn't stay in one place long enough to identify herself as native to a particular town. Instead she became a native of every town she slept in, as if the entire southern United States, from the depressed suburban wastelands the singer briefly inhabited to the lockers in which she stashed her books for a few months at a time—to the interchangeable series of bedrooms where she slept to the highways that connected one house to another—all became home. "My main memory of growing up is visual," Chan has said. "We had this old run-down graveyard behind our house [in North Carolina]. I remember running over a mud bridge through a tobacco patch in bare feet. God, now, that's pretty Southern." As an adult, Chan has come to realize how deeply her upbringing united her with the South. "I still love going back," the singer has said of the areas she lived in as a child. "It's part of me, and I don't even realize it when I'm gone."

Leamon's job kept him away from home for long stretches of time, but when he was around he brought stability to the household and paid attention to the kids. Leamon remembers several family vacations, including one to Topsail Island on the North Carolina coast. "It was a little place, real small, just a strip of land with water between it. We'd go there, get a hotel room, and play on the beach. It had one little restaurant. We'd also drive up in the mountains, to Banner Elk [a resort town in western North Carolina], and get a cabin where the ski resorts were. The kids would have their music in the back, listening to that, and Myra and I would be up front talking."

These moments of familial unity were few. "What kind of parents do they make? Shitty parents," Dr. Ewing says of schizophrenics. "Sometimes they can get up and make lunch for their kids and send them off to school, but what they can't really do is make emotional connection and understand what the kid really needs. And they also might be painting satanic symbols on the wall and chanting about the devil instead of changing diapers, who knows. One man put his two toddlers in the melting bucket at the steel plant because he believed that was the only way to save them from the devil. The range is huge. But mostly it would be sort of like they were absent."

Sometimes Myra's behavior would be limited to carelessness or basic neglect. "She'd just cut up some vegetables and say, 'Here's dinner,' " Lenny remembers. But when Myra was drinking, her temperament would shift from passive to aggressive. Chan has been uniformly vague about Myra's mental health problems. When she talks about her mom, she'll describe her as bipolar or simply crazy, then go into harrowing detail about growing up in fear of her mother's volatile mood swings. "When you're raised by a bipolar person, you have to be afraid," Chan has recalled. "If you turn the knob on the door when you come home from school too loudly, you're fucking in trouble, you know? I got shit kicked out of me. I was always afraid."

"One minute she can be as nice as can be towards you and you think everything is cool, and the next minute she flies off the handle," Lenny remembers. "She'd yell. You'd be stunned. Okay, what did I do? After a while, you're walking on eggshells—Okay, I have to do everything exactly the way Mom wants it done, 'cause I don't want her to yell at me." Leamon describes Myra's mood swings as directly connected to her drinking. "I don't know if Myra knows she needs help," Leamon muses. "Don't know if she knows she has a problem. Maybe she does and doesn't want to accept it. There's something there that's obviously bothering her, and she's not a drunk or anything, but when she does have a few drinks, a couple of beers, her personality changes—she'd get kind of manic. That brought along a lot of the problems, why they didn't get along. She would holler at them."

Chan learned to be submissive in order to survive. By the time she was in middle school, Chan had internalized the idea that she was always wrong, and this notion has haunted her into adulthood. Anyone who has seen Cat Power live, or has had even a five-minute conversation with Chan, has heard her say, "I'm sorry," or ask, "Are you mad at me?" at least once. She repeats these phrases like mantras, a dubious habit that her critics point to when they argue she's the cynical architect of her own mad image. But Chan's compulsive apologizing is as much a well-honed survival mechanism as it is cunning self-deprecation. Chan needed to be an emotional chameleon in order to get through life in new school after new school, and in order to manage her mother. If joy and effervescence were in order, that's what she would deliver. If absolute quiet and withdrawn submission was required, she would embody it. And when prostrate apology was necessary, that's what she would give.

Even though Chan was ill equipped as a kid to understand her mother's mental illness, she intuited enough that she began to fear not only her mother's unpredictable mood swings but also the demons that brought them on. "Because my mom was unstable growing up, it's been a fear of mine since I was a little girl—that they were going to take me away," the singer has said. Growing up with a mentally ill parent taught Chan to be afraid of her own mind.

In contrast to the instability Chan associated with her mother, Charlie Marshall, the charming almost rock star, was easy to idealize. Chan's perspective on her dad and on her parents' split has evolved since she was a kid, but she spent most of her adolescence and much of her twenties stubbornly worshiping him. Not only was he the cool parent, with the good taste in music, easy warmth, and relatively mellow personality, but he was also not there—and his absence made him easy to romanticize. "I was so trained as a child to accept him because he was never around," Chan has remembered. Father and daughter also had a special affinity for each other beyond the usual absentee-parent idealization: Charlie is a musician, and Chan always loved music.

Seeing their dad was so rare that when Charlie did get time with Miranda and Chan, it was treated like a holiday. "I'd go pick them up and I'd have 'em for the whole day," Charlie remembers. "We'd go to the mall and Myra would put pretty dresses on them both and they'd have brand-new shoes if we were doing something special, going to the movies or whatever. I'd hold Miranda's hand in my left hand and I'd have Chan's in my right and Chan would be almost like tap-dancing, she'd have so much energy. She's like a little bunny rabbit, and Miranda would be walking with me and we'd be talking, and Chan'd be just like bouncing like a rabbit." On these outings Charlie would treat the girls to an ice-cream cone, though Chan couldn't have the real thing because of her food allergies. "She had to have sherbet," Charlie remembers. "So I would get sherbet too. Miranda would have the ice cream and she'd be gloating right and left. I asked Chan later, I said, 'You knew all those years that I hated sherbet.' She said, 'Yeah, I knew it, Dad—it didn't make it any better!' "

Very early some weekend mornings, Charlie remembers Myra dropping the girls off unannounced at his house then driving away, leaving them to timidly knock on their father's door, hoping he would wake up and let them in. This sort of behavior angered his second wife, Sandy, with whom Charlie has another daughter, Ivy Elizabeth, born in 1981. "The kids didn't know what to do," Charlie remembers of these moments. "Sandy would be yelling at me, and the kids, they're caught right in the middle. In a broken home you have the continuance of life A or life B and the kids, they're out there somewhere in the ozone and they don't know what their place is or what they're supposed to do. It's not their fault."

As Chan grew up, she continued her emotional chameleon act at home with her mom while idealizing a father she barely saw and sustaining what few friendships she was able to forge at her string of new schools. Outwardly Chan was participating in childhood, but inwardly she was learning to turn to herself for real companionship. The more comfortable Chan got with the idea that she could only truly count on herself, the more time she spent in her own head, and the more active she became creatively. "I would write stories," the singer has said. "That was the only way I could say something." Chan's entire life was defined by other people's needs and expectations. She had to be docile around Mom, charming around Dad, willfully gregarious at each new school. But walking home from the bus or during study hall or alone in the room she shared with her sister late at night, Chan could tell herself the truth.

Chan wrote poems and mysteries and other short stories, and she also started writing music. When she was in fourth grade and living in McLeansville, North Carolina, Chan Marshall wrote her first real song. "I had this neighbor who had a piano," Chan has said. "I'd only seen pianos in church or in my dad's apartment, and I was never allowed to touch instruments. I grew up in a house that had alcoholism problems, and there are different codes of living when you grow up like that. I didn't go to other people's houses much." Chan was compelled by the piano: She wanted to have it all to herself, and one day she got the chance. "My neighbor's parents weren't home, and she was watching TV," Chan has remembered. "So I snuck into her den and I played this song. I called it 'Windows.' "

It's not an exaggeration to say that this moment changed Chan's life. The uninhibited written expression of her own thoughts was consoling, but music was even better — it was beyond words. "I felt like I had a secret," the singer has said of her emotional reaction to writing that first song. "Like I had made a life for myself." Instantly, music became a source of relief from the rest of her life. "Growing up with this nonsocietal structure, you have no real guidelines to follow. You either go to church and, like my grandmother, you believe in God and hope for something to keep yourself sane and positive, to keep continuing the struggle. Or you turn to alcohol and drugs or mental unstableness. So that's why I write . . . exercise communication. Did the music help me break that cycle? Shit yeah."

Music is the only element as integral to Chan's childhood as addiction and instability. Her father always had instruments around the house, and there were musicians around all the time, and her mom had a good voice and would sing to the girls. Church music was the foundation onto which the rest of Chan's musical influences were laid. On top of pensive, plaintive hymns and raucous gospel revivals came Myra's British bands and the blues, old soul, and classic rock that her dad and stepdad loved.

Chan used to sit cross-legged before Charlie's crates of old blues and classic-rock records. She would spend hours DJing for herself, playing tracks by James Brown, Billie Holiday, Eartha Kitt, and Creedence. This was Charlie's music, and it became Chan's music as well. "Something serious happened when I found the Buddy Holly and the first Rolling Stones record," Chan has said. "Playing those records, something happened to me." Chan was particularly taken with a Dylan record she found in her father's collection. "He was all alone on that blue cover," the singer has said. "I didn't know nothing about alone music. It felt like he was singing to me."

Chan talks most often about her father's influence on her musical taste, but Lenny remembers his sister expressing interest in Leamon's records as well. "I'm certainly not gonna say that Chan got all of her influences from my father," Lenny says. "But he had an old record collection—Eric Clapton, Otis Redding, the Rolling Stones. He used to play them every day in the morning, and in the evening when he got home from work. I think she commandeered some of his records, and I think some of her interest in the blues came from my father's records."

Chan's connection to Southern blues was reinforced by the fact that these songs—unlike any of the friends she made at the various schools she attended or the rooms she inhabited for a few months at a time, or the bookstores, cafés, and record stores she frequented in one town or the next—were always with her during her nomadic childhood. "I didn't know anybody, 'cause I went to a different school every year, so they were always my favorite songs," the singer has said of the tracks she heard at her parents' houses. "The heart of the music and the simplicity of it— I'd go to all these different schools and nobody had ever heard about it, so I couldn't have a relationship with any peers who knew old soul."

At home by herself at night, it was to her soul and blues heroes that Chan turned for comfort—but she was also a normal American teenager growing up in the eighties. She loved Duran Duran and Madonna and watched a lot of MTV. "As far as dressing, she would go through phases," Lenny remembers. "For one portion she loved Madonna, who was just coming out with 'Borderline' and 'Papa Don't Preach.' Then she would go through other phrases. Her favorite movie for a while was *The Breakfast Club* with Molly Ringwald and Judd Nelson. She watched that movie ad nauseam. She related to the Molly Ringwald character. She also really liked *Fast Times at Ridgemont High* and was really into *Less Than Zero*."

Chan embraced mainstream pop culture, but she was also tapped into the sounds of the underground. Miranda was part of Chan's connection to indie music—she gave her a cassette of Hüsker Dü's 1983 EP *Metal Circus* when they were teenagers—but it was really radio that opened Chan's eyes to the kinds of bands that were her forebears in indie rock. "I remember when I discovered college radio," the singer has said. "I was fourteen. I was in my room and my mom had given me this radio. I'd turn on the radio and tape stuff. [R.E.M.'s] 'Radio Free Europe'—I was like, that's so cool! Then the next song was like Concrete Blonde, then the Cure, then the Go-Go's, and I had all this music on this one tape. I'd listen to that or I'd listen to the radio and tape more songs. I learned that there was this other music, and it's not like Billy Idol, and it's not like 'What's Love Got to Do with It' or all the eighties stuff, like Kaja-googoo or Debbie Gibson. There's more out there."

5.

Daddy's Girl

As a child Chan witnessed firsthand what the life of a professional musician was like, and she hated it. The drug use,
the drinking, the sleeping around, and the blinding lust for
fame all repulsed her. She fantasized about rising above the

derelict rock 'n' roll circumstances of her birth and becoming a teacher or a vet, something "normal," she had said. Yet the people who made the music Chan loved—Billie Holiday, Bob Dylan, Eartha Kitt, Buddy Holly—had her deepest respect and admiration. Perhaps some of them lived depraved lives, but they rose above it to create sounds that penetrated her soul and made her life more bearable. This juxtaposition between music as an instrument of good and music as a gateway to evil continues to be one of the most fundamental conflicts in her life.

As the relationship continued to deteriorate between Chan and her mom, Chan began to project onto Charlie all the qualities of an ideal parent with even more intensity than she had as a little girl. The more Chan and Myra fought, the more appealing Charlie became, and the more Chan felt compelled to stand up to her mother until the situation reached a crisis point. In 1984, when Chan was in sixth grade and her sister was in eighth grade, Myra packed up the girls' things and moved them to Atlanta to live with their father.

"Basically, how can I put this to be politically correct," Lenny says, struggling. "She left home because her and my mother—oh, man, I don't know how to put this. She has a little bit of an alcohol problem. My mom would always give us a hard time. When she would drink she had a hard time getting along with anybody. Charlyn was just tired of it. So she went to Atlanta and moved in with Charlie. Miranda went with her. It was a breath of fresh air, a lot of independence. At that point Charlie's not used to being a father so he's like, 'How do I do this?' Charlyn had free rein to do whatever she wanted. She didn't like school that much. She just wanted to basically be free and live life."

"Myra calls me up and says, 'I'm bringing the kids down today,' " Charlie remembers. "She just brings them by and drops them off at my house. They don't know what's going on, it was the middle of the school year. They stayed for about a month that time." During this visit, Charlie registered the girls at school, but before long they were homesick for their life back in Greensboro, where Myra was still living. "Miranda came home from school one day and said, 'Dad, can I call Mom?'" Charlie remembers. "I knew what they were going to talk about. She missed her friends up in North Carolina."

Back in Greensboro, an uneasy peace between Chan and her mom was reached. Then, just as things seemed semi-settled, another family crisis occurred when Lenny was diagnosed with cerebral palsy. "In my case, Charlyn kind of had, I wouldn't say resentment, but they [Miranda and Chan] were teenagers when I was going through a lot of my physical trouble. They didn't know how to react to it. I was getting a lot of attention that might have been focused on them. I spent years in the hospital. I had about three or four surgeries." Leamon concurs. "The time we had to spend in hospitals and going to treatment centers, probably not enough attention was given to the girls."

Lenny is articulate, funny, and soft-spoken but direct. He says he feels lucky that in spite of his disability, which has put him in a wheelchair, he has been able to establish such a full life for himself. "I go to college, I drive, I work," he says. "I've been fortunate enough to do all those things. Some people can't. I have a day job and I own two companies— a vending company, and I run the e-commerce portion of my father's business. I also work at the Wal-Mart here [in Atlanta]. I'm the switchboard operator. I handle all the inbound and outbound calls. If you heard some of the people, you'd be laughing all day."

Lenny worries that, as used to living with his cerebral palsy as he is, the disease has kept him from being closer to Chan. "For whatever reason, we're kind of distant," he says quietly. "I love my sister to death. Any time she calls me, I'm there." Lenny is very aware of the fact that

Chan rarely mentions him in interviews. "I don't really know why she doesn't talk about me that much," he says. "I don't think she'd be ashamed. She says that she knew I'd been through a lot and didn't want me to have to deal with any questions. The other side of that is that she travels a lot. She's taken Miranda's kids on the road a couple of times, taken them to stay with her in Miami. She maybe feels responsible if anything happened to me if she took me, too."

Lenny's diagnosis was hard on the entire family, especially Myra. "My mom felt guilty," Lenny remembers. "You're a mother and you have a child that's born not the way you want them to be born, have an early life you don't want them to have, you kind of bear that burden." Myra assuaged her guilt by focusing all her energy on making Lenny well. Not only did Miranda and Chan get lost in the shadows, but they also had to pick up the slack around the house. "With my physical limitations, sometimes Miranda and Charlyn were left to care for me," Lenny remembers. "When I was younger I didn't have a lot of independent skills. When they were left to care for me, it kind of threw Chan for a loop. She didn't know a lot of stuff to do. She didn't want to hurt me. She was very distant. That's one memory that I have. She always took care of me, but was always real hesitant. She didn't want to cause me harm."

By the time she started ninth grade at Ragsdale High School in Greensboro, North Carolina, Chan was old enough to understand that Myra was not mentally well, which meant that she had even less respect for her mother's authority than your typical teenager. "My mom sent me to an acting workshop when I was in high school 'cause I wouldn't go to a therapist," Chan has said. "She was convinced that we [the girls] needed a shrink when actually she needed a fucking doctor." Chan was enraged by her mom's hypocritical expectation that she behave like a normal child when Myra was anything but a normal mother.

The entrenched conflict between Myra and Chan extended to Chan's body image and sense of herself as a young woman. The singer has always had a girly personality. Yet for years Chan wore her hair brutally short and shrouded herself in shapeless work clothes. As a child she thought of herself as ugly and made sure her appearance reflected that perception. "My mom told me that I was stupid and that I was ugly because I wasn't feminine," Chan has remembered. "I felt so awkward being a girl. All the girls at school were mean and beautiful." Lenny doesn't remember a lot of boys calling or stopping by. "If she had boys, she didn't have them around the house," he recalls. "She was probably worried that Myra would have caused conflict. She didn't want to have any problems with my mom. She laid low."

"I was, like, constantly suicidal and not having friends," the singer has since said of her state of mind in early high school. By then Chan had also discovered what her parents liked about drinking and taking drugs. "I started taking LSD and smoking all the pot I could get and drinking anything I could drink," she has recalled. "I'd get high all day and all night."

Things got so bad at Myra's that Chan was afraid to come home. She took to waiting out her mother's rages elsewhere. "My mom always had dogs," the singer has said. "I had my last dog when I was fourteen or fifteen, and we had a real connection. I would come home from school and there was so much shit going on I would get in the doghouse with him. It felt like he was my only friend." When Chan's relationship with her mother once again became unbearable, the singer turned to her father to rescue her. And unlike previous times when Chan moved out of her mom's house, this time she never came back. "Her mom called and she put Chan on the line," Charlie remembers. "She said, 'Dad, can I come live with you?' " She didn't speak to her mother again for more than six years.

If there was a specific incident between Chan and her mom that pre-cipitated the move, Chan didn't tell her father about it. "I asked Chan what happened a couple times," Charlie remembers. "She would just put it off as, 'She's crazy! She's crazy!' " As frank as Chan can be about her mother's tirades, you get the sense that she kept the worst of what hap-pened to herself. Even once Chan was living with her father, she still didn't reveal the most explicit details. "I know that time with her mother constituted a lot of the demons Chan fights today," Charlie says. "Chan has been totally afraid of her mom her entire life. You think of a suckling child, and that's the one connection they have with life, and to be afraid of that person that brings you into life, I mean, what a scary experience."

The trauma of finally leaving her mother's house was intense, but Chan got a second chance at a semistable adolescence in Atlanta. When she left North Carolina in the spring of 1988 Chan pulled out of tenth grade midyear, so in the fall she reenrolled as a sophomore at Campbell High School in Smyrna, Georgia. Six months after Chan moved in with her dad, Miranda joined them and, for the first time since Myra and Char-lie were married, the Marshall girls were living permanently under their father's roof. Charlie celebrated his fortieth birthday by quitting rock 'n' roll (again), and resigned himself to working regular jobs in between play-ing happy-hour piano gigs that got him home in time for dinner.

At sixteen years old, Chan was a suburban punk. The popular kids peg-rolled their acid-washed jeans and drove around in Camaros, the the-ater kids wore dark eyeliner and listened to the Smiths, and the city kids dealt drugs and snuck into hip-hop clubs on school nights. Chan hung out with the rock kids. "She was another alternative kid that was into some pretty sedate punk rock," recalls Loring Kemp, Chan's schoolmate at Campbell and now an Atlanta-based writer. "We were the type of kids who would write 'Violent Femmes' on our notebook. There were parties, and people smoked pot and did acid, but we weren't a rough inner-city crowd." The boys wore fauxhawks and trench coats; the girls bought used T-shirts and Levi's from the Salvation Army and wore them with black Doc Martens.

Chan had been to so many new schools over the years that adjusting to one more new one was routine. She experimented with drugs, she drank, she smoked, she had lots of friends, but she was never really part of the cool crowd. In some ways, outsider status was Chan's choice; she didn't like the exclusivity that came along with popularity, and shunned it. "It wasn't that she wasn't popular," Lenny recalls. "I believe she was popular. She basically was the way she is now. She didn't like a lot of clique-ish activity. She liked people that were real. Not phony." In other ways, however, Chan would have liked to feel more confident. "I always wanted to be like Madonna," the singer has confessed. "I wouldn't, like, show my boobs and wear that black bustier, but she made me feel sexy."

As with most people who don't assimilate well in high school, Chan's inability to fit in was a good sign. As she grew up, the singer continued to keep up with trends in pop culture and pop music. In particular, she was a fan of British postpunk bands like the Cure and the Psychedelic Furs, whose singles she bought in the import section of her local record store. But the blues played on repeat in her subconscious. When Chan started writing songs as Cat Power, her deep connection to traditional music would authenticate her as the female, indie-rock Robert Johnson, but as a teenager it defined her as painfully unlike everyone else. "I never met anyone in school who knew who Eartha Kitt or James Brown was," Chan has said.

6.

"The Piano Is Not a Toy"

While Chan attended Campbell High, she and her sister lived with their father in his apartment, and they had a good routine. On a typical evening Charlie would come home around eight, fresh off his cocktail-lounge gig, to find

Chan on the phone in her room. "I said, 'There's only one rule about that phone,' " Charlie remembers, laughing. " 'You do your homework, and then you can talk on it.' " Chan found a way around this. "I'd kind of sneak home and catch her on the phone while doing her homework with the TV going and a CD playing," her father remembers, chuckling. "I would say, 'Well, I know you're probably tuned into one of them.'

"Out of the seven days of the week, we each got to pick what we would have for dinner," Charlie remembers. "Everybody else had to agree, and then we could pick a movie. Chan had her movies that she loved. I really didn't care for Whoopi Goldberg at the time, and she made me watch *The Color Purple*. Now it's one of my favorite movies!"

Occasionally Charlie would take the girls to the record store, where they would sort through the stacks and beg their father to buy them the newest new-wave single. "They'd always go to the back of the store where they kept the black-and-whites—that's what I called imports," Charlie remembers. "The girls were fans of the Cure when they first came out. I said, 'Yeah, they're a really good band. They need one crossover hit and they'd be even bigger.' Both girls looked at me like, 'They don't need a crossover hit—they're fine just the way they are!' "

With Chan and her father finally living in the same house, Charlie had the chance to encourage his daughter's interest in his chosen profession. He could have taught her how to play guitar, he could have let her in on his own songwriting process. Music could have become an indelible bond between the two of them. Instead, Charlie was so intensely territorial about his work and forbidding about sharing his instruments that he made Chan feel she wasn't worthy of following in his footsteps.

"My dad was always writing songs," Chan has recalled. "But if you ever wanted to touch the guitar or piano, 'Uh-uh-uh-uh-uh.' There would be this huge, what's the word? Soliloquy about, 'The guitar is not a toy. The guitar is a musical instrument.' " Instead of perceiving his professional life as an inspiration, an interest they had in common, Charlie gave Chan the impression that music was his, not hers. "My father never encouraged me to be interested in music in a personal way," she has said. "Because he was a musician, he thought it was his territory."

Chan's increasing curiosity about her dad's music clashed with his resentment of her interest. "When I was in tenth grade, he had a baby grand," Chan remembered. "He'd come home and I'd be figuring it out. I liked music like every teenager. It was this massive thing, and it just made sense to me." Chan felt a natural affinity for the piano, but instead of developing an organic relationship with the instrument, she heard her father's admonishing words in her head: "The piano is not a toy." When Charlie left the house, Chan relished the opportunity to beat the crap out of her dad's prize. "I'd kind of bang on it," the singer has recalled. "It really made me rebellious."

Before Chan moved in with her dad, music was still a private pleasure and solace giver, but living with him corrupted the purity of her connection to writing and singing songs. It was also the beginning of her lifelong inferiority complex regarding her skills as a musician. "When he was gone I'd always play it to prove that this thing isn't so powerful. It's just a piano. It's supposed to be messed with, and there's no right or wrong," Chan has said. "That maybe created my rebellion to not learn to play."

Chan's father says he doesn't remember this. In fact, he has no memory of Chan writing songs or displaying any particular interest in playing instruments, but if she had, Charlie says, he would absolutely have encouraged her. "She never asked me about how to chord the guitar, so I never taught her how to play the guitar," he says. "Don't get me wrong, she loved music and she had her own little collections of music and everything, but she didn't seem interested in the instruments, not really." And if she had? "Well, I've always told the girls that these instruments are professional instruments, they're not to be played with. If they were abusing them, that was not allowed." Sensing that he might be coming across as cruel, he tells this story to clarify: "I got a little baby kitty. She loved to get into the piano. I hated cat hair in there, so one time when she got in the actual frame of the piano, I closed the front of it and I banged on it. I opened the lid and she jumped out. She never got back in."

Charlie Marshall wanted to be a rock star but ended up playing standards for tourists in cocktail lounges. The idea that his daughter had even the faintest desire, much less the necessary talent, to achieve what he couldn't troubled him. Chan is a born empathizer, always seeing the reason behind the mistake. She understood the source of her father's pain and accepted it even though it meant enduring his jealousy. "It was his dream. Since he was a little boy and he'd go tap-dance on people's porches in Alabama. He had very high expectations. He's a Capricorn. Very workaholic," she has said.

All these years later, Charlie's relationship with Chan exists, but the two are not close. Ever the dutiful daughter, Chan makes a point to invite her father to see her play when she's in Atlanta, and he'll usually come, accompanied by a date. But when he talks about those shows, there is an almost sociopathic lack of paternal pride in his voice. The primary thing Charlie sees when he watches his daughter onstage is that she has something he wants. "I was just blown away," Charlie says of a performance he saw at the Earl in Atlanta. "I mean, there's eighty-five, ninety kids, and they just sit right in the middle of the floor. She comes out onstage and you can hear a pin drop. The places I work, the people are eating and they're making so much noise. I said, 'God, it would be great to have this.'"

In spite of how Chan's complex and dark relationship with her father has played out over the years, her life has never been as normal as it was when she lived with him. "I really got my act together for a while and almost finished high school," the singer has remembered. "I told her that for each A she got, I'd give her fifty dollars," Charlie remembers. "Well, the first six weeks of the first semester, she had all A's and one B! Of course, that didn't continue, she was basically rehashing what she had done the year before. But a promise is a promise."

Chan blames pot smoking and her tendency to skip school for the fact that she flunked tenth grade and was forced to repeat it. "I went back. I did it over, and I made really good grades the next tenth grade," she remembers. Things were temporarily looking up. She had righted herself at school, was living a semistable life with her father, and was looking toward possibly graduating high school and getting one step closer to the legitimate, conventional life she desired. Then Charlie pulled the rug out from under her once again. "In the middle of eleventh grade, my dad kicked me out of the house because he went to live with his girlfriend," Chan has remembered. "He said that I could work and go to school."

A handful of credits shy of graduation, Chan found herself alone with no money, no parental support, and no place to live. It's hard to understand how any father could justify this choice, but Charlie has an explanation. "They had a curfew—they had to be home by twelve o'clock," he recalls in a calm, measured voice. "About three times in a row they didn't come home on time, so I told them that they were going to have to move out." Charlie believes this was the right decision. "They were a little bit upset at first, but then they realized that they were on their own. They were free. As a parent sometimes you have to do what's best."

Even after her father threw her out, effectively demolishing Chan's chance to graduate from high school, the singer still felt a stubborn sense of loyalty to her dad. "I was so angry at him, but I protected him so much," she has remembered. In a way, this move was nothing new. Charlie never seemed to be a reliable presence in Chan's life, even when she was a little girl. For all of Myra's faults, she stuck around to raise her children. Charlie seemed to operate as if parenthood was a hobby, one you could take up in your downtime and drop when things got too hard. When Charlie kicked Chan out of his house, it only reinforced what her childhood had already taught her about herself: namely, that she was worthless. "I was kind of shocked," Chan has said of her dad's decision. "But I was like, Who gives a fuck? I'm not gonna be anybody anyway."

7.

Cabbagetown

In 1881, construction began on the Fulton Bag and Cotton Mills, a factory located near the railroad tracks in east Atlanta. Heading into the turn of the century, textile production in the South emerged as a major industry and the mill expanded several times, bringing in workers, including Chan's great-great-grandparents, from South Georgia and the Appalachian mountains to live and work there. The insular neighborhood that was built to house them became known as Cabbagetown. "It got the name because you could smell the cabbage cooking," Leamon says. "That was all they could afford."

After World War II, changes in the business rendered the mill's products increasingly obsolete, but the majority of its workers stayed in Cabbagetown until the mill finally closed for good in 1977. Afterward, most of the workers scattered in search of new work, while those who stayed watched Cabbagetown fall into disrepair. In the 1980s and 1990s, a loose-knit community of backwater punks, painters, sculptors, drug dealers, drug doers, and musicians like Chan took refuge in this curious little neighborhood of modest two-story shotgun homes sitting side by side on narrow, uneven streets. These artists sought the same stability and willful isolation that mill families enjoyed one hundred years prior.

Cabbagetown's geography reinforces the sense of remoteness prized by those who live there. Railroad tracks separate the neighborhood from the leafy neighborhood of Inman Park to the north. South of Cabbagetown is East Atlanta, a formerly rough neighborhood where much of the city's recent music renaissance is taking place; to the west is Oakland Cemetery, and to the south is Grant Park. Even now there is a discernible sensory shift that takes place when you cross underneath the graffiti-decorated Krog Street Bridge and move south from the grand Victorians and established suburban splendor of Inman Park, under the railroad tracks, and into Cabbagetown. The air becomes thicker and more stagnant. The delicate camellia roses smell sweeter. The cicadas are louder on a summer night. The elms seem taller, their roots deeper, the expanse of their branches wider and more stately. Local women sip coffee and stop to gossip with each other on the way to get the mail. A young man takes off his T-shirt to hose off his balcony revealing intricate, almost refined full-body tattoos. Children languidly ride their bikes around the narrow, shady streets, their calls to one another drowned out by that thick, still air as they race each other up the small hilly alley that connects Cameron Street to Berean Avenue, the very street where Chan's great-grandparents made their home, and where Chan would live, decades later, in the late nineties.

Olivier Alary, the French musician who performs under the name Ensemble and who recorded the song "Disown, Delete" with Chan at Zero Return Studio in Atlanta, remembers Chan giving him a tour through Cabbagetown. "This old lady that had no teeth had this really angry dog that was swinging on the rocking chair," Alary remembers. "She kept saying, 'He's a bad dog!' It really felt like we were stuck in two centuries ago. Really flowery and really dirty. We saw a dog attached with a rope, not a leash, and he had two really trashy white kids playing in mud. It reeked of poverty."

There's a deep, cultural richness to Cabbagetown that makes outsiders feel distinctly foreign. You don't know this place. It's not that people are unfriendly. They will politely rise up out of their rocking chairs to give you thoughtful directions if you ask, they will talk to you about their personal histories, they will tell you how they first found themselves in this little pocket of bohemia, but they aren't going to think about you again once you're on your way: The residents of Cabbagetown are emotionally, creatively, and spiritually self-sufficient. In many ways, the Cabbagetown art scene that embraced Chan when she moved out of her dad's place was a real-world incarnation of the elusive countercultural nirvana the singer's parents idealized and longed for but failed to achieve. For Chan, coming to Cabbagetown was like finally coming home.

In 1991, by the time Chan moved out of her father's house and started her life in Atlanta, Cabbagetown had a real rock scene going. Bands like the Jody Grind, DQE (Dairy Queen Empire), and Magic Bone were rehearsing in backyards and playing shows in abandoned storefronts. These groups had little in common in terms of their sound, but they shared a sense of disenfranchisement from the mainstream music scene and the desire to live and work somewhere cheap and weird. Like Berlin in the 1970s, Brooklyn in the 1990s, or Montreal in the 2000s, the combination of affordable housing, good, cheap drugs, and a sense of brotherhood in debauchery brought the squat artists to Cabbagetown where they happily subsisted on ramen and Camels in exchange for inspiration and a place to shoot up, get laid, or sleep it off.

The Cabbagetown scene's unofficial vanguard was Benjamin Smoke, a flamboyantly gay poet and musician from rural Georgia who fronted two of the era's most significant bands, the Opal Foxx Quartet and Smoke. As potent as Benjamin's musical contribution to the scene was, his influence as a personality was almost more significant. He was a totally mesmerizing diva with a bawdy, deranged sense of humor, a sweet disposition, and a gift for inspiring others to act on their baser instincts. He was the undisputed queen of Cabbagetown, and he significantly influenced the other musicians and artists living and working in Atlanta in the late eighties and early nineties, including Chan.

Bill Taft, a veteran of the Atlanta rock scene since 1982, when he first moved to the city from Ohio, remembers the first time he saw Benjamin perform, right before he joined the lineup that was to become Benjamin's first brilliant band, the Opal Foxx Quartet. "Benjamin was playing at the Little Five Points Pub, and I got to hear him one night," Taft remembers. "It was the greatest, most wonderful thing I'd ever heard. It was hilarious, it was tragic, it was old-timey post-post-modern, just the strangest contradictions and juxtapositions. It was this punk-rock-showtune-cabaret-mindfuck. So I said, 'You need a guitar player, I'll play guitar with you.' "

Chan arrived in Atlanta with her spirit broken. After a childhood spent shape-shifting to suit a new town, a new school, a new incarnation of her mother's disease, Chan finally pulled her life together and made good grades at the same school for an entire year, all to be tossed out of her father's house on a whim. She thought very little of her prospects and even less of herself. If Chan had moved to New York City at nineteen, she would have been lost for good. She didn't have enough faith in herself at that point to survive in a place that measures success based on quantifiable accomplishment. The singer needed to live somewhere low-key, where people were being creative out of a sense of inspiration rather than duty. She needed to be somewhere where making music was an option, not an obligation. Chan needed Cabbagetown.

Just as she would later with the East Village and the Lower East Side of New York, both gloriously derelict and inspired places back in the nineties, Chan managed to catch Cabbagetown in its cultural sweet spot, after most of the scary drug dealers moved out but before the espresso drinkers moved in.

In the new millennium, Cabbagetown has exploded into a relatively expensive, gentrified enclave of well-to-do artists and professional people. Judy Ibbotson, a petite, gentle woman with a messy ponytail and the tough, tanned skin of a sun-worshipper, was Chan's landlord in the late 1990s. Today the old mill where Chan's great-grandparents worked has been turned into posh condos with enviably high ceilings, but in 1989, when Ibbotson moved to Cabbagetown, the neighborhood was still scary in a poetic way. It was the "home of go-carts and kids who go to jail early and whose parents use inhalants," Benjamin Smoke once said.

When the hillbillies moved out of Cabbagetown, they left their instruments for the young artists moving in. The most important bands to come out of the Cabbagetown music scene embodied a modern punk-rock ethos but conveyed a resounding sense of kinship with those who inhabited the neighborhood before them. "Everyone was in love with Burroughs and this sense of art and making something greater than four dumb drunk guys playing rock 'n' roll," local writer and promoter Henry Owings remembers. "Bringing in things like cellos and violins. And stripping things down, building things up, bringing in a horn, bringing in a harp. Making things that were more of a throwback to what this community was like in the twenties and thirties."

The apartment Ibbotson rented to Chan for $200 now goes for up-wards of $700. The house is a run-down, pale-yellow, glorified shack set close to the road, with porches both upstairs and downstairs. Out back there's a hilly backyard overgrown with bindweed, the delicate white flowers of balloon vine, and a giant oak tree that supports an unstable-looking tree house. Chan lived on the ground floor and used to appear barefoot on the porch on summer afternoons with a big box of Popsicles under her arm. Like the den mother of the neighborhood, she would pass out the frozen treats to the collection of scruffy kids who rode their bikes in an endless loop around the narrow streets.

"When we were living next door to each other, I kept seeing her out-side giving little riff-raff kids in Cabbagetown candy," Loring Kemp re-members. "The Cabbagetown kids were little badasses that were just mean, and she's like the pied piper! I would look out the window at eight o'clock in the morning and she'd be standing there with a line of kids. I always thought that part of the struggle she was having onstage and per-forming is that there's a big part of her that wants to be settled and wants to have a family, wants to be a housewife. She has goals in her personal life that don't agree with what she does professionally."

"Cabbagetown is now a shadow of what it was," laments Henry Owings, who has been living in Atlanta since 1997 and publishes the eviscerating music and culture magazine *Chunklet*. "Real estate prices rising and uptight gay couples coming in, and some would say improving, but I would say they ruin the character of Cabbagetown. It's really depressing because at one time it was everything to me. You just always knew that [in Cabbagetown] you're around your brethren, you're around your constituency. And they were weirdoes, too. When gentrification happened, all the weirdoes just kind of scattered. That sense of community, that specialness, is gone."

With Granny Lil's devotion to gospel, Leamon's taste in classic rock, Myra's worship of British-invasion music, and Charlie's love for the blues, Chan's musical roots were already deep by the time she started living on her own—but the singer's move to Cabbagetown solidified her connection with the sounds of the old South. In Cabbagetown Chan was surrounded by other people who were drawn to Americana and whose art reflected a modern interpretation of it. Chan fit in right away. Bill Taft remembers meeting Chan through her then-roommate Robert Hayes, who was Taft's bandmate at the time. "I was playing in a band called the Jody Grind—Robert Hayes was the bass player, Kelly Hogan was the singer," Taft remembers. "Kelly and I are practicing with Robert, Robert needs a place to stay, he gets a row house next to Kelly. Then Chan needs a place to stay, so Chan is living with Robert, and from there it just kind of went on." Chan became close with the Jody Grind, began going to shows at the Unicorn, the Little Five Points Pub, and Dottie's, and absorbed the scene's relaxed but dedicated music-making ethic.

When she first arrived in Atlanta Chan gravitated immediately toward artists, but it would take her years before she'd actually admit that she too wanted to make a living through art. "She obviously comes from a musical family," recalls Loring Kemp. "But I don't recall that she had any ambitions to become a songwriter or a singer." Instead Chan concentrated on getting her bearings. Paying rent, paying bills, having enough money to eat, getting creative about how to survive without a vocation, a high school diploma, or any family support: Those were her priorities. "She's very independent," Lenny says with pride. "She was always very independent. Working, thinking, having her own ideas."

By the time she was nearing twenty years old, Chan had come into her own. She was still a consummate tomboy, but she had traded in her Doc Martens for quirky, androgynously sexy men's shoes, and her short hair showed off her freckles and increasingly defined, postadolescent features. Chan still shopped at the Salvation Army for used Levi's, but she developed a more tactile relationship with her physical appearance, experimenting with makeup and cutting up clothes to suit a vision she had in her head.

Chan's first job in Atlanta was as a dishwasher at Fellini's Pizza, the unofficial day-job provider for the city's would-be rock stars. "I worked at Fellini's Pizza for three years, six days a week," Chan has said. "I learned how to make pizzas by watching the guys do it, and I always wanted to make it. One time they let me, and it was really inspiring." Fellini's is now a thriving local chain that employs well-scrubbed high school kids in mall-punk attire, but when Chan was working there it was dingy, dank, and proudly seedy.

"Now you go into Fellini's and it's actually kinda fancy," Jeff Clark, editor of the Atlanta-based music monthly *Stomp and Stammer*, marvels. "Back in the day, you would go into the one in Little Five and there was all kinds of graffiti on the walls. It was filthy. It was a little hole-in-the-wall shack." The transformation Fellini's has undergone reflects the makeover Atlanta experienced in the last twenty years. "These places were really just very lo-fi, but as they've grown and expanded," Clark explains, "they make money. It's legit now. That's the way Atlanta has changed, too. Cabbagetown at the time was a very low-rent, run-down, forgotten neighborhood where a bunch of poor people lived."

For Chan, working at Fellini's was like going to indie-rock college, a trade school for how to play music and also a social club, because everybody in the local scene came through Fellini's for a slice. Kristi Cameron, an old friend of Chan's who is now a senior editor at *Metropolis* magazine in New York City, first met Chan when she was working behind the counter. "I walked into Fellini's with a friend of mine," Cameron recalls. "I don't know if it's possible for a person to be searingly friendly, but that's what Chan was." Cameron, who has a reserved demeanor, was taken aback by the undiluted warmth and open confidence emanating off this counter girl. "She was completely imprinted on me at that time. I can remember weird tiny details, like cat-eye eyeliner, and that she was wearing a white thermal-underwear T-shirt that she had cut into a tank top, and she had a kind of twenties bob with bangs. Chan is not forthcoming, but she's very intimate with other people immediately."

Fellini's (d)evolution from hole-in-the-wall dive to slick multi-outpost franchise means that the store's founder, Clay Harper, now leads a very nice life. One of the employees at Criminal Records, the local independent record shop down the block, suggests contacting the tattooed rocker turned mogul at his French chalet. Back in the early nineties, Harper was just another struggling musician, flitting from band to band, living paycheck to paycheck. Harper's music career peaked with the Coolies, a cheeky Atlanta-based group who in the eighties released *Dig?*, an album of all-Paul (Simon and Anka) covers. Harper found that his business acumen outweighed his musical talent, started a chain of punk-rock pizza joints, and hired other aspiring artists to man the registers and bake the pies.

"Just about every musician in the nineties and late eighties worked at Fellini's. It was like a requirement," explains Kemp. Fellini's was so grungy that one former employee and local rocker, who now works at Criminal Records, says that he dared eat only the cheese slices because he knew the guys who topped the pizzas—and was revolted by where their hands might have been. "She was in the right place, because everyone she worked with there had a difficult history," Clay Harper has said. "She had a lot of life and character. And she was good for business because she was also cute."

Chan started off as a dishwasher and quickly moved up front, where she served beer and slices and sweet-talked the customers. "The dynamic back then was that you had one girl running the cash register, and then had the guys making the pizza," Kemp remembers. "It was very 'keep the girls up front.' " This gig at the pizza store earned Chan her first fans, as word spread very quickly that there was a new, foxy girl working the register at the Fellini's in Little Five. Before Chan played a single note in public, before her lyrics altered the life of a single fan, before it ever occurred to her that music could be her future, Chan experienced her first brush with fame as the hot pizza slinger at Fellini's.

Eric Levin, the shy rock geek who founded Criminal Records, remembers dispatching his teenage clerk to Fellini's to see if Chan was working. "I would send Lillian down there to see if she was working before I would go down," Levin remembers over coffee at Aurora, the local java house next door to Criminal Records. At the time, Chan was a younger, more tomboyish, less glamorous version of the rock vixen she is today. She dressed in battered jeans and loose-fitting work shirts, wore her hair short, and had the cherubic flushed cheeks of a teenager, but the singer was already a heartbreaker. "At that point you know when somebody's out of your league," Levin says, blushing. "She was the complete . . . like, 'Oh my God, she's the girl at Fellini's Pizza.' She was out of everybody's league." Even in her late teens, her ears ringing with the sound of her mother degrading her femininity, Chan was already aware of her power over men.

Levin was a hard-core Fellini's enthusiast. In fact, it was thanks to the pizza joint that he moved to Atlanta from Daytona, Florida, in the first place. "Daytona was a culturally bereft tourist town," Levin explains. "I came up here. I'd never been. The first weekend that I visited, I ended up at that pizza place at about two in the morning and they were playing Sonic Youth really loud. In my experience, the only place you would hear Sonic Youth loud was in my car or in my bedroom. It was really a cultural shock. I moved up two weeks later." Kemp, Chan's friend from high school who also worked at Fellini's, remembers the job as an excuse to play your favorite records all day and hang out with your friends. "We got free rein," she remembers. "During the day shift it was dead. It was bums coming in with one hundred pennies to get a slice." Chan knew more about the blues and old soul than any of her friends, but she'd never been exposed to the do-it-yourself indie-rock ethos that her fellow Fellini's employees and the bands they loved represented.

Working at Fellini's was fun. Chan and her sister lived in an apartment nearby in Little Five Points, and Chan was able to walk to work. "She loved Little Five Points," Lenny recalls. "I'd go to Fellini's. She worked in California Pizza Kitchen too." At work Chan hung out with affably grungy dudes, charmed the customers, and socialized with the local punks and degenerates who lived on the restaurant's famous dollar slices. Once Chan was comfortable at work (and had heard enough Sonic

Youth, Big Black, and early Pavement records to develop a thing for indie rock), she started to attend her coworkers' gigs. She soon realized that her father's approach to living and working as a musician wasn't the only way to go about it. Some of her new friends were trained musicians, but most were like Benjamin, proudly unschooled. Benjamin's philosophy, which he imparted to Chan, was the polar opposite of Charlie Marshall's. "Just because I couldn't play or sing didn't mean I couldn't be in a band," Benjamin once said.

Through these new friends, Chan started to view the life of a professional musician as respectable. She admired her friends' dedication to playing music: They may have been self-taught, but they worked at it like they deserved to play, like they loved to play. A local Atlanta band might play two shows a night, work on melodies or lyrics while baking pizzas during the day, then do it all again the next evening. The more time Chan spent with her rocker coworkers, the more conceivable writing and recording her own music started to seem. "My friends would be like, 'Let's play music,' but I really didn't know how to play," Chan has remembered. "We'd jam drunk, in the living room, like people do. It was fun. It didn't mean anything and it didn't make any sense, but that was perfect."

In 1992, after living and working in Atlanta for more than two years, Chan purchased a used Silvertone guitar from her friend Flat Duo Jets frontman Dexter Romweber. It came with an amp, which could have been useful if Chan ever picked up the instrument. Instead she used the instrument "like a vase or a plant," she has said. "It'd just sit in my corner like, Oh, it looks really great," she remembers. "Then I'd call my friend or go to work. I didn't feel like it was me to play music." For an entire year the beautiful guitar sat in a corner. Eventually Chan picked it up and plucked at it for a few minutes, humming a little before promptly returning it to its spot in the corner. Gradually the few minutes that she spent tinkering turned into hours, and before long she had written a handful of songs.

Living out on her own and working at Fellini's gave Chan confidence. Soon she even mustered up the courage to play some of her songs for her father. "I had no idea she was even getting into music until she sent me something," Charlie remembers. "She was always scribbling on papers, and Miranda and Chan were always playing their music and singing to' gether, but I never knew that she was writing songs." Charlie reacted to his daughter's guitar playing by telling her to get better at it. "I said, 'If you really want to develop as a guitar player, you need to learn to chord and to pick with an acoustic,' " Charlie recalls. After giving her this minilecture about the value of professional musicianship, Charlie handed his daughter a Takamine (sometimes called a "baby guitar") that had been sitting in his music room for six months and that he thought Chan would find easier to write on than the grown-up Silvertone she was toting around. "I said, 'This is such an excellent way to write, because you can take it anywhere.' " Chan gave the guitar away.

One of the first people who ever heard Chan's original songs was Jody Grind bass player Robert Hayes, who worked with Chan at Fellini's. Hayes needed a roommate, so Chan moved into his place in Cabbagetown, which meant that he was around anytime she felt brave enough to play for someone besides her plants. Hayes was intrigued by his roommate's songwriting style, but immediately noticed her debili' tating shyness. "I remember Robert saying, 'Well, Chan wants to be a singer,' or, 'Chan wants to write songs,' but there was something very hesitant about her playing," Bill Taft recalls. At this point Chan's music sounded a lot like the early Cat Power recordings, particularly the "Headlights" single and *Dear Sir* (out in 1995). The tracks were very elemental, featuring just a few simple chords and a repetitive, almost droning lyrical refrain. Chan would play these songs sitting in a chair with her body folded over the instrument and her gaze fixed firmly on the old man's dress shoes on her feet.

"Robert would describe it as, 'Well, Chan sang another one of her songs,' " Taft remembers, laughing. " 'She set up in the kitchen and I had to stand in the living room, she wouldn't let me be in the room with her. I thought it was pretty good, then she just put down her guitar and went for a walk.' " Chan's spare near-dirges were performed in a sort of trance, as if the singer were channeling the woes of generations. By comparison to this early material, *Myra Lee*, Cat Power's second album (which contains such uplifting tracks as "We All Die"), seems sunny. To everyone who heard Chan play, it was clear that this girl had a singular voice and that she wrote remarkable songs—but since she initially wouldn't play outside the confines of her kitchen, it took time before Chan found herself in a position to work constructively on honing her skills as a songwriter.

Even at the precipice of Chan Marshall's career, when she was playing songs for an audience that consisted of her roomate and a couple of alley cats, the singer wasn't sure she wanted to be there. "I always felt like, 'Me? No.' It always felt pretentious," she said later. After enough time spent tinkering with her guitar on her own, and a few silly, drunken jam sessions with her Fellini's friends, Chan became slightly less horrified by the notion of playing music in public. But as her initial hang-ups faded, new ones took their place. "All my friends were in bands, but none of them were girls," the singer has remembered.

Grace Braun, frontwoman of the rootsy punk cult band DQE, describes the marginalization that came with being the chick in an Atlanta rock band. "It's hard to be the girl that's at the front of the stage because there are expectations," Braun explains. "She's a girl. She's gonna sing all soft and pretty and quiet, we can turn her all the way down. She won't be able to play guitar. She's a girl, so we'll just turn her guitar down in the mix. It's not just me, it's a lot of women in the city."

In spite of her chronic shyness, deep-set insecurities, and the fact that she was female, Chan persevered and started playing regular gigs with a couple of friends. Her first real bandmate was drummer Glen Thrasher, a local musician, tastemaker, and founder of the influential *Destroy All Music* fanzine. Benjamin Smoke inspired Chan to shrug off her father's rules about music, but it was Glen who really showed her how to defy them. "He was my mentor," Chan has said of Thrasher. "He looked out for me and protected me and told me things about life and he liked me and respected me not sexually. I really looked up to that."

Thrasher's laid-back but serious approach to musicmaking eased the paralyzing effects of Charlie Marshall's influence; with Glen in her corner, Chan began to see performing as requiring neither the formal training she felt ashamed of not having nor the desire to be a famous rock star, which she found distasteful. "He didn't know how to play drums, but he'd play," Chan explained. "It encouraged me because I didn't know how to play. With the other boys there was a real agenda to have a band, and it was almost embarrassing to me. It seemed so small-minded to me. Like, ugh, how obvious, how corny. So we'd just make sounds."

With the confidence honed through practicing with Glen, Chan quickly added a few more players to her makeshift band including guitarists Mark Moore and Damon Moore (who are not related). With a couple of gigs booked for this yet-unnamed group, Mark Moore called up Chan at Fellini's and demanded that she, as the lead singer and frontwoman of this casual collection of players, come up with something. "There was a line of people," Chan has recalled. "Mark was yellin', 'We need a name!' This old man came in wearing a Cat Diesel Power cap. I was like, 'Cat Power!' and hung up the phone." That was it. Cat Power was born.

The name made absolutely no sense. First of all, Chan is a dog person. (Her chronic allergies kept her from having pets as a child, but she now has a French bulldog named Mona.) Secondly, the phrase "Cat Power" is conventionally associated with CAT, the logo and abbreviation for Caterpillar farm machinery. CAT POWER is displayed prominently, in all its yellow-and-black glory, on T-shirts and trucker caps (like the one worn by the Fellini's customer) advertising the company's tractors, bull-dozers, and other machines. "Cat Power" represents hard labor, dirty fingernails, greasy-spoon diners at truck stops, long nights on the road, burlap, flannel shirts, dusty back roads, horse feed. It means early morn-ings, calloused hands, sweat, the smell of hay, Wrangler jeans, and coun-try music. The name seemed impossibly ill suited to the enigmatic, fragile songstress with the dark soul who selected it.

Chan has since said she regrets naming her band so impulsively. "I didn't think about it," Chan has said. "I never thought that this would be what I would be doing." In fact, Chan says, she chose the name Cat Power out of defiance at being bossed around by her bandmates. "The guys said, 'You're the lead singer.' 'Why am I the lead singer?' 'Because you're the girl,' " Chan has remembered. "I was so angry that I was just kidding [about suggesting the name], kind of like, 'Fuck you.' But I wish I'd actually thought about it, because it doesn't mean anything."

In hindsight the name seems uncannily apt; it's intriguing but reveals almost nothing about the artist behind it, which is perfect for a woman who wants to hide in the public eye. Cat Power has been both a straight-up blues-rock group and a willfully weird chick folk singer; it's been a Memphis soul revue and an austere guitar group. Even the name's gritty association with farm machinery, which initially seemed so in-congruous with the ethereal elegies Chan was writing, now feels like a necessary representation of this sleek Chanel model's workingman past.

8.

We Formed a Band

After a few rotating lineup changes, Cat Power became a trio with Mark Moore on guitar, Glen Thrasher on drums, and Chan on vocals. Though Chan was close with Moore (they allegedly dated for a while), it was her continued friendship with Thrasher that propelled the band forward. Thrasher, a slight, pale, spectacle-wearing rock boy, was one of the most influential people in Atlanta's music scene and vital to Chan's development as a singer and songwriter.

His role as a local guru has largely passed, but Thrasher still acts as if he's behind an intellectual velvet rope. Numerous attempts were made to interview him for this book, and though he would respond to e-mails and suggest he might talk, Thrasher mostly just explained why I wasn't qualified to speak to him or write about Chan.

"Glen is a piece of work," Henry Owings, *Chunklet* founder and long-time Atlanta scenester says, shaking his head. "He's kind of a throwback to that total weird agro artsy-fartsy confrontational asshole grating dick in Cabbagetown: For every real polite person like Ben from Smoke, there's a Glen Thrasher, where it'd be like, 'Wow. You're a fucking dick.' "

It's unfortunate that Glen's bitterness has become so deep-seated, because his accomplishments are impressive. He grew up in Atlanta and began venturing into the city's derelict neighborhoods when he was a teenager, seeking out new music, new art, new material for *Lowlife*, the zine he published from 1984 to 1992. Gerard Cosloy, Matador Records cofounder and the man who would eventually sign Chan, admired Thrasher's writing and first read about Cat Power in an issue of *Lowlife*. During the 1980s, Glen also cohosted an experimental radio show, *Destroy All Music*, that featured expertly selected sets showcasing the local bands that were Cat Power's forebears.

Thrasher put on annual debauchery-filled *Destroy All Music* festivals, which allowed the bands he promoted on air to get together and play live. The gleefully chaotic, performance-art-meets-rock shows he hosted inspired many of the artists who shaped the Atlanta music scene in the 1990s. "Destroy All Music was three or four nights of noise improvisers, and punk-folk groups would play," Bill Taft, who played in both of Benjamin Smoke's bands as well as other local influential groups like the Jody Grind, remembers. "They'd sing their songs, they'd roll around on the floor, all their instruments were covered in fur, they'd eat glass—they wouldn't eat glass, but it was like that. None of their songs had verses or choruses, and they were all very focused moments of emotion, very intense dirges. It exorcised demons."

Glen Thrasher had an uncommonly refined ear for scouting exceptional musicians like Chan, as well as the organizational skills to unite a handful of disparate groups into a genuine musical movement. "I really can't stress enough that Glen is very modest," says Grace Braun, whom he also nurtured. "He can be quite curmudgeonly when he feels like it but unlike some people in the city, I've never heard him stand up and say, 'I did this and I made this person and I am the reason why they are famous.' "

"The first time I saw her she had Glen Thrasher playing drums, which is basically how she started out—it was just her and him," Jeff Clark of *Stomp and Stammer* remembers. "She had just been playing a very short time, a matter of months. It was in the basement of the Dark Horse Tavern." The Dark Horse Tavern used to host Brunch That Hurts, a series of comically debauched events featuring hangover-curing cocktails and lots of local rock bands. "Everybody would play around two P.M.," remembers Kemp. "Everybody was hungover, and whoever kinda showed up to play, played. There were people who showed up there who hadn't been to sleep."

These early Cat Power sets consisted of a mixture of the spare anti-songs Marshall had been writing on her Silvertone, plus a collection of covers—mostly old blues standards and songs by Bob Dylan. "She didn't really play that many shows before she left, but she'd gotten a lot of good press, and everyone started talking about Cat Power and Chan and how cool it was," Clark remembers. "There was nobody else doing anything like what Chan was doing."

Though Cat Power was jockeying for position amid a sea of other respected local bands, it's worth mentioning that with the exception of the Rock*A*Teens, who had a record deal with Merge and were somewhat known outside the Atlanta area, none of the major Cabbagetown rockers ever made it. The entire scene existed in a vacuum, with all the breakups, make-ups, and rises and falls in favor noticed only by those who were directly involved. "The Cabbagetown scene was more about being a freak on drugs, being an artiste smoke-and-mirrors jazz heroin freak something-or-another," says another Southerner, Charles Aaron. "Playing music was only a small part of whatever your personal transformative performance and your freak-outsider persona is. The music produced out of that was very much of its time."

Cat Power was one of the most interesting bands playing in Atlanta in the early 1990s, but Chan didn't serve as an emissary for the entire Atlanta music scene. In fact, though Cat Power earned a decent following before moving to New York in 1992, those outside of the Cabbagetown family (and probably some of those within it) had not made up their minds about Chan's talent by the time she left. To some she was still just the cute girl from Fellini's. "I remember buying the first single and then going to see her at the Atomic or the Shoebox in Athens in 1994," Owings remembers. "It just didn't leave an impression. Shortly after that, [Sonic Youth drummer and Cat Power advocate Steve Shelley] put out [Cat Power's second album] Myra Lee. I remember listening to it and I was like, I think this is great. But then she played here and in Athens all the time, and it never connected."

Before the legendarily unhinged Cat Power shows began in the late

1990s, Chan was already exhibiting unusual behavior onstage, and her fellow Atlantans didn't know what to make of it. "I went to the Earl, and I paid my ten dollars," local journalist Chad Radford remembers of his first Cat Power show. "The place was packed with people sitting on the floor Indian style. She starts a song, and then stops. Then she starts playing again, and while she's playing, she starts crying. I'm just like, what the fuck's this? She's like, 'I'm so sorry you people came to see me play, and paid all this money.' " Chad was horrified by the nonperformance he was seeing from this heavily hyped local artist. "I'm just like, 'Are you kidding me?' " he remembers. "People in the audience were like, 'You can do it!' And I'm like, 'God, what the hell did I just walk into?' I stayed for about ten songs before I got so frustrated I just got up and walked out. I was just thinking and thinking and thinking about how terrible it was, but then it dawned on me that any artist that could make a person react so strongly has really created something special. If you can piss somebody off so much that they're going to storm out, you've done a good thing. That's punk rock!"

For someone like Owings, a promoter and well-versed rock geek with a low tolerance for bullshit, even before Chan started getting famous, Cat Power's shows seemed maddeningly disconnected from the recorded music. "She would just be onstage, doubled over with her hair in her face, mumbling songs," Owings remembers. The *Chunklet* founder's love affair with Southern culture has been long and passionate, but he was never a Cabbagetown insider, and as such he was not part of the built-in musical family Chan felt close to. Around Owings and other nonintimates, Chan displayed a pathological shyness that her Fellini's coworkers and bandmates didn't see. "She was always sort of insecure, shy," Owings remembers. "Any time you would ever talk to her, it would either end in her crying or walking off and then crying. When I first moved to town, I was putting on a show at Under the Couch and she came to it. I was with [journalist and Chan's friend] Steve Dollar and I said something. I say a lot of semicrass things, but I mean them in the most respectful, friendly, jovial way. I was fucking with her in this way and I remember her tearing up and then walking away. She wasn't even performing. I mean, we were just talking."

Over the years, when Cat Power would come back to Atlanta to play, Chan drew a wide audience of interested music fans, many of whom never heard her perform during her Cabbagetown days and were curious about what they had been missing. "The first time I saw her was opening for Liz Phair at the Center Stage Theater," Steve Dollar, who works as a journalist, remembers. "I hadn't even heard about her. I just remember it being really, you know, offbeat, and people not digging it too much. There was a whole disjunction between a certain buzz about her that was completely not matching up with her performance." Dollar has a reputation among his friends for dragging people to shows they later regret paying for, and his first Cat Power gig was a perfect example. Everyone he brought with him was pissed off by the end of the show.

As Cat Power became more successful, it would have been understandable if some of the musicians Chan left behind resented her for breaking free. In the eyes of Chan's hometown peers, other bands were equally if not more worthy of fame and glory. "All of us thought, 'We're gonna be genius millionaires traveling the world, playing music,' " Bill Taft, who played in almost every important Cabbagetown band besides Cat Power, remembers. "She was right up there, she was like us. It was just like, There's Benjamin, there's Chan, you know, There's Kelly [Hogan], there's Grace [Braun] and DQE. So for me the question is not so much, Why is Chan so successful? but Why isn't Grace? Or Glen?"

In spite of the fact that Cat Power was the only commercial success to emerge from the Cabbagetown scene, Chan is mostly adored by her old friends from home, and even those who didn't know her personally respect her for maintaining her roots and not projecting haughty attitude when she comes back to town. "That's what's so fascinating to me about her," Kemp explains. "There were a lot of people that really struggled musically here and that wanted to do more, but you don't find the kind of resentment that you find with the Black Crowes, for instance. You just don't come across people who have anything bad to say about her. That cannot be said for the few that made it out of Atlanta." Jeff Clark of *Stomp and Stammer* agrees. "Everyone was always very proud and happy for her. There was not any hometown resentment. When she comes back to town she always hangs out with her old friends. It's not like she's on any kind of star trip."

Chan has as much affection for her hometown as it has for her. After recording *Moon Pix* in the winter of 1998, the singer returned to Atlanta and rented an apartment, and later she bought the modest Cabbagetown home that she still owns and put it to good use entertaining old friends, letting her collection of nomadic new ones crash there, enjoying the closest thing to a real home she'd ever had. Kemp giggles remembering the time that Chan breezed into town, called everyone she knew, and demanded that they appear that evening at her place for an impromptu black-tie cocktail party. "She wanted all the girls to wear dresses and I kept telling her, 'I'm coming straight from work and I have jeans on,' " Kemp remembers, giggling. "She kept prank-calling me and telling me it was the telephone company."

The court jester in Chan first came alive in Atlanta. She was always a charmer, but as a kid she needed that charm to survive. It was in Atlanta that Chan first learned to enjoy the jovial side of her personality and to let her friends in on it as well. There are few people close to Chan who don't comment on how funny she is and on how starkly that side of her personality contrasts with her public image as the indie princess of darkness. In the 2000s, Chan has spent more time on the road or camped out in other cities than she has in Atlanta, but in many ways the singer has never really left the city of her birth. Even after she moved to Miami in 2003, Chan kept her house in Cabbagetown, and she always comes back, even if it's just for a day or two at a time.

Lots of her local friends remember a particularly wild, comedic Christmas party the singer held in 2005. "We got a frantic phone call from Chan," Taft remembers. "We *had* to come to her Christmas party in Cabbagetown, and I had to bring the children. So we go over there, and it's a great party. She spent an hour in her living room playing Frisbee with my daughter. It was totally fun and not at all, you know, 'I'm an artist and I don't have time for doing anything except being creative.' It was like a church social."

Tradition is important to Chan. She was born in Atlanta, she performed her first show in Atlanta, and she still considers the city, and Cabbagetown in particular, to be a kind of home. She comes back when she needs to remember herself. "I saw people that we went to high school with at that party," Kemp remembers. "There's something about the South that is so easy for her. Here in Atlanta, there's a comfort for her that can't be found anywhere else."

As deep as Chan's connection is to the South in general and to Atlanta in particular, something drove her to leave. Chan absolutely could have made a career as a musician in Atlanta. Everybody else she knew there did. Though some of her former bandmates, like Glen Thrasher, are no longer playing, the majority of the scene's key personalities are still making music. Rock*A*Teens frontman (and Chan's former boyfriend) Chris Lopez now plays in Tenement Halls with Bill Taft. Kelly Hogan is still releasing records as a solo artist, and Grace Braun is working on new music. They're all still playing music, but none of them has a modeling contract with Chanel or a condo on Miami Beach. For all her disgust at what Chan has called the "obvious" reality of starting a rock band and aiming for fame, there was something in her that propelled her to do exactly that, and to succeed at it where most of her peers failed.

"She's a product of this crazy little artist enclave and look at what it did to her," Aaron points out. "She's an enigma. She's got a look. Atlanta has always been like that. It's never been about the music necessarily. The only thing that ever came out of the Atlanta punk scene were the drag queens. There's never been a good Atlanta punk band, but there's been tons of great Atlanta drag queens. RuPaul. Lady Bunny. They all moved to New York. They were all weird personalities acting out, kitschy, druggy, weird. I sort of see her as someone who was a child of all that but was really savvy about turning it into a more conventional career. I look at her as a real weirdo, but also as someone who moved to New York and crafted this persona for herself, like a torch singer who came out of this freaky underworld."

Thrasher has said that the band moved to New York in September 1992 because "it seemed like the thing to do at the time." It was the thing to do. Though there was a staggering amount of great music happening in Atlanta, no one outside of the Cabbagetown scene seemed to know about it. "Everybody had the sense that nothing was gonna happen for them if they remained here in Atlanta," Kemp remembers, and Clark agrees, "By that point she had the idea that maybe she could do it, and moving to New York would be a step in the right direction." As obvious as it seems that moving was the only choice Chan had if she wanted to make something of Cat Power, ambition is not the reason she gives when asked why she left Atlanta. According to Chan, she left to get away from the drugs and the death. Benjamin Smoke was the scene's most notorious addict, but his drug of choice was speed. Everyone else was doing heroin.

Like every other major urban area in America in the 1990s, in Atlanta heroin was cheap, extremely high quality, and easy to get. Dollar, who lived and worked in Atlanta during the late eighties and early nineties, sums up the arrival of heroin on the scene this way: "People started dying." For all the ink that has been spilled discussing Chan and her myriad addictions, when she first started her career in music she was unequivocally antidrug. Between her dad's acid trips, her mom's heavy drinking, and the collection of strung-out musicians she saw sleeping it off on her family's couch, Chan was the last person who would fall for the idea that drug use was romantic, part of a larger bohemian life that led to the making of good art. And when her friends started dying, Chan's hatred of drug use intensified.

Damon Moore, who played in an early version of Cat Power, died of an overdose in 1996. Allen Page, the drummer from Dirt and Opal Foxx Quartet, was another prominent casualty. A few of Atlanta's most well-known addicts survived heroin and are now in recovery including Coleman Lewis, who played guitar in Smoke, and Glen Thrasher, Chan's mentor. "He was one of the biggest heroin addicts in Atlanta," Jeff Clark says, and Chan's friend Steve Dollar, then an Atlanta-area journalist, puts it even more succinctly: "I'm surprised he's still alive, he was this ghostlike figure." Watching her friends overdose and knowing her mentor could easily be next, it's no wonder Chan developed such a violent aversion to hard drug use.

Tim Foljahn, Chan's future band mate, remembers the singer talking about her aversion to drug use. "Even for those days, heroin had rolled through Atlanta and just decimated the whole hipster population," he recalls. "It took like fifty percent. It was just really heavy. Even if some of those people were just her acquaintances, she still knew a lot of people that had died. She was sick of it."

Even without the booze, heroin overdoses, speed, needle swapping, and HIV infection that came with it, Cabbagetown rockers were prone to tragic deaths. Deacon Lunchbox, Chan's roommate Robert Hayes, and Rob Clayton, the drummer in the Jody Grind, were all killed in a car accident in 1992. The trio was driving in a rented van in Montgomery, Alabama, when a drunk driver crossed the I-65 median and hit them head-on. "I think you're safer serving your country in Iraq than playing music," Taft surmises. "I'm amazed at the number of funerals I've been to over the years." Grace Braun agrees. "My friend Mary died recently," she says. "She was eighty, and I was like, 'This is the best funeral I've ever been to, because she died of old age.' " Clark points out that it's not just the loss of life, it's the fact that so many of the deceased were crucial figures. "There's been a few people over the years that have grown to be a centerpiece of the scene, and all of them end up dying—it's really weird."

All that death and loss disturbed Chan. She had grown up around similar types of self-destructive behavior and she didn't like it, so she decided to leave Atlanta. "Everyone started doin' heroin and becoming a junkie," Chan has said when asked why she left home. "I wanted to escape." As much emotional sense as this rationale makes, it's also a ludicrous argument. The last place you'd want to move to avoid heroin in the early 1990s would have been New York City. Glen himself made this point in a post on his blog. "I don't think the move had anything to do with drugs," the former drummer wrote. "Although I am sure Chan was not thrilled with all the drugs her friends in Atlanta were using at the time. If Chan wanted to move away from drugs, why would she move to New York?" Furthermore, why would she bring with her Glen Thrasher, who was one of Atlanta's most notorious heroin addicts? "It's odd that she would say she wanted to get away from drugs, then take Glen up to New York," Clark muses.

Drug use and death weren't all Chan was running from. In 1992, at the age of twenty, Chan got pregnant and had an abortion. She would have had a son. Though she had good reason for making this decision (no real place to live, no steady job, an uncertain relationship with the child's would-be father), the experience has haunted Chan ever since. "It's the biggest mistake I ever made," she has said more than a decade later. Then, around the same time Chan was dealing with the aftermath of the abortion and her friends' deaths, the singer's sister, Miranda, was diagnosed with schizophrenia.

"Oh, Lord, Mandy," Leamon exclaims. "All of a sudden she was dating this North Carolina boy named Dean. She went to California. Something happened. Three days later they found her wandering around the airport. Brought her back to North Carolina. She was hallucinating. Out of it. Seeing things. Pregnant. Went to the hospital and had the baby. Had a real tough time. Couldn't figure out—decided some guy she was hanging around with drugged her. She's had a tough time ever since."

Ironically, considering Chan's mom's lifelong resistance to treating her own disease, Myra was instrumental in getting Miranda the help she needed. Much as Granny Lil did for Myra when she needed help with her young children, Myra committed herself to taking care of Miranda and her newborn son, Ian. "My mom actually helped her get into treatment," Lenny remembers. "Mandy stayed with my mom. She had Ian and my mom helped raise him. I think my mom understood." "My oldest daughter, she actually takes the medication," Charlie says. "It tends to make you put on weight, is the problem. She would get off the medication because she'd say, 'Dad, I'm getting fat.' But if you have to take your mental health with twenty pounds extra, then you do."

Chan had many good reasons to leave Atlanta (friends' deaths, heightened drug use, the future of her career), but the best one was that she already knew what life awaited her if she stayed. Chan was not speaking to her mother. She had a residual blind devotion to her dad, but he had betrayed her when he threw her out of his house. She had just aborted a child and discovered that her maternal, reliable older sister had the same disease that plagued her mother. Her new family, the assortment of pizza slingers, record-store geeks, local writers, and fellow musicians she had befriended, already seemed tainted by the shadow of drugs and death. If she'd stayed in Atlanta, Chan would likely have ended up living an indie-rock version of the barefoot-and-pregnant cliché she desperately wanted to avoid. In what would become a pattern for Chan throughout her life, she looked at her circumstances, gathered strength she didn't even know she had, severed ties with almost everyone she knew as if she were amputating a gangrened limb, and moved away.

9.

New York, New York

When Chan arrived in New York City in the early fall of 1992, she added herself to the long and illustrious list of people drawn to New York in search of a new self. She settled into life on the Lower East Side, which was then a forgotten urban wasteland. The scene was dirtier than it is now. For example, those few locals whose buildings haven't yet been outfitted with sleek washers and driers use the Laundromat on Third Street between Avenues B and C. Back in 1992, when Chan moved to New York, the place was like a take-out joint for drugs, where you could openly buy ten-dollar packets of heroin and cocaine. In the early 1990s, Manhattan's Lower East Side was still a genuinely dangerous place where homeless people, drug dealers, and addicts mingled with an influx of artists willing to brave the crack-vial-and-syringe-littered streets and constant threat of muggings for the sake of cheap rent and space to create.

Downtown Manhattan's drug scene was so in sync with the art and indie-music world that the heroin sold at the Laundromat came in glassine bags stamped with pop-culturally literate, darkly witty brand names like Tango and Cash, Eyewitness News, and Bad Lieutenant. This irreverent smack was so much a part of the local culture that indie-rock godheads Pavement wrote a song about waiting in line to buy it. On "Mercy Snack: The Laundromat," the B-side to the signature Matador band's 1992 single "Summer Babe," frontman Stephen Malkmus sings: "I'm jonesin' for a mercy snack . . . I've been down to the Laundromat."

By the late 2000s the Lower East Side has become a well-scrubbed theme park for hipster culture. Rivington Street, the artery that runs from the Bowery all the way to the East River in New York's Lower East Side, now features Schiller's, a high-end (masquerading as elegantly low-end) French bistro often mentioned on Page Six, a handful of bars where you can buy a fifteen-dollar martini, and multiple vintage-clothing stores frequented by the Olsen twins. But Tim Foljahn, Chan's friend and former Cat Power guitarist, remembers the neighborhood differently. "There were guys selling drugs on every corner," Foljahn says, shaking his head at how long ago it seems. "You'd see people not just by the methadone clinics, but all over the Lower East Side at the cop spots. I remember being down the Lower East Side and seeing people getting chased by somebody with a knife. That stuff was just happening." Foljahn is particularly amused/horrified by the real estate terminology used to describe areas that in the early nineties were all considered universally desolate. "Where Café Gitane is: 'Nolita,' " the guitarist scoffs, making air quotes and referencing one of eastern Soho's sceneiest cafés (frequented by the likes of David Bowie and Iman). "That was like no-man's-land—there was stuff blowing down the street."

People like Chan who were drawn to New York by instinct, looking for other damaged but hopeful creative souls, mourn the loss of the feeling of promise and possibility that came with the neighborhood's wantonness. "I don't wanna say there's a lot of white people running around with Fendi bands and stuff," Chan has said of the changes she sees in her neighborhood. "It's like a college town. I'm not trying to put it down. But a lot of people came to New York not to go to school. A lot of people came here as survivalists. Misfits. Outsiders. Characters. Because they felt displaced in whatever small town they were living in. If you're a poet, you had like a congregation of hope."

Life was difficult for the aspiring artists that moved to Manhattan's Lower East Side and East Village neighborhoods in the early nineties. Rent was cheap. (A walk-up on Thirteenth and Avenue A used to cost $700 a month. Now the same awkwardly arranged series of almost-rooms rents for about $2,500.) Any jobs available were of the low-income, retail variety. Before Craigslist and the myriad online job sites we have now, the jobless used to line up in front of the newsstand on Astor Place waiting for the *Village Voice* to come out every Tuesday night, hoping to get first look at the classifieds. This scene—hipsters scouring actual, physical newsprint for information about housing or work—looked like a breadline in Russia, with rent-controlled hovels and bartending gigs being doled out instead of stale onion rolls.

Most scenesters worked several tedious gigs to pay for guitar strings, canvases, loft space, rice and beans, cigarettes, or drugs—whatever it was that they needed in order to get by. In exchange for engaging in this relentless, debilitating struggle, the LES masses received inspiration. Those who survived in the Lower East Side were rewarded with a powerful and useful sense of romance about their derelict lives. In the 1990s, struggle defined these kids, some of whom hid their privileged backgrounds and posh art-school educations in order to feel romantically used by the world and (ideally) make work reflecting that sensation. Everything from what to eat for dinner to how to get your clothes clean to how to pay the rent to how to create felt like a struggle, and struggle felt good.

Stewart Lupton, lead singer and songwriter in Jonathan Fire*Eater, the most inspired garage-rock band in New York during the mid-nineties, remembers meeting Chan during this time. When originally contacted via MySpace regarding a potential interview about Chan for this book, Stewart responded with a Byronesque poem in which he suggested that any interview be conducted over oysters and champagne, because that was "the common fare of the period." Stewart and Chan first met at one of the clubs, bars, and playhouses that dotted Ludlow Street before the investment bankers moved in. "All of the sudden, this girl was constantly apologizing to me and I didn't know why," the singer remembers. "I really wanted to forgive her for whatever she was apologizing for, so I did, and we became friends." Lupton, who is now performing with a new group, the Child Ballads, says that this era in downtown

New York City history still haunts him. "I have an abiding, puzzling love for that woman and those years," he mused. "A microcosm of its own. I feel like a part of me is still suspended in that petri dish."

For Chan, the notion of redemption through strife was deeply appealing. Her childhood had left her believing she was illegitimate, not literally but figuratively. She felt unworthy of love, unworthy of having money, unworthy of success or recognition. Hard work became the aspiring singer's welcome penance. "Chan was the hardest-working kid on the Lower East Side," Foljahn remembers. "Everybody else was pretty slack, but she was working three or four jobs at all times. Nobody ever had any money, but she did because she was working four jobs. She was always at work, and then going to shows when she wasn't at work." Chan remembers the life she first led in New York as difficult but rewarding. "It was hard to find a job," Chan remembered. "The economy was different. It was dirtier. A lot more drugs. A lot more homeless people. There was a struggle, but in that struggle you were forced to be amongst reality and see reality." The fight to survive instilled a sense of resiliency and competence in Chan, which she needed if she was ever going to break out and admit to herself and the world that she wanted to play music for a living. "The voices that come out during a period of struggle, they're remarkable. There's a fearlessness," Chan explained. "When I was younger, there was struggle. And that's when I started writing songs, 'cause I didn't have a job and I didn't know anybody."

Chan may not have known very many people when she first arrived in New York, but she was surrounded by other survivalists who were her philosophical soulmates even if she wasn't aware of them. In a pre-Internet world, entire relationships were built on a shared love of Pavement's *Trigger Cut* EP, or the fact that you'd seen each other more than once at the same ABC No Rio show, or that you tended to hit the

Odessa diner on Avenue A around the same time each afternoon for disco fries and coffee. The Lower East Side was a village in the same way that the West Village was in the 1960s. When gentrification hit in the early 2000s and the neighborhood became upscale so went the last place on Manhattan with any truly bohemian feel.

If you take the F train down to Second Avenue on a Saturday night, you can do a walking tour of places Chan frequented when she moved to the city. Max Fish, the Lower East Side's most storied dive bar, which had Cat Power's *What Would the Community Think* on the juke-box from its release in 1996 through much of the rest of the nineties, is still there. You can count on it for a cheap cocktail and decent music, but from Thursday through Saturday nights it's overrun by slick bridge-and-tunnel kids looking to channel a night in the life of a grimy urban hip-ster. The Pink Pony Café is still serving strong coffee, hangover-abating omelets, and hair-of-the-dog cocktails during the day, but the theater spaces and boarded-up storefronts that used to surround it on Ludlow Street have been replaced with boutiques, sleek, sterile clubs, and gour-met delis pimping New Zealand–lamb-and-mint-jelly sandwiches and Vitamin Water. Other downtown institutions like Katz's, Veselka (a sur-viving source of good borscht and pierogi), Lucy's, Holiday Bar, and Ni-agra still open their doors, but the community of misfits Chan knew has dissipated.

"If I had come here now, maybe I would have gotten a job at a trendy place. I'd have been a bartender. Life might have been easier," the singer has said. "Now the way New York is, you don't see those characters, you don't find that inspiration to survive in the struggle because you don't see other people surviving struggle. You see people already secure. You see younger people who have the fortune of coming from a family who can afford to pay NYU's tuition. When I come back here and see my old friends, we still go to the same places, they still have that history of reality that's getting paved over and repainted. That's life. Things change. I'll always love New York for what it stands for. I knew there were smart people who lived here. People who were artists. People who came from all over the world. It helped me."

10.

Survival

_____

Through a friend of a friend, Chan was able to sublet a room in a communal-style apartment house on Third Street owned by Seth Tobocman, a political activist known for publishing leftist radical comic World War III Illustrated.

Chan was paying about fifty dollars a month when she first moved in; almost twenty years later, she still rents the same room for a slightly increased rate. Chan's roommates were mostly political activists like Seth, and as a result the hallways of their shared living space were blanketed in pamphlets and flyers. "It was really just a room," Foljahn recalls. "The guy who owned the apartment was an old Red. He was an old rebel, old-school Lower East Side, and very cool. There was always propaganda-type stuff up on the walls." Foljahn remembers Chan's room as tiny but packed. "She had a little window," Foljahn remembers. "The room was stacked with books and records and suitcases and weird art. It was all kind of old-lady stuff."

After Chan got settled, she spent much of September and October walking around the city in her beat-up brown oxfords, wearing layers of men's flannel shirts to protect her against the biting fall air. "I had this romantic idea that I'd come to New York and be a baker," Chan has remembered. "I wasn't good at baking, but I kept passing a bakery on Mott Street and wishing I could work there—the flour, the silence, the smell. You get to be alone." Baking bread was one of the only jobs Chan didn't work in her first years in New York. She waited tables at a restaurant on First Avenue and First Street called the Levy, and she unloaded trucks in the Meatpacking District for twenty-five dollars a day. "The way that I had been living was potatoes and rice," Chan has said. "Or stealing cans of tuna from Key Foods." She also took a job organizing the apartment of a woman with obsessive-compulsive disorder. Days spent arranging things according to someone else's hyper-particular system appealed to Chan. "I used to be a maid for this woman," the singer remembered. "She had all these little pills and things in the right spaces. I love organizing."

At first Chan was focused purely on not starving. She lined up as much work as possible, paid her bills on time, spent her money sparingly, and kept her head down. After she had been in New York for a few months, she started to relax somewhat. On a rare day off, she would hit the Salvation Army and pick up a new work shirt or pair of used jeans. She would sit alone with an after-work beer at SoHo burger outpost Fanelli's on Prince Street. Slowly but surely it began to sink in that she was actually making it in New York City. "I was the first person in my family to ever leave the South," Chan has explained. "I thought, 'I went to New York, I could go to Europe!' None of my family had ever been."

Chan has a very generous, warm, and giving side. She's passed out keys to her New York and Atlanta homes to most of her friends in case they are in town and need a place to stay, and she loves giving people gifts, from trinkets she'd bring home from Australia or Japan for Judy Ibbotson's son to birthday and Christmas presents for all her friends. But at the same time, Chan is very protective of what's hers, an instinct honed through growing up poor. "She's tough, she's really tough," Foljahn says. "That's the thing that people don't realize. She's been through some really hard shit in her life, and she will survive. Whatever happened when she was coming up was gnarly shit, and she's got a real vicious—like, 'That's my bowl'—instinct, I've seen that. It can snap. She can get angry with someone if they're taking her shit, and then she'll turn around and give it to somebody else who doesn't have any."

As Chan became more comfortable in New York City, her thoughts returned to making music. She and Glen started attending rock shows and, just as she had done back in Atlanta, Chan let the onstage bravery of other performers serve as inspiration to her. Of the shows that Chan saw in her first few years in New York, experimental punk and free-jazz at the gloriously dilapidated club ABC No Rio on Rivington Street made the most significant impression. "The lights were superbright, and there was a naked girl and some guy beating metal," Chan has said of her first experience there. "It was so inspiring."

"She developed in that community in Cabbagetown," Charles Aaron says, "but she needed to be somewhere else. She needed to be in a musical community. It could have been Athens—someplace where there are a lot of great musicians and a lot of clubs, a lot of working people, a lot of people who are better than you." Inspiration and challenge are exactly what Chan found in New York City. Once again Chan was drawn to artists who displayed no attachment to conventional attitudes about performance. When she arrived in New York, Chan was battling the idea that making and playing music was off-limits, that it required skill and formal training she didn't have. The shows she saw with Glen during her first two years in New York helped chip away at that ideology.

"I come from rock 'n' roll—my dad's a musician, it's this whole thing," Chan has explained. "Seeing Anthony Braxton playing noise jazz excited me because there was no social projection. People would just sit there and sometimes they wouldn't even pay attention. I was like, 'Man, these people don't care what they're doing.' That was what originally stimulated me to play—just making stuff up and not knowing what you're doing and there's so much energy and you make a million mistakes, but it felt really exciting and strange and wrong."

Once her taste for seeing live music was renewed, Chan couldn't get enough. She saw shows at the old Knitting Factory on Houston and at venues Cat Power would later play like the Cooler on West Fourteenth Street and CBGB. "You ended up at CB's and CB's Gallery a lot," Tim Foljahn says. "Brownie's, the Mercury Lounge a little bit, there was the Pyramid, and the Continental Divide was happening." Foljahn has particularly good memories of the Meatpacking District's two-hundred-capacity venue the Cooler, which he describes as a "mainstay" throughout much of the 1990s. "It was an old meat locker, and when it started out it was really great," the guitarist remembers. "It was about half jazz bands, and you'd go in the back and there'd be a cooler full of beer and there'd be nuts—you had like a back room where you could be, and it was just so deluxe. Then, of course, the nuts went away and then the beer went away and everything just got coked up and weird, but it was always a good club."

Foljahn also remembers a certain lawless attitude about when and where performances took place on the Lower East Side. If you found a space that had enough power outlets to support a few amplifiers and enough room to hold a cramped trio and a few fans, you had yourself a venue. "People were doing shows in weird spots," Foljahn remembers. "I saw shows in Two Boots [Alphabet City's premiere pizza joint]." Foljahn remembers playing his first show as Two Dollar Guitar with Blonde Redhead at the Levy on First Avenue and First Street, where Chan worked when she first arrived in New York. "You could still get away with that 'Oh, we're going to start having bands now' attitude. People don't really do that anymore."

While Chan was absorbing the sounds of the city, she and Glen began playing shows as Cat Power. The first one took place at a warehouse in Brooklyn, which Gerard Cosloy, who would later sign Cat Power to Matador Records, attended. These early gigs were really bizarre, and willfully so. Chan wanted her performances to channel that same defiant antiperformance ethos that she so admired in the avant-garde artists she'd been following. At Cat Power's second show, a random saxophonist and a naked, screaming Japanese girl were also in the lineup. "It was inspiring because these people weren't judging you—maybe they weren't even listening," Chan remembered. "I knew I was naïve and I knew I didn't want people looking at me. Those experiences [seeing those shows], they helped me feel confident that maybe I didn't know what I was doing, but that didn't mean it was wrong."

Chan didn't know it at the time, but before she'd ever released her first Cat Power single, before she'd signed a record deal or entered a recording studio or been on tour or headlined a show, she had already converted one of Cat Power's most ardent and influential fans in Matador's cofounder. Cosloy first heard about Cat Power in Glen Thrasher's zine, Lowlife. Before Chan relocated to New York from Atlanta, Gerard and Glen developed a grudgingly respectful relationship based on their mutual involvement in fanzine culture. "I had a correspondence relationship with Glen," Cosloy recalls. "At first it was kind of adversarial, and then over time kind of more, 'Well, this is what you do, and this is what I do, and I kind of like what you do even though I wouldn't do it myself.' I got to know him that way and he moved to New York and I remember hearing from him that he moved here and that he had a band. And his band was called Cat Power. So I was instantly curious."

Cat Power's first New York show was held in a huge loft that doubled as the apartment of the label head's former bandmate Michael Pavlak. Gerard's then-girlfriend, Vicki Wheeler, booked all Bicycle shows—most of which were held at Michael's pad. "She put on a lot of good shows," Gerard remembers. "Many people who are today superduper famous played some of their first New York shows in Michael's apartment, and Cat Power was one of those shows. Glen was playing drums, I think Mark Moore was playing guitar, and Chan was playing guitar. My first reaction to it was they were doing something extremely skeletal. Kind of intense. Kind of spooky. The material was definitely very good and very interesting."

"I was completely terrified," Chan said later of this show. "We played in an art gallery, and everybody was a part of the old no-wave

scene in New York. So they're all experienced and intellectual and talented and I'm really dumb. I don't know anything about music. So it
was pretty miserable, actually. Then [Glen] introduced me to his friend
Gerard from Matador, but I didn't know anything, so I was just like,
'Nice to meet you.' "

Even at these early Cat Power shows, Chan was already projecting a
mysterious charisma. "It was really hard to get a handle on what was up
with Chan," Cosloy remembers. "She had a presence but it was sort of
like an accidental apologetic presence, because she didn't make a lot of
eye contact with the audience, she turned away from the crowd a lot,
didn't make much conversation in between songs. But it really worked.
I mean, I thought they were really, really good. And it was definitely a
band that I wanted to see again ASAP."

Charles Aaron didn't agree. "I was at that show and she was terrible," the *Spin* editor remembers. "It was ridiculous! She didn't turn
around. Stood next to the drummer. Didn't face the crowd. There was
no music happening. She was the first or second person on the bill. This
weird girl from Atlanta. Yeah, whatever. Here's yet another thing that
Vicki and Gerard are going to tell me I have to watch out for before
there's even any evidence that it's worth a shit. It took her a long time
to develop into something."

Matador Records was founded in 1989 by a nineteen-year-old New
York rock geek named Chris Lombardi. After working on the fledgling
label by himself for a few years, he asked Gerard Cosloy, Boston-based
DJ, *Conflict* founder, and then head of Homestead Records, a venerated
noise-rock label, to help him run it. Lombardi had the level head required
to run the business, but he needed someone with serious scouting abilities and a reputation for tastemaking. Cosloy was perfect.

While in charge of Homestead, Cosloy helped put out some of the most influential underground records of the nineties, including Big Black's *Atomizer*, Sonic Youth's *Bad Moon Rising*, and Dinosaur Jr.'s very first album, *Dinosaur*. These albums would later be recognized as part of the golden age of indie rock, but at the time they were adored by a relatively small but passionate contingent of the listening public. These difficult-to-please egghead-rock boys and girls were exactly the people Lombardi needed to court as customers. From the very beginning, the key roles performed by Matador's two central figures were established: Lombardi provided the money and business savvy, Cosloy brought the cred.

"I was really obsessed with some bands Matador had," explains Mary Timony, frontwoman for droning noise rockers Helium, who were signed to Matador. "At that point, the label you were on really defined you more than it does now. You would meet people at the label who were really cool, and we got to tour with other bands. Even if it was just going to the record store to look for seven-inches or going to people's shows and buying their merch because that was the only place you could find it, there was a certain level of excitement."

Beautiful and enigmatic Timony was as poised as anyone to become the queen of 1990s indie rock, and for a time the New York zeitgeist definers were as giddy about her as they became about Cat Power. "I remember Vicki Wheeler being the same way about Mary Timony when Helium first came along," Aaron remembers. "Really being, 'Oh my God, this is an incredibly important woman who is very mysterious and inscrutable and is going to have a big impact.' In the beginning I was really skeptical about that, but I grew to love that band. She had a lot of charisma and she was beautiful and she was weird. There was a cult of personality around her. I listened to her records. Wrote about some of those records, and to this day, I think she's as talented as Chan."

Cosloy's reputation as an unimpeachable arbiter of cool established Matador's initial authority, but it was the bands he and Chris signed once the label was up and running that solidified the label's influence. "Their first breakout thing was Teenage Fanclub, followed by Pavement," Jim Greer, former *Spin* editor and sometime member of Matador band Guided by Voices remembers. "That's pretty good right there. And Liz Phair was pretty close with that, too. It wasn't even just those bands, but some of the lesser-known ones that still had a lot of credibility and critical acclaim. Hardly any sales, but lots of critical acclaim. I'd have to put down a lot of that to Gerard, it's just his ear."

When Cosloy joined Lombardi to head up Matador Records in 1990, they were looking ahead to years spent scouting new underground talent, shepherding along their albums, and exposing artists they admired to a savvy if relatively small audience. That's what independent record labels were about in the late eighties and early nineties: They couldn't compete in terms of distribution and sales with any of the so-called Big Four corporate labels, but they made up with taste for what they lacked in market share. As it turns out, mere months before Chan moved to New York—and two short years after Lombardi founded Matador Records in his bedroom—indie "cred," and the people who embodied it, especially Chan Marshall, would become the most powerful forces in mainstream music.

11.

Indie Goes Mainstream

On September 24, 1991, Geffen Records released Nirvana's second album and major label debut Nevermind. By January of the following year, it had replaced Michael Jackson's Dangerous in the number-one spot on the Billboard chart.

In this one instant, an entire musical, social, and political culture that had been proudly on the fringe for the better part of a decade suddenly became mainstream. *Nevermind*'s breakout single, "Smells Like Teen Spirit," was playing in your neighborhood drugstore, grocery store, convenience store, and minimart. Your grandparents had read articles about its impact in arts sections of their local newspapers, and progressive teachers were letting students write papers about the horror of high school life as revealed in the "Teen Spirit" video. Weird Al released a parody ("Smells Like Nirvana"), and fashion designers started sending flannel-influenced collections down the Paris runways. Nirvana and the alternative culture they represented was everywhere. Bands that never had to consider heretofore impossible issues like fame and wealth were suddenly facing major moral dilemmas.

"Signing to a major label was the most uncool thing you could do," Timony remembers of the pre-Nirvana era. "But after Nirvana broke, major labels were snapping up a bunch of these bands that were around." A generation of indie-rock bands who had formed under the pretense that they would be forever ignored by the mainstream instantly became commercially viable.

"It was because of Nirvana and the post-Nirvana feeding frenzy," Jim Greer, who was working at *Spin* in 1991, remembers. "A lot of bands who normally wouldn't have had any commercial expectations all of a sudden had what turned out to be in most cases unrealistic commercial expectations. It went from the highest you could ever hope for was to be as successful as the Pixies, which was 250,000 records. That was huge. That was enormous. People like Sonic Youth were jealous of the Pixies' level of success. Then after Nirvana happened, and a few other bands came along and sold a million records, in their wake there was an expectation."

Greer remembers going with Guided by Voices frontman Robert Pollard to a meeting at Atlantic Records when the band was entertaining offers from various major labels. "It was funny because Danny Goldberg, head of Atlantic then, he was like, 'You know, Stephen Malkmus wouldn't even come see me and meet me,' " Jim remembers, laughing. "And Bob's like, 'I want a gold record!' " In a post-Nirvana world it was suddenly conceivable that Guided by Voices, an extremely lo-fi revolving cast of beer-soaked Midwestern garage rockers led by a retired school teacher, not one of them cute or clean, could sell a million records easy.

In a post-Nirvana world, artists like Chicago-based singer-songwriter Liz Phair began their careers believing that wit, irony, and snark were not necessarily impediments to mammoth success. When Phair started out, she had none of Chan's hang-ups about fame, and when she went shopping for record labels she looked explicitly for a company that offered both strong indie credibility and the corporate vision necessary to turn her into a gigantic rock star. "What's the best indie label, just give me top of the line," Phair remembers asking her friend and future producer Brad Wood when she was searching for a home for the songs that would become her landmark 1993 debut, *Exile in Guyville*. Wood had a one-word answer for her: Matador.

A cassette called *Girly Sound* filled with Phair's spare, confrontational rants was circulating on what she calls the "underground railroad of indie-music exchange," and eventually landed on Cosloy's desk at Matador. Initially Phair was intimidated by Matador's reputation as supreme-cool hunters, so when Cosloy and Lombardi came to Chicago to visit her, the pressure to impress them was intense. "Chris wanted to know if there was any cocaine to buy in the 'hood," Phair remembers. "I didn't know how to get any, but I drove them to the bad part of town

and I acted like I knew what I was doing, and we ended up buying baking soda. He was really pissed, I was kind of humiliated. I was like,
'Wow, there goes my cool facade.' "

Lombardi and Cosloy overlooked Phair's drug-scoring naïveté, and
on June 22, 1993, Matador Records released Liz Phair's debut album,
Exile in Guyville, which was largely based on those early *Girly Sounds*
recordings. In early 1994, eight or so months after the album came out,
Guyville made a brief appearance on the *Billboard* chart, having sold more
than 200,000 copies, but its cultural dominance far outweighed its sales.
If you were cool, had ever been cool, or aspired to one day become cool,
you owned a copy of this record.

Phair and Matador had a huge indie-rock hit on their hands, but they
looked at it as merely the first step of a grand scheme to make tons of
money selling really good music to the mainstream. The label started out
as a home for great bands, but now that great bands were making great
big piles of cash, they wanted in on it. "Gerard and Chris saw themselves as minitycoons," Phair explains. "You felt like they were gonna do
big things, and that's what we had in common. It wasn't like they were
just really selfless and they loved these pure acts, and then when they
got successful they thought they'd make something of it. They wanted
to be moguls from the get-go, and that's what I loved about them—they
absolutely carried themselves like tycoons before they were."

Cat Power wasn't even signed to Matador when *Exile in Guyville*
came out, and Chan Marshall did not become a marquee Matador artist
until the late 1990s and early 2000s, but she has followed a path Phair
forged, both as the first female star of indie rock and as Matador's first
flagship female artist. The two women couldn't be more different as musicians—Liz Phair is a distinctly nineties wry social commentator with
a preternatural ear for the perfect pop song, and Chan is an eraless,

haunted blues singer—but in many ways Chan has the career Matador Records envisioned for Liz Phair.

One of the many side effects of Nirvana's success was that indie labels, not just bands, were being scouted by the Big Four. Matador was no exception and in 1993, they partnered with Atlantic Records. It was during this general era that Phair first remembers hearing about Cat Power. "She would have been the other girl." Phair's first impression of Chan was as a rebel who refused to change her style in order to maximize her marketability. "They were still looking at it through those ambitious eyes," Phair recalls, "like, 'Let's make another Liz Phair.' She was not quite playing ball. I vaguely remember there being this inability on their part to wrangle her the way they wanted."

Phair's deep respect for Chan's independence comes from her very personal understanding of how hard it is to stay grounded when, as a woman in the music business, every day someone new is telling you who you need to become if you want to be successful. Ever since the 1993 release of *Guyville*, Phair has been battling industry pressure to retreat into the prison of any number of women-in-rock archetypes—and in some instances, her willingness to listen to others over herself made for ultimately bad career decisions. Phair doesn't just admire Chan's independent spirit, she thinks it's the essence of Chan's allure. "She kept growing, and her appeal kept growing," Phair marvels, "despite or maybe because of this kind of wild-horse thing. That's a beautiful thing. It's maddening, but it's beautiful."

12.

Headlights

By December of 1992, Chan was making it all work. Cat Power played the occasional show, which was fun, and Chan continued to explore the LES scene, stomping through the first snow of the year in work boots and Levi's to see shows down on the Lower East Side. Glen got a day job working in an office at Cardozo Law School with his friend local scenester Rick Brown. Through Brown they met Bob Bannister, an accomplished guitarist who played in several local bands and who also worked at Cardozo during the day. "I was putting out a fanzine at the time called *On Site*, so I knew Glen from his fanzine," Bannister remembers. "Although we had more likely traded barbs than anything else, because that was the fanzine culture."

During their days at Cardozo, Glen told Rick Brown and Bob Bannister about Chan, and about the music the two of them were working on. After checking out a Cat Power show in person, Bannister joined the band as a guitarist. "I started playing, and we did a show as a trio at ABC No Rio, then we did a show at CBGB," Bannister remembers. This gig at CB's was a big deal for Chan. When she found out Cat Power had been booked at the legendary venue, she called up all her bandmates from back home and recruited several of them to join her onstage—including Fletcher Liegerot, Damon Moore, and Mark Moore, who had moved back to Atlanta mere weeks after he, Thrasher, and Chan first showed up. "It was December 10, 1992," Bob remembers. "All of Chan's friends that she'd been playing with in Atlanta were so excited that she was playing at CBGB that they all drove up to the show."

Before he moved up to New York, Glen Thrasher became friends with the New York–based noise rockers God Is My Co-Pilot, a band founded by husband-and-wife duo Sharon Topper and Craig Flanagin. In addition to playing in God Is My Co-Pilot, Craig ran his own small label, The Making of Americans. After seeing a couple Cat Power shows, he offered to record a single with the band. In early 1993, Chan, Glen, and Bob headed into a small studio in SoHo to record "Headlights," with Craig as the producer. The studio was owned by Don Fury, a seasoned producer and veteran of the eighties hardcore punk scene, who served as engineer during the recording sessions. "I only knew or liked six songs. It felt so strange. I was so suspicious," Chan remembered of her first time in the studio. "Microphones and headphones plugged in, and the guy is in that room turning buttons, and I felt like it was so unnatural and didn't make sense."

Three years before recording "Headlights," Chan was making Robert Hayes stand in the garden while she played for an audience of one in her Cabbagetown kitchen. By the time Cat Power was recording "Headlights" Chan's confidence had grown, but the experience of physically being in a studio triggered her ever-present sense of inadequacy. "I was really uptight and scared and embarrassed," she has said. "Like, Oh, I sound like shit and I can't play and it's really dark and they're all looking at me through that glass thing and I don't like how it feels." Chan found the studio environment sterile and threatening, and she heard exactly the kind of stiff amateurism in the "Headlights" single that she feared would emerge. "I had no idea what I was doing, and I'm not really happy with how it came out," Chan has said. "It sounds too trapped."

The single does have a certain cornered quality to it, as if Chan is singing in an interrogation room, but it also reveals the remote intimacy in Chan's vocals and the obscure but weirdly familiar style of her songwriting, both of which would become Cat Power hallmarks. The song is built around a series of repetitive phrases like "Get up around eight," "Last thing I remember," and "It's cold as hell," which reflects a style of songwriting Tim Foljahn noticed years later when he would help her record Cat Power's first three albums, *Dear Sir*, *Myra Lee*, and *What Would the Community Think*. "She would write a repetitive, looping line and then improv over it," Tim remembers. "It would become a stuck improvisation, but it would be this very lyrical thing." The "Headlights" single displays another of Cat Power's hallmark themes: merging a sense of dread with joy. The song sounds droning and repetitive, but the cover of the single features a photo of a young Chan Marshall, about six, dressed in a loose sundress and standing arms entwined, eyes closed, face blissfully lifted to the sky. The image was the perfect contrast to the anguished sounds contained inside the sleeve.

Part of Chan's discomfort with the recording process resulted from inexperience, but being in the studio with professionally trained musicians also triggered memories of her father telling her that making music required a sophistication she lacked. Chan's exposure to the loose Cabbagetown rockers and the wild free-jazz artists in downtown New York had made her more comfortable with her lack of professional performance experience, but once she entered the studio, a sense of familiar shame came rushing back. "Glen was like, 'Let's just try it,' " Chan has said of her friend's attempt to calm her down while recording. "When it was done, I couldn't breathe and just ran away," Chan remembered. "It was like getting closer to people I didn't know, and that was so intimidating to me, so I just left."

Guitarist Bob Bannister remembers Chan being unnecessarily hard on herself, but is quick to point out that her frustrations, while extreme, were not totally unfounded. Chan is a perfectionist, and recording live music is an inherently imperfect enterprise. A take that most people might hear as exquisitely vulnerable, Chan would hear as an embarrassing mess. "She was on the edge of that artistic sensitivity," Bannister acknowledges. "But you can hear what she was reacting to, which is that she didn't hit a note quite right or her voice cracked a bit. In a music that's more about expressiveness than virtuosity, it seems to me that nuances like that are not only not a problem, they're often good."

In recent years, Chan has attributed her self-sabotaging tendencies to her problems with alcohol, but at these early recording sessions, she didn't need whiskey to trigger her descent. "She's become legendary for being unstable, but it didn't strike me as that extreme," Bannister says of Chan's drinking. "I never saw any particular sign of excessive drinking or any drug use whatsoever." Foljahn concurs: The guitarist would go on to play with Cat Power through the conclusion of the *What Would the Community Think* tour and would see her exhibit plenty of alarming behavior, but he also says that he's never seen her drunk. "She was very careful with the booze, and that's when I was drinking a lot, so it was weird 'cause I'd be getting trashed and she wouldn't be," Foljahn remembers. "I remember being in Atlanta with her and her being like, 'No, I've got to keep it to a couple of beers because I don't want to get out of control.' She'd just come out of that scene where everybody was so fucked-up, and she'd just had it with that stuff."

God Is My Co-Pilot pressed five hundred copies of "Headlights" and distributed it on their Making of Americans label. The single, with its melancholy but melodic sound, boosted interest in Cat Power and attendance at the band's shows. Things were starting to go well for Chan and her fledgling music career: She had survived her first recording session relatively unscathed, people were responding to the tracks she recorded, and Cat Power shows were drawing fans.

"With that Glen guy, she evolved into a normal indie-rock act," Aaron says. "I don't think anything she'd been doing before was substantial in any way. She created something powerful for a wider audience. Something that could be packaged and sold. It's smart. She's talented. I would never have figured that she would have done anything like that. I just figured she was another one of those you-had-to-be-on-drugs-and-live-in-a-squat people."

Shortly after "Headlights" was released, Glen abruptly moved back to Atlanta. Glen was the one who inspired Chan to put Cat Power together in the first place. He helped Chan gain enough confidence to get onstage and perform back in Atlanta. He spearheaded the band's move to New York, and once there, he got Chan onstage and into a recording studio. Glen was Chan's greatest early champion and her most influential early collaborator, and his departure, especially for a woman with deep connections to the older men in her life, felt like abandonment.

The reasons why Glen left actually had very little to do with Chan and very much to do with his heroin addiction. "Glen went back to Atlanta totally independently of Chan," Bannister asserts. "He certainly didn't have a falling-out with her. It was entirely his own problems that caused him to leave. He was having trouble in New York." In addition to Thrasher's ongoing battle with addiction, Bannister also remembers the drummer struggling with the strain of trying to live an artist's life in an expensive city. "A lot of the things you can do to be involved in the life of the music scene, like putting out fanzines, putting on shows— these things are fun, but make you no money," Bannister explains. "They are easier to do in a city where the cost of living is much lower."

Thrasher's departure left Chan at a complete loss. "My drummer got addicted to heroin and left town," Chan has said, glossing over the fact that Glen was already an addict when they moved to New York. "So I just stopped playing music altogether, because he was the one who wanted us to play." With Thrasher back in Atlanta, any plan to turn Cat Power into a true ensemble evaporated, and Chan went through a period of deep confusion about what she was doing in New York. For the first time since she willed herself out of her father's house and into a real life of her own, Chan was forced to look at where she was, who she was, and what she was doing with her life. She no longer had Glen and their band to justify her presence in New York, and the choice to stay in the city had to be hers alone.

"It was real difficult during those first two years," Chan has said. "I moved to New York to get away from different things about Atlanta. I had my ex-boyfriend [Mark Moore] and a good friend of mine [Thrasher]. My good friend went insane and my ex-boyfriend got fucked up and left two or three weeks after I got there. I didn't know anybody and didn't have any money. But I didn't want to go back to Atlanta, and there was nowhere else I wanted to go."

In the wake of Thrasher's departure from New York, Chan was facing some of the toughest months of her life. For years, her insecurities about playing music for a living had been tempered by Thrasher, and before that, by her Cabbagetown friends, who made it easy for her to try out the idea of being a rock star without having to truly commit to a career in music. But New York City is not a place for the uncertain. It has a way of demanding a yes-or-no answer out of the aspiring artists who flock to it. After Thrasher left, Chan alone remained to define Cat Power's future. Would she stay and stand alone behind her music for the first time in her life? Or would she retreat back to safer territory? This conflict wore on Chan.

By the following summer, she was still lost. She had her life in New York established, could pay her rent, and had made a few friends, but she hadn't done anything with Cat Power since Thrasher moved away. Her dad invited her to take a road trip along with Miranda and Chan's half sister, Ivy, from Atlanta to Pensacola, Florida. Chan accepted. They all met up in Atlanta, then piled into Charlie's truck for the five-hour drive. Chan was being her usual gregarious self, telling her sisters jokes and bugging her dad to pull over at every secondhand store they passed so she could add to her collection of weird trinkets and beat-up jeans.

At one point the group made a pit stop at a fast-food joint. Hours later, Chan realized that she had left her wallet at the restaurant. "It was a little Roy Rogers billfold," Charlie remembers. "She was freaking out. She said, 'No, it's got my health card in there, it's got this, it's got that!' She was freaking out!" They were already several hundred miles away, so Charlie calmed Chan down, called the restaurant on his car phone, and arranged to have the wallet mailed to his daughter the following day. But the experience disturbed him. "I could see that she had inherited some of the schizophrenia or paranoia from her mom," he says. "The craziness in your family makes you crazy."

If Myra has schizophrenia, Chan has a better chance of developing it than the average person, but that doesn't mean she will. "Schizophrenia is genetically inherited, although it's not simple; the propensity for it is inherited," Dr. Ewing says. "Your risk of having schizophrenia if nobody in your family had it is about one percent. If one of your parents had it, it's about ten percent. If both your parents had it, it's about thirty percent. The accordance among identical twins is fifty percent." From a medical standpoint, even if Myra has the disease, Chan's chances of developing it are still pretty slim, but according to Charlie, both of Myra's daughters always seemed right up on the edge of sanity. "I could always tell both of the kids had inherited that from their mom," Charlie says. "I think my family has it some, too."

13.

The Next Liz Phair

After Glen Thrasher returned to Atlanta, Chan unoffi-
cially disbanded Cat Power. She didn't play any shows for
almost a year. Instead she focused on working. She got a
new job at Todd's Copy, an artists' hangout on Mott

Street, and suspended her pursuit of a professional career in music. Todd Jorgensen, the founder of Todd's Copy, originally worked at Jamie's Canvas in SoHo. Jamie's big draw for the artists living downtown in the late seventies and early eighties was that it was home to Todd's color Xerox machine, the only one in the neighborhood. Now that we have a Kinko's on every corner, it seems absurd that the presence of one such machine could have spawned an entire artists' community, but that's kind of what happened. "That was the go-to place for the SoHo art scene," Sonic Youth frontman and longtime New Yorker Thurston Moore says of Jamie's Canvas. "It was this intense thing, that you could go there and actually get a color Xerox."

When Todd decided to establish his own store, he took the copier with him, and all the artists who'd gotten accustomed to using it followed. Todd's Copy quickly became like a bustling Parisian café with color Xeroxes and roller balls for sale instead of coffee and croissants. "I knew it was a great place to be because in the eighties, all the artists would go there and do their work there—so you got to sort of hang with people like Jean-Michel Basquiat," Moore remembers. "You were always helping these guys out. It was this downtown scene. Glen Brodko would hang out there, Jim Jarmusch."

One day in the summer of 1994, Chan came home from work to discover that Cat Power was scheduled to play at CBGB's. "The people in God Is My Co-Pilot booked my first solo show in New York without me knowing about it," Chan has said. "I hadn't done any music at all for a year. Then one day I got home and saw there was a message on my answering machine from my friend saying I had a solo show to play at CBGB's Gallery. I checked the paper and there it was: 'Cat Power solo.' So you see, everyone's more responsible for my music than I am." Sharon and Craig of God Is My Co-Pilot were indeed once again instrumental in getting Chan's music out of her and into the world, but Chan could have chosen not to play. Instead she showed up and performed by herself for the first time ever. A few days later, Gerard Cosloy booked Cat Power to open for Liz Phair.

"I got home [and] there was a message from Gerard saying, 'Hey, Chan, would you like to open up for Liz Phair in two nights? You'll get paid two hundred dollars,'" Chan has remembered. "I was thinking, 'Wow. I've never made more than fifty bucks at most.' I didn't know who Liz Phair was. I had never heard her music. I had seen her on the cover of *Rolling Stone*. I thought, She's got to be good if she's on Matador and all these people like her. She's got to be talented, right? Wrong! I don't like Liz Phair. But that's the night I met Steve Shelley and Tim Foljahn. And that's the night Steve asked if we could put out a record."

Opening for Liz Phair in New York City was about as big a gig as Cat Power could have landed, and it exposed her to exactly the audience that would form her base: namely, girl rock geeks looking for a new personal hero, and dude rock geeks looking for a new crush. Phair doesn't remember this performance; she was still adjusting to the extreme transformation from sheltered suburbanite with a dirty mind to Gen-X poster girl, and was often paralyzed by extreme preshow jitters, not unlike Chan. "I was such an inexperienced performer," Phair recalls. "I would have been completely consumed with, 'Oh my God, I'm gonna get stoned,' and I'm sure that's what happened. Some friend was shoving me out, and so I probably missed what the hell else was going on."

While Phair was managing her own performance demons, Chan was dealing with the fact that most of the crowd mistook one beautiful brunette singer-songwriter for the other. "I heard the one guy say, 'My professor plays your CD all the time,'" Chan remembers. "I was like, 'I'm not Liz Phair!' It was so uncomfortable. That's one of my favorite stories. They liked me because they thought I was her." Chan was nervous, but in retrospect she was pleased with herself for pulling it together and delivering a solid show. "I was totally shaky and sweating," the singer has said. "But I did a really good job and I was professional and I finished every song. I was done, I walked off, and I looked out the curtain and the room was spiraling and people are standing up, and Gerard is like, 'That was great! Do you want to go back on?' And I was like, 'Nooo!' "

Though Chan remembers meeting Tim Foljahn and Steve Shelley for the first time at the Liz Phair show, Foljahn says they met in the spring of 1994 at a show by all-girl postpunk rockers the Raincoats. "Steve was playing with the Raincoats," Foljahn remembers. "This kid was warming up before the show. I looked over and honestly, beautiful kid, but I wasn't sure if it was a boy or a girl. Really short hair and the mackinaw coat and the little black shoes with the white socks. Really cool looking." Chan looked cool; she also looked nervous, and Foljahn decided to try to ease her pain by striking up a conversation with her.

Foljahn, Shelley, and the girls in the Raincoats were all planning to go out to dinner before the show, so they invited Chan to come along. "It was nice because the Raincoats, the lady rockers, were really nice to her," Foljahn remembers. "We went to this place where they would come and make guacamole right at your table." After enjoying a rowdy dinner fueled by margaritas and tableside guac, everybody went back to the club and played. This was the first and last time Tim ever remembers seeing Chan play solo, and he was totally mesmerized by her. "It was just like, Wow," he remembers. "Really, really beautiful and interesting. It was just her in this big place, wherever it was, and there was something really compelling about her songs." By the end of dinner, Foljahn had a raging crush on Chan; by the end of her set he was in love with her music. The two exchanged phone numbers and started hanging out.

At the time, Thurston Moore was playing solo material with Shelley and Foljahn: Together they recorded Moore's first solo album, 1995's *Psychic Hearts*. Moore's bandmates started talking about this cute new singer-songwriter they'd met, but what he didn't realize was that he and Chan already knew each other. "While we were hanging out doing *Psychic Hearts* stuff, we were rehearsing at this underground rehearsal joint on Mott Street between Houston and Prince," Moore recalls. "I remember Tim and Steve going over to Todd's and I was like, 'Why are you going over to Todd's Xerox shop?' and he's like, 'Well, there's this girl who works over there that Tim is really into, this kind of Southern girl.' "

That's when it occurred to Moore he'd already met Foljahn's crush. "I realized who he was talking about because I had gone in there and she was working, and Todd embarrassed her in front of me. He said, 'Oh, this girl is a big fan of yours.' I could see that she was mortified that he said that, you know? So I felt kind of sorry for her. But I didn't think anything of it. I thought she was just some kid working there. Then when Tim said he was going to see this girl there, I was like, 'You know, there is this kind of cute girl who was working there.' "

Chan did have a thing for Thurston. Ever since the rock boys at Fellini's introduced her to Sonic Youth back in the early nineties, Chan associated the band with the kind of integrity in musicmaking that she wanted to embody. "Rock 'n' roll was never a moneymaker to emotional, educated people," Chan has said. "Sonic Youth was coming from an underground place which is not purchasable. Thurston and Lee being poets foremost and Kim being an actual artist, they weren't a band, they were really individual people that did everything." In these new friends—Shelley, Moore, and Foljahn—Chan found a replacement for the community of fellow misfits she lost when her Cabbagetown friends left New York. Before long the singer was rehearsing with a new lineup of Cat Power featuring Foljahn on guitar and Shelley on drums.

When Steve Shelley, a bona fide member of a famous rock band, joined Cat Power, the group's profile got a big boost. His presence in the band also strengthened the quality of Cat Power's live performances. With Shelley and Foljahn onstage behind Chan, she relaxed and started to develop a distinctive stage presence. She showcased this new co-quettish confidence at a show at the Cooler in the fall of 1994, an event that everyone in town wanted to say they had seen. "The most signifi-cant thing I heard was about the Cooler show," Moore remembers. "Supposedly different people played, and then she came out and did this thing and the whole room just froze. Her voice and how she was singing and all of a sudden you knew there was something going on here. There was a buzz just from that show, and I immediately felt like, 'Oh, wow, I wish I'd seen that.' "

By late 1994, Cat Power was one of the most-discussed new artists in New York City. This was mostly a good thing for Chan. It meant that she could live the life of a professional musician if she wanted to. But Chan was still wary of that lifestyle, and the increased attention she was suddenly getting made it seem as if the decision had already been made for her. It also triggered her latent self-destructive tendencies. The more expectant the Cat Power audience grew, the more paralyzing Chan's in-security about her abilities became. "The audience started getting dif-ferent, like more of a rock audience," she has said. "They didn't get that we were just making shit up. People started looking cooler and acting cooler, and that made it more uncomfortable."

After hearing about Cat Power's performance at the Cooler, Moore vowed to see the band's next show, which took place at Brownie's. "I got up really close so I could check it out. I was bowled over by it," the Sonic Youth frontman remembers. "I thought she was fantastic, especially in light of the fact that only about a ninth of the audience was paying attention. Everybody else was just, like, socializing. What really got me was that she was singing a solid foot away from the mike and it was creating this atmosphere where it was just all this reverb. She wasn't singing forcibly to compensate for the crowd noise, but it sounded beautiful. Afterward I was like, 'That's such a radical thing—having all that reverb and then singing a foot away from the microphone just created this really, really weird, eerie kind of vibe. It was great.' And she said, 'Well, I didn't tell them to put the reverb on it.' I found out the sound guy was doing whatever he could to get her voice amplified, so he was just adding all this effect. So it was this system of errors creating this wonderful thing."

Moore found Chan's performance style odd but not disturbing. "She seemed a little nervous," Moore remembers. "But it wasn't the leaving-the-stage kind of nervous, it was sort of like throwing the set list away and fooling around." At this point, Chan used her time onstage to try out provocative performance techniques she'd seen at her favorite avant-garde rock shows. Instead of facing the audience, Chan would play a show with her back to the crowd, willfully disregarding the idea that she was there to entertain or even play actual music. "What was going on was a transaction," Chan has said of the shows she saw that inspired her early performance style. "There was no judgment. Only for that moment did that experience exist. So when it was our turn to play, I'd play with my back to the audience. We were creating a little world of our own."

These early Cat Power shows marked the beginning of a careerlong argument Chan has with herself—which has played out onstage in a very public and sometimes harrowing way—about whether or not she wants to be up there singing in the first place. In his brilliant 2008 memoir, *Black Postcards*, former Galaxie 500 and Luna singer Dean Wareham recalls seeing Cat Power around this time:

> Chan Marshall seemed in good form when we arrived at the show, playing the piano and singing beautiful. But things quickly went downhill. She stopped singing and started rambling incoherently. "I'm so tired. I'm so tired." She asked her soundwoman which song she should do. "Give me a song, baby . . . no, not that one. I already did that one." She picked up her guitar and strummed a few chords, then started talking again. "I *love* Vincent Gallo. I'm sooo tired. Someone bring me four shots of whiskey! And I don't care what it is, but there must be no ice and the first four letters of the whiskey must be G-L-E-N." "Play a song," one fan shouted. "You are not invited to my world," she told him. "I love everyone, but I do not like you . . . but I forgive you." The following night we performed at the hard club. People were still buzzing about the Cat Power show. It may have been a fiasco, but if people can't stop talking about your show, then surely you have done something right.

Chan's professional music life began as an after-school project, something she convinced herself she wasn't serious about so that she could pursue it without pressure or expectation. In Cabbagetown, this was easy. No one knew how to play. That was the point. In New York it was the same thing at first. Chan saw art-school grads and street kids colliding onstage in debauched celebrations of lack of training, lack of artifice, lack of expectation. But in the back of her head, all along, Chan heard Eartha Kitt, she heard James Brown, she heard Bob Dylan. She heard music that is all about knowing exactly what you're doing, and doing it extremely well, and it was *this* sound that the singer wanted to emulate. Chan could turn her back to the audience show after show, she could mumble into her mike, she could shroud her face in long brown hair, but none of that would turn her into a freewheeling performance artist. Chan Marshall is a traditional songwriter and a perfectionist. As hard as she tried to free herself from other people's expectations, life in New York City was teaching her that the most imposing ones were those she set for herself.

14.

Suddenly Cool

By the fall of 1994 the second incarnation of Cat Power, featuring Steve Shelley on drums, Tim Foljahn on guitar, and Chan on vocals, was well established as a hot new band to see in New York. The natural next step was to go back into the studio and record an album that would allow them to capitalize on their hype. In December of 1994, Cat Power went to the Mott Street space where they had been rehearsing and where Moore, Shelley, and Foljahn had worked on *Psychic Hearts*. Fueled by deli coffee and Italian takeout from restaurants down the block in Little Italy, in one day the trio recorded all twenty tracks that would become the first two Cat Power records, *Dear Sir* and *Myra Lee*.

The plan was straightforward: get in there, let Chan emote into the mike, improvise some complementary drums and guitar, and put out the album. "I said, 'I think your stuff is simple, and Steve and I can just sort of stay out of the way and let you do your thing,' " Foljahn remembers. The Mott Street studio place, with its moist concrete walls, stained cof-fee mugs, discarded beer cans, and assorted music equipment piled in corners, was as lo-fi as it got. "Literally it was the third subbasement," Foljahn recalls. "It was so New York."

Tim remembers the session as mellow and quick. Chan described it as anxiety-ridden. As during the "Headlights" session, Chan's lack of ex-perience in the studio and her uncertainty about how to incorporate other musicians into any of her songs made things extremely hard. "I guess I'm happy with the two albums," Chan told a reporter in 1996. "Most of the time Steve and Tim ended up looking at each other like, 'What do we do?' I wasn't sure what to tell them, since I had never re-ally written songs with a band in mind."

Dear Sir came out first, in October 1995 on Runt Records, a small Italian label. It's a raw, sometimes disturbing record that showcases Chan's ability to deliver incredibly personal songs that also feel remote and unknowable. The album is short: The track list has nine songs in-cluding two covers, "The Sleepwalker," written by Chris Matthews, and a harrowing version of the Tom Waits/Kathleen Brennan ballad

"Yesterday Is Here." Chan has always found sanctity in performing other people's songs. Those who attended her early shows would have heard lots of covers, and Chan had recorded a version of Peter Lofton's "Fun" (a live staple at the time) during the recording session for "Headlights," although it doesn't appear as a B-side to the single.

Dear Sir is an inconsistent record. "Itchyhead" is an initially compelling track because of Chan's anodyne but sirenesque vocals and the spare style of the recording, but the song never takes the listener much past despair. This is a pattern demonstrated by many of the songs on the album: They start off as oppressively dark, with Chan's voice hiding timidly in its lower registers before careening (with Shelley and Foljahn in tow) into a realm of sonic anguish so intense it's uncomfortable.

Yet there are several exquisite moments. A new recording of Cat Power's first single, "Headlights," concludes the album with a punch of appealingly skuzzy mid-nineties guitar-rock charm (even if the misery it conveys is abrasive in its intensity), and "Rockets," the second track on *Dear Sir*, is one of the best Cat Power songs of the 1990s. Chan has undersold this song as "just a hymn," but it's really the first Cat Power recording to display the delicate weirdness that would become Chan's hallmark as an artist for much of the next decade. "Where is the night so warm and so strange/That no one is afraid/Of themselves?" Chan asks wistfully, while Tim's guitar churns urgently behind her. "Here, pick up, dig, dig out those weeds/Out of your happy-go-lucky fields/Of such polluted thinking," she then sings with renewed vigor, as if this command, while not a real answer to the question she's just posed, is one appropriate response.

Dear Sir includes one of Cat Power's most notorious songs, "Mr. Gallo," which was supposedly inspired by filmmaker, former Todd's Copy employee, and Chan's alleged onetime lover, Vincent Gallo. The song has a depressive sort of girl-sings-about-boy-who-loves-girl-who-might-love-boy appeal that suits the subject. "She had men's shoes on, a nonmatching set, and both of them on the wrong foot," Gallo has said of the first time he saw Chan, when she was still working at Todd's. "She wasn't kidding. It was no joke. I thought, Oh, that girl is the greatest."

Chan has laughed off Gallo's account of their first meeting. "He was articulating his sense of humor," Chan has said. "My shit was fucking dorky. I was eccentric when I was twenty years old, let's face it." Gallo has gone on to say that he's flattered by the attention Chan gave him on her first album. "I like Cat Power, especially the song 'Mr. Gallo,' " the filmmaker told a reporter in 1997. "I would like any band that did a song about me." Gallo went on to boast about how madly in love with him Chan must have been to write such a song. "That good-looking Cat Power chick, Chan Marshall, wrote some nasty words," he's said. "What could she do? She loved me. I would've done the same thing if I loved me. Anyway, that chick's a superstar. I should've stayed with her."

While neither Chan nor Gallo has been explicit about what exactly went on between them, it's at least as likely that she ended things with him as it is that he ended things with her. "That was fascinating," Foljahn says of the Chan-Vincent romance. "At that time he seemed like this older guy that was all hooked up and was kind of stalking her. He'd show up at Todd's and be like, 'We gotta go out! We gotta go out! We gotta make it happen, you and me!' That's how he operates. I've been with other girls when he's hitting on them, and that's his thing."

Dear Sir didn't have much of a commercial impact, but it's an intriguing album that kept music-industry insiders interested. *Dear Sir* ensured that already-committed Cat Power fans would stay loyal through the release of the next album, *Myra Lee*, which Steve Shelley put out on his Smells Like Records label in March 1996. Shelley's involvement with Cat Power went a long way toward getting Chan noticed not just in New York, but all over the country. When Chan recorded the "Headlights" single, people back home in Atlanta knew about it and passed copies around—it was their friend's band. But when Shelley joined the band and then put out *Myra Lee* on his label, it was seen as his public endorsement of Chan, which bolstered the band's reputation and helped insulate Chan against increasingly vocal detractors.

"Over time she was developing a following," Gerard Cosloy remembers. "But there were people in town who were like, 'Forget it, get lost.' Chan is a love-her-or-hate-her songwriter. For those that are moved by her music, her genius seems obvious, but for those who aren't, she comes across as elevator music for self-indulgent, whiny hipsters." But even those who adore Cat Power's music were amazed by how quickly Chan's obscure lyrics and restrictively simple sound connected with a devoted, passionate audience. "I was surprised everyone else picked up on it," *Stomp and Stammer* editor Jeff Clark says. "I never thought that it was something that was going to be welcomed by a very wide audience. Some of those early albums I don't really understand."

Chan has not explicitly explained why she named the second Cat Power album after her mother, but she did begin speaking to Myra again for the first time in several years around the time *Myra Lee* came out. Back home in Greensboro, Chan's mom wasn't doing very well. Leamon and Myra had been married for thirteen years, but nearly every one of them was turbulent. The drama finally got to be too much, and in 1993 they got divorced. "They had a passionate love affair, or a psycho love affair, you could say," Lenny recalls. "They divorced when I was thirteen. I left when I was fourteen. I got out of there as soon as I could." Lenny went to live with his father in Columbia, South Carolina, and

Myra stayed in Greensboro. "She wasn't working a lot," Lenny recalls. "It was basically alimony and Mom's social-security check. I know that sounds bad. I'm just being honest."

To this day Lenny still has a hard time keeping up a good relationship with his mother. "I can't be around my mom," he says frankly. "Twenty minutes around her and I'm uneasy." He talks to her on the phone all the time, though, which he finds easier than seeing Myra face-to-face. "Charlyn is different from me," he says. "Charlyn can be around her, but she can't talk to her on the phone. It's completely flipped. Sometimes we get together for the holidays. Charlyn would go, but I wouldn't because it's uncomfortable. I love travel, but I wouldn't want to be around her. I was like, 'Hey, Merry Christmas, I'll see you when I see you.' "

Though *Myra Lee* was recorded at the same time as *Dear Sir*, the album feels more confident and less muddled than Cat Power's debut. *Myra Lee* sounds as if it was written and recorded by moonlight on a rickety old porch in the Deep South during a dark night of the soul. For those who missed it on *Dear Sir*, "Rockets" is included in the track list, but this time it has much more competition for the listener's attention. For the duration of her career, Chan has insisted that where others hear deep hopelessness and sorrow in her songs, she hears redemption. On *Myra Lee*'s second track, "We All Die," Chan showcases her ability to find promise in despair. The song's title is almost comically depressing, but the propulsive nature of the simple guitar/drums and Chan's repeating (unironic) lyrical refrain "All the lies aside/I believe I am the/Luckiest person alive" give the song a sense of defiant resiliency that, beginning with *Myra Lee*, is a recurring theme in much of Cat Power's music. On her second album Chan again chose to include a cover amid her original songs: Hank Williams's "Still in Love," which the singer transforms into a forlorn but romantic ballad. "Ice Water," with lyrics like "I feel just like/Some great big disease," is a good example of the awkward, personal confessional that would make legions of self-loathing adolescent girls latch onto Chan as their messiah.

In spite of Chan's insistence that her songs are not supposed to be debilitatingly sad, she admits that her early material was born out of incredible pain. "I know what I was thinking about then," she has said of the time she spent writing her first two albums. "I don't need those songs to remind me." Chan's early songs are confessionals in a genuinely religious sense, as if every lyric she wrote is a prayer for salvation from the memory that inspired it. Chan would suffer in the years to come from sharing so much personal pain with strangers, who often feel a sense of ownership over the songs.

All artists face concern about revealing too much of themselves in their art. You want your work to be personal, but not so intimate that in sharing the inspiration behind the art, you cease to own it. For Chan this has been a huge problem. Songwriting saved her from the emotional hell she was living in as a child; it made her feel as if she had a secret, an ace in the hole against the world. When she decided to share her music with strangers, she had to share her secret, and she's spent most of her career grappling with that reality. Through most of the 1990s, Cat Power continued to record songs that were often mysterious but never willfully masked.

Eventually, Chan adjusted her songwriting style in order to protect herself from excruciating emotional exposure. On the early albums, though, you're tapped directly into Chan's soul without filters or obfuscation. "Confused, wondering what the hell you're doing. Everything seems so desperate and empty and just lost," the singer has said, describing what she hears when she plays her early records. "I'm so glad I'm not there anymore."

Myra Lee was first released until March 1996, a year and two months after it was recorded alongside *Dear Sir* in that dank studio on Mott Street. Between the December 1994 recording of the first two Cat Power albums and the release of *Myra Lee* in early '96, the band played in New York as much as possible; they also went on tour for the first time. Chan may have moved to New York City in the summer of 1992, but she's never really left Atlanta. Even during her early years in New York, the singer would borrow a friend's car or scrape together enough Todd's Copy paychecks or waitressing tips to buy a bus ticket home. After recording with Shelley and Foljahn, Chan finally had a real band to-gether, and the practical entrepreneur in her began pairing trips home with minitours.

"She'd need to get to Atlanta," Foljahn remembers. "So we'd tour our way down there in some weird vehicle." Packed into a friend's wood-paneled station wagon or VW. bus, the band would head south, stop-ping to play shows at dive bars and small clubs between New York and Atlanta. Most every time Chan visited Atlanta, whether she was with or without her band, she would play a few local shows. Kristi Cameron remembers seeing Chan perform solo at Dottie's, a storied old Atlanta bar and sometime venue where the singer briefly worked back in her Cabbagetown days. "Dottie's was this totally trashy Southern country bar," Cameron remembers. "One of our friends started working as a bar-tender there and she started booking her friend's bands. She totally walks that line between redneck and whatever that Southern music-scene thing is."

After an entire childhood spent on the move, Chan easily adapted to touring life. She had her favorite clothes—beat-up Levi's, beaded bracelets, and work shirts—but besides something to wear, books, and a few records, Chan didn't need much stuff. She was perfectly at home in the passenger seat of a rented van on the way to her next gig. One of Chan's only on-the-road rules was that someone else had to drive: that way, she could focus on changing the radio station every few minutes, or read out loud to whoever was listening. "She would sit in the back and tell jokes and sing and read," Foljahn remembers. "She used to joke about wanting to go to McDonald's. She was always very interested in food." During these road trips, Foljahn also discovered Chan's capacity to perfectly mimic any song on the radio, which is ironic considering that she would later become famous for her virtually unrecognizable covers. "Riding in the car with her, she could do a whole Michael Jackson song any time she wanted to," the guitarist recalls. "She can do those songs for fun, but she would hit it every time. It was a little weird."

Chan isn't shy about expressing her opinion, and while she was cooped up in the car for hours on end with a bunch of boys, she was even more forceful. Decisions about where to eat, what radio station to listen to, and what time to pull over and sleep were often made by her. And yet every time she'd choose KFC over Burger King, or country over classic rock, she couldn't resist asking her favorite question: "Are you mad at me?" Foljahn got so bored with this refrain that he started answering yes each time she asked. "Her catchphrase was, 'I'm sorry, are you mad at me?' " Tim recalls. "She would start the conversation with that, and then you'd go from there. So when we were driving around, I'd be like, 'Yes, Chan, I'm really mad at you. Please don't talk to me.' That would sort of slow it down. She'd laugh."

Chan's trademark question is more than the old habit of a trained-to-be-submissive Southern girl: It's a manipulation technique. "That's the whole trick with people who ask, 'Are you mad at me?' It gets them instantly off the hook," the guitarist explains. "It's funny that she would always go, 'Are you mad at me?' because *she* was always mad at *me*,"

Chan's friend and former landlord Judy Ibbotson recalls. "She left a washer and dryer at her apartment when she moved out. Well, my insurance guy every now and then comes around and he said, 'You have to move that washer and dryer because it's a fire hazard.' I thought she'd abandoned it, 'cause it'd been a year and a half. So I gave it away. And then she's mad at me. She should have told me! I had to get it off the porch!"

By the time Shelley and Foljahn returned from a handful of trips on the road with Chan, they had new insight into the problems that came along with her compelling eccentricities. "Steve came back from that tour and he was like, 'I don't know how much longer I can do this,' " Moore remembers. "It became problematic because Steve has a classic Midwestern work ethic. He goes out and he wants to do the job the best he can, and he does it and it's great, and you can always depend on him. Chan was having a lot of issues about what her own value was as a performer."

This uncertainty about her worth manifested itself in a series of obnoxious onstage behaviors. Chan would begin songs and then abruptly end them, leaving the band unsure of what to play. She would perform with her back to the audience and compulsively apologize to the crowd for mistakes only she could hear. "It was very frustrating for the band," Foljahn recalls. "She would just stop playing a song. It annoyed the shit out of Steve, so I would kind of get annoyed along with him. You'd think, Why? Why? It was going so well! Why are we doing this? It's a whole different kind of frustration than I've had in any other band because you know she can do it if she wants to. That's the thing."

Even at this early stage in the evolution of Cat Power, Chan was already displaying some of the tics that would later aggravate her critics, alienate some of her most devoted followers, and compel a new group of voyeuristic fans to start attending her shows. "I'm not quite sure what happened, but Steve and Tim were in this rolling-of-the-eyes kind of thing when they came back," Moore remembers. "But they also had a sense of humor about it. They didn't really know what to think of it, but they did know that it was a little bit of a mess sometimes—more so than they were accustomed to, and it got a little weirder and weirder each time." In spite of their growing concern about Chan's mental state and frustration with the impact it had on her performance style, Shelley and Foljahn continued to play with Chan, and in February 1996 they recorded *What Would the Community Think* with her, then toured behind the album through the end of 1996.

15

What Would the Community Think

Between the October 1995 release of Dear Sir and the March 1996 release of Myra Lee, Cat Power finally signed a deal with Matador Records. Though Gerard Cosloy was interested in Chan and her music from the very beginning, not everyone at the label felt the same way. Some of the New York City-based tastemakers who saw Chan perform solo in the period between Glen Thrasher's spring 1993 departure and the following year, when she started playing with Steve Shelley and Tim Foljahn, had already decided she was overrated at best and a manipulative, crazy sympathy seeker at worst. "For people who are kind of into the whole 'set lists, thank you, good night, discernable beginning, middle, end,' it was a little hard to get a handle on," Cosloy explains.

"I saw a lot of bad shows where she never looked up," Charles Aaron recalls. "Why did I keep seeing her? Because I kept hearing about Chan: 'She's beautiful. She's enigmatic. She's poetic. She's mysterious. Nobody really knows where she's from. Her father's an itinerant bluesman!' I was from the South, so I had this interest in figuring out whether she was a fraud or not. And I more or less thought she was kind of a fraud for a long time. I thought everybody else was looking for this beautiful creature of the blues who was from the swamps."

Chan's onstage presence has always been divisive; for some it breeds intimacy, for others it smacks of artifice. But it wasn't just her polarizing nature as an artist that kept Matador from signing her until nearly four years after Cosloy first saw her perform. It was also the fact that both Matador and Chan are particular to the point of snobbery about the company they keep. "I didn't really know her well enough at that point to understand where she was coming from, how serious she was or wasn't," Cosloy remembers. "She was the least talkative person in that band. I met her a couple of times, but it was months and months before we ever had anything approaching a conversation."

In addition to Chan's evident shyness, Matador's own unspoken rules about courting artists delayed the consummation. "I was interested almost immediately, but at the time Matador was in a weird state of flux.

Still is, really," Cosloy ruminates. "We're weird in a passive-aggressive way in that on one hand, if an artist doesn't approach us, we don't know if they wanna be on the label. But on the other hand, we don't like it when we get approached. Sometimes it is just better not to be in this whole snipping, scouting thing and just let stuff happen naturally. In those days we were much bigger on letting stuff happen naturally. Those days it really was more about, like, we're gonna put out records by our friends, by people that we get to know, people we socialize with. It had less to do with Chan needing to convince us over however many years that she was ready for a record deal—it was more a matter of us getting to know her and vice versa."

It was also a matter of Chris Lombardi being convinced that Cat Power's austere music and elemental performances would one day translate to record and ticket sales. As a general rule, Gerard explains, Matador doesn't sign an artist unless he and Chris are in agreement, but sometimes that takes a while. "There are occasions where one of us might initiate a relationship with a band or be the one that's suggested it or whatever, but there's never a project where I'm the one who did—we just don't do that," Cosloy explains. "At that point in time I had the earlier relationship with Chan, and Chris hadn't seen some of those early shows. By the time he did see her, he liked what he heard, but there were a lot of questions about the nature of the performances, and how far could this go."

If Lombardi was cautious about investing in Cat Power, other people at the label were blatantly horrified that Matador was even considering it. "I don't want to bad-mouth anyone by name," Cosloy says, "but when we signed her, she had a number of big fans and friends in the office, but there were other people in our company who were just like, 'You've got to be kidding. Do you really think you're gonna sell this?'

Let's just say those people are no longer with us. They're alive, but they were wrong."

After the first two albums came out, it became clear that a small contingent of indulgent New York City hipsters weren't the only ones who heard something intriguing in Cat Power. As general interest in the band grew, the risks associated with investing in Chan diminished. "I don't want to make it sound like our thing is completely altruistic, because it isn't," Cosloy allows. "We were aware that the Italian label Runt was putting something out. We were aware that there was a growing relationship with Steve Shelley and that records were going to come out. There was a sense that there was something else going on commercially that would make things a little bit easier for us, but we had no way of knowing how far that would go."

Though *Myra Lee* was slated to be released on Smells Like Records in early 1996, Chan's new label wanted to release Cat Power's Matador Records debut as soon as possible, so it booked studio time for the band. In early February, a month before *Myra Lee* was in stores, Chan and Cat Power guitarist Tim Foljahn made the long drive from New York City down to Memphis to start recording Cat Power's third album at Easley Studios. They were supposed to meet up with Shelley, who was flying in from elsewhere.

At this point Shelley was serving as more than Cat Power's drummer. As the head of the label about to release the band's next album, Shelley was the singer's de facto manager, producer, and marketer. He set up the studio session that resulted in *Dear Sir* and *Myra Lee*, he played drums on both albums, toured in support of them, and kept Chan on task, whether in the studio or on the road. No one was a bigger Cat Power advocate than Steve. The March 1996 release of *Myra Lee* suggested that Cat Power had found a semihome on Steve's label, so when

Steve found out that Chan had signed with Matador, he had the right to be miffed—and he was, sort of.

"I remember being with Steve and him getting a phone call, he was talking to her," Moore recalls. "He said, 'Oh, congratulations,' and then he hung up the phone and said, 'Matador wants to sign Cat Power, and she's going to go for it.' He was sort of like, 'I invested a lot of energy and money into making these records and doing these tours,' but at the same time, he also understood the opportunity. He was on the fence with how he felt about it emotionally." As a music fan and businessman, Steve wanted to maintain his professional connection to Cat Power, but as a sane person looking to stay that way, he was better off letting Chan go. "Somebody swooped in, and that's never a good feeling," Moore acknowledges, "but the conflict was like, 'Well, it's a little emotionally draining to begin with, so . . .' "

Chan's account of Matador's courtship is characteristically vivid but nonspecific. "When I moved to New York I heard of Railroad Jerk, a Matador band," she said in 1998. "I didn't know anything. I had no conscience of the music business. I started seeing bands, kept seeing bands, and I saw Gerard from Matador. Nice guy. It just happened organically." Whatever consternation Steve felt as a result of Chan's decision to split for another label, it didn't stop him from recording Cat Power's third album, *What Would the Community Think*, expressly for Matador. "She recorded it for us," Cosloy says unequivocally. "It was one of these things that Chris and I had been talking about off and on for more than a year. I finally mentioned it to Chan one night after a show: 'Would you be interested in doing something with us?' It was not like a long negotiation or a series of business meetings. It was a pretty quick conversation."

After signing with Matador, Chan bought an old green-and-white Volkswagen bus that ran well but had no heat. This was the vehicle she and Foljahn drove down to Memphis that cold, dark February of 1996. "We were freezing," Foljahn remembers of the pair's trip down the Eastern Seaboard. "Chan got sick, she had a cold." The singer's voice sounds much more open and expressive on *Community* than it does on either of the first two Cat Power records, but according to Foljahn, Chan was too sick to relax and sing properly. "In a rehearsal room playing with her then, it was like playing with a sax player," Foljahn recalls. "She was loud and clear—it was very much, Whoa! Very strong." Chan's illness contributed to a detachment in the vocals that wasn't characteristic of her singing at the time.

The *Community* sessions marked the first time that Chan worked in a professional recording space. Easley Studios was cofounded by producers Doug Easley and Davis McCain in the early nineties, and it immediately became a respite-giving recording location for some of the most influential bands of the era. A greatest-hits list of the albums recorded there includes Pavement's *Wowee Zowee*, Sonic Youth's *Washing Machine*, Wilco's *A.M.*, the White Stripes' *White Blood Cells*, Loretta Lynn's *Van Lear Rose*, and Modest Mouse's *Good News for People Who Love Bad News*. Jeff Buckley was at Easley recording songs for what was supposed to be his second full-length album in late May of 1997 when he disappeared and was eventually found drowned in the Mississippi River. (The material he recorded was released on 1998's *Sketches [For My Sweetheart the Drunk]*.)

Tragically, the studio burned down in an electrical fire in March 2005.

With Easley Studios' storied history and Chan's relative lack of recording experience on her mind, the twenty-four-year-old singer entered the *Community* sessions haunted yet again by the idea that she had no right to be there. According to Chan, she was so unprepared to make the album that she barely got it together to tell her band when and where to show up. "I knew I had this huge journey, and I wasn't prepared for the journey," the singer has said. "Much less was I prepared to make a record. The night before we were supposed to leave, Tim calls, and he's like, 'Chan, we don't know what's going on, I guess we're not going?' I just hadn't called them." Chan dealt with her apprehension by holding herself to super-rigid standards once the recording session started. "She was tentative," Tim recalls. "She thought that doubling her vocals was cheating. 'Can you do that?' she said. 'I don't think that's cool. That's a special effect!' "

As long as she kept things minimal, Chan felt safe. She felt like a good person—as if through making brutally spare sounds, she was doing penance for not being professionally trained. "She didn't want any studio trickery," Foljahn recalls. "She was figuring out what it was like to be in a real studio, how to play studios. She always knew how to play the mike, and she always knew how to do a lot of things that were pretty subtle, but I think she was probably daunted. She realized that there was so much more that could be done [in the studio as compared to playing live], and she didn't have those ideas yet."

Though Chan's experience in a professional recording studio of Easley's caliber was minimal, she did enter the *Community* sessions aware of the fact that the songs she recorded would actually become an album, a notion that escaped her when recording *Dear Sir* and *Myra Lee*. "When I recorded with Steve and Tim, I actually didn't think that anyone was going to hear those recordings," Chan has said, referring to her first two albums. "We were recording for the Italian record. I didn't know that the other songs were going to be used for Steve's record, but people have heard those records." As wary as Chan was of the entire in-the-studio experience, her desire to achieve creative satisfaction on her third album gave her the courage she needed to battle back some of her insecurities and fight to make sure that what she heard in her head made it onto tape. "I am," Chan said, when asked if she was happy with the way Community turned out. "I got to do things, I got to direct it a little. The other times we just pressed record—this time I got to branch out and figure out where I thought it should go."

At Easley, Chan was impressive in ways she wasn't even aware of. Foljahn remembers that the engineers and studio techs were stunned by her ability to cut her vocals and guitar in one take, with no drama or ceremony about it. He also noticed that though Chan presents herself as a neophyte, her in-the-studio decisions revealed a deep knowledge of sound and song structure. "Chan's a very musical person," Foljahn explains. "She'd go over to the piano midsession and just figure something out. She didn't have a lot of experience, but she has a lot of skills—I don't want to say they are innate because I think that plays them down. I think she's listened very carefully to a lot of music."

What Would the Community Think was released on September 10, 1996. It's the only Cat Power album that really reflects Chan's life in New York. The abstract, fractured look of the cover, with its muted blue and gray tones, feels disjointed, moody, and undone but elegant, like the Lower East Side at night. The sonic tone of the album is disjointed but homogeneous, like an urban environment where anguish, joy, anger, and romance all merge in a dense collection of sound. The Chan Marshall you hear on Community is different from the one you met on Myra Lee or Dear Sir, more expressive, angrier, and even darker. She also emerges as a real singer.

Sonically, Community is an understated, cool guitar-rock record that sounds both timeless and distinctly nineties. ("I was thinking, why didn't we put a bass on that song?" Foljahn says of Community's lead single, "Nude as the News." "But it was the nineties, you didn't need a bass player!") Lyrically, the album is an aggressive, moody testament to Chan's ability to write songs that are disturbing and soothing at the same time. It opens with "In This Hole," a fraught meditation on meaninglessness. ("In this hole that we have fixed/We get further and further and further for what?") With that uplifting beginning, the album takes you through "Good Clean Fun," a rhythmic dirge in which Chan laments the disillusionment of a relationship ("It seems I have nothing to give/It seems you have nothing to give"). And the album's title track is an ethereal folk ballad that hints at an as-yet-unexplored richness within Chan's voice.

From there, the album continues to display an impressive range of almost unbearably depressing songs ("Taking People," "Water and Air") alongside traditional tracks that sound ageless, like covers of old hymns or blues standards. On "They Tell Me," for example, Chan sings the following lyrics with the collected sorrow of the generations of struggling Southerners who preceded her: "Maybe if I pray to the Lord above/I'll get some sleep/But the Lord don't give a shit about me." As she had on both of her first two records, Chan also included covers on *What Would the Community Think*. She does a version of "The Fate of the Human Carbine," an angry singsong track written by Peter Jeffries, as well as a cover of the Smog tune "Bathysphere," which was written by reclusive folk-rock poet Bill Callahan, whom Chan met and started dating in early 1996.

The most compelling song on *What Would the Community Think* is also the most famous. "Nude as the News," with its understated but urgent guitar sound, open, engaged vocals, and totally bizarre lyrics, became Cat Power's first hit. The song could be heard on college-radio stations nationwide, and in New York City during the late fall of 1996 it seemed like no one was playing anything else. The album was on constant rotation at Sounds and Kim's record stores on Saint Marks Place in the East Village, vinyl copies were on the turntables at crowded loft parties in then-scary, arty Williamsburg, Brooklyn, and "Nude as the News" was the most frequently selected track on the jukebox at Lower East Side dive Max Fish. The song was released as a single (the B-side of which was a cover of Sonic Youth's "Schizophrenia" retitled "Schizophrenia's Weighted Me Down") and was featured in Cat Power's first-ever music video.

Chan says that the phrase "nude as the news" is straightforward. "It just means reality. Like, Oops, there it is. That's all," the singer has said. But the secret meaning behind the song has been one of the greatest mysteries to die-hard Cat Power fans. The song seems to be about everything from a hot crush ("I still have a flame gun/For the cute cute cute ones") to ominous guys ("/ . . . in the cold light/There's a very big man"). For more than ten years, fans were free to speculate about the secret meaning of every line, but in an August 2007 interview with famed rock critic Greil Marcus published in *Interview* magazine, Chan confirmed that the song is really about the abortion she'd had when she was twenty and a conversation with Patti Smith.

"One song I've always wanted to ask you about is 'Nude as the News,' " Marcus asked Chan in the piece. "There is something wonderfully psychotic about that song." "I've never told anybody what that song's about . . . I wrote it when I was young," she responded.

> When I was making it up in my mind, I was feeling remorseful, I'd had an abortion when I was twenty. I felt guilt and the shame about that—which I still feel, but I've forgiven myself. I'd just seen Patti Smith perform for the first time—knowing that she had two children, her being a figure of feminine strength for me, connecting with her strength, wanting to

have it or work up to it and to fulfill my need for that strength, which I didn't have when I wrote that song. So it meant that I carry the soul of that child in me forever. I'm not real educated. There's a lot of societal anger: no education about when you get pregnant. There's self-hatred. I'm not the enemy; society didn't force me to have the abortion. But it's years of stories meshed into one triumphant one: I can carry the soul with me, hopefully, in my mind or my heart. Carry the soul with me. I've never told anybody this. So there it is, for the world to see.

In this same piece, Chan goes on to describe the two sides of herself as represented in "Nude as the News." One side is weak and the other is strong. In Chan's mind, her weaker self is the one that felt she had no choice but to terminate her pregnancy. The strong self is the one that knew she had two options and chose the one that wouldn't turn her into a hopelessly young mom.

The protective second self ... made me get the abortion, ... made me get out of certain situations in my past, ... helped me survive, and get away from the would-be father of the child. The first self ... the child's self, the weak self, the dependent self, the naïve self, didn't have the strength.... The second self is like the stronger me, the woman me, rationalizing with human rights and women's rights, telling the child in me that it's going to be okay, having to be stronger than I am, in a way.

"Nude as the News" is the first Cat Power song that plainly reveals the deep conflict (in this case it's between strength and weakness, but in other songs it takes different forms) at the center of Chan's music and her soul. With the release of this song, and the album on which it appears, an entirely new breed of intensely dedicated Cat Power fan emerged. They heard the conflict at the core of Chan's sound, at the core of her soul, really, and they related to it.

What Would the Community Think is not a soothing record. It's actually Cat Power's most violent, angry work, a deranged epic filled with sadness, guilt, and defiance, a combination that worked like a salve on Chan's self-loathing teenaged fans. At first it wasn't a problem that Cat Power's new converts expected her to be at least as miserable as they were, because she was. Eventually, though, the pressure to consistently articulate Community levels of anguish became a problem for Chan, which was a problem for her Community-era fans, who needed her to be permanently sad.

Chan has never been very comfortable with the expectation of intimacy between artists and fan. It's precisely because her songs are so personal that Chan is mystified by why other people relate to them so completely. To her, the songs are intrinsically connected to memories or experiences that are so private as to be uninteresting to anyone but her. As a child, Chan's only real friends were the voices she heard coming out of her record player, but she has never been able to sense the parallel between how she felt about Billie Holiday or Smokey Robinson and how Cat Power fans feel about Chan Marshall.

Chan also thinks that her music is misinterpreted; she doesn't understand why everybody thinks her songs are so sad. "They're not sad, they're triumphant," the singer has insisted. She will admit to feeling sad when writing some of the tracks on Community (and cites "King Rides By" as an example), but she insists that even in those moments, the song is always about accepting pain and celebrating the fact that you're strong

Chan in May of 1999. MARK WHITELEY

Chan applies her makeup backstage in Brussels during a tour stop in 2007. STEFANO GIOVANNINI

The elegant desolation
of Cabbagetown train tracks
in Atlanta, Georgia. ELIZABETH GOODMAN

Chan takes a pensive cigarette break while shooting a video with the Dirty Three in Williamsburg, Brooklyn, circa 2005 or 2006. STEFANO GIOVANNINI

At a Kinko's in Miami, Chan examines old photos of her younger, more androgynous self while preparing for an art show at Max Fish in New York City. STEFANO GIOVANNINI

Chan swings her guitar around during soundcheck at Irving Plaza during the Greatest tour. STEFANO GIOVANNINI

Chan onstage

with guitarist Judah Bauer during
a festival in Georgia in 2007.
STEFANO GIOVANNINI

Chan plays guitar backstage
at the Bowery Ballroom in 2003.
STEFANO GIOVANNINI

Chan shares the crowd's enthusiasm during a 2007 show at McCarren Park Pool in Brooklyn, New York. STEFANO GIOVANNINI

enough to survive it. "That one's sad. Some of them are sad, but also at the same time, that one included, there's a thing about realization and acceptance, which is kind of a triumph. So they don't seem that sad. It's accepting something to yourself, and that gives you some kind of strength."

More than a decade after she first played *What Would the Community Think* in her childhood bedroom, Appel still finds the album consoling. Chan doesn't get the same kind of satisfaction out of her early records. All the singer hears in *Community* is a series of grotesque technical inadequacies and the pain that inspired her to write the songs in the first place. "On those early albums, I was just a kid, dude—I didn't know how to sing. I didn't know what I was doing," Chan has explained. "I can't listen to them now. I have a friend in France who's a fan of *What Would the Community Think*. She put it on and it was excruciating for me. All I hear is memories of what I was going through then. I can't. It's ridiculous."

16.

Europe

The What Would the Community Think *recording process* *was more fulfilling for* Chan *than her previous in-the-* *studio experiences, but the pacing felt rushed and discom-* *bobulated.* Chan *recorded the album in February 1996, a* few months after Miranda gave birth to her second child, Audrey. Chan was in a hurry to finish the record and head back to North Carolina to meet her new niece. She wanted to get there as soon as possible because she knew she'd be off again soon, first to Austin, Texas, for the annual South by Southwest music conference, then to Atlanta, then on to her first real national tour. Chan was always good at living out of a suitcase, but she wasn't ready for the extreme transience she was about to experience.

At first it wasn't obvious that all this travel was taking a toll on Chan's mental health. After all, this was a girl whose dream was to get out of Georgia, and now she was scheduled to travel all over the entire United States before heading to Europe. First Chan headed home, where Cat Power played a resounding hometown gig with the Rock*A*Teens at Dottie's in Atlanta. After touring down South, Cat Power headed north to Chicago, where they played at the famed indie-rock club Lounge Ax. Then they flew to London and began a European tour that included several shows in France, where Cat Power has a particularly fervent fan base. It was during this final leg of the *Community* tour, in the late summer of 1996, that Chan started to unravel emotionally.

"The playing thing was just really horrible for her," Foljahn remembers. "She really didn't enjoy it. She didn't want to come out of the bathroom, she didn't want to do the show. There were scenes in the hotel room where she was just really tore up. It was inconsolable, suicidal sadness." At the time, Foljahn, like most of the other people Chan was around, was into the debauched touring life. The party started in the afternoon at the hotel room and continued at soundcheck, then at dinner, during the gig, at the after-party, and started again the next morning in a new city. The fact that she was there, in France, or Germany, or Spain, playing songs about abortion and abuse and neglect to a series of rooms full of strangers, was starting to dawn on Chan. The more she tried to process what was happening around her, the less able she was to carry on performing and the more entrenched the emotional rift between her and everyone else became.

Chan's reaction to fame was a combination of self-loathing and defiance: Why do all of these people care about me? Why should I care about them? "There's the inferiority and the superiority, and they always go together," Foljahn explains. "You've got this total insecurity, across-the-board insecurity, and yet this total belief in her talent because she knows how good she is and she kind of always did."

While Chan was struggling with her sense of worth as an artist, Cat Power's popularity was exploding. With every copy of *Community* sold—each one representative of Chan's triumphant success as a professional musician—the singer became more disturbed by exactly what she was selling and exactly what her fans thought they were buying.

"I did an interview in Paris when I was twenty-four years old," Chan remembered. "I didn't want to do the interview so I shoved towels in all my clothes and put them under the bed so it looked like I was asleep. I didn't understand this whole process of being interviewed, having my photo taken, just for art, just for a song. I thought, The song is there, I gave you the song. It's on a CD. You can have it. Thank you for giving me the present of being able to have a CD. It's an honor. When the interviewer came in, she thought, She's sleeping. Hearing her wondering what was wrong, I felt like an idiot. I pulled the covers down and said, 'I'm here.' I felt so bad. She was seventeen and had a fanzine in France. She started crying: 'Thank you. Your songs helped me. I was going to kill myself. I didn't know what to do. I played your record to help me.' "

The idea that Chan might have something in common with her fans was a revelation for her. "You realize, 'Fuck, I'm not alone. There are a lot

of people like us. Displaced. Emotional. Sensitive. Aware. Compassionate. Interested in the world.' " Chan still couldn't process that what she
meant to that seventeen-year-old French girl was what Bob Dylan meant
to her. But for every one of the times Chan felt a beneficent union with
her fans, there was another instance in which things didn't go so well.
The fans wanted to tell Chan about their own abortions, child-abusing
mothers, absent fathers, violent households, alcoholic relatives, to show
her that she had helped them accept the horror of experiences similar to
the ones she sings about. They felt better after unburdening themselves
to her, but she felt worse, like a priest who's heard too many confessions.
"The intensely autobiographical nature of her songs was freaking her out,"
Foljahn surmises. "She was thinking, What the hell am I doing? Why am
I doing this? Why am I singing such a personal thing to all these people?"

At this point Chan had yet to cultivate the Cat Power fan base specif-
ically drawn to her manic onstage behavior, but even before the tour
reached Europe, even before her most famously deranged shows took
place a few years later, Chan was already paying close attention to the
way an audience would react to her onstage emotional disintegration.

"I was with Man or Astro-man? and we went to Knoxville, Tennessee," Atlanta-based promoter Henry Owings remembers. "The lineup
was a package tour of Guv'ner and Cat Power and Man or Astro-man?,
who were at the peak of their crazy spazoid sci-fi powers. They were
headlining, Guv'ner was first, and Chan was in the middle." The order
of this lineup was ill-advised. Guv'ner's loud, angular sound amps the
crowd up for a rowdy rock show, not a girl with an acoustic guitar and
a fear of getting too close to the mike. "These kids from Knoxville want
to see the rock band," Owings remembers. "Chan goes up there and gets
through fragments of two songs, three songs, four songs, five songs,
whatever it is. She came offstage, took her guitar off, went upstairs to

this big wide empty room, and went over to the farthest corner, and from the other side of the room you could hear her whimpering and sobbing. Man or Astro-man? are like, 'What the fuck just happened? Was she *raped?*' "

Performing live brought out raw anguish in Chan, and she noticed, subconsciously, that this was fascinating to other people. Whether she knew it at the time or not, even in these catastrophic moments onstage—which began in these early years as a real, genuine, emotional reaction to unresolved issues with fame, performance, and the notion of audience—Chan was training herself to play up the chaos in her own head for performance's sake. "If you have a really low opinion of yourself that's really deep-seated, and then people say, 'Oh my God! You're so fragile, I love you! You're so complicated! When you broke down like that, I was really moved,' imagine what that does to you," *New York Times* music critic Ben Ratliff, who has written about Cat Power, asks. "It's like, 'Whoa! Well, I'm still worthless, but that thing that I did. . . .' " Chan's onstage breakdowns have never been contrived, but that doesn't mean that she isn't aware of how compelling they are.

She was and would continue to be justifiably criticized for flagrantly disregarding any sense of showmanship, but for a woman who refused to think of herself as a professional performer, the idea that she was responsible for delivering something polished onstage completely mystified her. And since her audience drew closer to her with every erratic sob, there was no reason for Chan to dry her tears. "When I write songs, it's for personal reasons," she has said. "Like the reason you might get a haircut or move out of town, it's because you don't want to look at negative images anymore, so you do something in your own life to change the situation. I wrote songs. I'm not trying to say anything to anyone. Whatever's there is a subconscious buildup."

Sometimes Chan's accounts of how she was sold into rock-star slavery are merely self-abdicating: "I gave my music to other people because they asked for it," she has said. "Steve Shelley wanted it for his label, Gerard Cosloy wanted it for Matador, and Mark Moore, who first put a microphone in front of my face, wanted to have a band." Other times, her explanations are so plainly false they're obnoxious. "What I do anyone could do," she has said.

Chan's modesty is a cover for her fear that she is actually the sole architect of her own fame. If Cat Power's success is somebody else's fault, then Chan gets to come along for the ride all the while complaining that she never wanted to be there in the first place. During the *Community* tour, this shell game imploded. "Her dream was happening," Foljahn says, "and she just didn't think she deserved it. There was that tension between whatever had gone on in her childhood and this reality that she could become this thing that she wanted to become, and I think it was painful for her."

Like most teenagers, Chan aspired to be the exact opposite of her parents, but to be a rebel in the Marshall family meant living a quiet, suburban life. If either of Charlie and Myra's kids defied their parents it was Miranda, who got married, had kids, and became a nurse. For Chan, Cat Power's success represented her failure as a human being. "I don't like to think of it as a career," the singer has said of making music. "There's so many other things I'd like to do, go work on a boat in Alaska, or teach kids their A to Z's. Music keeps me away from other things I'd like to do."

After she wrapped up the *Community* tour, Chan went back for a few months to New York, where she tried to reenter her prefame life. She went to other people's shows, enjoyed not having to work a day job, and played hostess to friends from out of town.

17.

Let's Move to the Country

Before **What Would the Community Think**'s release in September 1996, Chan was dealing with her first major what-am-I-doing-with-my-life breakdown. The singer would face many of these in the future, and all of them would center around the same central conflict: How can you be a rock star *and* a homemaker? A public figure and a private citizen? A sophisticated, well-traveled independent woman and a good Southern housewife? How can you be Cat Power and Chan Marshall all at once?

In the late fall of 1996, Chan arrived home in New York, back from her first major international tour. She tried to reconnect with her pre-*Community* life. That didn't work. "I like the fact that when I first moved here, I didn't know anybody," she has said of New York. "I like the fact that there were so many people and I was just one of the people. But now I can't concentrate. I'm always a nervous wreck and I'm always freaking out. It seems like everyone I talk to I'm always saying 'I'm sorry' to, because inside my head I'm thinking I'm going insane and I can't really express that, so I just say, 'I'm sorry.' What I really want to say is, 'I have to go, 'cause I can't concentrate.' "

Still unsure of what to do, Chan decided to play a few shows in New York. With Foljahn and Shelley behind her, Cat Power took the stage at the Knitting Factory for what would turn out to be her last performance for more than a year. This show should have been a homecoming celebration: Chan was playing in support of a successful record, had just returned from a whirlwind European tour, and was standing onstage with people she trusted. Yet midsong, midset, the singer looked out onto the range of expectant faces in the crowd and started screaming. At first the moment was interesting, another one of crazy Chan's crazy tics. Then it became mildly alarming, then disturbing, then totally harrowing. An alarmed murmur rose from the crowd, and Shelley and Foljahn stopped trying to keep the song going and looked at each other, unsure of what to do. When Chan finally stopped howling, she mumbled something inaudible into her mike and attempted to play again before the soundman finally cut her off.

When Chan talks about this show, she explains that she couldn't get off the stage because she couldn't admit that the performance was beyond salvation. "When things go wrong, I usually play for a long time," the singer has said. This paradox—that the worse things went, the longer Chan would play—became the dominant pattern in Cat Power shows for the next ten years. And its emergence reflected the larger conflict Chan was feeling about being onstage in the first place. Foljahn noticed it, Moore noticed it: Anyone who was around could see that Chan wasn't yet ready to succeed. She wasn't ready to deal with what success would mean about her worth as a person, what that would say about her talent as an artist, and the ways in which it would force her to admit that as much as she loathed rock stardom, she had become a rock star. Instead of contending with all of this, Chan decided to disappear for a while.

"I went to have fun," Chan has said of the trip to South Africa she took in early 1997. "But the first two weeks in Cape Town were such a nightmare that I ended up leaving and going to Johannesburg and then going to Durban and then farther out into the bush. That's where I saw the stuff that made me not want to make music anymore. I didn't think music was important. You can't feel like, when you're playing your songs and people are asking you questions and you're getting a photo shoot— you can't feel special or talented. It makes me think of what someone else doesn't have."

In addition to being struck by the contrast between her life and the lives of the locals, Chan also claims to have had a mystical experience while in Africa that really disturbed her. Apparently, she had a strange conversation with a Zulu shaman just as she was getting off the plane in Cape Town. "Twelve days later, I had to track him down because I was seeing people who weren't really there. I could no longer tell the difference between reality and what I thought was hell," Chan has said. She spoke to this shaman one more time and he explained a dream she had four years prior, which brought her a sense of relief and resolution. Chan has referred to this experience as a "spiritual episode," but is upset by the suggestion that it was something more menacing. "A friend of mine called it a psychotic episode, which hurt me more than I can say," the singer has said. "My problem is that other people's idea of reality is not mine."

Chan returned to New York, but didn't stay very long. She soon took off for the Pacific Northwest. "It's really pretty and clean and it's gonna be spring," the singer told a reporter before she left for Portland, Oregon, where her sometimes boyfriend, Truman's Water bassist Kirk Branstetter, was living. "I want a nice, quiet time." As with most of Chan's lurches toward the quiet life, her move to Oregon worked for a few months. She babysat, hung out with the guys from the band, and focused on inhaling clean air, smelling spring flowers, and purifying herself of all the evil dirty rock sins she had committed over the last year. Ultimately the city took to Chan more than she took to it: "I would go out there later and people would be talking to me about her," Foljahn remembers. "I think Chan had a good time out there, but it didn't last very long."

In the mid-nineties, Chan's dating life was as unwieldy as her professional life. She was always on the road or traveling on her own, and she wasn't sure whether she was going to continue making music or give it all up for a simpler life. In Bill Callahan, a poet Chan met in 1996, she found a reason to focus. By the late spring of 1997, Callahan, a handsome but somber-looking guy with a slight build and a knowing stare, was the only man left in Chan's life.

Callahan, who recorded music under the name Smog, was born in

June 1966 in Silver Spring, Maryland, a large suburb of Washington, D.C. He was a quiet child with an elaborate inner life he rarely shared. His brief forays into traditional teenage society included archery lessons, a stint on the middle school cross-country team, and hours spent skateboarding on the yellow slalom board he got at Sears. Callahan's musical heroes include John Lee Hooker and James Brown, but he was into the romance of discovering any kind of new music. "I made my way through just about everything as a kid," the singer has said. And when asked which artists first grabbed his attention, he said, "The transistor radio held to the ear late into the night."

In 1988, Bill used a four-track to record a series of homemade cassettes under the name Smog. From the very beginning, Bill was into brutally spare music: Smog's debut album *Sewn to the Sky* (released in 1990) showcases serrated, almost violent instrumentals played with a willful lack of artistry on junk-shop instruments. Callahan also was interested in music made without any of the usual frivolous adornments like an in-tune guitar or a hook. Callahan also had a predilection for wandering. In 1988 he moved to Georgia, then back to Maryland. Around the time *Sewn to the Sky* came out, Bill was off to New Hampshire, and in 1992, just after *Forgotten Foundation*, his debut album for indie label Drag City, came out, Bill moved to California, where he lived in San Francisco and Sacramento. All told, Callahan has lived in more than twenty cities in his life. He currently resides in Austin, Texas, though only he knows for how long.

According to Callahan, Chan decided to cover the Smog song "Bathysphere" on *What Would the Community Think* after she saw Callahan perform it live. "I liked her version," the reclusive singer-songwriter has said of the cover. "I think she's got a good voice, something that should be emanating from a minaret." Chan's choice to put a Smog cover on her album was the indie-rocker equivalent of passing Callahan a note in study hall, and it worked. For all Chan's insecurity and evident shyness, she's also boy-crazy, and tends to aggressively go after the men that she wants. "She's kind of a dude about the boys," Foljahn explains, laughing. "She's got a flame gun for the cute ones. She's on it."

Both Chan and Callahan have been careful not to openly discuss the details of their relationship (that's what postbreakup albums are for), and it's hard to pinpoint exactly when things between them went from like to love, but by the time Cat Power was on the European leg of the *Community* tour, the two were hanging out in Spain as a couple. The relationship continued through Cat Power's return to the States, and though it took her a few months to conclude she'd had enough of the music business, it was Callahan to whom Chan turned when she decided it was time to try out her real dream of becoming a wife and mother. In the spring of 1997 Chan left Portland and met Callahan in Prosperity, South Carolina, where the couple rented a modest two-story white clapboard house off Highway 51. Both vowed to end their nomadic ways.

Prosperity is a remote town of about a thousand people located in northwestern South Carolina. There is a slow, sticky feel to the place that makes porch swinging and iced-tea drinking seem like biological imperatives. In the parking lot of the Piggy Wiggly just outside town, a buxom teenage blonde in a hot-pink John Deere T-shirt makes out with a boy through the open window of his pickup truck. A few cars down, a mother in her twenties wrestles watermelons and twin toddlers into the backseat of a station wagon, the dashboard of which is cluttered with religious figurines. On a Sunday afternoon, Town Square Antiques, which sells everything from costume jewelry to beat-up old dressers to vintage housecoats, is just about the only place open. Down Main Street you'll find the BP station advertising HOT DOGS, PROPANE, BOILED P-NUTS, while teenagers congregate to drink soda pop, crush aluminum cans, and watch the cars go by.

Prosperity feels remote but not rural. The state highway that leads you to Main Street and the town's center features one Baptist or Lutheran church for every tractor-repair shop and fireworks depot. Life here is not bucolic. There's no livestock in sight, no produce stands or wide expanses of well-groomed farmland, and the houses in the area are modest suburban homes set close to the road, featuring mailboxes decorated with tacky floral contact paper. On the town's Web site, the mayor boasts that employment in the Prosperity area is steady, with the Georgia-Pacific sawmill and plywood plant, an auto-parts plant, and a frozen-bread-product producer nearby.

The small house that Chan and Bill lived in sits about five minutes outside of town. It's close enough to Highway 51 that the sound of cars whizzing by is constant. On the other side of the street is a vast expanse of deep-green land, overgrown with weeds. Next door is Ackerman's, a used-car depot that advertises with the slogan "We buy wrecks." Behind the house is more overgrown land dotted with discarded tractor parts, rusty from exposure to the elements. Prosperity isn't charming, it's oppressive.

The young couple moved to Prosperity in the late spring of 1997, when Chan was twenty-five and Bill was thirty. The plan was simple: Chan was going to quit making music and domesticate, and Bill was going to be the head of the couple's fledgling household. As the man, Bill would continue making Smog albums and touring so he could pull in decent money from royalties and live shows, while Chan would stay home and be a good wife and eventually a good mother as well. "My travels are over/My travels are through/Let's move to the country/Just me and you," he sings on "Let's Move to the Country," the opening track on

Knock Knock, a 1999 Smog album that is widely believed to chronicle the trajectory of his relationship with Chan.

The couple began their project with the same sense of optimism conveyed in this song. This was Bill's chance to stop moving long enough to actually invest in a real life with someone other than himself. It was Chan's chance to break out of the family business and pursue the life she'd always idealized: as a mother and a wife. "I said, 'I'm gonna be a housewife,' " Chan remembered. "I'm gonna play with deers. I'm gonna learn to cook. I'm gonna wear dresses and try to be normal." She's great at living out of a suitcase, but Chan actually has quite a few skills that recommend her to housewifery. From hot summer afternoons in Cabbagetown spent passing out Popsicles to neighborhood kids to the years Chan spent working in New York City restaurants, she has always found satisfaction in serving others, and she's always been a pretty decent cook. "She worked at all these fabulous restaurants," Foljahn says. "I remember once she made this thing with corn and sun-dried tomatoes . . . and she'd use good olive oil, and it was all very fancy and really good."

The plan worked for a while. When Bill wasn't on tour, Chan busied herself tending to him and to their home. When he was away she took walks, listened to records, and read.

"Chan moved into a little house in South Carolina with Bill," her stepdad, Leamon, remembers. "I met Bill. He was neat. He was quiet. . . . Didn't get to know him that well. I went out there to visit. Me and Lenny, or me and someone. They had a little farmhouse. We walked around the property, strummed the guitar a little while, she showed us the house, we had a light lunch, sandwiches and stuff." For a while the pair was really happy. They even bickered like a blissfully devoted married couple. "It was funny the things she had to complain about when she got back from South Carolina," Foljahn remembers. "They were all funny-old-married-people things like that he just wanted to cook the same thing all the time. She would cook all these fabulous things and he would just want to make vegetable stir-fry."

When they were both home at the same time, they would do silly couple stuff like take up odd projects or try out new recipes on each other. "One day, when I lived in the country, I just got bored," Chan has remembered. "My boyfriend and I went to Wal-Mart and bought some paints 'cause we found all this paper in the recycling bin at the dump. So we bought yellow, blue, red, and white. For eight hours—I made dinner in between paintings—I just made a bunch of paintings and never did it again. It's kinda how it is with songwriting. 'Oh, I feel like playin' the guitar. Oh, look. I have four new songs. I'm tired. I wanna go out to eat or something.' "

On the surface, Bill Callahan and Chan Marshall seem to be polar opposites. In person, Chan is a hipster Southern belle. Warm and pathologically social, Chan is the sort of person who can make ten friends in ten minutes in a roomful of complete strangers. She's also a huge flirt and a bit of a scenester. Foljahn remembers being at clubs and bars in New York with Chan in the early nineties and listening to her go on and on about whatever semifamous indie-rock sex object was in the room at the time. "We'd go someplace because she had a crush on Jon Spencer," the guitarist remembers. "She'd go, 'Oh, there he is!' Or Malkmus or whatever. She knew all these people, she knew everybody on the scene." Bill, on the other hand, is a total recluse, known for his unapologetically ornery personality in interviews, coal-black sense of humor, and his hermetic tendencies. It's not unreasonable to wonder: Besides lo-fi rock music, what did these two have in common?

For starters, Bill is as girl-crazy as Chan is boy-crazy. Besides Chan, his past girlfriends include zany journalist and zine-culture icon Lisa

"Suckdog" Carver and freak-folk harpist Joanna Newsom. Though Bill doesn't share Chan's almost predatory flirting style, his lyrics are sexually explicit, bawdy, aggressive, and sometimes violent. The sexualized vitriol certain Smog lyrics reveal has even led some people to call him a misogynist, but it's more that Bill's way of relaying truths about people and relationships often involves sex. In Smog songs, everybody is who they are in bed.

On "Dress Sexy at My Funeral," off *Dongs of Sevotion*, Callahan sings: "Dress sexy at my funeral my good wife/ . . . Wear your blouse undone to here/And your skirt split up to there/ . . . /Tell them about the time we did it/ . . . /On the railroad tracks with the gravel in your back/ . . . And in the graveyard where my body now rests." This is one of the Smog lyrics that scandalizes some listeners, but it's important to note that however seething his anger at women may be in this and other songs, he applies the same lewd examination style to himself. On "To Be of Use," a heartbreaking track off 1997's *Red Apple Falls*, Callahan uses sex as a metaphor to describe his desire to be of some use in life. "Most of my fantasies are of/Making someone else come/Most of my fantasies are of/To be of use/To be of some hard, simple, undeniable use."

Chan's old married life was blissful so long as Bill was around, but in May 1997 *Red Apple Falls* was released and the singer went out on the road to support it. This meant that Chan spent a lot of time alone. Locals remember seeing her making the twenty-minute walk along the rusty train tracks from her house into Prosperity, where she'd browse at the junk shop, sit under the gazebo in the main square, or eat lunch by herself at the Back Porch, the local watering hole. Surprisingly, other than vague memories, Chan didn't make much of an impression on her neighbors. In New York City, or Atlanta, or most other places Chan has lived over the years, she can't walk down the street without greeting people she knows from way back, people she met yesterday or doesn't know at all but wants to talk to anyway. In Prosperity, though, she barely made a ripple.

Chan Marshall is an urban pioneer who left the oppression and backwater degeneracy she associated with the South for the Northeast. If all she wanted was a family, she could have stayed in Atlanta, married young, and started having babies like both her sister and her mother did, but something drove her to pursue more than that. Yet when she achieved fame, success, and a career in music, she immediately longed for the life she left at home. This conflict still has not been settled in Chan's life, and when she was twenty-five it was even more unresolved. Chan managed to stay in Prosperity for the better part of a year. But in the fall of 1997, when Bill left for tour, Chan freaked out.

"I was in South Carolina by myself for an entire month," Chan has said. "There's no sounds or lights, just crickets and darkness. It's an old house, and if you're in a bad state of mind, you sometimes see things that aren't there and you go crazy." Chan battled back the darkness by sequestering herself in her farmhouse, turning on all the lights, and staying awake. After several days of self-induced sleeplessness, she started hallucinating. She also started writing songs.

In one deranged night Chan wrote six of the eleven dense, emotionally fraught tracks that would appear on Cat Power's next album, *Moon Pix*, including "No Sense," "Metal Heart," "Say," "Cross Bones Style," and "You May Know Him." The idea of an artist toiling away all night in a fit of inspiration is romantic, but it does not describe Chan's experience. It's not as though she finally found her muse; Chan literally thought she was going crazy. "I got woken up by someone in the field behind my house in South Carolina," Chan has said. "The earth started shaking, and dark spirits were smashing up against every window of my house. I woke up and had my kitten next to me . . . and I started praying to God to help me."

Something was coaxing Chan out into the field. "A voice was telling me my past would be forgotten if I would just meet him—whoever he was—in the field," she has said. "And I woke up screaming, 'No! I won't meet you!' And I knew who it was: the sneaky old serpent. My nightmare was surrounding my house like a tornado. So I just ran and got my guitar because I was trying to distract myself. I had to turn on the lights and sing to God. I got a tape recorder and recorded the next sixty minutes. And I played these long changes, into six different songs. That's where I got the record."

Chan often talks about being visited in her dreams by ghosts. "I feel like there's some sort of spectral sort of existence that follows me around," the singer has said. "I feel kind of haunted by it. I feel like there's a power and energy that really wants in." At first light the following morning, Chan jumped into her truck and drove straight to New York, a twelve-hour trip. "I told my friends, 'I thought I saw these demons in my house. It was pretty insane. But they were real and I know you think I'm crazy, but I could see them,' " the singer has remembered. "And they were like, 'Chan, you're insane, you need some help.' So I went back home the next day. And then when I got home the very next day, two friends of mine both died on the same day. And then that woke me up. And I was like, 'Oh, I'm not crazy.' "

Whatever it was that happened on that deranged, stormy summer night in Prosperity, whatever it was that took place between Chan and her shaman back in Africa, she put all of it into the songs she wrote for *Moon Pix*. And as soon as she came out of her hallucinatory haze, Chan contacted Matador and asked them to get her into the studio. "I woke up and I was like, 'Oh, hey Matador? How are y'all doing?' " the singer has said. " 'Ummmm, would y'all pay for my ticket to Australia so I can get the fuck out of where I'm at?' "

In total, Chan was only away from touring and recording for less than a year. For her it was a huge break from her *Community*-era life, but for the fans and for the people at Matador, Chan was hardly even gone. The break did symbolize a serious attempt to retire from the music business, but Chan was never so sure it would work that she severed ties with her record label. In fact, Cosloy had no idea Chan was considering quitting. "She never said, 'I don't want to play music anymore,' " he says. "In my experience, somebody saying, 'I'm gonna move to wherever and buy a house with Bill Callahan,' that's not such a strange thing. Saying, 'I'm gonna move to wherever and have kids with Bill Callahan,' that's happened to people I know about five times."

18.

Moon Pix

Matt Voigt, a warm, laid-back Australian in his mid-thirties, was at home in Melbourne enjoying a mellow Christmas holiday on December 30, 1997, when he got a phone call from the owner of Sing Sing studios, where he works as a sound engineer. "He said, 'Well, this American lady has come in and she wants to record an album,' " Voigt remembers. " 'Can you start on New Year's Day?' I was like, 'Well, no, not on New Year's Day,' so we decided to start the next day. She just walked in off the street, basically."

Chan was in town staying with her friend Jim White of the Australian instrumental rock trio the Dirty Three, but she hadn't made any formal plans to record until she arrived in Melbourne and played White the songs she'd written in South Carolina. Chan, White, and Mick Turner, also of the Dirty Three, demoed most of the tracks that would appear on *Moon Pix*, and some of these original, incredibly spare recordings made it onto the album. "She did a few songs in Jim's bathroom in his home," Voigt remembers. "One of the tracks that made it directly onto the album was 'Peking Saint'—that one was done in Jim's bathroom with one mike."

Jim White is a heroic figure to many of the renowned musicians who have worked with him. PJ Harvey likened his drumming to ballet dancing; Joanna Newsom has described him as a "player" who can "cling, with a palpable, high-stakes looseness and gorgeous blind faith, to the downbeat." All ornate praise from harpists aside, White has been absolutely crucial to Cat Power's evolution. Chan has always relied on older, saner male drummers to keep her focused both onstage and in life. Back in Cabbagetown it was Glen Thrasher. In New York it was Steve Shelley. And beginning with the recording of *Moon Pix*, it was Jim White.

After working out the arrangements with White prior to pressing record, Chan entered Sing Sing studios on January 2 as confident as she ever had been about the album she was about to make. In the past, Chan's in-the-studio philosophy involved working up the courage to show up, closing her eyes, and just playing, hoping that whatever came out wouldn't horrify her the next day. During the *Community* sessions Chan started to get a sense of the creative possibilities involved in record-ing versus playing live, but she was tentative about exploring them; she didn't want to feel as if her albums were inauthentic because they were bolstered by in-the-studio trickery. This time, Chan decided she was over all of that. "The first thing she said when she came in was, 'I want a drum beat, and I want it to kind of sound like this,'" Voigt remembers. Chan pulled out a copy of the Beastie Boys' *Liscensed to Ill* and played "Paul Revere." The subtle but uncredited sample courses throughout *Moon Pix*'s opening track, "American Flag." "So we got the drum beat from the Beastie Boys album. We reversed the loop and slowed it down, and then she played on top of that." They spent an entire day recording "American Flag."

Chan's experimentation with samples and multiple vocal loops was re-flective of a larger shift in her attitude toward making music. She still felt insecure, but she was no longer willing to be intimidated or bossed around. In the early years of her career, Chan dealt with plenty of pa-tronizing sound dudes and dictatorial studio engineers, and between them and her condescending father, the singer had enough of men telling her what to do with her music. By the time she showed up at Sing Sing, Chan had gained enough confidence to dictate her own terms, and she never let anyone boss her around onstage or in the studio again. "She had a strong idea of what she wanted to do," Voigt remembers. "My role was just to get her ideas onto the tape. I would come up with the odd idea, and if she liked it, then that was great, but it was all her show."

For Chan, there's a certain judgmental objectification that goes along with being condescended to by studio guys, and she's extremely sensitive to it. "In the same way as when someone on the street kind of looks you up and down and laughs, it's the same kind of vibe," the singer has said. "It's like, 'Fuck off! What do I fucking care if you think I don't know what fucking feedback sounds like?' I definitely get mad, angry, and aggressive, and I don't like getting aggressive."

Moon Pix took less than a week to record, and another handful of days to mix. In the evenings, after the day's work was done, Chan and the Dirty Three guys would head out into the city to eat dinner and drink, but while they were in the studio, it was all business. Chan's old insecurities did creep into the sessions whenever she had to record alone. "If you've seen her live in shows, you know how much she apologizes and stops playing," Voigt says. "Well, it was exactly the same in the studio. She'd be at the point of tears and then start crying and say how sorry she was and stop."

Voigt reacted to this with the same bewilderment most people feel when Chan starts picking apart what seems to anyone else like an exquisitely vulnerable performance. "I was just like, 'I've just heard the most amazing voice ever! What are you apologizing for?' " Voigt remembers. "I suppose it comes down to her feeling so vulnerable that when she does open up and sing, it's very emotional for her." Voigt remembers a direct connection between Chan's stability in the studio and White's presence. "When Jim was there, she was a bit more stable," Voigt recalls. "Jim had ideas of how the tracks should be, and he offered lots of positive suggestions. Chan just listened and they went ahead and did it. Jim gave her confidence that it was all going to be okay."

The *Moon Pix* sessions marked Chan's first attempt to really be the boss in the studio, but that doesn't mean she was happy with the results. "It was either tears and apologies or, 'Oh, well, that's okay, let's move on,' " Voigt remembers. Chan wasn't thrilled with the way *Moon Pix* came out, but she did see the record as a step forward for her in terms of bridging the gap between what she heard in her head and what actually appears on the record. "Maybe *happy* is not the right word, *interested* is," the singer has since said. "I'm becoming a woman, and as a person I'm changing and getting better and better. I don't consider myself a qualified musician, but I know I've become really involved with the whole fabric [of a record]."

On *Moon Pix*, Chan finally recorded something approximating the ideal she had in mind. Nearly everybody else who listened to the album heard a masterpiece. Before *Moon Pix* came out in September 1998, Cat Power was an enigmatic indie-rock phenomenon drawing the attention of a small collection of die-hard fans and zine-reading hipsters in New York, Los Angeles, Atlanta, and Europe. After *Moon Pix*, Cat Power was a star. "*Moon Pix* is when I started to become aware of Cat Power," *Saturday Night Live* cast member and longtime Cat Power fan Fred Armisen remembers. Like many of the Cat Power fans who discovered the band through *Moon Pix*, Fred was first drawn to the album via the cover shot, taken by Roe Ethridge, which shows an angelic-looking Chan peering out from behind a flowering plant. "Sometimes a record cover is enough. You look at the picture and you go, 'Oh, something interesting is happening here.' It spoke to you."

Moon Pix is the first Cat Power album that shows Chan's face on the cover. Anyone who'd heard of the band and wondered who or what was responsible for the haunting, remote music it made now saw, in this untamed creature peering inquisitively from behind a flowering bush, the face behind the voice. With the release of *Moon Pix*, Chan's beauty officially became associated with her music. "The new Cat Power record is proof positive that Marshall is the coolest [girl] on the planet," a Pitchfork reviewer enthused before adding that Chan has it "goin' on."

Dear Sir and *Myra Lee*, while clear and confident in brief moments, are marred by Chan's lack of in-the-studio experience. *Community* is a moody, aggressive album in which we glimpse the painful realities beneath Chan's anger but never really see them up close. Just as we see Chan's face, unobscured for the first time, on the cover of *Moon Pix*, so is she more exposed than ever on this album. So much so that it's often difficult to listen to. In reviews of the album, the only thing more commented on than Chan's sex appeal was the cringe-inducing nature of her songs. Ben French, founder of the rock-criticism website Nude as the News (named after the Cat Power song), described *Moon Pix* as "one of the best (and worst?) albums of the decade" and wrote that the experience of listening to it was torturous but enjoyable. "Marshall rips your heart out, slowly, through the course of forty-five minutes. *Moon Pix* is a rare exploration of absolute misery, perfect music for the lonely loser in all of us, but too dark for an everyday listen. [The album is] a strange, and dark, accomplishment, but a tremendous feat nonetheless."

When *Moon Pix* hit stores on September 22, 1998, it also propelled Cat Power to an entirely new level of fame. The album's mournful sensibility connected with a generation of idealists who were contending with the fact that the optimism and excitement they felt at the beginning of the decade had devolved into a sense of dread. River Phoenix was dead. So was Kurt Cobain. Those people still making money on lofty ideas for websites were watching themselves turn into the vacant yuppies they started playing computer games to escape. Those who were no longer making money on the Web had even bigger problems. And as if it wasn't depressing enough that your heroes were dead and the drugs no longer worked, along came the Y2K scare, which gave a firm date for apocalypse: January 1, 2000. The world seemed to be ending, and Cat Power released the soundtrack to its destruction.

Moon Pix is a melancholic gem, filled with spare songs that begin to take shape only to disintegrate in elegant, multilayered waves. Lyrically the album retreads Cat Power's usual themes of heartache, disappointment, and redemption through pain, but sonically it conveys a hypnotic, eerie spirituality, like goth church music. The album's general tone is so cloistered and dark, it's comical to imagine Chan and her team capturing these shadowy sounds in the middle of Australia's summer, but that's what happened. "It's a melancholy, ethereal winter album," engineer Matt Voigt affirms, "but it was quite nice weather. It was bright outside, but we pretended it was raining."

The literal sound of rain appears on "Say," a breakup song that conveys the sense of resigned solitude that appears throughout the album.

From the opening line of the album, "My friend," uttered like a siren's wail over the trembling, syncopated Beastie Boys drum beat, Chan's voice announces itself as open, present, and powerful. For the duration of the album it never wavers. On the understated, lunar-themed hymn "No Sense," Chan's voice leads us like a spiritual tour guide through the emotions of the song. "Cross Bones Style" is the "Nude as the News" of *Moon Pix*: It's the most propulsive, overtly catchy song, and it was the album's most prominent single. In Cat Power tradition, *Moon Pix* also includes one cover song, "Moonshiner," a traditional blues tune that Bob Dylan popularized. On "Metal Heart," the loose, uncertain arrangement allows Chan's voice to emerge as the strongest, most constant entity in Cat Power's world, a North Star for lost souls.

"Metal Heart" gets at the central sorrow of this album, and of her life. When she sings, "Metal heart you're not hiding/Metal heart you're not worth a thing," it's as if she's speaking with resignation to her own unfeeling heart, which has once again failed to allow her the simple life she's always dreamed of. "It's damned if you don't and it's damned if you do/Be true 'cause they'll lock you up in a sad, sad zoo," she further laments. On *Jukebox*, Cat Power's second album of covers, released in early 2008, the singer reinvented "Metal Heart" as a defiant send-off to the defeated person she was when she wrote it. In her review of the album, *Rolling Stone* senior editor Melissa Maerz described the new version as "a dramatic, crashing-drums-and-piano love letter to the old, fragile Marshall who wrote it." So completely does "Metal Heart" represent the emotionally crippled but forward-looking Chan Marshall of the 1990s that the artist herself chose the song to herald the rein-vention she's undertaken both professionally and personally in her mid-thirties.

The album drew the attention of a new breed of culturally clued-in celebrities like zeitgeist fashion designer Marc Jacobs. It also attracted a higher level of critical attention. Greil Marcus, arguably the preeminent music and pop-cultural critic of his generation, was one of the fans Chan earned after the release of *Moon Pix*. It was her take on "Moonshiner" that drew him in. In a column in *Interview* magazine, Marcus compared Cat Power's cover of the song with the Dylan version that inspired it. "Marshall's version is clean but weird," Marcus wrote. " 'I've been a moonshiner/For seventeen long years,' she sings, sounding at once ab-solutely convincing and not a day over seventeen herself." Marcus wasn't quite as convinced by Chan's original compositions—he refers to the original songs on *Moon Pix* as "drifting" and rife with "unclear pat-terns"—but he was impressed both by Chan's version of "Moonshiner" and by her willingness to take it on in the first place.

"Dylan's version is one of the best things he's ever recorded," Marcus explains from his home in Berkeley, California. "Cat Power is able to take a definitive performance of an old folk song, the kind of performance you would think, Well, no one needs to sing this anymore, and sing it as if she just discovered the song, as if she overheard it somewhere, as if she wrote it herself." This piqued Marcus's interest. "I felt that she had an ability to get inside of someone else's song, of a song she'd learned from someone else's recording, that both captured the song but also seemed to comment on the person who'd originally sung it. There seemed to be an intelligence at work in her music, a thoughtfulness that wasn't oppressive, wasn't, 'I'm so smart.' " After hearing *Moon Pix*, Marcus immediately put Cat Power on his radar as an artist whose career he would diligently follow. "She very quickly became someone to whom I was always going to listen, whether I liked what she did or not."

Moon Pix's lone piano track, "Colors and the Kids," stands out alongside "American Flag" and "Metal Heart" as a true highlight. It is lyrically direct. "It must be the colors/And the kids/That keep me alive/'Cause the music is boring me to death," Chan sings plainly. The song goes on to address everything from a wistful romanticizing of a past relationship (". . . I'd wanna go right away/To a January night/I built a shack with an old friend/He was someone I could learn from") to the exhaustion and alienation from friends that comes with the pressures of always being on the road ("It's so hard to go in the city/'Cause you wanna say hello to everybody").

"Colors and the Kids" also showcases the ways in which Chan's breakup with Bill Callahan works as a recurrent theme throughout *Moon Pix*. Neither Chan nor Bill has enumerated the details of their split, but looking back, Chan has said that a torturous breakup in 1998 triggered her self-destructive impulses: "I lost the love of my life in 1998 to another woman. He was the first person who loved me who I loved." Indeed, Cat Power and Smog fans alike have pored over both artists' post-breakup albums (*Moon Pix* and Smog's *Knock Knock*) for clues to what exactly happened. While neither record draws the listener a map, each adheres to the same loose theme: two strong-willed, independent personalities coming to terms with the fact that as much as they'd like to, they aren't ready to settle down.

Knock Knock begins with a declaration to move to the country, "Let's Move to the Country," and ends with two successive songs about the relief of being unattached, "Hit the Ground Running" and "I Could Drive Forever." The last song on that album, "Left Only with Love," is a warm and seemingly heartfelt wish-you-well send-off to an ex-girlfriend in which Bill sings, "You did what was right to do/And I hope you find your husband/And a father to your children/'Cause I'm left only with love for you."

Chan is less direct, but there are plenty of moments on *Moon Pix* in which she appears to be addressing Bill or pondering the disillusion of a relationship. On "Colors and the Kids," Chan indulges in heart-breaking wishful thinking about what could have been, singing, "I could stay here/Become someone different/I could stay here/Become someone better." On "He Turns Down," Chan engages the listener (or herself) in a rhetorical dialogue about staying in a relationship longer than you should: "Holding on for someone/Feels like holding on too long/Have you ever held on." It's also about feeling abandoned by the one you love: "It's not me, I am pretending/I'm not saved, he turned me down/He turns down."

As emotive as Chan and Callahan were in their respective sonic send-offs to each other, the most intense feelings were yet to come. Chan ex-

posed herself on *Moon Pix*, and in revealing her pain there was the im-
plicit hope that it would lessen. But the success of *Moon Pix* propelled
the singer into what would become a seemingly endless tour that kept
her rootless, off-kilter, and emotionally stunted. The wounds we hear
Chan describing in harrowing detail on *Moon Pix* would not heal for a
long while.

19.

"Is She Okay?"

Between the recording of Moon Pix in the winter of 1998 and the album's September release, Chan went back to New York City and tried to establish a new life. As spring turned to summer, she still wasn't settled. Word had gotten back to her that Bill Callahan might be seeing someone else. The idea that he might have moved on so quickly underscored just how badly their experimental domesticity had failed. Now there Chan was, back in her one-room apartment on East Third, with months and months of touring commitments and the loneliness of road life stretching before her. "I had to go on tour," she has said. "That's when the drinking started. I had a bottle of scotch backstage at that point. A year later, my rider had a bottle of scotch and a case of beer for every show."

After hearing *Moon Pix*, Matador knew they had an important record on their hands, and they got behind the album with an extensive (for an indie label) promotional campaign that included shooting a music video for the single. Chan has described "Cross Bones Style" as "the real dance song" on *Moon Pix*, which made it the ideal candidate. Ever obsessed with Madonna, Chan got excited about filming a Material Girl–inspired clip. "I'm thinking of doing a full-on 'Lucky Star'–style video," the singer said at the time. "Like Madonna, dancing in a white room. I'm sure I'll chicken out, though." "Cross Bones Style" was never released as a single, but she did make the video with her close friend Brett Vapnek directing. It features Chan and a bunch of friends doing funny approximations of angular dance moves while Chan, wearing a red dress and neckerchief that looks like it's choking her, pretends to play guitar. In other shots, Chan wears her late-nineties uniform of baggy jeans and conservative black button-down, against which her aggressively rosy lip gloss and eye makeup seems awkward.

The stress of touring behind a successful record took a significant psychological toll. By day she traveled from city to city in a sparse tour bus, looking forward to the next night she'd spend in a real bed. At night she drank, played her show, then drank some more. Through years spent in New York or on the road, Chan had collected a set of friends scattered around the world. At almost every tour stop, there was someone she needed to catch up with, so she'd rally with whiskey and nicotine and stay out until last call, then do it all again the next night. The alcohol kept her going into the wee hours of each morning, it allowed her to nod off to sleep at dawn, and it helped her contend with the residual awkwardness she felt onstage, which deepened as she became more successful and began to play to larger and more demanding audiences.

As the child of a wannabe rockstar and an alcoholic, Chan has never bought into the false romance of a Dionysian lifestyle. She wasn't the sort of drinker who had a few too many at the after-party; Chan drank to survive. "I've always been accountable," the singer has said. "I've always been very professional, believe it or not. Even though people think my shows have been . . . but as a friend, a person, a lover, a girlfriend, I've always been right there. Drinking was more of a way to continue traveling. To keep going to the next show, keep meeting people in different cities. It was a way for me to be calm."

By the time Chan was touring behind *Moon Pix*, her bouts of onstage lunacy were well-known, and most of Chan's hard-core fans believed they'd already witnessed the worst of their hero's psychological unraveling. They had not. In the months after *Moon Pix* was released, Chan's live shows transformed from merely weird and sometimes boring to harrowing displays of self-destruction and almost nightly antiperformances.

These raw shows became so notorious that they drew in a whole new group of Cat Power fan and critic: those who actually wanted to see the grotesque spectacle of public evisceration. Many who didn't buy the authenticity of Chan's breakdowns accused her of delivering performances that were nothing more than despicable manipulations of the artist-audience relationship.

From Jim Morrison in Miami in 1969 to the Sex Pistols at Winterland to Guns N' Roses in Toronto in 1992 to Amy Winehouse at the MTV Europe Awards in 2008, most notoriously unstable artists have a show that represents their darkest period, when all their demons emerge onstage for every last audience member to see. Cat Power's took place on January 4, 1999, at the Bowery Ballroom in New York City. Lucky for her, it was pre-YouTube, or the clip would still be passed around for the sheer shock value alone. The gig was part of a series of sold-out dates Chan played during that leg of the relentless *Moon Pix* tour. In addition to the core fans who were there for the music, Cat Power's audience now also included those who were there for the voyeuristic thrill of watching a performer's psyche dismantle onstage.

A severe winter chill has descended on the city, but the faithful bundle up and brave the stinging air outside for the promise of emotional warmth inside. It's after eleven before Chan appears onstage, not that you can see beneath the sheets of matted hair hanging over her face and the deliberately underlit stage. Fans are politely quiet when she first steps in front of the mike, but there's a sense of giddy anticipation in the crowd. Four months after the release of *Moon Pix*, Chan's adopted hometown is finally going to hear her perform material from an album that's being heralded as Cat Power's first masterpiece.

If there's a set list, no one's following it. Instead, Chan halfheartedly starts songs, then stops a quarter of the way through before calling off the band, which includes two of Chan's ex-boyfriends, Mark Moore on guitar and Chris Lopez on drums. "They hate me," she tells the audience in a loud whisper, her first comprehensible words of the evening. If she does manage to string together multiple seconds of coherent singing and playing, she'll stop anyway so that she can chastise herself for mistakes only she can hear. Chan mutters vicious descriptions of her own failures into the floor, then manically apologizes to the crowd, and finally, during a brutally aborted performance of "Cross Bones Style," the show disintegrates completely. Chan climbs off the stage and shuffles, hair over her eyes, baggy clothes barely shifting, her movements are so ponderous, out into the audience, where she crumples into a fetal position and rocks, head between her knees.

Her band is totally appalled. They storm off the stage, amps screeching and cymbals awkwardly banging against snare. Chan continues to press her face into the moist wood of the beer-soaked floor and wonders aloud what it would be like to be slashed by a machete. The crowd splits into two sets: Half is as revolted as the band by Chan's display of unabashedly sensationalized melodrama, the other half empathizes with the fragile singer and starts to come up, one by one, to reassuringly pet her head as if she is a wounded jungle creature in need of consolation.

New York Times critic Ben Ratliff was in the audience that night. Even though ten years have passed since the show, Ratliff's memory of Chan's performance of "Cross Bones Style" incites a combination of bafflement and rage. "She did this thing that on one level was part of what I found nauseating, but was also something that I had never seen before," he remembers. "She went into the audience and kept singing the song. She got down on the floor and put her nose and her forehead on the floor and people were patting her on the back, trying to make her feel better. I just thought, Ughh, you know? Like, No! You know? This is terrible! Doing this thing and ultimately *seeking* comfort like that from her fans, I found nauseating."

"I really didn't mind that they did that," Chan has said of her fans' physical intimacy. "Because I felt like I was already dead—that I wasn't even there anymore, or something. . . . When the fans were patting my back, I already felt like I'd been murdered, so it didn't bother me. As for the band, I've never talked to them about it and to this day I'm sure they still think that I'm crazy and out of control, and which is, you know, fine because it's not how I see myself, or how I feel. In fact the greatest misconception about me is that people think I'm crazy. I surely am not."

The following day, Ratliff's piece ran in the *New York Times*. He described the set as "staggering for its inversion of standard rock-performance ethics," before going on to indict Chan for not holding up her end of the bargain between audience and artist. "Gone was the idea of exultation, or of showing what one can do," Ratliff wrote. "In its place was outrageously passive-aggressive behavior and nonmusicianship."

It was a big deal for a paper as influential as the *New York Times* to be covering a show by this long-toiling local artist. The paper's presence reflected the reaches of Chan's new fame, but by melting down in front of Ratliff, Chan ensured she would now be at least as well-known for her self-destruction as for her music. No matter what their reaction, everyone who saw this show came away from it with the same question on their minds: Is she really crazy? After the Bowery show, this question would be alluded to in every Cat Power review, in every feature written about Chan. After this show, talking about Chan's mental state would become the primary way of talking about Cat Power.

"I really, really had a hard time with it," Ratliff recalls, still visibly disturbed by it all these years later. "In fact, when it was over, instead of just getting on the subway and going home, I walked about forty blocks thinking about it, because I didn't want to be complicit in any way with the fundamental bullshittiness of it, you know? I had such trouble with it. And yet it wasn't something that I felt like just cancel-ing the review and saying, 'It was a waste of time. Let's not deal with it.' Clearly there was something there that she had and nobody else had that was unique and special."

Ratliff was most troubled by the juxtaposition between Chan's evi-dent ability and her unwillingness to display it. "She was dealing with her own gifts in such a funny way," he recalls. "She was being really hide-and-seek with them. She'd make it clear that she could sing, and then it was like she forgot how. She would make it clear that she knew how to play chords, and then she would forget how. I felt like on one level it was sad, and on one level it was very manipulative. I felt like the audience was being manipulated, and I couldn't stand it.

"I listened to *Moon Pix* again and I just kept being drawn back to the moments on that record where she proves that she can sing," he explains almost ten years after writing the review. "Those are like, 'All right, she's got my trust.' Then it kind of drifts for a while, and then she sings a beautiful note. She has a kind of froggy, nasal voice that she can put on, and, man, it's good." For Ratliff, the frustrating thing about Chan is that she has the goods and won't give them up, which makes her failures obnoxious rather than endearing. "Have you ever had a schoolmate who goes around the class eliciting sympathy by saying, 'Oh my God. I'm going to fail this test so bad. I'm so stupid'? Then the person gets an A plus, and you knew all along that they would?" Ratliff asks. "That's the reaction that I had: 'I don't know what, clinically, is happening with you, but I think that you deserve to be ignored right now.' "

Chan is not one of those artists who avoids her own press. And even if she tried not to pay attention to what's being written about her, her family would keep her up to date. Myra buys lots of music magazines, and Granny Lil keeps track of what family secrets Chan is revealing in print.

She has even chastised her granddaughter for speaking so bluntly about Myra's alcoholism. As harsh as the *Times* review was, it actually remains one of Chan's favorite pieces of writing about Cat Power. "My booking agent faxed it to me while I was on tour," the singer remembered. "He was like, 'Be prepared, it's really bad.' He thought it was a huge deal." For Chan, a bad review is one that mislabels her as dumb or worthless or entitled. A critic that expects more of Chan than she's giving is one she appreciates, one who respects Chan more than she respects herself. "I was like, 'Oh, man, is he saying that I'm a stupid bitch with no sense of humor and I'm poor white trash and I don't have a vocabulary and I stand funny and I'm dumb?' " Chan has said. "It was a completely objective opinion about what he thought. I e-mailed my booking agent and was like, 'This isn't bad. It's realistic. It's good!' A personal attack from someone you don't know—negative, mean, maliciousness is bad. If you want to have an opinion, that's good."

Chan has been asked about what exactly happened that cold, still winter night at the Bowery Ballroom and she's offered an explanation that only deepens the mystery surrounding the show. "This guy was there who I had known for a long time," the singer has said. "He was on drugs and telling me crazy stuff. He had a gun and was trying to tease me that he had power. I thought he was going to shoot me." Chan has had several stalkers over the years, including one in France and an American girl who has been following her more recently. This guy could very well have been another stalker with a particularly dangerous profile. Chan has said that several months later, he shot both of his parents and himself.

As genuinely scary as this scenario sounds, it doesn't really explain Chan's demented behavior. Why didn't she call security? Or the cops? Why didn't she make a beeline for the nearest taxi and get the hell out of there? If someone is holding a gun to your head and therefore endangering you, them, and every single one of the five-hundred-plus people packed into the Bowery, you might react in any number of ways, but what most wouldn't do is go onstage and attempt to play a rock show for two hours.

Some would say this sort of scenario is definitive proof that Chan Marshall is a manipulative crackpot who stages breakdowns like mercenary performance-art pieces designed to bring in the ticket sales. Others, like Chan's former labelmate Mary Timony, say that anyone who interprets Chan's onstage behavior as contrived is missing the point. "Telling the audience that she feels uncomfortable—that's really a way of bringing them into her," Timony says. "To some people that's a construct, but that's because they don't understand it. I don't think she intended it to be this thing to make people interested in her. She lets people see her insecurities, and that makes people feel close to her, like she's opening up to them."

As completely as these devoted fans are on her side, Chan may sometimes wish they were more like the haters, who, at the very least, don't expect her to heal their wounds. During her first few years as a professional musician, Chan learned to deal with the Cat Power–obsessed French girls, the occasional crushed-out rocker boy, and the newly packed venues, but nothing prepared her for the type of fan that started showing up at her shows during the *Moon Pix* tour. "There was this Japanese woman," Chan remembered. "She was totally trembling. She wouldn't look at me. She was just like, 'I want to tell you that you help me,' and she started bawling and turned away. I gave her this hug and started bawling with her because I knew what she was going to say. I know how she felt. She started telling me stuff that happened, her eyes were just pouring out. She really was, like, looking for something to help her get out of her suicidal thoughts."

Most of the time Chan found these encounters stimulating; they reminded her that although she was not living the domesticated life she dreamed of as a kid, her music was making an impact on the lives of tens of thousands of strangers. "Those kinds of things are really amazing," Chan explained, "because that person who's shedding that, it's good for them. It makes me feel good when I see them so open as a human and not as zipped-up. That makes me cry, the human spirit, feeling like, Okay, we're not alone. They help me get through what I can't make sense of."

Cat Power's most heartbreaking songs convey intimacy through obscurity: "Nude as the News," "Metal Heart," "Rockets," these songs are all rife with an emotional density, the details of which are hidden in plain sight. These are the songs that bring fans the world over to their knees, made prostrate by the overwhelming sensation of being understood by someone in a way they never have before. Chan shares a communal sense of abject sadness with her fans, but there is a vast rift between the truth about her own personal emotional reality and what fans perceive via her songs. "It's almost like I'm making a connection with something that is not even there," Chan has said of her relationship with fans. "It's okay because they don't know what I'm talking about, really. They don't have the images I have. They have their own images, which is good."

Chan is able to look at the beneficial side of these encounters, appreciate them for the connection they represent between her music and its audience, and protect herself with the notion that although Cat Power fans feel they know her personally, there is always distance between what they perceive and who Chan Marshall really is. After a year on the road filled with countless moments like this, a year in which Chan looked into the eyes of hundreds of people who hear her every exhale as the word of their own personal messiah, that distance started to seem insufficient. It became increasingly difficult for Chan Marshall to separate herself from Cat Power, and this contributed to her drinking, which contributed to her erratic stage behavior, which ultimately (and ironically) alienated a core group of her original, most loyal fans.

Ultimately, only Chan knows the complex emotional realities behind her erratic onstage personae. Only she knows why she continues to stand night after night beneath the lights even though being there torments her. Only she knows what drives her to appeal equally to the two factions of her fan base—rubberneckers looking for the train wreck, and lost souls looking for a soul mate. What we know is that every time Chan crawls into the crowd and plucks her way through "Cross Bones Style" with her nose pressed to the floor, as she did at the Bowery that night, the fans reach out to console her because they believe she needs it. They believe they know exactly what it's like to feel as she does, and they long to reciprocally console her the way her music has consoled them. They believe they are sharing something pure with their idol. If they are, then both Chan and the crowd are experiencing an exquisite moment of redemption. If they aren't, then it's a cruel fraud.

"I Just Saw Jesus in Times Square"

Beginning around the Moon Pix tour, when she was in her mid- to late twenties, Chan became increasingly troubled by the idea that, like her sister and her mother, she was going to develop schizophrenia. As a child, Chan had nightmarish visions of her mother being hauled away by men in white coats. As she got older, Chan started to fear that this time around, they were coming for her.

The onset of schizophrenia is usually in late adolescence, after the frontal lobes are fully formed, but, because so little is really understood about the brain mechanics that are involved, there is no real maximum age of onset. If you have a genetic predisposition for schizophrenia, you are going to live your whole life at risk of developing it. "She worried about getting it. I know that worried her constantly," Judy Ibbotson says. "And she worried about her mom and sister. And she worried about the little ones [Chan's niece and nephew] being in that situation." Right before Chan left for the *Moon Pix* tour, she had to deal with a family emergency involving her mother. "She left with a day's notice," Ibbotson remembers. "She said she had to get up to North Carolina because something had happened."

By this time, Miranda was managing her disease well and enjoying her life as a wife and mother as well as her career as a nurse. But according to her son, Myra was still entrenched in what has become a lifelong battle against accepting help for her mental problems. "She has been diagnosed," Lenny says, "but refuses to acknowledge it or take her medication." Just as she did as a younger woman, and just as she does now, Lenny and Leamon agree that Myra found it difficult to keep a steady job. "Myra worked for a while at Coca-Cola, did bookkeeping, she had a few jobs," Leamon recalls. "She would work, then get mad at them, cuss them out, and get fired."

Chan began the *Moon Pix* tour worried about her family and afraid of this hateful disease that rendered both her mother and sister unable to trust their own thoughts. The idea that she too could wake up on any given morning and be crazy festered in Chan's mind throughout the duration of her time on the road. By the time she got back to New York, she was hallucinating.

Matthew Shipp is a celebrated underground jazz pianist who has been living in Alphabet City since 1984. He first met Chan in 1995. "I was standing in Bell Atlantic paying my bill at their office on Thirteenth Street, and there was this girl in back of me," Shipp recalls. "She taps me on the shoulder and says, 'Are you a jazz pianist?' I said, 'Yeah.' She goes, 'I just read an article about you.' I'm thinking to myself, 'God, this girl's really cute.' She must have been reading my mind because she goes, 'I'm friends with your wife, and I live next door to you.' " After that, Shipp started seeing Chan all over their neighborhood. They would bump into each other on the street and head down to Max Fish, or to sandwich-and-coffee outpost the Pink Pony, for a beer or a snack.

Around 1999, Shipp noticed a deterioration in Chan's psychological state. "She said she saw Jesus in Midtown," Shipp states unequivocally. "This was the late nineties. I was seeing Chan around a lot, and it seemed to me that she was on drugs. I've talked to all kinds of delusional people, but this was really scary, and I can't put my hand on exactly why. I remember thinking she was finished. She was talking about how she saw Jesus. Then she saw a vision of Satan, and then she talked to Satan and Jesus came and rescued her. With a straight face I said, 'Chan, are you all right?' And she said, 'Yeah, yeah, I'm all right. Why?' "

Not that Chan was in the mental state to appreciate this at the time, but the fact that she was having visions indicates she probably wasn't suffering from the same mental illness as her mom and sister. "Schizophrenics rarely have visual hallucinations," Dr. Ewing explains. "If somebody is having vivid, well-formed hallucinations—not just the dark shadow in the corner of the room, but something that looks like the real thing—you don't think about schizophrenia. In bipolar disorder, there are visions and hallucinations. You see a lot more bi-polar in families with schizophrenia."

Obsession with religion is something a lot of schizophrenics experi-ence in their auditory hallucinations, and similar visual sensations can accompany the manic phase of bipolar disorder. "God is sending them messages, expecting things of them," Dr. Ewing says of common schiz-ophrenic delusions. "Sometimes they think they are God and have some kind of special mission. That's more suggestive of a manic psychosis, the real religious overtones. If they bring in somebody naked, you pretty much don't need to know anything else. They're manic. [I] took care of a lovely young girl—[she] decided she needed to preach to the poor, but a real honest girl didn't hide behind clothing, so she gave her clothes away."

Just as Chan seemed to be careening out of control mentally, she started pulling herself together professionally. The singer has always had the financial wits of a girl who grew up worrying about the electricity getting shut off. Now that Chan makes a good living, she'll spend a few thousand dollars at a time on Louis Vuitton luggage or Chanel gloves, but she's still a relatively frugal person. Even during the *Moon Pix* tour, when she was never in one city for more than a few days, Chan always paid her bills on time. "She would send a check with a letter or a post-card, so it was always fun to get her rent," Ibbotson remembers. "She'd always write a note, and she told me if I needed it beforehand there was her best friend I could call."

While she was torturing herself over the idea that she might be crazy, Chan was designing a pale-pink-and-off-white color scheme for the walls of her Atlanta apartment, diligently paying her bills at both her Atlanta and New York residences, and pestering Matt Shipp for advice about how to make real money as a musician. "She was always stopping me and asking me questions about the business of jazz," Shipp remembers. "A jazz musician who has much less of a name than an indie-rock star can make a better living. She was struck by that, and was always asking me questions about the structure of touring. It seemed so cool to her that a jazz musician could go to Europe, do festivals because they're subsidized by governments. Not long after that, she got a really good manager. She was making the switch to Triple A."

Chan likes to think of signing with Matador and the events that followed as a series of coincidences that could have happened to anybody. "When you don't know that many people, and the few people you know and like tell you they want to put your record out, you start to think, 'Hmmmm. . . .' I was naïve," Chan has said. "If you don't know any better and people tell you to jump off a bridge. . . ." But even in the relatively early years of her career, friends like Shipp found this doe-eyed-ingenue act difficult to reconcile with the obvious careerist in Chan.

"She knows what she's doing," Shipp says with a sly smile. "On some levels, I think she's an extremely calculating person." Looking back, Shipp, who clearly adores Chan and respects her as a songwriter and singer, is also extremely skeptical about the idea that she happened upon success. "Anybody who can keep that type of profile that long—you have to be making some right moves," he says. "You can't make that many mistakes. I've never told her this, but she really knows what she's doing. I never used to know why she was asking me things or what she was processing, but she was taking in all the right information."

Chan not only disagrees with this impression of her as an ambitious, driven tycoon, she is actively offended by it. "My friend Terry says, 'Oh, I just think it's great. You know, you always knew that you wanted to be a singer, and wanted to be famous,' " Chan said at the time. "I'm just like, 'What?' I felt so insulted because that's not true. That's not the way that I am. She had it all wrong, and she's my friend, and things like that drive me insane." And yet in the post-*Moon Pix* era, when the Gap called, Chan didn't find their offer to model for them insulting. Later, when Cingular wanted her to record a special cover of the Nerves' "Hanging on the Telephone" for one of their ads, Chan wasn't offended enough to say no. And in 2008, when Lincoln asked her to record a version of David Bowie's "Space Oddity" especially for them, Chan had no problem doing it.

For all of Chan's evident business acumen, she also has a flighty, fiscally carefree side that concerns some of her friends. Chan routinely walks around with thousands of dollars in cash loose in the bottom of her purse and has a hard time keeping track of her credit cards, ID, and keys. Matt Shipp remembers walking on lower Broadway with Chan in the post-*Moon Pix* era and watching as she casually dropped fifty bucks on makeup in under ten minutes. A mere drop in the bucket for a rock star, but the mindlessness of Chan's spending alarmed Shipp.

As Cat Power's renown has grown, she's traded up from Sephora to even more upscale brands—and though she still walks around barefoot in rolled-up five-dollar used 501s, her family members have taken note. "I think everybody's a little concerned about her finances. Everybody wants her to be able to function financially after this is over," Lenny says. "She can't tour forever. I think she's made some unwise choices. She's just trying to live her life trying to find balance. But stayin' at the Ritz? There are cheaper alternatives. Then again, she's the one putting in the work. I'm hoping that her catalog and other things will help her sustain her life."

As Chan became more and more savvy about the music business, her relationship with Matador transformed from the traditional arrangement, in which the artist makes the art and the label does everything else, to something more complex. "[It's only] very recently that there's been any sort of weirdness, like serious weirdness about the working relationship," Cosloy says. "Chan pays a lot more attention to the day-to-day business of being Cat Power than she might have ten or twelve years ago." Consequently, Cosloy explains, the label is under more scrutiny from her than in the past. "Back in those days it was very much, Let the record label do its own thing. Now there's much more checks and balances. We have to go back to her much more often and say, 'What do you think of this? What do you think of this? What do you think of this?' There are occasional disagreements regarding money or contracts or what's the next thing to do, but at the end of the day she's the boss. At the end of the day, we work for her."

Cosloy also points out that Matador has benefited from Chan's acute understanding of how best to run the business of Cat Power. "Chan knows a lot more about the music business than a lot of other artists," Cosloy says. "She's seen a lot of funny stuff go down. And she honestly is trying to think of what would be fun or interesting or would look cool—she just presumes that her fans will get it, and so will everybody else, and nine times out of ten she's right."

21.

Bangs

Chan always had style. In the early nineties, when she was living in Cabbagetown, she dressed like an elegant trucker in cut-off T-shirts and eyeliner. When she moved to New York City, Chan adopted her own interpretation of the era's popular androgynous look, shaving her head and wearing work shirts, baggy Levi's, and the intentionally drab men's dress shoes worn by all the cool indie-rock chicks. After *Moon Pix* was released, Chan started dressing less like a stylish construction worker and more like a glamorous hipster. The first symbol of this shift was a simple haircut. The cover of *Moon Pix* features a dreamy, freckle-faced, shaggy-haired young girl peering out tentatively from behind a flowering tree. By the following year, Chan had grown out her hair and was wearing a shorter version of the dramatic eye-skimming bangs and long, straight mane she's now identified with—a style similar to Nico during her iconic tenure in the Velvet Underground; urban retro-chic.

Her transformation from tomboy to glamazon was also reflected in her new boyfriend, Daniel Currie, a twenty-two-year-old model and bartender Chan met on a street corner downtown in the spring of 1999, shortly after returning to New York. "I'm so much older, and I was thinking, 'You're so fucking cute and interesting,' " the singer has said of this first encounter. "When we kissed, he didn't think that I liked him."

With his shaggy dark hair, wiry frame, refined bone structure, and pink, cupid's-bow lips, Currie looked the part of the elegantly disheveled heroin-chic New York hipster—but he is actually a Southern boy from the Atlanta suburbs. In fact, he was born in the same hospital as Chan, Crawford Long. Chan relentlessly sought balance between her traditional self and the rock-star New Yorker within; in Daniel, she found a partner who shared this juxtaposition. Soon the new couple was inseparable. "I'm so engulfed with my relationship," Chan had said shortly after meeting Daniel. "I just want to be with him every day."

Though Currie had plenty of creative aspirations, they were at best casually directed. The forms of art he routinely practiced included skateboarding, putting up drywall, and bartending. Currie was young, his professional life yet to be established. Chan, on the other hand, was in the middle of a career upswing, so the young couple both committed to Cat Power and took their affair on the road. As the nineties came to an end, Cat Power was still touring, though not ostensibly in support of one particular album. *Moon Pix* had vaulted Chan's career to a new level that guaranteed her an audience whenever she decided to play. Matador was starting to make noise about a new record, but Chan was too in love to care.

Chan and Currie traveled the world together, enjoying the dizzying romance of endless travel made all the more intense by brand-new love. By day they would explore the exotic cities on Cat Power's itinerary, and at night Chan would play shows and Currie would hang out backstage, sometimes selling merch for his girlfriend or helping to load and unload gear. Chan was technically working, with money from Matador coming in to pay for the tour expenses as ticket sales increased both the company's and Chan's bank balances. Despite all her attempts to become a dutiful homemaker, Chan was once again the guy in her relationship and her partner, Currie, was along for the ride.

By the time the couple returned to New York, they were so used to a life that revolved around Cat Power, it was easy to continue along that path. Currie would work when he could, but mostly he followed his girlfriend around, waiting for her while she attended business meetings and coming along every time she had to go to the West Coast for press, or out on tour for a few weeks. Currie and Chan would also go home to Atlanta together, where they'd stay in Chan's house in Cabbagetown and visit with old friends and family. For the young couple this plan worked, but Chan's judgmental city friends were skeptical of the directionless pretty boy who'd infiltrated her life.

Compared to Bill Callahan, who had an intense personality, was older than Chan, and was more professionally accomplished than she was while they were dating, Currie was like a puppy, a giggling, silly partner in crime for Chan. Thurston Moore remembers meeting Currie outside the New York office of Chan's booking agent, Jim Romeo. "She was seeing this guy for quite a while, this sort of young male-model-looking guy," Moore remembers. "I remember going to her booking agent's place, and she was up there Xeroxing some stuff. I met him out in the street, like he was waiting for something. He had his little leather cap on. She goes, 'Did you meet my boyfriend?' I was like, 'Oh, yeah, yeah.' She goes, 'Isn't he cute? He's cute, isn't he?' I was like, 'Yeah, cute is a good word for it.' "

Like the Mafia, Lower East Side hipsters had a code in the 1990s. It was fine to bartend and wait tables in order to support your burgeoning career as a guitarist, but Currie's apparent lack of ambition to do any-thing other than follow his girlfriend around seemed utterly pathetic.

"I met him in California," Tim Foljahn says of Currie. "He was very sweet. It was just funny because he was such a model, which was mind-blowing because in that crowd, the dudes don't even have the balls to go out with a model. The remnants of the nineties, the whole thing has its own form of stuck-up weirdness. So everybody was being kind of weird about him, you know, because he's different. He wasn't a misan-thropic hipster. He was totally tan and hip and wearing this nice bathrobe. Everything looked fancier on him—he looked like a model!" Currie's Southern warmth and lack of neuroses turned off many of Chan's proudly cynical city friends, but it's exactly what drew the singer to him in the first place. "It wasn't complex," Chan has said of the four years she spent with Currie. "It's like when someone is with you in it, and it's a reciprocated love. I'd never felt that before."

Chan never introduced Bill Callahan to her father (though her step-father met him), but Charlie Marshall met Currie several times. "He and

Chan just looked like two little kids together," Charlie remembers. "In a lot of ways, that's what love is: You just peel back all the layers, and this is me, that's you, and we're in love." The couple even talked about marriage. "Saying 'We're getting married' is kind of an explanation for your idea of the future," Chan has said. "But did we want to marry each other? Yes, we did."

When they weren't running around Paris or London or giggling while trying on crappy sunglasses at some dusty truck stop while touring America, Currie and Chan were in New York, palling around with the city's coolest young artists. With her stylish haircut, new rock-star status, and model boyfriend by her side, Chan finally had a way into the fashion world that had always compelled her. "Back when I started hanging out with her at her place, you know, trying to kiss her, the most shocking thing was that there were all these fashion magazines around," Foljahn remembers. "She knew every model's name! I didn't know anything about any of this stuff, and I didn't even know anybody who knew anything about this stuff."

Chan's new friends included designers and fashion personalities like photographer Terry Richardson; Marc Jacobs, who was then perfectly in touch with the indie aesthetic and modernized vintage style; and French fashion house Balenciaga's new savant designer, Nicolas Ghesquiere. Like Chan, these artists made careers out of their ability to channel unique perspectives on underground pop culture into collections with mass appeal. In Chan these fashion leaders saw inspiring authenticity, which, for all the fantasy associated with couture, is the central element of style. In them, Chan saw her Lower East Side brethren with swankier apartments and better champagne in their fridges.

"She became really connected with these high-profile French fashion guys," Thurston Moore remembers. "She is certainly a beautiful and interesting-looking person, but they were sort of fascinated with her aesthetic. She does have a sense of style that is really personal, and it is very intriguing to these guys. Marc's [Jacobs] long-standing boyfriend, Pierre Bailey, is a photographer. I know he shot her live. She was making that scene."

Charles Aaron remembers that Chan was popular with the distinctly Lower East Side (and distinctly hard-to-impress) fashion kids, including designers Built by Wendy and those who hung out at the small, exclusive Ludlow Street boutique TG170. "The hippest people, all the most tastemaking music people, all the most tastemaking fashion people in the mid-nineties, those people who were the indie-fashion people then became more mainstream, were into her," he remembers. "They were all obsessed with Chan: She was the One.

"I remember going to a Knitting Factory show and sitting in the balcony with all those people and just thinking. This is fucking horrible," Aaron continues. "She can't sing. She's either scared or untalented, I can't tell which. She's phoning it in with her fake twang, and all these people who design cool jeans and belts are like gaga over her. She was very charismatic, though. In general. Even offstage, she might have had more than onstage. She would make albums that I didn't really listen to that much. I didn't get it. But she had a cult of personality."

Fashion designer Benjamin Cho remembers the first time he met Chan, in 1998. "I was at a photo shoot doing hair and makeup for [English fashion magazine] *Dazed and Confused*," Cho recalls. "Their shoot was running late, so I was just waiting there. She came off set and we were talking and having a really great time being silly. I thought she was a model. At the time so many models looked like her, because she's really beautiful but kind of masculine. She had short hair then."

Chan's appeal as a fashion muse comes from the same juxtaposition between transparency and mystery that makes her music so compelling. Chan is beautiful, but in a regular way. She can pull off false eyelashes, liquid eyeliner, and couture gowns like she's been playing dress-up in socialites' closets since childhood, but you can always see the shorn, Carhartt-wearing country girl beneath the makeup. "She's this indie girl, but when I go visit her in Miami, we're at the pool at the Delano ordering drinks, and she's in a Chanel bikini," Cho laughs. "You can do that if you don't give a shit. It's very punk. There's nothing punk about faking it. It's not like she's doing this to be on the best-dressed list. It's very natural. There's no desperation. Desperation makes people boring. All those starlets in Us Weekly are so boring."

When Chan describes her personal style, it's clear she enjoys mixing clothes that reflect both her down-home roots and her appreciation of glamour. "I'll buy army-navy, or go to the thrift store for old Levi's, and then I'll get an Eres Bra and Cosabella underwear," the singer has said of her approach to shopping. "Salvation Army jeans, a friend's band's T-shirt, and a Chanel fanny pack."

When they first met, Cho didn't realize Chan was there to shoot promo photos, but after they talked for a while she mentioned that she was in a band called Cat Power. Cho remembers that the name was vaguely familiar, but was more impressed by the gregarious personality he'd just met than by her notoriety. The pair stayed in touch. "I was really into letter writing back then," he remembers. "So I wrote her this letter and sent it to her in Georgia. And then I was at another photo shoot and she walks in. It was so random, I just kept seeing her at photo shoots. Then Moon Pix came out and I was like, 'Oh my motherfucking God, what a fantastic album.' So I used 'American Flag' in my first show, and we've remained really close. I consider her like family even though I never really see her."

For the most part, Chan's biological family is not a stabilizing force in her life. The family she counts on to be there for her when she's in trouble is her vast network of friends. "Chan puts a lot of importance on her friends," says Loring Kemp. "The way that she grew up, living with her dad and going back and forth with her mom, she has always created family. That's what I see in Atlanta with her friends, and that's where it comes from. Anybody from a single-parent home, especially a female that's being raised during her teenage years by a male, she creates a family around her."

22.

The Covers Record

Fan response to Moon Pix *was extremely positive, and Chan's zany, headline-grabbing tour for the record brought her new attention, as did endorsements like the Gap ads and Chan's new friendships within the fashion world. The* result of all this was that there were a lot of expectations riding on the next Cat Power album, and a lot of pressure to put it out sooner rather than later.

Theoretically, this shouldn't have been a problem. Chan never really stops writing, and she generally records a new song every couple of months. She travels so much that it's easy for her to pop into a studio in Dublin, or Sevilla, or Buenos Aires, and record a song she wrote last week. She does this so often that not even her label is sure how many Cat Power tracks are actually out there on tape. "Usually what happens is, I'll play it four times early on and be like, Is this something I don't want to remember?" Chan has said of her approach to writing. "If it's something I want to remember, I have to play it four more times because I have to remember it. Because in the time it takes for me to look under my bed to find the tape recorder, I lose all the lyrics and the music. Then a couple months later I'll be like, what is this? And then I'll remember. The trick is remembering it and testing yourself, without the cassette, if the song still resonates with you. The ones that come out are the ones I remember, so there's a lot of them that are like, No, no, no, no, no."

During the tail end of 1999, Chan was following her usual recording pattern—except that every time she got behind a studio mike, she found herself working on covers instead of new songs. "Even when I was younger, nervous, uncomfortably and emotionally disabled, I always felt more freedom singing covers because it's not really my material," Chan has said. "Before I put out The Covers Record, I had all these songs. I thought that was going to be the record, but I put out The Covers Record because I felt like I had a bad thing in my stomach. It wasn't time for that. I felt something telling me to do The Covers Record. I had this love for a lot of those songs, and they made me feel joyous. I didn't want to do the other songs."

Around this time, Chan embarked on an unusual tour, one that allowed her to stay as out of sight as possible and solidified her commitment to releasing an all-covers album. She scheduled a series of dates in which she performed solo, on a spooky black stage, while the silent film *The Passion of Joan of Arc* played on the wall behind her. She routinely sat to the side of the stage, lit only by the delicate rays of light reflecting off the screen, and played mostly covers as Joan of Arc, played by French actress Renée Jeanne Falconetti, martyred herself. "I want to be personless," Chan explained of the impulse to hide in plain sight onstage. Like many of the performances Chan would give during the *Covers Record* era, without the deranged craziness to occupy the audience, there was nothing left to hold their attention. "The *Joan of Arc* shows were just a way for her to get people distracted from looking at her," Chan's old friend from Atlanta, Steve Dollar, surmises. "So she could sort of evaporate. I went. I saw it. I don't know if it was really, like, great, you know? It was just her sort of doing her songs with *Joan of Arc* playing in the background."

Chan decided to record *The Covers Record* because she felt safer playing other people's songs than she did playing her own, but Chan's all-covers shows, both before and after the album's release, were not necessarily less unhinged. Henry Owings was booking the Echo Lounge in Atlanta during this tour and remembers being driven to a state of abject fury by Chan's self-defeating apathy. "Chan wanted to do, sit-down, two shows in one night: rows of chairs in the club, people watching the movie, and her on a mini–grand piano onstage, playing along with the music. We'd never projected a movie in there, so we were making this makeshift screen of bedsheets on the back wall. Both shows were already sold out, and there was a line, and it was drizzling outside. Showtime was about twenty minutes away, and I was a bundle of nerves. I was like, 'I just want to get this fucking done,' because she had made a couple of little jabs, a couple of little comments where she was talking about how I wasn't able to get the screen up right, or this piano needs to be moved, or we need to move these chairs closer, and it was kind of ticking me off.

"She's doing the soundcheck," Owings continues, "and twenty minutes from doors opening, she's hunched over on the piano bench, and I'm frantically trying to get this goddamn screen up. I'm like, 'Could somebody give me a hand here, please? I need to get this up.' And she just said: 'I don't even know why you're bothering. The show's gonna suck anyway.' At this point I throw the staple gun down, and I'm looking at her, and I am thumping her chest: 'If you're gonna say that, do you want me to go outside and tell everyone that the show's gonna suck? Because I don't have time for this.' I threw the staple gun, and I walked out, and I never came back, and I just let her rot on the vine. I understand the stress of her being the only one there. I get it. But there also comes a certain amount of professionalism, even in the roughest sense of the word that I've become accustomed to. Be it with some dirgey metal band or a girl on acoustic guitar. You don't say shit like that."

By this time, Chan was still in the midst of her second professional identity crisis. She was compelled yet again by the idea of settling down, starting a family, and living what she routinely terms "a normal life," but the success of *Moon Pix*, not to mention her own unquiet creative mind, would not allow it. Both *The Covers Record* and *The Passion of Joan of Arc* tour were attempts to have it both ways, to remain a professional, performing musician by trade without sacrificing her sanity. "I just want to chill out. I can't rock. I don't want to rock anymore," she said at the time. "I mean, I do later, maybe, but right now I'm just taking it as it comes."

Musicians will traditionally do a covers album to fulfill one last release of their recording contract, or because they have no other ideas, or because they are lazy, or because they are vain and want to show off their impressive ability to improve on someone else's songs, or because they genuinely want to pay tribute to another artist. There are many standard reasons, but none of them apply to Chan. For her it was about hiding—from her fans, from her critics, and from herself. The last Cat Power album was incredibly personal, and it transformed Chan into the type of star whose fans needed something from her. The tour almost killed her, but she made it through, and by the late 1990s she had a nice boyfriend and some money and didn't want to go back to the way things had been before. She didn't want to record songs that would land her in a fetal position during every show.

During the *Moon Pix* tour, when Chan managed to actually play her songs, the arrangements were very traditionally rock 'n' roll, especially for Cat Power. According to Chan, this was part of the problem. "I changed a lot of the chords to make them more rockin'," Chan had said. She found herself turning to the security of cover songs when the pressure to rock out became too intense. "Every now and then I'd say, 'Please don't play. I'm going to do this one right now,' " Chan has said. "I needed some grounding because I felt like rock was so *raaargh vroomagh*. I was like, 'Nuh, nuh, nuh, no.' By the end . . . I'd say, 'Relax.' Because I felt like what I was giving, I wasn't feeling. You know, having to be like 'Yeeaaahhh.' It was just like, 'God damn, shut up!' "

We saw Chan's face for the first time on the cover of *Moon Pix*, but the abstract sculpture that adorns *The Covers Record* reinforces the idea that Chan's gone underground again, only to be glimpsed as a shadow behind, to borrow Greil Marcus's word, the scrim of her music. *Moon Pix* featured a full band and the most experimental production of Chan's career. On *Covers*, the singer is once again alone with her songs, mostly backing herself on guitar or piano. She practically recorded the record alone as well. "I ended up in the studio recording with this young man at this place called Night Owl Studios across from Penn Station," Chan remembers. "I did most of the songs there just very, very, very, very quickly, and there's like four songs that are from different recording sessions."

What started as an intuition telling her not to release her new songs turned into an official plan when Chan met with Chris Lombardi in New York to discuss the progress of her new album. "I remember talking to her about this other record," Lombardi has said, "and she was just like, 'Oh, I don't want to do that, but I want to put these covers out.' " According to legend, Lombardi drafted a new contract on the spot, which he allegedly wrote down on a Post-it. Chan supposedly looked over the proposed advance and promptly demanded that he double it. For years, hard-core Cat Power fans have been lusting after the so-called lost Cat Power album that wasn't released as a result of this conversation, but Cosloy says it doesn't exist, or if it does, Matador doesn't have it. "She may have been recording things periodically," Cosloy explains. "But at no point did she submit an album to us in between *Moon Pix* and *The Covers Record*. That didn't happen."

Some of the songs Chan shelved in order to release *The Covers Record* ended up on future Cat Power albums. (For example, "He War," which appears on *You Are Free*, was written during this period.) "I have two CDs of stuff that I haven't released," Chan told a reporter before *The Covers Record* came out in 2000. "I'm saving them because, at the time, I was—I don't know. I feel funny about some of it, emotionally, personally, I don't know if I want to release it." The tracks she chooses never to record are likely to remain lost forever, because she doesn't typically test out new songs when playing live. "The ones that I haven't brought in the studio or ever played again are the first songs that I ever wrote," Chan has said. "They are either on a cassette or I know them and I'll never play them again. Or I've forgotten them."

The majority of the songs selected for *The Covers Record* were chosen simply because they popped into Chan's head onstage when she couldn't bear to play another one of her raw and personal tracks. She would look down at the set list taped next to her pedal board, and even though it might have said "Nude as the News," Chan would find herself playing Smog's "Red Apples" instead. Earlier that year Chan had a piano delivered to her house in Atlanta, and this also affected the song choice for *The Covers Record*, which features much more piano playing than any of the previous Cat Power albums. Chan's version of the Velvet Underground's "I Found a Reason" emerged out of a session spent tinkering around on her new instrument one lazy Atlanta afternoon.

The song choice on *Covers* also reflects Chan's roots as a country girl who first learned to sing in church. The songs that soothed her as a child continue to bring her comfort as an adult. When asked why she included a cover of the folk classic "Salty Dog" on her album, Chan makes a direct connection to one of the tapes her grandmother made of her singing when she was a little girl. "I have one that she found," Chan has said. "Me and my sister are both singing . . . 'Salty Dog' . . . When she gave me that tape, I didn't cry, but it was, 'Oh my God, listen to that little hick.' I loved to fucking sing. It was great. That comes from my dad. My dad used to make us sing when we were babies. Meanwhile, he's smoking grass right in front of us."

As elegant and spare as Chan's piano playing is, she of course considers herself to be a grossly inadequate player, still no better than the ignorant kid her dad warned to stay away from the keys. "I want people to know that I am not proud of my piano playing," Chan has said. "It's embarrassing to people's intelligence when I play piano." Chan has described looking out into the audience and counting the faces of the people she's sure can outplay her, because "growing up, everyone took piano lessons." When she toured behind The Covers Record, Chan's solution to this problem was to play in near darkness. "I don't want [the audience] to see my hands," Chan has explained. "It's a very bizarre feeling knowing that they can't see me, but my fucking hands are in the light."

At first listen, it's startling to hear some of the more familiar songs Chan chose to include on Covers ("Wild as the Wind" or "I Found a Reason," for example) reduced to spare parts, and in moments the effect goes beyond jarring and into the realm of brilliant reinvention. Moby Grape's longing-tinged, jangly folk-rock romp, "Naked if I Want To," becomes a gorgeous ode to redemption. Chan strips the Rolling Stones' "(I Can't Get No) Satisfaction" of all its aggressive bravado, revealing a plaintive elegy at the song's core.

"For 'Satisfaction,' I was at home in Atlanta for a few weeks, and I was just playin' around with this acoustic guitar my dad had given me," Chan has said. "A friend of mine had given me this old cassette. I can't remember the actual record the Stones did that song on. And my tape player wasn't working. And my truck was in the shop, so I just started playing it. I never knew how to cover songs, literally, technically. Nina Simone [["Wild Is the Wind"]]—the same thing. I was in the studio last summer, recording some other songs. And the piano was there, and I know the song, and I didn't bring the tape with me or anything, so I just sat down and was figuring out, like, okay, just make it up. This is how I want it. Never did I think, I have a list."

Most of the tracks on The Covers Record, however, feel frustratingly unfocused and casual, as if Chan was teaching piano lessons and needed something to play, so she learned these tunes. There's none of the delicate sorrow, none of the defeated optimism, none of the stark intimacy that fans and critics had come to expect from this deranged, redemptive performer.

What the album lacks in depth and personality it makes up somewhat in rock-geek credibility, because the song selection proves how complete Chan's knowledge of music history is. The singer's insecurities about her education as an artist go back to her father convincing her that music was another subject in school she wasn't smart enough to understand, but Chan can keep up with the snootiest of record-store clerks. "She was schooled," Foljahn says. "The guys she hung out with, Mark Moore and these other Atlanta people, they had vast record collections. She had all the Dylan bootlegs before a lot of people that I knew in New York. She listened to record-collector stuff."

Stewart Lupton first bonded with Chan over a mutual love for obscure Americana. "We were into old folk music like the Harry Smith anthology," Lupton remembers. "Everything that Dylan copped. I could start a line and she could finish it. She knows her stuff. I always sought her out when I saw her just 'cause she's fun to talk to. It's fun to have a friend where you can break into song, and she was fun to talk Dylan with." The pair even discussed doing a cover of Dylan's "Dark Eyes," the last (and woefully underappreciated) track on *Empire Burlesque*, which Dylan performed as a duet with Patti Smith during the pair's 1993 tour. "It is so beautiful and inscrutable, so many wormholes opening and closing," Lupton enthuses in an e-mail about the live version of this track. "His penchant/curiosity for prostitutes, New Orleans, and the tiny hurricanes of romance and fate, the coattails of Destiny disappearing around a crowded street corner, the velocity of it all. If your aim is true it will moisten your eyes. I have been whispering in Chan's ear the notion of recording our own version. It feels like the next right thing to do."

Matador abided by Chan's request and released *The Covers Record* in March 2000, but the label didn't consider the album a major priority. They knew Chan had stockpiled original songs, presumed an album of new material couldn't be far behind, and wanted to wait until they had it in hand before leveraging the post-*Moon Pix* buzz for a big Cat Power promotion campaign. This decision turned out to be a massive mistake. "This is where the ugly record-company stuff comes in," Cosloy explains. "There was a thought on our part that there was going to be a new album very shortly after the covers album. We made a miscalculation, and to this day it's something that's never really been resolved between us and Chan."

Chan was not pleased. "The whole record label and the booking agent, they think, 'This isn't a very big record. It's just kinda like a little thing she's doing. It's her side project,' " the singer has said of *Covers*. "I'm like, No, it's not. . . . This is probably the most important stuff that I've ever . . . tried to do. But the thing is that they're making it seem like it's actually smaller than what I've done. And in the past I never cared about what I did, and now they're sayin' that it's smaller than what I've done, and I actually loved it. It's all marketing and motives."

Chan had finally made an album she liked, but it was still very important to her to insist that, even if she was a musician, she wasn't really a rock star. And *Covers* represented her defiance of the expectation that she should be. So when Matador didn't get this, they became the enemy. "If I were a ballet dancer, I'd probably be doing some ballet somewhere. If I were a monkey, or if I worked with monkeys, I would be hangin' out with monkeys all the time. . . . Since I'm a musician, I happen to play for people," Chan has explained. "My dad is a musician.

I grew up always going to see him play. Since I'm a musician, it just seemed natural that I would play, too. . . . I'm not like Prince, or Beck, or Blues Explosion, you now . . . that like have fun and trip around and jump off their amps and say, 'Fuck yeah!' and all that, and 'All right!' and actually put 'All right!' and 'Yeah!' in their lyrics. I'm not like that. . . . I know that people want to see the rock, and I can't give it to 'em."

The fact that *The Covers Record* was so personally significant to Chan even though she didn't write the songs made it even more insulting when Matador chose to back-burner the record. And from a business standpoint, Chan was furious because she knew her fan base better than any professional marketer, and she was sure the album would connect. "It wasn't that we didn't think the covers album was brilliant," Cosloy insists. "We thought it was amazing. We were big fans of her ability to take somebody else's stuff and render it unrecognizable but also remind you why the material was so great in the first place. She's really great at stripping that stuff down and getting to the absolute heart of it. She was good at that way before *The Covers Record*."

The label's concern was capitalizing on the momentum they saw after *Moon Pix* came out. "Our feeling was, we've got a lot of momentum, we're coming off of a very successful project with *Moon Pix*," Cosloy says. "This is a covers record. We've been stressing for so long that this woman is a genius songwriter. She *is* a genius songwriter, let's not go crazy and try to triple the sales with the covers album, because if we fall short and then we've got a new album eight months later—we're very conscious of trying to space things out properly.

"We consciously went out with a very muted campaign for *The Covers Record*," Cosloy admits. "We spent very, very little money on display advertising. We decided: We're going to lowball this and let it find its audience, and over time it did very, very well, but I think that move may have been interpreted on her part as a lack of confidence on our part in her or the record. For her it's an important record. She actually believes that that was a great album, which it was."

Chan saw The Covers Record as a serious album, but the reviews shared Matador's assessment that it was a novelty designed to tide fans over before a proper follow-up to Moon Pix. "While we await her next album of new material, due next winter," Rolling Stone's Rob Sheffield wrote in his review, "The Covers Record provides a stopgap fix of her unnerving, cold-blooded voice and shaky acoustic guitar." Old-school Cat Power fans were equally puzzled by the album, which features only one song penned by Chan, "In This Hole," which was itself a cover of the track that originally appeared on What Would the Community Think.

Surprisingly, for a collection of new fans, some of them the most venerated rock critics in the world, The Covers Record represented the best of Cat Power. Writing for The New Yorker in 2007, Sasha Frere-Jones praised what he heard as Chan's improved vocal abilities. "Something, probably cigarettes, had rubbed some texture into her voice, and she had learned how to manipulate her breathy middle range," he wrote. "She had found the place, between an incantation and a whisper, where her voice wanted to settle, and revealed herself to be a conjurer, like Nina Simone and Patti Smith: someone who could bring a song home, not through force but by teasing and delaying words, and by resisting standard line readings." Frere-Jones also commented on what Chan herself already knew: that as a covers artist, she brings a strength and confidence to the music that doesn't exist when she plays her own compositions. "The Covers Record also provided Marshall with songs that she needed but hadn't been able to write: personal but poetically indirect, intimate but still odd."

"I think her songwriting is very dodgy. I don't think it really holds together," Greil Marcus says. "I think her songs are opportunities or plat-forms for her to find a way into some kind of emotional nakedness, but nevertheless preserve that sense of distance and sarcasm and doubt." This gift, to inhabit songs as if they're rented hotel rooms you tem-porarily call home, impressed Marcus and others like him who had never heard anything all that commanding in Cat Power's original songs but found themselves obsessed with the covers album. "I listened to *The Covers Record* pretty early and really liked that. Particularly 'Sea of Love' and 'Paths of Victory.' There is anonymity in her music where you don't have to wrestle with the sense of a real person. It's all fictional."

23.

You Are Free

After the release of **The Covers Record** in March 2000, Chan continued to tour relentlessly. Her life consisted of long stretches on the road, typically with Currie in tow, followed by a month or so spent visiting her family in North

Carolina and checking in with friends in Atlanta and New York, all of which was fueled by a constant supply of whatever booze she could find—scotch, beer, tequila—a lit Parliament in her hand at all times: Chan, she woke up with whiskey and went to sleep with wine.

Thurston Moore remembers Chan coming to visit him and his family in Greenfield, Massachusetts, in 2002. "We wanted to raise money for our daughter's school because they had no revenue, so we told the school that we would do a benefit for them," Moore remembers. "We had some local musicians play, Sonic Youth played, and Kim [Gordon, Moore's wife and Sonic Youth's bassist] asked Chan to play. She played solo and stayed at our place." With Chan living in their home, it was hard for Moore and Gordon to miss her alarming behavior. "She was nipping at the bottle," Moore recalls. "I could tell she needed her cigarettes and she needed her alcohol."

Because Matador underpromoted *The Covers Record*, Chan was faced with almost instant pressure, after its release, to come out with a new album. A year passed, then eighteen months, another tour, another trip to Paris, to Mexico, to Miami, another series of evasive phone conversations about when she might enter the studio, and yet nothing had come of it. With her whiskey and her cigarettes reassuringly within reach and Currie by her side, Chan had all the fuel she needed to procrastinate. "All I did was hang out with my boyfriend," Chan has said of the time that passed between *The Covers Record* and *You Are Free*. "I just tried to have fun on my off days with my boyfriend. Go to a snowy mountain and ride those skimobile things, or swimming topless."

Finally, in early 2002, Chan relented and began looking for an engineer to help her record the next Cat Power album. She was characteristically adamant that whomever she worked with understand his or her role: push the right button at the right moment, while Chan alone would determine what the songs should sound like. After lamenting the difficulty she was having finding a qualified but suitably compliant person to work with, a friend recommended Seattle-based superproducer Adam Kasper. "I got an e-mail [from Adam] saying: 'Engineer, producer, whatever you want,' " Chan has said. "I was like, 'Hmmm . . . sounds a little too friendly,' because I didn't know him at all. I'd never met him before. So I e-mailed him back, and I was like, 'I'm not interested in a producer, I only want an engineer, and I want to get that straight, so if you're interested, fine, if you're not, you're not.' "

It took a lot of back-and-forth before Chan was convinced that Kasper was the right man for the job. "I really wanted a good engineer," Chan recalled. "Someone I could really talk to in the studio. Every time I've tried to do that, it's some guy who is like, 'What you don't realize here is that you're going to have a lot of feedback.' I have to deal with that so much being a girl. That shit pisses me off so much!" By this stage in her career, Chan's pathological fear of being outmatched in the studio was manifesting itself as paranoid bossiness.

"I was looking for somebody who would let me do what I wanted to do," Chan explained. "I only sit in a room with someone who presses knobs because I don't really know how to do it. I'd love to do that by myself, but I need to have someone in there. Someone who will just shut the fuck up." Kasper insisted that he could be that guy, and eventually Chan believed him. In fact, she came to trust the producer so completely that she almost abandoned her strict rules against high-concept recording to work with Kasper on a polished, traditional Motown album, much like what she would later create with *The Greatest*. "Adam and I talked about him actually doing production, like *producing*, in a Sam Cooke–ish,

R&B kind of way. Like old Marvin Gaye," Chan recalled. But the singer wasn't yet ready to relinquish that much control. "I don't know. It's like you can't be yourself if someone's directing you. You can't, it doesn't make sense," she has said. "If you have someone directing you, you lose all your stuff. I just hate that fucking idea, it sounds so gross to me."

Chan's hesitance to expose herself to outside influences extended to her work with other musicians. Outside of her most trusted bandmates (Steve Shelley, Tim Foljahn, Glen Thrasher, Jim White), at this point in her career Chan rarely worked with other artists. On *You Are Free*, she warily broke this rule and let Kasper recruit complete strangers for the record. One of the first calls Kasper made was to composer David Campbell, who has worked with everyone from Maroon 5 to Air to Alanis Morissette to Wilco—and also happens to be Beck's father. "Adam Kasper called me," Campbell remembers. "The way he painted it, he was helping her do the record, but I mean, he produced the record. He was being modest." Kasper sent Campbell versions of "Werewolf" and "Good Woman," the two tracks on which Kasper and Chan decided they wanted string arrangements. Then, once Campbell had worked on some ideas, he invited Chan and Kasper to come to his house in Los Angeles so that he could play them his compositions.

Considering Chan's caution about working with strangers, she was very cool about letting Campbell do his work. "Sometimes artists get very directly involved in the creation of an arrangement," he explains, "but in this case they kind of left it to me to come up with what I felt." Before Campbell played his compositions for Chan and Kasper, he sensed that she was nervous. "She was excited and apprehensive and all kinds of cool emotions," Campbell remembers. The composer noticed Chan's shyness, which he attributed to her lack of experience working with others. "I'm not sure how many times she'd ever done this kind of process, maybe she never had," he recalls. "It was new territory."

Even though Chan trusted Kasper, she still disagreed with him all the time. "There were times in the studio when I freaked out," Chan has said. "We'd get in fights and the next day it would be okay." Resolutions to their disagreements came quickly, but the battles were intense. "Adam did try to talk me out and talk me into things a lot," Chan has said. "We did have arguments, and there were times I know he questioned being my friend ever again." Kasper has worked with Queens of the Stone Age, R.E.M., and Nirvana, and was producing both Pearl Jam's *Riot Act* and the Foo Fighters' *One by One* during the time *You Are Free* was made. Demand for the producer's time was very high, so Chan had to fly to meet him during his odd days off. In exchange for working on Kasper's schedule, Chan got to record in the fancy, well-appointed Seattle studio spaces Kasper was using for the Pearl Jam and Foo Fighters records. "I worked on his schedule," Chan has said. "He does a lot of big-money stuff, so the studios he was getting were really amazing—amazing amps, amazing guitars, amazing mikes, amazing spaces—really organic, strange, interesting places. When he had off time, we'd go in and then try to remember what we did, like, two months ago and pull that tape up. I'd be like, 'Uh, no, I wanna do something new,' and then I'd write a new song. So it basically worked like that—every few months getting together and essentially writing new songs."

Chan was less emotionally stable in 2003 than she had been in 1993, but she was infinitely more confident in the studio. *You Are Free* was on track to be the first semislick Cat Power album ever, recorded in a posh studio with fancy guest stars. In addition to Campbell, Pearl Jam frontman Eddie Vedder and Foo Fighters lead singer and Nirvana drummer Dave Grohl make significant contributions to *You Are Free*. Both of these artists had already been vocal about their adoration of Cat Power, Grohl having once referred to Chan's voice as "the most satisfying orgasm I could imagine."

Both Grohl and Vedder obviously were and still are more famous than Chan, which was, in part, why appearing on her record was good for their careers. Being associated with Cat Power gave both of these icons of nineties alternative rock the sheen of contemporary relevance.

The benefit for Chan was that she got to collaborate with two supremely gifted musicians who would attract even more attention to her new record. Yet in typical look-at-me-wait-don't-look-at-me conflict, Chan didn't want anyone to talk about the fact that famous people were appearing on her record. In the liner notes, both musicians are referred to only by their initials, a desperate attempt as coyness that's so ineffective it's almost parody.

If Chan really wanted to keep Vedder and Grohl's work secret, she should have made that super-clear to them. Via a post on the Foo Fighters website, Grohl announced that he was on the new Cat Power album, and Vedder mentioned it in an interview with *The Onion* that ran in November 2002. "I've been listening to Cat Power for a number of years now, and I think she's gonna come out with a new one [record] next year," Vedder said. "I added a couple of things to her record. We actually got in a room and sang together, and that was one of the highlights of last year—or was it this year? This year, I think. It might be under a pseudonym, though. That might be a secret. [*Laughs.*]"

The presence of these bold-name collaborators is just one of the ways in which *You Are Free* represents an important milestone in the evolution of Cat Power. Though Chan would resist it mightily throughout the year or so she worked with Kasper, the singer was no longer the reserved, naïve tomboy who gave fans a mainline to her soul on albums like *What Would the Community Think* and *Moon Pix*. Chan looked completely different, now that she was a shaggy-haired beauty with gowns in her closet and a model on her arm, but more importantly, her songwriting was different. The songs Chan was writing were no longer the brutally spare dirges she'd recorded throughout the 1990s. The singer had moved on.

Using *The Covers Record* as a much-needed hiatus from singing about exactly what she felt, Chan was able to hold onto that idea even as she wrote new, original songs for *You Are Free*. There's little doubt that in most of Cat Power's post-*Covers* work, she is still singing about herself, but she has yet to make another record as directly confessional as any of the four albums that preceded it. *You Are Free* is all about intimacy by proxy.

"I went to a lot of different kinds of schools: the inner-city school, the cornfield school, the rich-but-fucked-up-kids school," Chan has said. "The human condition is always the same. It doesn't matter what kind of person you meet. It is always the same stories everywhere. That is always really depressing. Not depressing. But things happen to innocent kids by adults and by society, because society controls children and what they're supposed to think and do and say. I think it is really disgusting that things like that aren't talked about more openly. In the adult world, they keep it hidden. That is really hard for people in society, especially for children. Nobody protects their beautiful differences. They want to keep differences under wraps so everybody can be the same."

Before *You Are Free*, Chan hadn't spent more than a week recording any one Cat Power album, so this system of working intensely for a day or two, then letting the songs sit untouched for months at a time, was new for her. "After a year there were like forty different songs," Chan has said. "I was going a little insane." Of the forty songs Chan and Kasper recorded, only fourteen made it onto the album. Kasper helped

Chan narrow down the collection, but it still felt a little as though Chan was choosing with her eyes closed. "At some point, you don't know what you're doing," she has said. "There's no formula. It's like when you're brushing your teeth and then you're over there on one tooth and you think, What makes you wanna go over to that tooth?"

The lack of a strict recording schedule allowed Chan to luxuriate in a seemingly limitless series of sonic options. In the past, the singer had only a few days of relatively low-rent studio time in which to bang out an entire record. She went in with a handful of prewritten songs, recorded her album, and went home. This time, because she was working with Kasper, Chan had time to be a rock star, which befitted the glossier, more produced album she was creating. "Sometimes I would show up, fly into a place, and have four or five days open but just work on one day," Chan has recalled. "We'd sit there with two bottles of scotch, packs of cigarettes, laughing and listening to old songs and going, 'This is so stupid! Ooh, ooh, ooh! I have an idea! Is the tape rolling?' Sometimes it was like, 'What are we doing?'

"All your songs are completely stripped-down at first, and that's the way they sound to you," Chan has explained, "but then you get into the studio and you try a little bit of this, then a little bit of this, 'cause you got time on your hands, 'cause it's a fucking free studio." All that free time made Chan uneasy. "I felt like I was making a mess because I don't [normally] do it this way," the singer has said. "Usually you put the amp in the same place and you record in three days. The difficult thing was the idea of the songs lingering. . . . The difficult thing was never fucking getting around to finishing it because we had so much liberty." Chan struggled during the recording of *You Are Free* to relax into the idea that building her songs out from their most basic structure could improve rather than ruin them.

Though Chan entered the recording process with more than an album's worth of original songs written in the previous four years, many of the most stunning tracks on *You Are Free*, like "Evolution," "I Don't Blame You," "Names," and "Maybe Not," were composed in spare moments of quiet downtime that Chan carved out for herself in between recording tracks that never made the album. "Those were written because I was just alone in a hotel room or in a studio," Chan has said. "I'm not around instruments. I used to have a piano [at her house in Atlanta], but I was never around to play it. I wrote a lot of songs on it, which aren't on this record. I wanted to put the fresher ones, the ones I was writing in between recording all these other songs that I had. Those songs are more special in a way to me because they are fresher. 'Speak for Me' was just me, literally, playing around."

The opening track on *You Are Free*, "I Don't Blame You," was the last song Chan wrote for the record. The plaintive, resigned track sets the entire pained but peaceful tone of the album. "I sat there while everybody was playing pool, Ping-Pong, and getting stoned while we were mixing and transferring tape," Chan has said. "I was in there singing that song. We'd been drinking all night. I was remembering somebody, and I was just sitting there. I don't want to forget a song, so I have to play it over and over and over. I must have played it twenty times. I got so completely delirious that when Adam walked in, he was laughing at me." Chan realized she'd accidentally written another song for the album. "I asked, 'Can I record this song real quick?'" Chan remembered. "I'm glad that I did it, 'cause I could have just forgotten it."

"I Don't Blame You" is about a performer trying to break out of the prison of audience expectations. It opens with Chan watching a wild-eyed rocker going through the motions onstage and ends with a declaration: "They never owned it/And you never owed it to them anyway."

Given Chan's own issues with audience, she addresses her rock star as a kindred spirit. She's not singing to herself, necessarily, but she intimately understands her subject's plight. Many people have speculated that Kurt Cobain, or perhaps Elliott Smith—both of whom struggled to reconcile their integrity with their success and both of whom committed suicide—inspired "I Don't Blame You," but Chan has kept her muse's identity a secret.

Cat Power fans have always read into Chan's lyrics and related directly to emotions she's expressing. It was a you-feel-this-and-I-do-too direct connection. Suddenly, in songs like "I Don't Blame You," Chan was using the structure of observing someone else's suffering to express personal emotions. Instead of being in the spotlight, she put herself in the audience with the fans, relating to something she's hearing and seeing onstage. Maybe she is the secret subject of "I Don't Blame You," maybe she's not. But the meaning, the intimacy, is the same regardless. "It's not about me," Chan has said. "That person who is going insane? I empathize. It is a performer, but there are lots of performers who have come before that person. I don't want to mention who, because there is so much bullshit surrounding that person."

One of the most striking songs on *You Are Free* is "Names," an elegy to innocents damaged by the heartless world. The song is classic Cat Power in that its heartbreaking narrative is accentuated by the spare, unadorned arrangement and delivery, but it represents the same shift in Chan's writing style: Once again, the listener feels close to Chan not as the subject of the song but as its conduit. The song describes the basic life stories of five people—Perry, Naomi, Sheryl, Donovan, and Charles—whom Chan knew during her childhood. The stories told in the song are of lives marred by abuse, abandonment, exploitation, and sorrow. The song conveys Chan's empathy for these people, but the stories she's telling are not her own. "They're people at different schools I would go to," Chan explains. "I was always moving around. Sometimes when you're the new person at school, you are kind of an outsider because nobody knows who you are, and people gravitate towards you.

"I wasn't very close friends with the first one," Chan said of "Perry," a ten-year-old boy with learning difficulties who was apparently abused by his dad. ("His father was a very mean man/His father burned his skin/His father sent him to his death," she sings in the song.) "I really liked him because he was slow. He was in special education, and everyone would throw spitballs and put boogers on his desk. They were very cruel to him, beat him up and pull his pants down and called him retarded. It was terrible. He rode the bus with me." Moving from town to town as a child allied Chan for life with other outsiders. She gravitates toward people who knew what it was like to exist on the fringe, for whatever reason—mental retardation, a destructive home life, sexual abuse. Chan's own inescapable sense of foreignness, even in her adult life, allows her to relate to the lost souls of the world. "I was at the piano," Chan remembered of her experience writing "Names." "I don't know what made me think of one of my friends. I was in another place and felt kind of disconnected. I'm not really close with my family or anything. My friends, they're my, you know, they're my friends. I felt kind of that same feeling of being not the new kid, but like, 'Where am I?' "

Chan recorded John Lee Hooker's "Keep on Runnin'" in honor of the singer and guitarist who passed away right after she had a dream about him. "I was on the wings, he was, like, playing onstage, sitting there with a guitar and a mike in front of thousands of people," the singer has said. "All of a sudden I notice he's looking at me, and he motions for me to come onstage with him. I look around, certain he's not talking to me, but he looks right at me and says, 'C'mon, I'm gonna sing 'Maudie,' and I want you to sing it with me.' I'm really nervous, but I go onstage and sing with him. He keeps winking at me—his eyes are really sparkly and moist and he's got these incredible dimples. I sang with him but felt so uncomfortable and awkward standing there. When I woke up, I was so excited I got to hang out with him and make him laugh. Oddly, we were supposed to play on the same bill at this festival, but he canceled the day of the show and didn't even show up. So I thought that was why I had the dream about him, then he passed away a little while after."

Eddie Vedder's most significant role comes on *You Are Free*'s most personal track, "Good Woman." The song is vintage Chan in that it's directly about her: "I want to be a good woman," Chan sings. With aching candor, "Good Woman" describes an impossible scenario between two people in love. "I want to be a good woman/And I want for you to be a good man/And this is why I will be leaving/And this is why I can't see you no more," Chan sings, with Vedder's trembling baritone echoing her.

It was particularly important to Chan to include a male voice on this song because it's meant to represent the trauma inflicted on both people in a doomed relationship. "That's what I wanted," Chan has said. "That's a decision I made when I was listening to it. I didn't want to be alone in that. Men have suffered as well. The disconnection between men and women is the reason for problem marriages, abused children, neglected love, mistrust, lies, and infidelity. That missed connection is why that song was written. The person who sang on that song [Eddie Vedder], I was thinking, It would be great if you could lend your [voice] because it would really help the flip side of what's important about men and women in relationships."

Campbell, who did the string arrangements on the Michael Hurley song "Werewolf," another cover, says that Chan had a very clear idea of what she wanted to hear. "There are a lot of projects where they haven't made decisions yet," he explains. "This was more like, 'Here's the vision—add to it.' The sound of her voice and guitar just seemed to want some other colors wafting around in the background." Campbell was impressed by Chan's vision, and by how little the final version of the song differed from the rough tracks. "The way you hear her vocal and guitar on the final album, that's exactly how I remember it when they gave it to me. The whole concept sonically of the thing had that kind of ambient feel, like she's in a distant place, and that's exactly how they gave it to me."

When the recording sessions for Campbell's string arrangements took place, Chan came down to L.A. to hang out even though her vocals were already done. "We did it at the Boat," Campbell remembers, "which is this really cool studio in Silver Lake owned by the Dust Brothers. It used to be a gospel radio station in the thirties, and they built this little building that somehow looks like a ship—it has a little porthole, it has a little bridge on the front." The atmosphere in the studio was loose but businesslike. "In the world of recording albums, string sessions tend to be a bit more staid—there's no groupies or strippers," Campbell jokes. "But there was a little bit of drinking going on. It was a good vibe."

Dave Grohl played drums on a few songs on *You Are Free*. "Shaking Paper" is a dense track made foreboding by the relentlessness of Grohl's lulling snare work. Chan has called the song her "favorite with drums" off the album. "When my friend"—Chan refused to refer to either Vedder or Grohl by name in interviews about the album— "was playing, I got to get exactly what I heard in my head," she said. "It was really kind of physically painful for him to do. It is the same thing for four minutes—I felt guilty for it but I'm so happy, because he was doing exactly what I heard."

The most atypical track on *You Are Free* is "Free," a rollicking, almost-pop song that features the lyric "Don't be in love with the autograph" and counts as Cat Power's first overtly antifame tune. "It's like 'Kill your idols,' " Chan has said of the song's meaning. "Enjoy what you have yourself and what you can create. You don't have to look at a television, just . . . grass roots. Look around, enjoy art. Look to what you have, 'cause things look differently if you look at them all long enough. Just forget what you're supposed to know."

The fan and critical reaction to *You Are Free* was generally positive, but after the recording sessions were over, Chan was left with serious reservations about whether or not stepping outside of her comfort zone, working with other musicians, and building her songs out beyond their original spare formula was a good idea. In her head, most of her songs sound and should sound as basic as possible, and any attempt at elaboration obscured their meaning. "I liked 'Free' better when there's nothing on it but [the guitar]," Chan has said. She feels the same way about "He War," which she wrote before *The Covers Record* came out, and which was about her then boyfriend Daniel Currie. "It sounds so different now, which I don't like," Chan has said of the version included on *You Are Free*. "I hate that. It doesn't sound the way it used to sound because I hadn't played it in so long, but I knew if I didn't put 'He War' out, it would never come out."

This conflict—between wanting to grow as a musician and use the studio tools at her disposal versus feeling fundamentally most comfortable with spare, simple production—has been raging in Chan's mind since the beginning of her career. Some part of her will always be most at home playing an acoustic guitar barefoot in her Cabbagetown back-yard for an audience of none, because even though she's grown to like some aspects of it, she genuinely never really believed making music would be her life. "There's a certain energy some songs have to me, but there's some I don't want to touch with a ten-foot pole," Chan has said. "That's how I felt about some songs that were recorded with a band. It was always improv—I didn't want to practice because I was really shy about playing with other people. I kind of got manipulated into doing it. I feel like I murdered some of the songs by having a band on them."

In spite of all this, Chan has acknowledged that some of her collaborations on *You Are Free* worked out well. "One of the guys in the studio put the piano for 'Evolution' into a chamber," the singer remembered. "It makes the sound tremble, rather than a reverb or an echo. It's like a shaking sound. That we kept on the record. The tamborino on 'Baby Doll'—the tamborino guy was just practicing at the beginning of the song. 'Well, maybe we should just not put it in the song and leave it on the record as an intro,' 〚we thought〛. That was definitely not what it was supposed to be."

If following up *Moon Pix* with a mellow album filled with other people's songs and a tour spent onstage in the dark wasn't enough of a declaration against fame, Chan's reaction to the press surrounding *You Are Free* made obvious her intense hatred of celebrity. Kasper's presence on *You Are Free* already drew a new level of attention to the record, but when word got out that both Eddie Vedder and Dave Grohl would appear on the album, that's all the journalists, critics, and fans wanted to talk to her about. Chan enjoyed working with these men, but she resented the attention it brought to the album; it reinforced her initial wariness about inviting anyone new into the Cat Power realm. "You think, 'Oh, he's your friend,' " Chan has said of Kasper, "but you don't want that to be the projection of the interview, the projection of the record, the projection of the magazine or the label in the bio. You don't want that to be a fucking part of it, because it's so manipulative!"

The more interviews she did to promote the record, the more questions she was asked about her famous collaborators, the more irate Chan became that anyone cared. "This publicity machine, it makes me sick," she has raged. "They need a name. I just wanna get away from that. I don't want those things to be talked about at all." The entire experience of working with famous musicians reminded Chan of the way she initially perceived the music business when her father was chasing rock stardom with the Brick Wall. Fame, money, power: All of it struck Chan then as grotesque and cheap, everything that made her want to avoid the music business in the first place.

As justifiably marginalized as it made Chan feel to have so much attention placed on two guys who barely played on her album, her outrage could also be viewed as astounding naïveté or, if one were given to cynicism, false protestation. After all, no one forced her to recruit two of the most famous musicians in rock, with tens of millions of albums sold between them, to appear on her record. Chan is, by many accounts, very willful. She doesn't get bossed around easily, and by this time, ten years into her career, she knew how to handle herself. Chan must have expected that she would be fielding lots of questions about Vedder and Grohl, but pretended that she could control the tenor of the press response to suit her I'm-just-playing-with-my-pals spin on the album and avoid the hype that superstar collaborations inevitably invite.

24.
Fame

The public response to You Are Free was astounding. Fans who pledged their allegiance to the cult of Chan after hearing Moon Pix remained fascinated by Cat Power four and a half years later, and in that interim the singer had also established an entirely new, entirely mainstream fan base thanks to *The Covers Record*. Both groups of fans—the original Cat Power obsessives, and the new, soccer-mom-and-dad, NPR-listening yuppie contingent— were all super-primed for a new album.

"It's interesting to talk to people outside of New York once she started touring," Charles Aaron recalls. "People genuinely saw something in her without all this New York mystique and mystery and bullshit. Like, my wife sort of liked Cat Power from *You Are Free*—that's the album where I felt like this is a real artist. The song 'You Are Free' is a song I would put on a mix tape for years and years and years."

You Are Free was released on February 18, 2003. The reviews were largely positive. Reviewing for *Rolling Stone*, Kelefa Sanneh called the album Chan's "most beautiful" and remarked on the evolution of songwriting revealed within its fourteen tracks. "There are gaunt rock songs and ramshackle ballads," Sanneh wrote, "all painted with bold, sure strokes that belie her ambivalence." Online music magazine Pitchfork gave the album an 8.9 out of ten, praising the first half for its "stunning variety and intrigue," while suggesting that the track list could have used some editing: "As the old adage goes, ten songs is an album, and in this case, fourteen is a few too many." Greil Marcus, who has made it clear that he prefers Chan's covers to her original compositions, was nonetheless impressed by what he heard. "I like *You Are Free* enormously," he says. "It's completely alive and ambitious and expansive. It lives up to the title. I think of it as this little drama where a person is trying to convince herself that, yes, she *is* free."

As the first album of the post-*Covers* era, *You Are Free* was all but universally hailed as something different and unexpected from an artist whom many assumed had already released her best material. "Honestly, by the time *You Are Free* came out, I was surprised it was that good,"

Aaron says. "I really liked it. I took the time out to listen to it because I felt like she was a whole different person in a way. I didn't connect with that other person, who was kind of like a performance artist.

"I don't know if the shows were great," Aaron continues. "They were still totally all over the place. But I didn't feel like I was buying into some little novella, some little play that we all were gonna be in, some psychodrama being played out. Clearly she'd learned how to sing. She'd learned how to write songs. I had it on record. I never really had it in person."

In addition to receiving good reviews, *You Are Free* also attracted attention because it represented a new and extremely appealing chapter in the singer's saga. Chan Marshall's life was always at least as interesting as Cat Power's music, but for much of the early part of her career there was only the depressing part of the story to tell. Now that the ultimate damaged Southern belle was reaching for freedom armed with a slick new sound and an even slicker haircut, her narrative had a Hollywood-ending sheen to it. Interested but previously unconvinced music fans no longer needed to get sad with Chan; *You Are Free* allowed them to celebrate with her.

Around the release of *You Are Free*, Chan was profiled in *New York* magazine, *Rolling Stone*, and, most famously, in *The New Yorker*, which ran a tasteful but risqué portrait of the singer by celebrated photographer and cultural icon Richard Avedon. The photo features Chan in full hippie-vixen mode, arms full of miscellaneous bracelets, breasts barely covered by a Bob Dylan T-shirt, and a patch of pubic hair peeking out from beneath the fly of her unbuttoned Levi's. The vision of indie rock's cult heroine exposed in such a prestigious magazine hammered home Chan's emerging image as the genre's critically respected pinup girl.

The Avedon shoot took place in New York, and Chan had to fly in for it. The singer's body was so destroyed from relentless partying that she couldn't walk off the plane by herself: She had to be taken out of the airport in a wheelchair. A few days later, she showed up at Avedon's studio in New York, blitzed, grinning and giggling, but unable to button her jeans. "The reason why my fly's undone is because it hurt so bad, because I was killing my organs," Chan has said. "I didn't have time to zip up. I guess he didn't realize my pants were undone because he was eighty years old." Once again Chan's self-abuse directly advanced her career. "The first pubic hairs ever to be published in *The New Yorker*," Chan has said. "My grandmother shit a brick.

"He took me upstairs to his apartment. It was like a museum," Chan remembered. "It was modest—eight hundred square feet, maybe, all open-floor with a kitchen. He had a portrait of Marilyn. . . . He had all these photos from Africa. He had pictures of his wife and his son and books upon books. It was just a mesh of collectible things from all over the world. He opened up a bottle of champagne and we sat in the garden and I smoked. He was so accommodating. He was running around doing everything for me—so handsome, such an open-minded person. We talked about Dylan and a lot about the civil-rights era. He was just a wealth of knowledge."

The photo is absolutely stunning: A weird combination of rude and refined, it shows a tanned Chan with her hair pulled back, beaming from behind puffy, messily made-up eyes. She looks beautiful. She looks iconic. She looks supremely fucked-up. "Never in a million years did I think I'd open up *The New Yorker* one day and there she'd be, flashing pubic hair with a Bob Dylan T-shirt on," Steve Dollar says, laughing. "I had dinner with her one night in New York after the Avedon thing. She had a huge dinner with her friends and had a couple beers and was quite jolly. I was impressed by the amount of food she ate. She's totally, like, carnivorous.

"They spent a lot of time talking about Martin Luther King," Dollar says. "She's obsessed with him. She once said she felt like because of Martin Luther King, Atlanta had this aura over it that would protect it. Avedon was the sixties, and she liked hanging out with him because he knew all those people that were her idols." Chan recalled. "He was talking to me about Malcolm X, Martin Luther King Junior, Bob Dylan, Janis Joplin," she has remembered. "He said, 'I was doing fashion just to pay for trips to Cambodia and Vietnam. Something about your music shows me that you understand things, and I just want to talk to you.' I told him about the show that I was doing for Janis Joplin's birthday in Central Park. He said, 'I would love to come. I loved Janis so much. She was a great girl. Such a sweetheart.' He came to the show, this eighty-year-old man rocking out to Big Brother and the Holding Company and me."

Even as Chan grew more comfortable with her professional accomplishments, with the idea of herself as someone who makes music for a living, she remained stubbornly committed to the desire to abandon it. Soon after *You Are Free* came out, Chan again started talking about how exhausting the transient touring life is and how nice it would be to have a reason to give it up. "I've been traveling for like four years straight, so I'm not living anywhere," the singer said at the time. "There's a big map in my mind, and I don't know dates and I don't know days, but I know cities and I know the amount of time I'm supposed to be in each place. Home? No, I don't have a home yet. As I get older I don't know what I'm going to do. Thirty wasn't a big deal, but when I'm forty I'm going to be so much more tired of doing this than I am now. It's really wearing me out, traveling and playing shows. I don't have any routine. I'm lucky if I brush my teeth twice a day."

Chan's previous fantasies about abandoning musicmaking to domesticate involved visions of her and a boyfriend blissfully baking pies and frolicking barefoot in country streams somewhere, but as she got older, she started thinking in more concrete terms about motherhood and marriage. "If I could change what I'm doing, I would probably want to be a mom," Chan has said. "I don't want to be like this. I don't want to be alone. I'd love to have someone, you know. I'd love to, I mean, I'm just like the next guy, but I'm not because I can't stop being this way." Chan sees touring and making albums as a perverse affliction, something she can't find the will to quit, but starting a family might force her to change. "If I ever get pregnant, I'll probably stop," Chan explained. "If it happened, I would be excited. I think that would ground me and force me to stop playing music and wandering around. I would still make songs, but I would have a focus."

Chan has always lived a nomadic lifestyle, but in the months leading up to and following the release of *You Are Free* she made a renewed effort to plant roots, this time in Miami, where an old friend had recently moved. "One of her best friends is this girl Jenny Lee, who now lives in Miami," Loring Kemp recalls. "They've been friends since middle school and they're still very close." Chan first started visiting Miami regularly in 1999, and by the time she decided she liked it enough to stay, Jenny had moved up to New York. But the singer's love affair with the laid-back eclecticism of the place had already sunk in.

In 2003 Chan bought a small condo on Ocean Drive in South Beach and officially made Miami her home. "I can work on things that I couldn't do while I was touring. Things like physical health, sleep, not drinking, stuff like that," Chan has said of her attraction to Florida. She's also an avid sun worshipper and loves the ocean, so her condo, which is right by the water, gave Chan easy access to a mellow, beachcomber sort of life that she found very restorative. Just as Chan was reaching for a saner lifestyle in Florida, one that might eventually support the marriage and family life she craved, her relationship with Currie began to unravel.

Chan wrote "He War" in the late 1990s, around the same time she met Daniel; by the winter of 2003, a few months before *You Are Free* came out, Chan found herself in a speedboat, chasing Currie through placid Miami waters while her friend Brett Vapnek filmed the entire chase for the "He War" video. The clip isn't meant to be metaphorical: Chan and Currie play themselves, and the desperate sense of irreversible disconnection conveyed by the video reflects exactly what was going on between them at the time.

After countless trips back to Atlanta together, Chan had gotten to know Currie's family well. When the pair separated, the singer mourned the loss of her adopted family. Well after the breakup, Charlie Marshall remembers his daughter fretting about how to get Christmas presents to the Curries. "We were flying back to Atlanta on the plane together," Charlie recalls. "She wanted me to go bring Daniel and his sister and mother their Christmas presents. I said, 'Well, sweetheart, when I get into Atlanta I pick up my car and I drive to Alabama, and I see my folks in Alabama for their Christmas—that's a lot of driving and flying.' I think she was upset that she had to do it herself. I think she didn't want to see them right then."

Chan has not been very forthcoming about what caused the couple's breakup, but both she and Currie were totally wrecked in the aftermath. For years following their split Chan would refer to Currie as the love of her life, and she has suggested that the stress of losing him sparked a drinking and drugging tailspin that nearly killed her. Because she's the one in the public eye, Chan has had more opportunity to describe the effect the split had on her, but according to Currie's mother, Winnie, her son has never really recovered from his relationship with Chan. "I will say this, he is very screwed-up because of her," Mrs. Currie reveals. "She was a lot older and he was a pretty young guy in New York. He's still screwed-up. I don't know what will happen to Daniel. It probably would have been better for him had he never met her. It's not that we don't like her, we do, but for him it was bad." Daniel's mother hesitates to say more about the details of her son's relationship with Chan, but tells me that he called me at least once, ready to tell his own story. "He got your machine," Winnie explains, "but he didn't leave a message." Repeated attempts to contact Daniel went otherwise unanswered.

Out of pain and frustration resulting from the breakup, Chan trashed the elegant Silvertone guitar that once decorated her glorified squat in Cabbagetown. "It was either that or jump out the window," she has said. The couple's breakup took the better part of a year, but in those first torturous, emotionally unstable months, Chan had even less reason to stay in one place—so she embarked on a lengthy tour that continued off and on for two full years.

Cat Power's output during this period was as all over the place as Chan's mind. In 2004 Matador put out Cat Power's one and only critical flop, *Speaking for Trees*, a CD/DVD combo that featured Chan at her hiding-from-fame-while-simultaneously-courting-it worst. The crux of the release is a two-hour Cat Power solo concert performed in the woods and shot by Chan's friend Mark Borthwick, whose ample skills as a still photographer don't translate to film. The reviews on the Amazon.com page for this release have titles like "not all experiments work," "the most boring film ever," and "apparently Chan likes 'shrooms." The songs Chan plays, which include her own material as well as covers, are compelling, but the audio is poor, the bursts of blinding sunlight and deafening sound of crickets are supremely distracting, the singer's face is almost completely obscured throughout, and ultimately the Chan-gets-lost-in-nature sensibility feels self-indulgent and contrived.

Speaking for Trees does contain an excellent original Cat Power tune, "From Fur City," which Chan wrote in tribute to her friend Benjamin Smoke. The poet laureate of Cabbagetown eventually contracted HIV from using dirty needles. On January 29, 1999, he died from an AIDS-related infection. Chan attended his memorial.

Though she resented it mightily, working on *You Are Free* with other established musicians opened Chan up to future collaborations. The audio CD portion of *SFT* contains an eighteen-minute song, "Willie Deadwilder," recorded with then up-and-coming guitarist M. Ward. And that same year, Chan lent her vocals to the track "I've Been Thinking" on the Handsome Boy Modeling School's album *White People*. In addition to working with other artists Chan was on the road, writing songs and popping into the studio on her off days to record them. In 2005 Cat Power did an Australian tour supporting Nick Cave and appeared at the Meltdown festival, directed that year by Patti Smith. During these gigs Chan started to play some of these new songs, many of which would appear on her next album.

At this point in her career, Chan was living the relatively good life on the road. She stayed in hotels with actual lobbies and was routinely invited to glitzy parties and events in nearly every major city she played. But she was extremely lonely. Chan muted the isolation of a life set at highway rest stops and after-parties with as much alcohol as she could swallow. "In the morning I would go to the minibar and get Jack Daniel's and do that all day long," Chan has said of her post–*You Are Free* life. "Obviously I was really unhappy, but I wasn't goin' to let myself know that, so I made sure I was drunk for every minute of every fuckin' day. I was a mess. But again, it was the best time of my life. I don't remember anything."

When Chan was later asked what part of sobriety she finds most difficult, she said it's remembering things she did when she was drunk. "Like taking my shirt off at the Chateau Marmont," she has said. "Or hanging out all night with these homeless Muslim guys in Spain. Realizing that I put myself at risk." Chan's under-the-influence antics got her banned, like some imploding starlet, from the Chateau. "All these photographs in the *New York Times* were really disturbing me," the singer has remembered. "The election was coming up. There were all these mosques and synagogues being bombed—just really depressing images, and I kept cutting them out and sticking them all over. I had heavy traffic coming in and out of my hotel room. At the pool I was just clearly shit-faced, getting people in the pool to sing along and running around topless. I pulled Kirsten Dunst's top down at one point. You know, just drunk—someone who doesn't realize their actions until they get reminded."

Chan embraced perpetual drunkenness like a warm fog that brought cozy familiarity to every chilly, bleak hotel room. It also ensured the singer wouldn't have to focus on any ugly memories. "Shane MacGowan is probably the happiest person on the planet because he can keep himself in a bubble," Chan has said of the famously dissolute, toothless frontman for the Pogues. "But imagine what he could do if someone could get him sober. Live longer. Survive. Write fucking books. In the bubble you're never gonna fall in love, never gonna settle down.

"Drugs and alcohol were part of my growing up," the singer has said. "The people I was around were of the sixties. There was that sense of rebellion. Then the seventies hit and it was all about cocaine. The reefer was always around, and so was alcohol. It just got darker and darker, but I thought I'd never have a problem with alcohol. And then I stopped and asked myself: Why am I drinking two bottles of wine at dinner or half a bottle of scotch? I never really thought, When something bad happens, you go to the bar and turn off your emotions. I never realized that I'd gotten to the point of such depression."

As vocal as Chan has been about her drinking problem and her family's history of substance abuse, a remarkable number of the singer's close friends don't buy her as an alcoholic. "I know musicians who had severe substance or alcohol problems," Steve Dollar says. "A certain amount of drinking is just maintenance, then there's people doing destructive drinking. I don't really see her like that, though. She doesn't seem like an out-of-control person. But then again, it's not like there weren't a lot of people that were pretty blacked-out down in Atlanta, so you could, in fact, seem to be pretty okay by comparison."

Jeff Clark and Loring Kemp are similarly perplexed by the notion of their friend as an out-of-control addict. "To me or Jeff, it wasn't obvious," Kemp says. "I don't remember seeing her falling-down drunk or doing anything outrageous. I remember her having a good time, but never anything that would ring alarm bells. As eccentric as she can be, she's a very, very smart and together person. She really loves life and all the experiences she can have doing this. I can't ever imagine her allowing herself to go down that road."

The fact that many of Chan's close friends didn't pick up on her drinking problem is, in a way, a sign of exactly how bad it was. Chan is the first to admit that she's a master of disguising what's really going on with her for the benefit of other people in her life; she had to be in order to survive her childhood. "Chan Marshall, me, has always taken care of herself," the singer has said, speaking about herself in the third person. "Chan has never been an addict. Chan's had friends who are dead because of their promiscuity with drug use. Chan would never be a junkie. Chan's mom was an alcoholic; she would never do that. Chan was always in control."

The singer also points out that though she was an excessive drinker, she could hold her liquor. "I wasn't a sloppy drunk. I could have a fifth of scotch and still be carrying on a rational conversation, doing dishes or whatever, and never slurring," she has explained. "The amount that you drink enables you to drink more. If you have one drink on Monday, you can have two on Tuesday, and then three on Wednesday. By the time you hit Saturday, you're up to ten drinks. You feel like shit on Sunday, so you have a drink, and then two on Monday. When that happens, depression stays in your blood."

The Greatest

Chan may have a preternaturally developed sense of her own appeal, but by accident or by design, she was still not as famous as she could have been. The singer's bluesy vocal style, her high profile in areas outside of music, and the fact that Cat Power's songs became more mainstream as her career progressed suggested that every minivan in America should have had *The Covers Record* or *You Are Free* in its CD changer. The fact that they didn't frustrated the label guys who'd put a decade-plus into coaching Chan from a howling androgynous banshee to a polished star. "Obviously there is still a slight nagging feeling on our part that compared to her level of celebrity, we wish more records were being sold," Cosloy allows. "We wouldn't be human if we didn't sit around every now and then and say, 'Well, gee, how come she doesn't sell as many records as Norah Jones?'"

In February 2002, Jones, a little-known jazz vocalist, released her debut album, *Come Away with Me*. By June, Jones's second single, "Don't Know Why," was as ubiquitous as Avril Lavigne's bratty summer hit "Complicated." Jones was neither a pop star nor a merely palatable Lilith girl: She has a moody voice that's not dissimilar to Chan's and a sober, pensive style. Yet *Come Away with Me* eventually reached the top of the *Billboard* chart, cleaned up at the 2003 Grammies with five wins, and to date has sold more than twenty million copies, making it the best-selling studio album of the decade thus far. The singer's next album, 2004's *Feels Like Home*, sold a million copies in its first week of release, firmly establishing the Norah Jones business model as one to emulate. No singer in contemporary music was as well positioned to capitalize on Jones's success as Chan, and Cat Power's next album, 2006's *The Greatest*, was designed to do exactly that.

In the three-plus years that passed between *You Are Free* and the summer of 2005, when Chan entered the studio to record *The Greatest*, she was as cagey with Matador as she was with the press about where she was and with whom she was recording. In spring of 2005, Chris Lombardi began the long process of locating Chan and locking her into a specific time and place where she would record the next Cat Power album. In the ten years Chan had been making music professionally, everyone from the most die-hard Cat Power fans to skeptical critics to the executives at her label had wondered aloud why Chan hadn't yet made the traditional soul record her honey-toned voice always seemed best suited for.

Lombardi was at the top of the list of people who wanted to see Cat Power make an old-school, Muscle Shoals–style album that would finally take advantage, commercially, of Chan's voice. Lombardi and a small Matador team tracked Chan down in Barcelona, took her out for a giant Spanish meal, and, legend has it, by the time they were enjoying their postmeal kava, Cat Power was scheduled to record in June with Al Green's band at Ardent Studios in Memphis. "Everyone wanted a band," Chan has recalled. "It was: 'Where's the rock 'n' roll? Where's the band?' " It has been suggested that Chan refused to record unless Lombardi got her Al Green's players, assuming this would be impossible, but Cosloy says negotiations weren't quite that theatrical. "As far as Chan saying, 'Get me Al Green's band or I won't make the record,' I don't think that's true. That might be a slight exaggeration."

Robert Gordon, a renowned Memphis-based journalist who knows all the old-time blues players in the area, put Chan in touch with the performers who would record *The Greatest* with her. "Gordon was the one who got Teenie and the other players together," Cosloy says, referring to legendary songwriter and guitarist Teenie Hodges. "Musically, the record, it's all Chan, and the band are obviously awesome and great players, but Robert and Chris especially did a lot of heavy lifting as far as just getting a record together."

"When planning the recording of her latest album . . . Chan Marshall (aka Cat Power) phoned me for assistance," Gordon wrote as part of an introduction to an interview he did with Chan for *Stop Smiling*. "She wanted to record in Memphis with a Memphis group and a Memphis sound, and wondered if I could help put together a band. Her call renewed an acquaintanceship we'd struck up during her previous Memphis sessions, for *What Would the Community Think*, a decade earlier."

Hodges, Al Green's guitarist and cowriter of some of the legend's most famous hits, including "Take Me to the River" and "Love and Happiness," got the call from Gordon before he'd ever heard of Cat Power. "Robert called me one day to see if I would be interested in recording Cat Power," Hodges remembers. "He said, 'Have you ever heard of her? Heard her play or sing?' I said, 'No, I've never heard of her before tonight.' " Gordon set up a meeting between Stuart Sikes, who would produce the album, Chan, and Hodges at a restaurant in Memphis. At first the meal felt like a bad first date. "Rob and I are sitting next to each other," Hodges remembers. "Chan went back to the other side of the table, and Rob said, 'Chan, you come over and sit by Teenie.' " But soon Chan warmed up, and twenty minutes later the whole group decided to go straight from the restaurant to the studio to try out a few ideas.

In addition to working with Al Green, Mabon "Teenie" Hodges also recorded and toured with his brothers, bassist Leroy "Flick" Hodges and keyboardist Charles Hodges, as the Hi Rhythm Section. They worked as the in-house band on many songs released by legendary Memphis soul and rockabilly label Hi Records. The group's ability to conjure both sorrow and warmth with simple, deeply emotive playing provided the backdrop for some of the greatest soul records ever, including Al Green classics "Let's Stay Together" and "Here I Am (Come and Take Me)" as well as the Ann Peebles song "I Can't Stand the Rain" (later made even more famous by Missy Elliott) and O. V. Wright's "A Nickel and a Nail."

Today Hodges is a physically fragile man with a flirtatious wit that belies his poor health. He suffers from emphysema, which seriously impairs his breathing and has affected his ability to tour, record, and even spend time outside during the warmer months. As a kid, however, the legendary bluesman was a promising baseball player and had dreams of becoming a professional catcher before an early growth spurt proved to be the only one he'd ever experience—and he was forced to admit he was too short and too thin for the professional leagues.

The Greatest was a full-blown studio record with sophisticated production and senior players backing Chan up, and this scared her to death. The rest of the world was impressed by the fame quotient of her You Are Free collaborators, but to Chan, Vedder and Grohl and Kasper were just grown-up kids like her, with their roots firmly planted in indie rock. The idea of working with the Memphis players was much more daunting because these people were Chan's heroes. They made the music that kept her company as a girl when things were bad. Faced with the reality of directing her musical idols in the studio, all of Chan's old hang-ups reappeared.

June in Memphis is best spent sipping iced tea and waiting for fall, but Chan and her players (who would later tour with her as the Memphis Rhythm Band) assembled at Ardent Studios every morning and got right to work, recording each track on The Greatest in a one-take session. This meant that the band had to be extremely well rehearsed, yet comfortable enough with each other to keep the sound from feeling uptight. Chan's approach to accomplishing this was to stay drunk all day.

"I was bad," the singer has said. "I always had my fifth of scotch, but I didn't realize that I always had that. I thought it was normal. I didn't realize I was a mess." Chan needed to communicate with her musicians, but she wasn't sure how to do it. "The recording process was intense," the singer has said. "You know, white girl from Georgia asking these legendary musicians if they'd be interested in recording. Teenie would be like, 'Now, what key is this song in?' and I'd be like, 'I don't know anything about keys.' "

Hodges quickly became Chan's friend and supporter in the studio, serving as a conduit between Chan's vision for the songs and the rest of the musicians. "All I need is a music sheet, not numbered chords with a number chart," Hodges explains. "That's the way we do it in Memphis and Nashville. The person to start that process was Reggie Young with the Memphis Boys. Reggie was my mentor for playing guitar, so we adopted that style. Once we got her in the studio, I'd just tell her, 'Just play it on the guitar or the piano, and as you play it, I'll write it out.' "

"He'd be like, 'Okay, just play it,' " Chan has said. " 'I'd play and he'd mark down the Nashville number system.' " Each number represents a chord, making it easier to write out the basic structure of a song. "That's the way poor people learned to play because," she says, adopting a Deep South accent, "they don't have no *con-serrr-va-tory*." Hodges was crucial to making Chan feel comfortable enough in the studio that she was able to communicate her ideas to the rest of the players. "Teenie would be like, 'See that note you played? That's the key. It's always gonna come back to that note,' " Chan has said. Teaching Chan the Nashville number system was one way Hodges kept the singer relaxed in the studio. He also helped her stay drunk. "The first day when we went to the studio, she said, 'I'd sure like to have a drink, but I can't because if my boyfriend knew it, he'd kill me,' " Hodges remembers. "I said something like, 'I won't tell. I've got some corn liquor.' So she took a drink of it, and from that day and for the next three days, she drank and drank."

"We would get into the studio and I would play a song. They'd listen to it, and then Teenie would say, 'Now, Chan, was that 5-5-1-5 or 5-1-1-5?' " the singer has remembered. "I would just sit there silent and kinda start tearing up and sort of try and hide under the piano. And they would look at each other like, 'Oh yeah—right,' and then go into the corner and work it out."

"Chan would say, 'Oh, my songs are so simple!' " producer Stuart Sikes has said. "But no one there was like, 'Well, this is too easy!' Everybody really got into it. They were there for three days and would come back to see what was going on, everyone who recorded on it—even the horn guys would sneak back in. And after we did it, they all individually told me how much they liked it."

Hodges helped Chan explain what she heard in her head to the rest of the band, but in the songwriting department, the self-described white girl from Georgia didn't need much help. "Reminded me of Bob Dylan," the bluesman says of Chan's songs. "He's a great poet, but she sings better." Chan's understanding of simplicity in songwriting particularly impressed Hodges. "The more simple the better, because people will understand where you're coming from," the guitarist explains.

"Everything Smokey Robinson writes is simple," Hodges continues. "Everything Stevie Wonder writes is simple. Everything Al Green writes is simple. Simplicity is the answer. Most people try to play a hundred notes, whereas you should maybe only play six—but you've got to find the right notes to play." If comparing Chan to Dylan, one of the singer's most revered heroes, isn't high enough praise, Hodges took the compliment even further. "People ask me, 'Who does she remind me of?' " he says. "I say, 'She reminds me of Chan.' Nobody else. That's just her. She's original."

The *Greatest* sessions were very traditional. Each track was recorded in a single take, and the entire album was completed in three days, not including rehearsal time and mixing. This is how Hodges likes to work. "Even doing Al Green's stuff—to do a whole album would take three

days." On each of the three days the players recorded songs from morning to night, and at the end of the third day the album was finished. The
pace was hard on Chan, and she was unable to relax and really sing the
way she would have liked. "I was tracking live while playing the guitar
or the piano, depending on the song, with these legendary people. So
my voice wasn't really open on that record," Chan has said.

The arrangement and execution of the *Greatest* tracks was finalized
in the studio with the Memphis Rhythm Band, but Chan had been
working on the songs they recorded for more than two years. "I usually
write when I'm alone with a piano or a guitar and I get that feeling like
you're hungry for a cookie or chocolate or something," Chan has said.
"It's almost a feeling of emotion. If I'm not near an instrument I'll just
go and write, but if I am near an instrument, then I just start playing and
the melody just comes, and then those are the words, but I never really
write with something in mind. It's usually something that I'm thinking
about, but whatever's in my subconscious comes out, and that's what
the song will translate as."

Chan wrote many of the songs on *The Greatest* sitting by herself at
the piano in her living room in Cabbagetown. "In Atlanta I wrote 'Lived
in Bars' and 'The Greatest' on my piano," she remembered, "on the same
street in Cabbagetown where my grandfather brought his thirteen-year-
old bride." Chan actually wrote a third song that completes the triplet
but has not yet recorded it. "*The Greatest* is about the workingman,
about families in the South. Poor. No education. Working, always working," the singer has said. "It's about trying to stay alive and have respect
for yourself. Everyone in the history of the world suffers and gets
through things."

"I have no idea how she connects with a song. She's a mystery," Ensemble frontman and Chan collaborator Olivier Alary says. "I helped her

move a piano back into her house. We were waiting for a guy to take the piano because it was very heavy. The piano was on the porch, and it was dark and hot, and all the crickets, and I was like, 'Please play that song 'Evolution.' Sitting next to her on the piano—in the studio you hear a voice through the speakers, but there sitting next to her, I really felt it was not her singing, it was ghosts singing. She doesn't have the same speaking voice as the singing voice. It was otherworldly."

The album's title track, "The Greatest," is the first song, and it sets the tone of redemption through pain for the entire album. Warm, gentle piano opens the track before Chan's voice comes in, inviting and sorrowful at once. "Once I wanted to be the greatest/Two fists of solid rock/With brains that could explain any feeling," Chan sings over lilting piano and mellifluous steel guitar. This image of fists clenched in defense against the world became an effigy for the entire album. A pair of golden boxing gloves on a chain decorates the album's cover, and when she played the album live, Chan would frequently dance around onstage as though she was sparring with (and clobbering) an unseen demon. "The boxer is an element of strength, concentration, and setting a goal for yourself," the singer has explained. " 'The Greatest' is an homage to humanity. It's important, I think, to have a statement of intent."

Not all of the tracks on *The Greatest* are about battling back against the world: Some are about love, both lost and found. "That's about my ex-boyfriend," Chan has said of "Empty Shell." "The breakup of this love of my life was right after the album [*You Are Free*] had come out. I came over to London, and after soundcheck I was writing it. It was a really painful time." The optimistic love song on the record is "Could We," which Chan wrote after realizing that she could be drawn to new boys even after losing someone she thought was the one. "I was so happy," the singer has said of how she felt writing it. "I had separated from someone, and we all know what that can be like. Then the spring of last year, something happened. In spring there's the birds and the bees and everything's sweet and new life and fresh, and I started dating again."

The promise relayed on "Could We" does not carry over to the other love songs on *The Greatest*. "Where Is My Love," for example, is meant to be taken literally, and was inspired by the singer's sadness at not having yet settled down to start a family. "I have five best girlfriends," Chan has said. "One of them would always start singing, 'Where is my love—where is *myyyyy* love?' when we were twenty-three and drunk on the street. I wrote that song for her, but once I sat down and started to play it, I started bawling. I realized it rings true for me too. I don't have any kids, and all of my friends have babies. I don't have a husband. I think about it."

One of the most impressive songs on *The Greatest* is "Willie," six minutes of classic-style soul that Chan wrote during a three-hour cab ride from Tallahassee to Pensacola, Florida, to visit Granny Lil. As opposed to several of the other songs on *The Greatest*, which are short and spare, sometimes containing only one repeating line, "Willie" is a robust, fully fleshed-out narrative. "The driver's name was Willie," Chan has said. "He was an older gentleman. I was in a really good mood and trying to talk to him." Initially Willie wasn't interested in chatting, but three hours is a long time, and before long the driver had told Chan his entire life story.

The pair made a detour to Willie's girlfriend's trailer to drop something off. "She was beautiful," the singer has recalled, "with bleach-blond hair and a white T-shirt and cut-off blue-jean shorts and barefoot. When she started coming closer, I could see his face changing, and he got real happy." After visiting Willie's girlfriend and hearing all about his plans to propose, Chan made the driver pull over so she could grab her guitar out of the trunk. She sketched out the basic lyrics and structure of the song during the rest of the ride. "There'd be stretches when we weren't talking, and I'd be singin' the melody in my head, writing everything down," Chan has said. "We'd stop to get gas and the song would still be playing in my mind."

The Greatest is the first Cat Power album that Chan actually owned up to liking. "I feel protective about it," the singer has said. "I've never felt that way before." She considers it her first real album, the beginning of an era. "Technically it's my seventh record, but I feel like it's my first," the singer has said of The Greatest. "When I was just starting out, I was nineteen and just experimenting with writing songs and playing guitar and singing—it was just a hobby."

When The Greatest was released on January 20, 2006, it was heralded as the most fully realized album of Cat Power's career. Reviewers commented on a new and welcome sense of self-confidence within the songs that somehow didn't obscure Chan's trademark vulnerability. Rolling Stone contributing editor Christian Hoard wrote in his review that the most remarkable aspect of The Greatest is "how much Marshall accomplishes without ever straining," and his magazine placed the album at number six on its list of the best albums of 2006. Reviewing the record for Spin, critic Will Hermes was so inspired, he went crazy with the redemption metaphors: "On The Greatest, she rises like a wounded but unbowed lioness and conjures the uncertainty of the human condition with a new certainty." The Greatest was also awarded the 2006 Shortlist Music Prize, an award given to albums that have sold fewer than one million copies and have therefore not been certified Gold. Cat Power won over albums by Tom Waits, Regina Spektor, and Girl Talk, making Chan the first woman ever to win the award. Cat

Power fans new and old agreed with the critics and bought a record number of copies in the first week of release. Their enthusiasm pushed *The Greatest* to number thirty-four on the *Billboard* chart, by far Cat Power's highest charting ever.

Everyone involved wanted to celebrate victory, so they heralded the album as the great soul record Chan had been working toward all along. However, in many ways *The Greatest* is a subpar Cat Power album. The songwriting is not as consistently strong as on *Moon Pix* or *You Are Free;* "Where Is My Love" and "The Moon" are both half-baked non-songs built around trite refrains. Chan's greatest gift as a musician is her unparalleled voice, but you can actually hear more of it on *Moon Pix* or *You Are Free* than on *The Greatest*, where the stylized production sometimes gets in the way.

Even on the songs where Chan's voice and the arrangements mesh perfectly ("The Greatest," "Willie"), the result is not nearly as satisfying as one might expect. Since Chan first started performing, it has always seemed a no-brainer to pair her rich, Georgia-inflected voice with a stellar R&B band, but something got lost in the perfection of the match. Part of the intrigue of Cat Power has always been the disconnection in Chan's music. Her best work is unsettling in a good way, off-kilter and unbalanced most of the time, then strong and clear for brief, fleeting moments. As with an eclipse, the power of the best Cat Power songs comes from sensing that the perfection within them can't last.

"She never makes the record I want her to make," Tim Foljahn says. "I like the Memphis record, but there's always too much between me and her voice. That record sounds good, but I've heard her sing, and her voice has so much going on that you don't need much else. When you start layering all those textures behind her, it's distracting." Greil Marcus puts it more directly. "*The Greatest* never did anything for me," he says. "It seemed ornate and gussied up. I didn't get it. I didn't get the title, and it didn't make me care. I've gone back to it at various times to see if it would communicate differently, and it hasn't so far."

Other critics were harsher, affirming Chan's worst fears about her inadequacies as a musician by implying that she wasn't fit to stand onstage with the likes of the Memphis players. "I like the *Greatest* album, but I think it would be better without them," Charles Aaron says of Chan's band. "I don't want to have to think about them interacting with her. They're slumming! And I've been around her as she talks to people. There's no communication on a serious level happening. That's not a nice thing to say. But I feel like . . . they worked with *Al Green*, you know? She's Cat Power. I'm sorry, that's just not the same ballgame."

When Chan delivered *The Greatest* to Matador, her label was thrilled. After ten years of nurturing this shy, self-sabotaging artist, Matador finally had the record in hand that could make Cat Power a big star. But then, with a major national tour set to start on February 11, a press release went out on February 6 announcing that all scheduled Cat Power dates in the United States were canceled due to unspecified health reasons. Days later, Matador announced the further cancellations scheduled to take place in Europe. The label declined to elaborate "out of respect for Chan's privacy," but the general consensus was that Chan Marshall had finally cracked up. Which, according to her, is exactly what happened. "I was at the end of my rope," the singer has said. "I was done. I was cooked. I was so cooked."

26.

Trying to Die

In the thirty-four years Chan lived before her Miami hospitalization, the singer had been running from mental illness, alcoholism, and self-loathing. All it took was the right series of events to trigger a psychotic break. "It took a period of two and a half years of touring around the world over and over and over," Chan has said of the circumstances that finally did her in. The singer went straight from the road-warrior lifestyle into the studio, then back home to Miami. With eight members in Chan's Memphis Rhythm Band, the *Greatest* tour was shaping up to be the most ambitious of Cat Power's career. The singer could have used a quiet fall reading novels at the beach before getting back on the road in the winter. But Matador, eager to capitalize on what it saw as its marquee artist's crowning achievement, launched a major promotional campaign in advance of the album's January release.

"I was really stressed out from all the press that I told Matador that I didn't want to do for the album," Chan said, looking back. "I wanted to take three months off to recuperate from destroying myself for the last three and a half years. Just let the album ride on reviews and kick-ass, outstanding performances. They said no. So I just got out of my mind, saying yes to every fuckin' interview they gave me from every fuckin' country. I also started doing cocaine."

The singer has always had a habit of disappearing on friends and family, but this time she systematically cut off contact with everyone she knew and started making plans for what they would do without her. "I alienated everyone around me," she has said. "I was becoming an alcoholic in Miami and literally lying in bed for a year. Getting out of bed was for getting the Mexican-food delivery, or receiving a shipment of boxes of alcohol—beer, wines, scotch, tequila . . . whatever."

In a typical display of Chan's ever-conflicting personalities, as she was setting herself up for suicide by alcohol, she was also making preparations for surviving the depression. Before Chan cut off contact with her friends, she started distancing herself from those who had drug, alcohol, and mental-illness problems that triggered hers. "There was this girl, a poet, a writer from Texas, that I knew that I had to stay away from," the singer explained. "I knew her since we were fourteen years old. I was still drinking all the fucking time. She was still on drugs. I knew something was gonna happen even though I was in a bubble, sloppy and always drunk. I didn't say, 'Look, you're on dope and I can't fucking hang out with you.' But I said, 'Look, you're on dope and it hurts me.' I had to find that fine line."

Weeks before her hospitalization, Chan was scheduled to do another round of press before beginning the tour. She had just returned to Miami from Nashville, where she shot the video for the album's first single, "Living Proof," with her old friend, the reclusive film director and Marc Jacobs model Harmony Korine. On the plane back home, Chan got so wasted that a friend had to help her navigate the trip.

Back in Miami, she was met by her UK press representative, a British journalist from *Dazed and Confused*, and an American photographer sent to shoot the singer for a Cat Power feature. The plan was to have drinks at a local bar, then do the interview and photo shoot the follow-ing day. "We went to this bar, but I couldn't cope with being out of the house," Chan later remembered. "I couldn't cope with life or people; I couldn't smile, talk, or bullshit; I couldn't fake it anymore, so I left. I said to myself, I'm just gonna go home, take all these new pills the doctor gave me to be happy, drink all of that shit in my home, then I'll be dead and I won't have to deal with the interview." That's when Mary J. Blige showed up.

Chan has always been a Blige fanatic. She told one interviewer that if she were in a cover band, it would be a Mary J. Blige version. And it's not hard to see why: The two women have a lot in common. In addition to being beautiful and having vocal talent, a dark childhood, and un-tamed independence, Blige shares Chan's struggle with alcohol and drug abuse. The R&B singer has been open in interviews about the horrors she's endured battling addiction, abusive relationships, and the prison of depression. Chan has described Blige as one of the most beautiful women on earth, and covered Mary's song "Deep Inside" during one of the Cat Power Peel Sessions. On this night in Miami, when Chan was calcu-lating how much booze it would take to drink herself to death, she saw a flyer for Blige's 2005 record *The Breakthrough*. "Just because of that stupid postcard of Mary's face, I forgot about everything I'd been plan-ning and started focusing on Mary," Chan remembered. "I'd been read-ing interviews and she said she'd quit smoking pot, doing drugs, and drinking. That she'd fallen in love and was writing all these new songs. I love Mary so much, so I thought, I'm just gonna go home, go to bed, forget what I felt, and tomorrow will be okay."

The next day, Chan got up and industriously prepared for the arrival of the British journalists by ordering from the liquor store she had on speed dial. The singer knew she would need to be drinking all day, so she wanted everyone else to be as well. Wine, she has said she remembers thinking, seemed more "socially acceptable" than her usual hard-liquor buffet, so she got a case of it. The *Dazed and Confused* team showed up along with Chan's UK publicist, and for a while everything was going okay. "I was giving everyone wine, so I thought it was okay for me to drink," Chan has said. "The photographer was taking pictures and she was like, 'Oh, could you play this harmonica?' That was it. I just started bawling. I couldn't stand the camera being in my fucking face and my home was a mess because I didn't give a shit about myself. Something snapped and I was like, 'I don't want to be a fucking monkey and play the fucking harmonica.' I went into the bathroom, locked the door."

At first Chan's guests waited. They had another glass of wine and spoke calmly to her through the locked bathroom door, trying not to overreact to the singer's scary behavior. But when two hours had passed without Chan saying anything, the singer's publicist crouched softly in front of the door and made one last attempt to talk her down.

Chan continued to sit, knees to her chest, crying, but managed to find voice enough to ask everyone to leave. The singer stayed there, rocking back and forth on the cold, grimy tile floor, and listened to the muted, alarmed murmurs of her guests. Then she heard the gentle clangs of the photographer dismantling her lights and zipping up camera bags. When at last Chan heard the click of her front door lock sliding into place, the singer unwrapped her arms from around her knees, stretched out her stiff legs, and got up. She left all the lights off, waited until the sunlight faded from behind her shades, and, when it was fully dark outside, Chan went to get the newspaper.

This trip to the corner store was the last Chan saw of the outside world for ten days. The lead story in the *New York Times* that day reported that militant political group Hamas won the majority of parliamentary seats in Palestine's elections. Even for a sane person, this was not good news. But in Chan's fragile mental state, the idea that terrorists were the chosen representatives of a majority of the people in this volatile region seemed like a sure sign of the impending apocalypse. The singer went home, bolted the door, arranged her supplies of drugs and alcohol, and prepared to die.

"I decided I was going to fast and pray to God about Hamas winning," Chan has said. "I closed my windows and shut my blinds. The coke I had was gone by day two. Then I started drinking all the alcohol I could find. By the last three days it was just water and no sleep at all." At this point her behavior became increasingly ritualistic. Chan selected the proper music for her death, Miles Davis's soundtrack to Louis Malle's 1955 film *Ascenseur pour l'échafaud*, which she played on repeat. Chan then got dressed in what she has described as a "respectable" outfit. "I put on a dress. It was a Marc Jacobs dress from 1999," she has recalled. "It was dark blue, and it was from the chest to just above the ankle."

Next Chan put together a makeshift will. "I made piles of stuff for all my friends and family members," the singer has explained. "Little pieces of me, little things I owned. I was preparing for when they found my body, that there would be a story for each friend who came to go through my stuff." The last thing Chan had to do was attempt some sort of final peacemaking gesture toward her mother. "I sent my mom an e-mail that morning. I said, 'I forgive you for everything, everything was so hard on you.' That kind of spawned the ready-to-go feeling. I was ready to take all my antidepressants and OD."

At this point Chan was mostly cut off from the world. Hundreds of e-mails sat unread in her inbox detailing the minutia of her forthcoming tour, she hadn't showered in more than a week, and she wasn't answering text messages, usually her primary form of communication with friends. On Chan's tenth day of isolation, however, her friend Brett Vapnek—the New York–based filmmaker who directed several Cat Power videos—managed to get through to Chan on the phone. What Vapnek heard on the other end of the line worried her so much she called her sister Susanna, who immediately got a cab to the airport. "The day I went down to Miami, my sister had talked to Chan in the morning and said she didn't sound totally coherent," Susanna, a painter, has said. "I got a really bad feeling. I knew she was down there to isolate herself. That definitely seemed like a sign of depression to me."

Chan has referred to the painter, also from Georgia, as her "Psychic Sis" because of their close connection. And the name seems appropriate considering that Susanna got on that plane based purely on intuition.

The old friends hadn't spoken in more than a year, and Susanna wasn't even sure where Chan's apartment was. All she had to guide her was the return address on a card Chan had sent. "Psychic Sis had a bad feeling the day I wanted to kill myself," Chan has said. "She's the one that canceled the tour. She's the one that heard my prayers, basically." When Susanna showed up at Chan's apartment, the singer was so far gone, she didn't recognize her friend's voice and refused to open the door. After the painter started crying, Chan relented.

Inside, Susanna was confronted with a death shrine. Chan hadn't opened the shades or windows in ten days and all her houseplants were withering from lack of sunlight. Every available surface was covered with empty liquor bottles and overflowing ashtrays, each butt smoked all the way down to the filter. The air inside the apartment was thick with the mingling smoke of cigarettes and incense, which the singer was furiously burning and waving at the evil spirits she saw in the room. Chan's hair was matted in clumps against her scalp. The pupils of her hazel eyes were wide and darted back and forth as she tried to reconcile her friend's real-life physical presence with the visions and voices that had been her only company for ten days. "I was thinking crazy thoughts," Chan has said. " 'Satan's here, coming to take me to hell.' I was really scared. I had been praying to God to send someone to help me."

Susanna immediately realized that Chan would need to be hospitalized. Concealing her sorrow, she bathed her friend, changed the sheets on Chan's bed, and convinced her to sleep for a few hours. Then, quietly sobbing, Susanna called her mom. Chan heard the painter crying in the other room and started to worry that her friend was in trouble. "I was like, 'Are you okay?' " Chan has said. "She was like, 'Yeah, but my stomach hurts. Please will you come with me to the emergency room?' " Susanna and Chan took a short cab ride from the Miami Beach condo to the Mount Sinai Medical Center. The voices in Chan's head told her that Susanna's illness was a ruse, but the singer's concern for her friend drowned them out. "I started focusing on her, like, 'Oh my God, Susanna's going to die.' I was holding her hand," Chan has said. "The illogical part of me was still hearing voices: 'You've lost your mind, you're suicidal, and Susanna knows.' "

Chan expected Vapnek to tell the attending nurse about her unbearable stomachache, but instead Chan watched Vapnek break down as she explained Chan's condition. "Susanna doesn't cry," Chan has said. "I thought, Look how much pain she's in, and it's not because of her stomach, it's because of me. I felt like a kid, like I'd done something wrong, that I'd been bad." Chan would spend the next few months thinking about how much pain her self-destruction had caused to those who love her, but at this point she was incapable of rationally comprehending what was going on. "The doctor came over and I just went with it, because I felt shameful and guilty," Chan has said. The singer now realized they weren't at the hospital for Susanna, but she still didn't understand that she, Chan Marshall, was the only patient. "The doctor said, 'We might need to keep you here for a few days,' and I was like, 'Oh, okay, we're both going to spend the night. It will be like a party,' " Chan has remembered.

After the singer was dressed in hospital clothes, her possessions catalogued and stored, Susanna watched as the nightmare Chan had been running from since childhood came true. "The people in white coats took me through these hallways," Chan has said. "Through the security doors, with this bright light on, and through this doorway. I said, 'There's only one bed in here. I'll sleep on the floor, Susanna can sleep on the bed. Do you have blankets?' As I turned around, the doors shut and I saw Susanna waving. I was like, 'The joke's on me.' I thought I was in hell."

"Look, if she's banging her head, if she's attacking you with furniture, you tackle her and put her in the padded room," Dr. Ewing continues. "If in the padded room she's trying to scratch her eyes out, you tie her down with leather straps. If she cries and sits and rocks, you leave her alone. If she's not sleeping, you give her something to make her sleep. If she's withdrawing from alcohol, you check her blood pressure and pulse. A lot of modern-day fucked-up hospitals, they'd start her on one of every psychotropic known to man and charge money for it. I would start by just containing her. Something is wrong here. This is fucked-up. We don't want you to die. Tell me about it. What's going on here. Don't know what her diagnosis is, but a good working hypothesis is alcoholism. That'd be a really good start."

During Chan's first night in the hospital and for most of the first three days of her stay at the Mount Sinai Medical Center, she was hearing voices and seeing visions. Chan has called it the most difficult night of her entire life. "I heard a lion growling in the corner of my room," she has said. "I sat with that lion motherfucker in the corner and this vampire guy came over to my bed squeaking like he was really sick. I could feel the warmth of his breath. I asked God to please stay with me and help me."

The delusions were so intense that Chan says she kept her eyes closed for the entire next day, during which she stayed in her room, refusing to eat or take the medication her doctors were prescribing, drinking glass after glass of milk instead. "Susanna would try to come in and try to feed me, but I was afraid the food had chemical drugs in it," the singer has said. "I kept imagining I would barf the drugs up and I didn't wanna barf."

Chan stayed awake for days preceding her hospitalization in part because she was afraid to sleep, worried that if she did the creatures she was keeping at bay with incense and scotch would overtake her like body-snatchers. By the second night in the hospital, Chan became convinced she had to escape. "It was like *The Exorcist*," she has said. "I realized, 'Okay, I've got to get my spirit out of here because I'm in hell.' So I jumped off the bed and hit the wall, trying to let my spirit out, but it didn't work. That's when reality hit me: 'You're in the hospital, dumb-ass.' " On the third day Chan started to reconnect with reality. She started watching the other patients in her ward, all of whom were in various stages of psychosis, and concluded that she wasn't sick in the same way.

That night, sitting quietly in the locked ward of a mental hospital while her fellow patients raved, Chan started thinking about how she got there. The singer knew she wasn't irretrievably crazy, but her circumstances forced her to accept that she wasn't quite sane, either. "The third night, I opened the door and was like, 'Okay, if I'm not in hell, then I'll leave it up to God to put me wherever I need to be and I'll accept that place.' " That's when Chan started working on getting better. "The doctor came in and said, 'Please, can you tell me what's the most destructive thing in your life which causes you to be unhappy?' " Chan has remembered. "It took me a long time to say it, but eventually I admitted: 'I think I have a drinking problem.' When I heard myself say that, I was suddenly really awake."

Although she has described facing her abuse of alcohol as a watershed moment in treatment, she never quit drinking completely and doesn't consider herself an alcoholic. "It wasn't that I was an alcoholic, it was my lifestyle—the depression of drinking every day and not having a home," she has said. "If you're an alcoholic, it's because you're depressed. That's it. There's something you're trying to avoid. And once you quit all that shit, you're looking at it, and you're forced to remember things clearly. How you reacted, what you did . . . you're forced to be strong in a way."

Once Chan decided she wasn't crazy and didn't belong in the hospital, she went about proving it to her doctors. She started showing up for meals, conversing with other patients and nurses, eating, and, as the singer has put it, demonstrating that she "knows how to open the utensils pack." While these were all good signs, Chan was still unwell. She started to remember the events that led up to her hospitalization. Seeing visions? Hearing voices? Being dragged away by men in white coats? Could a person who went through all that ever trust her own mind again? "On the fourth day I woke up and was like, shit, Susanna is not coming back," Chan has said. "Maybe Susanna is just part of your split personality. Maybe everyone is part of your split personality. Maybe your mom doesn't exist. Maybe you aren't really you. Maybe you're really seventy-five years old and you're homeless with cancer and you're on a respirator, and when you open your eyes you're going to see that you're dying."

Chan was now well enough to understand that while she was locked away in her tomb of an apartment, much of what she perceived as real—the satanic demons and cackling voices—was only in her head. This brought comfort, but it also brought terror: Maybe even the progress she was making in the hospital was just another piece of an epic hallucination. "I got out of bed and went right up to the mirror," she has said. "At this point I was raw. I hadn't seen myself. I hadn't brushed my hair. And I looked, and I looked like me. Like the inside of me. Like a little kid. When I saw my face, all I wanted to do was protect that person."

Over the years, Chan has held her father more accountable for the mistakes he made as a parent and has become more forgiving of her mom.

"As an adult, as a woman, realizing my mom's position—when she had us and he left us. Left her. Now I'm really angry at him," Chan said. "I've never been angry at him before, and I think he knows that I'm angry, and I think he thinks it's funny. It breaks my heart. My inner child, I'm almost petting her head and telling her, It's okay, that I'm gonna take care of you now, and that man really didn't love you and it's not your fault."

Gazing into that hospital mirror, the singer was overcome with the urge to protect all incarnations of Chan Marshall—inner child and adult, sane person and insane person. "I was like, What would a sane person do?" the singer has remembered. "I brushed my teeth and combed my hair. I went to the counter and I was like, 'I think I'm supposed to ask for medication.' And that was it. That was the day." Chan considers this exchange between her mind and her reflection to be the turning point in her recovery. After that, she accepted treatment. "On the fifth day I actually gained happiness," Chan has explained. "I felt excited to get up to go brush my teeth, excited to go have breakfast, excited to watch TV. The Super Bowl was on and the Rolling Stones were playing. I'd never seen them play before—I had tickets when I was sixteen, but I sold them for drugs." For the first time in years, Chan was awake, coherent, and genuinely excited to be alive.

"On the sixth day the doctor's like, 'How are you feeling today, Charlyn?' " the singer has said. "I said, 'I'm feeling fine, I'm just, you know, a little scared because the people keep screaming at night and stuff.' " At this point Chan was mentally well enough to be terrified of her deranged wardmates. "I was literally scared shitless every day I was there. I was next door to this guy who was terribly, horribly, physically violent, and the doors don't have locks on them. I would always be last at breakfast, and I'd always have to sit in front of him. Then he started sitting with me. He would say things like, 'I'm going to make you suck my dick, you're gonna suck my dick.' "

Chan has said that her doctors initially thought she would be hospitalized for at least a month, but instead they discharged her within a week. "I learned really quickly: 'Chan, you're not crazy. Remember?' I just snapped out of it," the singer has said. "Because I reacted so well to the medication, and thank God I did, on the sixth day the doctor said, 'So are you having any strange thoughts this morning?' " Chan remembered. "I was like, No. He's like, 'Okay. I think I'm going to let you go tomorrow.' "

27

No More Drama

While Chan was institutionalized, her record label and booking agent dealt with the professional fallout from her breakdown. The entire Greatest tour, meant to include months of dates in both America and the UK, was completely canceled, costing Matador a reported $100,000 and putting the entire Memphis Rhythm Band out of work. Meanwhile, *The Greatest* was garnering the best reviews of Cat Power's career, which, combined with Chan's apparent collapse, put interest in the singer at an all-time high. Yet with no star available to promote the album, Matador had no way to capitalize on this perfect publicity storm.

Gerard Cosloy is reticent to discuss the label's specific reaction to Chan's hospitalization ("To answer that question would be like me publicly saying I think she has a problem," he said when asked), and it seems clear that the label did not get involved in Chan's recovery beyond canceling the tour and giving her ample recovery time. But Cosloy has clearly given a lot of thought to what he considers the appropriate relationship between troubled artist and record label. "I've worked with a lot of artists over the years who had issues—personal issues, needle issues, alcohol issues," Cosloy muses. "We always do the very best we can to help people out, but we can't force someone to do anything. It's all very tricky because our actual job description involves exploiting people. I mean, it says in the contract, 'Exploitation of your likeness, exploitation of your masters.' Exploitation, that's really what it's about."

In the wake of Kurt Cobain's death, there was a lot of talk in the music industry about how far that exploitation should go. "After Kurt killed himself there was certainly a sense that he had been overly pressed by people who didn't have his best interest at heart," Jim Greer remembers. "Every person is different," Cosloy says, sighing. "I would never, ever want to see somebody continuing to perform, write, record, whatever, if they needed to do something else to get their stuff together. On the other hand, I'm also not sure it's our role to say, 'Hey, you're in no condition to do this.' I mean, who the fuck are we?"

Cosloy has dealt with plenty of self-abusing rock stars in his twenty

years in the music business and he has, on occasion, felt the need to con-
front them about destructive behavior. Cosloy and Lombardi once pulled
aside Guided by Voices visionary and lead lush Bob Pollard to discuss his
drinking. "There was a point in time where we thought that Bob's booz-
ing was affecting the quality of the performances and was detrimental
overall to getting business done for GBV," Cosloy recalls. "He didn't
take kindly to that suggestion, to say the least."

The fact that Matador was willing to go there when they deemed it
necessary lends credence to Cosloy's claim that he never really worried
about Chan—or at least didn't worry that her substance abuse would
affect her productivity (though it obviously did). Today Cosloy stands by
the label's decision not to intervene. "At some point you have to make
a decision: Are you in a partnership with a trustworthy, reasonable, rational adult?" Cosloy asks. "On that level of things, I feel pretty good
about Chan Marshall as a rational, reasonable, responsible adult."

When Chan left Mount Sinai, she was much closer to the coherent
version of herself that Cosloy sees, but she was not cured. Her psychotic
break was over, but the singer was just beginning to understand the circumstances that brought it on. When she got back to her apartment in
Miami Beach, Chan discovered that Susanna Vapnek had purged the
place of all remnants of the singer's breakdown. "Susanna had taken all
my clothes to the Laundromat or the dry cleaners and washed everything. It was like walking into my second chance," Chan has said. She
settled into her newly sparkling pad and was preparing to make a fruit
salad when she realized that her kitchen knives were missing. "Susanna
had hidden them the night I was cuckoo and had forgotten about them,"
the singer said. "We started laughing hysterically. She was like, 'Let me
cut that for you.' I was like, 'I'm not going back there, don't worry
about it.'"

Susanna stuck around for a few days, watching Chan for any signs of lingering danger. But eventually the painter had to get back to her life in New York, and Chan was alone once again. The singer hesitated to jump back into the chaos of her old life, and with all Cat Power business on pause, she was able to stay close to home and concentrate on taking good care of herself. "I remember contacting Stefano [a mutual close friend and photographer whose work appears in this book] and asking him, 'What's going on?' because I was concerned," Thurston Moore says. "I said, 'Well, is there anything I could do? Could I talk to her?' He said, 'She's not talking to anybody, but she does answer her text messages,' so I texted her and asked if she needed anything. She wrote back, 'Thanks, I'll be okay, I've just got to figure some things out.' "

For the first time since she was a teenager, Chan had nowhere she had to be, nobody around to occupy her attention, and no substances to distract her from her thoughts. "I hadn't had time off since I lived in South Carolina in 1996–97, so it was really weird to wake up in the same place," Chan has said. "I thought, What the fuck am I going to do with myself?" The prospect of all that unstructured time alone—especially in contrast to the regimented life she'd been living as a touring musician—was intimidating, but Chan embraced it.

She started listening closely to her body and mind, relying on intuition and instinct to guide every moment of her day. She ate what she wanted to eat when she wanted to eat it. She slept when she wanted for as long as she wanted. She read all the books she'd been buying for years but never had time to read. She spent hours trying on clothes in her closet, many of them forgotten purchases with the tags still on. She scrubbed her apartment. She wrote in a journal. She woke up early and swam in the ocean before breakfast. She experimented in the kitchen. She bought the Winsor Pilates DVD from television and started exercising every day with a neighbor. She made tea. She went out dancing with her girlfriends. She hosted dinner parties.

The singer relished relearning how to live. "If I wanted to, I could wake up at six, swim in the ocean till seven thirty, lay around and read on the beach," Chan recalled. "I could do whatever I wanted. I didn't have to go be on a plane. I didn't have to be at soundcheck. I didn't have to do an interview. I didn't have to rush to see my four best friends in New York in one hour before I have to fly to Paris to do another show. I could come back from the beach, sleep till four. I could get in a taxi, go see two movies, and on the way home go to a bookstore and buy a couple of books. I could write an eight-page letter to a friend on a typewriter, to someone I was only able to hang out with at soundcheck in Portland. I could go see a therapist, talk about something that happened when I was eighteen. The world was open.

"If you drink every day, I highly recommend trying not doing it for a while," Chan has said since becoming semisober. "Being on the road, touring, the many bars . . . you meet so many different strangers. I drank to create a bubble so I wouldn't really have to be there all the time. And alcoholism runs in my family. I thought, 'Oh, it'll never affect me. I've got a control on it.' But there's a good aspect: It helped me understand alcoholics I've known my whole life. It helped me understand their perspective and the crazy things they do that were often hurtful—traumatizing at times. It helped me understand I can't take it personally, even though it's really hard to accept sometimes."

Chan didn't participate in an organized recovery program like Alcoholics Anonymous, but during the months that followed her hospitalization she continued to see her doctors and follow a vaguely twelve-stepesque plan. "I received a letter from her," Moore remembers. "I think she wrote to a lot of people apologizing for her behavior and saying how she has discovered herself. It really looked like a letter that somebody wanted to write as part of a program." Stewart Lupton didn't receive a letter from Chan, but he got a similar sense that she was out there in the world, making amends. "I hadn't talked to her in a while when I saw her with the Memphis crew," he remembers. "But getting the record was like talking to her. I knew some sea change had happened, and I couldn't stop listening to it. Don't tell her that, 'cause she'll apologize."

At home, away from the spotlight and alone for the first time in years with her guitar and her musical instincts, Chan started reconnecting with the songs she loved as a child. She wore out records by Buddy Holly, Billie Holiday, Aretha Franklin, Patsy Cline, and Hank Williams, playing certain tracks on repeat and tinkering with her own interpretations of her favorite songs. Many of these cuts would later appear on the singer's second covers album, *Jukebox*, which would be released in 2008.

Winter gave way to spring, and soon summer was looming. Cat Power had not played a single show since the previous fall and hadn't been out on a proper tour in more than a year. The band still hadn't performed a single song off *The Greatest* since the album's acclaimed release. But Chan was starting to feel that familiar roving impulse. She called up Matador, announced that she was ready to return to her life as a rock 'n' roll star, and that summer, six months after *The Greatest* came out, Cat Power and her Memphis Rhythm Band finally hit the road in support of a reissued, repackaged version of the album.

At Mount Sinai Hospital, Chan didn't find God, sanity, or the strength to combat debilitating addiction: She found that she actually likes herself, and that realization jump-started her will to live. "Having traveled around drinking, drinking, drinking, being in bars and stuff, I now see myself at thirty-four versus twenty-four, [when I was] feeling inferior for many different reasons," Chan mused. "Being a Southern female uneducated poor person, they're shackles. I accepted them and thought that I was less 'cause I was a woman. Less 'cause I was uneducated. Less 'cause I come from the South. Who I thought I was then, who I was then—I see myself, all the things I thought I knew then. I feel like I know myself more now than I did then. I can trust myself more, and that makes me feel like I'm not a piece of shit. That makes me feel good."

Conclusion

In the summer of 2007 I interviewed Nick Cave for Rolling Stone. He and his deranged blues-rocking side project, Grinderman (whose signature song is titled "No Pussy Blues"), were in New York City to open (along with Porter

Wagoner) for the White Stripes at the Detroit duo's first-ever gig at Madison Square Garden. We met at the decidedly un-rock 'n' roll hour of ten thirty a.m. at a hotel that should have been the Chelsea (New York's most famous home away from home for debauched poets) but was actually the Holiday Inn type hotel just next door. I was extremely nervous. Cave is a whip-smart musical visionary with a reputation for torturing journalists who don't impress him. My only comfort was that a friend and fellow journalist once confused him with Nick Drake during their interview, so I knew the bar had been set very low.

After meeting him in the lobby, I had the thrilling experience of riding in an uncomfortably small hotel elevator with the recently showered Australian rock star (black hair still wet, vintage Hawaiian shirt clinging to his chest). We got off on the sixth floor, arranged ourselves awkwardly on the scratchy floral bedspread in one of the band members' rooms, and talked for twenty minutes. When the interview was over, I rode the elevator back down to the lobby with Cave and the bearded Grinderman violinist Warren Ellis, who also plays with Australian group and occasional Cat Power collaborators the Dirty Three. Cave leaned against the elevator door, arms crossed, managing to glare and smirk at me at the same time. Ellis was friendlier. I mentioned that I was working on a book about Cat Power and asked Ellis, then Cave, if he would consider being interviewed for it. "You're doing a book on Cat Power?" Cave said from behind comically cheap-looking mirrored aviators. "Yes," I said, quivering. "An entire book?" Cave asked. "I mean, I could see doing a *pamphlet*."

On September 15, 2008, Nick Cave and the Bad Seeds sold out approximately eighteen hundred seats at the Hollywood Bowl. The legendary venue is one of the largest the band has ever played. It's speculated that the secret to their sudden box office success wasn't a renewed interest in diabolical Australian geniuses, great as Cave and his band's new album *Dig, Lazarus, Dig!!!* was. It wasn't even the promise that Cave would wear that filmy Hawaiian shirt onstage. It was the fact that they shared the bill with Spiritualized, and more crucially, Cat Power. She did the same thing for Interpol at MSG earlier in the year.

Boys could slag her off, underestimate her, or imply that she was not ready for the full-book treatment, but when they had arenas to fill they were more than happy to capitalize on some of that dubious charisma. Soon Cat Power will be filling these venues herself.

In a post-*Greatest* world, anything is possible for Chan Marshall. It was as if she compiled one of those things-to-do-before-you-die lists self-help books advocate, then tackled each and every item on it. Chan hasn't yet made it to painter, baker, or schoolteacher, but she did cover visual performer, professional model, actress, activist, and mother, albeit to a little French bulldog named Mona.

In 2006, Chan told the *New York Times* that she was going to audition to be a cast member on *Saturday Night Live*. This from a woman whose sunniest album includes a song based around the refrain "I hate myself and I want to die" (which she stole from Kurt Cobain, a man equally famous for his optimism). In frenzied moments of passionate motivation, Chan had no doubt made similar grandiose proclamations, but in the past nobody was really listening. This time everybody's ears were perked.

"People were like, Did you hear this? Chan wants to be on *Saturday Night Live*," Fred Armisen remembers. (Armisen is a real live *SNL* cast member who plays Barack Obama on the show, has directed music videos, and can be seen opening for Jeff Tweedy's solo tour in the Wilco documentary *I Am Trying to Break Your Heart*.) "People blew it out of proportion. As I talked to her, I was like, Well, she's just saying that she can do characters and she can do impressions and stuff. Which she can, really well. It's like me saying, 'I play such great drums, I could totally be in the Shins!' Then it's like: Fred Armisen has made an announcement that he's gonna play in the Shins."

There are lots of opportunities available to Chan now that she is a genuine icon in a world full of TMZ-minted celebrities, and she's taken advantage of many of them. After meeting Chan at the Mercer Hotel in New York City, Chanel designer Karl Lagerfeld offered her a job as the face of the label's new jewelry line. In the fall of 2006 Chan and her new players, the Dirty Delta Blues Band, performed in Paris at Chanel's spring show. Chan also lent her voice to the musical excursions of her new fellow model friends, including Jack White's wife, Karen Elson, with whom Chan sang a version of "Je T'aime (Moi Non Plus)" for a 2005 Serge Gainsbourg tribute album.

In the winter of 2007 Chan collaborated with multimedia artist Doug Aitken for an installation at the MOMA, which featured Tilda Swinton and Donald Sutherland among her fellow performers. And supermodel and sometimes girlfriend to Pete Doherty Irina Lazareanu says that Chan will appear on her forthcoming album. In 2007 she appeared as Jude Law's girlfriend in her first feature film, Wong Kar-wai's *My Blueberry Nights*, and in the fall of 2007 Chan had her first solo art show at Max Fish down on the Lower East Side, her old stomping grounds.

With the spoils of her new projects, Chan bought a new, splashier two-story condo in Miami. With a coat of fresh paint and lots of light, Chan's spare, airy, peaceful home is filled with framed photos of the Rolling Stones and Dylan and toys for Mona, to whom she openly coos in a throaty baby voice.

In 2007, almost ten years after Chan made that disturbing and inspiring first trip to Africa, the singer tried to go back, though civil war in Kenya forced her to cancel part of her journey. Chan also started working with various relief organizations and reached out to her fans, encouraging them to give to people affected by the cyclone that hit India in November 2007.

In April of 2007 Chan finally met Bob Dylan. "At last we meet," Chan's hero supposedly said to her backstage at his show in Paris. "I love you," Chan responded. Dylan's alleged response? "I like the sound of that. At least somebody does." She wrote "Song to Bobby," the one new original composition on *Jukebox*, about this encounter—one she'd been waiting for her entire life.

Even with all these new distractions, Cat Power's musical prominence was only increasing. Chan's version of "Sea of Love," off the original covers record, was featured prominently in 2008's Oscar-winning sleeper blockbuster and pop-cultural phenomenon *Juno*. And the elder statesmen of rock, many of whom, like Cave, had remained skeptical of this fragile Southern singer, started to invite Chan to their lunch tables.

The singer was among the list of collaborators Yoko Ono invited to record versions of Ono's songs for 2007's *Yes, I'm a Witch*. "I cannot believe what she did," the venerated Ono enthuses. "To pick 'Revelations,' it's a very difficult one. This song was the kind of song that was buried because the nature of it is not pop. She brought it out. For her to do this was really an honor for me. I'm thankful to her. She gave a big, beautiful moment for this song." After working with Chan, Ono perceived the singer as a potent artistic force. "She's big now, and also a very powerful person and singer-songwriter."

Still, when Chan's take on David Bowie's "Space Oddity" began blaring out of TV sets across America as part of a Lincoln car commercial, it felt like it was high time Cat Power got back to real work. The singer's next album of original songs has yet to be released, but *Jukebox*, another collection of covers that came out on January 22, 2008, suggests that Chan is poised to mutate once again.

Like the original covers record, two years separate *Jukebox* from its predecessor in the Cat Power canon. Like *Covers*, Chan decided to make *Jukebox* after she had already written most of a new album of original material that she was not yet emotionally ready to release. Like *Covers*, *Jukebox* features mostly cover songs except for one of Chan's old tunes ("American Flag," originally off *Moon Pix*) revamped to reflect the changes in the composer and one new original ("Song to Bobby"). And like *Covers*, a new level of Chan's celebrity cachet preceded the recording of *Jukebox*.

Like training wheels on a child's bike, *The Covers Record* helped Chan navigate the transition from confessional tomboy to mysterious glamour girl. *Jukebox* works in exactly the same way. It marks a shift in Chan from successful, record-selling celebrity to someone else; someone we will get to know in the coming years.

"I have to say, I'm more excited to hear her next album than any album she's ever made," concedes Charles Aaron, who has spent fifteen years waiting to love a Cat Power record. "The fact that she can get up there and not embarrass herself with those Memphis guys impressed me enough to want to take her seriously. And the Memphis-horns thing is cool, but just make a Cat Power indie-rock album with all the best people who are your peers, and write some really good songs, and maybe we can finally see her for who she really is. I'm tired of having an attitude about Cat Power. It felt like a weight. Now I know with one hundred percent certainty that she's got great music in her. Maybe I'd missed something before because of all the nonsense."

In the time since Chan was released from the hospital and announced she was sober, the singer has definitely started drinking again. At first it was a thimble of vodka in her OJ in honor of a friend's birthday. Then it was a beer with food. Then the ritualized postshow glass of wine. Then the occasional beer or two (or four) while relaxing in her hotel room. Chan Marshall's demons will never die. Within her there will always be a struggle between the two opposing sides of her conflicting personality. She will always want to stay home *and* go out, to dress like a dude *and* wear couture. She will always want to be Cat Power and Chan Marshall, Gatsby and Jay Gatz. Yet even as she's added a drink or two to her postbreakdown regimen, she hasn't foregone the fruit salad and mint tea.

Most important, when Chan invariably loses her way again, she knows how to get back to where she is now. All she has to do is sing. "Who doesn't love singing songs, making music?" she asked. "It's the one chain they can't break. My dad was a singer, my mom was a singer, my stepdad was in bands, my grandma was a singer in church. We were always singing. I have that cassette of me singing 'The Gambler' when I was six, and it's the way I'm singing now. It's the same shit. I spent all these years learning to play guitar, learning to express myself musically. Listening to that tape, my Southern little voice, it broke my heart because I didn't have to spend all this fucking time trying to find . . . I'm Southern, you know what I mean? Six years old. It was there, but I didn't know it. It was repressed."

Acknowledgments

So here's the thing, writing a book is really hard. Surprisingly, this didn't occur to me until I was way into the process. I imagined I'd spend much of my time wearing expensive lipstick and elegantly disheveled clothing while typing on a sleek Mac in a downtown café. Instead I found myself up at four in the morning in not entirely clean Old Navy pajamas, pacing and scribbling on purple note cards. The entirety of this book might have remained scrawled in deranged-person speak were it not for the help of the following people:

My parents, Anne and Russell Goodman, deserve infinite thanks for their enduring patience and grace during this process. Not only did they offer the important perspective of smart people outside of the indie-hipster realm, but they also provided sanctuary at home when I needed to just focus and write in front of the fire while someone else cooked dinner.

Marc Spitz's input as a writer who's been here before was absolutely invaluable. In addition to reading multiple drafts, he performed really ghetto tasks like transcribing stray interview tapes and fetching me bottles of red wine, bags of cheap chocolate, and 90s Tom Cruise whenever I needed to fortify myself. He also forced me to leave the house and act like a human being when things got really bad. Most of all though, he believed in my ability to pull this off. Thank you Marc.

Maureen Callahan read my early drafts, listened to me ramble on about every great and disastrous interview, and served as a crucial voice of measured reason during my innumerable crises. She is my hero. And not just because no one knows how old she is.

Jacob Goodman was always there to calm me down or get me psyched with incomprehensible Russian phrases memorized from *The Hunt for Red October*. Thanks J.

Ruth Goodman: You have been a part of this book in so many ways. Thank you for sticking by me nana.

Niki Kanodia: Thank you for standing serenely by while I disappeared time and time again to work on this project. You are an enduring friend.

I've been working on this book for the entire time Kate Cafaro has known me, and yet she still likes me. The girl is clearly both a saint and a lunatic, but I couldn't have done it without her. Literally. She printed out the final version on the morning it was due.

Thanks to my two basset hounds, Joni Mitchell and Jerry Orbach, for never, ever, not even once respecting my writing process and, in fact, actively trying to keep this book from happening by stepping on the computer or spilling things or eating magazines I needed or demanding to be fed/played with/taken out just when I was coming to some kind of important point.

Thanks to Jillian Peña and Ariel Ashe—I never wanted sisters because girls are evil, but if I had to have a couple you two would be at the top of my list.

John Gray always treats me like I'm better than I am, which makes me strive to prove him right. Thank you.

Many thanks to Sharon, Elani, and Valerie Rager for always making me keep my heels down. Somehow all those lessons in and out of the ring are part of this book.

Heaps of thanks in the form of good green-chili stew to my agent Jim Fitzgerald. Thanks to Anne Garrett as well.

Thank you to everyone at Random House who worked on this book. In particular, Carrie Thornton, Brandi Bowles, Erin LaCour, Lindsey Moore, and most especially Brett Valley, whose response to having this project dropped on his desk was to buy me a dirty martini. That's just classy.

Thanks to fellow writers and friends who helped me in innumerable ways: Jenny Eliscu, Jaan Uhelszki, Mark Binelli, Rob Sheffield, David Modigliani, Charles Aaron, Sia Michel, Imran Ahmed, Nathan Deuel, Irina Aleksander, Nick Damski, Tyler Gray, Sophie Schulte-Hillen, Melissa Maerz, James Barber, Tracy Pepper, David Swanson, and Antony Ellis.

Thanks so much to everyone at *Blender*, especially Joe Levy, Rob Tannenbaum, and Nora Haynes.

Thanks to the people at Taos Creek Cabins, Sugar Magnolia Bed and Breakfast in Atlanta, and Bikram's Yoga Downtown in Albuquerque—all places where I worked out parts of this book.

Thanks to President Bartlet and his cabinet for making me feel like it would all be okay.

Thanks to Carlo Vogel and Dave Townsend for your help behind the scenes.

Thank you to everyone who agreed to speak to me—on and off the record.

And finally, thank you Adderall.

Sources

Als, Hilton. "Wayward Girl." *The New Yorker*, August 18, 2003.

Armisen, Fred, with Brandon Stousuy. "Interview: Cat Power." *Pitchfork*, November 13, 2006.

Ashare, Matt. "Southern Accents." *The Phoenix*, September 1, 2006.

Blackman, Guy. "The Power of One." *The Age*, January 15, 2006.

Cohen, Jem. "Smoke Gets In Your Eyes." *Flagpole*, November 29, 2000.

Cohen, Jonathan. "Reality Check." *Nude as the News*, February 19, 2003.

Dark, Jane. "Gray Line—Off Rhyme." *Village Voice*, September 29, 1998.

Dornan, Matt. "Cat Power." *Comes With A Smile*, Winter 1998/1999.

Eliscu, Jenny. "Are You Mad at Me?" *Rolling Stone*, April 3, 2003.

Ellis, Suzanne. "Cat Power Exposes Her Metal Heart." *City News*, February 13, 2008.

Erber, Thomas. "Cat Power: La Voix Et Son Trouble." *Officiel*, August 2007.

French, Ben. "Moon Pix." *Nude as the News*.

Frere-Jones, Sasha. "Wonder Woman." *The New Yorker*, December 10, 2007.

Fritch, Matthew. "Cat Power: The Comeback Story." *Magnet*, January/February 2007.

Gordon, Robert. "Lived In Bars." *Stop Smiling*, October 27, 2006.

Hiatt, Brian. "Soul Kitten." *Rolling Stone*, February 7, 2008.

Holland, Jools. "Cat Power." *Later . . . with Jools Holland*, February 1, 2008.

Keller, Jason. "Cat Power." *NOW Toronto*, February 7–14, 2008.

Kelley, Trevor. "Cat Power: Ordinary People." *Harp*, January/February 2006.

Kellner, Amy. "Cat Power." *Index*, September/October 1998.

Knowles, David. "Nine Lives." *Men's Vogue*, October 2007.

Lagambina, Gregg. "The Soul of Cat Power: A Ghost Story in Twelve Short Chapters." *Filter*, Winter 2006.

Lao, Linette. "Interview with Chan Marshall." *Crimewave*, Winter 1996/1997.

Larocca, Amy. "Folk Heroine." *New York Magazine*, August 27, 2001.

Lee, Carol. "Happily Ever After." *Paper*, May 1, 2007.

Maerz, Melissa. "The Spin Interview: Cat Power." *Spin*, December 2006.

Magnet magazine. "The Year In Music: Cat Power." January/February 1999.

Marcus, Greil. "Cat Power." *Interview*, August 2007.

Marcus, Greil. "What Goes Under the Covers—Cover Bands." *Interview*, January 1999.

McCormick, Neil. "Cat Power: Dazzling Talent Who Emerged From the Dark." *Telegraph*, April 23, 2007.

Miller, Dustin. "Fragile Powerful." *Oyster*, August/September 2006.

Miller, Winter. "9 Lives and Counting: Cat Power Sobers Up." *New York Times*, September 20, 2006.

O'Hara, Gail. "Cat Power: The Chickfactor Interview." *Chickfactor*, 1997.

Peisner, David. "The Cat's Table." *Creative Loafing*, 1998.

Perez, Rodrigo. "Interview: Cat Power." *Pitchfork*, January 3, 2003.

Power, Cat. "Insound Presents a Night With Cat Power." *Insound*.

Power, Cat. Interview by *ITW*, February 2008.

Power, Cat. Interview by *A Key to the Social Club*, June 2000.

Power, Cat. Interview by *NOW Toronto*, October 22–28, 1998.

Power, Cat. Interview by *Nude as the News*, February 2006.

Power, Cat. Interview by *Nylon*, March 2003.

Power, Cat. Interview by *Much Music*.

Power, Cat. Interview by *PRIMS*.

Power, Cat. Interview by Sharlene Chu. *MTV News*.

Ratliff, Ben. "Performance Anxiety: Hiding Onstage." *New York Times*, January 5, 1999.

Reardon, Ben. "Angels Have White Wings." *i-D*, May 2007.

Romero, Michele. "Meow Miss." *Entertainment Weekly*, February 7, 2003.

Rosenblum-Sorgenfrei, Lars, and Gabriel of *Sonic Noise*. "Cat Power." *Ink Blot Magazine*, 1999.

Sarig, Roni. "Cat's Meow." *Creative Loafing*, March 12, 2003.

Segal, Victoria. "Chan Speaks." *Mojo*, January 2006.

Shipp, Matt. "Paranormaltown Flyer." *Stomp and Stammer*, October 1998.

Soft Focus. "Chan Marshall." *VBS.TV*, 2008.

Sokol, Brett. "The Year of the Cat." *Ocean Drive*, December 2006.

Spitz, Marc. "Redemption Songs." *Uncut*, December 2006.

Stacey, Dave. "Cat Power." *Mommy & I Are One*, Summer 1996.

Thrasher, Glen. glenthrasher.blogspot.com, December 26, 2006.

Tignor, Steve. "Cat Power and the Glory." *Puncture*, Summer 1996.

Trong, Stephanie. "Cat Power." *Venuszine*, December 1, 2006.

Uhelszki, Jaan. "Cat Power: Beauty Secrets." *Harp*, December 2006.

Uhelszki, Jaan. "Cat Power: Freebird." *Harp*, February 2003.

Uhelszki, Jaan. "Chan Marshall (aka Cat Power), 31, New York City, NY." *Harp*, July/August 2005.

Usinger, Mike. "The Cult of Cat Power." *Straight.com*, August 24, 2006.

Van Meter, William. "I'm A Survivor." *New York* magazine, January 14, 2006.

Wagner, Alex. "The Last Call." *Fader*, January 2008.

Wappler, Margaret. "Bill Callahan: The Rising." *Fader*, April 2007.

Wareham, Dean. *Black Postcards: A Rock & Roll Romance*. New York: Penguin Press, 2008.

West, Naomi. "Cat's Whiskers." *Telegraph*, February 14, 2003.

NEW INTERNATIONAL VERSION

HOLY BIBLE

ZONDERVAN®

NIV Outreach New Testament
Published by Zondervan
Grand Rapids, Michigan 49546, USA

Printed in the United States of America

N101210

18 19 20 21 22 23 24 25 /SGM/ 20 19 18 17 16 15 14 13 12 11 10 9 8 7 6 5

A portion of the purchase price of your NIV® Bible is provided to Biblica so together we support the mission of *Transforming lives through God's Word.*

Biblica provides God's Word to people through translation, publishing and Bible engagement in Africa, Asia Pacific, Europe, Latin America, Middle East, and North America. Through its worldwide reach, Biblica engages people with God's Word so that their lives are transformed through a relationship with Jesus Christ.

Table of Contents

The New Testament

Preface

The goal of the New International Version (NIV) is to enable English-speaking people from around the world to read and hear God's eternal Word in their own language. Our work as translators is motivated by our conviction that the Bible is God's Word in written form. We believe that the Bible contains the divine answer to the deepest needs of humanity, sheds unique light on our path in a dark world and sets forth the way to our eternal well-being. Out of these deep convictions, we have sought to recreate as far as possible the experience of the original audience—blending transparency to the original text with accessibility for the millions of English speakers around the world. We have prioritized accuracy, clarity and literary quality with the goal of creating a translation suitable for public and private reading, evangelism, teaching, preaching, memorizing and liturgical use. We have also sought to preserve a measure of continuity with the long tradition of translating the Scriptures into English.

The complete NIV Bible was first published in 1978. It was a completely new translation made by over a hundred scholars working directly from the best available Hebrew, Aramaic and Greek texts. The translators came from the United States, Great Britain, Canada, Australia and New Zealand, giving the translation an international scope. They were from many denominations and churches—including Anglican, Assemblies of God, Baptist, Brethren, Christian Reformed, Church of Christ, Evangelical Covenant, Evangelical Free, Lutheran, Mennonite, Methodist, Nazarene, Presbyterian, Wesleyan and others. This breadth of denominational and theological perspective helped to safeguard the translation from sectarian bias. For these reasons, and by the grace of God, the NIV has gained a wide readership in all parts of the English-speaking world.

The work of translating the Bible is never finished. As good as they are, English translations must be regularly updated so that they will continue to communicate accurately the meaning of God's Word. Updates are needed in order to reflect the latest developments in our understanding of the biblical world and its languages and to keep pace with changes in English usage. Recognizing, then, that the NIV would retain its ability to communicate God's Word accurately only if it were regularly updated, the original translators established the Committee on Bible Translation (CBT). The Committee is a self-perpetuating group of biblical scholars charged with keeping abreast of advances in biblical scholarship and changes in English and issuing periodic updates to the NIV. The CBT is an independent, self-governing body and has sole responsibility for the NIV text. The Committee mirrors the original group of translators in its diverse international and denominational makeup and in its unifying commitment to the Bible as God's inspired Word.

In obedience to its mandate, the Committee has issued periodic updates to the NIV. An initial revision was released in 1984. A more thorough revision process was completed in 2005, resulting in the separately published TNIV. The updated NIV you now have in your hands builds on both the original NIV and the TNIV and represents the latest effort of the Committee to articulate God's unchanging Word in the way the original authors might have said it had they been speaking in English to the global English-speaking audience today.

Translation Philosophy

The Committee's translating work has been governed by three widely accepted principles about the way people use words and about the way we understand them.

First, the meaning of words is determined by the way that users of the language actually use them at any given time. For the biblical languages, therefore, the Committee utilizes the best and most recent scholarship on the way Hebrew, Aramaic and Greek words were being used in biblical times. At the same time, the Committee carefully studies the state of modern English. Good translation is like good communication: one must know the target audience so that the appropriate choices can be made about which English words to use to represent the original words of Scripture. From its inception, the NIV has had as its target the general English-speaking population all over the world, the "International" in its title reflecting this concern. The aim of the Committee is to put the Scriptures into natural English that will communicate effectively with the broadest possible audience of English speakers.

Modern technology has enhanced the Committee's ability to choose the right English words to convey the meaning of the original text. The field of computational linguistics harnesses the power of computers to provide broadly applicable and current data about the state of the language. Translators can now access huge databases of modern English to better understand the current meaning and usage of key words. The Committee utilized this resource in preparing the 2011 edition of the NIV. An area of especially rapid and significant change in English is the way certain nouns and pronouns are used to refer to human beings. The Committee therefore requested experts in computational linguistics at Collins Dictionaries to pose some key questions about this usage to its database of English—the largest in the world, with over 4.4 billion words, gathered from several English-speaking countries and including both spoken and written English. (The Collins Study, called "The Development and Use of Gender Language in Contemporary English," can be accessed at http://www.thenivbible. com/about-the-niv/about-the-2011-edition/.) The study revealed that the most popular words to describe the human race in modern U.S. English were "humanity," "man" and "mankind." The Committee then used this data in the updated NIV, choosing from among these three words (and occasionally others also) depending on the context.

A related issue creates a larger problem for modern translations: the move away from using the third-person masculine singular pronouns—"he/him/his"—to refer to men and women equally. This usage does persist in some forms of English, and this revision therefore occasionally uses these pronouns in a generic sense. But the tendency, recognized in day-to-day usage and confirmed by the Collins study, is away from the generic use of "he," "him" and "his." In recognition of this shift in language and in an effort to translate into the natural English that people are actually using, this revision of the NIV generally uses other constructions when the biblical text is plainly addressed to men and women equally. The reader will encounter especially frequently a "they," "their" or "them" to express a generic singular idea. Thus, for instance, Mark 8:36 reads: "What good is it for someone to gain the whole world, yet forfeit their soul?" This generic use of the "distributive" or "singular" "they/them/their" has been used for many centuries by respected writers of English and has now become established as standard English, spoken and written, all over the world.

A second linguistic principle that feeds into the Committee's translation work is that meaning is found not in individual words, as vital as they are, but in larger clusters: phrases, clauses, sentences, discourses. Translation is not, as many people think, a matter of word substitution: English word x in place of Hebrew word y. Translators must first determine the meaning of the words of the biblical languages in the context of the passage and then select English words that accurately communicate that meaning to modern listeners and readers. This means that accurate translation will not always reflect the exact structure of the original language. To be sure, there is debate over the degree to which translators should try to preserve the "form" of the original text in English. From the beginning, the NIV has taken a mediating position on this issue. The manual produced when the translation that became the NIV was first being planned states: "If the Greek or Hebrew syntax has a good parallel in modern English, it should be used. But if there is no good parallel, the English syntax appropriate to the meaning of the original is to be chosen." It is fine, in other words, to carry over the form of the biblical languages into English—but not at the expense of natural expression. The principle that meaning resides in larger clusters of words means that the Committee has not insisted on a "word-for-word" approach to translation. We certainly believe that every word of Scripture is inspired by God and therefore to be carefully studied to determine what God is saying to us. It is for this reason that the Committee labors over every single word of the original texts, working hard to determine how each of those words contributes to what the text is saying. Ultimately, however, it is how these individual words function in combination with other words that determines meaning.

A third linguistic principle guiding the Committee in its translation work is the recognition that words have a spectrum of meaning. It is popular to define a word by using another word, or "gloss," to substitute for it. This substitute word is then sometimes called the "literal" meaning of a word. In fact, however, words have a range of possible meanings. Those meanings will vary depending on the context, and words in one language will usually not occupy the same semantic range as words in another language. The Committee therefore studies each original word of Scripture in its context to identify its meaning in a particular verse and then chooses an appropriate English word (or phrase) to represent it. It is impossible, then, to translate any given Hebrew, Aramaic or Greek word with the same English word all the time. The Committee does try to translate related occurrences of a word in the original languages with the same English word in order to preserve the connection for the English reader. But the Committee generally privileges clear natural meaning over a concern with consistency in rendering particular words.

Textual Basis

For the Old Testament the standard Hebrew text, the Masoretic Text as published in the latest edition of Biblia Hebraica, has been used throughout. The Masoretic Text tradition contains marginal notations that offer variant readings. These have sometimes been followed instead of the text itself. Because such instances involve variants within the Masoretic tradition, they have not been indicated in the textual notes. In a few cases, words in the basic consonantal text have been divided differently than in the Masoretic Text. Such cases are usually indicated in the textual footnotes. The Dead Sea Scrolls contain biblical texts that represent an earlier stage of the transmission of the Hebrew text. They have been consulted, as have been the Samaritan Pentateuch and the ancient scribal traditions concerning deliberate textual changes. The translators also consulted the more important early versions. Readings from these versions, the Dead Sea Scrolls and the scribal traditions were occasionally followed where the Masoretic Text seemed doubtful and where accepted principles of textual criticism showed that one or more of these textual witnesses appeared to provide the correct reading. In rare cases, the translators have emended the Hebrew text where it appears to have become corrupted at an even earlier stage of its transmission. These departures from the Masoretic Text are also indicated in the textual footnotes. Sometimes the vowel indicators (which are later additions to the basic consonantal text) found in the Masoretic Text did not, in the judgment of the translators, represent the correct vowels for the original text. Accordingly, some words have been read with a different set of vowels. These instances are usually not indicated in the footnotes.

The Greek text used in translating the New Testament has been an eclectic one, based on the latest editions of the Nestle-Aland/United Bible Societies' Greek New Testament. The translators have made their choices among the variant readings in accordance with widely accepted principles of New Testament textual criticism. Footnotes call attention to places where uncertainty remains.

The New Testament authors, writing in Greek, often quote the Old Testament from its ancient Greek version, the Septuagint. This is one reason why some of the Old Testament quotations in the NIV New Testament are not identical to the corresponding passages in the NIV Old Testament. Such quotations in the New Testament are indicated with the footnote "(see Septuagint)."

Footnotes and Formatting

Footnotes in this version are of several kinds, most of which need no explanation. Those giving alternative translations begin with "Or" and generally introduce the alternative with the last word preceding it in the text, except when it is a single-word alternative. When poetry is quoted in a footnote a slash mark indicates a line division.

It should be noted that references to diseases, minerals, flora and fauna, architectural details, clothing, jewelry, musical instruments and other articles cannot always be identified with precision. Also, linear measurements and measures of capacity can only be approximated (see the Table of Weights and Measures). Although Selah, used mainly in the Psalms, is probably a musical term, its meaning is uncertain. Since it may interrupt reading and distract the reader, this word has not been kept in the English text, but every occurrence has been signaled by a footnote.

As an aid to the reader, sectional headings have been inserted. They are not to be regarded as part of the biblical text and are not intended for oral reading. It is the Committee's hope that these headings may prove more helpful to the reader than the traditional chapter divisions, which were introduced long after the Bible was written.

Sometimes the chapter and/or verse numbering in English translations of the Old Testament differs from that found in published Hebrew texts. This is particularly the case in the Psalms, where the traditional titles are included in the Hebrew verse numbering. Such differences are indicated in the footnotes at the bottom of the page. In the New Testament, verse numbers that marked off portions of the traditional English text not supported by the best Greek manuscripts now appear in brackets, with a footnote indicating the text that has been omitted (see, for example, Matthew 17:[21]).

Mark 16:9–20 and John 7:53—8:11, although long accorded virtually equal status with the rest of the Gospels in which they stand, have a questionable standing in the textual history of the New Testament, as noted in the bracketed annotations with which they are set off. A different typeface has been chosen for these passages to indicate their uncertain status.

Basic formatting of the text, such as lining the poetry, paragraphing (both prose and poetry), setting up of (administrative-like) lists, indenting letters and lengthy prayers within narratives and the insertion of sectional headings, has been the work of the Committee. However, the choice between single-column and double-column formats has been left to the publishers. Also the issuing of "red-letter" editions is a publisher's choice—one that the Committee does not endorse.

The Committee has again been reminded that every human effort is flawed—including this revision of the NIV. We trust, however, that many will find in it an improved representation of the Word of God, through which they hear his call to faith in our Lord Jesus Christ and to service in his kingdom. We offer this version of the Bible to him in whose name and for whose glory it has been made.

The Committee on Bible Translation

The
New Testament

Matthew

The Genealogy of Jesus the Messiah

1 This is the genealogy[a] of Jesus the Messiah[b] the son of David, the son of Abraham:

[2] Abraham was the father of Isaac,
Isaac the father of Jacob,
Jacob the father of Judah and his brothers,
[3] Judah the father of Perez and Zerah, whose mother was Tamar,
Perez the father of Hezron,
Hezron the father of Ram,
[4] Ram the father of Amminadab,
Amminadab the father of Nahshon,
Nahshon the father of Salmon,
[5] Salmon the father of Boaz, whose mother was Rahab,
Boaz the father of Obed, whose mother was Ruth,
Obed the father of Jesse,
[6] and Jesse the father of King David.

David was the father of Solomon, whose mother had been Uriah's wife,
[7] Solomon the father of Rehoboam,
Rehoboam the father of Abijah,
Abijah the father of Asa,
[8] Asa the father of Jehoshaphat,
Jehoshaphat the father of Jehoram,
Jehoram the father of Uzziah,
[9] Uzziah the father of Jotham,
Jotham the father of Ahaz,
Ahaz the father of Hezekiah,
[10] Hezekiah the father of Manasseh,
Manasseh the father of Amon,
Amon the father of Josiah,
[11] and Josiah the father of Jeconiah[c] and his brothers at the time of the exile to Babylon.

[12] After the exile to Babylon:
Jeconiah was the father of Shealtiel,
Shealtiel the father of Zerubbabel,
[13] Zerubbabel the father of Abihud,
Abihud the father of Eliakim,
Eliakim the father of Azor,
[14] Azor the father of Zadok,
Zadok the father of Akim,
Akim the father of Elihud,
[15] Elihud the father of Eleazar,
Eleazar the father of Matthan,
Matthan the father of Jacob,
[16] and Jacob the father of Joseph, the husband of Mary, and Mary was the mother of Jesus who is called the Messiah.

[17] Thus there were fourteen generations in all from Abraham to David, fourteen from David to the exile to Babylon, and fourteen from the exile to the Messiah.

Joseph Accepts Jesus as His Son

[18] This is how the birth of Jesus the Messiah came about[d]: His mother Mary was pledged to be married to Joseph, but before they came together, she was found to be pregnant through the Holy Spirit. [19] Because Joseph her husband was faithful to the law, and yet[e] did not want to expose her to public disgrace, he had in mind to divorce her quietly.

[20] But after he had considered this, an angel of the Lord appeared to him in a dream and said, "Joseph son of David, do not be afraid to take Mary home as your wife, because what is conceived in her is from the Holy Spirit. [21] She will give birth to a son, and you are to give him the name Jesus,[f] because he will save his people from their sins."

[22] All this took place to fulfill what the Lord had said through the prophet: [23] "The virgin will conceive and give birth to a son, and they will call him Immanuel"[g] (which means "God with us").

[24] When Joseph woke up, he did what the angel of the Lord had commanded him and took Mary home as his wife. [25] But he did not consummate their marriage until she gave birth to a son. And he gave him the name Jesus.

The Magi Visit the Messiah

2 After Jesus was born in Bethlehem in Judea, during the time of King Herod, Magi[h] from the east came to Jerusalem [2] and asked, "Where is the one who has been born king of the Jews? We saw his star when it rose and have come to worship him."

[3] When King Herod heard this he was disturbed, and all Jerusalem with him. [4] When he had called together all the people's chief priests and teachers of the law, he asked them where the Messiah was to be born. [5] "In Bethlehem in Judea," they replied, "for this is what the prophet has written:

[6] "'But you, Bethlehem, in the land of Judah, are by no means least among the rulers of Judah;
for out of you will come a ruler who will shepherd my people Israel.'[i]"

[7] Then Herod called the Magi secretly and found out from them the exact time the star had appeared. [8] He sent them to Bethlehem and said, "Go and search carefully for the child. As soon as you find him, report to me, so that I too may go and worship him."

---

[a] 1 Or is an account of the origin   [b] 1 Or Jesus Christ. Messiah (Hebrew) and Christ (Greek) both mean Anointed One; also in verse 18.   [c] 11 That is, Jehoiachin; also in verse 12   [d] 18 Or The origin of Jesus the Messiah was like this   [e] 19 Or was a righteous man and   [f] 21 Jesus is the Greek form of Joshua, which means the LORD saves.   [g] 23 Isaiah 7:14   [h] 1 Traditionally wise men   [i] 6 Micah 5:2,4

[9]After they had heard the king, they went on their way, and the star they had seen when it rose went ahead of them until it stopped over the place where the child was. [10]When they saw the star, they were overjoyed. [11]On coming to the house, they saw the child with his mother Mary, and they bowed down and worshiped him. Then they opened their treasures and presented him with gifts of gold, frankincense and myrrh. [12]And having been warned in a dream not to go back to Herod, they returned to their country by another route.

The Escape to Egypt

[13]When they had gone, an angel of the Lord appeared to Joseph in a dream. "Get up," he said, "take the child and his mother and escape to Egypt. Stay there until I tell you, for Herod is going to search for the child to kill him."

[14]So he got up, took the child and his mother during the night and left for Egypt, [15]where he stayed until the death of Herod. And so was fulfilled what the Lord had said through the prophet: "Out of Egypt I called my son."[a]

[16]When Herod realized that he had been outwitted by the Magi, he was furious, and he gave orders to kill all the boys in Bethlehem and its vicinity who were two years old and under, in accordance with the time he had learned from the Magi. [17]Then what was said through the prophet Jeremiah was fulfilled:

[18]"A voice is heard in Ramah,
    weeping and great mourning,
Rachel weeping for her children
    and refusing to be comforted,
    because they are no more."[b]

The Return to Nazareth

[19]After Herod died, an angel of the Lord appeared in a dream to Joseph in Egypt [20]and said, "Get up, take the child and his mother and go to the land of Israel, for those who were trying to take the child's life are dead."

[21]So he got up, took the child and his mother and went to the land of Israel. [22]But when he heard that Archelaus was reigning in Judea in place of his father Herod, he was afraid to go there. Having been warned in a dream, he withdrew to the district of Galilee, [23]and he went and lived in a town called Nazareth. So was fulfilled what was said through the prophets, that he would be called a Nazarene.

John the Baptist Prepares the Way

3 In those days John the Baptist came, preaching in the wilderness of Judea [2]and saying, "Repent, for the kingdom of heaven has come near." [3]This is he who was spoken of through the prophet Isaiah:

"A voice of one calling in the wilderness,
'Prepare the way for the Lord,
    make straight paths for him.'"[c]

[4]John's clothes were made of camel's hair, and he had a leather belt around his waist. His food was locusts and wild honey. [5]People went out to him from Jerusalem and all Judea and the whole region of the Jordan. [6]Confessing their sins, they were baptized by him in the Jordan River.

[7]But when he saw many of the Pharisees and Sadducees coming to where he was baptizing, he said to them: "You brood of vipers! Who warned you to flee from the coming wrath? [8]Produce fruit in keeping with repentance. [9]And do not think you can say to yourselves, 'We have Abraham as our father.' I tell you that out of these stones God can raise up children for Abraham. [10]The ax is already at the root of the trees, and every tree that does not produce good fruit will be cut down and thrown into the fire.

[11]"I baptize you with[d] water for repentance. But after me comes one who is more powerful than I, whose sandals I am not worthy to carry. He will baptize you with[d] the Holy Spirit and fire. [12]His winnowing fork is in his hand, and he will clear his threshing floor, gathering his wheat into the barn and burning up the chaff with unquenchable fire."

The Baptism of Jesus

[13]Then Jesus came from Galilee to the Jordan to be baptized by John. [14]But John tried to deter him, saying, "I need to be baptized by you, and do you come to me?"

[15]Jesus replied, "Let it be so now; it is proper for us to do this to fulfill all righteousness." Then John consented.

[16]As soon as Jesus was baptized, he went up out of the water. At that moment heaven was opened, and he saw the Spirit of God descending like a dove and alighting on him. [17]And a voice from heaven said, "This is my Son, whom I love; with him I am well pleased."

Jesus Is Tested in the Wilderness

4 Then Jesus was led by the Spirit into the wilderness to be tempted[e] by the devil. [2]After fasting forty days and forty nights, he was hungry. [3]The tempter came to him and said, "If you are the Son of God, tell these stones to become bread."

[4]Jesus answered, "It is written: 'Man shall not live on bread alone, but on every word that comes from the mouth of God.'[f]"

[5]Then the devil took him to the holy city and had him stand on the highest point of the temple. [6]"If you are the Son of God," he said, "throw yourself down. For it is written:

"'He will command his angels concerning you,
    and they will lift you up in their hands,
    so that you will not strike your foot
        against a stone.'[g]"

[7]Jesus answered him, "It is also written: 'Do not put the Lord your God to the test.'[h]"

---

[a] 15 Hosea 11:1   [b] 18 Jer. 31:15   [c] 3 Isaiah 40:3
mean *tested*.   [f] 4 Deut. 8:3   [g] 6 Psalm 91:11,12
[d] 11 Or *in*   [e] 1 The Greek for *tempted* can also
[h] 7 Deut. 6:16

⁸Again, the devil took him to a very high mountain and showed him all the kingdoms of the world and their splendor. ⁹"All this I will give you," he said, "if you will bow down and worship me."

¹⁰Jesus said to him, "Away from me, Satan! For it is written: 'Worship the Lord your God, and serve him only.'ᵃ"

¹¹Then the devil left him, and angels came and attended him.

Jesus Begins to Preach

¹²When Jesus heard that John had been put in prison, he withdrew to Galilee. ¹³Leaving Nazareth, he went and lived in Capernaum, which was by the lake in the area of Zebulun and Naphtali— ¹⁴to fulfill what was said through the prophet Isaiah:

¹⁵"Land of Zebulun and land of Naphtali,
   the Way of the Sea, beyond the
      Jordan,
   Galilee of the Gentiles—
¹⁶the people living in darkness
   have seen a great light;
on those living in the land of the shadow
      of death
   a light has dawned."ᵇ

¹⁷From that time on Jesus began to preach, "Repent, for the kingdom of heaven has come near."

Jesus Calls His First Disciples

¹⁸As Jesus was walking beside the Sea of Galilee, he saw two brothers, Simon called Peter and his brother Andrew. They were casting a net into the lake, for they were fishermen. ¹⁹"Come, follow me," Jesus said, "and I will send you out to fish for people." ²⁰At once they left their nets and followed him.

²¹Going on from there, he saw two other brothers, James son of Zebedee and his brother John. They were in a boat with their father Zebedee, preparing their nets. Jesus called them, ²²and immediately they left the boat and their father and followed him.

Jesus Heals the Sick

²³Jesus went throughout Galilee, teaching in their synagogues, proclaiming the good news of the kingdom, and healing every disease and sickness among the people. ²⁴News about him spread all over Syria, and people brought to him all who were ill with various diseases, those suffering severe pain, the demon-possessed, those having seizures, and the paralyzed; and he healed them. ²⁵Large crowds from Galilee, the Decapolis,ᶜ Jerusalem, Judea and the region across the Jordan followed him.

Introduction to the Sermon on the Mount

5 Now when Jesus saw the crowds, he went up on a mountainside and sat down. His disciples came to him, ²and he began to teach them.

The Beatitudes

He said:

³ "Blessed are the poor in spirit,
   for theirs is the kingdom of heaven.
⁴Blessed are those who mourn,
   for they will be comforted.
⁵Blessed are the meek,
   for they will inherit the earth.
⁶Blessed are those who hunger and thirst
      for righteousness,
   for they will be filled.
⁷Blessed are the merciful,
   for they will be shown mercy.
⁸Blessed are the pure in heart,
   for they will see God.
⁹Blessed are the peacemakers,
   for they will be called children of God.
¹⁰Blessed are those who are persecuted
      because of righteousness,
   for theirs is the kingdom of heaven.

¹¹"Blessed are you when people insult you, persecute you and falsely say all kinds of evil against you because of me. ¹²Rejoice and be glad, because great is your reward in heaven, for in the same way they persecuted the prophets who were before you.

Salt and Light

¹³"You are the salt of the earth. But if the salt loses its saltiness, how can it be made salty again? It is no longer good for anything, except to be thrown out and trampled underfoot.

¹⁴"You are the light of the world. A town built on a hill cannot be hidden. ¹⁵Neither do people light a lamp and put it under a bowl. Instead they put it on its stand, and it gives light to everyone in the house. ¹⁶In the same way, let your light shine before others, that they may see your good deeds and glorify your Father in heaven.

The Fulfillment of the Law

¹⁷"Do not think that I have come to abolish the Law or the Prophets; I have not come to abolish them but to fulfill them. ¹⁸For truly I tell you, until heaven and earth disappear, not the smallest letter, not the least stroke of a pen, will by any means disappear from the Law until everything is accomplished. ¹⁹Therefore anyone who sets aside one of the least of these commands and teaches others accordingly will be called least in the kingdom of heaven, but whoever practices and teaches these commands will be called great in the kingdom of heaven. ²⁰For I tell you that unless your righteousness surpasses that of the Pharisees and the teachers of the law, you will certainly not enter the kingdom of heaven.

Murder

²¹"You have heard that it was said to the people long ago, 'You shall not murder,ᵈ and anyone who murders will be subject to

---

ᵃ 10 Deut. 6:13   ᵇ 16 Isaiah 9:1,2   ᶜ 25 That is, the Ten Cities   ᵈ 21 Exodus 20:13

judgment.' ²²But I tell you that anyone who is angry with a brother or sister^(a,b) will be subject to judgment. Again, anyone who says to a brother or sister, 'Raca,'^c is answerable to the court. And anyone who says, 'You fool!' will be in danger of the fire of hell.

²³"Therefore, if you are offering your gift at the altar and there remember that your brother or sister has something against you, ²⁴leave your gift there in front of the altar. First go and be reconciled to them; then come and offer your gift.

²⁵"Settle matters quickly with your adversary who is taking you to court. Do it while you are still together on the way, or your adversary may hand you over to the judge, and the judge may hand you over to the officer, and you may be thrown into prison. ²⁶Truly I tell you, you will not get out until you have paid the last penny.

Adultery

²⁷"You have heard that it was said, 'You shall not commit adultery.'^d ²⁸But I tell you that anyone who looks at a woman lustfully has already committed adultery with her in his heart. ²⁹If your right eye causes you to stumble, gouge it out and throw it away. It is better for you to lose one part of your body than for your whole body to be thrown into hell. ³⁰And if your right hand causes you to stumble, cut it off and throw it away. It is better for you to lose one part of your body than for your whole body to go into hell.

Divorce

³¹"It has been said, 'Anyone who divorces his wife must give her a certificate of divorce.'^e ³²But I tell you that anyone who divorces his wife, except for sexual immorality, makes her the victim of adultery, and anyone who marries a divorced woman commits adultery.

Oaths

³³"Again, you have heard that it was said to the people long ago, 'Do not break your oath, but fulfill to the Lord the vows you have made.' ³⁴But I tell you, do not swear an oath at all: either by heaven, for it is God's throne; ³⁵or by the earth, for it is his footstool; or by Jerusalem, for it is the city of the Great King. ³⁶And do not swear by your head, for you cannot make even one hair white or black. ³⁷All you need to say is simply 'Yes' or 'No'; anything beyond this comes from the evil one.^f

Eye for Eye

³⁸"You have heard that it was said, 'Eye for eye, and tooth for tooth.'^g ³⁹But I tell you, do not resist an evil person. If anyone slaps you on the right cheek, turn to them the other cheek also. ⁴⁰And if anyone wants to sue you and take your shirt, hand over your coat as well. ⁴¹If anyone forces you to go one mile, go with them two miles. ⁴²Give to the one who asks you, and do not turn away from the one who wants to borrow from you.

Love for Enemies

⁴³"You have heard that it was said, 'Love your neighbor^h and hate your enemy.' ⁴⁴But I tell you, love your enemies and pray for those who persecute you, ⁴⁵that you may be children of your Father in heaven. He causes his sun to rise on the evil and the good, and sends rain on the righteous and the unrighteous. ⁴⁶If you love those who love you, what reward will you get? Are not even the tax collectors doing that? ⁴⁷And if you greet only your own people, what are you doing more than others? Do not even pagans do that? ⁴⁸Be perfect, therefore, as your heavenly Father is perfect.

Giving to the Needy

6 "Be careful not to practice your righteousness in front of others to be seen by them. If you do, you will have no reward from your Father in heaven.

²"So when you give to the needy, do not announce it with trumpets, as the hypocrites do in the synagogues and on the streets, to be honored by others. Truly I tell you, they have received their reward in full. ³But when you give to the needy, do not let your left hand know what your right hand is doing, ⁴so that your giving may be in secret. Then your Father, who sees what is done in secret, will reward you.

Prayer

⁵"And when you pray, do not be like the hypocrites, for they love to pray standing in the synagogues and on the street corners to be seen by others. Truly I tell you, they have received their reward in full. ⁶But when you pray, go into your room, close the door and pray to your Father, who is unseen. Then your Father, who sees what is done in secret, will reward you. ⁷And when you pray, do not keep on babbling like pagans, for they think they will be heard because of their many words. ⁸Do not be like them, for your Father knows what you need before you ask him.

⁹"This, then, is how you should pray:

"'Our Father in heaven,
  hallowed be your name,
¹⁰your kingdom come,
  your will be done,
    on earth as it is in heaven.
¹¹Give us today our daily bread.
¹²And forgive us our debts,
    as we also have forgiven our debtors.
¹³And lead us not into temptation,^i
    but deliver us from the evil one.^i'

---

^a 22 The Greek word for *brother or sister* (*adelphos*) refers here to a fellow disciple, whether man or woman; also in verse 23.   ^b 22 Some manuscripts *brother or sister without cause*
^c 22 An Aramaic term of contempt   ^d 27 Exodus 20:14   ^e 31 Deut. 24:1   ^f 37 Or *from evil*
^g 38 Exodus 21:24; Lev. 24:20; Deut. 19:21   ^h 43 Lev. 19:18   ^i 13 The Greek for *temptation* can also mean *testing.*   ^i 13 Or *from evil*; some late manuscripts *one, / for yours is the kingdom and the power and the glory forever. Amen.*

[14]For if you forgive other people when they sin against you, your heavenly Father will also forgive you. [15]But if you do not forgive others their sins, your Father will not forgive your sins.

Fasting

[16]"When you fast, do not look somber as the hypocrites do, for they disfigure their faces to show others they are fasting. Truly I tell you, they have received their reward in full. [17]But when you fast, put oil on your head and wash your face, [18]so that it will not be obvious to others that you are fasting, but only to your Father, who is unseen; and your Father, who sees what is done in secret, will reward you.

Treasures in Heaven

[19]"Do not store up for yourselves treasures on earth, where moths and vermin destroy, and where thieves break in and steal. [20]But store up for yourselves treasures in heaven, where moths and vermin do not destroy, and where thieves do not break in and steal. [21]For where your treasure is, there your heart will be also.

[22]"The eye is the lamp of the body. If your eyes are healthy,[a] your whole body will be full of light. [23]But if your eyes are unhealthy,[b] your whole body will be full of darkness. If then the light within you is darkness, how great is that darkness!

[24]"No one can serve two masters. Either you will hate the one and love the other, or you will be devoted to the one and despise the other. You cannot serve both God and money.

Do Not Worry

[25]"Therefore I tell you, do not worry about your life, what you will eat or drink; or about your body, what you will wear. Is not life more than food, and the body more than clothes? [26]Look at the birds of the air; they do not sow or reap or store away in barns, and yet your heavenly Father feeds them. Are you not much more valuable than they? [27]Can any one of you by worrying add a single hour to your life[c]? [28]"And why do you worry about clothes? See how the flowers of the field grow. They do not labor or spin. [29]Yet I tell you that not even Solomon in all his splendor was dressed like one of these. [30]If that is how God clothes the grass of the field, which is here today and tomorrow is thrown into the fire, will he not much more clothe you—you of little faith? [31]So do not worry, saying, 'What shall we eat?' or 'What shall we drink?' or 'What shall we wear?' [32]For the pagans run after all these things, and your heavenly Father knows that you need them. [33]But seek first his kingdom and his righteousness, and all these things will be given to you as well. [34]Therefore do not worry about tomorrow, for tomorrow will worry about itself. Each day has enough trouble of its own.

Judging Others

7 "Do not judge, or you too will be judged. [2]For in the same way you judge others, you will be judged, and with the measure you use, it will be measured to you.

[3]"Why do you look at the speck of sawdust in your brother's eye and pay no attention to the plank in your own eye? [4]How can you say to your brother, 'Let me take the speck out of your eye,' when all the time there is a plank in your own eye? [5]You hypocrite, first take the plank out of your own eye, and then you will see clearly to remove the speck from your brother's eye.

[6]"Do not give dogs what is sacred; do not throw your pearls to pigs. If you do, they may trample them under their feet, and turn and tear you to pieces.

Ask, Seek, Knock

[7]"Ask and it will be given to you; seek and you will find; knock and the door will be opened to you. [8]For everyone who asks receives; the one who seeks finds; and to the one who knocks, the door will be opened.

[9]"Which of you, if your son asks for bread, will give him a stone? [10]Or if he asks for a fish, will give him a snake? [11]If you, then, though you are evil, know how to give good gifts to your children, how much more will your Father in heaven give good gifts to those who ask him! [12]So in everything, do to others what you would have them do to you, for this sums up the Law and the Prophets.

The Narrow and Wide Gates

[13]"Enter through the narrow gate. For wide is the gate and broad is the road that leads to destruction, and many enter through it. [14]But small is the gate and narrow the road that leads to life, and only a few find it.

True and False Prophets

[15]"Watch out for false prophets. They come to you in sheep's clothing, but inwardly they are ferocious wolves. [16]By their fruit you will recognize them. Do people pick grapes from thornbushes, or figs from thistles? [17]Likewise, every good tree bears good fruit, but a bad tree bears bad fruit. [18]A good tree cannot bear bad fruit, and a bad tree cannot bear good fruit. [19]Every tree that does not bear good fruit is cut down and thrown into the fire. [20]Thus, by their fruit you will recognize them.

True and False Disciples

[21]"Not everyone who says to me, 'Lord, Lord,' will enter the kingdom of heaven, but only the one who does the will of my Father who is in heaven. [22]Many will say to me on that day, 'Lord, Lord, did we not prophesy in your name and in your name drive out demons and in your name perform many miracles?' [23]Then I will tell them plainly, 'I never knew you. Away from me, you evildoers!'

---

[a] 22 The Greek for *healthy* here implies *generous.*
[c] 27 Or *single cubit to your height*
[b] 23 The Greek for *unhealthy* here implies *stingy.*

The Wise and Foolish Builders

24"Therefore everyone who hears these words of mine and puts them into practice is like a wise man who built his house on the rock. 25The rain came down, the streams rose, and the winds blew and beat against that house; yet it did not fall, because it had its foundation on the rock. 26But everyone who hears these words of mine and does not put them into practice is like a foolish man who built his house on sand. 27The rain came down, the streams rose, and the winds blew and beat against that house, and it fell with a great crash."

28When Jesus had finished saying these things, the crowds were amazed at his teaching, 29because he taught as one who had authority, and not as their teachers of the law.

Jesus Heals a Man With Leprosy

8 When Jesus came down from the mountainside, large crowds followed him. 2A man with leprosy*a* came and knelt before him and said, "Lord, if you are willing, you can make me clean."

3Jesus reached out his hand and touched the man. "I am willing," he said. "Be clean!" Immediately he was cleansed of his leprosy. 4Then Jesus said to him, "See that you don't tell anyone. But go, show yourself to the priest and offer the gift Moses commanded, as a testimony to them."

The Faith of the Centurion

5When Jesus had entered Capernaum, a centurion came to him, asking for help. 6"Lord," he said, "my servant lies at home paralyzed, suffering terribly."

7Jesus said to him, "Shall I come and heal him?"

8The centurion replied, "Lord, I do not deserve to have you come under my roof. But just say the word, and my servant will be healed. 9For I myself am a man under authority, with soldiers under me. I tell this one, 'Go,' and he goes; and that one, 'Come,' and he comes. I say to my servant, 'Do this,' and he does it."

10When Jesus heard this, he was amazed and said to those following him, "Truly I tell you, I have not found anyone in Israel with such great faith. 11I say to you that many will come from the east and the west, and will take their places at the feast with Abraham, Isaac and Jacob in the kingdom of heaven. 12But the subjects of the kingdom will be thrown outside, into the darkness, where there will be weeping and gnashing of teeth."

13Then Jesus said to the centurion, "Go! Let it be done just as you believed it would." And his servant was healed at that moment.

Jesus Heals Many

14When Jesus came into Peter's house, he saw Peter's mother-in-law lying in bed with a fever. 15He touched her hand and the fever left her, and she got up and began to wait on him.

16When evening came, many who were demon-possessed were brought to him, and he drove out the spirits with a word and healed all the sick. 17This was to fulfill what was spoken through the prophet Isaiah:

"He took up our infirmities
  and bore our diseases."*b*

The Cost of Following Jesus

18When Jesus saw the crowd around him, he gave orders to cross to the other side of the lake. 19Then a teacher of the law came to him and said, "Teacher, I will follow you wherever you go."

20Jesus replied, "Foxes have dens and birds have nests, but the Son of Man has no place to lay his head."

21Another disciple said to him, "Lord, first let me go and bury my father."

22But Jesus told him, "Follow me, and let the dead bury their own dead."

Jesus Calms the Storm

23Then he got into the boat and his disciples followed him. 24Suddenly a furious storm came up on the lake, so that the waves swept over the boat. But Jesus was sleeping. 25The disciples went and woke him, saying, "Lord, save us! We're going to drown!"

26He replied, "You of little faith, why are you so afraid?" Then he got up and rebuked the winds and the waves, and it was completely calm.

27The men were amazed and asked, "What kind of man is this? Even the winds and the waves obey him!"

Jesus Restores Two Demon-Possessed Men

28When he arrived at the other side in the region of the Gadarenes,*c* two demon-possessed men coming from the tombs met him. They were so violent that no one could pass that way. 29"What do you want with us, Son of God?" they shouted. "Have you come here to torture us before the appointed time?"

30Some distance from them a large herd of pigs was feeding. 31The demons begged Jesus, "If you drive us out, send us into the herd of pigs."

32He said to them, "Go!" So they came out and went into the pigs, and the whole herd rushed down the steep bank into the lake and died in the water. 33Those tending the pigs ran off, went into the town and reported all this, including what had happened to the demon-possessed men. 34Then the whole town went out to meet Jesus. And when they saw him, they pleaded with him to leave their region.

Jesus Forgives and Heals a Paralyzed Man

9 Jesus stepped into a boat, crossed over and came to his own town. 2Some men brought to him a paralyzed man, lying on a mat. When Jesus saw their faith, he said to the man, "Take heart, son; your sins are forgiven."

---

a 2 The Greek word traditionally translated *leprosy* was used for various diseases affecting the skin.   *b* 17 Isaiah 53:4 (see Septuagint)   *c* 28 Some manuscripts *Gergesenes*; other manuscripts *Gerasenes*

³At this, some of the teachers of the law said to themselves, "This fellow is blaspheming!"

⁴Knowing their thoughts, Jesus said, "Why do you entertain evil thoughts in your hearts? ⁵Which is easier: to say, 'Your sins are forgiven,' or to say, 'Get up and walk'? ⁶But I want you to know that the Son of Man has authority on earth to forgive sins." So he said to the paralyzed man, "Get up, take your mat and go home." ⁷Then the man got up and went home. ⁸When the crowd saw this, they were filled with awe; and they praised God, who had given such authority to man.

The Calling of Matthew

⁹As Jesus went on from there, he saw a man named Matthew sitting at the tax collector's booth. "Follow me," he told him, and Matthew got up and followed him.

¹⁰While Jesus was having dinner at Matthew's house, many tax collectors and sinners came and ate with him and his disciples. ¹¹When the Pharisees saw this, they asked his disciples, "Why does your teacher eat with tax collectors and sinners?"

¹²On hearing this, Jesus said, "It is not the healthy who need a doctor, but the sick. ¹³But go and learn what this means: 'I desire mercy, not sacrifice.'ᵃ For I have not come to call the righteous, but sinners."

Jesus Questioned About Fasting

¹⁴Then John's disciples came and asked him, "How is it that we and the Pharisees fast often, but your disciples do not fast?"

¹⁵Jesus answered, "How can the guests of the bridegroom mourn while he is with them? The time will come when the bridegroom will be taken from them; then they will fast. ¹⁶"No one sews a patch of unshrunk cloth on an old garment, for the patch will pull away from the garment, making the tear worse. ¹⁷Neither do people pour new wine into old wineskins. If they do, the skins will burst; the wine will run out and the wineskins will be ruined. No, they pour new wine into new wineskins, and both are preserved."

Jesus Raises a Dead Girl and Heals a Sick Woman

¹⁸While he was saying this, a synagogue leader came and knelt before him and said, "My daughter has just died. But come and put your hand on her, and she will live." ¹⁹Jesus got up and went with him, and so did his disciples.

²⁰Just then a woman who had been subject to bleeding for twelve years came up behind him and touched the edge of his cloak. ²¹She said to herself, "If I only touch his cloak, I will be healed."

²²Jesus turned and saw her. "Take heart, daughter," he said, "your faith has healed you." And the woman was healed at that moment.

²³When Jesus entered the synagogue leader's house and saw the noisy crowd and people playing pipes, ²⁴he said, "Go away. The girl is not dead but asleep." But they laughed at him. ²⁵After the crowd had been put outside, he went in and took the girl by the hand, and she got up. ²⁶News of this spread through all that region.

Jesus Heals the Blind and the Mute

²⁷As Jesus went on from there, two blind men followed him, calling out, "Have mercy on us, Son of David!"

²⁸When he had gone indoors, the blind men came to him, and he asked them, "Do you believe that I am able to do this?"

"Yes, Lord," they replied.

²⁹Then he touched their eyes and said, "According to your faith let it be done to you"; ³⁰and their sight was restored. Jesus warned them sternly, "See that no one knows about this." ³¹But they went out and spread the news about him all over that region.

³²While they were going out, a man who was demon-possessed and could not talk was brought to Jesus. ³³And when the demon was driven out, the man who had been mute spoke. The crowd was amazed and said, "Nothing like this has ever been seen in Israel."

³⁴But the Pharisees said, "It is by the prince of demons that he drives out demons."

The Workers Are Few

³⁵Jesus went through all the towns and villages, teaching in their synagogues, proclaiming the good news of the kingdom and healing every disease and sickness. ³⁶When he saw the crowds, he had compassion on them, because they were harassed and helpless, like sheep without a shepherd. ³⁷Then he said to his disciples, "The harvest is plentiful but the workers are few. ³⁸Ask the Lord of the harvest, therefore, to send out workers into his harvest field."

Jesus Sends Out the Twelve

10 Jesus called his twelve disciples to him and gave them authority to drive out impure spirits and to heal every disease and sickness.

²These are the names of the twelve apostles: first, Simon (who is called Peter) and his brother Andrew; James son of Zebedee, and his brother John; ³Philip and Bartholomew; Thomas and Matthew the tax collector; James son of Alphaeus, and Thaddaeus; ⁴Simon the Zealot and Judas Iscariot, who betrayed him.

⁵These twelve Jesus sent out with the following instructions: "Do not go among the Gentiles or enter any town of the Samaritans. ⁶Go rather to the lost sheep of Israel. ⁷As you go, proclaim this message: 'The kingdom of heaven has come near.' ⁸Heal the sick, raise the dead, cleanse those who have leprosy,ᵇ drive out demons. Freely you have received; freely give.

ᵃ 13 Hosea 6:6 ᵇ 8 The Greek word traditionally translated *leprosy* was used for various diseases affecting the skin.

⁹"Do not get any gold or silver or copper to take with you in your belts— ¹⁰no bag for the journey or extra shirt or sandals or a staff, for the worker is worth his keep. ¹¹Whatever town or village you enter, search there for some worthy person and stay at their house until you leave. ¹²As you enter the home, give it your greeting. ¹³If the home is deserving, let your peace rest on it; if it is not, let your peace return to you. ¹⁴If anyone will not welcome you or listen to your words, leave that home or town and shake the dust off your feet. ¹⁵Truly I tell you, it will be more bearable for Sodom and Gomorrah on the day of judgment than for that town.

¹⁶"I am sending you out like sheep among wolves. Therefore be as shrewd as snakes and as innocent as doves. ¹⁷Be on your guard; you will be handed over to the local councils and be flogged in the synagogues. ¹⁸On my account you will be brought before governors and kings as witnesses to them and to the Gentiles. ¹⁹But when they arrest you, do not worry about what to say or how to say it. At that time you will be given what to say, ²⁰for it will not be you speaking, but the Spirit of your Father speaking through you.

²¹"Brother will betray brother to death, and a father his child; children will rebel against their parents and have them put to death. ²²You will be hated by everyone because of me, but the one who stands firm to the end will be saved. ²³When you are persecuted in one place, flee to another. Truly I tell you, you will not finish going through the towns of Israel before the Son of Man comes.

²⁴"The student is not above the teacher, nor a servant above his master. ²⁵It is enough for students to be like their teachers, and servants like their masters. If the head of the house has been called Beelzebul, how much more the members of his household!

²⁶"So do not be afraid of them, for there is nothing concealed that will not be disclosed, or hidden that will not be made known. ²⁷What I tell you in the dark, speak in the daylight; what is whispered in your ear, proclaim from the roofs. ²⁸Do not be afraid of those who kill the body but cannot kill the soul. Rather, be afraid of the One who can destroy both soul and body in hell. ²⁹Are not two sparrows sold for a penny? Yet not one of them will fall to the ground outside your Father's care.ᵃ ³⁰And even the very hairs of your head are all numbered. ³¹So don't be afraid; you are worth more than many sparrows.

³²"Whoever acknowledges me before others, I will also acknowledge before my Father in heaven. ³³But whoever disowns me before others, I will disown before my Father in heaven.

³⁴"Do not suppose that I have come to bring peace to the earth. I did not come to bring peace, but a sword. ³⁵For I have come to turn

" 'a man against his father,
   a daughter against her mother,

a daughter-in-law against her mother-in-law—
³⁶ a man's enemies will be the members of his own household.'ᵇ

³⁷"Anyone who loves their father or mother more than me is not worthy of me; anyone who loves their son or daughter more than me is not worthy of me. ³⁸Whoever does not take up their cross and follow me is not worthy of me. ³⁹Whoever finds their life will lose it, and whoever loses their life for my sake will find it.

⁴⁰"Anyone who welcomes you welcomes me, and anyone who welcomes me welcomes the one who sent me. ⁴¹Whoever welcomes a prophet as a prophet will receive a prophet's reward, and whoever welcomes a righteous person as a righteous person will receive a righteous person's reward. ⁴²And if anyone gives even a cup of cold water to one of these little ones who is my disciple, truly I tell you, that person will certainly not lose their reward."

Jesus and John the Baptist

11 After Jesus had finished instructing his twelve disciples, he went on from there to teach and preach in the towns of Galilee.ᶜ

²When John, who was in prison, heard about the deeds of the Messiah, he sent his disciples ³to ask him, "Are you the one who is to come, or should we expect someone else?"

⁴Jesus replied, "Go back and report to John what you hear and see: ⁵The blind receive sight, the lame walk, those who have leprosyᵈ are cleansed, the deaf hear, the dead are raised, and the good news is proclaimed to the poor. ⁶Blessed is anyone who does not stumble on account of me."

⁷As John's disciples were leaving, Jesus began to speak to the crowd about John: "What did you go out into the wilderness to see? A reed swayed by the wind? ⁸If not, what did you go out to see? A man dressed in fine clothes? No, those who wear fine clothes are in kings' palaces. ⁹Then what did you go out to see? A prophet? Yes, I tell you, and more than a prophet. ¹⁰This is the one about whom it is written:

" 'I will send my messenger ahead of you,
   who will prepare your way before you.'ᵉ

¹¹Truly I tell you, among those born of women there has not risen anyone greater than John the Baptist; yet whoever is least in the kingdom of heaven is greater than he. ¹²From the days of John the Baptist until now, the kingdom of heaven has been subjected to violence,ᶠ and violent people have been raiding it. ¹³For all the Prophets and the Law prophesied until John. ¹⁴And if you are willing to accept it, he is the Elijah who was to come. ¹⁵Whoever has ears, let them hear.

¹⁶"To what can I compare this generation? They are like children sitting in the marketplaces and calling out to others:

ᵃ 29 Or will; or knowledge   ᵇ 36 Micah 7:6   ᶜ 1 Greek in their towns   ᵈ 5 The Greek word traditionally translated leprosy was used for various diseases affecting the skin.   ᵉ 10 Mal. 3:1   ᶠ 12 Or been forcefully advancing

17 " 'We played the pipe for you,
        and you did not dance;
    we sang a dirge,
        and you did not mourn.'

18 For John came neither eating nor drinking, and they say, 'He has a demon.' 19 The Son of Man came eating and drinking, and they say, 'Here is a glutton and a drunkard, a friend of tax collectors and sinners.' But wisdom is proved right by her deeds."

Woe on Unrepentant Towns

20 Then Jesus began to denounce the towns in which most of his miracles had been performed, because they did not repent. 21 "Woe to you, Chorazin! Woe to you, Bethsaida! For if the miracles that were performed in you had been performed in Tyre and Sidon, they would have repented long ago in sackcloth and ashes. 22 But I tell you, it will be more bearable for Tyre and Sidon on the day of judgment than for you. 23 And you, Capernaum, will you be lifted to the heavens? No, you will go down to Hades.[a] For if the miracles that were performed in you had been performed in Sodom, it would have remained to this day. 24 But I tell you that it will be more bearable for Sodom on the day of judgment than for you."

The Father Revealed in the Son

25 At that time Jesus said, "I praise you, Father, Lord of heaven and earth, because you have hidden these things from the wise and learned, and revealed them to little children. 26 Yes, Father, for this is what you were pleased to do.

27 "All things have been committed to me by my Father. No one knows the Son except the Father, and no one knows the Father except the Son and those to whom the Son chooses to reveal him.

28 "Come to me, all you who are weary and burdened, and I will give you rest. 29 Take my yoke upon you and learn from me, for I am gentle and humble in heart, and you will find rest for your souls. 30 For my yoke is easy and my burden is light."

Jesus Is Lord of the Sabbath

12 At that time Jesus went through the grainfields on the Sabbath. His disciples were hungry and began to pick some heads of grain and eat them. 2 When the Pharisees saw this, they said to him, "Look! Your disciples are doing what is unlawful on the Sabbath."

3 He answered, "Haven't you read what David did when he and his companions were hungry? 4 He entered the house of God, and he and his companions ate the consecrated bread—which was not lawful for them to do, but only for the priests. 5 Or haven't you read in the Law that the priests on Sabbath duty in the temple desecrate the Sabbath and yet are innocent? 6 I tell you that something greater than the temple is here. 7 If you had known what these words mean, 'I desire mercy, not sacrifice,'[b] you would not have condemned the innocent. 8 For the Son of Man is Lord of the Sabbath."

9 Going on from that place, he went into their synagogue, 10 and a man with a shriveled hand was there. Looking for a reason to bring charges against Jesus, they asked him, "Is it lawful to heal on the Sabbath?"

11 He said to them, "If any of you has a sheep and it falls into a pit on the Sabbath, will you not take hold of it and lift it out? 12 How much more valuable is a person than a sheep! Therefore it is lawful to do good on the Sabbath."

13 Then he said to the man, "Stretch out your hand." So he stretched it out and it was completely restored, just as sound as the other. 14 But the Pharisees went out and plotted how they might kill Jesus.

God's Chosen Servant

15 Aware of this, Jesus withdrew from that place. A large crowd followed him, and he healed all who were ill. 16 He warned them not to tell others about him. 17 This was to fulfill what was spoken through the prophet Isaiah:

18 "Here is my servant whom I have chosen,
        the one I love, in whom I delight;
    I will put my Spirit on him,
        and he will proclaim justice to the
            nations.
19 He will not quarrel or cry out;
        no one will hear his voice in the streets.
20 A bruised reed he will not break,
        and a smoldering wick he will not snuff
            out,
    till he has brought justice through to
            victory.
21   In his name the nations will put their
            hope."[c]

Jesus and Beelzebul

22 Then they brought him a demon-possessed man who was blind and mute, and Jesus healed him, so that he could both talk and see. 23 All the people were astonished and said, "Could this be the Son of David?"

24 But when the Pharisees heard this, they said, "It is only by Beelzebul, the prince of demons, that this fellow drives out demons."

25 Jesus knew their thoughts and said to them, "Every kingdom divided against itself will be ruined, and every city or household divided against itself will not stand. 26 If Satan drives out Satan, he is divided against himself. How then can his kingdom stand? 27 And if I drive out demons by Beelzebul, by whom do your people drive them out? So then, they will be your judges. 28 But if it is by the Spirit of God that I drive out demons, then the kingdom of God has come upon you.

29 "Or again, how can anyone enter a strong man's house and carry off his possessions unless he first ties up the strong man? Then he can plunder his house.

30 "Whoever is not with me is against me, and whoever does not gather with me scatters.

---

a 23 That is, the realm of the dead   b 7 Hosea 6:6   c 21 Isaiah 42:1-4

³¹And so I tell you, every kind of sin and slander can be forgiven, but blasphemy against the Spirit will not be forgiven. ³²Anyone who speaks a word against the Son of Man will be forgiven, but anyone who speaks against the Holy Spirit will not be forgiven, either in this age or in the age to come.

³³"Make a tree good and its fruit will be good, or make a tree bad and its fruit will be bad, for a tree is recognized by its fruit. ³⁴You brood of vipers, how can you who are evil say anything good? For the mouth speaks what the heart is full of. ³⁵A good man brings good things out of the good stored up in him, and an evil man brings evil things out of the evil stored up in him. ³⁶But I tell you that everyone will have to give account on the day of judgment for every empty word they have spoken. ³⁷For by your words you will be acquitted, and by your words you will be condemned."

The Sign of Jonah

³⁸Then some of the Pharisees and teachers of the law said to him, "Teacher, we want to see a sign from you."

³⁹He answered, "A wicked and adulterous generation asks for a sign! But none will be given it except the sign of the prophet Jonah. ⁴⁰For as Jonah was three days and three nights in the belly of a huge fish, so the Son of Man will be three days and three nights in the heart of the earth. ⁴¹The men of Nineveh will stand up at the judgment with this generation and condemn it; for they repented at the preaching of Jonah, and now something greater than Jonah is here. ⁴²The Queen of the South will rise at the judgment with this generation and condemn it; for she came from the ends of the earth to listen to Solomon's wisdom, and now something greater than Solomon is here.

⁴³"When an impure spirit comes out of a person, it goes through arid places seeking rest and does not find it. ⁴⁴Then it says, 'I will return to the house I left.' When it arrives, it finds the house unoccupied, swept clean and put in order. ⁴⁵Then it goes and takes with it seven other spirits more wicked than itself, and they go in and live there. And the final condition of that person is worse than the first. That is how it will be with this wicked generation."

Jesus' Mother and Brothers

⁴⁶While Jesus was still talking to the crowd, his mother and brothers stood outside, wanting to speak to him. ⁴⁷Someone told him, "Your mother and brothers are standing outside, wanting to speak to you."

⁴⁸He replied to him, "Who is my mother, and who are my brothers?" ⁴⁹Pointing to his disciples, he said, "Here are my mother and my brothers. ⁵⁰For whoever does the will of my Father in heaven is my brother and sister and mother."

The Parable of the Sower

13 That same day Jesus went out of the house and sat by the lake. ²Such large crowds gathered around him that he got into a boat and sat in it, while all the people stood on the shore. ³Then he told them many things in parables, saying: "A farmer went out to sow his seed. ⁴As he was scattering the seed, some fell along the path, and the birds came and ate it up. ⁵Some fell on rocky places, where it did not have much soil. It sprang up quickly, because the soil was shallow. ⁶But when the sun came up, the plants were scorched, and they withered because they had no root. ⁷Other seed fell among thorns, which grew up and choked the plants. ⁸Still other seed fell on good soil, where it produced a crop—a hundred, sixty or thirty times what was sown. ⁹Whoever has ears, let them hear."

¹⁰The disciples came to him and asked, "Why do you speak to the people in parables?"

¹¹He replied, "Because the knowledge of the secrets of the kingdom of heaven has been given to you, but not to them. ¹²Whoever has will be given more, and they will have an abundance. Whoever does not have, even what they have will be taken from them. ¹³This is why I speak to them in parables:

"Though seeing, they do not see;
    though hearing, they do not hear or
        understand.

¹⁴In them is fulfilled the prophecy of Isaiah:

"'You will be ever hearing but never
        understanding;
    you will be ever seeing but never
        perceiving.
¹⁵For this people's heart has become
        calloused;
    they hardly hear with their ears,
    and they have closed their eyes.
Otherwise they might see with their eyes,
    hear with their ears,
    understand with their hearts
and turn, and I would heal them.'ᵃ

¹⁶But blessed are your eyes because they see, and your ears because they hear. ¹⁷For truly I tell you, many prophets and righteous people longed to see what you see but did not see it, and to hear what you hear but did not hear it.

¹⁸"Listen then to what the parable of the sower means: ¹⁹When anyone hears the message about the kingdom and does not understand it, the evil one comes and snatches away what was sown in their heart. This is the seed sown along the path. ²⁰The seed falling on rocky ground refers to someone who hears the word and at once receives it with joy. ²¹But since they have no root, they last only a short time. When trouble or persecution comes because of the word, they quickly fall away. ²²The seed falling among the thorns refers to someone who hears the word, but the worries of this life and the deceitfulness of wealth choke the word, making it unfruitful. ²³But the seed falling on good soil refers

---

ᵃ 15 Isaiah 6:9,10 (see Septuagint)

to someone who hears the word and understands it. This is the one who produces a crop, yielding a hundred, sixty or thirty times what was sown."

The Parable of the Weeds

²⁴Jesus told them another parable: "The kingdom of heaven is like a man who sowed good seed in his field. ²⁵But while everyone was sleeping, his enemy came and sowed weeds among the wheat, and went away. ²⁶When the wheat sprouted and formed heads, then the weeds also appeared.

²⁷"The owner's servants came to him and said, 'Sir, didn't you sow good seed in your field? Where then did the weeds come from?'

²⁸"'An enemy did this,' he replied.

"The servants asked him, 'Do you want us to go and pull them up?'

²⁹"'No,' he answered, 'because while you are pulling the weeds, you may uproot the wheat with them. ³⁰Let both grow together until the harvest. At that time I will tell the harvesters: First collect the weeds and tie them in bundles to be burned; then gather the wheat and bring it into my barn.'"

The Parables of the Mustard Seed and the Yeast

³¹He told them another parable: "The kingdom of heaven is like a mustard seed, which a man took and planted in his field. ³²Though it is the smallest of all seeds, yet when it grows, it is the largest of garden plants and becomes a tree, so that the birds come and perch in its branches."

³³He told them still another parable: "The kingdom of heaven is like yeast that a woman took and mixed into about sixty pounds*a* of flour until it worked all through the dough."

³⁴Jesus spoke all these things to the crowd in parables; he did not say anything to them without using a parable. ³⁵So was fulfilled what was spoken through the prophet:

"I will open my mouth in parables,
I will utter things hidden since the
creation of the world."*b*

The Parable of the Weeds Explained

³⁶Then he left the crowd and went into the house. His disciples came to him and said, "Explain to us the parable of the weeds in the field."

³⁷He answered, "The one who sowed the good seed is the Son of Man. ³⁸The field is the world, and the good seed stands for the people of the kingdom. The weeds are the people of the evil one, ³⁹and the enemy who sows them is the devil. The harvest is the end of the age, and the harvesters are angels.

⁴⁰"As the weeds are pulled up and burned in the fire, so it will be at the end of the age. ⁴¹The Son of Man will send out his angels, and they will weed out of his kingdom everything that causes sin and all who do evil. ⁴²They will throw them into the blazing furnace, where there will be weeping and gnashing of teeth. ⁴³Then the righteous will shine like the sun in the kingdom of their Father. Whoever has ears, let them hear.

The Parables of the Hidden Treasure and the Pearl

⁴⁴"The kingdom of heaven is like treasure hidden in a field. When a man found it, he hid it again, and then in his joy went and sold all he had and bought that field.

⁴⁵"Again, the kingdom of heaven is like a merchant looking for fine pearls. ⁴⁶When he found one of great value, he went away and sold everything he had and bought it.

The Parable of the Net

⁴⁷"Once again, the kingdom of heaven is like a net that was let down into the lake and caught all kinds of fish. ⁴⁸When it was full, the fishermen pulled it up on the shore. Then they sat down and collected the good fish in baskets, but threw the bad away. ⁴⁹This is how it will be at the end of the age. The angels will come and separate the wicked from the righteous ⁵⁰and throw them into the blazing furnace, where there will be weeping and gnashing of teeth.

⁵¹"Have you understood all these things?" Jesus asked.

"Yes," they replied.

⁵²He said to them, "Therefore every teacher of the law who has become a disciple in the kingdom of heaven is like the owner of a house who brings out of his storeroom new treasures as well as old."

A Prophet Without Honor

⁵³When Jesus had finished these parables, he moved on from there. ⁵⁴Coming to his hometown, he began teaching the people in their synagogue, and they were amazed. "Where did this man get this wisdom and these miraculous powers?" they asked. ⁵⁵"Isn't this the carpenter's son? Isn't his mother's name Mary, and aren't his brothers James, Joseph, Simon and Judas? ⁵⁶Aren't all his sisters with us? Where then did this man get all these things?" ⁵⁷And they took offense at him.

But Jesus said to them, "A prophet is not without honor except in his own town and in his own home."

⁵⁸And he did not do many miracles there because of their lack of faith.

John the Baptist Beheaded

14 At that time Herod the tetrarch heard the reports about Jesus, ²and he said to his attendants, "This is John the Baptist; he has risen from the dead! That is why miraculous powers are at work in him."

³Now Herod had arrested John and bound him and put him in prison because of Herodias, his brother Philip's wife, ⁴for John had

---

a 33 Or about 27 kilograms   *b 35* Psalm 78:2

been saying to him: "It is not lawful for you to have her." [5]Herod wanted to kill John, but he was afraid of the people, because they considered John a prophet.

[6]On Herod's birthday the daughter of Herodias danced for the guests and pleased Herod so much [7]that he promised with an oath to give her whatever she asked. [8]Prompted by her mother, she said, "Give me here on a platter the head of John the Baptist." [9]The king was distressed, but because of his oaths and his dinner guests, he ordered that her request be granted [10]and had John beheaded in the prison. [11]His head was brought in on a platter and given to the girl, who carried it to her mother. [12]John's disciples came and took his body and buried it. Then they went and told Jesus.

Jesus Feeds the Five Thousand

[13]When Jesus heard what had happened, he withdrew by boat privately to a solitary place. Hearing of this, the crowds followed him on foot from the towns. [14]When Jesus landed and saw a large crowd, he had compassion on them and healed their sick.

[15]As evening approached, the disciples came to him and said, "This is a remote place, and it's already getting late. Send the crowds away, so they can go to the villages and buy themselves some food."

[16]Jesus replied, "They do not need to go away. You give them something to eat."

[17]"We have here only five loaves of bread and two fish," they answered.

[18]"Bring them here to me," he said. [19]And he directed the people to sit down on the grass. Taking the five loaves and the two fish and looking up to heaven, he gave thanks and broke the loaves. Then he gave them to the disciples, and the disciples gave them to the people. [20]They all ate and were satisfied, and the disciples picked up twelve basketfuls of broken pieces that were left over. [21]The number of those who ate was about five thousand men, besides women and children.

Jesus Walks on the Water

[22]Immediately Jesus made the disciples get into the boat and go on ahead of him to the other side, while he dismissed the crowd. [23]After he had dismissed them, he went up on a mountainside by himself to pray. Later that night, he was there alone, [24]and the boat was already a considerable distance from land, buffeted by the waves because the wind was against it.

[25]Shortly before dawn Jesus went out to them, walking on the lake. [26]When the disciples saw him walking on the lake, they were terrified. "It's a ghost," they said, and cried out in fear.

[27]But Jesus immediately said to them: "Take courage! It is I. Don't be afraid."

[28]"Lord, if it's you," Peter replied, "tell me to come to you on the water."

[29]"Come," he said.

Then Peter got down out of the boat, walked on the water and came toward Jesus. [30]But when he saw the wind, he was afraid and, beginning to sink, cried out, "Lord, save me!"

[31]Immediately Jesus reached out his hand and caught him. "You of little faith," he said, "why did you doubt?"

[32]And when they climbed into the boat, the wind died down. [33]Then those who were in the boat worshiped him, saying, "Truly you are the Son of God."

[34]When they had crossed over, they landed at Gennesaret. [35]And when the men of that place recognized Jesus, they sent word to all the surrounding country. People brought all their sick to him [36]and begged him to let the sick just touch the edge of his cloak, and all who touched it were healed.

That Which Defiles

15 Then some Pharisees and teachers of the law came to Jesus from Jerusalem and asked, [2]"Why do your disciples break the tradition of the elders? They don't wash their hands before they eat!"

[3]Jesus replied, "And why do you break the command of God for the sake of your tradition? [4]For God said, 'Honor your father and mother'[a] and 'Anyone who curses their father or mother is to be put to death.'[b] [5]But you say that if anyone declares that what might have been used to help their father or mother is 'devoted to God,' [6]they are not to 'honor their father or mother' with it. Thus you nullify the word of God for the sake of your tradition. [7]You hypocrites! Isaiah was right when he prophesied about you:

[8] "'These people honor me with their lips,
    but their hearts are far from me.
[9] They worship me in vain;
    their teachings are merely human
      rules.'[c]

[10]Jesus called the crowd to him and said, "Listen and understand. [11]What goes into someone's mouth does not defile them, but what comes out of their mouth, that is what defiles them."

[12]Then the disciples came to him and asked, "Do you know that the Pharisees were offended when they heard this?"

[13]He replied, "Every plant that my heavenly Father has not planted will be pulled up by the roots. [14]Leave them; they are blind guides.[d] If the blind lead the blind, both will fall into a pit."

[15]Peter said, "Explain the parable to us."

[16]"Are you still so dull?" Jesus asked them. [17]"Don't you see that whatever enters the mouth goes into the stomach and then out of the body? [18]But the things that come out of a person's mouth come from the heart, and these defile them. [19]For out of the heart come evil thoughts—murder, adultery, sexual immorality, theft, false testimony, slander. [20]These are what defile a person; but eating with unwashed hands does not defile them."

[a] 4 Exodus 20:12; Deut. 5:16   [b] 4 Exodus 21:17; Lev. 20:9   [c] 9 Isaiah 29:13   [d] 14 Some manuscripts blind guides of the blind

The Faith of a Canaanite Woman

²¹Leaving that place, Jesus withdrew to the region of Tyre and Sidon. ²²A Canaanite woman from that vicinity came to him, crying out, "Lord, Son of David, have mercy on me! My daughter is demon-possessed and suffering terribly."

²³Jesus did not answer a word. So his disciples came to him and urged him, "Send her away, for she keeps crying out after us."

²⁴He answered, "I was sent only to the lost sheep of Israel."

²⁵The woman came and knelt before him. "Lord, help me!" she said.

²⁶He replied, "It is not right to take the children's bread and toss it to the dogs."

²⁷"Yes it is, Lord," she said. "Even the dogs eat the crumbs that fall from their master's table."

²⁸Then Jesus said to her, "Woman, you have great faith! Your request is granted." And her daughter was healed at that moment.

Jesus Feeds the Four Thousand

²⁹Jesus left there and went along the Sea of Galilee. Then he went up on a mountainside and sat down. ³⁰Great crowds came to him, bringing the lame, the blind, the crippled, the mute and many others, and laid them at his feet; and he healed them. ³¹The people were amazed when they saw the mute speaking, the crippled made well, the lame walking and the blind seeing. And they praised the God of Israel.

³²Jesus called his disciples to him and said, "I have compassion for these people; they have already been with me three days and have nothing to eat. I do not want to send them away hungry, or they may collapse on the way."

³³His disciples answered, "Where could we get enough bread in this remote place to feed such a crowd?"

³⁴"How many loaves do you have?" Jesus asked.

"Seven," they replied, "and a few small fish."

³⁵He told the crowd to sit down on the ground. ³⁶Then he took the seven loaves and the fish, and when he had given thanks, he broke them and gave them to the disciples, and they in turn to the people. ³⁷They all ate and were satisfied. Afterward the disciples picked up seven basketfuls of broken pieces that were left over. ³⁸The number of those who ate was four thousand men, besides women and children. ³⁹After Jesus had sent the crowd away, he got into the boat and went to the vicinity of Magadan.

The Demand for a Sign

16 The Pharisees and Sadducees came to Jesus and tested him by asking him to show them a sign from heaven.

²He replied, "When evening comes, you say, 'It will be fair weather, for the sky is red,' ³and in the morning, 'Today it will be stormy, for the sky is red and overcast.' You know how to interpret the appearance of the sky, but you cannot interpret the signs of the times.ᵃ ⁴A wicked and adulterous generation looks for a sign, but none will be given it except the sign of Jonah." Jesus then left them and went away.

The Yeast of the Pharisees and Sadducees

⁵When they went across the lake, the disciples forgot to take bread. ⁶"Be careful," Jesus said to them. "Be on your guard against the yeast of the Pharisees and Sadducees."

⁷They discussed this among themselves and said, "It is because we didn't bring any bread."

⁸Aware of their discussion, Jesus asked, "You of little faith, why are you talking among yourselves about having no bread? ⁹Do you still not understand? Don't you remember the five loaves for the five thousand, and how many basketfuls you gathered? ¹⁰Or the seven loaves for the four thousand, and how many basketfuls you gathered? ¹¹How is it you don't understand that I was not talking to you about bread? But be on your guard against the yeast of the Pharisees and Sadducees." ¹²Then they understood that he was not telling them to guard against the yeast used in bread, but against the teaching of the Pharisees and Sadducees.

Peter Declares That Jesus Is the Messiah

¹³When Jesus came to the region of Caesarea Philippi, he asked his disciples, "Who do people say the Son of Man is?"

¹⁴They replied, "Some say John the Baptist; others say Elijah; and still others, Jeremiah or one of the prophets."

¹⁵"But what about you?" he asked. "Who do you say I am?"

¹⁶Simon Peter answered, "You are the Messiah, the Son of the living God."

¹⁷Jesus replied, "Blessed are you, Simon son of Jonah, for this was not revealed to you by flesh and blood, but by my Father in heaven. ¹⁸And I tell you that you are Peter,ᵇ and on this rock I will build my church, and the gates of Hadesᶜ will not overcome it. ¹⁹I will give you the keys of the kingdom of heaven; whatever you bind on earth will beᵈ bound in heaven, and whatever you loose on earth will beᵈ loosed in heaven." ²⁰Then he ordered his disciples not to tell anyone that he was the Messiah.

Jesus Predicts His Death

²¹From that time on Jesus began to explain to his disciples that he must go to Jerusalem and suffer many things at the hands of the elders, the chief priests and the teachers of the law, and that he must be killed and on the third day be raised to life.

²²Peter took him aside and began to rebuke him. "Never, Lord!" he said. "This shall never happen to you!"

ᵃ 2,3 Some early manuscripts do not have *When evening comes . . . of the times.*   ᵇ 18 The Greek word for *Peter* means *rock.*   ᶜ 18 That is, the realm of the dead   ᵈ 19 Or *will have been*

23Jesus turned and said to Peter, "Get behind me, Satan! You are a stumbling block to me; you do not have in mind the concerns of God, but merely human concerns."

24Then Jesus said to his disciples, "Whoever wants to be my disciple must deny themselves and take up their cross and follow me. 25For whoever wants to save their life*a* will lose it, but whoever loses their life for me will find it. 26What good will it be for someone to gain the whole world, yet forfeit their soul? Or what can anyone give in exchange for their soul? 27For the Son of Man is going to come in his Father's glory with his angels, and then he will reward each person according to what they have done.

28"Truly I tell you, some who are standing here will not taste death before they see the Son of Man coming in his kingdom."

The Transfiguration

17 After six days Jesus took with him Peter, James and John the brother of James, and led them up a high mountain by themselves. 2There he was transfigured before them. His face shone like the sun, and his clothes became as white as the light. 3Just then there appeared before them Moses and Elijah, talking with Jesus.

4Peter said to Jesus, "Lord, it is good for us to be here. If you wish, I will put up three shelters—one for you, one for Moses and one for Elijah."

5While he was still speaking, a bright cloud covered them, and a voice from the cloud said, "This is my Son, whom I love; with him I am well pleased. Listen to him!"

6When the disciples heard this, they fell facedown to the ground, terrified. 7But Jesus came and touched them. "Get up," he said. "Don't be afraid." 8When they looked up, they saw no one except Jesus.

9As they were coming down the mountain, Jesus instructed them, "Don't tell anyone what you have seen, until the Son of Man has been raised from the dead."

10The disciples asked him, "Why then do the teachers of the law say that Elijah must come first?"

11Jesus replied, "To be sure, Elijah comes and will restore all things. 12But I tell you, Elijah has already come, and they did not recognize him, but have done to him everything they wished. In the same way the Son of Man is going to suffer at their hands." 13Then the disciples understood that he was talking to them about John the Baptist.

Jesus Heals a Demon-Possessed Boy

14When they came to the crowd, a man approached Jesus and knelt before him. 15"Lord, have mercy on my son," he said. "He has seizures and is suffering greatly. He often falls into the fire or into the water. 16I brought him to your disciples, but they could not heal him."

17"You unbelieving and perverse genera-tion," Jesus replied, "how long shall I stay with you? How long shall I put up with you? Bring the boy here to me." 18Jesus rebuked the demon, and it came out of the boy, and he was healed at that moment.

19Then the disciples came to Jesus in private and asked, "Why couldn't we drive it out?"

20He replied, "Because you have so little faith. Truly I tell you, if you have faith as small as a mustard seed, you can say to this mountain, 'Move from here to there,' and it will move. Nothing will be impossible for you." [21]*b*

Jesus Predicts His Death a Second Time

22When they came together in Galilee, he said to them, "The Son of Man is going to be delivered into the hands of men. 23They will kill him, and on the third day he will be raised to life." And the disciples were filled with grief.

The Temple Tax

24After Jesus and his disciples arrived in Capernaum, the collectors of the two-drachma temple tax came to Peter and asked, "Doesn't your teacher pay the temple tax?"

25"Yes, he does," he replied.

When Peter came into the house, Jesus was the first to speak. "What do you think, Simon?" he asked. "From whom do the kings of the earth collect duty and taxes—from their own children or from others?"

26"From others," Peter answered.

"Then the children are exempt," Jesus said to him. 27"But so that we may not cause offense, go to the lake and throw out your line. Take the first fish you catch; open its mouth and you will find a four-drachma coin. Take it and give it to them for my tax and yours."

The Greatest in the Kingdom of Heaven

18 At that time the disciples came to Jesus and asked, "Who, then, is the greatest in the kingdom of heaven?"

2He called a little child to him, and placed the child among them. 3And he said: "Truly I tell you, unless you change and become like little children, you will never enter the kingdom of heaven. 4Therefore, whoever takes the lowly position of this child is the greatest in the kingdom of heaven. 5And whoever welcomes one such child in my name welcomes me.

Causing to Stumble

6"If anyone causes one of these little ones—those who believe in me—to stumble, it would be better for them to have a large millstone hung around their neck and to be drowned in the depths of the sea. 7Woe to the world because of the things that cause people to stumble! Such things must come, but woe to the person through whom they come! 8If your hand or your foot causes you to stumble, cut it off and throw it away. It is better for you to

---

a 25 The Greek word means either *life* or *soul*; also in verse 26.   *b* 21 Some manuscripts include here words similar to Mark 9:29.

enter life maimed or crippled than to have two hands or two feet and be thrown into eternal fire. [9]And if your eye causes you to stumble, gouge it out and throw it away. It is better for you to enter life with one eye than to have two eyes and be thrown into the fire of hell.

The Parable of the Wandering Sheep

[10]"See that you do not despise one of these little ones. For I tell you that their angels in heaven always see the face of my Father in heaven. [11]*a*

[12]"What do you think? If a man owns a hundred sheep, and one of them wanders away, will he not leave the ninety-nine on the hills and go to look for the one that wandered off? [13]And if he finds it, truly I tell you, he is happier about that one sheep than about the ninety-nine that did not wander off. [14]In the same way your Father in heaven is not willing that any of these little ones should perish.

Dealing With Sin in the Church

[15]"If your brother or sister*b* sins,*c* go and point out their fault, just between the two of you. If they listen to you, you have won them over. [16]But if they will not listen, take one or two others along, so that 'every matter may be established by the testimony of two or three witnesses.'*d* [17]If they still refuse to listen, tell it to the church; and if they refuse to listen even to the church, treat them as you would a pagan or a tax collector.

[18]"Truly I tell you, whatever you bind on earth will be*e* bound in heaven, and whatever you loose on earth will be*e* loosed in heaven. [19]"Again, truly I tell you that if two of you on earth agree about anything they ask for, it will be done for them by my Father in heaven. [20]For where two or three gather in my name, there am I with them."

The Parable of the Unmerciful Servant

[21]Then Peter came to Jesus and asked, "Lord, how many times shall I forgive my brother or sister who sins against me? Up to seven times?"

[22]Jesus answered, "I tell you, not seven times, but seventy-seven times.*f*

[23]"Therefore, the kingdom of heaven is like a king who wanted to settle accounts with his servants. [24]As he began the settlement, a man who owed him ten thousand bags of gold*g* was brought to him. [25]Since he was not able to pay, the master ordered that he and his wife and his children and all that he had be sold to repay the debt.

[26]"At this the servant fell on his knees before him. 'Be patient with me,' he begged, 'and I will pay back everything.' [27]The servant's master took pity on him, canceled the debt and let him go.

[28]"But when that servant went out, he found one of his fellow servants who owed him a hundred silver coins.*h* He grabbed him and began to choke him. 'Pay back what you owe me!' he demanded.

[29]"His fellow servant fell to his knees and begged him, 'Be patient with me, and I will pay it back.'

[30]"But he refused. Instead, he went off and had the man thrown into prison until he could pay the debt. [31]When the other servants saw what had happened, they were outraged and went and told their master everything that had happened.

[32]"Then the master called the servant in. 'You wicked servant,' he said, 'I canceled all that debt of yours because you begged me to. [33]Shouldn't you have had mercy on your fellow servant just as I had on you?' [34]In anger his master handed him over to the jailers to be tortured, until he should pay back all he owed.

[35]"This is how my heavenly Father will treat each of you unless you forgive your brother or sister from your heart."

Divorce

19 When Jesus had finished saying these things, he left Galilee and went into the region of Judea to the other side of the Jordan. [2]Large crowds followed him, and he healed them there.

[3]Some Pharisees came to him to test him. They asked, "Is it lawful for a man to divorce his wife for any and every reason?"

[4]"Haven't you read," he replied, "that at the beginning the Creator 'made them male and female,'*i* [5]and said, 'For this reason a man will leave his father and mother and be united to his wife, and the two will become one flesh'*j*? [6]So they are no longer two, but one flesh. Therefore what God has joined together, let no one separate."

[7]"Why then," they asked, "did Moses command that a man give his wife a certificate of divorce and send her away?"

[8]Jesus replied, "Moses permitted you to divorce your wives because your hearts were hard. But it was not this way from the beginning. [9]I tell you that anyone who divorces his wife, except for sexual immorality, and marries another woman commits adultery."

[10]The disciples said to him, "If this is the situation between a husband and wife, it is better not to marry."

[11]Jesus replied, "Not everyone can accept this word, but only those to whom it has been given. [12]For there are eunuchs who were born that way, and there are eunuchs who have been made eunuchs by others—and there are those who choose to live like eunuchs for the sake of the kingdom of heaven. The one who can accept this should accept it."

---

a 11 Some manuscripts include here the words of Luke 19:10.   *b* 15 The Greek word for *brother or sister* (*adelphos*) refers here to a fellow disciple, whether man or woman; also in verses 21 and 35.
c 15 Some manuscripts *sins against you*   *d* 16 Deut. 19:15   *e* 18 Or *will have been*   *f* 22 Or *seventy times seven*   *g* 24 Greek *ten thousand talents*; a talent was worth about 20 years of a day laborer's wages.   *h* 28 Greek *a hundred denarii*; a denarius was the usual daily wage of a day laborer (see 20:2).   *i* 4 Gen. 1:27   *j* 5 Gen. 2:24

The Little Children and Jesus

¹³Then people brought little children to Jesus for him to place his hands on them and pray for them. But the disciples rebuked them. ¹⁴Jesus said, "Let the little children come to me, and do not hinder them, for the kingdom of heaven belongs to such as these." ¹⁵When he had placed his hands on them, he went on from there.

The Rich and the Kingdom of God

¹⁶Just then a man came up to Jesus and asked, "Teacher, what good thing must I do to get eternal life?"

¹⁷"Why do you ask me about what is good?" Jesus replied. "There is only One who is good. If you want to enter life, keep the commandments."

¹⁸"Which ones?" he inquired.

Jesus replied, "'You shall not murder, you shall not commit adultery, you shall not steal, you shall not give false testimony, ¹⁹honor your father and mother,'ᵃ and 'love your neighbor as yourself.'ᵇ"

²⁰"All these I have kept," the young man said. "What do I still lack?"

²¹Jesus answered, "If you want to be perfect, go, sell your possessions and give to the poor, and you will have treasure in heaven. Then come, follow me."

²²When the young man heard this, he went away sad, because he had great wealth.

²³Then Jesus said to his disciples, "Truly I tell you, it is hard for someone who is rich to enter the kingdom of heaven. ²⁴Again I tell you, it is easier for a camel to go through the eye of a needle than for someone who is rich to enter the kingdom of God."

²⁵When the disciples heard this, they were greatly astonished and asked, "Who then can be saved?"

²⁶Jesus looked at them and said, "With man this is impossible, but with God all things are possible."

²⁷Peter answered him, "We have left everything to follow you! What then will there be for us?"

²⁸Jesus said to them, "Truly I tell you, at the renewal of all things, when the Son of Man sits on his glorious throne, you who have followed me will also sit on twelve thrones, judging the twelve tribes of Israel. ²⁹And everyone who has left houses or brothers or sisters or father or mother or wifeᶜ or children or fields for my sake will receive a hundred times as much and will inherit eternal life. ³⁰But many who are first will be last, and many who are last will be first.

The Parable of the Workers in the Vineyard

20 "For the kingdom of heaven is like a landowner who went out early in the morning to hire workers for his vineyard. ²He agreed to pay them a denariusᵈ for the day and sent them into his vineyard.

³"About nine in the morning he went out and saw others standing in the marketplace doing nothing. ⁴He told them, 'You also go and work in my vineyard, and I will pay you whatever is right.' ⁵So they went.

"He went out again about noon and about three in the afternoon and did the same thing. ⁶About five in the afternoon he went out and found still others standing around. He asked them, 'Why have you been standing here all day long doing nothing?'

⁷"'Because no one has hired us,' they answered.

"He said to them, 'You also go and work in my vineyard.'

⁸"When evening came, the owner of the vineyard said to his foreman, 'Call the workers and pay them their wages, beginning with the last ones hired and going on to the first.'

⁹"The workers who were hired about five in the afternoon came and each received a denarius. ¹⁰So when those came who were hired first, they expected to receive more. But each one of them also received a denarius. ¹¹When they received it, they began to grumble against the landowner. ¹²'These who were hired last worked only one hour,' they said, 'and you have made them equal to us who have borne the burden of the work and the heat of the day.'

¹³"But he answered one of them, 'I am not being unfair to you, friend. Didn't you agree to work for a denarius? ¹⁴Take your pay and go. I want to give the one who was hired last the same as I gave you. ¹⁵Don't I have the right to do what I want with my own money? Or are you envious because I am generous?'

¹⁶"So the last will be first, and the first will be last."

Jesus Predicts His Death a Third Time

¹⁷Now Jesus was going up to Jerusalem. On the way, he took the Twelve aside and said to them, ¹⁸"We are going up to Jerusalem, and the Son of Man will be delivered over to the chief priests and the teachers of the law. They will condemn him to death ¹⁹and will hand him over to the Gentiles to be mocked and flogged and crucified. On the third day he will be raised to life!"

A Mother's Request

²⁰Then the mother of Zebedee's sons came to Jesus with her sons and, kneeling down, asked a favor of him.

²¹"What is it you want?" he asked.

She said, "Grant that one of these two sons of mine may sit at your right and the other at your left in your kingdom."

²²"You don't know what you are asking," Jesus said to them. "Can you drink the cup I am going to drink?"

"We can," they answered.

²³Jesus said to them, "You will indeed drink from my cup, but to sit at my right or left is not for me to grant. These places belong to

---

ᵃ 19 Exodus 20:12-16; Deut. 5:16-20   ᵇ 19 Lev. 19:18   ᶜ 29 Some manuscripts do not have or wife.
ᵈ 2 A denarius was the usual daily wage of a day laborer.

those for whom they have been prepared by my Father."

²⁴When the ten heard about this, they were indignant with the two brothers. ²⁵Jesus called them together and said, "You know that the rulers of the Gentiles lord it over them, and their high officials exercise authority over them. ²⁶Not so with you. Instead, whoever wants to become great among you must be your servant, ²⁷and whoever wants to be first must be your slave— ²⁸just as the Son of Man did not come to be served, but to serve, and to give his life as a ransom for many."

Two Blind Men Receive Sight

²⁹As Jesus and his disciples were leaving Jericho, a large crowd followed him. ³⁰Two blind men were sitting by the roadside, and when they heard that Jesus was going by, they shouted, "Lord, Son of David, have mercy on us!"

³¹The crowd rebuked them and told them to be quiet, but they shouted all the louder, "Lord, Son of David, have mercy on us!"

³²Jesus stopped and called them. "What do you want me to do for you?" he asked.

³³"Lord," they answered, "we want our sight."

³⁴Jesus had compassion on them and touched their eyes. Immediately they received their sight and followed him.

Jesus Comes to Jerusalem as King

21 As they approached Jerusalem and came to Bethphage on the Mount of Olives, Jesus sent two disciples, ²saying to them, "Go to the village ahead of you, and at once you will find a donkey tied there, with her colt by her. Untie them and bring them to me. ³If anyone says anything to you, say that the Lord needs them, and he will send them right away."

⁴This took place to fulfill what was spoken through the prophet:

⁵ "Say to Daughter Zion,
  'See, your king comes to you,
gentle and riding on a donkey,
  and on a colt, the foal of a donkey.' "ᵃ

⁶The disciples went and did as Jesus had instructed them. ⁷They brought the donkey and the colt and placed their cloaks on them for Jesus to sit on. ⁸A very large crowd spread their cloaks on the road, while others cut branches from the trees and spread them on the road. ⁹The crowds that went ahead of him and those that followed shouted,

"Hosannaᵇ to the Son of David!"

"Blessed is he who comes in the name of the Lord!"ᶜ

"Hosannaᵇ in the highest heaven!"

¹⁰When Jesus entered Jerusalem, the whole city was stirred and asked, "Who is this?"

¹¹The crowds answered, "This is Jesus, the prophet from Nazareth in Galilee."

Jesus at the Temple

¹²Jesus entered the temple courts and drove out all who were buying and selling there. He overturned the tables of the money changers and the benches of those selling doves. ¹³"It is written," he said to them, " 'My house will be called a house of prayer,'ᵈ but you are making it 'a den of robbers.'ᵉ"

¹⁴The blind and the lame came to him at the temple, and he healed them. ¹⁵But when the chief priests and the teachers of the law saw the wonderful things he did and the children shouting in the temple courts, "Hosanna to the Son of David," they were indignant.

¹⁶"Do you hear what these children are saying?" they asked him.

"Yes," replied Jesus, "have you never read,

" 'From the lips of children and infants
  you, Lord, have called forth your
    praise'ᶠ?"

¹⁷And he left them and went out of the city to Bethany, where he spent the night.

Jesus Curses a Fig Tree

¹⁸Early in the morning, as Jesus was on his way back to the city, he was hungry. ¹⁹Seeing a fig tree by the road, he went up to it but found nothing on it except leaves. Then he said to it, "May you never bear fruit again!" Immediately the tree withered.

²⁰When the disciples saw this, they were amazed. "How did the fig tree wither so quickly?" they asked.

²¹Jesus replied, "Truly I tell you, if you have faith and do not doubt, not only can you do what was done to the fig tree, but also you can say to this mountain, 'Go, throw yourself into the sea,' and it will be done. ²²If you believe, you will receive whatever you ask for in prayer."

The Authority of Jesus Questioned

²³Jesus entered the temple courts, and, while he was teaching, the chief priests and the elders of the people came to him. "By what authority are you doing these things?" they asked. "And who gave you this authority?"

²⁴Jesus replied, "I will also ask you one question. If you answer me, I will tell you by what authority I am doing these things. ²⁵John's baptism—where did it come from? Was it from heaven, or of human origin?"

They discussed it among themselves and said, "If we say, 'From heaven,' he will ask, 'Then why didn't you believe him?' ²⁶But if we say, 'Of human origin'—we are afraid of the people, for they all hold that John was a prophet."

²⁷So they answered Jesus, "We don't know."

Then he said, "Neither will I tell you by what authority I am doing these things.

ᵃ 5 Zech. 9:9   ᵇ 9 A Hebrew expression meaning "Save!" which became an exclamation of praise; also in verse 15   ᶜ 9 Psalm 118:25;26   ᵈ 13 Isaiah 56:7   ᵉ 13 Jer. 7:11   ᶠ 16 Psalm 8:2 (see Septuagint)

The Parable of the Two Sons

28"What do you think? There was a man who had two sons. He went to the first and said, 'Son, go and work today in the vineyard.'

29"'I will not,' he answered, but later he changed his mind and went.

30"Then the father went to the other son and said the same thing. He answered, 'I will, sir,' but he did not go.

31"Which of the two did what his father wanted?"

"The first," they answered.

Jesus said to them, "Truly I tell you, the tax collectors and the prostitutes are entering the kingdom of God ahead of you. 32For John came to you to show you the way of righteousness, and you did not believe him, but the tax collectors and the prostitutes did. And even after you saw this, you did not repent and believe him.

The Parable of the Tenants

33"Listen to another parable: There was a landowner who planted a vineyard. He put a wall around it, dug a winepress in it and built a watchtower. Then he rented the vineyard to some farmers and moved to another place. 34When the harvest time approached, he sent his servants to the tenants to collect his fruit.

35"The tenants seized his servants; they beat one, killed another, and stoned a third. 36Then he sent other servants to them, more than the first time, and the tenants treated them the same way. 37Last of all, he sent his son to them. 'They will respect my son,' he said.

38"But when the tenants saw the son, they said to each other, 'This is the heir. Come, let's kill him and take his inheritance.' 39So they took him and threw him out of the vineyard and killed him.

40"Therefore, when the owner of the vineyard comes, what will he do to those tenants?"

41"He will bring those wretches to a wretched end," they replied, "and he will rent the vineyard to other tenants, who will give him his share of the crop at harvest time."

42Jesus said to them, "Have you never read in the Scriptures:

"'The stone the builders rejected
has become the cornerstone;
the Lord has done this,
and it is marvelous in our eyes'*a*?

43"Therefore I tell you that the kingdom of God will be taken away from you and given to a people who will produce its fruit. 44Anyone who falls on this stone will be broken to pieces; anyone on whom it falls will be crushed."*b*

45When the chief priests and the Pharisees heard Jesus' parables, they knew he was talking about them. 46They looked for a way to arrest him, but they were afraid of the crowd because the people held that he was a prophet.

The Parable of the Wedding Banquet

22 Jesus spoke to them again in parables, saying: 2"The kingdom of heaven is like a king who prepared a wedding banquet for his son. 3He sent his servants to those who had been invited to the banquet to tell them to come, but they refused to come.

4"Then he sent some more servants and said, 'Tell those who have been invited that I have prepared my dinner: My oxen and fattened cattle have been butchered, and everything is ready. Come to the wedding banquet.'

5"But they paid no attention and went off—one to his field, another to his business. 6The rest seized his servants, mistreated them and killed them. 7The king was enraged. He sent his army and destroyed those murderers and burned their city.

8"Then he said to his servants, 'The wedding banquet is ready, but those I invited did not deserve to come. 9So go to the street corners and invite to the banquet anyone you find.' 10So the servants went out into the streets and gathered all the people they could find, the bad as well as the good, and the wedding hall was filled with guests.

11"But when the king came in to see the guests, he noticed a man there who was not wearing wedding clothes. 12He asked, 'How did you get in here without wedding clothes, friend?' The man was speechless.

13"Then the king told the attendants, 'Tie him hand and foot, and throw him outside, into the darkness, where there will be weeping and gnashing of teeth.'

14"For many are invited, but few are chosen."

Paying the Imperial Tax to Caesar

15Then the Pharisees went out and laid plans to trap him in his words. 16They sent their disciples to him along with the Herodians. "Teacher," they said, "we know that you are a man of integrity and that you teach the way of God in accordance with the truth. You aren't swayed by others, because you pay no attention to who they are. 17Tell us then, what is your opinion? Is it right to pay the imperial tax*c* to Caesar or not?"

18But Jesus, knowing their evil intent, said, "You hypocrites, why are you trying to trap me? 19Show me the coin used for paying the tax." They brought him a denarius, 20and he asked them, "Whose image is this? And whose inscription?"

21"Caesar's," they replied.

Then he said to them, "So give back to Caesar what is Caesar's, and to God what is God's."

22When they heard this, they were amazed. So they left him and went away.

Marriage at the Resurrection

23That same day the Sadducees, who say there is no resurrection, came to him with a

---

a 42 Psalm 118:22,23   *b* 44 Some manuscripts do not have verse 44.   *c* 17 A special tax levied on subject peoples, not on Roman citizens

question. 24"Teacher," they said, "Moses told us that if a man dies without having children, his brother must marry the widow and raise up offspring for him. 25Now there were seven brothers among us. The first one married and died, and since he had no children, he left his wife to his brother. 26The same thing happened to the second and third brother, right on down to the seventh. 27Finally, the woman died. 28Now then, at the resurrection, whose wife will she be of the seven, since all of them were married to her?"

29Jesus replied, "You are in error because you do not know the Scriptures or the power of God. 30At the resurrection people will neither marry nor be given in marriage; they will be like the angels in heaven. 31But about the resurrection of the dead—have you not read what God said to you, 32'I am the God of Abraham, the God of Isaac, and the God of Jacob'ᵃ? He is not the God of the dead but of the living."

33When the crowds heard this, they were astonished at his teaching.

The Greatest Commandment

34Hearing that Jesus had silenced the Sadducees, the Pharisees got together. 35One of them, an expert in the law, tested him with this question: 36"Teacher, which is the greatest commandment in the Law?"

37Jesus replied: "'Love the Lord your God with all your heart and with all your soul and with all your mind.'ᵇ 38This is the first and greatest commandment. 39And the second is like it: 'Love your neighbor as yourself.'ᶜ 40All the Law and the Prophets hang on these two commandments."

Whose Son Is the Messiah?

41While the Pharisees were gathered together, Jesus asked them, 42"What do you think about the Messiah? Whose son is he?"

"The son of David," they replied.

43He said to them, "How is it then that David, speaking by the Spirit, calls him 'Lord'? For he says,

44 "'The Lord said to my Lord:
  "Sit at my right hand
until I put your enemies
  under your feet."'ᵈ

45If then David calls him 'Lord,' how can he be his son?" 46No one could say a word in reply, and from that day on no one dared to ask him any more questions.

A Warning Against Hypocrisy

23 Then Jesus said to the crowds and to his disciples: 2"The teachers of the law and the Pharisees sit in Moses' seat. 3So you must be careful to do everything they tell you. But do not do what they do, for they do not practice what they preach. 4They tie up heavy, cumbersome loads and put them on other people's shoulders, but they themselves are not willing to lift a finger to move them.

5"Everything they do is done for people to see: They make their phylacteriesᵉ wide and the tassels on their garments long; 6they love the place of honor at banquets and the most important seats in the synagogues; 7they love to be greeted with respect in the marketplaces and to be called 'Rabbi' by others.

8"But you are not to be called 'Rabbi,' for you have one Teacher, and you are all brothers. 9And do not call anyone on earth 'father,' for you have one Father, and he is in heaven. 10Nor are you to be called instructors, for you have one Instructor, the Messiah. 11The greatest among you will be your servant. 12For those who exalt themselves will be humbled, and those who humble themselves will be exalted.

Seven Woes on the Teachers of the Law and the Pharisees

13"Woe to you, teachers of the law and Pharisees, you hypocrites! You shut the door of the kingdom of heaven in people's faces. You yourselves do not enter, nor will you let those enter who are trying to. [14]ᶠ

15"Woe to you, teachers of the law and Pharisees, you hypocrites! You travel over land and sea to win a single convert, and when you have succeeded, you make them twice as much a child of hell as you are.

16"Woe to you, blind guides! You say, 'If anyone swears by the temple, it means nothing; but anyone who swears by the gold of the temple is bound by that oath.' 17You blind fools! Which is greater: the gold, or the temple that makes the gold sacred? 18You also say, 'If anyone swears by the altar, it means nothing; but anyone who swears by the gift on the altar is bound by that oath.' 19You blind men! Which is greater: the gift, or the altar that makes the gift sacred? 20Therefore, anyone who swears by the altar swears by it and by everything on it. 21And anyone who swears by the temple swears by it and by the one who dwells in it. 22And anyone who swears by heaven swears by God's throne and by the one who sits on it.

23"Woe to you, teachers of the law and Pharisees, you hypocrites! You give a tenth of your spices—mint, dill and cumin. But you have neglected the more important matters of the law—justice, mercy and faithfulness. You should have practiced the latter, without neglecting the former. 24You blind guides! You strain out a gnat but swallow a camel.

25"Woe to you, teachers of the law and Pharisees, you hypocrites! You clean the outside of the cup and dish, but inside they are full of greed and self-indulgence. 26Blind Pharisee! First clean the inside of the cup and dish, and then the outside also will be clean.

27"Woe to you, teachers of the law and Pharisees, you hypocrites! You are like

---

ᵃ 32 Exodus 3:6   ᵇ 37 Deut. 6:5   ᶜ 39 Lev. 19:18   ᵈ 44 Psalm 110:1   ᵉ 5 That is, boxes containing Scripture verses, worn on forehead and arm   ᶠ 14 Some manuscripts include here words similar to Mark 12:40 and Luke 20:47.

whitewashed tombs, which look beautiful on the outside but on the inside are full of the bones of the dead and everything unclean. [28]In the same way, on the outside you appear to people as righteous but on the inside you are full of hypocrisy and wickedness.

[29]"Woe to you, teachers of the law and Pharisees, you hypocrites! You build tombs for the prophets and decorate the graves of the righteous. [30]And you say, 'If we had lived in the days of our ancestors, we would not have taken part with them in shedding the blood of the prophets.' [31]So you testify against yourselves that you are the descendants of those who murdered the prophets. [32]Go ahead, then, and complete what your ancestors started!

[33]"You snakes! You brood of vipers! How will you escape being condemned to hell? [34]Therefore I am sending you prophets and sages and teachers. Some of them you will kill and crucify; others you will flog in your synagogues and pursue from town to town. [35]And so upon you will come all the righteous blood that has been shed on earth, from the blood of righteous Abel to the blood of Zechariah son of Berekiah, whom you murdered between the temple and the altar. [36]Truly I tell you, all this will come on this generation.

[37]"Jerusalem, Jerusalem, you who kill the prophets and stone those sent to you, how often I have longed to gather your children together, as a hen gathers her chicks under her wings, and you were not willing. [38]Look, your house is left to you desolate. [39]For I tell you, you will not see me again until you say, 'Blessed is he who comes in the name of the Lord.'[a]"

The Destruction of the Temple and Signs of the End Times

24 Jesus left the temple and was walking away when his disciples came up to him to call his attention to its buildings. [2]"Do you see all these things?" he asked. "Truly I tell you, not one stone here will be left on another; every one will be thrown down."

[3]As Jesus was sitting on the Mount of Olives, the disciples came to him privately. "Tell us," they said, "when will this happen, and what will be the sign of your coming and of the end of the age?"

[4]Jesus answered: "Watch out that no one deceives you. [5]For many will come in my name, claiming, 'I am the Messiah,' and will deceive many. [6]You will hear of wars and rumors of wars, but see to it that you are not alarmed. Such things must happen, but the end is still to come. [7]Nation will rise against nation, and kingdom against kingdom. There will be famines and earthquakes in various places. [8]All these are the beginning of birth pains.

[9]"Then you will be handed over to be persecuted and put to death, and you will be hated by all nations because of me. [10]At that time many will turn away from the faith and will betray and hate each other, [11]and many

false prophets will appear and deceive many people. [12]Because of the increase of wickedness, the love of most will grow cold, [13]but the one who stands firm to the end will be saved. [14]And this gospel of the kingdom will be preached in the whole world as a testimony to all nations, and then the end will come.

[15]"So when you see standing in the holy place 'the abomination that causes desolation,'[b] spoken of through the prophet Daniel—let the reader understand— [16]then let those who are in Judea flee to the mountains. [17]Let no one on the housetop go down to take anything out of the house. [18]Let no one in the field go back to get their cloak. [19]How dreadful it will be in those days for pregnant women and nursing mothers! [20]Pray that your flight will not take place in winter or on the Sabbath. [21]For then there will be great distress, unequaled from the beginning of the world until now—and never to be equaled again.

[22]"If those days had not been cut short, no one would survive, but for the sake of the elect those days will be shortened. [23]At that time if anyone says to you, 'Look, here is the Messiah!' or, 'There he is!' do not believe it. [24]For false messiahs and false prophets will appear and perform great signs and wonders to deceive, if possible, even the elect. [25]See, I have told you ahead of time.

[26]"So if anyone tells you, 'There he is, out in the wilderness,' do not go out; or, 'Here he is, in the inner rooms,' do not believe it. [27]For as lightning that comes from the east is visible even in the west, so will be the coming of the Son of Man. [28]Wherever there is a carcass, there the vultures will gather.

[29]"Immediately after the distress of those days

> " 'the sun will be darkened,
>   and the moon will not give its light;
> the stars will fall from the sky,
>   and the heavenly bodies will be
>   shaken.'[c]

[30]"Then will appear the sign of the Son of Man in heaven. And then all the peoples of the earth[d] will mourn when they see the Son of Man coming on the clouds of heaven, with power and great glory.[e] [31]And he will send his angels with a loud trumpet call, and they will gather his elect from the four winds, from one end of the heavens to the other.

[32]"Now learn this lesson from the fig tree: As soon as its twigs get tender and its leaves come out, you know that summer is near. [33]Even so, when you see all these things, you know that it[f] is near, right at the door. [34]Truly I tell you, this generation will certainly not pass away until all these things have happened. [35]Heaven and earth will pass away, but my words will never pass away.

The Day and Hour Unknown

[36]"But about that day or hour no one knows, not even the angels in heaven, nor the Son,[g]

---

a 39 Psalm 118:26   *b 15* Daniel 9:27; 11:31; 12:11   *c 29* Isaiah 13:10; 34:4   *d 30* Or *the tribes of the land*   *e 30* See Daniel 7:13-14.   *f 33* Or *he*   *g 36* Some manuscripts do not have *nor the Son*.

but only the Father. ³⁷As it was in the days of Noah, so it will be at the coming of the Son of Man. ³⁸For in the days before the flood, people were eating and drinking, marrying and giving in marriage, up to the day Noah entered the ark; ³⁹and they knew nothing about what would happen until the flood came and took them all away. That is how it will be at the coming of the Son of Man. ⁴⁰Two men will be in the field; one will be taken and the other left. ⁴¹Two women will be grinding with a hand mill; one will be taken and the other left.

⁴²"Therefore keep watch, because you do not know on what day your Lord will come. ⁴³But understand this: If the owner of the house had known at what time of night the thief was coming, he would have kept watch and would not have let his house be broken into. ⁴⁴So you also must be ready, because the Son of Man will come at an hour when you do not expect him.

⁴⁵"Who then is the faithful and wise servant, whom the master has put in charge of the servants in his household to give them their food at the proper time? ⁴⁶It will be good for that servant whose master finds him doing so when he returns. ⁴⁷Truly I tell you, he will put him in charge of all his possessions. ⁴⁸But suppose that servant is wicked and says to himself, 'My master is staying away a long time,' ⁴⁹and he then begins to beat his fellow servants and to eat and drink with drunkards. ⁵⁰The master of that servant will come on a day when he does not expect him and at an hour he is not aware of. ⁵¹He will cut him to pieces and assign him a place with the hypocrites, where there will be weeping and gnashing of teeth.

The Parable of the Ten Virgins

25 "At that time the kingdom of heaven will be like ten virgins who took their lamps and went out to meet the bridegroom. ²Five of them were foolish and five were wise. ³The foolish ones took their lamps but did not take any oil with them. ⁴The wise ones, however, took oil in jars along with their lamps. ⁵The bridegroom was a long time in coming, and they all became drowsy and fell asleep.

⁶"At midnight the cry rang out: 'Here's the bridegroom! Come out to meet him!'

⁷"Then all the virgins woke up and trimmed their lamps. ⁸The foolish ones said to the wise, 'Give us some of your oil; our lamps are going out.'

⁹"'No,' they replied, 'there may not be enough for both us and you. Instead, go to those who sell oil and buy some for yourselves.'

¹⁰"But while they were on their way to buy the oil, the bridegroom arrived. The virgins who were ready went in with him to the wedding banquet. And the door was shut.

¹¹"Later the others also came. 'Lord, Lord,' they said, 'open the door for us!'

¹²"But he replied, 'Truly I tell you, I don't know you.'

¹³"Therefore keep watch, because you do not know the day or the hour.

The Parable of the Bags of Gold

¹⁴"Again, it will be like a man going on a journey, who called his servants and entrusted his wealth to them. ¹⁵To one he gave five bags of gold, to another two bags, and to another one bag,^a each according to his ability. Then he went on his journey. ¹⁶The man who had received five bags of gold went at once and put his money to work and gained five bags more. ¹⁷So also, the one with two bags of gold gained two more. ¹⁸But the man who had received one bag went off, dug a hole in the ground and hid his master's money.

¹⁹"After a long time the master of those servants returned and settled accounts with them. ²⁰The man who had received five bags of gold brought the other five. 'Master,' he said, 'you entrusted me with five bags of gold. See, I have gained five more.'

²¹"His master replied, 'Well done, good and faithful servant! You have been faithful with a few things; I will put you in charge of many things. Come and share your master's happiness!'

²²"The man with two bags of gold also came. 'Master,' he said, 'you entrusted me with two bags of gold; see, I have gained two more.'

²³"His master replied, 'Well done, good and faithful servant! You have been faithful with a few things; I will put you in charge of many things. Come and share your master's happiness!'

²⁴"Then the man who had received one bag of gold came. 'Master,' he said, 'I knew that you are a hard man, harvesting where you have not sown and gathering where you have not scattered seed. ²⁵So I was afraid and went out and hid your gold in the ground. See, here is what belongs to you.'

²⁶"His master replied, 'You wicked, lazy servant! So you knew that I harvest where I have not sown and gather where I have not scattered seed? ²⁷Well then, you should have put my money on deposit with the bankers, so that when I returned I would have received it back with interest.

²⁸"'So take the bag of gold from him and give it to the one who has ten bags. ²⁹For whoever has will be given more, and they will have an abundance. Whoever does not have, even what they have will be taken from them. ³⁰And throw that worthless servant outside, into the darkness, where there will be weeping and gnashing of teeth.'

The Sheep and the Goats

³¹"When the Son of Man comes in his glory, and all the angels with him, he will sit on his glorious throne. ³²All the nations will be gathered before him, and he will separate the people one from another as a shepherd separates the sheep from the goats. ³³He will

---

^a 15 Greek *five talents . . . two talents . . . one talent*; also throughout this parable; a talent was worth about 20 years of a day laborer's wage.

put the sheep on his right and the goats on his left.

34"Then the King will say to those on his right, 'Come, you who are blessed by my Father; take your inheritance, the kingdom prepared for you since the creation of the world. 35For I was hungry and you gave me something to eat, I was thirsty and you gave me something to drink, I was a stranger and you invited me in, 36I needed clothes and you clothed me, I was sick and you looked after me, I was in prison and you came to visit me.'

37"Then the righteous will answer him, 'Lord, when did we see you hungry and feed you, or thirsty and give you something to drink? 38When did we see you a stranger and invite you in, or needing clothes and clothe you? 39When did we see you sick or in prison and go to visit you?'

40"The King will reply, 'Truly I tell you, whatever you did for one of the least of these brothers and sisters of mine, you did for me.'

41"Then he will say to those on his left, 'Depart from me, you who are cursed, into the eternal fire prepared for the devil and his angels. 42For I was hungry and you gave me nothing to eat, I was thirsty and you gave me nothing to drink, 43I was a stranger and you did not invite me in, I needed clothes and you did not clothe me, I was sick and in prison and you did not look after me.'

44"They also will answer, 'Lord, when did we see you hungry or thirsty or a stranger or needing clothes or sick or in prison, and did not help you?'

45"He will reply, 'Truly I tell you, whatever you did not do for one of the least of these, you did not do for me.'

46"Then they will go away to eternal punishment, but the righteous to eternal life."

The Plot Against Jesus

26 When Jesus had finished saying all these things, he said to his disciples, 2"As you know, the Passover is two days away—and the Son of Man will be handed over to be crucified."

3Then the chief priests and the elders of the people assembled in the palace of the high priest, whose name was Caiaphas, 4and they schemed to arrest Jesus secretly and kill him. 5"But not during the festival," they said, "or there may be a riot among the people."

Jesus Anointed at Bethany

6While Jesus was in Bethany in the home of Simon the Leper, 7a woman came to him with an alabaster jar of very expensive perfume, which she poured on his head as he was reclining at the table.

8When the disciples saw this, they were indignant. "Why this waste?" they asked. 9"This perfume could have been sold at a high price and the money given to the poor."

10Aware of this, Jesus said to them, "Why are you bothering this woman? She has done

a beautiful thing to me. 11The poor you will always have with you,a but you will not always have me. 12When she poured this perfume on my body, she did it to prepare me for burial. 13Truly I tell you, wherever this gospel is preached throughout the world, what she has done will also be told, in memory of her."

Judas Agrees to Betray Jesus

14Then one of the Twelve—the one called Judas Iscariot—went to the chief priests 15and asked, "What are you willing to give me if I deliver him over to you?" So they counted out for him thirty pieces of silver. 16From then on Judas watched for an opportunity to hand him over.

The Last Supper

17On the first day of the Festival of Unleavened Bread, the disciples came to Jesus and asked, "Where do you want us to make preparations for you to eat the Passover?"

18He replied, "Go into the city to a certain man and tell him, 'The Teacher says: My appointed time is near. I am going to celebrate the Passover with my disciples at your house.'" 19So the disciples did as Jesus had directed them and prepared the Passover.

20When evening came, Jesus was reclining at the table with the Twelve. 21And while they were eating, he said, "Truly I tell you, one of you will betray me."

22They were very sad and began to say to him one after the other, "Surely you don't mean me, Lord?"

23Jesus replied, "The one who has dipped his hand into the bowl with me will betray me. 24The Son of Man will go just as it is written about him. But woe to that man who betrays the Son of Man! It would be better for him if he had not been born."

25Then Judas, the one who would betray him, said, "Surely you don't mean me, Rabbi?"
Jesus answered, "You have said so."

26While they were eating, Jesus took bread, and when he had given thanks, he broke it and gave it to his disciples, saying, "Take and eat; this is my body."

27Then he took a cup, and when he had given thanks, he gave it to them, saying, "Drink from it, all of you. 28This is my blood of theb covenant, which is poured out for many for the forgiveness of sins. 29I tell you, I will not drink from this fruit of the vine from now on until that day when I drink it new with you in my Father's kingdom."

30When they had sung a hymn, they went out to the Mount of Olives.

Jesus Predicts Peter's Denial

31Then Jesus told them, "This very night you will all fall away on account of me, for it is written:

"'I will strike the shepherd,
    and the sheep of the flock will be
        scattered.'c

---

a 11 See Deut. 15:11.   b 28 Some manuscripts *the new*   c 31 Zech. 13:7

32But after I have risen, I will go ahead of you into Galilee."

33Peter replied, "Even if all fall away on account of you, I never will."

34"Truly I tell you," Jesus answered, "this very night, before the rooster crows, you will disown me three times."

35But Peter declared, "Even if I have to die with you, I will never disown you." And all the other disciples said the same.

Gethsemane

36Then Jesus went with his disciples to a place called Gethsemane, and he said to them, "Sit here while I go over there and pray." 37He took Peter and the two sons of Zebedee along with him, and he began to be sorrowful and troubled. 38Then he said to them, "My soul is overwhelmed with sorrow to the point of death. Stay here and keep watch with me."

39Going a little farther, he fell with his face to the ground and prayed, "My Father, if it is possible, may this cup be taken from me. Yet not as I will, but as you will."

40Then he returned to his disciples and found them sleeping. "Couldn't you men keep watch with me for one hour?" he asked Peter. 41"Watch and pray so that you will not fall into temptation. The spirit is willing, but the flesh is weak."

42He went away a second time and prayed, "My Father, if it is not possible for this cup to be taken away unless I drink it, may your will be done."

43When he came back, he again found them sleeping, because their eyes were heavy. 44So he left them and went away once more and prayed the third time, saying the same thing.

45Then he returned to the disciples and said to them, "Are you still sleeping and resting? Look, the hour has come, and the Son of Man is delivered into the hands of sinners. 46Rise! Let us go! Here comes my betrayer!"

Jesus Arrested

47While he was still speaking, Judas, one of the Twelve, arrived. With him was a large crowd armed with swords and clubs, sent from the chief priests and the elders of the people. 48Now the betrayer had arranged a signal with them: "The one I kiss is the man; arrest him." 49Going at once to Jesus, Judas said, "Greetings, Rabbi!" and kissed him.

50Jesus replied, "Do what you came for, friend."[a]

Then the men stepped forward, seized Jesus and arrested him. 51With that, one of Jesus' companions reached for his sword, drew it out and struck the servant of the high priest, cutting off his ear.

52"Put your sword back in its place," Jesus said to him, "for all who draw the sword will die by the sword. 53Do you think I cannot call on my Father, and he will at once put at my disposal more than twelve legions of angels? 54But how then would the Scriptures be fulfilled that say it must happen in this way?"

55In that hour Jesus said to the crowd, "Am I leading a rebellion, that you have come out with swords and clubs to capture me? Every day I sat in the temple courts teaching, and you did not arrest me. 56But this has all taken place that the writings of the prophets might be fulfilled." Then all the disciples deserted him and fled.

Jesus Before the Sanhedrin

57Those who had arrested Jesus took him to Caiaphas the high priest, where the teachers of the law and the elders had assembled. 58But Peter followed him at a distance, right up to the courtyard of the high priest. He entered and sat down with the guards to see the outcome.

59The chief priests and the whole Sanhedrin were looking for false evidence against Jesus so that they could put him to death. 60But they did not find any, though many false witnesses came forward.

Finally two came forward 61and declared, "This fellow said, 'I am able to destroy the temple of God and rebuild it in three days.'"

62Then the high priest stood up and said to Jesus, "Are you not going to answer? What is this testimony that these men are bringing against you?" 63But Jesus remained silent.

The high priest said to him, "I charge you under oath by the living God: Tell us if you are the Messiah, the Son of God."

64"You have said so," Jesus replied. "But I say to all of you: From now on you will see the Son of Man sitting at the right hand of the Mighty One and coming on the clouds of heaven."[b]

65Then the high priest tore his clothes and said, "He has spoken blasphemy! Why do we need any more witnesses? Look, now you have heard the blasphemy. 66What do you think?"

"He is worthy of death," they answered.

67Then they spit in his face and struck him with their fists. Others slapped him 68and said, "Prophesy to us, Messiah. Who hit you?"

Peter Disowns Jesus

69Now Peter was sitting out in the courtyard, and a servant girl came to him. "You also were with Jesus of Galilee," she said.

70But he denied it before them all. "I don't know what you're talking about," he said.

71Then he went out to the gateway, where another servant girl saw him and said to the people there, "This fellow was with Jesus of Nazareth."

72He denied it again, with an oath: "I don't know the man!"

73After a little while, those standing there went up to Peter and said, "Surely you are one of them; your accent gives you away."

74Then he began to call down curses, and he swore to them, "I don't know the man!"

Immediately a rooster crowed. 75Then Peter remembered the word Jesus had spoken: "Before the rooster crows, you will disown

---

a 50 Or *"Why have you come, friend?"*   *b* 64 See Psalm 110:1; Daniel 7:13.

me three times." And he went outside and wept bitterly.

Judas Hangs Himself

27 Early in the morning, all the chief priests and the elders of the people made their plans how to have Jesus executed. ²So they bound him, led him away and handed him over to Pilate the governor.

³When Judas, who had betrayed him, saw that Jesus was condemned, he was seized with remorse and returned the thirty pieces of silver to the chief priests and the elders. ⁴"I have sinned," he said, "for I have betrayed innocent blood."

"What is that to us?" they replied. "That's your responsibility."

⁵So Judas threw the money into the temple and left. Then he went away and hanged himself.

⁶The chief priests picked up the coins and said, "It is against the law to put this into the treasury, since it is blood money." ⁷So they decided to use the money to buy the potter's field as a burial place for foreigners. ⁸That is why it has been called the Field of Blood to this day. ⁹Then what was spoken by Jeremiah the prophet was fulfilled: "They took the thirty pieces of silver, the price set on him by the people of Israel, ¹⁰and they used them to buy the potter's field, as the Lord commanded me."ᵃ

Jesus Before Pilate

¹¹Meanwhile Jesus stood before the governor, and the governor asked him, "Are you the king of the Jews?"

"You have said so," Jesus replied.

¹²When he was accused by the chief priests and the elders, he gave no answer. ¹³Then Pilate asked him, "Don't you hear the testimony they are bringing against you?" ¹⁴But Jesus made no reply, not even to a single charge—to the great amazement of the governor.

¹⁵Now it was the governor's custom at the festival to release a prisoner chosen by the crowd. ¹⁶At that time they had a well-known prisoner whose name was Jesusᵇ Barabbas. ¹⁷So when the crowd had gathered, Pilate asked them, "Which one do you want me to release to you: Jesus Barabbas, or Jesus who is called the Messiah?" ¹⁸For he knew it was out of self-interest that they had handed Jesus over to him.

¹⁹While Pilate was sitting on the judge's seat, his wife sent him this message: "Don't have anything to do with that innocent man, for I have suffered a great deal today in a dream because of him."

²⁰But the chief priests and the elders persuaded the crowd to ask for Barabbas and to have Jesus executed.

²¹"Which of the two do you want me to release to you?" asked the governor.

"Barabbas," they answered.

²²"What shall I do, then, with Jesus who is called the Messiah?" Pilate asked.

They all answered, "Crucify him!"

²³"Why? What crime has he committed?" asked Pilate.

But they shouted all the louder, "Crucify him!"

²⁴When Pilate saw that he was getting nowhere, but that instead an uproar was starting, he took water and washed his hands in front of the crowd. "I am innocent of this man's blood," he said. "It is your responsibility!"

²⁵All the people answered, "His blood is on us and on our children!"

²⁶Then he released Barabbas to them. But he had Jesus flogged, and handed him over to be crucified.

The Soldiers Mock Jesus

²⁷Then the governor's soldiers took Jesus into the Praetorium and gathered the whole company of soldiers around him. ²⁸They stripped him and put a scarlet robe on him, ²⁹and then twisted together a crown of thorns and set it on his head. They put a staff in his right hand. Then they knelt in front of him and mocked him. "Hail, king of the Jews!" they said. ³⁰They spit on him, and took the staff and struck him on the head again and again. ³¹After they had mocked him, they took off the robe and put his own clothes on him. Then they led him away to crucify him.

The Crucifixion of Jesus

³²As they were going out, they met a man from Cyrene, named Simon, and they forced him to carry the cross. ³³They came to a place called Golgotha (which means "the place of the skull"). ³⁴There they offered Jesus wine to drink, mixed with gall; but after tasting it, he refused to drink it. ³⁵When they had crucified him, they divided up his clothes by casting lots. ³⁶And sitting down, they kept watch over him there. ³⁷Above his head they placed the written charge against him: THIS IS JESUS, THE KING OF THE JEWS.

³⁸Two rebels were crucified with him, one on his right and one on his left. ³⁹Those who passed by hurled insults at him, shaking their heads ⁴⁰and saying, "You who are going to destroy the temple and build it in three days, save yourself! Come down from the cross, if you are the Son of God!" ⁴¹In the same way the chief priests, the teachers of the law and the elders mocked him. ⁴²"He saved others," they said, "but he can't save himself! He's the king of Israel! Let him come down now from the cross, and we will believe in him. ⁴³He trusts in God. Let God rescue him now if he wants him, for he said, 'I am the Son of God.'" ⁴⁴In the same way the rebels who were crucified with him also heaped insults on him.

The Death of Jesus

⁴⁵From noon until three in the afternoon darkness came over all the land. ⁴⁶About three in the afternoon Jesus cried out in a loud

---

ᵃ 10 See Zech. 11:12,13; Jer. 19:1-13; 32:6-9.   ᵇ 16 Many manuscripts do not have Jesus; also in verse 17.

voice, *"Eli, Eli,[a] lema sabachthani?"* (which means "My God, my God, why have you forsaken me?").[b] [47]When some of those standing there heard this, they said, "He's calling Elijah."

[48]Immediately one of them ran and got a sponge. He filled it with wine vinegar, put it on a staff, and offered it to Jesus to drink. [49]The rest said, "Now leave him alone. Let's see if Elijah comes to save him."

[50]And when Jesus had cried out again in a loud voice, he gave up his spirit.

[51]At that moment the curtain of the temple was torn in two from top to bottom. The earth shook, the rocks split [52]and the tombs broke open. The bodies of many holy people who had died were raised to life. [53]They came out of the tombs after Jesus' resurrection and[c] went into the holy city and appeared to many people.

[54]When the centurion and those with him who were guarding Jesus saw the earthquake and all that had happened, they were terrified, and exclaimed, "Surely he was the Son of God!"

[55]Many women were there, watching from a distance. They had followed Jesus from Galilee to care for his needs. [56]Among them were Mary Magdalene, Mary the mother of James and Joseph,[d] and the mother of Zebedee's sons.

The Burial of Jesus

[57]As evening approached, there came a rich man from Arimathea, named Joseph, who had himself become a disciple of Jesus. [58]Going to Pilate, he asked for Jesus' body, and Pilate ordered that it be given to him. [59]Joseph took the body, wrapped it in a clean linen cloth, [60]and placed it in his own new tomb that he had cut out of the rock. He rolled a big stone in front of the entrance to the tomb and went away. [61]Mary Magdalene and the other Mary were sitting there opposite the tomb.

The Guard at the Tomb

[62]The next day, the one after Preparation Day, the chief priests and the Pharisees went to Pilate. [63]"Sir," they said, "we remember that while he was still alive that deceiver said, 'After three days I will rise again.' [64]So give the order for the tomb to be made secure until the third day. Otherwise, his disciples may come and steal the body and tell the people that he has been raised from the dead. This last deception will be worse than the first."

[65]"Take a guard," Pilate answered. "Go, make the tomb as secure as you know how." [66]So they went and made the tomb secure by putting a seal on the stone and posting the guard.

Jesus Has Risen

28 After the Sabbath, at dawn on the first day of the week, Mary Magdalene and the other Mary went to look at the tomb.

[2]There was a violent earthquake, for an angel of the Lord came down from heaven and, going to the tomb, rolled back the stone and sat on it. [3]His appearance was like lightning, and his clothes were white as snow. [4]The guards were so afraid of him that they shook and became like dead men.

[5]The angel said to the women, "Do not be afraid, for I know that you are looking for Jesus, who was crucified. [6]He is not here; he has risen, just as he said. Come and see the place where he lay. [7]Then go quickly and tell his disciples: 'He has risen from the dead and is going ahead of you into Galilee. There you will see him.' Now I have told you."

[8]So the women hurried away from the tomb, afraid yet filled with joy, and ran to tell his disciples. [9]Suddenly Jesus met them. "Greetings," he said. They came to him, clasped his feet and worshiped him. [10]Then Jesus said to them, "Do not be afraid. Go and tell my brothers to go to Galilee; there they will see me."

The Guards' Report

[11]While the women were on their way, some of the guards went into the city and reported to the chief priests everything that had happened. [12]When the chief priests met with the elders and devised a plan, they gave the soldiers a large sum of money, [13]telling them, "You are to say, 'His disciples came during the night and stole him away while we were asleep.' [14]If this report gets to the governor, we will satisfy him and keep you out of trouble." [15]So the soldiers took the money and did as they were instructed. And this story has been widely circulated among the Jews to this very day.

The Great Commission

[16]Then the eleven disciples went to Galilee, to the mountain where Jesus had told them to go. [17]When they saw him, they worshiped him; but some doubted. [18]Then Jesus came to them and said, "All authority in heaven and on earth has been given to me. [19]Therefore go and make disciples of all nations, baptizing them in the name of the Father and of the Son and of the Holy Spirit, [20]and teaching them to obey everything I have commanded you. And surely I am with you always, to the very end of the age."

---

[a] 46 Some manuscripts *Eloi, Eloi*   [b] 46 Psalm 22:1   [c] 53 Or *tombs, and after Jesus' resurrection*
they   [d] 56 Greek *Joses,* a variant of *Joseph*

Mark

John the Baptist Prepares the Way

1 The beginning of the good news about Jesus the Messiah,[a] the Son of God,[b] ²as it is written in Isaiah the prophet:

"I will send my messenger ahead of you,
   who will prepare your way"[c]—
³"a voice of one calling in the
      wilderness,
'Prepare the way for the Lord,
   make straight paths for him.'"[d]

⁴And so John the Baptist appeared in the wilderness, preaching a baptism of repentance for the forgiveness of sins. ⁵The whole Judean countryside and all the people of Jerusalem went out to him. Confessing their sins, they were baptized by him in the Jordan River. ⁶John wore clothing made of camel's hair, with a leather belt around his waist, and he ate locusts and wild honey. ⁷And this was his message: "After me comes the one more powerful than I, the straps of whose sandals I am not worthy to stoop down and untie. ⁸I baptize you with[e] water, but he will baptize you with[e] the Holy Spirit."

The Baptism and Testing of Jesus

⁹At that time Jesus came from Nazareth in Galilee and was baptized by John in the Jordan. ¹⁰Just as Jesus was coming up out of the water, he saw heaven being torn open and the Spirit descending on him like a dove. ¹¹And a voice came from heaven: "You are my Son, whom I love; with you I am well pleased." ¹²At once the Spirit sent him out into the wilderness, ¹³and he was in the wilderness forty days, being tempted[f] by Satan. He was with the wild animals, and angels attended him.

Jesus Announces the Good News

¹⁴After John was put in prison, Jesus went into Galilee, proclaiming the good news of God. ¹⁵"The time has come," he said. "The kingdom of God has come near. Repent and believe the good news!"

Jesus Calls His First Disciples

¹⁶As Jesus walked beside the Sea of Galilee, he saw Simon and his brother Andrew casting a net into the lake, for they were fishermen. ¹⁷"Come, follow me," Jesus said, "and I will send you out to fish for people." ¹⁸At once they left their nets and followed him.

¹⁹When he had gone a little farther, he saw James son of Zebedee and his brother John in a boat, preparing their nets. ²⁰Without delay he called them, and they left their father Zebedee in the boat with the hired men and followed him.

Jesus Drives Out an Impure Spirit

²¹They went to Capernaum, and when the Sabbath came, Jesus went into the synagogue and began to teach. ²²The people were amazed at his teaching, because he taught them as one who had authority, not as the teachers of the law. ²³Just then a man in their synagogue who was possessed by an impure spirit cried out, ²⁴"What do you want with us, Jesus of Nazareth? Have you come to destroy us? I know who you are—the Holy One of God!"

²⁵"Be quiet!" said Jesus sternly. "Come out of him!" ²⁶The impure spirit shook the man violently and came out of him with a shriek.

²⁷The people were all so amazed that they asked each other, "What is this? A new teaching—and with authority! He even gives orders to impure spirits and they obey him." ²⁸News about him spread quickly over the whole region of Galilee.

Jesus Heals Many

²⁹As soon as they left the synagogue, they went with James and John to the home of Simon and Andrew. ³⁰Simon's mother-in-law was in bed with a fever, and they immediately told Jesus about her. ³¹So he went to her, took her hand and helped her up. The fever left her and she began to wait on them.

³²That evening after sunset the people brought to Jesus all the sick and demon-possessed. ³³The whole town gathered at the door, ³⁴and Jesus healed many who had various diseases. He also drove out many demons, but he would not let the demons speak because they knew who he was.

Jesus Prays in a Solitary Place

³⁵Very early in the morning, while it was still dark, Jesus got up, left the house and went off to a solitary place, where he prayed. ³⁶Simon and his companions went to look for him, ³⁷and when they found him, they exclaimed: "Everyone is looking for you!"

³⁸Jesus replied, "Let us go somewhere else—to the nearby villages—so I can preach there also. That is why I have come." ³⁹So he traveled throughout Galilee, preaching in their synagogues and driving out demons.

Jesus Heals a Man With Leprosy

⁴⁰A man with leprosy[g] came to him and begged him on his knees, "If you are willing, you can make me clean."

---

[a] 1 Or *Jesus Christ. Messiah* (Hebrew) and *Christ* (Greek) both mean *Anointed One.*   [b] 1 Some manuscripts do not have *the Son of God.*   [c] 2 Mal. 3:1   [d] 3 Isaiah 40:3   [e] 8 Or *in*   [f] 13 The Greek for *tempted* can also mean *tested.*   [g] 40 The Greek word traditionally translated *leprosy* was used for various diseases affecting the skin.

[41]Jesus was indignant.[a] He reached out his hand and touched the man. "I am willing," he said. "Be clean!" [42]Immediately the leprosy left him and he was cleansed.

[43]Jesus sent him away at once with a strong warning: [44]"See that you don't tell this to anyone. But go, show yourself to the priest and offer the sacrifices that Moses commanded for your cleansing, as a testimony to them." [45]Instead he went out and began to talk freely, spreading the news. As a result, Jesus could no longer enter a town openly but stayed outside in lonely places. Yet the people still came to him from everywhere.

Jesus Forgives and Heals a Paralyzed Man

2 A few days later, when Jesus again entered Capernaum, the people heard that he had come home. [2]They gathered in such large numbers that there was no room left, not even outside the door, and he preached the word to them. [3]Some men came, bringing to him a paralyzed man, carried by four of them. [4]Since they could not get him to Jesus because of the crowd, they made an opening in the roof above Jesus by digging through it and then lowered the mat the man was lying on. [5]When Jesus saw their faith, he said to the paralyzed man, "Son, your sins are forgiven."

[6]Now some teachers of the law were sitting there, thinking to themselves, [7]"Why does this fellow talk like that? He's blaspheming! Who can forgive sins but God alone?"

[8]Immediately Jesus knew in his spirit that this was what they were thinking in their hearts, and he said to them, "Why are you thinking these things? [9]Which is easier: to say to this paralyzed man, 'Your sins are forgiven,' or to say, 'Get up, take your mat and walk'? [10]But I want you to know that the Son of Man has authority on earth to forgive sins." So he said to the man, [11]"I tell you, get up, take your mat and go home." [12]He got up, took his mat and walked out in full view of them all. This amazed everyone and they praised God, saying, "We have never seen anything like this!"

Jesus Calls Levi and Eats With Sinners

[13]Once again Jesus went out beside the lake. A large crowd came to him, and he began to teach them. [14]As he walked along, he saw Levi son of Alphaeus sitting at the tax collector's booth. "Follow me," Jesus told him, and Levi got up and followed him.

[15]While Jesus was having dinner at Levi's house, many tax collectors and sinners were eating with him and his disciples, for there were many who followed him. [16]When the teachers of the law who were Pharisees saw him eating with the sinners and tax collectors, they asked his disciples: "Why does he eat with tax collectors and sinners?"

[17]On hearing this, Jesus said to them, "It is not the healthy who need a doctor, but the sick. I have not come to call the righteous, but sinners."

Jesus Questioned About Fasting

[18]Now John's disciples and the Pharisees were fasting. Some people came and asked Jesus, "How is it that John's disciples and the disciples of the Pharisees are fasting, but yours are not?"

[19]Jesus answered, "How can the guests of the bridegroom fast while he is with them? They cannot, so long as they have him with them. [20]But the time will come when the bridegroom will be taken from them, and on that day they will fast.

[21]"No one sews a patch of unshrunk cloth on an old garment. Otherwise, the new piece will pull away from the old, making the tear worse. [22]And no one pours new wine into old wineskins. Otherwise, the wine will burst the skins, and both the wine and the wineskins will be ruined. No, they pour new wine into new wineskins."

Jesus Is Lord of the Sabbath

[23]One Sabbath Jesus was going through the grainfields, and as his disciples walked along, they began to pick some heads of grain. [24]The Pharisees said to him, "Look, why are they doing what is unlawful on the Sabbath?"

[25]He answered, "Have you never read what David did when he and his companions were hungry and in need? [26]In the days of Abiathar the high priest, he entered the house of God and ate the consecrated bread, which is lawful only for priests to eat. And he also gave some to his companions."

[27]Then he said to them, "The Sabbath was made for man, not man for the Sabbath. [28]So the Son of Man is Lord even of the Sabbath."

Jesus Heals on the Sabbath

3 Another time Jesus went into the synagogue, and a man with a shriveled hand was there. [2]Some of them were looking for a reason to accuse Jesus, so they watched him closely to see if he would heal him on the Sabbath. [3]Jesus said to the man with the shriveled hand, "Stand up in front of everyone."

[4]Then Jesus asked them, "Which is lawful on the Sabbath: to do good or to do evil, to save life or to kill?" But they remained silent.

[5]He looked around at them in anger and, deeply distressed at their stubborn hearts, said to the man, "Stretch out your hand." He stretched it out, and his hand was completely restored. [6]Then the Pharisees went out and began to plot with the Herodians how they might kill Jesus.

Crowds Follow Jesus

[7]Jesus withdrew with his disciples to the lake, and a large crowd from Galilee followed. [8]When they heard about all he was doing, many people came to him from Judea, Jerusalem, Idumea, and the regions across the

---

[a] 41 Many manuscripts *Jesus was filled with compassion*

Jordan and around Tyre and Sidon. ⁹Because of the crowd he told his disciples to have a small boat ready for him, to keep the people from crowding him. ¹⁰For he had healed many, so that those with diseases were pushing forward to touch him. ¹¹Whenever the impure spirits saw him, they fell down before him and cried out, "You are the Son of God." ¹²But he gave them strict orders not to tell others about him.

Jesus Appoints the Twelve

¹³Jesus went up on a mountainside and called to him those he wanted, and they came to him. ¹⁴He appointed twelve*a* that they might be with him and that he might send them out to preach ¹⁵and to have authority to drive out demons. ¹⁶These are the twelve he appointed: Simon (to whom he gave the name Peter), ¹⁷James son of Zebedee and his brother John (to them he gave the name Boanerges, which means "sons of thunder"), ¹⁸Andrew, Philip, Bartholomew, Matthew, Thomas, James son of Alphaeus, Thaddaeus, Simon the Zealot ¹⁹and Judas Iscariot, who betrayed him.

Jesus Accused by His Family and by Teachers of the Law

²⁰Then Jesus entered a house, and again a crowd gathered, so that he and his disciples were not even able to eat. ²¹When his family*b* heard about this, they went to take charge of him, for they said, "He is out of his mind." ²²And the teachers of the law who came down from Jerusalem said, "He is possessed by Beelzebul! By the prince of demons he is driving out demons."

²³So Jesus called them over to him and began to speak to them in parables: "How can Satan drive out Satan? ²⁴If a kingdom is divided against itself, that kingdom cannot stand. ²⁵If a house is divided against itself, that house cannot stand. ²⁶And if Satan opposes himself and is divided, he cannot stand; his end has come. ²⁷In fact, no one can enter a strong man's house without first tying him up. Then he can plunder the strong man's house. ²⁸Truly I tell you, people can be forgiven all their sins and every slander they utter, ²⁹but whoever blasphemes against the Holy Spirit will never be forgiven; they are guilty of an eternal sin."

³⁰He said this because they were saying, "He has an impure spirit."

³¹Then Jesus' mother and brothers arrived. Standing outside, they sent someone in to call him. ³²A crowd was sitting around him, and they told him, "Your mother and brothers are outside looking for you."

³³"Who are my mother and my brothers?" he asked.

³⁴Then he looked at those seated in a circle around him and said, "Here are my mother and my brothers! ³⁵Whoever does God's will is my brother and sister and mother."

The Parable of the Sower

4 Again Jesus began to teach by the lake. The crowd that gathered around him was so large that he got into a boat and sat in it out on the lake, while all the people were along the shore at the water's edge. ²He taught them many things by parables, and in his teaching said: ³"Listen! A farmer went out to sow his seed. ⁴As he was scattering the seed, some fell along the path, and the birds came and ate it up. ⁵Some fell on rocky places, where it did not have much soil. It sprang up quickly, because the soil was shallow. ⁶But when the sun came up, the plants were scorched, and they withered because they had no root. ⁷Other seed fell among thorns, which grew up and choked the plants, so that they did not bear grain. ⁸Still other seed fell on good soil. It came up, grew and produced a crop, some multiplying thirty, some sixty, some a hundred times."

⁹Then Jesus said, "Whoever has ears to hear, let them hear."

¹⁰When he was alone, the Twelve and the others around him asked him about the parables. ¹¹He told them, "The secret of the kingdom of God has been given to you. But to those on the outside everything is said in parables ¹²so that,

"'they may be ever seeing but never perceiving,
    and ever hearing but never understanding;
otherwise they might turn and be forgiven!'*c*

¹³Then Jesus said to them, "Don't you understand this parable? How then will you understand any parable? ¹⁴The farmer sows the word. ¹⁵Some people are like seed along the path, where the word is sown. As soon as they hear it, Satan comes and takes away the word that was sown in them. ¹⁶Others, like seed sown on rocky places, hear the word and at once receive it with joy. ¹⁷But since they have no root, they last only a short time. When trouble or persecution comes because of the word, they quickly fall away. ¹⁸Still others, like seed sown among thorns, hear the word; ¹⁹but the worries of this life, the deceitfulness of wealth and the desires for other things come in and choke the word, making it unfruitful. ²⁰Others, like seed sown on good soil, hear the word, accept it, and produce a crop—some thirty, some sixty, some a hundred times what was sown."

A Lamp on a Stand

²¹He said to them, "Do you bring in a lamp to put it under a bowl or a bed? Instead, don't you put it on its stand? ²²For whatever is hidden is meant to be disclosed, and whatever is concealed is meant to be brought out into the open. ²³If anyone has ears to hear, let them hear."

²⁴"Consider carefully what you hear," he

---

a 14 Some manuscripts *twelve—designating them apostles—*   *b* 21 Or *his associates*   *c* 12 Isaiah 6:9,10

continued. "With the measure you use, it will be measured to you—and even more. 25Whoever has will be given more; whoever does not have, even what they have will be taken from them."

The Parable of the Growing Seed

26He also said, "This is what the kingdom of God is like. A man scatters seed on the ground. 27Night and day, whether he sleeps or gets up, the seed sprouts and grows, though he does not know how. 28All by itself the soil produces grain—first the stalk, then the head, then the full kernel in the head. 29As soon as the grain is ripe, he puts the sickle to it, because the harvest has come."

The Parable of the Mustard Seed

30Again he said, "What shall we say the kingdom of God is like, or what parable shall we use to describe it? 31It is like a mustard seed, which is the smallest of all seeds on earth. 32Yet when planted, it grows and becomes the largest of all garden plants, with such big branches that the birds can perch in its shade."

33With many similar parables Jesus spoke the word to them, as much as they could understand. 34He did not say anything to them without using a parable. But when he was alone with his own disciples, he explained everything.

Jesus Calms the Storm

35That day when evening came, he said to his disciples, "Let us go over to the other side." 36Leaving the crowd behind, they took him along, just as he was, in the boat. There were also other boats with him. 37A furious squall came up, and the waves broke over the boat, so that it was nearly swamped. 38Jesus was in the stern, sleeping on a cushion. The disciples woke him and said to him, "Teacher, don't you care if we drown?"

39He got up, rebuked the wind and said to the waves, "Quiet! Be still!" Then the wind died down and it was completely calm.

40He said to his disciples, "Why are you so afraid? Do you still have no faith?"

41They were terrified and asked each other, "Who is this? Even the wind and the waves obey him!"

Jesus Restores a Demon-Possessed Man

5 They went across the lake to the region of the Gerasenes.a 2When Jesus got out of the boat, a man with an impure spirit came from the tombs to meet him. 3This man lived in the tombs, and no one could bind him anymore, not even with a chain. 4For he had often been chained hand and foot, but he tore the chains apart and broke the irons on his feet. No one was strong enough to subdue him. 5Night and day among the tombs and in the hills he would cry out and cut himself with stones.

6When he saw Jesus from a distance, he ran and fell on his knees in front of him. 7He shouted at the top of his voice, "What do you want with me, Jesus, Son of the Most High God? In God's name don't torture me!" 8For Jesus had said to him, "Come out of this man, you impure spirit!"

9Then Jesus asked him, "What is your name?"

"My name is Legion," he replied, "for we are many." 10And he begged Jesus again and again not to send them out of the area.

11A large herd of pigs was feeding on the nearby hillside. 12The demons begged Jesus, "Send us among the pigs; allow us to go into them." 13He gave them permission, and the impure spirits came out and went into the pigs. The herd, about two thousand in number, rushed down the steep bank into the lake and were drowned.

14Those tending the pigs ran off and reported this in the town and countryside, and the people went out to see what had happened. 15When they came to Jesus, they saw the man who had been possessed by the legion of demons, sitting there, dressed and in his right mind; and they were afraid. 16Those who had seen it told the people what had happened to the demon-possessed man—and told about the pigs as well. 17Then the people began to plead with Jesus to leave their region.

18As Jesus was getting into the boat, the man who had been demon-possessed begged to go with him. 19Jesus did not let him, but said, "Go home to your own people and tell them how much the Lord has done for you, and how he has had mercy on you." 20So the man went away and began to tell in the Decapolisb how much Jesus had done for him. And all the people were amazed.

Jesus Raises a Dead Girl and Heals a Sick Woman

21When Jesus had again crossed over by boat to the other side of the lake, a large crowd gathered around him while he was by the lake. 22Then one of the synagogue leaders, named Jairus, came, and when he saw Jesus, he fell at his feet. 23He pleaded earnestly with him, "My little daughter is dying. Please come and put your hands on her so that she will be healed and live." 24So Jesus went with him.

A large crowd followed and pressed around him. 25And a woman was there who had been subject to bleeding for twelve years. 26She had suffered a great deal under the care of many doctors and had spent all she had, yet instead of getting better she grew worse. 27When she heard about Jesus, she came up behind him in the crowd and touched his cloak, 28because she thought, "If I just touch his clothes, I will be healed." 29Immediately her bleeding stopped and she felt in her body that she was freed from her suffering.

30At once Jesus realized that power had gone out from him. He turned around in the crowd and asked, "Who touched my clothes?"

31"You see the people crowding against

---

a 1 Some manuscripts Gadarenes; other manuscripts Gergesenes   b 20 That is, the Ten Cities

you," his disciples answered, "and yet you can ask, 'Who touched me?' "

³²But Jesus kept looking around to see who had done it. ³³Then the woman, knowing what had happened to her, came and fell at his feet and, trembling with fear, told him the whole truth. ³⁴He said to her, "Daughter, your faith has healed you. Go in peace and be freed from your suffering."

³⁵While Jesus was still speaking, some people came from the house of Jairus, the synagogue leader. "Your daughter is dead," they said. "Why bother the teacher anymore?"

³⁶Overhearing[a] what they said, Jesus told him, "Don't be afraid; just believe."

³⁷He did not let anyone follow him except Peter, James and John the brother of James. ³⁸When they came to the home of the synagogue leader, Jesus saw a commotion, with people crying and wailing loudly. ³⁹He went in and said to them, "Why all this commotion and wailing? The child is not dead but asleep." ⁴⁰But they laughed at him.

After he put them all out, he took the child's father and mother and the disciples who were with him, and went in where the child was. ⁴¹He took her by the hand and said to her, "Talitha koum!" (which means "Little girl, I say to you, get up!"). ⁴²Immediately the girl stood up and began to walk around (she was twelve years old). At this they were completely astonished. ⁴³He gave strict orders not to let anyone know about this, and told them to give her something to eat.

A Prophet Without Honor

6 Jesus left there and went to his hometown, accompanied by his disciples. ²When the Sabbath came, he began to teach in the synagogue, and many who heard him were amazed.

"Where did this man get these things?" they asked. "What's this wisdom that has been given him? What are these remarkable miracles he is performing? ³Isn't this the carpenter? Isn't this Mary's son and the brother of James, Joseph,[b] Judas and Simon? Aren't his sisters here with us?" And they took offense at him.

⁴Jesus said to them, "A prophet is not without honor except in his own town, among his relatives and in his own home." ⁵He could not do any miracles there, except lay his hands on a few sick people and heal them. ⁶He was amazed at their lack of faith.

Jesus Sends Out the Twelve

Then Jesus went around teaching from village to village. ⁷Calling the Twelve to him, he began to send them out two by two and gave them authority over impure spirits.

⁸These were his instructions: "Take nothing for the journey except a staff—no bread, no bag, no money in your belts. ⁹Wear sandals but not an extra shirt. ¹⁰Whenever you enter a house, stay there until you leave that town. ¹¹And if any place will not welcome you or listen to you, leave that place and shake the dust off your feet as a testimony against them."

¹²They went out and preached that people should repent. ¹³They drove out many demons and anointed many sick people with oil and healed them.

John the Baptist Beheaded

¹⁴King Herod heard about this, for Jesus' name had become well known. Some were saying,[c] "John the Baptist has been raised from the dead, and that is why miraculous powers are at work in him."

¹⁵Others said, "He is Elijah."

And still others claimed, "He is a prophet, like one of the prophets of long ago."

¹⁶But when Herod heard this, he said, "John, whom I beheaded, has been raised from the dead!"

¹⁷For Herod himself had given orders to have John arrested, and he had him bound and put in prison. He did this because of Herodias, his brother Philip's wife, whom he had married. ¹⁸For John had been saying to Herod, "It is not lawful for you to have your brother's wife." ¹⁹So Herodias nursed a grudge against John and wanted to kill him. But she was not able to, ²⁰because Herod feared John and protected him, knowing him to be a righteous and holy man. When Herod heard John, he was greatly puzzled[d]; yet he liked to listen to him.

²¹Finally the opportune time came. On his birthday Herod gave a banquet for his high officials and military commanders and the leading men of Galilee. ²²When the daughter of[e] Herodias came in and danced, she pleased Herod and his dinner guests.

The king said to the girl, "Ask me for anything you want, and I'll give it to you." ²³And he promised her with an oath, "Whatever you ask I will give you, up to half my kingdom."

²⁴She went out and said to her mother, "What shall I ask for?"

"The head of John the Baptist," she answered.

²⁵At once the girl hurried in to the king with the request: "I want you to give me right now the head of John the Baptist on a platter."

²⁶The king was greatly distressed, but because of his oaths and his dinner guests, he did not want to refuse her. ²⁷So he immediately sent an executioner with orders to bring John's head. The man went, beheaded John in the prison, ²⁸and brought back his head on a platter. He presented it to the girl, and she gave it to her mother. ²⁹On hearing of this, John's disciples came and took his body and laid it in a tomb.

Jesus Feeds the Five Thousand

³⁰The apostles gathered around Jesus and reported to him all they had done and taught. ³¹Then, because so many people were coming and going that they did not even have a chance to eat, he said to them, "Come with me by yourselves to a quiet place and get some rest."

---

a 36 Or *Ignoring*   *b 3* Greek *Joses,* a variant of *Joseph*   *c 14* Some early manuscripts *saying*   *d 20* Some early manuscripts *he did many things*   *e 22* Some early manuscripts *When his daughter*

³²So they went away by themselves in a boat to a solitary place. ³³But many who saw them leaving recognized them and ran on foot from all the towns and got there ahead of them. ³⁴When Jesus landed and saw a large crowd, he had compassion on them, because they were like sheep without a shepherd. So he began teaching them many things.

³⁵By this time it was late in the day, so his disciples came to him. "This is a remote place," they said, "and it's already very late. ³⁶Send the people away so that they can go to the surrounding countryside and villages and buy themselves something to eat."

³⁷But he answered, "You give them something to eat."

They said to him, "That would take more than half a year's wages*a*! Are we to go and spend that much on bread and give it to them to eat?"

³⁸"How many loaves do you have?" he asked. "Go and see."

When they found out, they said, "Five—and two fish."

³⁹Then Jesus directed them to have all the people sit down in groups on the green grass. ⁴⁰So they sat down in groups of hundreds and fifties. ⁴¹Taking the five loaves and the two fish and looking up to heaven, he gave thanks and broke the loaves. Then he gave them to his disciples to distribute to the people. He also divided the two fish among them all. ⁴²They all ate and were satisfied, ⁴³and the disciples picked up twelve basketfuls of broken pieces of bread and fish. ⁴⁴The number of the men who had eaten was five thousand.

Jesus Walks on the Water

⁴⁵Immediately Jesus made his disciples get into the boat and go on ahead of him to Bethsaida, while he dismissed the crowd. ⁴⁶After leaving them, he went up on a mountainside to pray.

⁴⁷Later that night, the boat was in the middle of the lake, and he was alone on land. ⁴⁸He saw the disciples straining at the oars, because the wind was against them. Shortly before dawn he went out to them, walking on the lake. He was about to pass by them, ⁴⁹but when they saw him walking on the lake, they thought he was a ghost. They cried out, ⁵⁰because they all saw him and were terrified.

Immediately he spoke to them and said, "Take courage! It is I. Don't be afraid." ⁵¹Then he climbed into the boat with them, and the wind died down. They were completely amazed, ⁵²for they had not understood about the loaves; their hearts were hardened.

⁵³When they had crossed over, they landed at Gennesaret and anchored there. ⁵⁴As soon as they got out of the boat, people recognized Jesus. ⁵⁵They ran throughout that whole region and carried the sick on mats to wherever they heard he was. ⁵⁶And wherever he went—into villages, towns or countryside— they placed the sick in the marketplaces. They begged him to let them touch even the edge of his cloak, and all who touched it were healed.

That Which Defiles

7 The Pharisees and some of the teachers of the law who had come from Jerusalem gathered around Jesus ²and saw some of his disciples eating food with hands that were defiled, that is, unwashed. ³(The Pharisees and all the Jews do not eat unless they give their hands a ceremonial washing, holding to the tradition of the elders. ⁴When they come from the marketplace they do not eat unless they wash. And they observe many other traditions, such as the washing of cups, pitchers and kettles.*b*)

⁵So the Pharisees and teachers of the law asked Jesus, "Why don't your disciples live according to the tradition of the elders instead of eating their food with defiled hands?"

⁶He replied, "Isaiah was right when he prophesied about you hypocrites; as it is written:

"'These people honor me with their lips,
    but their hearts are far from me.
⁷They worship me in vain;
    their teachings are merely human
        rules.'*c*

⁸You have let go of the commands of God and are holding on to human traditions."

⁹And he continued, "You have a fine way of setting aside the commands of God in order to observe*d* your own traditions! ¹⁰For Moses said, 'Honor your father and mother,'*e* and, 'Anyone who curses their father or mother is to be put to death.'*f* ¹¹But you say that if anyone declares that what might have been used to help their father or mother is Corban (that is, devoted to God)— ¹²then you no longer let them do anything for their father or mother. ¹³Thus you nullify the word of God by your tradition that you have handed down. And you do many things like that."

¹⁴Again Jesus called the crowd to him and said, "Listen to me, everyone, and understand this. ¹⁵Nothing outside a person can defile them by going into them. Rather, it is what comes out of a person that defiles them." [16]*g*

¹⁷After he had left the crowd and entered the house, his disciples asked him about this parable. ¹⁸"Are you so dull?" he asked. "Don't you see that nothing that enters a person from the outside can defile them? ¹⁹For it doesn't go into their heart but into their stomach, and then out of the body." (In saying this, Jesus declared all foods clean.)

²⁰He went on: "What comes out of a person is what defiles them. ²¹For it is from within, out of a person's heart, that evil thoughts come—sexual immorality, theft, murder, ²²adultery, greed, malice, deceit, lewdness, envy, slander, arrogance and folly. ²³All these evils come from inside and defile a person."

---

a 37 Greek *take two hundred denarii*   *b* 4 Some early manuscripts *pitchers, kettles and dining couches*   *c* 6,7 Isaiah 29:13   *d* 9 Some manuscripts *set up*   *e* 10 Exodus 20:12; Deut. 5:16
f 10 Exodus 21:17; Lev. 20:9   *g* 16 Some manuscripts include here the words of 4:23.

Jesus Honors a Syrophoenician Woman's Faith

²⁴Jesus left that place and went to the vicinity of Tyre.ᵃ He entered a house and did not want anyone to know it; yet he could not keep his presence secret. ²⁵In fact, as soon as she heard about him, a woman whose little daughter was possessed by an impure spirit came and fell at his feet. ²⁶The woman was a Greek, born in Syrian Phoenicia. She begged Jesus to drive the demon out of her daughter.

²⁷"First let the children eat all they want," he told her, "for it is not right to take the children's bread and toss it to the dogs."

²⁸"Lord," she replied, "even the dogs under the table eat the children's crumbs."

²⁹Then he told her, "For such a reply, you may go; the demon has left your daughter."

³⁰She went home and found her child lying on the bed, and the demon gone.

Jesus Heals a Deaf and Mute Man

³¹Then Jesus left the vicinity of Tyre and went through Sidon, down to the Sea of Galilee and into the region of the Decapolis.ᵇ ³²There some people brought to him a man who was deaf and could hardly talk, and they begged Jesus to place his hand on him.

³³After he took him aside, away from the crowd, Jesus put his fingers into the man's ears. Then he spit and touched the man's tongue. ³⁴He looked up to heaven and with a deep sigh said to him, *"Ephphatha!"* (which means "Be opened!"). ³⁵At this, the man's ears were opened, his tongue was loosened and he began to speak plainly.

³⁶Jesus commanded them not to tell anyone. But the more he did so, the more they kept talking about it. ³⁷People were overwhelmed with amazement. "He has done everything well," they said. "He even makes the deaf hear and the mute speak."

Jesus Feeds the Four Thousand

8 During those days another large crowd gathered. Since they had nothing to eat, Jesus called his disciples to him and said, ²"I have compassion for these people; they have already been with me three days and have nothing to eat. ³If I send them home hungry, they will collapse on the way, because some of them have come a long distance."

⁴His disciples answered, "But where in this remote place can anyone get enough bread to feed them?"

⁵"How many loaves do you have?" Jesus asked.

"Seven," they replied.

⁶He told the crowd to sit down on the ground. When he had taken the seven loaves and given thanks, he broke them and gave them to his disciples to distribute to the people, and they did so. ⁷They had a few small fish as well; he gave thanks for them also and told the disciples to distribute them. ⁸The people ate and were satisfied. Afterward the disciples picked up seven basketfuls of broken pieces that were left over. ⁹About four thousand were present. After he had sent them away, ¹⁰he got into the boat with his disciples and went to the region of Dalmanutha.

¹¹The Pharisees came and began to question Jesus. To test him, they asked him for a sign from heaven. ¹²He sighed deeply and said, "Why does this generation ask for a sign? Truly I tell you, no sign will be given to it." ¹³Then he left them, got back into the boat and crossed to the other side.

The Yeast of the Pharisees and Herod

¹⁴The disciples had forgotten to bring bread, except for one loaf they had with them in the boat. ¹⁵"Be careful," Jesus warned them. "Watch out for the yeast of the Pharisees and that of Herod."

¹⁶They discussed this with one another and said, "It is because we have no bread."

¹⁷Aware of their discussion, Jesus asked them: "Why are you talking about having no bread? Do you still not see or understand? Are your hearts hardened? ¹⁸Do you have eyes but fail to see, and ears but fail to hear? And don't you remember? ¹⁹When I broke the five loaves for the five thousand, how many basketfuls of pieces did you pick up?"

"Twelve," they replied.

²⁰"And when I broke the seven loaves for the four thousand, how many basketfuls of pieces did you pick up?"

They answered, "Seven."

²¹He said to them, "Do you still not understand?"

Jesus Heals a Blind Man at Bethsaida

²²They came to Bethsaida, and some people brought a blind man and begged Jesus to touch him. ²³He took the blind man by the hand and led him outside the village. When he had spit on the man's eyes and put his hands on him, Jesus asked, "Do you see anything?"

²⁴He looked up and said, "I see people; they look like trees walking around."

²⁵Once more Jesus put his hands on the man's eyes. Then his eyes were opened, his sight was restored, and he saw everything clearly. ²⁶Jesus sent him home, saying, "Don't even go intoᶜ the village."

Peter Declares That Jesus Is the Messiah

²⁷Jesus and his disciples went on to the villages around Caesarea Philippi. On the way he asked them, "Who do people say I am?"

²⁸They replied, "Some say John the Baptist; others say Elijah; and still others, one of the prophets."

²⁹"But what about you?" he asked. "Who do you say I am?"

Peter answered, "You are the Messiah."

³⁰Jesus warned them not to tell anyone about him.

ᵃ 24 Many early manuscripts *Tyre and Sidon go and tell anyone in*   ᵇ 31 That is, the Ten Cities   ᶜ 26 Some manuscripts

Jesus Predicts His Death

³¹He then began to teach them that the Son of Man must suffer many things and be rejected by the elders, the chief priests and the teachers of the law, and that he must be killed and after three days rise again. ³²He spoke plainly about this, and Peter took him aside and began to rebuke him.

³³But when Jesus turned and looked at his disciples, he rebuked Peter. "Get behind me, Satan!" he said. "You do not have in mind the concerns of God, but merely human concerns."

The Way of the Cross

³⁴Then he called the crowd to him along with his disciples and said: "Whoever wants to be my disciple must deny themselves and take up their cross and follow me. ³⁵For whoever wants to save their life*a* will lose it, but whoever loses their life for me and for the gospel will save it. ³⁶What good is it for someone to gain the whole world, yet forfeit their soul? ³⁷Or what can anyone give in exchange for their soul? ³⁸If anyone is ashamed of me and my words in this adulterous and sinful generation, the Son of Man will be ashamed of them when he comes in his Father's glory with the holy angels."

9 And he said to them, "Truly I tell you, some who are standing here will not taste death before they see that the kingdom of God has come with power."

The Transfiguration

²After six days Jesus took Peter, James and John with him and led them up a high mountain, where they were all alone. There he was transfigured before them. ³His clothes became dazzling white, whiter than anyone in the world could bleach them. ⁴And there appeared before them Elijah and Moses, who were talking with Jesus.

⁵Peter said to Jesus, "Rabbi, it is good for us to be here. Let us put up three shelters—one for you, one for Moses and one for Elijah." ⁶(He did not know what to say, they were so frightened.)

⁷Then a cloud appeared and covered them, and a voice came from the cloud: "This is my Son, whom I love. Listen to him!"

⁸Suddenly, when they looked around, they no longer saw anyone with them except Jesus.

⁹As they were coming down the mountain, Jesus gave them orders not to tell anyone what they had seen until the Son of Man had risen from the dead. ¹⁰They kept the matter to themselves, discussing what "rising from the dead" meant.

¹¹And they asked him, "Why do the teachers of the law say that Elijah must come first?"

¹²Jesus replied, "To be sure, Elijah does come first, and restores all things. Why then is it written that the Son of Man must suffer much and be rejected? ¹³But I tell you, Elijah has come, and they have done to him everything they wished, just as it is written about him."

Jesus Heals a Boy Possessed by an Impure Spirit

¹⁴When they came to the other disciples, they saw a large crowd around them and the teachers of the law arguing with them. ¹⁵As soon as all the people saw Jesus, they were overwhelmed with wonder and ran to greet him.

¹⁶"What are you arguing with them about?" he asked.

¹⁷A man in the crowd answered, "Teacher, I brought you my son, who is possessed by a spirit that has robbed him of speech. ¹⁸Whenever it seizes him, it throws him to the ground. He foams at the mouth, gnashes his teeth and becomes rigid. I asked your disciples to drive out the spirit, but they could not."

¹⁹"You unbelieving generation," Jesus replied, "how long shall I stay with you? How long shall I put up with you? Bring the boy to me."

²⁰So they brought him. When the spirit saw Jesus, it immediately threw the boy into a convulsion. He fell to the ground and rolled around, foaming at the mouth.

²¹Jesus asked the boy's father, "How long has he been like this?"

"From childhood," he answered. ²²"It has often thrown him into fire or water to kill him. But if you can do anything, take pity on us and help us."

²³"'If you can'?" said Jesus. "Everything is possible for one who believes."

²⁴Immediately the boy's father exclaimed, "I do believe; help me overcome my unbelief!"

²⁵When Jesus saw that a crowd was running to the scene, he rebuked the impure spirit. "You deaf and mute spirit," he said, "I command you, come out of him and never enter him again."

²⁶The spirit shrieked, convulsed him violently and came out. The boy looked so much like a corpse that many said, "He's dead." ²⁷But Jesus took him by the hand and lifted him to his feet, and he stood up.

²⁸After Jesus had gone indoors, his disciples asked him privately, "Why couldn't we drive it out?"

²⁹He replied, "This kind can come out only by prayer.*b*"

Jesus Predicts His Death a Second Time

³⁰They left that place and passed through Galilee. Jesus did not want anyone to know where they were, ³¹because he was teaching his disciples. He said to them, "The Son of Man is going to be delivered into the hands of men. They will kill him, and after three days he will rise." ³²But they did not understand what he meant and were afraid to ask him about it.

---

a 35 The Greek word means either *life* or *soul*; also in verses 36 and 37.   *b* 29 Some manuscripts *prayer and fasting*

33They came to Capernaum. When he was in the house, he asked them, "What were you arguing about on the road?" 34But they kept quiet because on the way they had argued about who was the greatest.

35Sitting down, Jesus called the Twelve and said, "Anyone who wants to be first must be the very last, and the servant of all."

36He took a little child whom he placed among them. Taking the child in his arms, he said to them, 37"Whoever welcomes one of these little children in my name welcomes me; and whoever welcomes me does not welcome me but the one who sent me."

Whoever Is Not Against Us Is for Us

38"Teacher," said John, "we saw someone driving out demons in your name and we told him to stop, because he was not one of us."

39"Do not stop him," Jesus said. "For no one who does a miracle in my name can in the next moment say anything bad about me, 40for whoever is not against us is for us. 41Truly I tell you, anyone who gives you a cup of water in my name because you belong to the Messiah will certainly not lose their reward.

Causing to Stumble

42"If anyone causes one of these little ones—those who believe in me—to stumble, it would be better for them if a large millstone were hung around their neck and they were thrown into the sea. 43If your hand causes you to stumble, cut it off. It is better for you to enter life maimed than with two hands to go into hell, where the fire never goes out. [44]a 45And if your foot causes you to stumble, cut it off. It is better for you to enter life crippled than to have two feet and be thrown into hell. [46]a 47And if your eye causes you to stumble, pluck it out. It is better for you to enter the kingdom of God with one eye than to have two eyes and be thrown into hell, 48where

"'the worms that eat them do not die,
    and the fire is not quenched.'b

49Everyone will be salted with fire.

50"Salt is good, but if it loses its saltiness, how can you make it salty again? Have salt among yourselves, and be at peace with each other."

Divorce

10 Jesus then left that place and went into the region of Judea and across the Jordan. Again crowds of people came to him, and as was his custom, he taught them.

2Some Pharisees came and tested him by asking, "Is it lawful for a man to divorce his wife?"

3"What did Moses command you?" he replied.

4They said, "Moses permitted a man to write a certificate of divorce and send her away."

5"It was because your hearts were hard that Moses wrote you this law," Jesus replied. 6"But at the beginning of creation God 'made them male and female.'c 7'For this reason a man will leave his father and mother and be united to his wife,d 8and the two will become one flesh.'e So they are no longer two, but one flesh. 9Therefore what God has joined together, let no one separate."

10When they were in the house again, the disciples asked Jesus about this. 11He answered, "Anyone who divorces his wife and marries another woman commits adultery against her. 12And if she divorces her husband and marries another man, she commits adultery."

The Little Children and Jesus

13People were bringing little children to Jesus for him to place his hands on them, but the disciples rebuked them. 14When Jesus saw this, he was indignant. He said to them, "Let the little children come to me, and do not hinder them, for the kingdom of God belongs to such as these. 15Truly I tell you, anyone who will not receive the kingdom of God like a little child will never enter it." 16And he took the children in his arms, placed his hands on them and blessed them.

The Rich and the Kingdom of God

17As Jesus started on his way, a man ran up to him and fell on his knees before him. "Good teacher," he asked, "what must I do to inherit eternal life?"

18"Why do you call me good?" Jesus answered. "No one is good—except God alone. 19You know the commandments: 'You shall not murder, you shall not commit adultery, you shall not steal, you shall not give false testimony, you shall not defraud, honor your father and mother.'f"

20"Teacher," he declared, "all these I have kept since I was a boy."

21Jesus looked at him and loved him. "One thing you lack," he said. "Go, sell everything you have and give to the poor, and you will have treasure in heaven. Then come, follow me."

22At this the man's face fell. He went away sad, because he had great wealth.

23Jesus looked around and said to his disciples, "How hard it is for the rich to enter the kingdom of God!"

24The disciples were amazed at his words. But Jesus said again, "Children, how hard it isg to enter the kingdom of God! 25It is easier for a camel to go through the eye of a needle than for someone who is rich to enter the kingdom of God."

26The disciples were even more amazed, and said to each other, "Who then can be saved?"

27Jesus looked at them and said, "With man

---

a 44,46 Some manuscripts include here the words of verse 48.   b 48 Isaiah 66:24   c 6 Gen. 1:27
d 7 Some early manuscripts do not have and be united to his wife.   e 8 Gen. 2:24   f 19 Exodus
20:12-16; Deut. 5:16-20   g 24 Some manuscripts is for those who trust in riches

this is impossible, but not with God; all things are possible with God."

²⁸Then Peter spoke up, "We have left everything to follow you!"

²⁹"Truly I tell you," Jesus replied, "no one who has left home or brothers or sisters or mother or father or children or fields for me and the gospel ³⁰will fail to receive a hundred times as much in this present age: homes, brothers, sisters, mothers, children and fields—along with persecutions—and in the age to come eternal life. ³¹But many who are first will be last, and the last first."

Jesus Predicts His Death a Third Time

³²They were on their way up to Jerusalem, with Jesus leading the way, and the disciples were astonished, while those who followed were afraid. Again he took the Twelve aside and told them what was going to happen to him. ³³"We are going up to Jerusalem," he said, "and the Son of Man will be delivered over to the chief priests and the teachers of the law. They will condemn him to death and will hand him over to the Gentiles, ³⁴who will mock him and spit on him, flog him and kill him. Three days later he will rise."

The Request of James and John

³⁵Then James and John, the sons of Zebedee, came to him. "Teacher," they said, "we want you to do for us whatever we ask."

³⁶"What do you want me to do for you?" he asked.

³⁷They replied, "Let one of us sit at your right and the other at your left in your glory."

³⁸"You don't know what you are asking," Jesus said. "Can you drink the cup I drink or be baptized with the baptism I am baptized with?"

³⁹"We can," they answered.

Jesus said to them, "You will drink the cup I drink and be baptized with the baptism I am baptized with, ⁴⁰but to sit at my right or left is not for me to grant. These places belong to those for whom they have been prepared."

⁴¹When the ten heard about this, they became indignant with James and John. ⁴²Jesus called them together and said, "You know that those who are regarded as rulers of the Gentiles lord it over them, and their high officials exercise authority over them. ⁴³Not so with you. Instead, whoever wants to become great among you must be your servant, ⁴⁴and whoever wants to be first must be slave of all. ⁴⁵For even the Son of Man did not come to be served, but to serve, and to give his life as a ransom for many."

Blind Bartimaeus Receives His Sight

⁴⁶Then they came to Jericho. As Jesus and his disciples, together with a large crowd, were leaving the city, a blind man, Bartimaeus (which means "son of Timaeus"), was sitting by the roadside begging. ⁴⁷When he heard that it was Jesus of Nazareth, he began to shout, "Jesus, Son of David, have mercy on me!"

⁴⁸Many rebuked him and told him to be quiet, but he shouted all the more, "Son of David, have mercy on me!"

⁴⁹Jesus stopped and said, "Call him."

So they called to the blind man, "Cheer up! On your feet! He's calling you." ⁵⁰Throwing his cloak aside, he jumped to his feet and came to Jesus.

⁵¹"What do you want me to do for you?" Jesus asked him.

The blind man said, "Rabbi, I want to see."

⁵²"Go," said Jesus, "your faith has healed you." Immediately he received his sight and followed Jesus along the road.

Jesus Comes to Jerusalem as King

11 As they approached Jerusalem and came to Bethphage and Bethany at the Mount of Olives, Jesus sent two of his disciples, ²saying to them, "Go to the village ahead of you, and just as you enter it, you will find a colt tied there, which no one has ever ridden. Untie it and bring it here. ³If anyone asks you, 'Why are you doing this?' say, 'The Lord needs it and will send it back here shortly.'"

⁴They went and found a colt outside in the street, tied at a doorway. As they untied it, ⁵some people standing there asked, "What are you doing, untying that colt?" ⁶They answered as Jesus had told them to, and the people let them go. ⁷When they brought the colt to Jesus and threw their cloaks over it, he sat on it. ⁸Many people spread their cloaks on the road, while others spread branches they had cut in the fields. ⁹Those who went ahead and those who followed shouted,

"Hosanna!ᵃ"

"Blessed is he who comes in the name of the Lord!"ᵇ

¹⁰"Blessed is the coming kingdom of our father David!"

"Hosanna in the highest heaven!"

¹¹Jesus entered Jerusalem and went into the temple courts. He looked around at everything, but since it was already late, he went out to Bethany with the Twelve.

Jesus Curses a Fig Tree and Clears the Temple Courts

¹²The next day as they were leaving Bethany, Jesus was hungry. ¹³Seeing in the distance a fig tree in leaf, he went to find out if it had any fruit. When he reached it, he found nothing but leaves, because it was not the season for figs. ¹⁴Then he said to the tree, "May no one ever eat fruit from you again." And his disciples heard him say it.

¹⁵On reaching Jerusalem, Jesus entered the temple courts and began driving out those who were buying and selling there. He overturned the tables of the money changers and

---

ᵃ 9 A Hebrew expression meaning "Save!" which became an exclamation of praise; also in verse 10
ᵇ 9 Psalm 118:25,26

the benches of those selling doves, [16]and would not allow anyone to carry merchandise through the temple courts. [17]And as he taught them, he said, "Is it not written: 'My house will be called a house of prayer for all nations'[a]? But you have made it 'a den of robbers.'[b]"

[18]The chief priests and the teachers of the law heard this and began looking for a way to kill him, for they feared him, because the whole crowd was amazed at his teaching.

[19]When evening came, Jesus and his disciples[c] went out of the city.

[20]In the morning, as they went along, they saw the fig tree withered from the roots. [21]Peter remembered and said to Jesus, "Rabbi, look! The fig tree you cursed has withered!"

[22]"Have faith in God," Jesus answered. [23]"Truly[d] I tell you, if anyone says to this mountain, 'Go, throw yourself into the sea,' and does not doubt in their heart but believes that what they say will happen, it will be done for them. [24]Therefore I tell you, whatever you ask for in prayer, believe that you have received it, and it will be yours. [25]And when you stand praying, if you hold anything against anyone, forgive them, so that your Father in heaven may forgive you your sins." [26][e]

The Authority of Jesus Questioned

[27]They arrived again in Jerusalem, and while Jesus was walking in the temple courts, the chief priests, the teachers of the law and the elders came to him. [28]"By what authority are you doing these things?" they asked. "And who gave you authority to do this?"

[29]Jesus replied, "I will ask you one question. Answer me, and I will tell you by what authority I am doing these things. [30]John's baptism—was it from heaven, or of human origin? Tell me!"

[31]They discussed it among themselves and said, "If we say, 'From heaven,' he will ask, 'Then why didn't you believe him?' [32]But if we say, 'Of human origin' . . . ." (They feared the people, for everyone held that John really was a prophet.)

[33]So they answered Jesus, "We don't know."

Jesus said, "Neither will I tell you by what authority I am doing these things."

The Parable of the Tenants

12 Jesus then began to speak to them in parables: "A man planted a vineyard. He put a wall around it, dug a pit for the winepress and built a watchtower. Then he rented the vineyard to some farmers and moved to another place. [2]At harvest time he sent a servant to the tenants to collect from them some of the fruit of the vineyard. [3]But they seized him, beat him and sent him away empty-handed. [4]Then he sent another servant to them; they struck this man on the head and treated him shamefully. [5]He sent still another, and that one they killed. He sent many

others; some of them they beat, others they killed.

[6]"He had one left to send, a son, whom he loved. He sent him last of all, saying, 'They will respect my son.'

[7]"But the tenants said to one another, 'This is the heir. Come, let's kill him, and the inheritance will be ours.' [8]So they took him and killed him, and threw him out of the vineyard.

[9]"What then will the owner of the vineyard do? He will come and kill those tenants and give the vineyard to others. [10]Haven't you read this passage of Scripture:

"'The stone the builders rejected
  has become the cornerstone;
[11]the Lord has done this,
  and it is marvelous in our eyes'[f]?"

[12]Then the chief priests, the teachers of the law and the elders looked for a way to arrest him because they knew he had spoken the parable against them. But they were afraid of the crowd; so they left him and went away.

Paying the Imperial Tax to Caesar

[13]Later they sent some of the Pharisees and Herodians to Jesus to catch him in his words. [14]They came to him and said, "Teacher, we know that you are a man of integrity. You aren't swayed by others, because you pay no attention to who they are; but you teach the way of God in accordance with the truth. Is it right to pay the imperial tax[g] to Caesar or not? [15]Should we pay or shouldn't we?"

But Jesus knew their hypocrisy. "Why are you trying to trap me?" he asked. "Bring me a denarius and let me look at it." [16]They brought the coin, and he asked them, "Whose image is this? And whose inscription?"

"Caesar's," they replied.

[17]Then Jesus said to them, "Give back to Caesar what is Caesar's and to God what is God's."

And they were amazed at him.

Marriage at the Resurrection

[18]Then the Sadducees, who say there is no resurrection, came to him with a question. [19]"Teacher," they said, "Moses wrote for us that if a man's brother dies and leaves a wife but no children, the man must marry the widow and raise up offspring for his brother. [20]Now there were seven brothers. The first one married and died without leaving any children. [21]The second one married the widow, but he also died, leaving no child. It was the same with the third. [22]In fact, none of the seven left any children. Last of all, the woman died too. [23]At the resurrection[h] whose wife will she be, since the seven were married to her?"

[24]Jesus replied, "Are you not in error because you do not know the Scriptures or the power of God? [25]When the dead rise, they will neither marry nor be given in marriage;

---

[a] 17 Isaiah 56:7   [b] 17 Jer. 7:11   [c] 19 Some early manuscripts came, Jesus   [d] 22,23 Some early manuscripts "If you have faith in God," Jesus answered, [23]"truly   [e] 26 Some manuscripts include here words similar to Matt. 6:15.   [f] 11 Psalm 118:22,23   [g] 14 A special tax levied on subject peoples, not on Roman citizens   [h] 23 Some manuscripts resurrection, when people rise from the dead,

they will be like the angels in heaven. 26Now about the dead rising—have you not read in the Book of Moses, in the account of the burning bush, how God said to him, 'I am the God of Abraham, the God of Isaac, and the God of Jacob'ᵃ? 27He is not the God of the dead, but of the living. You are badly mistaken!"

The Greatest Commandment

28One of the teachers of the law came and heard them debating. Noticing that Jesus had given them a good answer, he asked him, "Of all the commandments, which is the most important?"

29"The most important one," answered Jesus, "is this: 'Hear, O Israel: The Lord our God, the Lord is one.ᵇ 30Love the Lord your God with all your heart and with all your soul and with all your mind and with all your strength.'ᶜ 31The second is this: 'Love your neighbor as yourself.'ᵈ There is no commandment greater than these."

32"Well said, teacher," the man replied. "You are right in saying that God is one and there is no other but him. 33To love him with all your heart, with all your understanding and with all your strength, and to love your neighbor as yourself is more important than all burnt offerings and sacrifices."

34When Jesus saw that he had answered wisely, he said to him, "You are not far from the kingdom of God." And from then on no one dared ask him any more questions.

Whose Son Is the Messiah?

35While Jesus was teaching in the temple courts, he asked, "Why do the teachers of the law say that the Messiah is the son of David? 36David himself, speaking by the Holy Spirit, declared:

"'The Lord said to my Lord:
"Sit at my right hand
until I put your enemies
under your feet."'ᵉ

37David himself calls him 'Lord.' How then can he be his son?"

The large crowd listened to him with delight.

Warning Against the Teachers of the Law

38As he taught, Jesus said, "Watch out for the teachers of the law. They like to walk around in flowing robes and be greeted with respect in the marketplaces, 39and have the most important seats in the synagogues and the places of honor at banquets. 40They devour widows' houses and for a show make lengthy prayers. These men will be punished most severely."

The Widow's Offering

41Jesus sat down opposite the place where the offerings were put and watched the crowd putting their money into the temple treasury. Many rich people threw in large amounts. 42But a poor widow came and put in two very small copper coins, worth only a few cents.

43Calling his disciples to him, Jesus said, "Truly I tell you, this poor widow has put more into the treasury than all the others. 44They all gave out of their wealth; but she, out of her poverty, put in everything—all she had to live on."

The Destruction of the Temple and Signs of the End Times

13 As Jesus was leaving the temple, one of his disciples said to him, "Look, Teacher! What massive stones! What magnificent buildings!"

2"Do you see all these great buildings?" replied Jesus. "Not one stone here will be left on another; every one will be thrown down."

3As Jesus was sitting on the Mount of Olives opposite the temple, Peter, James, John and Andrew asked him privately, 4"Tell us, when will these things happen? And what will be the sign that they are all about to be fulfilled?"

5Jesus said to them: "Watch out that no one deceives you. 6Many will come in my name, claiming, 'I am he,' and will deceive many. 7When you hear of wars and rumors of wars, do not be alarmed. Such things must happen, but the end is still to come. 8Nation will rise against nation, and kingdom against kingdom. There will be earthquakes in various places, and famines. These are the beginning of birth pains.

9"You must be on your guard. You will be handed over to the local councils and flogged in the synagogues. On account of me you will stand before governors and kings as witnesses to them. 10And the gospel must first be preached to all nations. 11Whenever you are arrested and brought to trial, do not worry beforehand about what to say. Just say whatever is given you at the time, for it is not you speaking, but the Holy Spirit.

12"Brother will betray brother to death, and a father his child. Children will rebel against their parents and have them put to death. 13Everyone will hate you because of me, but the one who stands firm to the end will be saved.

14"When you see 'the abomination that causes desolation'ᶠ standing where itᵍ does not belong—let the reader understand—then let those who are in Judea flee to the mountains. 15Let no one on the housetop go down or enter the house to take anything out. 16Let no one in the field go back to get their cloak. 17How dreadful it will be in those days for pregnant women and nursing mothers! 18Pray that this will not take place in winter, 19because those will be days of distress unequaled from the beginning, when God created the world, until now—and never to be equaled again.

20"If the Lord had not cut short those days, no one would survive. But for the sake of the elect, whom he has chosen, he has shortened them. 21At that time if anyone says to you,

---

ᵃ 26 Exodus 3:6   ᵇ 29 Or The Lord our God is one Lord   ᶜ 30 Deut. 6:4,5   ᵈ 31 Lev. 19:18
ᵉ 36 Psalm 110:1   ᶠ 14 Daniel 9:27; 11:31; 12:11   ᵍ 14 Or he

'Look, here is the Messiah!' or, 'Look, there he is!' do not believe it. [22]For false messiahs and false prophets will appear and perform signs and wonders to deceive, if possible, even the elect. [23]So be on your guard; I have told you everything ahead of time.

[24]"But in those days, following that distress,

> "'the sun will be darkened,
>   and the moon will not give its light;
> [25]the stars will fall from the sky,
>   and the heavenly bodies will be
>   shaken.'[a]

[26]"At that time people will see the Son of Man coming in clouds with great power and glory. [27]And he will send his angels and gather his elect from the four winds, from the ends of the earth to the ends of the heavens.

[28]"Now learn this lesson from the fig tree: As soon as its twigs get tender and its leaves come out, you know that summer is near. [29]Even so, when you see these things happening, you know that it[b] is near, right at the door. [30]Truly I tell you, this generation will certainly not pass away until all these things have happened. [31]Heaven and earth will pass away, but my words will never pass away.

The Day and Hour Unknown

[32]"But about that day or hour no one knows, not even the angels in heaven, nor the Son, but only the Father. [33]Be on guard! Be alert[c]! You do not know when that time will come. [34]It's like a man going away: He leaves his house and puts his servants in charge, each with their assigned task, and tells the one at the door to keep watch.

[35]"Therefore keep watch because you do not know when the owner of the house will come back—whether in the evening, or at midnight, or when the rooster crows, or at dawn. [36]If he comes suddenly, do not let him find you sleeping. [37]What I say to you, I say to everyone: 'Watch!'"

Jesus Anointed at Bethany

14 Now the Passover and the Festival of Unleavened Bread were only two days away, and the chief priests and the teachers of the law were scheming to arrest Jesus secretly and kill him. [2]"But not during the festival," they said, "or the people may riot."

[3]While he was in Bethany, reclining at the table in the home of Simon the Leper, a woman came with an alabaster jar of very expensive perfume, made of pure nard. She broke the jar and poured the perfume on his head. [4]Some of those present were saying indignantly to one another, "Why this waste of perfume? [5]It could have been sold for more than a year's wages[d] and the money given to the poor." And they rebuked her harshly.

[6]"Leave her alone," said Jesus. "Why are you bothering her? She has done a beautiful thing to me. [7]The poor you will always have with you,[e] and you can help them any time you want. But you will not always have me. [8]She did what she could. She poured perfume on my body beforehand to prepare for my burial. [9]Truly I tell you, wherever the gospel is preached throughout the world, what she has done will also be told, in memory of her."

[10]Then Judas Iscariot, one of the Twelve, went to the chief priests to betray Jesus to them. [11]They were delighted to hear this and promised to give him money. So he watched for an opportunity to hand him over.

The Last Supper

[12]On the first day of the Festival of Unleavened Bread, when it was customary to sacrifice the Passover lamb, Jesus' disciples asked him, "Where do you want us to go and make preparations for you to eat the Passover?"

[13]So he sent two of his disciples, telling them, "Go into the city, and a man carrying a jar of water will meet you. Follow him. [14]Say to the owner of the house he enters, 'The Teacher asks: Where is my guest room, where I may eat the Passover with my disciples?' [15]He will show you a large room upstairs, furnished and ready. Make preparations for us there."

[16]The disciples left, went into the city and found things just as Jesus had told them. So they prepared the Passover.

[17]When evening came, Jesus arrived with the Twelve. [18]While they were reclining at the table eating, he said, "Truly I tell you, one of you will betray me—one who is eating with me."

[19]They were saddened, and one by one they said to him, "Surely you don't mean me?"

[20]"It is one of the Twelve," he replied, "one who dips bread into the bowl with me. [21]The Son of Man will go just as it is written about him. But woe to that man who betrays the Son of Man! It would be better for him if he had not been born."

[22]While they were eating, Jesus took bread, and when he had given thanks, he broke it and gave it to his disciples, saying, "Take it; this is my body."

[23]Then he took a cup, and when he had given thanks, he gave it to them, and they all drank from it.

[24]"This is my blood of the[f] covenant, which is poured out for many," he said to them. [25]"Truly I tell you, I will not drink again from the fruit of the vine until that day when I drink it new in the kingdom of God."

[26]When they had sung a hymn, they went out to the Mount of Olives.

Jesus Predicts Peter's Denial

[27]"You will all fall away," Jesus told them, "for it is written:

> "'I will strike the shepherd,
>   and the sheep will be scattered.'[g]

[28]But after I have risen, I will go ahead of you into Galilee."

---

[a] 25 Isaiah 13:10; 34:4   [b] 29 Or he   [c] 33 Some manuscripts *alert and pray*   [d] 5 Greek *than three hundred denarii*   [e] 7 See Deut. 15:11.   [f] 24 Some manuscripts *the new*   [g] 27 Zech. 13:7

²⁹Peter declared, "Even if all fall away, I will not."

³⁰"Truly I tell you," Jesus answered, "today—yes, tonight—before the rooster crows twice[a] you yourself will disown me three times."

³¹But Peter insisted emphatically, "Even if I have to die with you, I will never disown you." And all the others said the same.

Gethsemane

³²They went to a place called Gethsemane, and Jesus said to his disciples, "Sit here while I pray." ³³He took Peter, James and John along with him, and he began to be deeply distressed and troubled. ³⁴"My soul is overwhelmed with sorrow to the point of death," he said to them. "Stay here and keep watch."

³⁵Going a little farther, he fell to the ground and prayed that if possible the hour might pass from him. ³⁶"Abba,[b] Father," he said, "everything is possible for you. Take this cup from me. Yet not what I will, but what you will."

³⁷Then he returned to his disciples and found them sleeping. "Simon," he said to Peter, "are you asleep? Couldn't you keep watch for one hour? ³⁸Watch and pray so that you will not fall into temptation. The spirit is willing, but the flesh is weak."

³⁹Once more he went away and prayed the same thing. ⁴⁰When he came back, he again found them sleeping, because their eyes were heavy. They did not know what to say to him.

⁴¹Returning the third time, he said to them, "Are you still sleeping and resting? Enough! The hour has come. Look, the Son of Man is delivered into the hands of sinners. ⁴²Rise! Let us go! Here comes my betrayer!"

Jesus Arrested

⁴³Just as he was speaking, Judas, one of the Twelve, appeared. With him was a crowd armed with swords and clubs, sent from the chief priests, the teachers of the law, and the elders. ⁴⁴Now the betrayer had arranged a signal with them: "The one I kiss is the man; arrest him and lead him away under guard." ⁴⁵Going at once to Jesus, Judas said, "Rabbi!" and kissed him. ⁴⁶The men seized Jesus and arrested him. ⁴⁷Then one of those standing near drew his sword and struck the servant of the high priest, cutting off his ear.

⁴⁸"Am I leading a rebellion," said Jesus, "that you have come out with swords and clubs to capture me? ⁴⁹Every day I was with you, teaching in the temple courts, and you did not arrest me. But the Scriptures must be fulfilled." ⁵⁰Then everyone deserted him and fled.

⁵¹A young man, wearing nothing but a linen garment, was following Jesus. When they seized him, ⁵²he fled naked, leaving his garment behind.

Jesus Before the Sanhedrin

⁵³They took Jesus to the high priest, and all the chief priests, the elders and the teachers of the law came together. ⁵⁴Peter followed him at a distance, right into the courtyard of the high priest. There he sat with the guards and warmed himself at the fire.

⁵⁵The chief priests and the whole Sanhedrin were looking for evidence against Jesus so that they could put him to death, but they did not find any. ⁵⁶Many testified falsely against him, but their statements did not agree.

⁵⁷Then some stood up and gave this false testimony against him: ⁵⁸"We heard him say, 'I will destroy this temple made with human hands and in three days will build another, not made with hands.'" ⁵⁹Yet even then their testimony did not agree.

⁶⁰Then the high priest stood up before them and asked Jesus, "Are you not going to answer? What is this testimony that these men are bringing against you?" ⁶¹But Jesus remained silent and gave no answer.

Again the high priest asked him, "Are you the Messiah, the Son of the Blessed One?"

⁶²"I am," said Jesus. "And you will see the Son of Man sitting at the right hand of the Mighty One and coming on the clouds of heaven."

⁶³The high priest tore his clothes. "Why do we need any more witnesses?" he asked. ⁶⁴"You have heard the blasphemy. What do you think?"

They all condemned him as worthy of death. ⁶⁵Then some began to spit at him; they blindfolded him, struck him with their fists, and said, "Prophesy!" And the guards took him and beat him.

Peter Disowns Jesus

⁶⁶While Peter was below in the courtyard, one of the servant girls of the high priest came by. ⁶⁷When she saw Peter warming himself, she looked closely at him.

"You also were with that Nazarene, Jesus," she said.

⁶⁸But he denied it. "I don't know or understand what you're talking about," he said, and went out into the entryway.[c]

⁶⁹When the servant girl saw him there, she said again to those standing around, "This fellow is one of them." ⁷⁰Again he denied it.

After a little while, those standing near said to Peter, "Surely you are one of them, for you are a Galilean."

⁷¹He began to call down curses, and he swore to them, "I don't know this man you're talking about."

⁷²Immediately the rooster crowed the second time.[d] Then Peter remembered the word Jesus had spoken to him: "Before the rooster crows twice[a] you will disown me three times." And he broke down and wept.

Jesus Before Pilate

15 Very early in the morning, the chief priests, with the elders, the teachers of the law and the whole Sanhedrin, made their

---

[a] 30,72 Some early manuscripts do not have twice.   [b] 36 Aramaic for father   [c] 68 Some early manuscripts entryway and the rooster crowed   [d] 72 Some early manuscripts do not have the second time.

plans. So they bound Jesus, led him away and handed him over to Pilate.

[2]"Are you the king of the Jews?" asked Pilate.

"You have said so," Jesus replied.

[3]The chief priests accused him of many things. [4]So again Pilate asked him, "Aren't you going to answer? See how many things they are accusing you of."

[5]But Jesus still made no reply, and Pilate was amazed.

[6]Now it was the custom at the festival to release a prisoner whom the people requested. [7]A man called Barabbas was in prison with the insurrectionists who had committed murder in the uprising. [8]The crowd came up and asked Pilate to do for them what he usually did.

[9]"Do you want me to release to you the king of the Jews?" asked Pilate, [10]knowing it was out of self-interest that the chief priests had handed Jesus over to him. [11]But the chief priests stirred up the crowd to have Pilate release Barabbas instead.

[12]"What shall I do, then, with the one you call the king of the Jews?" Pilate asked them.

[13]"Crucify him!" they shouted.

[14]"Why? What crime has he committed?" asked Pilate.

But they shouted all the louder, "Crucify him!"

[15]Wanting to satisfy the crowd, Pilate released Barabbas to them. He had Jesus flogged, and handed him over to be crucified.

The Soldiers Mock Jesus

[16]The soldiers led Jesus away into the palace (that is, the Praetorium) and called together the whole company of soldiers. [17]They put a purple robe on him, then twisted together a crown of thorns and set it on him. [18]And they began to call out to him, "Hail, king of the Jews!" [19]Again and again they struck him on the head with a staff and spit on him. Falling on their knees, they paid homage to him. [20]And when they had mocked him, they took off the purple robe and put his own clothes on him. Then they led him out to crucify him.

The Crucifixion of Jesus

[21]A certain man from Cyrene, Simon, the father of Alexander and Rufus, was passing by on his way in from the country, and they forced him to carry the cross. [22]They brought Jesus to the place called Golgotha (which means "the place of the skull"). [23]Then they offered him wine mixed with myrrh, but he did not take it. [24]And they crucified him. Dividing up his clothes, they cast lots to see what each would get.

[25]It was nine in the morning when they crucified him. [26]The written notice of the charge against him read: THE KING OF THE JEWS.

[27]They crucified two rebels with him, one on his right and one on his left. [28][a] [29]Those who passed by hurled insults at him, shaking their heads and saying, "So! You who are going to destroy the temple and build it in three days, [30]come down from the cross and save yourself!" [31]In the same way the chief priests and the teachers of the law mocked him among themselves. "He saved others," they said, "but he can't save himself! [32]Let this Messiah, this king of Israel, come down now from the cross, that we may see and believe." Those crucified with him also heaped insults on him.

The Death of Jesus

[33]At noon, darkness came over the whole land until three in the afternoon. [34]And at three in the afternoon Jesus cried out in a loud voice, "*Eloi, Eloi, lema sabachthani?*" (which means "My God, my God, why have you forsaken me?").[b]

[35]When some of those standing near heard this, they said, "Listen, he's calling Elijah."

[36]Someone ran, filled a sponge with wine vinegar, put it on a staff, and offered it to Jesus to drink. "Now leave him alone. Let's see if Elijah comes to take him down," he said.

[37]With a loud cry, Jesus breathed his last.

[38]The curtain of the temple was torn in two from top to bottom. [39]And when the centurion, who stood there in front of Jesus, saw how he died,[c] he said, "Surely this man was the Son of God!"

[40]Some women were watching from a distance. Among them were Mary Magdalene, Mary the mother of James the younger and of Joseph,[d] and Salome. [41]In Galilee these women had followed him and cared for his needs. Many other women who had come up with him to Jerusalem were also there.

The Burial of Jesus

[42]It was Preparation Day (that is, the day before the Sabbath). So as evening approached, [43]Joseph of Arimathea, a prominent member of the Council, who was himself waiting for the kingdom of God, went boldly to Pilate and asked for Jesus' body. [44]Pilate was surprised to hear that he was already dead. Summoning the centurion, he asked him if Jesus had already died. [45]When he learned from the centurion that it was so, he gave the body to Joseph. [46]So Joseph bought some linen cloth, took down the body, wrapped it in the linen, and placed it in a tomb cut out of rock. Then he rolled a stone against the entrance of the tomb. [47]Mary Magdalene and Mary the mother of Joseph saw where he was laid.

Jesus Has Risen

16 When the Sabbath was over, Mary Magdalene, Mary the mother of James, and Salome bought spices so that they might go to anoint Jesus' body. [2]Very early on the first day of the week, just after sunrise, they were on their way to the tomb [3]and they asked each other, "Who will roll the stone away from the entrance of the tomb?"

---

a 28 Some manuscripts include here words similar to Luke 22:37.   *b 34* Psalm 22:1   *c 39* Some manuscripts *saw that he died with such a cry*   *d 40* Greek *Joses*, a variant of *Joseph*; also in verse 47

⁴But when they looked up, they saw that the stone, which was very large, had been rolled away. ⁵As they entered the tomb, they saw a young man dressed in a white robe sitting on the right side, and they were alarmed.

⁶"Don't be alarmed," he said. "You are looking for Jesus the Nazarene, who was crucified. He has risen! He is not here. See the place where they laid him. ⁷But go, tell his disciples and Peter, 'He is going ahead of you into Galilee. There you will see him, just as he told you.'"

⁸Trembling and bewildered, the women went out and fled from the tomb. They said nothing to anyone, because they were afraid.ᵃ

[The earliest manuscripts and some other ancient witnesses do not have verses 9–20.]

⁹When Jesus rose early on the first day of the week, he appeared first to Mary Magdalene, out of whom he had driven seven demons. ¹⁰She went and told those who had been with him and who were mourning and weeping. ¹¹When they heard that Jesus was alive and that she had seen him, they did not believe it.

¹²Afterward Jesus appeared in a different form to two of them while they were walking in the country. ¹³These returned and reported it to the rest; but they did not believe them either.

¹⁴Later Jesus appeared to the Eleven as they were eating; he rebuked them for their lack of faith and their stubborn refusal to believe those who had seen him after he had risen.

¹⁵He said to them, "Go into all the world and preach the gospel to all creation. ¹⁶Whoever believes and is baptized will be saved, but whoever does not believe will be condemned. ¹⁷And these signs will accompany those who believe: In my name they will drive out demons; they will speak in new tongues; ¹⁸they will pick up snakes with their hands; and when they drink deadly poison, it will not hurt them at all; they will place their hands on sick people, and they will get well."

¹⁹After the Lord Jesus had spoken to them, he was taken up into heaven and he sat at the right hand of God. ²⁰Then the disciples went out and preached everywhere, and the Lord worked with them and confirmed his word by the signs that accompanied it.

Luke

Introduction

1 Many have undertaken to draw up an account of the things that have been fulfilledᵇ among us, ²just as they were handed down to us by those who from the first were eyewitnesses and servants of the word. ³With this in mind, since I myself have carefully investigated everything from the beginning, I too decided to write an orderly account for you, most excellent Theophilus, ⁴so that you may know the certainty of the things you have been taught.

The Birth of John the Baptist Foretold

⁵In the time of Herod king of Judea there was a priest named Zechariah, who belonged to the priestly division of Abijah; his wife Elizabeth was also a descendant of Aaron. ⁶Both of them were righteous in the sight of God, observing all the Lord's commands and decrees blamelessly. ⁷But they were childless because Elizabeth was not able to conceive, and they were both very old.

⁸Once when Zechariah's division was on duty and he was serving as priest before God, ⁹he was chosen by lot, according to the custom of the priesthood, to go into the temple of the Lord and burn incense. ¹⁰And when the time for the burning of incense came, all the assembled worshipers were praying outside.

¹¹Then an angel of the Lord appeared to him, standing at the right side of the altar of incense. ¹²When Zechariah saw him, he was startled and was gripped with fear. ¹³But the angel said to him: "Do not be afraid, Zechariah; your prayer has been heard. Your wife Elizabeth will bear you a son, and you are to call him John. ¹⁴He will be a joy and delight to you, and many will rejoice because of his birth, ¹⁵for he will be great in the sight of the Lord. He is never to take wine or other fermented drink, and he will be filled with the Holy Spirit even before he is born. ¹⁶He will bring back many of the people of Israel to the Lord their God. ¹⁷And he will go on before the Lord, in the spirit and power of Elijah, to turn the hearts of the parents to their children and the disobedient to the wisdom of the righteous—to make ready a people prepared for the Lord."

¹⁸Zechariah asked the angel, "How can I be sure of this? I am an old man and my wife is well along in years."

¹⁹The angel said to him, "I am Gabriel. I

ᵃ 8 Some manuscripts have the following ending between verses 8 and 9, and one manuscript has it after verse 8 (omitting verses 9-20): *Then they quickly reported all these instructions to those around Peter. After this, Jesus himself also sent out through them from east to west the sacred and imperishable proclamation of eternal salvation. Amen.* ᵇ 1 Or *been surely believed*

stand in the presence of God, and I have been sent to speak to you and to tell you this good news. ²⁰And now you will be silent and not able to speak until the day this happens, because you did not believe my words, which will come true at their appointed time."

²¹Meanwhile, the people were waiting for Zechariah and wondering why he stayed so long in the temple. ²²When he came out, he could not speak to them. They realized he had seen a vision in the temple, for he kept making signs to them but remained unable to speak.

²³When his time of service was completed, he returned home. ²⁴After this his wife Elizabeth became pregnant and for five months remained in seclusion. ²⁵"The Lord has done this for me," she said. "In these days he has shown his favor and taken away my disgrace among the people."

The Birth of Jesus Foretold

²⁶In the sixth month of Elizabeth's pregnancy, God sent the angel Gabriel to Nazareth, a town in Galilee, ²⁷to a virgin pledged to be married to a man named Joseph, a descendant of David. The virgin's name was Mary. ²⁸The angel went to her and said, "Greetings, you who are highly favored! The Lord is with you."

²⁹Mary was greatly troubled at his words and wondered what kind of greeting this might be. ³⁰But the angel said to her, "Do not be afraid, Mary; you have found favor with God. ³¹You will conceive and give birth to a son, and you are to call him Jesus. ³²He will be great and will be called the Son of the Most High. The Lord God will give him the throne of his father David, ³³and he will reign over Jacob's descendants forever; his kingdom will never end."

³⁴"How will this be," Mary asked the angel, "since I am a virgin?"

³⁵The angel answered, "The Holy Spirit will come on you, and the power of the Most High will overshadow you. So the holy one to be born will be called*a* the Son of God. ³⁶Even Elizabeth your relative is going to have a child in her old age, and she who was said to be unable to conceive is in her sixth month. ³⁷For no word from God will ever fail."

³⁸"I am the Lord's servant," Mary answered. "May your word to me be fulfilled." Then the angel left her.

Mary Visits Elizabeth

³⁹At that time Mary got ready and hurried to a town in the hill country of Judea, ⁴⁰where she entered Zechariah's home and greeted Elizabeth. ⁴¹When Elizabeth heard Mary's greeting, the baby leaped in her womb, and Elizabeth was filled with the Holy Spirit. ⁴²In a loud voice she exclaimed: "Blessed are you among women, and blessed is the child you will bear! ⁴³But why am I so favored, that the mother of my Lord should come to me? ⁴⁴As soon as the sound of your greeting reached my ears, the baby in my womb leaped for joy.

⁴⁵Blessed is she who has believed that the Lord would fulfill his promises to her!"

Mary's Song

⁴⁶And Mary said:

"My soul glorifies the Lord
⁴⁷   and my spirit rejoices in God my
       Savior,
⁴⁸for he has been mindful
   of the humble state of his servant.
From now on all generations will call me
       blessed,
⁴⁹   for the Mighty One has done great
       things for me—
   holy is his name.
⁵⁰His mercy extends to those who fear him,
   from generation to generation.
⁵¹He has performed mighty deeds with his
       arm;
   he has scattered those who are proud in
       their inmost thoughts.
⁵²He has brought down rulers from their
       thrones
   but has lifted up the humble.
⁵³He has filled the hungry with good things
   but has sent the rich away empty.
⁵⁴He has helped his servant Israel,
   remembering to be merciful
⁵⁵to Abraham and his descendants forever,
   just as he promised our ancestors."

⁵⁶Mary stayed with Elizabeth for about three months and then returned home.

The Birth of John the Baptist

⁵⁷When it was time for Elizabeth to have her baby, she gave birth to a son. ⁵⁸Her neighbors and relatives heard that the Lord had shown her great mercy, and they shared her joy.

⁵⁹On the eighth day they came to circumcise the child, and they were going to name him after his father Zechariah, ⁶⁰but his mother spoke up and said, "No! He is to be called John."

⁶¹They said to her, "There is no one among your relatives who has that name."

⁶²Then they made signs to his father, to find out what he would like to name the child. ⁶³He asked for a writing tablet, and to everyone's astonishment he wrote, "His name is John." ⁶⁴Immediately his mouth was opened and his tongue set free, and he began to speak, praising God. ⁶⁵All the neighbors were filled with awe, and throughout the hill country of Judea people were talking about all these things. ⁶⁶Everyone who heard this wondered about it, asking, "What then is this child going to be?" For the Lord's hand was with him.

Zechariah's Song

⁶⁷His father Zechariah was filled with the Holy Spirit and prophesied:

⁶⁸"Praise be to the Lord, the God of Israel,
   because he has come to his people and
       redeemed them.

---

a 35 Or *So the child to be born will be called holy,*

[69] He has raised up a horn[a] of salvation
for us
in the house of his servant David
[70] (as he said through his holy prophets of
long ago),
[71] salvation from our enemies
and from the hand of all who hate us—
[72] to show mercy to our ancestors
and to remember his holy covenant,
[73] the oath he swore to our father
Abraham:
[74] to rescue us from the hand of our
enemies,
and to enable us to serve him without
fear
[75] in holiness and righteousness before
him all our days.

[76] And you, my child, will be called a
prophet of the Most High;
for you will go on before the Lord to
prepare the way for him,
[77] to give his people the knowledge of
salvation
through the forgiveness of their sins,
[78] because of the tender mercy of our God,
by which the rising sun will come to us
from heaven
[79] to shine on those living in darkness
and in the shadow of death,
to guide our feet into the path of peace."

[80] And the child grew and became strong in
spirit[b]; and he lived in the wilderness until he
appeared publicly to Israel.

The Birth of Jesus

2 In those days Caesar Augustus issued a decree that a census should be taken of the entire Roman world. [2](This was the first census that took place while[c] Quirinius was governor of Syria.) [3]And everyone went to their own town to register.

[4]So Joseph also went up from the town of Nazareth in Galilee to Judea, to Bethlehem the town of David, because he belonged to the house and line of David. [5]He went there to register with Mary, who was pledged to be married to him and was expecting a child. [6]While they were there, the time came for the baby to be born, [7]and she gave birth to her firstborn, a son. She wrapped him in cloths and placed him in a manger, because there was no guest room available for them.

[8]And there were shepherds living out in the fields nearby, keeping watch over their flocks at night. [9]An angel of the Lord appeared to them, and the glory of the Lord shone around them, and they were terrified. [10]But the angel said to them, "Do not be afraid. I bring you good news that will cause great joy for all the people. [11]Today in the town of David a Savior has been born to you; he is the Messiah, the Lord. [12]This will be a sign to you: You will find a baby wrapped in cloths and lying in a manger."

[13]Suddenly a great company of the heavenly host appeared with the angel, praising God and saying,

[14] "Glory to God in the highest heaven,
and on earth peace to those on whom
his favor rests."

[15]When the angels had left them and gone into heaven, the shepherds said to one another, "Let's go to Bethlehem and see this thing that has happened, which the Lord has told us about."

[16]So they hurried off and found Mary and Joseph, and the baby, who was lying in the manger. [17]When they had seen him, they spread the word concerning what had been told them about this child, [18]and all who heard it were amazed at what the shepherds said to them. [19]But Mary treasured up all these things and pondered them in her heart. [20]The shepherds returned, glorifying and praising God for all the things they had heard and seen, which were just as they had been told.

[21]On the eighth day, when it was time to circumcise the child, he was named Jesus, the name the angel had given him before he was conceived.

Jesus Presented in the Temple

[22]When the time came for the purification rites required by the Law of Moses, Joseph and Mary took him to Jerusalem to present him to the Lord [23](as it is written in the Law of the Lord, "Every firstborn male is to be consecrated to the Lord"[d]), [24]and to offer a sacrifice in keeping with what is said in the Law of the Lord: "a pair of doves or two young pigeons."[e]

[25]Now there was a man in Jerusalem called Simeon, who was righteous and devout. He was waiting for the consolation of Israel, and the Holy Spirit was on him. [26]It had been revealed to him by the Holy Spirit that he would not die before he had seen the Lord's Messiah. [27]Moved by the Spirit, he went into the temple courts. When the parents brought in the child Jesus to do for him what the custom of the Law required, [28]Simeon took him in his arms and praised God, saying:

[29] "Sovereign Lord, as you have promised,
you may now dismiss[f] your servant in
peace.
[30] For my eyes have seen your salvation,
[31] which you have prepared in the sight of
all nations:
[32] a light for revelation to the Gentiles,
and the glory of your people Israel."

[33]The child's father and mother marveled at what was said about him. [34]Then Simeon blessed them and said to Mary, his mother: "This child is destined to cause the falling and rising of many in Israel, and to be a sign that will be spoken against, [35]so that the thoughts of many hearts will be revealed. And a sword will pierce your own soul too."

[36]There was also a prophet, Anna, the

a 69 Horn here symbolizes a strong king.   b 80 Or in the Spirit   c 2 Or This census took place before   d 23 Exodus 13:2,12   e 24 Lev. 12:8   f 29 Or promised, / now dismiss

daughter of Penuel, of the tribe of Asher. She was very old; she had lived with her husband seven years after her marriage, [37]and then was a widow until she was eighty-four.[a] She never left the temple but worshiped night and day, fasting and praying. [38]Coming up to them at that very moment, she gave thanks to God and spoke about the child to all who were looking forward to the redemption of Jerusalem.

[39]When Joseph and Mary had done everything required by the Law of the Lord, they returned to Galilee to their own town of Nazareth. [40]And the child grew and became strong; he was filled with wisdom, and the grace of God was on him.

The Boy Jesus at the Temple

[41]Every year Jesus' parents went to Jerusalem for the Festival of the Passover. [42]When he was twelve years old, they went up to the festival, according to the custom. [43]After the festival was over, while his parents were returning home, the boy Jesus stayed behind in Jerusalem, but they were unaware of it. [44]Thinking he was in their company, they traveled on for a day. Then they began looking for him among their relatives and friends. [45]When they did not find him, they went back to Jerusalem to look for him. [46]After three days they found him in the temple courts, sitting among the teachers, listening to them and asking them questions. [47]Everyone who heard him was amazed at his understanding and his answers. [48]When his parents saw him, they were astonished. His mother said to him, "Son, why have you treated us like this? Your father and I have been anxiously searching for you."

[49]"Why were you searching for me?" he asked. "Didn't you know I had to be in my Father's house?"[b] [50]But they did not understand what he was saying to them.

[51]Then he went down to Nazareth with them and was obedient to them. But his mother treasured all these things in her heart. [52]And Jesus grew in wisdom and stature, and in favor with God and man.

John the Baptist Prepares the Way

3 In the fifteenth year of the reign of Tiberius Caesar—when Pontius Pilate was governor of Judea, Herod tetrarch of Galilee, his brother Philip tetrarch of Iturea and Traconitis, and Lysanias tetrarch of Abilene— [2]during the high-priesthood of Annas and Caiaphas, the word of God came to John son of Zechariah in the wilderness. [3]He went into all the country around the Jordan, preaching a baptism of repentance for the forgiveness of sins. [4]As it is written in the book of the words of Isaiah the prophet:

"A voice of one calling in the wilderness,
'Prepare the way for the Lord,
make straight paths for him.

[5]Every valley shall be filled in,
every mountain and hill made low.
The crooked roads shall become straight,
the rough ways smooth.
[6]And all people will see God's salvation.'"[c]

[7]John said to the crowds coming out to be baptized by him, "You brood of vipers! Who warned you to flee from the coming wrath? [8]Produce fruit in keeping with repentance. And do not begin to say to yourselves, 'We have Abraham as our father.' For I tell you that out of these stones God can raise up children for Abraham. [9]The ax is already at the root of the trees, and every tree that does not produce good fruit will be cut down and thrown into the fire."

[10]"What should we do then?" the crowd asked.

[11]John answered, "Anyone who has two shirts should share with the one who has none, and anyone who has food should do the same."

[12]Even tax collectors came to be baptized. "Teacher," they asked, "what should we do?"

[13]"Don't collect any more than you are required to," he told them.

[14]Then some soldiers asked him, "And what should we do?"

He replied, "Don't extort money and don't accuse people falsely—be content with your pay."

[15]The people were waiting expectantly and were all wondering in their hearts if John might possibly be the Messiah. [16]John answered them all, "I baptize you with[d] water. But one who is more powerful than I will come, the straps of whose sandals I am not worthy to untie. He will baptize you with[d] the Holy Spirit and fire. [17]His winnowing fork is in his hand to clear his threshing floor and to gather the wheat into his barn, but he will burn up the chaff with unquenchable fire." [18]And with many other words John exhorted the people and proclaimed the good news to them.

[19]But when John rebuked Herod the tetrarch because of his marriage to Herodias, his brother's wife, and all the other evil things he had done, [20]Herod added this to them all: He locked John up in prison.

The Baptism and Genealogy of Jesus

[21]When all the people were being baptized, Jesus was baptized too. And as he was praying, heaven was opened [22]and the Holy Spirit descended on him in bodily form like a dove. And a voice came from heaven: "You are my Son, whom I love; with you I am well pleased."

[23]Now Jesus himself was about thirty years old when he began his ministry. He was the son, so it was thought, of Joseph,

the son of Heli, [24]the son of Matthat,
the son of Levi, the son of Melki,
the son of Jannai, the son of Joseph,
[25]the son of Mattathias, the son of Amos,
the son of Nahum, the son of Esli,

the son of Naggai, 26the son of Maath,
the son of Mattathias, the son of Semein,
the son of Josek, the son of Joda,
27the son of Joanan, the son of Rhesa,
the son of Zerubbabel, the son of Shealtiel,
the son of Neri, 28the son of Melki,
the son of Addi, the son of Cosam,
the son of Elmadam, the son of Er,
29the son of Joshua, the son of Eliezer,
the son of Jorim, the son of Matthat,
the son of Levi, 30the son of Simeon,
the son of Judah, the son of Joseph,
the son of Jonam, the son of Eliakim,
31the son of Melea, the son of Menna,
the son of Mattatha, the son of Nathan,
the son of David, 32the son of Jesse,
the son of Obed, the son of Boaz,
the son of Salmon,a the son of Nahshon,
33the son of Amminadab, the son of Ram,b
the son of Hezron, the son of Perez,
the son of Judah, 34the son of Jacob,
the son of Isaac, the son of Abraham,
the son of Terah, the son of Nahor,
35the son of Serug, the son of Reu,
the son of Peleg, the son of Eber,
the son of Shelah, 36the son of Cainan,
the son of Arphaxad, the son of Shem,
the son of Noah, the son of Lamech,
37the son of Methuselah, the son of Enoch,
the son of Jared, the son of Mahalalel,
the son of Kenan, 38the son of Enosh,
the son of Seth, the son of Adam,
the son of God.

Jesus Is Tested in the Wilderness

4 Jesus, full of the Holy Spirit, left the Jordan and was led by the Spirit into the wilderness, 2where for forty days he was temptedc by the devil. He ate nothing during those days, and at the end of them he was hungry.
3The devil said to him, "If you are the Son of God, tell this stone to become bread."
4Jesus answered, "It is written: 'Man shall not live on bread alone.'d"
5The devil led him up to a high place and showed him in an instant all the kingdoms of the world. 6And he said to him, "I will give you all their authority and splendor; it has been given to me, and I can give it to anyone I want to. 7If you worship me, it will all be yours."
8Jesus answered, "It is written: 'Worship the Lord your God and serve him only.'e"
9The devil led him to Jerusalem and had him stand on the highest point of the temple. "If you are the Son of God," he said, "throw yourself down from here. 10For it is written:

" 'He will command his angels concerning
you
to guard you carefully;
11they will lift you up in their hands,
so that you will not strike your foot
against a stone.'f"

12Jesus answered, "It is said: 'Do not put the Lord your God to the test.'g"
13When the devil had finished all this tempting, he left him until an opportune time.

Jesus Rejected at Nazareth

14Jesus returned to Galilee in the power of the Spirit, and news about him spread through the whole countryside. 15He was teaching in their synagogues, and everyone praised him.
16He went to Nazareth, where he had been brought up, and on the Sabbath day he went into the synagogue, as was his custom. He stood up to read, 17and the scroll of the prophet Isaiah was handed to him. Unrolling it, he found the place where it is written:

18"The Spirit of the Lord is on me,
because he has anointed me
to proclaim good news to the poor.
He has sent me to proclaim freedom for
the prisoners
and recovery of sight for the blind,
to set the oppressed free,
19   to proclaim the year of the Lord's
favor."h

20Then he rolled up the scroll, gave it back to the attendant and sat down. The eyes of everyone in the synagogue were fastened on him. 21He began by saying to them, "Today this scripture is fulfilled in your hearing."
22All spoke well of him and were amazed at the gracious words that came from his lips. "Isn't this Joseph's son?" they asked.
23Jesus said to them, "Surely you will quote this proverb to me: 'Physician, heal yourself!' And you will tell me, 'Do here in your hometown what we have heard that you did in Capernaum.'"
24"Truly I tell you," he continued, "no prophet is accepted in his hometown. 25I assure you that there were many widows in Israel in Elijah's time, when the sky was shut for three and a half years and there was a severe famine throughout the land. 26Yet Elijah was not sent to any of them, but to a widow in Zarephath in the region of Sidon. 27And there were many in Israel with leprosyi in the time of Elisha the prophet, yet not one of them was cleansed—only Naaman the Syrian."
28All the people in the synagogue were furious when they heard this. 29They got up, drove him out of the town, and took him to the brow of the hill on which the town was built, in order to throw him off the cliff. 30But he walked right through the crowd and went on his way.

Jesus Drives Out an Impure Spirit

31Then he went down to Capernaum, a town in Galilee, and on the Sabbath he taught the people. 32They were amazed at his teaching, because his words had authority.
33In the synagogue there was a man

---

a 32 Some early manuscripts Sala   b 33 Some manuscripts Amminadab, the son of Admin, the son of Arni; other manuscripts vary widely.   c 2 The Greek for tempted can also mean tested.
d 4 Deut. 8:3   e 8 Deut. 6:13   f 11 Psalm 91:11,12   g 12 Deut. 6:16   h 19 Isaiah 61:1,2 (see Septuagint); Isaiah 58:6   i 27 The Greek word traditionally translated leprosy was used for various diseases affecting the skin.

possessed by a demon, an impure spirit. He cried out at the top of his voice, [34]"Go away! What do you want with us, Jesus of Nazareth? Have you come to destroy us? I know who you are—the Holy One of God!"

[35]"Be quiet!" Jesus said sternly. "Come out of him!" Then the demon threw the man down before them all and came out without injuring him.

[36]All the people were amazed and said to each other, "What words these are! With authority and power he gives orders to impure spirits and they come out!" [37]And the news about him spread throughout the surrounding area.

Jesus Heals Many

[38]Jesus left the synagogue and went to the home of Simon. Now Simon's mother-in-law was suffering from a high fever, and they asked Jesus to help her. [39]So he bent over her and rebuked the fever, and it left her. She got up at once and began to wait on them.

[40]At sunset, the people brought to Jesus all who had various kinds of sickness, and laying his hands on each one, he healed them. [41]Moreover, demons came out of many people, shouting, "You are the Son of God!" But he rebuked them and would not allow them to speak, because they knew he was the Messiah.

[42]At daybreak, Jesus went out to a solitary place. The people were looking for him and when they came to where he was, they tried to keep him from leaving them. [43]But he said, "I must proclaim the good news of the kingdom of God to the other towns also, because that is why I was sent." [44]And he kept on preaching in the synagogues of Judea.

Jesus Calls His First Disciples

5 One day as Jesus was standing by the Lake of Gennesaret,[a] the people were crowding around him and listening to the word of God. [2]He saw at the water's edge two boats, left there by the fishermen, who were washing their nets. [3]He got into one of the boats, the one belonging to Simon, and asked him to put out a little from shore. Then he sat down and taught the people from the boat.

[4]When he had finished speaking, he said to Simon, "Put out into deep water, and let down the nets for a catch."

[5]Simon answered, "Master, we've worked hard all night and haven't caught anything. But because you say so, I will let down the nets."

[6]When they had done so, they caught such a large number of fish that their nets began to break. [7]So they signaled their partners in the other boat to come and help them, and they came and filled both boats so full that they began to sink.

[8]When Simon Peter saw this, he fell at Jesus' knees and said, "Go away from me, Lord; I am a sinful man!" [9]For he and all his companions were astonished at the catch of fish they had taken, [10]and so were James and John, the sons of Zebedee, Simon's partners.

Then Jesus said to Simon, "Don't be afraid; from now on you will fish for people." [11]So they pulled their boats up on shore, left everything and followed him.

Jesus Heals a Man With Leprosy

[12]While Jesus was in one of the towns, a man came along who was covered with leprosy.[b] When he saw Jesus, he fell with his face to the ground and begged him, "Lord, if you are willing, you can make me clean."

[13]Jesus reached out his hand and touched the man. "I am willing," he said. "Be clean!" And immediately the leprosy left him.

[14]Then Jesus ordered him, "Don't tell anyone, but go, show yourself to the priest and offer the sacrifices that Moses commanded for your cleansing, as a testimony to them."

[15]Yet the news about him spread all the more, so that crowds of people came to hear him and to be healed of their sicknesses. [16]But Jesus often withdrew to lonely places and prayed.

Jesus Forgives and Heals a Paralyzed Man

[17]One day Jesus was teaching, and Pharisees and teachers of the law were sitting there. They had come from every village of Galilee and from Judea and Jerusalem. And the power of the Lord was with Jesus to heal the sick. [18]Some men came carrying a paralyzed man on a mat and tried to take him into the house to lay him before Jesus. [19]When they could not find a way to do this because of the crowd, they went up on the roof and lowered him on his mat through the tiles into the middle of the crowd, right in front of Jesus.

[20]When Jesus saw their faith, he said, "Friend, your sins are forgiven."

[21]The Pharisees and the teachers of the law began thinking to themselves, "Who is this fellow who speaks blasphemy? Who can forgive sins but God alone?"

[22]Jesus knew what they were thinking and asked, "Why are you thinking these things in your hearts? [23]Which is easier: to say, 'Your sins are forgiven,' or to say, 'Get up and walk'? [24]But I want you to know that the Son of Man has authority on earth to forgive sins." So he said to the paralyzed man, "I tell you, get up, take your mat and go home." [25]Immediately he stood up in front of them, took what he had been lying on and went home praising God. [26]Everyone was amazed and gave praise to God. They were filled with awe and said, "We have seen remarkable things today."

Jesus Calls Levi and Eats With Sinners

[27]After this, Jesus went out and saw a tax collector by the name of Levi sitting at his tax booth. "Follow me," Jesus said to him, [28]and Levi got up, left everything and followed him.

---

[a] 1 That is, the Sea of Galilee [b] 12 The Greek word traditionally translated *leprosy* was used for various diseases affecting the skin.

²⁹Then Levi held a great banquet for Jesus at his house, and a large crowd of tax collectors and others were eating with them. ³⁰But the Pharisees and the teachers of the law who belonged to their sect complained to his disciples, "Why do you eat and drink with tax collectors and sinners?"

³¹Jesus answered them, "It is not the healthy who need a doctor, but the sick. ³²I have not come to call the righteous, but sinners to repentance."

Jesus Questioned About Fasting

³³They said to him, "John's disciples often fast and pray, and so do the disciples of the Pharisees, but yours go on eating and drinking."

³⁴Jesus answered, "Can you make the friends of the bridegroom fast while he is with them? ³⁵But the time will come when the bridegroom will be taken from them; in those days they will fast."

³⁶He told them this parable: "No one tears a piece out of a new garment to patch an old one. Otherwise, they will have torn the new garment, and the patch from the new will not match the old. ³⁷And no one pours new wine into old wineskins. Otherwise, the new wine will burst the skins; the wine will run out and the wineskins will be ruined. ³⁸No, new wine must be poured into new wineskins. ³⁹And no one after drinking old wine wants the new, for they say, 'The old is better.'"

Jesus Is Lord of the Sabbath

6 One Sabbath Jesus was going through the grainfields, and his disciples began to pick some heads of grain, rub them in their hands and eat the kernels. ²Some of the Pharisees asked, "Why are you doing what is unlawful on the Sabbath?"

³Jesus answered them, "Have you never read what David did when he and his companions were hungry? ⁴He entered the house of God, and taking the consecrated bread, he ate what is lawful only for priests to eat. And he also gave some to his companions." ⁵Then Jesus said to them, "The Son of Man is Lord of the Sabbath."

⁶On another Sabbath he went into the synagogue and was teaching, and a man was there whose right hand was shriveled. ⁷The Pharisees and the teachers of the law were looking for a reason to accuse Jesus, so they watched him closely to see if he would heal on the Sabbath. ⁸But Jesus knew what they were thinking and said to the man with the shriveled hand, "Get up and stand in front of everyone." So he got up and stood there.

⁹Then Jesus said to them, "I ask you, which is lawful on the Sabbath: to do good or to do evil, to save life or to destroy it?"

¹⁰He looked around at them all, and then said to the man, "Stretch out your hand." He did so, and his hand was completely restored. ¹¹But the Pharisees and the teachers of the law were furious and began to discuss with one another what they might do to Jesus.

The Twelve Apostles

¹²One of those days Jesus went out to a mountainside to pray, and spent the night praying to God. ¹³When morning came, he called his disciples to him and chose twelve of them, whom he also designated apostles: ¹⁴Simon (whom he named Peter), his brother Andrew, James, John, Philip, Bartholomew, ¹⁵Matthew, Thomas, James son of Alphaeus, Simon who was called the Zealot, ¹⁶Judas son of James, and Judas Iscariot, who became a traitor.

Blessings and Woes

¹⁷He went down with them and stood on a level place. A large crowd of his disciples was there and a great number of people from all over Judea, from Jerusalem, and from the coastal region around Tyre and Sidon, ¹⁸who had come to hear him and to be healed of their diseases. Those troubled by impure spirits were cured, ¹⁹and the people all tried to touch him, because power was coming from him and healing them all.

²⁰Looking at his disciples, he said:

"Blessed are you who are poor,
  for yours is the kingdom of God.
²¹Blessed are you who hunger now,
  for you will be satisfied.
Blessed are you who weep now,
  for you will laugh.
²²Blessed are you when people hate you,
  when they exclude you and insult you
  and reject your name as evil,
    because of the Son of Man.

²³"Rejoice in that day and leap for joy, because great is your reward in heaven. For that is how their ancestors treated the prophets.

²⁴"But woe to you who are rich,
  for you have already received your
    comfort.
²⁵Woe to you who are well fed now,
  for you will go hungry.
Woe to you who laugh now,
  for you will mourn and weep.
²⁶Woe to you when everyone speaks well of
    you,
  for that is how their ancestors treated
    the false prophets.

Love for Enemies

²⁷"But to you who are listening I say: Love your enemies, do good to those who hate you, ²⁸bless those who curse you, pray for those who mistreat you. ²⁹If someone slaps you on one cheek, turn to them the other also. If someone takes your coat, do not withhold your shirt from them. ³⁰Give to everyone who asks you, and if anyone takes what belongs to you, do not demand it back. ³¹Do to others as you would have them do to you.

³²"If you love those who love you, what credit is that to you? Even sinners love those who love them. ³³And if you do good to those who are good to you, what credit is that to you? Even sinners do that. ³⁴And if you lend to those from whom you expect repayment,

what credit is that to you? Even sinners lend to sinners, expecting to be repaid in full. **35**But love your enemies, do good to them, and lend to them without expecting to get anything back. Then your reward will be great, and you will be children of the Most High, because he is kind to the ungrateful and wicked. **36**Be merciful, just as your Father is merciful.

Judging Others

37"Do not judge, and you will not be judged. Do not condemn, and you will not be condemned. Forgive, and you will be forgiven. **38**Give, and it will be given to you. A good measure, pressed down, shaken together and running over, will be poured into your lap. For with the measure you use, it will be measured to you."

39He also told them this parable: "Can the blind lead the blind? Will they not both fall into a pit? **40**The student is not above the teacher, but everyone who is fully trained will be like their teacher.

41"Why do you look at the speck of sawdust in your brother's eye and pay no attention to the plank in your own eye? **42**How can you say to your brother, 'Brother, let me take the speck out of your eye,' when you yourself fail to see the plank in your own eye? You hypocrite, first take the plank out of your eye, and then you will see clearly to remove the speck from your brother's eye.

A Tree and Its Fruit

43"No good tree bears bad fruit, nor does a bad tree bear good fruit. **44**Each tree is recognized by its own fruit. People do not pick figs from thornbushes, or grapes from briers. **45**A good man brings good things out of the good stored up in his heart, and an evil man brings evil things out of the evil stored up in his heart. For the mouth speaks what the heart is full of.

The Wise and Foolish Builders

46"Why do you call me, 'Lord, Lord,' and do not do what I say? **47**As for everyone who comes to me and hears my words and puts them into practice, I will show you what they are like. **48**They are like a man building a house, who dug down deep and laid the foundation on rock. When a flood came, the torrent struck that house but could not shake it, because it was well built. **49**But the one who hears my words and does not put them into practice is like a man who built a house on the ground without a foundation. The moment the torrent struck that house, it collapsed and its destruction was complete."

The Faith of the Centurion

7 When Jesus had finished saying all this to the people who were listening, he entered Capernaum. **2**There a centurion's servant, whom his master valued highly, was sick and about to die. **3**The centurion heard of Jesus and sent some elders of the Jews to him, asking him to come and heal his servant. **4**When they came to Jesus, they pleaded earnestly with him, "This man deserves to have you do this, **5**because he loves our nation and has built our synagogue." **6**So Jesus went with them.

He was not far from the house when the centurion sent friends to say to him: "Lord, don't trouble yourself, for I do not deserve to have you come under my roof. **7**That is why I did not even consider myself worthy to come to you. But say the word, and my servant will be healed. **8**For I myself am a man under authority, with soldiers under me. I tell this one, 'Go,' and he goes; and that one, 'Come,' and he comes. I say to my servant, 'Do this,' and he does it."

9When Jesus heard this, he was amazed at him, and turning to the crowd following him, he said, "I tell you, I have not found such great faith even in Israel." **10**Then the men who had been sent returned to the house and found the servant well.

Jesus Raises a Widow's Son

11Soon afterward, Jesus went to a town called Nain, and his disciples and a large crowd went along with him. **12**As he approached the town gate, a dead person was being carried out—the only son of his mother, and she was a widow. And a large crowd from the town was with her. **13**When the Lord saw her, his heart went out to her and he said, "Don't cry."

14Then he went up and touched the bier they were carrying him on, and the bearers stood still. He said, "Young man, I say to you, get up!" **15**The dead man sat up and began to talk, and Jesus gave him back to his mother.

16They were all filled with awe and praised God. "A great prophet has appeared among us," they said. "God has come to help his people." **17**This news about Jesus spread throughout Judea and the surrounding country.

Jesus and John the Baptist

18John's disciples told him about all these things. Calling two of them, **19**he sent them to the Lord to ask, "Are you the one who is to come, or should we expect someone else?"

20When the men came to Jesus, they said, "John the Baptist sent us to you to ask, 'Are you the one who is to come, or should we expect someone else?'"

21At that very time Jesus cured many who had diseases, sicknesses and evil spirits, and gave sight to many who were blind. **22**So he replied to the messengers, "Go back and report to John what you have seen and heard: The blind receive sight, the lame walk, those who have leprosy*a* are cleansed, the deaf hear, the dead are raised, and the good news is proclaimed to the poor. **23**Blessed is anyone who does not stumble on account of me."

24After John's messengers left, Jesus began

---

a 22 The Greek word traditionally translated *leprosy* was used for various diseases affecting the skin.

to speak to the crowd about John: "What did you go out into the wilderness to see? A reed swayed by the wind? [25]If not, what did you go out to see? A man dressed in fine clothes? No, those who wear expensive clothes and indulge in luxury are in palaces. [26]But what did you go out to see? A prophet? Yes, I tell you, and more than a prophet. [27]This is the one about whom it is written:

> " 'I will send my messenger ahead of you,
>   who will prepare your way before you.'[a]

[28]I tell you, among those born of women there is no one greater than John; yet the one who is least in the kingdom of God is greater than he."

[29](All the people, even the tax collectors, when they heard Jesus' words, acknowledged that God's way was right, because they had been baptized by John. [30]But the Pharisees and the experts in the law rejected God's purpose for themselves, because they had not been baptized by John.)

[31]Jesus went on to say, "To what, then, can I compare the people of this generation? What are they like? [32]They are like children sitting in the marketplace and calling out to each other:

> " 'We played the pipe for you,
>   and you did not dance;
> we sang a dirge,
>   and you did not cry.'

[33]For John the Baptist came neither eating bread nor drinking wine, and you say, 'He has a demon.' [34]The Son of Man came eating and drinking, and you say, 'Here is a glutton and a drunkard, a friend of tax collectors and sinners.' [35]But wisdom is proved right by all her children."

Jesus Anointed by a Sinful Woman

[36]When one of the Pharisees invited Jesus to have dinner with him, he went to the Pharisee's house and reclined at the table. [37]A woman in that town who lived a sinful life learned that Jesus was eating at the Pharisee's house, so she came there with an alabaster jar of perfume. [38]As she stood behind him at his feet weeping, she began to wet his feet with her tears. Then she wiped them with her hair, kissed them and poured perfume on them.

[39]When the Pharisee who had invited him saw this, he said to himself, "If this man were a prophet, he would know who is touching him and what kind of woman she is—that she is a sinner."

[40]Jesus answered him, "Simon, I have something to tell you."

"Tell me, teacher," he said.

[41]"Two people owed money to a certain moneylender. One owed him five hundred denarii,[b] and the other fifty. [42]Neither of them had the money to pay him back, so he forgave the debts of both. Now which of them will love him more?"

[43]Simon replied, "I suppose the one who had the bigger debt forgiven."

"You have judged correctly," Jesus said.

[44]Then he turned toward the woman and said to Simon, "Do you see this woman? I came into your house. You did not give me any water for my feet, but she wet my feet with her tears and wiped them with her hair. [45]You did not give me a kiss, but this woman, from the time I entered, has not stopped kissing my feet. [46]You did not put oil on my head, but she has poured perfume on my feet. [47]Therefore, I tell you, her many sins have been forgiven—as her great love has shown. But whoever has been forgiven little loves little."

[48]Then Jesus said to her, "Your sins are forgiven."

[49]The other guests began to say among themselves, "Who is this who even forgives sins?"

[50]Jesus said to the woman, "Your faith has saved you; go in peace."

The Parable of the Sower

8 After this, Jesus traveled about from one town and village to another, proclaiming the good news of the kingdom of God. The Twelve were with him, [2]and also some women who had been cured of evil spirits and diseases: Mary (called Magdalene) from whom seven demons had come out; [3]Joanna the wife of Chuza, the manager of Herod's household; Susanna; and many others. These women were helping to support them out of their own means.

[4]While a large crowd was gathering and people were coming to Jesus from town after town, he told this parable: [5]"A farmer went out to sow his seed. As he was scattering the seed, some fell along the path; it was trampled on, and the birds ate it up. [6]Some fell on rocky ground, and when it came up, the plants withered because they had no moisture. [7]Other seed fell among thorns, which grew up with it and choked the plants. [8]Still other seed fell on good soil. It came up and yielded a crop, a hundred times more than was sown."

When he said this, he called out, "Whoever has ears to hear, let them hear."

[9]His disciples asked him what this parable meant. [10]He said, "The knowledge of the secrets of the kingdom of God has been given to you, but to others I speak in parables, so that,

> " 'though seeing, they may not see;
>   though hearing, they may not
>   understand.'[c]

[11]"This is the meaning of the parable: The seed is the word of God. [12]Those along the path are the ones who hear, and then the devil comes and takes away the word from their hearts, so that they may not believe and be saved. [13]Those on the rocky ground are the ones who receive the word with joy when they hear it, but they have no root. They believe for a while, but in the time of testing they

---

[a] 27 Mal. 3:1   [b] 41 A denarius was the usual daily wage of a day laborer (see Matt. 20:2).
[c] 10 Isaiah 6:9

fall away. [14]The seed that fell among thorns stands for those who hear, but as they go on their way they are choked by life's worries, riches and pleasures, and they do not mature. [15]But the seed on good soil stands for those with a noble and good heart, who hear the word, retain it, and by persevering produce a crop.

A Lamp on a Stand

[16]"No one lights a lamp and hides it in a clay jar or puts it under a bed. Instead, they put it on a stand, so that those who come in can see the light. [17]For there is nothing hidden that will not be disclosed, and nothing concealed that will not be known or brought out into the open. [18]Therefore consider carefully how you listen. Whoever has will be given more; whoever does not have, even what they think they have will be taken from them."

Jesus' Mother and Brothers

[19]Now Jesus' mother and brothers came to see him, but they were not able to get near him because of the crowd. [20]Someone told him, "Your mother and brothers are standing outside, wanting to see you."

[21]He replied, "My mother and brothers are those who hear God's word and put it into practice."

Jesus Calms the Storm

[22]One day Jesus said to his disciples, "Let us go over to the other side of the lake." So they got into a boat and set out. [23]As they sailed, he fell asleep. A squall came down on the lake, so that the boat was being swamped, and they were in great danger.

[24]The disciples went and woke him, saying, "Master, Master, we're going to drown!"

He got up and rebuked the wind and the raging waters; the storm subsided, and all was calm. [25]"Where is your faith?" he asked his disciples.

In fear and amazement they asked one another, "Who is this? He commands even the winds and the water, and they obey him."

Jesus Restores a Demon-Possessed Man

[26]They sailed to the region of the Gerasenes,[a] which is across the lake from Galilee. [27]When Jesus stepped ashore, he was met by a demon-possessed man from the town. For a long time this man had not worn clothes or lived in a house, but had lived in the tombs. [28]When he saw Jesus, he cried out and fell at his feet, shouting at the top of his voice, "What do you want with me, Jesus, Son of the Most High God? I beg you, don't torture me!" [29]For Jesus had commanded the impure spirit to come out of the man. Many times it had seized him, and though he was chained hand and foot and kept under guard, he had broken his chains and had been driven by the demon into solitary places.

[30]Jesus asked him, "What is your name?"

"Legion," he replied, because many demons had gone into him. [31]And they begged Jesus repeatedly not to order them to go into the Abyss.

[32]A large herd of pigs was feeding there on the hillside. The demons begged Jesus to let them go into the pigs, and he gave them permission. [33]When the demons came out of the man, they went into the pigs, and the herd rushed down the steep bank into the lake and was drowned.

[34]When those tending the pigs saw what had happened, they ran off and reported this in the town and countryside, [35]and the people went out to see what had happened. When they came to Jesus, they found the man from whom the demons had gone out, sitting at Jesus' feet, dressed and in his right mind; and they were afraid. [36]Those who had seen it told the people how the demon-possessed man had been cured. [37]Then all the people of the region of the Gerasenes asked Jesus to leave them, because they were overcome with fear. So he got into the boat and left.

[38]The man from whom the demons had gone out begged to go with him, but Jesus sent him away, saying, [39]"Return home and tell how much God has done for you." So the man went away and told all over town how much Jesus had done for him.

Jesus Raises a Dead Girl and Heals a Sick Woman

[40]Now when Jesus returned, a crowd welcomed him, for they were all expecting him. [41]Then a man named Jairus, a synagogue leader, came and fell at Jesus' feet, pleading with him to come to his house [42]because his only daughter, a girl of about twelve, was dying.

As Jesus was on his way, the crowds almost crushed him. [43]And a woman was there who had been subject to bleeding for twelve years,[b] but no one could heal her. [44]She came up behind him and touched the edge of his cloak, and immediately her bleeding stopped.

[45]"Who touched me?" Jesus asked.

When they all denied it, Peter said, "Master, the people are crowding and pressing against you."

[46]But Jesus said, "Someone touched me; I know that power has gone out from me."

[47]Then the woman, seeing that she could not go unnoticed, came trembling and fell at his feet. In the presence of all the people, she told why she had touched him and how she had been instantly healed. [48]Then he said to her, "Daughter, your faith has healed you. Go in peace."

[49]While Jesus was still speaking, someone came from the house of Jairus, the synagogue leader. "Your daughter is dead," he said. "Don't bother the teacher anymore."

[50]Hearing this, Jesus said to Jairus, "Don't be afraid; just believe, and she will be healed."

---

[a] 26 Some manuscripts *Gadarenes*; other manuscripts *Gergesenes*; also in verse 37   [b] 43 Many manuscripts *years, and she had spent all she had on doctors*

51When he arrived at the house of Jairus, he did not let anyone go in with him except Peter, John and James, and the child's father and mother. 52Meanwhile, all the people were wailing and mourning for her. "Stop wailing," Jesus said. "She is not dead but asleep."

53They laughed at him, knowing that she was dead. 54But he took her by the hand and said, "My child, get up!" 55Her spirit returned, and at once she stood up. Then Jesus told them to give her something to eat. 56Her parents were astonished, but he ordered them not to tell anyone what had happened.

Jesus Sends Out the Twelve

9 When Jesus had called the Twelve together, he gave them power and authority to drive out all demons and to cure diseases, 2and he sent them out to proclaim the kingdom of God and to heal the sick. 3He told them: "Take nothing for the journey—no staff, no bag, no bread, no money, no extra shirt. 4Whatever house you enter, stay there until you leave that town. 5If people do not welcome you, leave their town and shake the dust off your feet as a testimony against them." 6So they set out and went from village to village, proclaiming the good news and healing people everywhere.

7Now Herod the tetrarch heard about all that was going on. And he was perplexed because some were saying that John had been raised from the dead, 8others that Elijah had appeared, and still others that one of the prophets of long ago had come back to life. 9But Herod said, "I beheaded John. Who, then, is this I hear such things about?" And he tried to see him.

Jesus Feeds the Five Thousand

10When the apostles returned, they reported to Jesus what they had done. Then he took them with him and they withdrew by themselves to a town called Bethsaida, 11but the crowds learned about it and followed him. He welcomed them and spoke to them about the kingdom of God, and healed those who needed healing.

12Late in the afternoon the Twelve came to him and said, "Send the crowd away so they can go to the surrounding villages and countryside and find food and lodging, because we are in a remote place here."

13He replied, "You give them something to eat."

They answered, "We have only five loaves of bread and two fish—unless we go and buy food for all this crowd." 14(About five thousand men were there.)

But he said to his disciples, "Have them sit down in groups of about fifty each." 15The disciples did so, and everyone sat down. 16Taking the five loaves and the two fish and looking up to heaven, he gave thanks and broke them. Then he gave them to the disciples to distribute to the people. 17They all ate and were satisfi... picked up twelve baske... that were left over.

Peter Declares That Jes...

18Once when Jesus w... and his disciples wer... them, "Who do the cr...

19They replied, "Som... others say Elijah; and still others, that one of the prophets of long ago has come back to life."

20"But what about you?" he asked. "Who do you say I am?"

Peter answered, "God's Messiah."

Jesus Predicts His Death

21Jesus strictly warned them not to tell this to anyone. 22And he said, "The Son of Man must suffer many things and be rejected by the elders, the chief priests and the teachers of the law, and he must be killed and on the third day be raised to life."

23Then he said to them all: "Whoever wants to be my disciple must deny themselves and take up their cross daily and follow me. 24For whoever wants to save their life will lose it, but whoever loses their life for me will save it. 25What good is it for someone to gain the whole world, and yet lose or forfeit their very self? 26Whoever is ashamed of me and my words, the Son of Man will be ashamed of them when he comes in his glory and in the glory of the Father and of the holy angels.

27"Truly I tell you, some who are standing here will not taste death before they see the kingdom of God."

The Transfiguration

28About eight days after Jesus said this, he took Peter, John and James with him and went up onto a mountain to pray. 29As he was praying, the appearance of his face changed, and his clothes became as bright as a flash of lightning. 30Two men, Moses and Elijah, appeared in glorious splendor, talking with Jesus. 31They spoke about his departure,a which he was about to bring to fulfillment at Jerusalem. 32Peter and his companions were very sleepy, but when they became fully awake, they saw his glory and the two men standing with him. 33As the men were leaving Jesus, Peter said to him, "Master, it is good for us to be here. Let us put up three shelters—one for you, one for Moses and one for Elijah." (He did not know what he was saying.)

34While he was speaking, a cloud appeared and covered them, and they were afraid as they entered the cloud. 35A voice came from the cloud, saying, "This is my Son, whom I have chosen; listen to him." 36When the voice had spoken, they found that Jesus was alone. The disciples kept this to themselves and did not tell anyone at that time what they had seen.

a 31 Greek exodos

Demon-Possessed Boy

...xt day, when they came down from ...ntain, a large crowd met him. [38]A man ...crowd called out, "Teacher, I beg you ...ok at my son, for he is my only child. [39]A ...irit seizes him and he suddenly screams; it ...hrows him into convulsions so that he foams at the mouth. It scarcely ever leaves him and is destroying him. [40]I begged your disciples to drive it out, but they could not."

[41]"You unbelieving and perverse generation," Jesus replied, "how long shall I stay with you and put up with you? Bring your son here."

[42]Even while the boy was coming, the demon threw him to the ground in a convulsion. But Jesus rebuked the impure spirit, healed the boy and gave him back to his father. [43]And they were all amazed at the greatness of God.

Jesus Predicts His Death a Second Time

While everyone was marveling at all that Jesus did, he said to his disciples, [44]"Listen carefully to what I am about to tell you: The Son of Man is going to be delivered into the hands of men." [45]But they did not understand what this meant. It was hidden from them, so that they did not grasp it, and they were afraid to ask him about it.

[46]An argument started among the disciples as to which of them would be the greatest. [47]Jesus, knowing their thoughts, took a little child and had him stand beside him. [48]Then he said to them, "Whoever welcomes this little child in my name welcomes me; and whoever welcomes me welcomes the one who sent me. For it is the one who is least among you all who is the greatest."

[49]"Master," said John, "we saw someone driving out demons in your name and we tried to stop him, because he is not one of us."

[50]"Do not stop him," Jesus said, "for whoever is not against you is for you."

Samaritan Opposition

[51]As the time approached for him to be taken up to heaven, Jesus resolutely set out for Jerusalem. [52]And he sent messengers on ahead, who went into a Samaritan village to get things ready for him; [53]but the people there did not welcome him, because he was heading for Jerusalem. [54]When the disciples James and John saw this, they asked, "Lord, do you want us to call fire down from heaven to destroy them[a]?" [55]But Jesus turned and rebuked them. [56]Then he and his disciples went to another village.

The Cost of Following Jesus

[57]As they were walking along the road, a man said to him, "I will follow you wherever you go."

[58]Jesus replied, "Foxes have dens and birds have nests, but the Son of Man has no place to lay his head."

[59]He said to another man, "Follow me."

But he replied, "Lord, first let me go and bury my father."

[60]Jesus said to him, "Let the dead bury their own dead, but you go and proclaim the kingdom of God."

[61]Still another said, "I will follow you, Lord; but first let me go back and say goodbye to my family."

[62]Jesus replied, "No one who puts a hand to the plow and looks back is fit for service in the kingdom of God."

Jesus Sends Out the Seventy-Two

10 After this the Lord appointed seventy-two[b] others and sent them two by two ahead of him to every town and place where he was about to go. [2]He told them, "The harvest is plentiful, but the workers are few. Ask the Lord of the harvest, therefore, to send out workers into his harvest field. [3]Go! I am sending you out like lambs among wolves. [4]Do not take a purse or bag or sandals; and do not greet anyone on the road.

[5]"When you enter a house, first say, 'Peace to this house.' [6]If someone who promotes peace is there, your peace will rest on them; if not, it will return to you. [7]Stay there, eating and drinking whatever they give you, for the worker deserves his wages. Do not move around from house to house.

[8]"When you enter a town and are welcomed, eat what is offered to you. [9]Heal the sick who are there and tell them, 'The kingdom of God has come near to you.' [10]But when you enter a town and are not welcomed, go into its streets and say, [11]'Even the dust of your town we wipe from our feet as a warning to you. Yet be sure of this: The kingdom of God has come near.' [12]I tell you, it will be more bearable on that day for Sodom than for that town.

[13]"Woe to you, Chorazin! Woe to you, Bethsaida! For if the miracles that were performed in you had been performed in Tyre and Sidon, they would have repented long ago, sitting in sackcloth and ashes. [14]But it will be more bearable for Tyre and Sidon at the judgment than for you. [15]And you, Capernaum, will you be lifted to the heavens? No, you will go down to Hades.[c]

[16]"Whoever listens to you listens to me; whoever rejects you rejects me; but whoever rejects me rejects him who sent me."

[17]The seventy-two returned with joy and said, "Lord, even the demons submit to us in your name."

[18]He replied, "I saw Satan fall like lightning from heaven. [19]I have given you authority to trample on snakes and scorpions and to overcome all the power of the enemy; nothing will harm you. [20]However, do not rejoice that the spirits submit to you, but rejoice that your names are written in heaven."

[21]At that time Jesus, full of joy through the Holy Spirit, said, "I praise you, Father, Lord of heaven and earth, because you have hidden

---

a 54 Some manuscripts *them, just as Elijah did*
c 15 That is, the realm of the dead
b 1 Some manuscripts *seventy*; also in verse 17

these things from the wise and learned, and revealed them to little children. Yes, Father, for this is what you were pleased to do.

²²"All things have been committed to me by my Father. No one knows who the Son is except the Father, and no one knows who the Father is except the Son and those to whom the Son chooses to reveal him."

²³Then he turned to his disciples and said privately, "Blessed are the eyes that see what you see. ²⁴For I tell you that many prophets and kings wanted to see what you see but did not see it, and to hear what you hear but did not hear it."

The Parable of the Good Samaritan

²⁵On one occasion an expert in the law stood up to test Jesus. "Teacher," he asked, "what must I do to inherit eternal life?"

²⁶"What is written in the Law?" he replied. "How do you read it?"

²⁷He answered, " 'Love the Lord your God with all your heart and with all your soul and with all your strength and with all your mind'ᵃ; and, 'Love your neighbor as yourself.'ᵇ"

²⁸"You have answered correctly," Jesus replied. "Do this and you will live."

²⁹But he wanted to justify himself, so he asked Jesus, "And who is my neighbor?"

³⁰In reply Jesus said: "A man was going down from Jerusalem to Jericho, when he was attacked by robbers. They stripped him of his clothes, beat him and went away, leaving him half dead. ³¹A priest happened to be going down the same road, and when he saw the man, he passed by on the other side. ³²So too, a Levite, when he came to the place and saw him, passed by on the other side. ³³But a Samaritan, as he traveled, came where the man was; and when he saw him, he took pity on him. ³⁴He went to him and bandaged his wounds, pouring on oil and wine. Then he put the man on his own donkey, brought him to an inn and took care of him. ³⁵The next day he took out two denariiᶜ and gave them to the innkeeper. 'Look after him,' he said, 'and when I return, I will reimburse you for any extra expense you may have.'

³⁶"Which of these three do you think was a neighbor to the man who fell into the hands of robbers?"

³⁷The expert in the law replied, "The one who had mercy on him."

Jesus told him, "Go and do likewise."

At the Home of Martha and Mary

³⁸As Jesus and his disciples were on their way, he came to a village where a woman named Martha opened her home to him. ³⁹She had a sister called Mary, who sat at the Lord's feet listening to what he said. ⁴⁰But Martha was distracted by all the preparations that had to be made. She came to him and asked, "Lord, don't you care that my sister has left me to do the work by myself? Tell her to help me!"

⁴¹"Martha, Martha," the Lord answered, "you are worried and upset about many things, ⁴²but few things are needed—or indeed only one.ᵈ Mary has chosen what is better, and it will not be taken away from her."

Jesus' Teaching on Prayer

11 One day Jesus was praying in a certain place. When he finished, one of his disciples said to him, "Lord, teach us to pray, just as John taught his disciples."

²He said to them, "When you pray, say:

" 'Father,ᵉ
hallowed be your name,
your kingdom come.ᶠ
³Give us each day our daily bread.
⁴Forgive us our sins,
for we also forgive everyone who sins
against us.ᵍ
And lead us not into temptation.ʰ' "

⁵Then Jesus said to them, "Suppose you have a friend, and you go to him at midnight and say, 'Friend, lend me three loaves of bread; ⁶a friend of mine on a journey has come to me, and I have no food to offer him.' ⁷And suppose the one inside answers, 'Don't bother me. The door is already locked, and my children and I are in bed. I can't get up and give you anything.' ⁸I tell you, even though he will not get up and give you the bread because of friendship, yet because of your shameless audacityⁱ he will surely get up and give you as much as you need.

⁹"So I say to you: Ask and it will be given to you; seek and you will find; knock and the door will be opened to you. ¹⁰For everyone who asks receives; the one who seeks finds; and to the one who knocks, the door will be opened.

¹¹"Which of you fathers, if your son asks forʲ a fish, will give him a snake instead? ¹²Or if he asks for an egg, will give him a scorpion? ¹³If you then, though you are evil, know how to give good gifts to your children, how much more will your Father in heaven give the Holy Spirit to those who ask him!"

Jesus and Beelzebul

¹⁴Jesus was driving out a demon that was mute. When the demon left, the man who had been mute spoke, and the crowd was amazed. ¹⁵But some of them said, "By Beelzebul, the prince of demons, he is driving out demons." ¹⁶Others tested him by asking for a sign from heaven.

¹⁷Jesus knew their thoughts and said to them: "Any kingdom divided against itself

---

ᵃ 27 Deut. 6:5   ᵇ 27 Lev. 19:18   ᶜ 35 A denarius was the usual daily wage of a day laborer (see Matt. 20:2).   ᵈ 42 Some manuscripts *but only one thing is needed*   ᵉ 2 Some manuscripts *Our Father in heaven*   ᶠ 2 Some manuscripts *come. May your will be done on earth as it is in heaven.*   ᵍ 4 Greek *everyone who is indebted to us*   ʰ 4 Some manuscripts *temptation, but deliver us from the evil one*   ⁱ 8 Or *yet to preserve his good name*   ʲ 11 Some manuscripts *for bread, will give him a stone? Or if he asks for*

will be ruined, and a house divided against itself will fall. [18]If Satan is divided against himself, how can his kingdom stand? I say this because you claim that I drive out demons by Beelzebul. [19]Now if I drive out demons by Beelzebul, by whom do your followers drive them out? So then, they will be your judges. [20]But if I drive out demons by the finger of God, then the kingdom of God has come upon you.

[21]"When a strong man, fully armed, guards his own house, his possessions are safe. [22]But when someone stronger attacks and overpowers him, he takes away the armor in which the man trusted and divides up his plunder.

[23]"Whoever is not with me is against me, and whoever does not gather with me scatters.

[24]"When an impure spirit comes out of a person, it goes through arid places seeking rest and does not find it. Then it says, 'I will return to the house I left.' [25]When it arrives, it finds the house swept clean and put in order. [26]Then it goes and takes seven other spirits more wicked than itself, and they go in and live there. And the final condition of that person is worse than the first."

[27]As Jesus was saying these things, a woman in the crowd called out, "Blessed is the mother who gave you birth and nursed you."

[28]He replied, "Blessed rather are those who hear the word of God and obey it."

The Sign of Jonah

[29]As the crowds increased, Jesus said, "This is a wicked generation. It asks for a sign, but none will be given it except the sign of Jonah. [30]For as Jonah was a sign to the Ninevites, so also will the Son of Man be to this generation. [31]The Queen of the South will rise at the judgment with the people of this generation and condemn them, for she came from the ends of the earth to listen to Solomon's wisdom; and now something greater than Solomon is here. [32]The men of Nineveh will stand up at the judgment with this generation and condemn it, for they repented at the preaching of Jonah; and now something greater than Jonah is here.

The Lamp of the Body

[33]"No one lights a lamp and puts it in a place where it will be hidden, or under a bowl. Instead they put it on its stand, so that those who come in may see the light. [34]Your eye is the lamp of your body. When your eyes are healthy,[a] your whole body also is full of light. But when they are unhealthy,[b] your body also is full of darkness. [35]See to it, then, that the light within you is not darkness. [36]Therefore, if your whole body is full of light, and no part of it dark, it will be just as full of light as when a lamp shines its light on you."

Woes on the Pharisees and the Experts in the Law

[37]When Jesus had finished speaking, a Pharisee invited him to eat with him; so he went in and reclined at the table. [38]But the Pharisee was surprised when he noticed that Jesus did not first wash before the meal.

[39]Then the Lord said to him, "Now then, you Pharisees clean the outside of the cup and dish, but inside you are full of greed and wickedness. [40]You foolish people! Did not the one who made the outside make the inside also? [41]But now as for what is inside you—be generous to the poor, and everything will be clean for you.

[42]"Woe to you Pharisees, because you give God a tenth of your mint, rue and all other kinds of garden herbs, but you neglect justice and the love of God. You should have practiced the latter without leaving the former undone.

[43]"Woe to you Pharisees, because you love the most important seats in the synagogues and respectful greetings in the marketplaces.

[44]"Woe to you, because you are like unmarked graves, which people walk over without knowing it."

[45]One of the experts in the law answered him, "Teacher, when you say these things, you insult us also."

[46]Jesus replied, "And you experts in the law, woe to you, because you load people down with burdens they can hardly carry, and you yourselves will not lift one finger to help them.

[47]"Woe to you, because you build tombs for the prophets, and it was your ancestors who killed them. [48]So you testify that you approve of what your ancestors did; they killed the prophets, and you build their tombs. [49]Because of this, God in his wisdom said, 'I will send them prophets and apostles, some of whom they will kill and others they will persecute.' [50]Therefore this generation will be held responsible for the blood of all the prophets that has been shed since the beginning of the world, [51]from the blood of Abel to the blood of Zechariah, who was killed between the altar and the sanctuary. Yes, I tell you, this generation will be held responsible for it all.

[52]"Woe to you experts in the law, because you have taken away the key to knowledge. You yourselves have not entered, and you have hindered those who were entering."

[53]When Jesus went outside, the Pharisees and the teachers of the law began to oppose him fiercely and to besiege him with questions, [54]waiting to catch him in something he might say.

Warnings and Encouragements

12 Meanwhile, when a crowd of many thousands had gathered, so that they were trampling on one another, Jesus began to speak first to his disciples, saying: "Be[c] on your guard against the yeast of the Pharisees, which is hypocrisy. [2]There is nothing concealed that will not be disclosed, or hidden that will not be made known. [3]What you have said in the dark will be heard in the daylight, and what you have whispered in the ear in

---

[a] 34 The Greek for *healthy* here implies *generous*.
[c] 1 Or *speak to his disciples, saying: "First of all, be*

[b] 34 The Greek for *unhealthy* here implies *stingy*.

the inner rooms will be proclaimed from the roofs.

⁴"I tell you, my friends, do not be afraid of those who kill the body and after that can do no more. ⁵But I will show you whom you should fear: Fear him who, after your body has been killed, has authority to throw you into hell. Yes, I tell you, fear him. ⁶Are not five sparrows sold for two pennies? Yet not one of them is forgotten by God. ⁷Indeed, the very hairs of your head are all numbered. Don't be afraid; you are worth more than many sparrows.

⁸"I tell you, whoever publicly acknowledges me before others, the Son of Man will also acknowledge before the angels of God. ⁹But whoever disowns me before others will be disowned before the angels of God. ¹⁰And everyone who speaks a word against the Son of Man will be forgiven, but anyone who blasphemes against the Holy Spirit will not be forgiven.

¹¹"When you are brought before synagogues, rulers and authorities, do not worry about how you will defend yourselves or what you will say, ¹²for the Holy Spirit will teach you at that time what you should say."

The Parable of the Rich Fool

¹³Someone in the crowd said to him, "Teacher, tell my brother to divide the inheritance with me."

¹⁴Jesus replied, "Man, who appointed me a judge or an arbiter between you?" ¹⁵Then he said to them, "Watch out! Be on your guard against all kinds of greed; life does not consist in an abundance of possessions."

¹⁶And he told them this parable: "The ground of a certain rich man yielded an abundant harvest. ¹⁷He thought to himself, 'What shall I do? I have no place to store my crops.'

¹⁸"Then he said, 'This is what I'll do. I will tear down my barns and build bigger ones, and there I will store my surplus grain. ¹⁹And I'll say to myself, "You have plenty of grain laid up for many years. Take life easy; eat, drink and be merry."'

²⁰"But God said to him, 'You fool! This very night your life will be demanded from you. Then who will get what you have prepared for yourself?'

²¹"This is how it will be with whoever stores up things for themselves but is not rich toward God."

Do Not Worry

²²Then Jesus said to his disciples: "Therefore I tell you, do not worry about your life, what you will eat; or about your body, what you will wear. ²³For life is more than food, and the body more than clothes. ²⁴Consider the ravens: They do not sow or reap, they have no storeroom or barn; yet God feeds them. And how much more valuable you are than birds! ²⁵Who of you by worrying can add a single hour to your life*a*? ²⁶Since you cannot

do this very little thing, why do you worry about the rest?

²⁷"Consider how the wild flowers grow. They do not labor or spin. Yet I tell you, not even Solomon in all his splendor was dressed like one of these. ²⁸If that is how God clothes the grass of the field, which is here today, and tomorrow is thrown into the fire, how much more will he clothe you—you of little faith! ²⁹And do not set your heart on what you will eat or drink; do not worry about it. ³⁰For the pagan world runs after all such things, and your Father knows that you need them. ³¹But seek his kingdom, and these things will be given to you as well.

³²"Do not be afraid, little flock, for your Father has been pleased to give you the kingdom. ³³Sell your possessions and give to the poor. Provide purses for yourselves that will not wear out, a treasure in heaven that will never fail, where no thief comes near and no moth destroys. ³⁴For where your treasure is, there your heart will be also.

Watchfulness

³⁵"Be dressed ready for service and keep your lamps burning, ³⁶like servants waiting for their master to return from a wedding banquet, so that when he comes and knocks they can immediately open the door for him. ³⁷It will be good for those servants whose master finds them watching when he comes. Truly I tell you, he will dress himself to serve, will have them recline at the table and will come and wait on them. ³⁸It will be good for those servants whose master finds them ready, even if he comes in the middle of the night or toward daybreak. ³⁹But understand this: If the owner of the house had known at what hour the thief was coming, he would not have let his house be broken into. ⁴⁰You also must be ready, because the Son of Man will come at an hour when you do not expect him."

⁴¹Peter asked, "Lord, are you telling this parable to us, or to everyone?"

⁴²The Lord answered, "Who then is the faithful and wise manager, whom the master puts in charge of his servants to give them their food allowance at the proper time? ⁴³It will be good for that servant whom the master finds doing so when he returns. ⁴⁴Truly I tell you, he will put him in charge of all his possessions. ⁴⁵But suppose the servant says to himself, 'My master is taking a long time in coming,' and he then begins to beat the other servants, both men and women, and to eat and drink and get drunk. ⁴⁶The master of that servant will come on a day when he does not expect him and at an hour he is not aware of. He will cut him to pieces and assign him a place with the unbelievers.

⁴⁷"The servant who knows the master's will and does not get ready or does not do what the master wants will be beaten with many blows. ⁴⁸But the one who does not know and does things deserving punishment will be beaten with few blows. From everyone who

a 25 Or single cubit to your height

has been given much, much will be demanded; and from the one who has been entrusted with much, much more will be asked.

Not Peace but Division

49"I have come to bring fire on the earth, and how I wish it were already kindled! 50But I have a baptism to undergo, and what constraint I am under until it is completed! 51Do you think I came to bring peace on earth? No, I tell you, but division. 52From now on there will be five in one family divided against each other, three against two and two against three. 53They will be divided, father against son and son against father, mother against daughter and daughter against mother, mother-in-law against daughter-in-law and daughter-in-law against mother-in-law."

Interpreting the Times

54He said to the crowd: "When you see a cloud rising in the west, immediately you say, 'It's going to rain,' and it does. 55And when the south wind blows, you say, 'It's going to be hot,' and it is. 56Hypocrites! You know how to interpret the appearance of the earth and the sky. How is it that you don't know how to interpret this present time?

57"Why don't you judge for yourselves what is right? 58As you are going with your adversary to the magistrate, try hard to be reconciled on the way, or your adversary may drag you off to the judge, and the judge turn you over to the officer, and the officer throw you into prison. 59I tell you, you will not get out until you have paid the last penny."

Repent or Perish

13 Now there were some present at that time who told Jesus about the Galileans whose blood Pilate had mixed with their sacrifices. 2Jesus answered, "Do you think that these Galileans were worse sinners than all the other Galileans because they suffered this way? 3I tell you, no! But unless you repent, you too will all perish. 4Or those eighteen who died when the tower in Siloam fell on them—do you think they were more guilty than all the others living in Jerusalem? 5I tell you, no! But unless you repent, you too will all perish."

6Then he told this parable: "A man had a fig tree growing in his vineyard, and he went to look for fruit on it but did not find any. 7So he said to the man who took care of the vineyard, 'For three years now I've been coming to look for fruit on this fig tree and haven't found any. Cut it down! Why should it use up the soil?'

8"'Sir,' the man replied, 'leave it alone for one more year, and I'll dig around it and fertilize it. 9If it bears fruit next year, fine! If not, then cut it down.'"

Jesus Heals a Crippled Woman on the Sabbath

10On a Sabbath Jesus was teaching in one of the synagogues, 11and a woman was there who had been crippled by a spirit for eighteen years. She was bent over and could not straighten up at all. 12When Jesus saw her, he called her forward and said to her, "Woman, you are set free from your infirmity." 13Then he put his hands on her, and immediately she straightened up and praised God.

14Indignant because Jesus had healed on the Sabbath, the synagogue leader said to the people, "There are six days for work. So come and be healed on those days, not on the Sabbath."

15The Lord answered him, "You hypocrites! Doesn't each of you on the Sabbath untie your ox or donkey from the stall and lead it out to give it water? 16Then should not this woman, a daughter of Abraham, whom Satan has kept bound for eighteen long years, be set free on the Sabbath day from what bound her?"

17When he said this, all his opponents were humiliated, but the people were delighted with all the wonderful things he was doing.

The Parables of the Mustard Seed and the Yeast

18Then Jesus asked, "What is the kingdom of God like? What shall I compare it to? 19It is like a mustard seed, which a man took and planted in his garden. It grew and became a tree, and the birds perched in its branches."

20Again he asked, "What shall I compare the kingdom of God to? 21It is like yeast that a woman took and mixed into about sixty pounds*a* of flour until it worked all through the dough."

The Narrow Door

22Then Jesus went through the towns and villages, teaching as he made his way to Jerusalem. 23Someone asked him, "Lord, are only a few people going to be saved?"

He said to them, 24"Make every effort to enter through the narrow door, because many, I tell you, will try to enter and will not be able to. 25Once the owner of the house gets up and closes the door, you will stand outside knocking and pleading, 'Sir, open the door for us.'

"But he will answer, 'I don't know you or where you come from.'

26"Then you will say, 'We ate and drank with you, and you taught in our streets.'

27"But he will reply, 'I don't know you or where you come from. Away from me, all you evildoers!'

28"There will be weeping there, and gnashing of teeth, when you see Abraham, Isaac and Jacob and all the prophets in the kingdom of God, but you yourselves thrown out. 29People will come from east and west and north and south, and will take their places at the feast in the kingdom of God. 30Indeed there are those who are last who will be first, and first who will be last."

Jesus' Sorrow for Jerusalem

31At that time some Pharisees came to Jesus and said to him, "Leave this place and go somewhere else. Herod wants to kill you."

a 21 Or about 27 kilograms

³²He replied, "Go tell that fox, 'I will keep on driving out demons and healing people today and tomorrow, and on the third day I will reach my goal.' ³³In any case, I must press on today and tomorrow and the next day—for surely no prophet can die outside Jerusalem!

³⁴"Jerusalem, Jerusalem, you who kill the prophets and stone those sent to you, how often I have longed to gather your children together, as a hen gathers her chicks under her wings, and you were not willing. ³⁵Look, your house is left to you desolate. I tell you, you will not see me again until you say, 'Blessed is he who comes in the name of the Lord.'ᵃ"

Jesus at a Pharisee's House

14 One Sabbath, when Jesus went to eat in the house of a prominent Pharisee, he was being carefully watched. ²There in front of him was a man suffering from abnormal swelling of his body. ³Jesus asked the Pharisees and experts in the law, "Is it lawful to heal on the Sabbath or not?" ⁴But they remained silent. So taking hold of the man, he healed him and sent him on his way.

⁵Then he asked them, "If one of you has a childᵇ or an ox that falls into a well on the Sabbath day, will you not immediately pull it out?" ⁶And they had nothing to say.

⁷When he noticed how the guests picked the places of honor at the table, he told them this parable: ⁸"When someone invites you to a wedding feast, do not take the place of honor, for a person more distinguished than you may have been invited. ⁹If so, the host who invited both of you will come and say to you, 'Give this person your seat.' Then, humiliated, you will have to take the least important place. ¹⁰But when you are invited, take the lowest place, so that when your host comes, he will say to you, 'Friend, move up to a better place.' Then you will be honored in the presence of all the other guests. ¹¹For all those who exalt themselves will be humbled, and those who humble themselves will be exalted."

¹²Then Jesus said to his host, "When you give a luncheon or dinner, do not invite your friends, your brothers or sisters, your relatives, or your rich neighbors; if you do, they may invite you back and so you will be repaid. ¹³But when you give a banquet, invite the poor, the crippled, the lame, the blind, ¹⁴and you will be blessed. Although they cannot repay you, you will be repaid at the resurrection of the righteous."

The Parable of the Great Banquet

¹⁵When one of those at the table with him heard this, he said to Jesus, "Blessed is the one who will eat at the feast in the kingdom of God."

¹⁶Jesus replied: "A certain man was preparing a great banquet and invited many guests. ¹⁷At the time of the banquet he sent his servant to tell those who had been invited, 'Come, for everything is now ready.'

¹⁸"But they all alike began to make excuses. The first said, 'I have just bought a field, and I must go and see it. Please excuse me.'

¹⁹"Another said, 'I have just bought five yoke of oxen, and I'm on my way to try them out. Please excuse me.'

²⁰"Still another said, 'I just got married, so I can't come.'

²¹"The servant came back and reported this to his master. Then the owner of the house became angry and ordered his servant, 'Go out quickly into the streets and alleys of the town and bring in the poor, the crippled, the blind and the lame.'

²²"'Sir,' the servant said, 'what you ordered has been done, but there is still room.'

²³"Then the master told his servant, 'Go out to the roads and country lanes and compel them to come in, so that my house will be full. ²⁴I tell you, not one of those who were invited will get a taste of my banquet.'"

The Cost of Being a Disciple

²⁵Large crowds were traveling with Jesus, and turning to them he said: ²⁶"If anyone comes to me and does not hate father and mother, wife and children, brothers and sisters—yes, even their own life—such a person cannot be my disciple. ²⁷And whoever does not carry their cross and follow me cannot be my disciple.

²⁸"Suppose one of you wants to build a tower. Won't you first sit down and estimate the cost to see if you have enough money to complete it? ²⁹For if you lay the foundation and are not able to finish it, everyone who sees it will ridicule you, ³⁰saying, 'This person began to build and wasn't able to finish.'

³¹"Or suppose a king is about to go to war against another king. Won't he first sit down and consider whether he is able with ten thousand men to oppose the one coming against him with twenty thousand? ³²If he is not able, he will send a delegation while the other is still a long way off and will ask for terms of peace. ³³In the same way, those of you who do not give up everything you have cannot be my disciples.

³⁴"Salt is good, but if it loses its saltiness, how can it be made salty again? ³⁵It is fit neither for the soil nor for the manure pile; it is thrown out.

"Whoever has ears to hear, let them hear."

The Parable of the Lost Sheep

15 Now the tax collectors and sinners were all gathering around to hear Jesus. ²But the Pharisees and the teachers of the law muttered, "This man welcomes sinners and eats with them."

³Then Jesus told them this parable: ⁴"Suppose one of you has a hundred sheep and loses one of them. Doesn't he leave the ninety-nine in the open country and go after the lost sheep until he finds it? ⁵And when he finds it, he joyfully puts it on his shoulders ⁶and goes

---

ᵃ 35 Psalm 118:26   ᵇ 5 Some manuscripts *donkey*

home. Then he calls his friends and neighbors together and says, 'Rejoice with me; I have found my lost sheep.' 7I tell you that in the same way there will be more rejoicing in heaven over one sinner who repents than over ninety-nine righteous persons who do not need to repent.

The Parable of the Lost Coin

8"Or suppose a woman has ten silver coins*a* and loses one. Doesn't she light a lamp, sweep the house and search carefully until she finds it? 9And when she finds it, she calls her friends and neighbors together and says, 'Rejoice with me; I have found my lost coin.' 10In the same way, I tell you, there is rejoicing in the presence of the angels of God over one sinner who repents."

The Parable of the Lost Son

11Jesus continued: "There was a man who had two sons. 12The younger one said to his father, 'Father, give me my share of the estate.' So he divided his property between them.

13"Not long after that, the younger son got together all he had, set off for a distant country and there squandered his wealth in wild living. 14After he had spent everything, there was a severe famine in that whole country, and he began to be in need. 15So he went and hired himself out to a citizen of that country, who sent him to his fields to feed pigs. 16He longed to fill his stomach with the pods that the pigs were eating, but no one gave him anything.

17"When he came to his senses, he said, 'How many of my father's hired servants have food to spare, and here I am starving to death! 18I will set out and go back to my father and say to him: Father, I have sinned against heaven and against you. 19I am no longer worthy to be called your son; make me like one of your hired servants.' 20So he got up and went to his father.

"But while he was still a long way off, his father saw him and was filled with compassion for him; he ran to his son, threw his arms around him and kissed him.

21"The son said to him, 'Father, I have sinned against heaven and against you. I am no longer worthy to be called your son.'

22"But the father said to his servants, 'Quick! Bring the best robe and put it on him. Put a ring on his finger and sandals on his feet. 23Bring the fattened calf and kill it. Let's have a feast and celebrate. 24For this son of mine was dead and is alive again; he was lost and is found.' So they began to celebrate.

25"Meanwhile, the older son was in the field. When he came near the house, he heard music and dancing. 26So he called one of the servants and asked him what was going on. 27'Your brother has come,' he replied, 'and your father has killed the fattened calf because he has him back safe and sound.'

28"The older brother became angry and refused to go in. So his father went out and pleaded with him. 29But he answered his father, 'Look! All these years I've been slaving for you and never disobeyed your orders. Yet you never gave me even a young goat so I could celebrate with my friends. 30But when this son of yours who has squandered your property with prostitutes comes home, you kill the fattened calf for him!'

31"'My son,' the father said, 'you are always with me, and everything I have is yours. 32But we had to celebrate and be glad, because this brother of yours was dead and is alive again; he was lost and is found.'"

The Parable of the Shrewd Manager

16 Jesus told his disciples: "There was a rich man whose manager was accused of wasting his possessions. 2So he called him in and asked him, 'What is this I hear about you? Give an account of your management, because you cannot be manager any longer.'

3"The manager said to himself, 'What shall I do now? My master is taking away my job. I'm not strong enough to dig, and I'm ashamed to beg— 4I know what I'll do so that, when I lose my job here, people will welcome me into their houses.'

5"So he called in each one of his master's debtors. He asked the first, 'How much do you owe my master?'

6"'Nine hundred gallons*b* of olive oil,' he replied.

"The manager told him, 'Take your bill, sit down quickly, and make it four hundred and fifty.'

7"Then he asked the second, 'And how much do you owe?'

"'A thousand bushels*c* of wheat,' he replied.

"He told him, 'Take your bill and make it eight hundred.'

8"The master commended the dishonest manager because he had acted shrewdly. For the people of this world are more shrewd in dealing with their own kind than are the people of the light. 9I tell you, use worldly wealth to gain friends for yourselves, so that when it is gone, you will be welcomed into eternal dwellings.

10"Whoever can be trusted with very little can also be trusted with much, and whoever is dishonest with very little will also be dishonest with much. 11So if you have not been trustworthy in handling worldly wealth, who will trust you with true riches? 12And if you have not been trustworthy with someone else's property, who will give you property of your own?

13"No one can serve two masters. Either you will hate the one and love the other, or you will be devoted to the one and despise the other. You cannot serve both God and money."

14The Pharisees, who loved money, heard all this and were sneering at Jesus. 15He said to them, "You are the ones who justify your-

---

a 8 Greek *ten drachmas*, each worth about a day's wages   *b* 6 Or about 3,000 liters   *c* 7 Or about 30 tons

selves in the eyes of others, but God knows your hearts. What people value highly is detestable in God's sight.

Additional Teachings

16"The Law and the Prophets were proclaimed until John. Since that time, the good news of the kingdom of God is being preached, and everyone is forcing their way into it. 17It is easier for heaven and earth to disappear than for the least stroke of a pen to drop out of the Law.

18"Anyone who divorces his wife and marries another woman commits adultery, and the man who marries a divorced woman commits adultery.

The Rich Man and Lazarus

19"There was a rich man who was dressed in purple and fine linen and lived in luxury every day. 20At his gate was laid a beggar named Lazarus, covered with sores 21and longing to eat what fell from the rich man's table. Even the dogs came and licked his sores.

22"The time came when the beggar died and the angels carried him to Abraham's side. The rich man also died and was buried. 23In Hades, where he was in torment, he looked up and saw Abraham far away, with Lazarus by his side. 24So he called to him, 'Father Abraham, have pity on me and send Lazarus to dip the tip of his finger in water and cool my tongue, because I am in agony in this fire.'

25"But Abraham replied, 'Son, remember that in your lifetime you received your good things, while Lazarus received bad things, but now he is comforted here and you are in agony. 26And besides all this, between us and you a great chasm has been set in place, so that those who want to go from here to you cannot, nor can anyone cross over from there to us.'

27"He answered, 'Then I beg you, father, send Lazarus to my family, 28for I have five brothers. Let him warn them, so that they will not also come to this place of torment.'

29"Abraham replied, 'They have Moses and the Prophets; let them listen to them.'

30"'No, father Abraham,' he said, 'but if someone from the dead goes to them, they will repent.'

31"He said to him, 'If they do not listen to Moses and the Prophets, they will not be convinced even if someone rises from the dead.'"

Sin, Faith, Duty

17 Jesus said to his disciples: "Things that cause people to stumble are bound to come, but woe to anyone through whom they come. 2It would be better for them to be thrown into the sea with a millstone tied around their neck than to cause one of these little ones to stumble. 3So watch yourselves.

"If your brother or sister[a] sins against you, rebuke them; and if they repent, forgive them.

4Even if they sin against you seven times in a day and seven times come back to you saying 'I repent,' you must forgive them."

5The apostles said to the Lord, "Increase our faith!"

6He replied, "If you have faith as small as a mustard seed, you can say to this mulberry tree, 'Be uprooted and planted in the sea,' and it will obey you.

7"Suppose one of you has a servant plowing or looking after the sheep. Will he say to the servant when he comes in from the field, 'Come along now and sit down to eat'? 8Won't he rather say, 'Prepare my supper, get yourself ready and wait on me while I eat and drink; after that you may eat and drink'? 9Will he thank the servant because he did what he was told to do? 10So you also, when you have done everything you were told to do, should say, 'We are unworthy servants; we have only done our duty.'"

Jesus Heals Ten Men With Leprosy

11Now on his way to Jerusalem, Jesus traveled along the border between Samaria and Galilee. 12As he was going into a village, ten men who had leprosy[b] met him. They stood at a distance 13and called out in a loud voice, "Jesus, Master, have pity on us!"

14When he saw them, he said, "Go, show yourselves to the priests." And as they went, they were cleansed.

15One of them, when he saw he was healed, came back, praising God in a loud voice. 16He threw himself at Jesus' feet and thanked him—and he was a Samaritan.

17Jesus asked, "Were not all ten cleansed? Where are the other nine? 18Has no one returned to give praise to God except this foreigner?" 19Then he said to him, "Rise and go; your faith has made you well."

The Coming of the Kingdom of God

20Once, on being asked by the Pharisees when the kingdom of God would come, Jesus replied, "The coming of the kingdom of God is not something that can be observed, 21nor will people say, 'Here it is,' or 'There it is,' because the kingdom of God is in your midst."[c]

22Then he said to his disciples, "The time is coming when you will long to see one of the days of the Son of Man, but you will not see it. 23People will tell you, 'There he is!' or 'Here he is!' Do not go running off after them. 24For the Son of Man in his day[d] will be like the lightning, which flashes and lights up the sky from one end to the other. 25But first he must suffer many things and be rejected by this generation.

26"Just as it was in the days of Noah, so also will it be in the days of the Son of Man. 27People were eating, drinking, marrying and being given in marriage up to the day Noah entered the ark. Then the flood came and destroyed them all.

---

a 3 The Greek word for *brother or sister* (*adelphos*) refers here to a fellow disciple, whether man or woman. b 12 The Greek word traditionally translated *leprosy* was used for various diseases affecting the skin. c 21 Or *is within you* d 24 Some manuscripts do not have *in his day*.

28"It was the same in the days of Lot. People were eating and drinking, buying and selling, planting and building. 29But the day Lot left Sodom, fire and sulfur rained down from heaven and destroyed them all.

30"It will be just like this on the day the Son of Man is revealed. 31On that day no one who is on the housetop, with possessions inside, should go down to get them. Likewise, no one in the field should go back for anything. 32Remember Lot's wife! 33Whoever tries to keep their life will lose it, and whoever loses their life will preserve it. 34I tell you, on that night two people will be in one bed; one will be taken and the other left. 35Two women will be grinding grain together; one will be taken and the other left." [36]a

37"Where, Lord?" they asked.

He replied, "Where there is a dead body, there the vultures will gather."

The Parable of the Persistent Widow

18 Then Jesus told his disciples a parable to show them that they should always pray and not give up. 2He said: "In a certain town there was a judge who neither feared God nor cared what people thought. 3And there was a widow in that town who kept coming to him with the plea, 'Grant me justice against my adversary.'

4"For some time he refused. But finally he said to himself, 'Even though I don't fear God or care what people think, 5yet because this widow keeps bothering me, I will see that she gets justice, so that she won't eventually come and attack me!'"

6And the Lord said, "Listen to what the unjust judge says. 7And will not God bring about justice for his chosen ones, who cry out to him day and night? Will he keep putting them off? 8I tell you, he will see that they get justice, and quickly. However, when the Son of Man comes, will he find faith on the earth?"

The Parable of the Pharisee and the Tax Collector

9To some who were confident of their own righteousness and looked down on everyone else, Jesus told this parable: 10"Two men went up to the temple to pray, one a Pharisee and the other a tax collector. 11The Pharisee stood by himself and prayed: 'God, I thank you that I am not like other people—robbers, evildoers, adulterers—or even like this tax collector. 12I fast twice a week and give a tenth of all I get.'

13"But the tax collector stood at a distance. He would not even look up to heaven, but beat his breast and said, 'God, have mercy on me, a sinner.'

14"I tell you that this man, rather than the other, went home justified before God. For all those who exalt themselves will be humbled, and those who humble themselves will be exalted."

The Little Children and Jesus

15People were also bringing babies to Jesus for him to place his hands on them. When the disciples saw this, they rebuked them. 16But Jesus called the children to him and said, "Let the little children come to me, and do not hinder them, for the kingdom of God belongs to such as these. 17Truly I tell you, anyone who will not receive the kingdom of God like a little child will never enter it."

The Rich and the Kingdom of God

18A certain ruler asked him, "Good teacher, what must I do to inherit eternal life?"

19"Why do you call me good?" Jesus answered. "No one is good—except God alone. 20You know the commandments: 'You shall not commit adultery, you shall not murder, you shall not steal, you shall not give false testimony, honor your father and mother.'b"

21"All these I have kept since I was a boy," he said.

22When Jesus heard this, he said to him, "You still lack one thing. Sell everything you have and give to the poor, and you will have treasure in heaven. Then come, follow me."

23When he heard this, he became very sad, because he was very wealthy. 24Jesus looked at him and said, "How hard it is for the rich to enter the kingdom of God! 25Indeed, it is easier for a camel to go through the eye of a needle than for someone who is rich to enter the kingdom of God."

26Those who heard this asked, "Who then can be saved?"

27Jesus replied, "What is impossible with man is possible with God."

28Peter said to him, "We have left all we had to follow you!"

29"Truly I tell you," Jesus said to them, "no one who has left home or wife or brothers or sisters or parents or children for the sake of the kingdom of God 30will fail to receive many times as much in this age, and in the age to come eternal life."

Jesus Predicts His Death a Third Time

31Jesus took the Twelve aside and told them, "We are going up to Jerusalem, and everything that is written by the prophets about the Son of Man will be fulfilled. 32He will be delivered over to the Gentiles. They will mock him, insult him and spit on him; 33they will flog him and kill him. On the third day he will rise again."

34The disciples did not understand any of this. Its meaning was hidden from them, and they did not know what he was talking about.

A Blind Beggar Receives His Sight

35As Jesus approached Jericho, a blind man was sitting by the roadside begging. 36When he heard the crowd going by, he asked what was happening. 37They told him, "Jesus of Nazareth is passing by."

---

a 36 Some manuscripts include here words similar to Matt. 24:40.   b 20 Exodus 20:12-16; Deut. 5:16-20

³⁸He called out, "Jesus, Son of David, have mercy on me!"

³⁹Those who led the way rebuked him and told him to be quiet, but he shouted all the more, "Son of David, have mercy on me!"

⁴⁰Jesus stopped and ordered the man to be brought to him. When he came near, Jesus asked him, ⁴¹"What do you want me to do for you?"

"Lord, I want to see," he replied.

⁴²Jesus said to him, "Receive your sight; your faith has healed you." ⁴³Immediately he received his sight and followed Jesus, praising God. When all the people saw it, they also praised God.

Zacchaeus the Tax Collector

19 Jesus entered Jericho and was passing through. ²A man was there by the name of Zacchaeus; he was a chief tax collector and was wealthy. ³He wanted to see who Jesus was, but because he was short he could not see over the crowd. ⁴So he ran ahead and climbed a sycamore-fig tree to see him, since Jesus was coming that way.

⁵When Jesus reached the spot, he looked up and said to him, "Zacchaeus, come down immediately. I must stay at your house today." ⁶So he came down at once and welcomed him gladly.

⁷All the people saw this and began to mutter, "He has gone to be the guest of a sinner."

⁸But Zacchaeus stood up and said to the Lord, "Look, Lord! Here and now I give half of my possessions to the poor, and if I have cheated anybody out of anything, I will pay back four times the amount."

⁹Jesus said to him, "Today salvation has come to this house, because this man, too, is a son of Abraham. ¹⁰For the Son of Man came to seek and to save the lost."

The Parable of the Ten Minas

¹¹While they were listening to this, he went on to tell them a parable, because he was near Jerusalem and the people thought that the kingdom of God was going to appear at once. ¹²He said: "A man of noble birth went to a distant country to have himself appointed king and then to return. ¹³So he called ten of his servants and gave them ten minas.ᵃ 'Put this money to work,' he said, 'until I come back.'

¹⁴"But his subjects hated him and sent a delegation after him to say, 'We don't want this man to be our king.'

¹⁵"He was made king, however, and returned home. Then he sent for the servants to whom he had given the money, in order to find out what they had gained with it.

¹⁶"The first one came and said, 'Sir, your mina has earned ten more.'

¹⁷"'Well done, my good servant!' his master replied. 'Because you have been trustworthy in a very small matter, take charge of ten cities.'

¹⁸"The second came and said, 'Sir, your mina has earned five more.'

¹⁹"His master answered, 'You take charge of five cities.'

²⁰"Then another servant came and said, 'Sir, here is your mina; I have kept it laid away in a piece of cloth. ²¹I was afraid of you, because you are a hard man. You take out what you did not put in and reap what you did not sow.'

²²"His master replied, 'I will judge you by your own words, you wicked servant! You knew, did you, that I am a hard man, taking out what I did not put in, and reaping what I did not sow? ²³Why then didn't you put my money on deposit, so that when I came back, I could have collected it with interest?'

²⁴"Then he said to those standing by, 'Take his mina away from him and give it to the one who has ten minas.'

²⁵"'Sir,' they said, 'he already has ten!'

²⁶"He replied, 'I tell you that to everyone who has, more will be given, but as for the one who has nothing, even what they have will be taken away. ²⁷But those enemies of mine who did not want me to be king over them—bring them here and kill them in front of me.'"

Jesus Comes to Jerusalem as King

²⁸After Jesus had said this, he went on ahead, going up to Jerusalem. ²⁹As he approached Bethphage and Bethany at the hill called the Mount of Olives, he sent two of his disciples, saying to them, ³⁰"Go to the village ahead of you, and as you enter it, you will find a colt tied there, which no one has ever ridden. Untie it and bring it here. ³¹If anyone asks you, 'Why are you untying it?' say, 'The Lord needs it.'"

³²Those who were sent ahead went and found it just as he had told them. ³³As they were untying the colt, its owners asked them, "Why are you untying the colt?"

³⁴They replied, "The Lord needs it."

³⁵They brought it to Jesus, threw their cloaks on the colt and put Jesus on it. ³⁶As he went along, people spread their cloaks on the road.

³⁷When he came near the place where the road goes down the Mount of Olives, the whole crowd of disciples began joyfully to praise God in loud voices for all the miracles they had seen:

³⁸"Blessed is the king who comes in the
    name of the Lord!"ᵇ

"Peace in heaven and glory in the
    highest!"

³⁹Some of the Pharisees in the crowd said to Jesus, "Teacher, rebuke your disciples!"

⁴⁰"I tell you," he replied, "if they keep quiet, the stones will cry out."

⁴¹As he approached Jerusalem and saw the city, he wept over it ⁴²and said, "If you, even you, had only known on this day what would bring you peace—but now it is hidden from your eyes. ⁴³The days will come upon you when your enemies will build an embankment against you and encircle you and hem

ᵃ 13 A mina was about three months' wages.   ᵇ 38 Psalm 118:26

you in on every side. 44They will dash you to the ground, you and the children within your walls. They will not leave one stone on another, because you did not recognize the time of God's coming to you."

Jesus at the Temple

45When Jesus entered the temple courts, he began to drive out those who were selling. 46"It is written," he said to them, "'My house will be a house of prayer'*a*; but you have made it 'a den of robbers.'*b*"

47Every day he was teaching at the temple. But the chief priests, the teachers of the law and the leaders among the people were trying to kill him. 48Yet they could not find any way to do it, because all the people hung on his words.

The Authority of Jesus Questioned

20 One day as Jesus was teaching the people in the temple courts and proclaiming the good news, the chief priests and the teachers of the law, together with the elders, came up to him. 2"Tell us by what authority you are doing these things," they said. "Who gave you this authority?"

3He replied, "I will also ask you a question. Tell me: 4John's baptism—was it from heaven, or of human origin?"

5They discussed it among themselves and said, "If we say, 'From heaven,' he will ask, 'Why didn't you believe him?' 6But if we say, 'Of human origin,' all the people will stone us, because they are persuaded that John was a prophet."

7So they answered, "We don't know where it was from."

8Jesus said, "Neither will I tell you by what authority I am doing these things."

The Parable of the Tenants

9He went on to tell the people this parable: "A man planted a vineyard, rented it to some farmers and went away for a long time. 10At harvest time he sent a servant to the tenants so they would give him some of the fruit of the vineyard. But the tenants beat him and sent him away empty-handed. 11He sent another servant, but that one also they beat and treated shamefully and sent away empty-handed. 12He sent still a third, and they wounded him and threw him out.

13"Then the owner of the vineyard said, 'What shall I do? I will send my son, whom I love; perhaps they will respect him.'

14"But when the tenants saw him, they talked the matter over. 'This is the heir,' they said. 'Let's kill him, and the inheritance will be ours.' 15So they threw him out of the vineyard and killed him.

"What then will the owner of the vineyard do to them? 16He will come and kill those tenants and give the vineyard to others."

When the people heard this, they said, "God forbid!"

17Jesus looked directly at them and asked, "Then what is the meaning of that which is written:

"'The stone the builders rejected has become the cornerstone'*c*?

18Everyone who falls on that stone will be broken to pieces; anyone on whom it falls will be crushed."

19The teachers of the law and the chief priests looked for a way to arrest him immediately, because they knew he had spoken this parable against them. But they were afraid of the people.

Paying Taxes to Caesar

20Keeping a close watch on him, they sent spies, who pretended to be sincere. They hoped to catch Jesus in something he said, so that they might hand him over to the power and authority of the governor. 21So the spies questioned him: "Teacher, we know that you speak and teach what is right, and that you do not show partiality but teach the way of God in accordance with the truth. 22Is it right for us to pay taxes to Caesar or not?"

23He saw through their duplicity and said to them, 24"Show me a denarius. Whose image and inscription are on it?"

"Caesar's," they replied.

25He said to them, "Then give back to Caesar what is Caesar's, and to God what is God's."

26They were unable to trap him in what he had said there in public. And astonished by his answer, they became silent.

The Resurrection and Marriage

27Some of the Sadducees, who say there is no resurrection, came to Jesus with a question. 28"Teacher," they said, "Moses wrote for us that if a man's brother dies and leaves a wife but no children, the man must marry the widow and raise up offspring for his brother. 29Now there were seven brothers. The first one married a woman and died childless. 30The second 31and then the third married her, and in the same way the seven died, leaving no children. 32Finally, the woman died too. 33Now then, at the resurrection whose wife will she be, since the seven were married to her?"

34Jesus replied, "The people of this age marry and are given in marriage. 35But those who are considered worthy of taking part in the age to come and in the resurrection from the dead will neither marry nor be given in marriage, 36and they can no longer die; for they are like the angels. They are God's children, since they are children of the resurrection. 37But in the account of the burning bush, even Moses showed that the dead rise, for he calls the Lord 'the God of Abraham, and the God of Isaac, and the God of Jacob.'*d* 38He is not the God of the dead, but of the living, for to him all are alive."

39Some of the teachers of the law respond-

a 46 Isaiah 56:7   *b 46* Jer. 7:11   *c 17* Psalm 118:22   *d 37* Exodus 3:6

ed, "Well said, teacher!" [40]And no one dared to ask him any more questions.

Whose Son Is the Messiah?

[41]Then Jesus said to them, "Why is it said that the Messiah is the son of David? [42]David himself declares in the Book of Psalms:

"'The Lord said to my Lord:
  "Sit at my right hand
[43]until I make your enemies
  a footstool for your feet."' [a]

[44]David calls him 'Lord.' How then can he be his son?"

Warning Against the Teachers of the Law

[45]While all the people were listening, Jesus said to his disciples, [46]"Beware of the teachers of the law. They like to walk around in flowing robes and love to be greeted with respect in the marketplaces and have the most important seats in the synagogues and the places of honor at banquets. [47]They devour widows' houses and for a show make lengthy prayers. These men will be punished most severely."

The Widow's Offering

21 As Jesus looked up, he saw the rich putting their gifts into the temple treasury. [2]He also saw a poor widow put in two very small copper coins. [3]"Truly I tell you," he said, "this poor widow has put in more than all the others. [4]All these people gave their gifts out of their wealth; but she out of her poverty put in all she had to live on."

The Destruction of the Temple and Signs of the End Times

[5]Some of his disciples were remarking about how the temple was adorned with beautiful stones and with gifts dedicated to God. But Jesus said, [6]"As for what you see here, the time will come when not one stone will be left on another; every one of them will be thrown down."

[7]"Teacher," they asked, "when will these things happen? And what will be the sign that they are about to take place?"

[8]He replied: "Watch out that you are not deceived. For many will come in my name, claiming, 'I am he,' and, 'The time is near.' Do not follow them. [9]When you hear of wars and uprisings, do not be frightened. These things must happen first, but the end will not come right away."

[10]Then he said to them: "Nation will rise against nation, and kingdom against kingdom. [11]There will be great earthquakes, famines and pestilences in various places, and fearful events and great signs from heaven.

[12]"But before all this, they will seize you and persecute you. They will hand you over to synagogues and put you in prison, and you will be brought before kings and governors, and all on account of my name. [13]And so you

will bear testimony to me. [14]But make up your mind not to worry beforehand how you will defend yourselves. [15]For I will give you words and wisdom that none of your adversaries will be able to resist or contradict. [16]You will be betrayed even by parents, brothers and sisters, relatives and friends, and they will put some of you to death. [17]Everyone will hate you because of me. [18]But not a hair of your head will perish. [19]Stand firm, and you will win life.

[20]"When you see Jerusalem being surrounded by armies, you will know that its desolation is near. [21]Then let those who are in Judea flee to the mountains, let those in the city get out, and let those in the country not enter the city. [22]For this is the time of punishment in fulfillment of all that has been written. [23]How dreadful it will be in those days for pregnant women and nursing mothers! There will be great distress in the land and wrath against this people. [24]They will fall by the sword and will be taken as prisoners to all the nations. Jerusalem will be trampled on by the Gentiles until the times of the Gentiles are fulfilled.

[25]"There will be signs in the sun, moon and stars. On the earth, nations will be in anguish and perplexity at the roaring and tossing of the sea. [26]People will faint from terror, apprehensive of what is coming on the world, for the heavenly bodies will be shaken. [27]At that time they will see the Son of Man coming in a cloud with power and great glory. [28]When these things begin to take place, stand up and lift up your heads, because your redemption is drawing near."

[29]He told them this parable: "Look at the fig tree and all the trees. [30]When they sprout leaves, you can see for yourselves and know that summer is near. [31]Even so, when you see these things happening, you know that the kingdom of God is near.

[32]"Truly I tell you, this generation will certainly not pass away until all these things have happened. [33]Heaven and earth will pass away, but my words will never pass away.

[34]"Be careful, or your hearts will be weighed down with carousing, drunkenness and the anxieties of life, and that day will close on you suddenly like a trap. [35]For it will come on all those who live on the face of the whole earth. [36]Be always on the watch, and pray that you may be able to escape all that is about to happen, and that you may be able to stand before the Son of Man."

[37]Each day Jesus was teaching at the temple, and each evening he went out to spend the night on the hill called the Mount of Olives, [38]and all the people came early in the morning to hear him at the temple.

Judas Agrees to Betray Jesus

22 Now the Festival of Unleavened Bread, called the Passover, was approaching, [2]and the chief priests and the teachers of the law were looking for some way to get rid of Jesus, for they were afraid of the people. [3]Then Satan entered Judas, called Iscariot, one of the

[a] 43 Psalm 110:1

Twelve. ⁴And Judas went to the chief priests and the officers of the temple guard and discussed with them how he might betray Jesus. ⁵They were delighted and agreed to give him money. ⁶He consented, and watched for an opportunity to hand Jesus over to them when no crowd was present.

The Last Supper

⁷Then came the day of Unleavened Bread on which the Passover lamb had to be sacrificed. ⁸Jesus sent Peter and John, saying, "Go and make preparations for us to eat the Passover."

⁹"Where do you want us to prepare for it?" they asked.

¹⁰He replied, "As you enter the city, a man carrying a jar of water will meet you. Follow him to the house that he enters, ¹¹and say to the owner of the house, 'The Teacher asks: Where is the guest room, where I may eat the Passover with my disciples?' ¹²He will show you a large room upstairs, all furnished. Make preparations there."

¹³They left and found things just as Jesus had told them. So they prepared the Passover.

¹⁴When the hour came, Jesus and his apostles reclined at the table. ¹⁵And he said to them, "I have eagerly desired to eat this Passover with you before I suffer. ¹⁶For I tell you, I will not eat it again until it finds fulfillment in the kingdom of God."

¹⁷After taking the cup, he gave thanks and said, "Take this and divide it among you. ¹⁸For I tell you I will not drink again from the fruit of the vine until the kingdom of God comes."

¹⁹And he took bread, gave thanks and broke it, and gave it to them, saying, "This is my body given for you; do this in remembrance of me."

²⁰In the same way, after the supper he took the cup, saying, "This cup is the new covenant in my blood, which is poured out for you.ᵃ ²¹But the hand of him who is going to betray me is with mine on the table. ²²The Son of Man will go as it has been decreed. But woe to that man who betrays him!" ²³They began to question among themselves which of them it might be who would do this.

²⁴A dispute also arose among them as to which of them was considered to be greatest. ²⁵Jesus said to them, "The kings of the Gentiles lord it over them; and those who exercise authority over them call themselves Benefactors. ²⁶But you are not to be like that. Instead, the greatest among you should be like the youngest, and the one who rules like the one who serves. ²⁷For who is greater, the one who is at the table or the one who serves? Is it not the one who is at the table? But I am among you as one who serves. ²⁸You are those who have stood by me in my trials. ²⁹And I confer on you a kingdom, just as my Father conferred one on me, ³⁰so that you may eat and drink at my table in my kingdom and sit on thrones, judging the twelve tribes of Israel.

³¹"Simon, Simon, Satan has asked to sift all of you as wheat. ³²But I have prayed for you, Simon, that your faith may not fail. And when you have turned back, strengthen your brothers."

³³But he replied, "Lord, I am ready to go with you to prison and to death."

³⁴Jesus answered, "I tell you, Peter, before the rooster crows today, you will deny three times that you know me."

³⁵Then Jesus asked them, "When I sent you without purse, bag or sandals, did you lack anything?"

"Nothing," they answered.

³⁶He said to them, "But now if you have a purse, take it, and also a bag; and if you don't have a sword, sell your cloak and buy one. ³⁷It is written: 'And he was numbered with the transgressors'ᵇ; and I tell you that this must be fulfilled in me. Yes, what is written about me is reaching its fulfillment."

³⁸The disciples said, "See, Lord, here are two swords."

"That's enough!" he replied.

Jesus Prays on the Mount of Olives

³⁹Jesus went out as usual to the Mount of Olives, and his disciples followed him. ⁴⁰On reaching the place, he said to them, "Pray that you will not fall into temptation." ⁴¹He withdrew about a stone's throw beyond them, knelt down and prayed, ⁴²"Father, if you are willing, take this cup from me; yet not my will, but yours be done." ⁴³An angel from heaven appeared to him and strengthened him. ⁴⁴And being in anguish, he prayed more earnestly, and his sweat was like drops of blood falling to the ground.ᶜ

⁴⁵When he rose from prayer and went back to the disciples, he found them asleep, exhausted from sorrow. ⁴⁶"Why are you sleeping?" he asked them. "Get up and pray so that you will not fall into temptation."

Jesus Arrested

⁴⁷While he was still speaking a crowd came up, and the man who was called Judas, one of the Twelve, was leading them. He approached Jesus to kiss him, ⁴⁸but Jesus asked him, "Judas, are you betraying the Son of Man with a kiss?"

⁴⁹When Jesus' followers saw what was going to happen, they said, "Lord, should we strike with our swords?" ⁵⁰And one of them struck the servant of the high priest, cutting off his right ear.

⁵¹But Jesus answered, "No more of this!" And he touched the man's ear and healed him.

⁵²Then Jesus said to the chief priests, the officers of the temple guard, and the elders, who had come for him, "Am I leading a rebellion, that you have come with swords and clubs? ⁵³Every day I was with you in the temple courts, and you did not lay a hand on me. But this is your hour—when darkness reigns."

ᵃ 19,20 Some manuscripts do not have given for you . . . poured out for you.   ᵇ 37 Isaiah 53:12   ᶜ 43,44 Many early manuscripts do not have verses 43 and 44.

Peter Disowns Jesus

⁵⁴Then seizing him, they led him away and took him into the house of the high priest. Peter followed at a distance. ⁵⁵And when some there had kindled a fire in the middle of the courtyard and had sat down together, Peter sat down with them. ⁵⁶A servant girl saw him seated there in the firelight. She looked closely at him and said, "This man was with him."

⁵⁷But he denied it. "Woman, I don't know him," he said.

⁵⁸A little later someone else saw him and said, "You also are one of them."

"Man, I am not!" Peter replied.

⁵⁹About an hour later another asserted, "Certainly this fellow was with him, for he is a Galilean."

⁶⁰Peter replied, "Man, I don't know what you're talking about!" Just as he was speaking, the rooster crowed. ⁶¹The Lord turned and looked straight at Peter. Then Peter remembered the word the Lord had spoken to him: "Before the rooster crows today, you will disown me three times." ⁶²And he went outside and wept bitterly.

The Guards Mock Jesus

⁶³The men who were guarding Jesus began mocking and beating him. ⁶⁴They blindfolded him and demanded, "Prophesy! Who hit you?" ⁶⁵And they said many other insulting things to him.

Jesus Before Pilate and Herod

⁶⁶At daybreak the council of the elders of the people, both the chief priests and the teachers of the law, met together, and Jesus was led before them. ⁶⁷"If you are the Messiah," they said, "tell us."

Jesus answered, "If I tell you, you will not believe me, ⁶⁸and if I asked you, you would not answer. ⁶⁹But from now on, the Son of Man will be seated at the right hand of the mighty God."

⁷⁰They all asked, "Are you then the Son of God?"

He replied, "You say that I am."

⁷¹Then they said, "Why do we need any more testimony? We have heard it from his own lips."

23 Then the whole assembly rose and led him off to Pilate. ²And they began to accuse him, saying, "We have found this man subverting our nation. He opposes payment of taxes to Caesar and claims to be Messiah, a king."

³So Pilate asked Jesus, "Are you the king of the Jews?"

"You have said so," Jesus replied.

⁴Then Pilate announced to the chief priests and the crowd, "I find no basis for a charge against this man."

⁵But they insisted, "He stirs up the people all over Judea by his teaching. He started in Galilee and has come all the way here."

⁶On hearing this, Pilate asked if the man was a Galilean. ⁷When he learned that Jesus was under Herod's jurisdiction, he sent him to Herod, who was also in Jerusalem at that time.

⁸When Herod saw Jesus, he was greatly pleased, because for a long time he had been wanting to see him. From what he had heard about him, he hoped to see him perform a sign of some sort. ⁹He plied him with many questions, but Jesus gave him no answer. ¹⁰The chief priests and the teachers of the law were standing there, vehemently accusing him. ¹¹Then Herod and his soldiers ridiculed and mocked him. Dressing him in an elegant robe, they sent him back to Pilate. ¹²That day Herod and Pilate became friends—before this they had been enemies.

¹³Pilate called together the chief priests, the rulers and the people, ¹⁴and said to them, "You brought me this man as one who was inciting the people to rebellion. I have examined him in your presence and have found no basis for your charges against him. ¹⁵Neither has Herod, for he sent him back to us; as you can see, he has done nothing to deserve death. ¹⁶Therefore, I will punish him and then release him." [¹⁷]ᵃ

¹⁸But the whole crowd shouted, "Away with this man! Release Barabbas to us!" ¹⁹(Barabbas had been thrown into prison for an insurrection in the city, and for murder.)

²⁰Wanting to release Jesus, Pilate appealed to them again. ²¹But they kept shouting, "Crucify him! Crucify him!"

²²For the third time he spoke to them: "Why? What crime has this man committed? I have found in him no grounds for the death penalty. Therefore I will have him punished and then release him."

²³But with loud shouts they insistently demanded that he be crucified, and their shouts prevailed. ²⁴So Pilate decided to grant their demand. ²⁵He released the man who had been thrown into prison for insurrection and murder, the one they asked for, and surrendered Jesus to their will.

The Crucifixion of Jesus

²⁶As the soldiers led him away, they seized Simon from Cyrene, who was on his way in from the country, and put the cross on him and made him carry it behind Jesus. ²⁷A large number of people followed him, including women who mourned and wailed for him. ²⁸Jesus turned and said to them, "Daughters of Jerusalem, do not weep for me; weep for yourselves and for your children. ²⁹For the time will come when you will say, 'Blessed are the childless women, the wombs that never bore and the breasts that never nursed!' ³⁰Then

> "'they will say to the mountains, "Fall on us!"
> and to the hills, "Cover us!"'ᵇ

³¹For if people do these things when the tree is green, what will happen when it is dry?"

³²Two other men, both criminals, were also led out with him to be executed. ³³When they

---

ᵃ 17 Some manuscripts include here words similar to Matt. 27:15 and Mark 15:6.   ᵇ 30 Hosea 10:8

came to the place called the Skull, they crucified him there, along with the criminals—one on his right, the other on his left. ³⁴Jesus said, "Father, forgive them, for they do not know what they are doing."ᵃ And they divided up his clothes by casting lots.

³⁵The people stood watching, and the rulers even sneered at him. They said, "He saved others; let him save himself if he is God's Messiah, the Chosen One."

³⁶The soldiers also came up and mocked him. They offered him wine vinegar ³⁷and said, "If you are the king of the Jews, save yourself."

³⁸There was a written notice above him, which read: THIS IS THE KING OF THE JEWS.

³⁹One of the criminals who hung there hurled insults at him: "Aren't you the Messiah? Save yourself and us!"

⁴⁰But the other criminal rebuked him. "Don't you fear God," he said, "since you are under the same sentence? ⁴¹We are punished justly, for we are getting what our deeds deserve. But this man has done nothing wrong."

⁴²Then he said, "Jesus, remember me when you come into your kingdom.ᵇ"

⁴³Jesus answered him, "Truly I tell you, today you will be with me in paradise."

The Death of Jesus

⁴⁴It was now about noon, and darkness came over the whole land until three in the afternoon, ⁴⁵for the sun stopped shining. And the curtain of the temple was torn in two. ⁴⁶Jesus called out with a loud voice, "Father, into your hands I commit my spirit."ᶜ When he had said this, he breathed his last.

⁴⁷The centurion, seeing what had happened, praised God and said, "Surely this was a righteous man." ⁴⁸When all the people who had gathered to witness this sight saw what took place, they beat their breasts and went away. ⁴⁹But all those who knew him, including the women who had followed him from Galilee, stood at a distance, watching these things.

The Burial of Jesus

⁵⁰Now there was a man named Joseph, a member of the Council, a good and upright man, ⁵¹who had not consented to their decision and action. He came from the Judean town of Arimathea, and he himself was waiting for the kingdom of God. ⁵²Going to Pilate, he asked for Jesus' body. ⁵³Then he took it down, wrapped it in linen cloth and placed it in a tomb cut in the rock, one in which no one had yet been laid. ⁵⁴It was Preparation Day, and the Sabbath was about to begin.

⁵⁵The women who had come with Jesus from Galilee followed Joseph and saw the tomb and how his body was laid in it. ⁵⁶Then they went home and prepared spices and perfumes. But they rested on the Sabbath in obedience to the commandment.

Jesus Has Risen

24 On the first day of the week, very early in the morning, the women took the spices they had prepared and went to the tomb. ²They found the stone rolled away from the tomb, ³but when they entered, they did not find the body of the Lord Jesus. ⁴While they were wondering about this, suddenly two men in clothes that gleamed like lightning stood beside them. ⁵In their fright the women bowed down with their faces to the ground, but the men said to them, "Why do you look for the living among the dead? ⁶He is not here; he has risen! Remember how he told you, while he was still with you in Galilee: ⁷'The Son of Man must be delivered over to the hands of sinners, be crucified and on the third day be raised again.' " ⁸Then they remembered his words.

⁹When they came back from the tomb, they told all these things to the Eleven and to all the others. ¹⁰It was Mary Magdalene, Joanna, Mary the mother of James, and the others with them who told this to the apostles. ¹¹But they did not believe the women, because their words seemed to them like nonsense. ¹²Peter, however, got up and ran to the tomb. Bending over, he saw the strips of linen lying by themselves, and he went away, wondering to himself what had happened.

On the Road to Emmaus

¹³Now that same day two of them were going to a village called Emmaus, about seven milesᵈ from Jerusalem. ¹⁴They were talking with each other about everything that had happened. ¹⁵As they talked and discussed these things with each other, Jesus himself came up and walked along with them; ¹⁶but they were kept from recognizing him.

¹⁷He asked them, "What are you discussing together as you walk along?"

They stood still, their faces downcast. ¹⁸One of them, named Cleopas, asked him, "Are you the only one visiting Jerusalem who does not know the things that have happened there in these days?"

¹⁹"What things?" he asked.

"About Jesus of Nazareth," they replied. "He was a prophet, powerful in word and deed before God and all the people. ²⁰The chief priests and our rulers handed him over to be sentenced to death, and they crucified him; ²¹but we had hoped that he was the one who was going to redeem Israel. And what is more, it is the third day since all this took place. ²²In addition, some of our women amazed us. They went to the tomb early this morning ²³but didn't find his body. They came and told us that they had seen a vision of angels, who said he was alive. ²⁴Then some of our companions went to the tomb and found it just as the women had said, but they did not see Jesus."

²⁵He said to them, "How foolish you are, and how slow to believe all that the prophets have spoken! ²⁶Did not the Messiah have to suffer these things and then enter his glory?" ²⁷And

ᵃ 34 Some early manuscripts do not have this sentence.   ᵇ 42 Some manuscripts *come with your kingly power*   ᶜ 46 Psalm 31:5   ᵈ 13 Or about 11 kilometers

beginning with Moses and all the Prophets, he explained to them what was said in all the Scriptures concerning himself.

²⁸As they approached the village to which they were going, Jesus continued on as if he were going farther. ²⁹But they urged him strongly, "Stay with us, for it is nearly evening; the day is almost over." So he went in to stay with them.

³⁰When he was at the table with them, he took bread, gave thanks, broke it and began to give it to them. ³¹Then their eyes were opened and they recognized him, and he disappeared from their sight. ³²They asked each other, "Were not our hearts burning within us while he talked with us on the road and opened the Scriptures to us?"

³³They got up and returned at once to Jerusalem. There they found the Eleven and those with them, assembled together ³⁴and saying, "It is true! The Lord has risen and has appeared to Simon." ³⁵Then the two told what had happened on the way, and how Jesus was recognized by them when he broke the bread.

Jesus Appears to the Disciples

³⁶While they were still talking about this, Jesus himself stood among them and said to them, "Peace be with you."

³⁷They were startled and frightened, thinking they saw a ghost. ³⁸He said to them, "Why are you troubled, and why do doubts rise in your minds? ³⁹Look at my hands and my feet. It is I myself! Touch me and see; a ghost does not have flesh and bones, as you see I have."

⁴⁰When he had said this, he showed them his hands and feet. ⁴¹And while they still did not believe it because of joy and amazement, he asked them, "Do you have anything here to eat?" ⁴²They gave him a piece of broiled fish, ⁴³and he took it and ate it in their presence.

⁴⁴He said to them, "This is what I told you while I was still with you: Everything must be fulfilled that is written about me in the Law of Moses, the Prophets and the Psalms."

⁴⁵Then he opened their minds so they could understand the Scriptures. ⁴⁶He told them, "This is what is written: The Messiah will suffer and rise from the dead on the third day, ⁴⁷and repentance for the forgiveness of sins will be preached in his name to all nations, beginning at Jerusalem. ⁴⁸You are witnesses of these things. ⁴⁹I am going to send you what my Father has promised; but stay in the city until you have been clothed with power from on high."

The Ascension of Jesus

⁵⁰When he had led them out to the vicinity of Bethany, he lifted up his hands and blessed them. ⁵¹While he was blessing them, he left them and was taken up into heaven. ⁵²Then they worshiped him and returned to Jerusalem with great joy. ⁵³And they stayed continually at the temple, praising God.

John

The Word Became Flesh

1 In the beginning was the Word, and the Word was with God, and the Word was God. ²He was with God in the beginning. ³Through him all things were made; without him nothing was made that has been made. ⁴In him was life, and that life was the light of all mankind. ⁵The light shines in the darkness, and the darkness has not overcome[a] it.

⁶There was a man sent from God whose name was John. ⁷He came as a witness to testify concerning that light, so that through him all might believe. ⁸He himself was not the light; he came only as a witness to the light.

⁹The true light that gives light to everyone was coming into the world. ¹⁰He was in the world, and though the world was made through him, the world did not recognize him. ¹¹He came to that which was his own, but his own did not receive him. ¹²Yet to all who did receive him, to those who believed in his name, he gave the right to become children of God— ¹³children born not of natural descent, nor of human decision or a husband's will, but born of God.

¹⁴The Word became flesh and made his dwelling among us. We have seen his glory, the glory of the one and only Son, who came from the Father, full of grace and truth.

¹⁵(John testified concerning him. He cried out, saying, "This is the one I spoke about when I said, 'He who comes after me has surpassed me because he was before me.'") ¹⁶Out of his fullness we have all received grace in place of grace already given. ¹⁷For the law was given through Moses; grace and truth came through Jesus Christ. ¹⁸No one has ever seen God, but the one and only Son, who is himself God and[b] is in closest relationship with the Father, has made him known.

John the Baptist Denies Being the Messiah

¹⁹Now this was John's testimony when the Jewish leaders[c] in Jerusalem sent priests and

---

[a] 5 Or understood   [b] 18 Some manuscripts but the only Son, who   [c] 19 The Greek term traditionally translated the Jews (hoi Ioudaioi) refers here and elsewhere in John's Gospel to those Jewish leaders who opposed Jesus; also in 5:10, 15, 16; 7:1, 11, 13; 9:22; 18:14, 28, 36; 19:7, 12, 31, 38; 20:19.

Levites to ask him who he was. [20]He did not fail to confess, but confessed freely, "I am not the Messiah."

[21]They asked him, "Then who are you? Are you Elijah?"

He said, "I am not."

"Are you the Prophet?"

He answered, "No."

[22]Finally they said, "Who are you? Give us an answer to take back to those who sent us. What do you say about yourself?"

[23]John replied in the words of Isaiah the prophet, "I am the voice of one calling in the wilderness, 'Make straight the way for the Lord.'"[a]

[24]Now the Pharisees who had been sent [25]questioned him, "Why then do you baptize if you are not the Messiah, nor Elijah, nor the Prophet?"

[26]"I baptize with[b] water," John replied, "but among you stands one you do not know. [27]He is the one who comes after me, the straps of whose sandals I am not worthy to untie."

[28]This all happened at Bethany on the other side of the Jordan, where John was baptizing.

John Testifies About Jesus

[29]The next day John saw Jesus coming toward him and said, "Look, the Lamb of God, who takes away the sin of the world! [30]This is the one I meant when I said, 'A man who comes after me has surpassed me because he was before me.' [31]I myself did not know him, but the reason I came baptizing with water was that he might be revealed to Israel."

[32]Then John gave this testimony: "I saw the Spirit come down from heaven as a dove and remain on him. [33]And I myself did not know him, but the one who sent me to baptize with water told me, 'The man on whom you see the Spirit come down and remain is the one who will baptize with the Holy Spirit.' [34]I have seen and I testify that this is God's Chosen One."[c]

John's Disciples Follow Jesus

[35]The next day John was there again with two of his disciples. [36]When he saw Jesus passing by, he said, "Look, the Lamb of God!"

[37]When the two disciples heard him say this, they followed Jesus. [38]Turning around, Jesus saw them following and asked, "What do you want?"

They said, "Rabbi" (which means "Teacher"), "where are you staying?"

[39]"Come," he replied, "and you will see."

So they went and saw where he was staying, and they spent that day with him. It was about four in the afternoon.

[40]Andrew, Simon Peter's brother, was one of the two who heard what John had said and who had followed Jesus. [41]The first thing Andrew did was to find his brother Simon and tell him, "We have found the Messiah" (that is, the Christ). [42]And he brought him to Jesus.

Jesus looked at him and said, "You are Simon son of John. You will be called Cephas" (which, when translated, is Peter[d]).

Jesus Calls Philip and Nathanael

[43]The next day Jesus decided to leave for Galilee. Finding Philip, he said to him, "Follow me."

[44]Philip, like Andrew and Peter, was from the town of Bethsaida. [45]Philip found Nathanael and told him, "We have found the one Moses wrote about in the Law, and about whom the prophets also wrote—Jesus of Nazareth, the son of Joseph."

[46]"Nazareth! Can anything good come from there?" Nathanael asked.

"Come and see," said Philip.

[47]When Jesus saw Nathanael approaching, he said of him, "Here truly is an Israelite in whom there is no deceit."

[48]"How do you know me?" Nathanael asked.

Jesus answered, "I saw you while you were still under the fig tree before Philip called you."

[49]Then Nathanael declared, "Rabbi, you are the Son of God; you are the king of Israel."

[50]Jesus said, "You believe[e] because I told you I saw you under the fig tree. You will see greater things than that." [51]He then added, "Very truly I tell you,[f] you[f] will see 'heaven open, and the angels of God ascending and descending on'[g] the Son of Man."

Jesus Changes Water Into Wine

2 On the third day a wedding took place at Cana in Galilee. Jesus' mother was there, [2]and Jesus and his disciples had also been invited to the wedding. [3]When the wine was gone, Jesus' mother said to him, "They have no more wine."

[4]"Woman,[h] why do you involve me?" Jesus replied. "My hour has not yet come."

[5]His mother said to the servants, "Do whatever he tells you."

[6]Nearby stood six stone water jars, the kind used by the Jews for ceremonial washing, each holding from twenty to thirty gallons.[i]

[7]Jesus said to the servants, "Fill the jars with water"; so they filled them to the brim.

[8]Then he told them, "Now draw some out and take it to the master of the banquet."

They did so, [9]and the master of the banquet tasted the water that had been turned into wine. He did not realize where it had come from, though the servants who had drawn the water knew. Then he called the bridegroom aside [10]and said, "Everyone brings out the choice wine first and then the cheaper wine after the guests have had too much to drink; but you have saved the best till now."

[11]What Jesus did here in Cana of Galilee was the first of the signs through which he revealed his glory; and his disciples believed in him.

---

[a] 23 Isaiah 40:3   [b] 26 Or in; also in verses 31 and 33 (twice)   [c] 34 See Isaiah 42:1; many manuscripts is the Son of God.   [d] 42 Cephas (Aramaic) and Peter (Greek) both mean rock.   [e] 50 Or Do you believe . . . ?   [f] 51 The Greek is plural.   [g] 51 Gen. 28:12   [h] 4 The Greek for Woman does not denote any disrespect.   [i] 6 Or from about 75 to about 115 liters

¹²After this he went down to Capernaum with his mother and brothers and his disciples. There they stayed for a few days.

Jesus Clears the Temple Courts

¹³When it was almost time for the Jewish Passover, Jesus went up to Jerusalem. ¹⁴In the temple courts he found people selling cattle, sheep and doves, and others sitting at tables exchanging money. ¹⁵So he made a whip out of cords, and drove all from the temple courts, both sheep and cattle; he scattered the coins of the money changers and overturned their tables. ¹⁶To those who sold doves he said, "Get these out of here! Stop turning my Father's house into a market!" ¹⁷His disciples remembered that it is written: "Zeal for your house will consume me."ᵃ

¹⁸The Jews then responded to him, "What sign can you show us to prove your authority to do all this?"

¹⁹Jesus answered them, "Destroy this temple, and I will raise it again in three days."

²⁰They replied, "It has taken forty-six years to build this temple, and you are going to raise it in three days?" ²¹But the temple he had spoken of was his body. ²²After he was raised from the dead, his disciples recalled what he had said. Then they believed the scripture and the words that Jesus had spoken.

²³Now while he was in Jerusalem at the Passover Festival, many people saw the signs he was performing and believed in his name.ᵇ ²⁴But Jesus would not entrust himself to them, for he knew all people. ²⁵He did not need any testimony about mankind, for he knew what was in each person.

Jesus Teaches Nicodemus

3 Now there was a Pharisee, a man named Nicodemus who was a member of the Jewish ruling council. ²He came to Jesus at night and said, "Rabbi, we know that you are a teacher who has come from God. For no one could perform the signs you are doing if God were not with him."

³Jesus replied, "Very truly I tell you, no one can see the kingdom of God unless they are born again.ᶜ"

⁴"How can someone be born when they are old?" Nicodemus asked. "Surely they cannot enter a second time into their mother's womb to be born!"

⁵Jesus answered, "Very truly I tell you, no one can enter the kingdom of God unless they are born of water and the Spirit. ⁶Flesh gives birth to flesh, but the Spiritᵈ gives birth to spirit. ⁷You should not be surprised at my saying, 'Youᵉ must be born again.' ⁸The wind blows wherever it pleases. You hear its sound, but you cannot tell where it comes from or where it is going. So it is with everyone born of the Spirit."ᶠ

⁹"How can this be?" Nicodemus asked.

¹⁰"You are Israel's teacher," said Jesus, "and do you not understand these things? ¹¹Very truly I tell you, we speak of what we know, and we testify to what we have seen, but still you people do not accept our testimony. ¹²I have spoken to you of earthly things and you do not believe; how then will you believe if I speak of heavenly things? ¹³No one has ever gone into heaven except the one who came from heaven—the Son of Man.ᵍ ¹⁴Just as Moses lifted up the snake in the wilderness, so the Son of Man must be lifted up,ʰ ¹⁵that everyone who believes may have eternal life in him."ⁱ

¹⁶For God so loved the world that he gave his one and only Son, that whoever believes in him shall not perish but have eternal life. ¹⁷For God did not send his Son into the world to condemn the world, but to save the world through him. ¹⁸Whoever believes in him is not condemned, but whoever does not believe stands condemned already because they have not believed in the name of God's one and only Son. ¹⁹This is the verdict: Light has come into the world, but people loved darkness instead of light because their deeds were evil. ²⁰Everyone who does evil hates the light, and will not come into the light for fear that their deeds will be exposed. ²¹But whoever lives by the truth comes into the light, so that it may be seen plainly that what they have done has been done in the sight of God.

John Testifies Again About Jesus

²²After this, Jesus and his disciples went out into the Judean countryside, where he spent some time with them, and baptized. ²³Now John also was baptizing at Aenon near Salim, because there was plenty of water, and people were coming and being baptized. ²⁴(This was before John was put in prison.) ²⁵An argument developed between some of John's disciples and a certain Jew over the matter of ceremonial washing. ²⁶They came to John and said to him, "Rabbi, that man who was with you on the other side of the Jordan—the one you testified about—look, he is baptizing, and everyone is going to him."

²⁷To this John replied, "A person can receive only what is given them from heaven. ²⁸You yourselves can testify that I said, 'I am not the Messiah but am sent ahead of him.' ²⁹The bride belongs to the bridegroom. The friend who attends the bridegroom waits and listens for him, and is full of joy when he hears the bridegroom's voice. That joy is mine, and it is now complete. ³⁰He must become greater; I must become less."ʲ

³¹The one who comes from above is above all; the one who is from the earth belongs to the earth, and speaks as one from the earth. The one who comes from heaven is above all. ³²He testifies to what he has seen and heard,

---

ᵃ 17 Psalm 69:9   ᵇ 23 Or *in him*   ᶜ 3 The Greek for *again* also means *from above*; also in verse 7.
ᵈ 6 Or *but spirit*   ᵉ 7 The Greek is plural.   ᶠ 8 The Greek for *Spirit* is the same as that for *wind*.
ᵍ 13 Some manuscripts *Man, who is in heaven*   ʰ 14 The Greek for *lifted up* also means *exalted*.
ⁱ 15 Some interpreters end the quotation with verse 21.   ʲ 30 Some interpreters end the quotation with verse 36.

but no one accepts his testimony. ³³Whoever has accepted it has certified that God is truthful. ³⁴For the one whom God has sent speaks the words of God, for God[a] gives the Spirit without limit. ³⁵The Father loves the Son and has placed everything in his hands. ³⁶Whoever believes in the Son has eternal life, but whoever rejects the Son will not see life, for God's wrath remains on them.

Jesus Talks With a Samaritan Woman

4 Now Jesus learned that the Pharisees had heard that he was gaining and baptizing more disciples than John— ²although in fact it was not Jesus who baptized, but his disciples. ³So he left Judea and went back once more to Galilee.

⁴Now he had to go through Samaria. ⁵So he came to a town in Samaria called Sychar, near the plot of ground Jacob had given to his son Joseph. ⁶Jacob's well was there, and Jesus, tired as he was from the journey, sat down by the well. It was about noon.

⁷When a Samaritan woman came to draw water, Jesus said to her, "Will you give me a drink?" ⁸(His disciples had gone into the town to buy food.)

⁹The Samaritan woman said to him, "You are a Jew and I am a Samaritan woman. How can you ask me for a drink?" (For Jews do not associate with Samaritans.[b])

¹⁰Jesus answered her, "If you knew the gift of God and who it is that asks you for a drink, you would have asked him and he would have given you living water."

¹¹"Sir," the woman said, "you have nothing to draw with and the well is deep. Where can you get this living water? ¹²Are you greater than our father Jacob, who gave us the well and drank from it himself, as did also his sons and his livestock?"

¹³Jesus answered, "Everyone who drinks this water will be thirsty again, ¹⁴but whoever drinks the water I give them will never thirst. Indeed, the water I give them will become in them a spring of water welling up to eternal life."

¹⁵The woman said to him, "Sir, give me this water so that I won't get thirsty and have to keep coming here to draw water."

¹⁶He told her, "Go, call your husband and come back."

¹⁷"I have no husband," she replied.

Jesus said to her, "You are right when you say you have no husband. ¹⁸The fact is, you have had five husbands, and the man you now have is not your husband. What you have just said is quite true."

¹⁹"Sir," the woman said, "I can see that you are a prophet. ²⁰Our ancestors worshiped on this mountain, but you Jews claim that the place where we must worship is in Jerusalem."

²¹"Woman," Jesus replied, "believe me, a time is coming when you will worship the Father neither on this mountain nor in Jerusalem. ²²You Samaritans worship what you do not know; we worship what we do know, for salvation is from the Jews. ²³Yet a time is coming and has now come when the true worshipers will worship the Father in the Spirit and in truth, for they are the kind of worshipers the Father seeks. ²⁴God is spirit, and his worshipers must worship in the Spirit and in truth."

²⁵The woman said, "I know that Messiah" (called Christ) "is coming. When he comes, he will explain everything to us."

²⁶Then Jesus declared, "I, the one speaking to you—I am he."

The Disciples Rejoin Jesus

²⁷Just then his disciples returned and were surprised to find him talking with a woman. But no one asked, "What do you want?" or "Why are you talking with her?"

²⁸Then, leaving her water jar, the woman went back to the town and said to the people, ²⁹"Come, see a man who told me everything I ever did. Could this be the Messiah?" ³⁰They came out of the town and made their way toward him.

³¹Meanwhile his disciples urged him, "Rabbi, eat something."

³²But he said to them, "I have food to eat that you know nothing about."

³³Then his disciples said to each other, "Could someone have brought him food?"

³⁴"My food," said Jesus, "is to do the will of him who sent me and to finish his work. ³⁵Don't you have a saying, 'It's still four months until harvest'? I tell you, open your eyes and look at the fields! They are ripe for harvest. ³⁶Even now the one who reaps draws a wage and harvests a crop for eternal life, so that the sower and the reaper may be glad together. ³⁷Thus the saying 'One sows and another reaps' is true. ³⁸I sent you to reap what you have not worked for. Others have done the hard work, and you have reaped the benefits of their labor."

Many Samaritans Believe

³⁹Many of the Samaritans from that town believed in him because of the woman's testimony, "He told me everything I ever did." ⁴⁰So when the Samaritans came to him, they urged him to stay with them, and he stayed two days. ⁴¹And because of his words many more became believers.

⁴²They said to the woman, "We no longer believe just because of what you said; now we have heard for ourselves, and we know that this man really is the Savior of the world."

Jesus Heals an Official's Son

⁴³After the two days he left for Galilee. ⁴⁴(Now Jesus himself had pointed out that a prophet has no honor in his own country.) ⁴⁵When he arrived in Galilee, the Galileans welcomed him. They had seen all that he had done in Jerusalem at the Passover Festival, for they also had been there.

⁴⁶Once more he visited Cana in Galilee, where he had turned the water into wine.

---

a 34 Greek *he*   *b* 9 Or *do not use dishes Samaritans have used*

And there was a certain royal official whose son lay sick at Capernaum. ⁴⁷When this man heard that Jesus had arrived in Galilee from Judea, he went to him and begged him to come and heal his son, who was close to death.

⁴⁸"Unless you people see signs and wonders," Jesus told him, "you will never believe."

⁴⁹The royal official said, "Sir, come down before my child dies."

⁵⁰"Go," Jesus replied, "your son will live."

The man took Jesus at his word and departed. ⁵¹While he was still on the way, his servants met him with the news that his boy was living. ⁵²When he inquired as to the time when his son got better, they said to him, "Yesterday, at one in the afternoon, the fever left him."

⁵³Then the father realized that this was the exact time at which Jesus had said to him, "Your son will live." So he and his whole household believed.

⁵⁴This was the second sign Jesus performed after coming from Judea to Galilee.

The Healing at the Pool

5 Some time later, Jesus went up to Jerusalem for one of the Jewish festivals. ²Now there is in Jerusalem near the Sheep Gate a pool, which in Aramaic is called Bethesdaᵃ and which is surrounded by five covered colonnades. ³Here a great number of disabled people used to lie—the blind, the lame, the paralyzed. [⁴]ᵇ ⁵One who was there had been an invalid for thirty-eight years. ⁶When Jesus saw him lying there and learned that he had been in this condition for a long time, he asked him, "Do you want to get well?"

⁷"Sir," the invalid replied, "I have no one to help me into the pool when the water is stirred. While I am trying to get in, someone else goes down ahead of me."

⁸Then Jesus said to him, "Get up! Pick up your mat and walk." ⁹At once the man was cured; he picked up his mat and walked.

The day on which this took place was a Sabbath, ¹⁰and so the Jewish leaders said to the man who had been healed, "It is the Sabbath; the law forbids you to carry your mat."

¹¹But he replied, "The man who made me well said to me, 'Pick up your mat and walk.' "

¹²So they asked him, "Who is this fellow who told you to pick it up and walk?"

¹³The man who was healed had no idea who it was, for Jesus had slipped away into the crowd that was there.

¹⁴Later Jesus found him at the temple and said to him, "See, you are well again. Stop sinning or something worse may happen to you." ¹⁵The man went away and told the Jewish leaders that it was Jesus who had made him well.

The Authority of the Son

¹⁶So, because Jesus was doing these things on the Sabbath, the Jewish leaders began to persecute him. ¹⁷In his defense Jesus said to them, "My Father is always at his work to this very day, and I too am working." ¹⁸For this reason they tried all the more to kill him; not only was he breaking the Sabbath, but he was even calling God his own Father, making himself equal with God.

¹⁹Jesus gave them this answer: "Very truly I tell you, the Son can do nothing by himself; he can do only what he sees his Father doing, because whatever the Father does the Son also does. ²⁰For the Father loves the Son and shows him all he does. Yes, and he will show him even greater works than these, so that you will be amazed. ²¹For just as the Father raises the dead and gives them life, even so the Son gives life to whom he is pleased to give it. ²²Moreover, the Father judges no one, but has entrusted all judgment to the Son, ²³that all may honor the Son just as they honor the Father. Whoever does not honor the Son does not honor the Father, who sent him.

²⁴"Very truly I tell you, whoever hears my word and believes him who sent me has eternal life and will not be judged but has crossed over from death to life. ²⁵Very truly I tell you, a time is coming and has now come when the dead will hear the voice of the Son of God and those who hear will live. ²⁶For as the Father has life in himself, so he has granted the Son also to have life in himself. ²⁷And he has given him authority to judge because he is the Son of Man.

²⁸"Do not be amazed at this, for a time is coming when all who are in their graves will hear his voice ²⁹and come out—those who have done what is good will rise to live, and those who have done what is evil will rise to be condemned. ³⁰By myself I can do nothing; I judge only as I hear, and my judgment is just, for I seek not to please myself but him who sent me.

Testimonies About Jesus

³¹"If I testify about myself, my testimony is not true. ³²There is another who testifies in my favor, and I know that his testimony about me is true.

³³"You have sent to John and he has testified to the truth. ³⁴Not that I accept human testimony; but I mention it that you may be saved. ³⁵John was a lamp that burned and gave light, and you chose for a time to enjoy his light.

³⁶"I have testimony weightier than that of John. For the works that the Father has given me to finish—the very works that I am doing—testify that the Father has sent me. ³⁷And the Father who sent me has himself testified concerning me. You have never heard his voice nor seen his form, ³⁸nor does his word dwell in you, for you do not believe the one he sent. ³⁹You studyᶜ the Scriptures diligently because you think that in them you have eternal life. These are the very Scriptures that

---

ᵃ 2 Some manuscripts *Bethzatha*; other manuscripts *Bethsaida*   ᵇ *3,4* Some manuscripts include here, wholly or in part, *paralyzed—and they waited for the moving of the waters. ⁴From time to time an angel of the Lord would come down and stir up the waters. The first one into the pool after each such disturbance would be cured of whatever disease they had.*   ᶜ *39* Or ³⁹*Study*

testify about me, 40yet you refuse to come to me to have life.

41"I do not accept glory from human beings, 42but I know you. I know that you do not have the love of God in your hearts. 43I have come in my Father's name, and you do not accept me; but if someone else comes in his own name, you will accept him. 44How can you believe since you accept glory from one another but do not seek the glory that comes from the only God*a*?

45"But do not think I will accuse you before the Father. Your accuser is Moses, on whom your hopes are set. 46If you believed Moses, you would believe me, for he wrote about me. 47But since you do not believe what he wrote, how are you going to believe what I say?"

Jesus Feeds the Five Thousand

6 Some time after this, Jesus crossed to the far shore of the Sea of Galilee (that is, the Sea of Tiberias), 2and a great crowd of people followed him because they saw the signs he had performed by healing the sick. 3Then Jesus went up on a mountainside and sat down with his disciples. 4The Jewish Passover Festival was near.

5When Jesus looked up and saw a great crowd coming toward him, he said to Philip, "Where shall we buy bread for these people to eat?" 6He asked this only to test him, for he already had in mind what he was going to do.

7Philip answered him, "It would take more than half a year's wages*b* to buy enough bread for each one to have a bite!"

8Another of his disciples, Andrew, Simon Peter's brother, spoke up, 9"Here is a boy with five small barley loaves and two small fish, but how far will they go among so many?"

10Jesus said, "Have the people sit down." There was plenty of grass in that place, and they sat down (about five thousand men were there). 11Jesus then took the loaves, gave thanks, and distributed to those who were seated as much as they wanted. He did the same with the fish.

12When they had all had enough to eat, he said to his disciples, "Gather the pieces that are left over. Let nothing be wasted." 13So they gathered them and filled twelve baskets with the pieces of the five barley loaves left over by those who had eaten.

14After the people saw the sign Jesus performed, they began to say, "Surely this is the Prophet who is to come into the world." 15Jesus, knowing that they intended to come and make him king by force, withdrew again to a mountain by himself.

Jesus Walks on the Water

16When evening came, his disciples went down to the lake, 17where they got into a boat and set off across the lake for Capernaum. By now it was dark, and Jesus had not yet joined them. 18A strong wind was blowing and the waters grew rough. 19When they had rowed about three or four miles,*c* they saw Jesus approaching the boat, walking on the water; and they were frightened. 20But he said to them, "It is I; don't be afraid." 21Then they were willing to take him into the boat, and immediately the boat reached the shore where they were heading.

22The next day the crowd that had stayed on the opposite shore of the lake realized that only one boat had been there, and that Jesus had not entered it with his disciples, but that they had gone away alone. 23Then some boats from Tiberias landed near the place where the people had eaten the bread after the Lord had given thanks. 24Once the crowd realized that neither Jesus nor his disciples were there, they got into the boats and went to Capernaum in search of Jesus.

Jesus the Bread of Life

25When they found him on the other side of the lake, they asked him, "Rabbi, when did you get here?"

26Jesus answered, "Very truly I tell you, you are looking for me, not because you saw the signs I performed but because you ate the loaves and had your fill. 27Do not work for food that spoils, but for food that endures to eternal life, which the Son of Man will give you. For on him God the Father has placed his seal of approval."

28Then they asked him, "What must we do to do the works God requires?"

29Jesus answered, "The work of God is this: to believe in the one he has sent."

30So they asked him, "What sign then will you give that we may see it and believe you? What will you do? 31Our ancestors ate the manna in the wilderness; as it is written: 'He gave them bread from heaven to eat.'*d*"

32Jesus said to them, "Very truly I tell you, it is not Moses who has given you the bread from heaven, but it is my Father who gives you the true bread from heaven. 33For the bread of God is the bread that comes down from heaven and gives life to the world."

34"Sir," they said, "always give us this bread."

35Then Jesus declared, "I am the bread of life. Whoever comes to me will never go hungry, and whoever believes in me will never be thirsty. 36But as I told you, you have seen me and still you do not believe. 37All those the Father gives me will come to me, and whoever comes to me I will never drive away. 38For I have come down from heaven not to do my will but to do the will of him who sent me. 39And this is the will of him who sent me, that I shall lose none of all those he has given me, but raise them up at the last day. 40For my Father's will is that everyone who looks to the Son and believes in him shall have eternal life, and I will raise them up at the last day."

41At this the Jews there began to grumble about him because he said, "I am the bread

---

a 44 Some early manuscripts *the Only One*   *b 7* Greek *take two hundred denarii*   *c 19* Or about 5 or 6 kilometers   *d 31* Exodus 16:4; Neh. 9:15; Psalm 78:24,25

that came down from heaven." [42]They said, "Is this not Jesus, the son of Joseph, whose father and mother we know? How can he now say, 'I came down from heaven'?"

[43]"Stop grumbling among yourselves," Jesus answered. [44]"No one can come to me unless the Father who sent me draws them, and I will raise them up at the last day. [45]It is written in the Prophets: 'They will all be taught by God.'[a] Everyone who has heard the Father and learned from him comes to me. [46]No one has seen the Father except the one who is from God; only he has seen the Father. [47]Very truly I tell you, the one who believes has eternal life. [48]I am the bread of life. [49]Your ancestors ate the manna in the wilderness, yet they died. [50]But here is the bread that comes down from heaven, which anyone may eat and not die. [51]I am the living bread that came down from heaven. Whoever eats this bread will live forever. This bread is my flesh, which I will give for the life of the world."

[52]Then the Jews began to argue sharply among themselves, "How can this man give us his flesh to eat?"

[53]Jesus said to them, "Very truly I tell you, unless you eat the flesh of the Son of Man and drink his blood, you have no life in you. [54]Whoever eats my flesh and drinks my blood has eternal life, and I will raise them up at the last day. [55]For my flesh is real food and my blood is real drink. [56]Whoever eats my flesh and drinks my blood remains in me, and I in them. [57]Just as the living Father sent me and I live because of the Father, so the one who feeds on me will live because of me. [58]This is the bread that came down from heaven. Your ancestors ate manna and died, but whoever feeds on this bread will live forever." [59]He said this while teaching in the synagogue in Capernaum.

Many Disciples Desert Jesus

[60]On hearing it, many of his disciples said, "This is a hard teaching. Who can accept it?"

[61]Aware that his disciples were grumbling about this, Jesus said to them, "Does this offend you? [62]Then what if you see the Son of Man ascend to where he was before! [63]The Spirit gives life; the flesh counts for nothing. The words I have spoken to you—they are full of the Spirit[b] and life. [64]Yet there are some of you who do not believe." For Jesus had known from the beginning which of them did not believe and who would betray him. [65]He went on to say, "This is why I told you that no one can come to me unless the Father has enabled them."

[66]From this time many of his disciples turned back and no longer followed him.

[67]"You do not want to leave too, do you?" Jesus asked the Twelve.

[68]Simon Peter answered him, "Lord, to whom shall we go? You have the words of eternal life. [69]We have come to believe and to know that you are the Holy One of God."

[70]Then Jesus replied, "Have I not chosen you, the Twelve? Yet one of you is a devil!" [71](He meant Judas, the son of Simon Iscariot, who, though one of the Twelve, was later to betray him.)

Jesus Goes to the Festival of Tabernacles

7 After this, Jesus went around in Galilee. He did not want[c] to go about in Judea because the Jewish leaders there were looking for a way to kill him. [2]But when the Jewish Festival of Tabernacles was near, [3]Jesus' brothers said to him, "Leave Galilee and go to Judea, so that your disciples there may see the works you do. [4]No one who wants to become a public figure acts in secret. Since you are doing these things, show yourself to the world." [5]For even his own brothers did not believe in him.

[6]Therefore Jesus told them, "My time is not yet here; for you any time will do. [7]The world cannot hate you, but it hates me because I testify that its works are evil. [8]You go to the festival. I am not[d] going up to this festival, because my time has not yet fully come." [9]After he had said this, he stayed in Galilee.

[10]However, after his brothers had left for the festival, he went also, not publicly, but in secret. [11]Now at the festival the Jewish leaders were watching for Jesus and asking, "Where is he?"

[12]Among the crowds there was widespread whispering about him. Some said, "He is a good man."

Others replied, "No, he deceives the people." [13]But no one would say anything publicly about him for fear of the leaders.

Jesus Teaches at the Festival

[14]Not until halfway through the festival did Jesus go up to the temple courts and begin to teach. [15]The Jews there were amazed and asked, "How did this man get such learning without having been taught?"

[16]Jesus answered, "My teaching is not my own. It comes from the one who sent me. [17]Anyone who chooses to do the will of God will find out whether my teaching comes from God or whether I speak on my own. [18]Whoever speaks on their own does so to gain personal glory, but he who seeks the glory of the one who sent him is a man of truth; there is nothing false about him. [19]Has not Moses given you the law? Yet not one of you keeps the law. Why are you trying to kill me?"

[20]"You are demon-possessed," the crowd answered. "Who is trying to kill you?"

[21]Jesus said to them, "I did one miracle, and you are all amazed. [22]Yet, because Moses gave you circumcision (though actually it did not come from Moses, but from the patriarchs), you circumcise a boy on the Sabbath. [23]Now if a boy can be circumcised on the Sabbath so that the law of Moses may not be broken, why are you angry with me for healing a man's whole body on the Sabbath? [24]Stop judging

---

[a] 45 Isaiah 54:13   [b] 63 Or *are Spirit*; or *are spirit*   [c] 1 Some manuscripts *not have authority*
[d] 8 Some manuscripts *not yet*

by mere appearances, but instead judge correctly."

Division Over Who Jesus Is

25At that point some of the people of Jerusalem began to ask, "Isn't this the man they are trying to kill? 26Here he is, speaking publicly, and they are not saying a word to him. Have the authorities really concluded that he is the Messiah? 27But we know where this man is from; when the Messiah comes, no one will know where he is from."

28Then Jesus, still teaching in the temple courts, cried out, "Yes, you know me, and you know where I am from. I am not here on my own authority, but he who sent me is true. You do not know him, 29but I know him because I am from him and he sent me."

30At this they tried to seize him, but no one laid a hand on him, because his hour had not yet come. 31Still, many in the crowd believed in him. They said, "When the Messiah comes, will he perform more signs than this man?"

32The Pharisees heard the crowd whispering such things about him. Then the chief priests and the Pharisees sent temple guards to arrest him.

33Jesus said, "I am with you for only a short time, and then I am going to the one who sent me. 34You will look for me, but you will not find me; and where I am, you cannot come."

35The Jews said to one another, "Where does this man intend to go that we cannot find him? Will he go where our people live scattered among the Greeks, and teach the Greeks? 36What did he mean when he said, 'You will look for me, but you will not find me,' and 'Where I am, you cannot come'?"

37On the last and greatest day of the festival, Jesus stood and said in a loud voice, "Let anyone who is thirsty come to me and drink. 38Whoever believes in me, as Scripture has said, rivers of living water will flow from within them."a 39By this he meant the Spirit, whom those who believed in him were later to receive. Up to that time the Spirit had not been given, since Jesus had not yet been glorified.

40On hearing his words, some of the people said, "Surely this man is the Prophet."

41Others said, "He is the Messiah."

Still others asked, "How can the Messiah come from Galilee? 42Does not Scripture say that the Messiah will come from David's descendants and from Bethlehem, the town where David lived?" 43Thus the people were divided because of Jesus. 44Some wanted to seize him, but no one laid a hand on him.

Unbelief of the Jewish Leaders

45Finally the temple guards went back to the chief priests and the Pharisees, who asked them, "Why didn't you bring him in?"

46"No one ever spoke the way this man does," the guards replied.

47"You mean he has deceived you also?" the Pharisees retorted. 48"Have any of the rulers or of the Pharisees believed in him? 49No! But this mob that knows nothing of the law—there is a curse on them."

50Nicodemus, who had gone to Jesus earlier and who was one of their own number, asked, 51"Does our law condemn a man without first hearing him to find out what he has been doing?"

52They replied, "Are you from Galilee, too? Look into it, and you will find that a prophet does not come out of Galilee."

[The earliest manuscripts and many other ancient witnesses do not have John 7:53—8:11.

A few manuscripts include these verses, wholly or in part, after John 7:36, John 21:25, Luke 21:38 or Luke 24:53.]

8 53Then they all went home, 1but Jesus went to the Mount of Olives.

2At dawn he appeared again in the temple courts, where all the people gathered around him, and he sat down to teach them. 3The teachers of the law and the Pharisees brought in a woman caught in adultery. They made her stand before the group 4and said to Jesus, "Teacher, this woman was caught in the act of adultery. 5In the Law Moses commanded us to stone such women. Now what do you say?" 6They were using this question as a trap, in order to have a basis for accusing him.

But Jesus bent down and started to write on the ground with his finger. 7When they kept on questioning him, he straightened up and said to them, "Let any one of you who is without sin be the first to throw a stone at her." 8Again he stooped down and wrote on the ground.

9At this, those who heard began to go away one at a time, the older ones first, until only Jesus was left, with the woman still standing there. 10Jesus straightened up and asked her, "Woman, where are they? Has no one condemned you?"

11"No one, sir," she said.

"Then neither do I condemn you," Jesus declared. "Go now and leave your life of sin."

Dispute Over Jesus' Testimony

12When Jesus spoke again to the people, he said, "I am the light of the world. Whoever follows me will never walk in darkness, but will have the light of life."

13The Pharisees challenged him, "Here you are, appearing as your own witness; your testimony is not valid."

14Jesus answered, "Even if I testify on my own behalf, my testimony is valid, for I know where I came from and where I am going. But you have no idea where I come from or where I am going. 15You judge by human standards; I pass judgment on no one. 16But if I do judge, my decisions are true, because I am not alone. I stand with the Father, who sent me. 17In your own Law it is written that the testimony of two

---

a 37,38 Or me. And let anyone drink 38who believes in me." As Scripture has said, "Out of him (or them) will flow rivers of living water."

witnesses is true. [18]I am one who testifies for myself; my other witness is the Father, who sent me."

[19]Then they asked him, "Where is your father?"

"You do not know me or my Father," Jesus replied. "If you knew me, you would know my Father also." [20]He spoke these words while teaching in the temple courts near the place where the offerings were put. Yet no one seized him, because his hour had not yet come.

Dispute Over Who Jesus Is

[21]Once more Jesus said to them, "I am going away, and you will look for me, and you will die in your sin. Where I go, you cannot come." [22]This made the Jews ask, "Will he kill himself? Is that why he says, 'Where I go, you cannot come'?"

[23]But he continued, "You are from below; I am from above. You are of this world; I am not of this world. [24]I told you that you would die in your sins; if you do not believe that I am he, you will indeed die in your sins."

[25]"Who are you?" they asked.

"Just what I have been telling you from the beginning," Jesus replied. "I have much to say in judgment of you. But he who sent me is trustworthy, and what I have heard from him I tell the world."

[27]They did not understand that he was telling them about his Father. [28]So Jesus said, "When you have lifted up[a] the Son of Man, then you will know that I am he and that I do nothing on my own but speak just what the Father has taught me. [29]The one who sent me is with me; he has not left me alone, for I always do what pleases him." [30]Even as he spoke, many believed in him.

Dispute Over Whose Children Jesus' Opponents Are

[31]To the Jews who had believed him, Jesus said, "If you hold to my teaching, you are really my disciples. [32]Then you will know the truth, and the truth will set you free."

[33]They answered him, "We are Abraham's descendants and have never been slaves of anyone. How can you say that we shall be set free?"

[34]Jesus replied, "Very truly I tell you, everyone who sins is a slave to sin. [35]Now a slave has no permanent place in the family, but a son belongs to it forever. [36]So if the Son sets you free, you will be free indeed. [37]I know that you are Abraham's descendants. Yet you are looking for a way to kill me, because you have no room for my word. [38]I am telling you what I have seen in the Father's presence, and you are doing what you have heard from your father.[b]"

[39]"Abraham is our father," they answered.

"If you were Abraham's children," said Jesus, "then you would[c] do what Abraham did. [40]As it is, you are looking for a way to kill me, a man who has told you the truth that I heard from God. Abraham did not do such things. [41]You are doing the works of your own father."

"We are not illegitimate children," they protested. "The only Father we have is God himself."

[42]Jesus said to them, "If God were your Father, you would love me, for I have come here from God. I have not come on my own; God sent me. [43]Why is my language not clear to you? Because you are unable to hear what I say. [44]You belong to your father, the devil, and you want to carry out your father's desires. He was a murderer from the beginning, not holding to the truth, for there is no truth in him. When he lies, he speaks his native language, for he is a liar and the father of lies. [45]Yet because I tell the truth, you do not believe me! [46]Can any of you prove me guilty of sin? If I am telling the truth, why don't you believe me? [47]Whoever belongs to God hears what God says. The reason you do not hear is that you do not belong to God."

Jesus' Claims About Himself

[48]The Jews answered him, "Aren't we right in saying that you are a Samaritan and demon-possessed?"

[49]"I am not possessed by a demon," said Jesus, "but I honor my Father and you dishonor me. [50]I am not seeking glory for myself; but there is one who seeks it, and he is the judge. [51]Very truly I tell you, whoever obeys my word will never see death."

[52]At this they exclaimed, "Now we know that you are demon-possessed! Abraham died and so did the prophets, yet you say that whoever obeys your word will never taste death. [53]Are you greater than our father Abraham? He died, and so did the prophets. Who do you think you are?"

[54]Jesus replied, "If I glorify myself, my glory means nothing. My Father, whom you claim as your God, is the one who glorifies me. [55]Though you do not know him, I know him. If I said I did not, I would be a liar like you, but I do know him and obey his word. [56]Your father Abraham rejoiced at the thought of seeing my day; he saw it and was glad."

[57]"You are not yet fifty years old," they said to him, "and you have seen Abraham!"

[58]"Very truly I tell you," Jesus answered, "before Abraham was born, I am!" [59]At this, they picked up stones to stone him, but Jesus hid himself, slipping away from the temple grounds.

Jesus Heals a Man Born Blind

9 As he went along, he saw a man blind from birth. [2]His disciples asked him, "Rabbi, who sinned, this man or his parents, that he was born blind?"

[3]"Neither this man nor his parents sinned,"

---

[a] 28 The Greek for *lifted up* also means *exalted*.   [b] 38 Or *presence. Therefore do what you have heard from the Father.*   [c] 39 Some early manuscripts *"If you are Abraham's children," said Jesus, "then*

said Jesus, "but this happened so that the works of God might be displayed in him. [4]As long as it is day, we must do the works of him who sent me. Night is coming, when no one can work. [5]While I am in the world, I am the light of the world."

[6]After saying this, he spit on the ground, made some mud with the saliva, and put it on the man's eyes. [7]"Go," he told him, "wash in the Pool of Siloam" (this word means "Sent"). So the man went and washed, and came home seeing.

[8]His neighbors and those who had formerly seen him begging asked, "Isn't this the same man who used to sit and beg?" [9]Some claimed that he was.

Others said, "No, he only looks like him."

But he himself insisted, "I am the man."

[10]"How then were your eyes opened?" they asked.

[11]He replied, "The man they call Jesus made some mud and put it on my eyes. He told me to go to Siloam and wash. So I went and washed, and then I could see."

[12]"Where is this man?" they asked him.

"I don't know," he said.

The Pharisees Investigate the Healing

[13]They brought to the Pharisees the man who had been blind. [14]Now the day on which Jesus made the mud and opened the man's eyes was a Sabbath. [15]Therefore the Pharisees also asked him how he had received his sight. "He put mud on my eyes," the man replied, "and I washed, and now I see."

[16]Some of the Pharisees said, "This man is not from God, for he does not keep the Sabbath."

But others asked, "How can a sinner perform such signs?" So they were divided.

[17]Then they turned again to the blind man, "What have you to say about him? It was your eyes he opened."

The man replied, "He is a prophet."

[18]They still did not believe that he had been blind and had received his sight until they sent for the man's parents. [19]"Is this your son?" they asked. "Is this the one you say was born blind? How is it that now he can see?"

[20]"We know he is our son," the parents answered, "and we know he was born blind. [21]But how he can see now, or who opened his eyes, we don't know. Ask him. He is of age; he will speak for himself." [22]His parents said this because they were afraid of the Jewish leaders, who already had decided that anyone who acknowledged that Jesus was the Messiah would be put out of the synagogue. [23]That was why his parents said, "He is of age; ask him."

[24]A second time they summoned the man who had been blind. "Give glory to God by telling the truth," they said. "We know this man is a sinner."

[25]He replied, "Whether he is a sinner or not, I don't know. One thing I do know. I was blind but now I see!"

[26]Then they asked him, "What did he do to you? How did he open your eyes?"

[27]He answered, "I have told you already and you did not listen. Why do you want to hear it again? Do you want to become his disciples too?"

[28]Then they hurled insults at him and said, "You are this fellow's disciple! We are disciples of Moses! [29]We know that God spoke to Moses, but as for this fellow, we don't even know where he comes from."

[30]The man answered, "Now that is remarkable! You don't know where he comes from, yet he opened my eyes. [31]We know that God does not listen to sinners. He listens to the godly person who does his will. [32]Nobody has ever heard of opening the eyes of a man born blind. [33]If this man were not from God, he could do nothing."

[34]To this they replied, "You were steeped in sin at birth; how dare you lecture us!" And they threw him out.

Spiritual Blindness

[35]Jesus heard that they had thrown him out, and when he found him, he said, "Do you believe in the Son of Man?"

[36]"Who is he, sir?" the man asked. "Tell me so that I may believe in him."

[37]Jesus said, "You have now seen him; in fact, he is the one speaking with you."

[38]Then the man said, "Lord, I believe," and he worshiped him.

[39]Jesus said,[a] "For judgment I have come into this world, so that the blind will see and those who see will become blind."

[40]Some Pharisees who were with him heard him say this and asked, "What? Are we blind too?"

[41]Jesus said, "If you were blind, you would not be guilty of sin; but now that you claim you can see, your guilt remains.

The Good Shepherd and His Sheep

10 "Very truly I tell you Pharisees, anyone who does not enter the sheep pen by the gate, but climbs in by some other way, is a thief and a robber. [2]The one who enters by the gate is the shepherd of the sheep. [3]The gatekeeper opens the gate for him, and the sheep listen to his voice. He calls his own sheep by name and leads them out. [4]When he has brought out all his own, he goes on ahead of them, and his sheep follow him because they know his voice. [5]But they will never follow a stranger; in fact, they will run away from him because they do not recognize a stranger's voice." [6]Jesus used this figure of speech, but the Pharisees did not understand what he was telling them.

[7]Therefore Jesus said again, "Very truly I tell you, I am the gate for the sheep. [8]All who have come before me are thieves and robbers, but the sheep have not listened to them. [9]I am the gate; whoever enters through me will be saved.[b] They will come in and go out, and find

---

[a] 38,39 Some early manuscripts do not have *Then the man said . . .* [39]*Jesus said.*   [b] 9 Or *kept safe*

pasture. [10]The thief comes only to steal and kill and destroy; I have come that they may have life, and have it to the full.

[11]"I am the good shepherd. The good shepherd lays down his life for the sheep. [12]The hired hand is not the shepherd and does not own the sheep. So when he sees the wolf coming, he abandons the sheep and runs away. Then the wolf attacks the flock and scatters it. [13]The man runs away because he is a hired hand and cares nothing for the sheep.

[14]"I am the good shepherd; I know my sheep and my sheep know me— [15]just as the Father knows me and I know the Father—and I lay down my life for the sheep. [16]I have other sheep that are not of this sheep pen. I must bring them also. They too will listen to my voice, and there shall be one flock and one shepherd. [17]The reason my Father loves me is that I lay down my life—only to take it up again. [18]No one takes it from me, but I lay it down of my own accord. I have authority to lay it down and authority to take it up again. This command I received from my Father."

[19]The Jews who heard these words were again divided. [20]Many of them said, "He is demon-possessed and raving mad. Why listen to him?"

[21]But others said, "These are not the sayings of a man possessed by a demon. Can a demon open the eyes of the blind?"

Further Conflict Over Jesus' Claims

[22]Then came the Festival of Dedication[a] at Jerusalem. It was winter, [23]and Jesus was in the temple courts walking in Solomon's Colonnade. [24]The Jews who were there gathered around him, saying, "How long will you keep us in suspense? If you are the Messiah, tell us plainly."

[25]Jesus answered, "I did tell you, but you do not believe. The works I do in my Father's name testify about me, [26]but you do not believe because you are not my sheep. [27]My sheep listen to my voice; I know them, and they follow me. [28]I give them eternal life, and they shall never perish; no one will snatch them out of my hand. [29]My Father, who has given them to me, is greater than all[b]; no one can snatch them out of my Father's hand. [30]I and the Father are one."

[31]Again his Jewish opponents picked up stones to stone him, [32]but Jesus said to them, "I have shown you many good works from the Father. For which of these do you stone me?"

[33]"We are not stoning you for any good work," they replied, "but for blasphemy, because you, a mere man, claim to be God."

[34]Jesus answered them, "Is it not written in your Law, 'I have said you are "gods" '[c]? [35]If he called them 'gods,' to whom the word of God came—and Scripture cannot be set aside— [36]what about the one whom the Father set apart as his very own and sent into the world? Why then do you accuse me of blasphemy because I said, 'I am God's Son'? [37]Do not believe me unless I do the works of my Father. [38]But if I do them, even though you do not believe me, believe the works, that you may know and understand that the Father is in me, and I in the Father." [39]Again they tried to seize him, but he escaped their grasp.

[40]Then Jesus went back across the Jordan to the place where John had been baptizing in the early days. There he stayed, [41]and many people came to him. They said, "Though John never performed a sign, all that John said about this man was true." [42]And in that place many believed in Jesus.

The Death of Lazarus

11 Now a man named Lazarus was sick. He was from Bethany, the village of Mary and her sister Martha. [2](This Mary, whose brother Lazarus now lay sick, was the same one who poured perfume on the Lord and wiped his feet with her hair.) [3]So the sisters sent word to Jesus, "Lord, the one you love is sick."

[4]When he heard this, Jesus said, "This sickness will not end in death. No, it is for God's glory so that God's Son may be glorified through it." [5]Now Jesus loved Martha and her sister and Lazarus. [6]So when he heard that Lazarus was sick, he stayed where he was two more days, [7]and then he said to his disciples, "Let us go back to Judea."

[8]"But Rabbi," they said, "a short while ago the Jews there tried to stone you, and yet you are going back?"

[9]Jesus answered, "Are there not twelve hours of daylight? Anyone who walks in the daytime will not stumble, for they see by this world's light. [10]It is when a person walks at night that they stumble, for they have no light."

[11]After he had said this, he went on to tell them, "Our friend Lazarus has fallen asleep; but I am going there to wake him up."

[12]His disciples replied, "Lord, if he sleeps, he will get better." [13]Jesus had been speaking of his death, but his disciples thought he meant natural sleep.

[14]So then he told them plainly, "Lazarus is dead, [15]and for your sake I am glad I was not there, so that you may believe. But let us go to him."

[16]Then Thomas (also known as Didymus[d]) said to the rest of the disciples, "Let us also go, that we may die with him."

Jesus Comforts the Sisters of Lazarus

[17]On his arrival, Jesus found that Lazarus had already been in the tomb for four days. [18]Now Bethany was less than two miles[e] from Jerusalem, [19]and many Jews had come to Martha and Mary to comfort them in the loss of their brother. [20]When Martha heard that Jesus was coming, she went out to meet him, but Mary stayed at home.

[21]"Lord," Martha said to Jesus, "if you had

---

[a] 22 That is, Hanukkah   [b] 29 Many early manuscripts *What my Father has given me is greater than all*   [c] 34 Psalm 82:6   [d] 16 *Thomas* (Aramaic) and *Didymus* (Greek) both mean *twin.*
[e] 18 Or *about 3 kilometers*

been here, my brother would not have died.
²²But I know that even now God will give you
whatever you ask."

²³Jesus said to her, "Your brother will rise
again."

²⁴Martha answered, "I know he will rise
again in the resurrection at the last day."

²⁵Jesus said to her, "I am the resurrection
and the life. The one who believes in me will
live, even though they die; ²⁶and whoever lives
by believing in me will never die. Do you believe this?"

²⁷"Yes, Lord," she replied, "I believe that
you are the Messiah, the Son of God, who is
to come into the world."

²⁸After she had said this, she went back
and called her sister Mary aside. "The Teacher is here," she said, "and is asking for you."
²⁹When Mary heard this, she got up quickly and went to him. ³⁰Now Jesus had not yet
entered the village, but was still at the place
where Martha had met him. ³¹When the Jews
who had been with Mary in the house, comforting her, noticed how quickly she got up
and went out, they followed her, supposing
she was going to the tomb to mourn there.

³²When Mary reached the place where
Jesus was and saw him, she fell at his feet and
said, "Lord, if you had been here, my brother
would not have died."

³³When Jesus saw her weeping, and the
Jews who had come along with her also weeping, he was deeply moved in spirit and troubled. ³⁴"Where have you laid him?" he asked.

"Come and see, Lord," they replied.

³⁵Jesus wept.

³⁶Then the Jews said, "See how he loved him!"
³⁷But some of them said, "Could not he who
opened the eyes of the blind man have kept
this man from dying?"

Jesus Raises Lazarus From the Dead

³⁸Jesus, once more deeply moved, came to
the tomb. It was a cave with a stone laid across
the entrance. ³⁹"Take away the stone," he said.

"But, Lord," said Martha, the sister of the
dead man, "by this time there is a bad odor,
for he has been there four days."

⁴⁰Then Jesus said, "Did I not tell you that if
you believe, you will see the glory of God?"

⁴¹So they took away the stone. Then Jesus
looked up and said, "Father, I thank you that
you have heard me. ⁴²I knew that you always
hear me, but I said this for the benefit of the
people standing here, that they may believe
that you sent me."

⁴³When he had said this, Jesus called in a
loud voice, "Lazarus, come out!" ⁴⁴The dead
man came out, his hands and feet wrapped
with strips of linen, and a cloth around his face.

Jesus said to them, "Take off the grave
clothes and let him go."

The Plot to Kill Jesus

⁴⁵Therefore many of the Jews who had come
to visit Mary, and had seen what Jesus did,
believed in him. ⁴⁶But some of them went to
the Pharisees and told them what Jesus had
done. ⁴⁷Then the chief priests and the Pharisees called a meeting of the Sanhedrin.

"What are we accomplishing?" they asked.
"Here is this man performing many signs. ⁴⁸If
we let him go on like this, everyone will believe in him, and then the Romans will come
and take away both our temple and our nation."

⁴⁹Then one of them, named Caiaphas, who
was high priest that year, spoke up, "You
know nothing at all! ⁵⁰You do not realize
that it is better for you that one man die for
the people than that the whole nation perish."

⁵¹He did not say this on his own, but as
high priest that year he prophesied that Jesus
would die for the Jewish nation, ⁵²and not only
for that nation but also for the scattered children of God, to bring them together and make
them one. ⁵³So from that day on they plotted
to take his life.

⁵⁴Therefore Jesus no longer moved about
publicly among the people of Judea. Instead
he withdrew to a region near the wilderness,
to a village called Ephraim, where he stayed
with his disciples.

⁵⁵When it was almost time for the Jewish
Passover, many went up from the country
to Jerusalem for their ceremonial cleansing
before the Passover. ⁵⁶They kept looking for
Jesus, and as they stood in the temple courts
they asked one another, "What do you think?
Isn't he coming to the festival at all?" ⁵⁷But
the chief priests and the Pharisees had giv-
en orders that anyone who found out where
Jesus was should report it so that they might
arrest him.

Jesus Anointed at Bethany

12 Six days before the Passover, Jesus came
to Bethany, where Lazarus lived, whom
Jesus had raised from the dead. ²Here a dinner was given in Jesus' honor. Martha served,
while Lazarus was among those reclining at
the table with him. ³Then Mary took about
a pint*a* of pure nard, an expensive perfume;
she poured it on Jesus' feet and wiped his feet
with her hair. And the house was filled with
the fragrance of the perfume.

⁴But one of his disciples, Judas Iscariot,
who was later to betray him, objected, ⁵"Why
wasn't this perfume sold and the money given
to the poor? It was worth a year's wages.*b*"
⁶He did not say this because he cared about
the poor but because he was a thief; as keeper
of the money bag, he used to help himself to
what was put into it.

⁷"Leave her alone," Jesus replied. "It was
intended that she should save this perfume for
the day of my burial. ⁸You will always have
the poor among you,*c* but you will not always
have me."

⁹Meanwhile a large crowd of Jews found out
that Jesus was there and came, not only because of him but also to see Lazarus, whom he
had raised from the dead. ¹⁰So the chief priests

---

a 3 Or about 0.5 liter   *b 5* Greek *three hundred denarii*   *c 8* See Deut. 15:11.

made plans to kill Lazarus as well, [11]for on account of him many of the Jews were going over to Jesus and believing in him.

Jesus Comes to Jerusalem as King

[12]The next day the great crowd that had come for the festival heard that Jesus was on his way to Jerusalem. [13]They took palm branches and went out to meet him, shouting,

"Hosanna![a]"

"Blessed is he who comes in the name of the Lord!"[b]

"Blessed is the king of Israel!"

[14]Jesus found a young donkey and sat on it, as it is written:

[15] "Do not be afraid, Daughter Zion;
see, your king is coming,
seated on a donkey's colt."[c]

[16]At first his disciples did not understand all this. Only after Jesus was glorified did they realize that these things had been written about him and that these things had been done to him.

[17]Now the crowd that was with him when he called Lazarus from the tomb and raised him from the dead continued to spread the word. [18]Many people, because they had heard that he had performed this sign, went out to meet him. [19]So the Pharisees said to one another, "See, this is getting us nowhere. Look how the whole world has gone after him!"

Jesus Predicts His Death

[20]Now there were some Greeks among those who went up to worship at the festival. [21]They came to Philip, who was from Bethsaida in Galilee, with a request. "Sir," they said, "we would like to see Jesus." [22]Philip went to tell Andrew; Andrew and Philip in turn told Jesus.

[23]Jesus replied, "The hour has come for the Son of Man to be glorified. [24]Very truly I tell you, unless a kernel of wheat falls to the ground and dies, it remains only a single seed. But if it dies, it produces many seeds. [25]Anyone who loves their life will lose it, while anyone who hates their life in this world will keep it for eternal life. [26]Whoever serves me must follow me; and where I am, my servant also will be. My Father will honor the one who serves me.

[27]"Now my soul is troubled, and what shall I say? 'Father, save me from this hour'? No, it was for this very reason I came to this hour. [28]Father, glorify your name!"

Then a voice came from heaven, "I have glorified it, and will glorify it again." [29]The crowd that was there and heard it said it had thundered; others said an angel had spoken to him.

[30]Jesus said, "This voice was for your benefit, not mine. [31]Now is the time for judgment on this world; now the prince of this world will be driven out. [32]And I, when I am lifted up[d] from the earth, will draw all people to myself." [33]He said this to show the kind of death he was going to die.

[34]The crowd spoke up, "We have heard from the Law that the Messiah will remain forever, so how can you say, 'The Son of Man must be lifted up'? Who is this 'Son of Man'?"

[35]Then Jesus told them, "You are going to have the light just a little while longer. Walk while you have the light, before darkness overtakes you. Whoever walks in the dark does not know where they are going. [36]Believe in the light while you have the light, so that you may become children of light." When he had finished speaking, Jesus left and hid himself from them.

Belief and Unbelief Among the Jews

[37]Even after Jesus had performed so many signs in their presence, they still would not believe in him. [38]This was to fulfill the word of Isaiah the prophet:

"Lord, who has believed our message
and to whom has the arm of the Lord
been revealed?"[e]

[39]For this reason they could not believe, because, as Isaiah says elsewhere:

[40] "He has blinded their eyes
and hardened their hearts,
so they can neither see with their eyes,
nor understand with their hearts,
nor turn—and I would heal them."[f]

[41]Isaiah said this because he saw Jesus' glory and spoke about him.

[42]Yet at the same time many even among the leaders believed in him. But because of the Pharisees they would not openly acknowledge their faith for fear they would be put out of the synagogue; [43]for they loved human praise more than praise from God.

[44]Then Jesus cried out, "Whoever believes in me does not believe in me only, but in the one who sent me. [45]The one who looks at me is seeing the one who sent me. [46]I have come into the world as a light, so that no one who believes in me should stay in darkness.

[47]"If anyone hears my words but does not keep them, I do not judge that person. For I did not come to judge the world, but to save the world. [48]There is a judge for the one who rejects me and does not accept my words; the very words I have spoken will condemn them at the last day. [49]For I did not speak on my own, but the Father who sent me commanded me to say all that I have spoken. [50]I know that his command leads to eternal life. So whatever I say is just what the Father has told me to say."

Jesus Washes His Disciples' Feet

13 It was just before the Passover Festival. Jesus knew that the hour had come for him to leave this world and go to the Father.

[a] 13 A Hebrew expression meaning "Save!" which became an exclamation of praise
[b] 13 Psalm 118:25,26   [c] 15 Zech. 9:9   [d] 32 The Greek for *lifted up* also means *exalted*.
[e] 38 Isaiah 53:1   [f] 40 Isaiah 6:10

Having loved his own who were in the world, he loved them to the end.

²The evening meal was in progress, and the devil had already prompted Judas, the son of Simon Iscariot, to betray Jesus. ³Jesus knew that the Father had put all things under his power, and that he had come from God and was returning to God; ⁴so he got up from the meal, took off his outer clothing, and wrapped a towel around his waist. ⁵After that, he poured water into a basin and began to wash his disciples' feet, drying them with the towel that was wrapped around him.

⁶He came to Simon Peter, who said to him, "Lord, are you going to wash my feet?"

⁷Jesus replied, "You do not realize now what I am doing, but later you will understand."

⁸"No," said Peter, "you shall never wash my feet."

Jesus answered, "Unless I wash you, you have no part with me."

⁹"Then, Lord," Simon Peter replied, "not just my feet but my hands and my head as well!"

¹⁰Jesus answered, "Those who have had a bath need only to wash their feet; their whole body is clean. And you are clean, though not every one of you." ¹¹For he knew who was going to betray him, and that was why he said not every one was clean.

¹²When he had finished washing their feet, he put on his clothes and returned to his place. "Do you understand what I have done for you?" he asked them. ¹³"You call me 'Teacher' and 'Lord,' and rightly so, for that is what I am. ¹⁴Now that I, your Lord and Teacher, have washed your feet, you also should wash one another's feet. ¹⁵I have set you an example that you should do as I have done for you. ¹⁶Very truly I tell you, no servant is greater than his master, nor is a messenger greater than the one who sent him. ¹⁷Now that you know these things, you will be blessed if you do them.

Jesus Predicts His Betrayal

¹⁸"I am not referring to all of you; I know those I have chosen. But this is to fulfill this passage of Scripture: 'He who shared my bread has turned[a] against me.'[b]

¹⁹"I am telling you now before it happens, so that when it does happen you will believe that I am who I am. ²⁰Very truly I tell you, whoever accepts anyone I send accepts me; and whoever accepts me accepts the one who sent me."

²¹After he had said this, Jesus was troubled in spirit and testified, "Very truly I tell you, one of you is going to betray me."

²²His disciples stared at one another, at a loss to know which of them he meant. ²³One of them, the disciple whom Jesus loved, was reclining next to him. ²⁴Simon Peter motioned to this disciple and said, "Ask him which one he means."

²⁵Leaning back against Jesus, he asked him, "Lord, who is it?"

²⁶Jesus answered, "It is the one to whom I will give this piece of bread when I have dipped it in the dish." Then, dipping the piece of bread, he gave it to Judas, the son of Simon Iscariot. ²⁷As soon as Judas took the bread, Satan entered into him.

So Jesus told him, "What you are about to do, do quickly." ²⁸But no one at the meal understood why Jesus said this to him. ²⁹Since Judas had charge of the money, some thought Jesus was telling him to buy what was needed for the festival, or to give something to the poor. ³⁰As soon as Judas had taken the bread, he went out. And it was night.

Jesus Predicts Peter's Denial

³¹When he was gone, Jesus said, "Now the Son of Man is glorified and God is glorified in him. ³²If God is glorified in him,[c] God will glorify the Son in himself, and will glorify him at once.

³³"My children, I will be with you only a little longer. You will look for me, and just as I told the Jews, so I tell you now: Where I am going, you cannot come.

³⁴"A new command I give you: Love one another. As I have loved you, so you must love one another. ³⁵By this everyone will know that you are my disciples, if you love one another."

³⁶Simon Peter asked him, "Lord, where are you going?"

Jesus replied, "Where I am going, you cannot follow now, but you will follow later."

³⁷Peter asked, "Lord, why can't I follow you now? I will lay down my life for you."

³⁸Then Jesus answered, "Will you really lay down your life for me? Very truly I tell you, before the rooster crows, you will disown me three times!

Jesus Comforts His Disciples

14 "Do not let your hearts be troubled. You believe in God[d]; believe also in me. ²My Father's house has many rooms; if that were not so, would I have told you that I am going there to prepare a place for you? ³And if I go and prepare a place for you, I will come back and take you to be with me that you also may be where I am. ⁴You know the way to the place where I am going."

Jesus the Way to the Father

⁵Thomas said to him, "Lord, we don't know where you are going, so how can we know the way?"

⁶Jesus answered, "I am the way and the truth and the life. No one comes to the Father except through me. ⁷If you really know me, you will know[e] my Father as well. From now on, you do know him and have seen him."

⁸Philip said, "Lord, show us the Father and that will be enough for us."

⁹Jesus answered: "Don't you know me, Philip, even after I have been among you such

---

a 18 Greek *has lifted up his heel*   b 18 Psalm 41:9   c 32 Many early manuscripts do not have *If God is glorified in him.*   d 1 Or *Believe in God*   e 7 Some manuscripts *If you really knew me, you would know*

a long time? Anyone who has seen me has seen the Father. How can you say, 'Show us the Father'? [10]Don't you believe that I am in the Father, and that the Father is in me? The words I say to you I do not speak on my own authority. Rather, it is the Father, living in me, who is doing his work. [11]Believe me when I say that I am in the Father and the Father is in me; or at least believe on the evidence of the works themselves. [12]Very truly I tell you, whoever believes in me will do the works I have been doing, and they will do even greater things than these, because I am going to the Father. [13]And I will do whatever you ask in my name, so that the Father may be glorified in the Son. [14]You may ask me for anything in my name, and I will do it.

Jesus Promises the Holy Spirit

[15]"If you love me, keep my commands. [16]And I will ask the Father, and he will give you another advocate to help you and be with you forever— [17]the Spirit of truth. The world cannot accept him, because it neither sees him nor knows him. But you know him, for he lives with you and will be[a] in you. [18]I will not leave you as orphans; I will come to you. [19]Before long, the world will not see me anymore, but you will see me. Because I live, you also will live. [20]On that day you will realize that I am in my Father, and you are in me, and I am in you. [21]Whoever has my commands and keeps them is the one who loves me. The one who loves me will be loved by my Father, and I too will love them and show myself to them."

[22]Then Judas (not Judas Iscariot) said, "But, Lord, why do you intend to show yourself to us and not to the world?"

[23]Jesus replied, "Anyone who loves me will obey my teaching. My Father will love them, and we will come to them and make our home with them. [24]Anyone who does not love me will not obey my teaching. These words you hear are not my own; they belong to the Father who sent me.

[25]"All this I have spoken while still with you. [26]But the Advocate, the Holy Spirit, whom the Father will send in my name, will teach you all things and will remind you of everything I have said to you. [27]Peace I leave with you; my peace I give you. I do not give to you as the world gives. Do not let your hearts be troubled and do not be afraid.

[28]"You heard me say, 'I am going away and I am coming back to you.' If you loved me, you would be glad that I am going to the Father, for the Father is greater than I. [29]I have told you now before it happens, so that when it does happen you will believe. [30]I will not say much more to you, for the prince of this world is coming. He has no hold over me, [31]but he comes so that the world may learn that I love the Father and do exactly what my Father has commanded me.

"Come now; let us leave.

The Vine and the Branches

15 "I am the true vine, and my Father is the gardener. [2]He cuts off every branch in me that bears no fruit, while every branch that does bear fruit he prunes[b] so that it will be even more fruitful. [3]You are already clean because of the word I have spoken to you. [4]Remain in me, as I also remain in you. No branch can bear fruit by itself; it must remain in the vine. Neither can you bear fruit unless you remain in me.

[5]"I am the vine; you are the branches. If you remain in me and I in you, you will bear much fruit; apart from me you can do nothing. [6]If you do not remain in me, you are like a branch that is thrown away and withers; such branches are picked up, thrown into the fire and burned. [7]If you remain in me and my words remain in you, ask whatever you wish, and it will be done for you. [8]This is to my Father's glory, that you bear much fruit, showing yourselves to be my disciples.

[9]"As the Father has loved me, so have I loved you. Now remain in my love. [10]If you keep my commands, you will remain in my love, just as I have kept my Father's commands and remain in his love. [11]I have told you this so that my joy may be in you and that your joy may be complete. [12]My command is this: Love each other as I have loved you. [13]Greater love has no one than this: to lay down one's life for one's friends. [14]You are my friends if you do what I command. [15]I no longer call you servants, because a servant does not know his master's business. Instead, I have called you friends, for everything that I learned from my Father I have made known to you. [16]You did not choose me, but I chose you and appointed you so that you might go and bear fruit—fruit that will last—and so that whatever you ask in my name the Father will give you. [17]This is my command: Love each other.

The World Hates the Disciples

[18]"If the world hates you, keep in mind that it hated me first. [19]If you belonged to the world, it would love you as its own. As it is, you do not belong to the world, but I have chosen you out of the world. That is why the world hates you. [20]Remember what I told you: 'A servant is not greater than his master.'[c] If they persecuted me, they will persecute you also. If they obeyed my teaching, they will obey yours also. [21]They will treat you this way because of my name, for they do not know the one who sent me. [22]If I had not come and spoken to them, they would not be guilty of sin; but now they have no excuse for their sin. [23]Whoever hates me hates my Father as well. [24]If I had not done among them the works no one else did, they would not be guilty of sin. As it is, they have seen, and yet they have hated both me and my Father. [25]But this is to fulfill what is written in their Law: 'They hated me without reason.'[d]

---

[a] 17 Some early manuscripts *and is*   [b] 2 The Greek for *he prunes* also means *he cleans.*   [c] 20 John 13:16   [d] 25 Psalms 35:19; 69:4

The Work of the Holy Spirit

26"When the Advocate comes, whom I will send to you from the Father—the Spirit of truth who goes out from the Father—he will testify about me. 27And you also must testify, for you have been with me from the beginning.

16 "All this I have told you so that you will not fall away. 2They will put you out of the synagogue; in fact, the time is coming when anyone who kills you will think they are offering a service to God. 3They will do such things because they have not known the Father or me. 4I have told you this, so that when their time comes you will remember that I warned you about them. I did not tell you this from the beginning because I was with you, 5but now I am going to him who sent me. None of you asks me, 'Where are you going?' 6Rather, you are filled with grief because I have said these things. 7But very truly I tell you, it is for your good that I am going away. Unless I go away, the Advocate will not come to you; but if I go, I will send him to you. 8When he comes, he will prove the world to be in the wrong about sin and righteousness and judgment: 9about sin, because people do not believe in me; 10about righteousness, because I am going to the Father, where you can see me no longer; 11and about judgment, because the prince of this world now stands condemned.

12"I have much more to say to you, more than you can now bear. 13But when he, the Spirit of truth, comes, he will guide you into all the truth. He will not speak on his own; he will speak only what he hears, and he will tell you what is yet to come. 14He will glorify me because it is from me that he will receive what he will make known to you. 15All that belongs to the Father is mine. That is why I said the Spirit will receive from me what he will make known to you."

The Disciples' Grief Will Turn to Joy

16Jesus went on to say, "In a little while you will see me no more, and then after a little while you will see me."

17At this, some of his disciples said to one another, "What does he mean by saying, 'In a little while you will see me no more, and then after a little while you will see me,' and 'Because I am going to the Father'?" 18They kept asking, "What does he mean by 'a little while'? We don't understand what he is saying."

19Jesus saw that they wanted to ask him about this, so he said to them, "Are you asking one another what I meant when I said, 'In a little while you will see me no more, and then after a little while you will see me'? 20Very truly I tell you, you will weep and mourn while the world rejoices. You will grieve, but your grief will turn to joy. 21A woman giving birth to a child has pain because her time has come; but when her baby is born she forgets the anguish because of her joy that a child is born into the world. 22So with you: Now is your time of grief, but I will see you again and you will rejoice, and no one will take away your joy. 23In that day you will no longer ask me anything. Very truly I tell you, my Father will give you whatever you ask in my name. 24Until now you have not asked for anything in my name. Ask and you will receive, and your joy will be complete.

25"Though I have been speaking figuratively, a time is coming when I will no longer use this kind of language but will tell you plainly about my Father. 26In that day you will ask in my name. I am not saying that I will ask the Father on your behalf. 27No, the Father himself loves you because you have loved me and have believed that I came from God. 28I came from the Father and entered the world; now I am leaving the world and going back to the Father."

29Then Jesus' disciples said, "Now you are speaking clearly and without figures of speech. 30Now we can see that you know all things and that you do not even need to have anyone ask you questions. This makes us believe that you came from God."

31"Do you now believe?" Jesus replied. 32"A time is coming and in fact has come when you will be scattered, each to your own home. You will leave me all alone. Yet I am not alone, for my Father is with me.

33"I have told you these things, so that in me you may have peace. In this world you will have trouble. But take heart! I have overcome the world."

Jesus Prays to Be Glorified

17 After Jesus said this, he looked toward heaven and prayed:

"Father, the hour has come. Glorify your Son, that your Son may glorify you. 2For you granted him authority over all people that he might give eternal life to all those you have given him. 3Now this is eternal life: that they know you, the only true God, and Jesus Christ, whom you have sent. 4I have brought you glory on earth by finishing the work you gave me to do. 5And now, Father, glorify me in your presence with the glory I had with you before the world began.

Jesus Prays for His Disciples

6"I have revealed you*a* to those whom you gave me out of the world. They were yours; you gave them to me and they have obeyed your word. 7Now they know that everything you have given me comes from you. 8For I gave them the words you gave me and they accepted them. They knew with certainty that I came from you, and they believed that you sent me. 9I pray for them. I am not praying for the world, but for those you have given me, for they are yours. 10All I have is yours, and all you have is mine. And glory has

---

a 6 Greek *your name*

come to me through them. ¹¹I will remain in the world no longer, but they are still in the world, and I am coming to you. Holy Father, protect them by the power of*a* your name, the name you gave me, so that they may be one as we are one. ¹²While I was with them, I protected them and kept them safe by*b* that name you gave me. None has been lost except the one doomed to destruction so that Scripture would be fulfilled.

¹³"I am coming to you now, but I say these things while I am still in the world, so that they may have the full measure of my joy within them. ¹⁴I have given them your word and the world has hated them, for they are not of the world any more than I am of the world. ¹⁵My prayer is not that you take them out of the world but that you protect them from the evil one. ¹⁶They are not of the world, even as I am not of it. ¹⁷Sanctify them by*c* the truth; your word is truth. ¹⁸As you sent me into the world, I have sent them into the world. ¹⁹For them I sanctify myself, that they too may be truly sanctified.

Jesus Prays for All Believers

²⁰"My prayer is not for them alone. I pray also for those who will believe in me through their message, ²¹that all of them may be one, Father, just as you are in me and I am in you. May they also be in us so that the world may believe that you have sent me. ²²I have given them the glory that you gave me, that they may be one as we are one— ²³I in them and you in me—so that they may be brought to complete unity. Then the world will know that you sent me and have loved them even as you have loved me.

²⁴"Father, I want those you have given me to be with me where I am, and to see my glory, the glory you have given me because you loved me before the creation of the world.

²⁵"Righteous Father, though the world does not know you, I know you, and they know that you have sent me. ²⁶I have made you*d* known to them, and will continue to make you known in order that the love you have for me may be in them and that I myself may be in them."

Jesus Arrested

18 When he had finished praying, Jesus left with his disciples and crossed the Kidron Valley. On the other side there was a garden, and he and his disciples went into it.

²Now Judas, who betrayed him, knew the place, because Jesus had often met there with his disciples. ³So Judas came to the garden, guiding a detachment of soldiers and some officials from the chief priests and the Pharisees. They were carrying torches, lanterns and weapons.

⁴Jesus, knowing all that was going to happen to him, went out and asked them, "Who is it you want?"

⁵"Jesus of Nazareth," they replied.

"I am he," Jesus said. (And Judas the traitor was standing there with them.) ⁶When Jesus said, "I am he," they drew back and fell to the ground.

⁷Again he asked them, "Who is it you want?"

"Jesus of Nazareth," they said.

⁸Jesus answered, "I told you that I am he. If you are looking for me, then let these men go." ⁹This happened so that the words he had spoken would be fulfilled: "I have not lost one of those you gave me."*e*

¹⁰Then Simon Peter, who had a sword, drew it and struck the high priest's servant, cutting off his right ear. (The servant's name was Malchus.)

¹¹Jesus commanded Peter, "Put your sword away! Shall I not drink the cup the Father has given me?"

¹²Then the detachment of soldiers with its commander and the Jewish officials arrested Jesus. They bound him ¹³and brought him first to Annas, who was the father-in-law of Caiaphas, the high priest that year. ¹⁴Caiaphas was the one who had advised the Jewish leaders that it would be good if one man died for the people.

Peter's First Denial

¹⁵Simon Peter and another disciple were following Jesus. Because this disciple was known to the high priest, he went with Jesus into the high priest's courtyard, ¹⁶but Peter had to wait outside at the door. The other disciple, who was known to the high priest, came back, spoke to the servant girl on duty there and brought Peter in.

¹⁷"You aren't one of this man's disciples too, are you?" she asked Peter.

He replied, "I am not."

¹⁸It was cold, and the servants and officials stood around a fire they had made to keep warm. Peter also was standing with them, warming himself.

The High Priest Questions Jesus

¹⁹Meanwhile, the high priest questioned Jesus about his disciples and his teaching.

²⁰"I have spoken openly to the world," Jesus replied. "I always taught in synagogues or at the temple, where all the Jews come together. I said nothing in secret. ²¹Why question me? Ask those who heard me. Surely they know what I said."

²²When Jesus said this, one of the officials nearby slapped him in the face. "Is this the way you answer the high priest?" he demanded.

²³"If I said something wrong," Jesus replied, "testify as to what is wrong. But if I spoke the truth, why did you strike me?" ²⁴Then Annas sent him bound to Caiaphas the high priest.

---

a 11 Or Father, keep them faithful to   b 12 Or kept them faithful to   c 17 Or them to live in accordance with   d 26 Greek your name   e 9 John 6:39

Peter's Second and Third Denials

²⁵Meanwhile, Simon Peter was still standing there warming himself. So they asked him, "You aren't one of his disciples too, are you?"

He denied it, saying, "I am not."

²⁶One of the high priest's servants, a relative of the man whose ear Peter had cut off, challenged him, "Didn't I see you with him in the garden?" ²⁷Again Peter denied it, and at that moment a rooster began to crow.

Jesus Before Pilate

²⁸Then the Jewish leaders took Jesus from Caiaphas to the palace of the Roman governor. By now it was early morning, and to avoid ceremonial uncleanness they did not enter the palace, because they wanted to be able to eat the Passover. ²⁹So Pilate came out to them and asked, "What charges are you bringing against this man?"

³⁰"If he were not a criminal," they replied, "we would not have handed him over to you."

³¹Pilate said, "Take him yourselves and judge him by your own law."

"But we have no right to execute anyone," they objected. ³²This took place to fulfill what Jesus had said about the kind of death he was going to die.

³³Pilate then went back inside the palace, summoned Jesus and asked him, "Are you the king of the Jews?"

³⁴"Is that your own idea," Jesus asked, "or did others talk to you about me?"

³⁵"Am I a Jew?" Pilate replied. "Your own people and chief priests handed you over to me. What is it you have done?"

³⁶Jesus said, "My kingdom is not of this world. If it were, my servants would fight to prevent my arrest by the Jewish leaders. But now my kingdom is from another place."

³⁷"You are a king, then!" said Pilate.

Jesus answered, "You say that I am a king. In fact, the reason I was born and came into the world is to testify to the truth. Everyone on the side of truth listens to me."

³⁸"What is truth?" retorted Pilate. With this he went out again to the Jews gathered there and said, "I find no basis for a charge against him. ³⁹But it is your custom for me to release to you one prisoner at the time of the Passover. Do you want me to release 'the king of the Jews'?"

⁴⁰They shouted back, "No, not him! Give us Barabbas!" Now Barabbas had taken part in an uprising.

Jesus Sentenced to Be Crucified

19 Then Pilate took Jesus and had him flogged. ²The soldiers twisted together a crown of thorns and put it on his head. They clothed him in a purple robe ³and went up to him again and again, saying, "Hail, king of the Jews!" And they slapped him in the face.

⁴Once more Pilate came out and said to the Jews gathered there, "Look, I am bringing him out to you to let you know that I find no basis for a charge against him." ⁵When Jesus came out wearing the crown of thorns and the purple robe, Pilate said to them, "Here is the man!"

⁶As soon as the chief priests and their officials saw him, they shouted, "Crucify! Crucify!"

But Pilate answered, "You take him and crucify him. As for me, I find no basis for a charge against him."

⁷The Jewish leaders insisted, "We have a law, and according to that law he must die, because he claimed to be the Son of God."

⁸When Pilate heard this, he was even more afraid, ⁹and he went back inside the palace. "Where do you come from?" he asked Jesus, but Jesus gave him no answer. ¹⁰"Do you refuse to speak to me?" Pilate said. "Don't you realize I have power either to free you or to crucify you?"

¹¹Jesus answered, "You would have no power over me if it were not given to you from above. Therefore the one who handed me over to you is guilty of a greater sin."

¹²From then on, Pilate tried to set Jesus free, but the Jewish leaders kept shouting, "If you let this man go, you are no friend of Caesar. Anyone who claims to be a king opposes Caesar."

¹³When Pilate heard this, he brought Jesus out and sat down on the judge's seat at a place known as the Stone Pavement (which in Aramaic is Gabbatha). ¹⁴It was the day of Preparation of the Passover; it was about noon.

"Here is your king," Pilate said to the Jews.

¹⁵But they shouted, "Take him away! Take him away! Crucify him!"

"Shall I crucify your king?" Pilate asked.

"We have no king but Caesar," the chief priests answered.

¹⁶Finally Pilate handed him over to them to be crucified.

The Crucifixion of Jesus

So the soldiers took charge of Jesus. ¹⁷Carrying his own cross, he went out to the place of the Skull (which in Aramaic is called Golgotha). ¹⁸There they crucified him, and with him two others—one on each side and Jesus in the middle.

¹⁹Pilate had a notice prepared and fastened to the cross. It read: JESUS OF NAZARETH, THE KING OF THE JEWS. ²⁰Many of the Jews read this sign, for the place where Jesus was crucified was near the city, and the sign was written in Aramaic, Latin and Greek. ²¹The chief priests of the Jews protested to Pilate, "Do not write 'The King of the Jews,' but that this man claimed to be king of the Jews."

²²Pilate answered, "What I have written, I have written."

²³When the soldiers crucified Jesus, they took his clothes, dividing them into four shares, one for each of them, with the undergarment remaining. This garment was seamless, woven in one piece from top to bottom. ²⁴"Let's not tear it," they said to one another. "Let's decide by lot who will get it."

This happened that the scripture might be fulfilled that said,

"They divided my clothes among them
   and cast lots for my garment."[a]

So this is what the soldiers did.

[25]Near the cross of Jesus stood his mother, his mother's sister, Mary the wife of Clopas, and Mary Magdalene. [26]When Jesus saw his mother there, and the disciple whom he loved standing nearby, he said to her, "Woman,[b] here is your son," [27]and to the disciple, "Here is your mother." From that time on, this disciple took her into his home.

The Death of Jesus

[28]Later, knowing that everything had now been finished, and so that Scripture would be fulfilled, Jesus said, "I am thirsty." [29]A jar of wine vinegar was there, so they soaked a sponge in it, put the sponge on a stalk of the hyssop plant, and lifted it to Jesus' lips. [30]When he had received the drink, Jesus said, "It is finished." With that, he bowed his head and gave up his spirit.

[31]Now it was the day of Preparation, and the next day was to be a special Sabbath. Because the Jewish leaders did not want the bodies left on the crosses during the Sabbath, they asked Pilate to have the legs broken and the bodies taken down. [32]The soldiers therefore came and broke the legs of the first man who had been crucified with Jesus, and then those of the other. [33]But when they came to Jesus and found that he was already dead, they did not break his legs. [34]Instead, one of the soldiers pierced Jesus' side with a spear, bringing a sudden flow of blood and water. [35]The man who saw it has given testimony, and his testimony is true. He knows that he tells the truth, and he testifies so that you also may believe. [36]These things happened so that the scripture would be fulfilled: "Not one of his bones will be broken,"[c] [37]and, as another scripture says, "They will look on the one they have pierced."[d]

The Burial of Jesus

[38]Later, Joseph of Arimathea asked Pilate for the body of Jesus. Now Joseph was a disciple of Jesus, but secretly because he feared the Jewish leaders. With Pilate's permission, he came and took the body away. [39]He was accompanied by Nicodemus, the man who earlier had visited Jesus at night. Nicodemus brought a mixture of myrrh and aloes, about seventy-five pounds.[e] [40]Taking Jesus' body, the two of them wrapped it, with the spices, in strips of linen. This was in accordance with Jewish burial customs. [41]At the place where Jesus was crucified, there was a garden, and in the garden a new tomb, in which no one had ever been laid. [42]Because it was the Jewish day of Preparation and since the tomb was nearby, they laid Jesus there.

The Empty Tomb

20 Early on the first day of the week, while it was still dark, Mary Magdalene went to the tomb and saw that the stone had been removed from the entrance. [2]So she came running to Simon Peter and the other disciple, the one Jesus loved, and said, "They have taken the Lord out of the tomb, and we don't know where they have put him!"

[3]So Peter and the other disciple started for the tomb. [4]Both were running, but the other disciple outran Peter and reached the tomb first. [5]He bent over and looked in at the strips of linen lying there but did not go in. [6]Then Simon Peter came along behind him and went straight into the tomb. He saw the strips of linen lying there, [7]as well as the cloth that had been wrapped around Jesus' head. The cloth was still lying in its place, separate from the linen. [8]Finally the other disciple, who had reached the tomb first, also went inside. He saw and believed. [9](They still did not understand from Scripture that Jesus had to rise from the dead.) [10]Then the disciples went back to where they were staying.

Jesus Appears to Mary Magdalene

[11]Now Mary stood outside the tomb crying. As she wept, she bent over to look into the tomb [12]and saw two angels in white, seated where Jesus' body had been, one at the head and the other at the foot.

[13]They asked her, "Woman, why are you crying?"

"They have taken my Lord away," she said, "and I don't know where they have put him." [14]At this, she turned around and saw Jesus standing there, but she did not realize that it was Jesus.

[15]He asked her, "Woman, why are you crying? Who is it you are looking for?"

Thinking he was the gardener, she said, "Sir, if you have carried him away, tell me where you have put him, and I will get him."

[16]Jesus said to her, "Mary."

She turned toward him and cried out in Aramaic, "Rabboni!" (which means "Teacher").

[17]Jesus said, "Do not hold on to me, for I have not yet ascended to the Father. Go instead to my brothers and tell them, 'I am ascending to my Father and your Father, to my God and your God.'"

[18]Mary Magdalene went to the disciples with the news: "I have seen the Lord!" And she told them that he had said these things to her.

Jesus Appears to His Disciples

[19]On the evening of that first day of the week, when the disciples were together, with the doors locked for fear of the Jewish leaders, Jesus came and stood among them and said, "Peace be with you!" [20]After he said this, he showed them his hands and side. The disciples were overjoyed when they saw the Lord. [21]Again Jesus said, "Peace be with you! As the Father has sent me, I am sending you." [22]And with that he breathed on them and said, "Receive the Holy Spirit. [23]If you forgive anyone's sins, their sins are forgiven; if you do not forgive them, they are not forgiven."

---

[a] 24 Psalm 22:18   [b] 26 The Greek for *Woman* does not denote any disrespect.   [c] 36 Exodus 12:46; Num. 9:12; Psalm 34:20   [d] 37 Zech. 12:10   [e] 39 Or about 34 kilograms

Jesus Appears to Thomas

24Now Thomas (also known as Didymus[a]), one of the Twelve, was not with the disciples when Jesus came. 25So the other disciples told him, "We have seen the Lord!"

But he said to them, "Unless I see the nail marks in his hands and put my finger where the nails were, and put my hand into his side, I will not believe."

26A week later his disciples were in the house again, and Thomas was with them. Though the doors were locked, Jesus came and stood among them and said, "Peace be with you!" 27Then he said to Thomas, "Put your finger here; see my hands. Reach out your hand and put it into my side. Stop doubting and believe."

28Thomas said to him, "My Lord and my God!"

29Then Jesus told him, "Because you have seen me, you have believed; blessed are those who have not seen and yet have believed."

The Purpose of John's Gospel

30Jesus performed many other signs in the presence of his disciples, which are not recorded in this book. 31But these are written that you may believe[b] that Jesus is the Messiah, the Son of God, and that by believing you may have life in his name.

Jesus and the Miraculous Catch of Fish

21 Afterward Jesus appeared again to his disciples, by the Sea of Galilee.[c] It happened this way: 2Simon Peter, Thomas (also known as Didymus[a]), Nathanael from Cana in Galilee, the sons of Zebedee, and two other disciples were together. 3"I'm going out to fish," Simon Peter told them, and they said, "We'll go with you." So they went out and got into the boat, but that night they caught nothing.

4Early in the morning, Jesus stood on the shore, but the disciples did not realize that it was Jesus.

5He called out to them, "Friends, haven't you any fish?"

"No," they answered.

6He said, "Throw your net on the right side of the boat and you will find some." When they did, they were unable to haul the net in because of the large number of fish.

7Then the disciple whom Jesus loved said to Peter, "It is the Lord!" As soon as Simon Peter heard him say, "It is the Lord," he wrapped his outer garment around him (for he had taken it off) and jumped into the water. 8The other disciples followed in the boat, towing the net full of fish, for they were not far from shore, about a hundred yards.[d] 9When they landed, they saw a fire of burning coals there with fish on it, and some bread.

10Jesus said to them, "Bring some of the fish you have just caught." 11So Simon Peter climbed back into the boat and dragged the net ashore. It was full of large fish, 153, but even with so many the net was not torn. 12Jesus said to them, "Come and have breakfast." None of the disciples dared ask him, "Who are you?" They knew it was the Lord. 13Jesus came, took the bread and gave it to them, and did the same with the fish. 14This was now the third time Jesus appeared to his disciples after he was raised from the dead.

Jesus Reinstates Peter

15When they had finished eating, Jesus said to Simon Peter, "Simon son of John, do you love me more than these?"

"Yes, Lord," he said, "you know that I love you."

Jesus said, "Feed my lambs."

16Again Jesus said, "Simon son of John, do you love me?"

He answered, "Yes, Lord, you know that I love you."

Jesus said, "Take care of my sheep."

17The third time he said to him, "Simon son of John, do you love me?"

Peter was hurt because Jesus asked him the third time, "Do you love me?" He said, "Lord, you know all things; you know that I love you."

Jesus said, "Feed my sheep. 18Very truly I tell you, when you were younger you dressed yourself and went where you wanted; but when you are old you will stretch out your hands, and someone else will dress you and lead you where you do not want to go." 19Jesus said this to indicate the kind of death by which Peter would glorify God. Then he said to him, "Follow me!"

20Peter turned and saw that the disciple whom Jesus loved was following them. (This was the one who had leaned back against Jesus at the supper and had said, "Lord, who is going to betray you?") 21When Peter saw him, he asked, "Lord, what about him?"

22Jesus answered, "If I want him to remain alive until I return, what is that to you? You must follow me." 23Because of this, the rumor spread among the believers that this disciple would not die. But Jesus did not say that he would not die; he only said, "If I want him to remain alive until I return, what is that to you?"

24This is the disciple who testifies to these things and who wrote them down. We know that his testimony is true.

25Jesus did many other things as well. If every one of them were written down, I suppose that even the whole world would not have room for the books that would be written.

---

a 24,2 Thomas (Aramaic) and Didymus (Greek) both mean twin.   b 31 Or may continue to believe
c 1 Greek Tiberias   d 8 Or about 90 meters

Acts

Jesus Taken Up Into Heaven

1 In my former book, Theophilus, I wrote about all that Jesus began to do and to teach ²until the day he was taken up to heaven, after giving instructions through the Holy Spirit to the apostles he had chosen. ³After his suffering, he presented himself to them and gave many convincing proofs that he was alive. He appeared to them over a period of forty days and spoke about the kingdom of God. ⁴On one occasion, while he was eating with them, he gave them this command: "Do not leave Jerusalem, but wait for the gift my Father promised, which you have heard me speak about. ⁵For John baptized with*a* water, but in a few days you will be baptized with*a* the Holy Spirit."

⁶Then they gathered around him and asked him, "Lord, are you at this time going to restore the kingdom to Israel?"

⁷He said to them: "It is not for you to know the times or dates the Father has set by his own authority. ⁸But you will receive power when the Holy Spirit comes on you; and you will be my witnesses in Jerusalem, and in all Judea and Samaria, and to the ends of the earth."

⁹After he said this, he was taken up before their very eyes, and a cloud hid him from their sight.

¹⁰They were looking intently up into the sky as he was going, when suddenly two men dressed in white stood beside them. ¹¹"Men of Galilee," they said, "why do you stand here looking into the sky? This same Jesus, who has been taken from you into heaven, will come back in the same way you have seen him go into heaven."

Matthias Chosen to Replace Judas

¹²Then the apostles returned to Jerusalem from the hill called the Mount of Olives, a Sabbath day's walk*b* from the city. ¹³When they arrived, they went upstairs to the room where they were staying. Those present were Peter, John, James and Andrew; Philip and Thomas, Bartholomew and Matthew; James son of Alphaeus and Simon the Zealot, and Judas son of James. ¹⁴They all joined together constantly in prayer, along with the women and Mary the mother of Jesus, and with his brothers.

¹⁵In those days Peter stood up among the believers (a group numbering about a hundred and twenty) ¹⁶and said, "Brothers and sisters,*c* the Scripture had to be fulfilled in which the Holy Spirit spoke long ago through David concerning Judas, who served as guide

for those who arrested Jesus. ¹⁷He was one of our number and shared in our ministry."

¹⁸(With the payment he received for his wickedness, Judas bought a field; there he fell headlong, his body burst open and all his intestines spilled out. ¹⁹Everyone in Jerusalem heard about this, so they called that field in their language Akeldama, that is, Field of Blood.)

²⁰"For," said Peter, "it is written in the Book of Psalms:

> " 'May his place be deserted;
> let there be no one to dwell in it,'*d*

and,

> " 'May another take his place of
> leadership.'*e*

²¹Therefore it is necessary to choose one of the men who have been with us the whole time the Lord Jesus was living among us, ²²beginning from John's baptism to the time when Jesus was taken up from us. For one of these must become a witness with us of his resurrection."

²³So they nominated two men: Joseph called Barsabbas (also known as Justus) and Matthias. ²⁴Then they prayed, "Lord, you know everyone's heart. Show us which of these two you have chosen ²⁵to take over this apostolic ministry, which Judas left to go where he belongs." ²⁶Then they cast lots, and the lot fell to Matthias; so he was added to the eleven apostles.

The Holy Spirit Comes at Pentecost

2 When the day of Pentecost came, they were all together in one place. ²Suddenly a sound like the blowing of a violent wind came from heaven and filled the whole house where they were sitting. ³They saw what seemed to be tongues of fire that separated and came to rest on each of them. ⁴All of them were filled with the Holy Spirit and began to speak in other tongues*f* as the Spirit enabled them.

⁵Now there were staying in Jerusalem God-fearing Jews from every nation under heaven. ⁶When they heard this sound, a crowd came together in bewilderment, because each one heard their own language being spoken. ⁷Utterly amazed, they asked: "Aren't all these who are speaking Galileans? ⁸Then how is it that each of us hears them in our native language? ⁹Parthians, Medes and Elamites; residents of Mesopotamia, Judea and Cappadocia, Pontus and Asia,*g* ¹⁰Phrygia and Pamphylia, Egypt and the parts of Libya near Cyrene; visitors from Rome ¹¹(both Jews and converts to Judaism); Cretans and Arabs—we hear

---

a 5 Or *in*   *b 12* That is, about 5/8 mile or about 1 kilometer   *c 16* The Greek word for *brothers and sisters (adelphoi)* refers here to believers, both men and women, as part of God's family; also in 6:3; 11:29; 12:17; 16:40; 18:18, 27; 21:7, 17; 28:14, 15.   *d 20* Psalm 69:25   *e 20* Psalm 109:8
f 4 Or *languages*; also in verse 11   *g 9* That is, the Roman province by that name

them declaring the wonders of God in our own tongues!" ¹²Amazed and perplexed, they asked one another, "What does this mean?"

¹³Some, however, made fun of them and said, "They have had too much wine."

Peter Addresses the Crowd

¹⁴Then Peter stood up with the Eleven, raised his voice and addressed the crowd: "Fellow Jews and all of you who live in Jerusalem, let me explain this to you; listen carefully to what I say. ¹⁵These people are not drunk, as you suppose. It's only nine in the morning! ¹⁶No, this is what was spoken by the prophet Joel:

¹⁷ᵃ 'In the last days, God says,
    I will pour out my Spirit on all people.
Your sons and daughters will prophesy,
    your young men will see visions,
    your old men will dream dreams.
¹⁸Even on my servants, both men and
        women,
    I will pour out my Spirit in those days,
        and they will prophesy.
¹⁹I will show wonders in the heavens above
        and signs on the earth below,
    blood and fire and billows of smoke.
²⁰The sun will be turned to darkness
        and the moon to blood
    before the coming of the great and
        glorious day of the Lord.
²¹And everyone who calls
    on the name of the Lord will be saved.'ᵃ

²²"Fellow Israelites, listen to this: Jesus of Nazareth was a man accredited by God to you by miracles, wonders and signs, which God did among you through him, as you yourselves know. ²³This man was handed over to you by God's deliberate plan and foreknowledge; and you, with the help of wicked men,ᵇ put him to death by nailing him to the cross. ²⁴But God raised him from the dead, freeing him from the agony of death, because it was impossible for death to keep its hold on him. ²⁵David said about him:

" 'I saw the Lord always before me.
    Because he is at my right hand,
    I will not be shaken.
²⁶Therefore my heart is glad and my tongue
        rejoices;
    my body also will rest in hope,
²⁷because you will not abandon me to the
        realm of the dead,
    you will not let your holy one see decay.
²⁸You have made known to me the paths of
        life;
    you will fill me with joy in your
        presence.'ᶜ

²⁹"Fellow Israelites, I can tell you confidently that the patriarch David died and was buried, and his tomb is here to this day. ³⁰But he was a prophet and knew that God had promised him on oath that he would place one of his descendants on his throne. ³¹Seeing what

was to come, he spoke of the resurrection of the Messiah, that he was not abandoned to the realm of the dead, nor did his body see decay. ³²God has raised this Jesus to life, and we are all witnesses of it. ³³Exalted to the right hand of God, he has received from the Father the promised Holy Spirit and has poured out what you now see and hear. ³⁴For David did not ascend to heaven, and yet he said,

" 'The Lord said to my Lord:
    "Sit at my right hand
³⁵until I make your enemies
    a footstool for your feet." 'ᵈ

³⁶"Therefore let all Israel be assured of this: God has made this Jesus, whom you crucified, both Lord and Messiah."

³⁷When the people heard this, they were cut to the heart and said to Peter and the other apostles, "Brothers, what shall we do?"

³⁸Peter replied, "Repent and be baptized, every one of you, in the name of Jesus Christ for the forgiveness of your sins. And you will receive the gift of the Holy Spirit. ³⁹The promise is for you and your children and for all who are far off—for all whom the Lord our God will call."

⁴⁰With many other words he warned them; and he pleaded with them, "Save yourselves from this corrupt generation." ⁴¹Those who accepted his message were baptized, and about three thousand were added to their number that day.

The Fellowship of the Believers

⁴²They devoted themselves to the apostles' teaching and to fellowship, to the breaking of bread and to prayer. ⁴³Everyone was filled with awe at the many wonders and signs performed by the apostles. ⁴⁴All the believers were together and had everything in common. ⁴⁵They sold property and possessions to give to anyone who had need. ⁴⁶Every day they continued to meet together in the temple courts. They broke bread in their homes and ate together with glad and sincere hearts, ⁴⁷praising God and enjoying the favor of all the people. And the Lord added to their number daily those who were being saved.

Peter Heals a Lame Beggar

3 One day Peter and John were going up to the temple at the time of prayer—at three in the afternoon. ²Now a man who was lame from birth was being carried to the temple gate called Beautiful, where he was put every day to beg from those going into the temple courts. ³When he saw Peter and John about to enter, he asked them for money. ⁴Peter looked straight at him, as did John. Then Peter said, "Look at us!" ⁵So the man gave them his attention, expecting to get something from them.

⁶Then Peter said, "Silver or gold I do not have, but what I do have I give you. In the name of Jesus Christ of Nazareth, walk." ⁷Taking him by the right hand, he helped him

---

ᵃ 21 Joel 2:28-32   ᵇ 23 Or of those not having the law (that is, Gentiles)   ᶜ 28 Psalm 16:8-11 (see Septuagint)   ᵈ 35 Psalm 110:1

up, and instantly the man's feet and ankles became strong. [8]He jumped to his feet and began to walk. Then he went with them into the temple courts, walking and jumping, and praising God. [9]When all the people saw him walking and praising God, [10]they recognized him as the same man who used to sit begging at the temple gate called Beautiful, and they were filled with wonder and amazement at what had happened to him.

Peter Speaks to the Onlookers

[11]While the man held on to Peter and John, all the people were astonished and came running to them in the place called Solomon's Colonnade. [12]When Peter saw this, he said to them: "Fellow Israelites, why does this surprise you? Why do you stare at us as if by our own power or godliness we had made this man walk? [13]The God of Abraham, Isaac and Jacob, the God of our fathers, has glorified his servant Jesus. You handed him over to be killed, and you disowned him before Pilate, though he had decided to let him go. [14]You disowned the Holy and Righteous One and asked that a murderer be released to you. [15]You killed the author of life, but God raised him from the dead. We are witnesses of this. [16]By faith in the name of Jesus, this man whom you see and know was made strong. It is Jesus' name and the faith that comes through him that has completely healed him, as you can all see.

[17]"Now, fellow Israelites, I know that you acted in ignorance, as did your leaders. [18]But this is how God fulfilled what he had foretold through all the prophets, saying that his Messiah would suffer. [19]Repent, then, and turn to God, so that your sins may be wiped out, that times of refreshing may come from the Lord, [20]and that he may send the Messiah, who has been appointed for you—even Jesus. [21]Heaven must receive him until the time comes for God to restore everything, as he promised long ago through his holy prophets. [22]For Moses said, 'The Lord your God will raise up for you a prophet like me from among your own people; you must listen to everything he tells you. [23]Anyone who does not listen to him will be completely cut off from their people.'[a]

[24]"Indeed, beginning with Samuel, all the prophets who have spoken have foretold these days. [25]And you are heirs of the prophets and of the covenant God made with your fathers. He said to Abraham, 'Through your offspring all peoples on earth will be blessed.'[b] [26]When God raised up his servant, he sent him first to you to bless you by turning each of you from your wicked ways."

Peter and John Before the Sanhedrin

4 The priests and the captain of the temple guard and the Sadducees came up to Peter and John while they were speaking to the people. [2]They were greatly disturbed because the apostles were teaching the people, proclaiming in Jesus the resurrection of the dead. [3]They seized Peter and John and, because it was evening, they put them in jail until the next day. [4]But many who heard the message believed; so the number of men who believed grew to about five thousand.

[5]The next day the rulers, the elders and the teachers of the law met in Jerusalem. [6]Annas the high priest was there, and so were Caiaphas, John, Alexander and others of the high priest's family. [7]They had Peter and John brought before them and began to question them: "By what power or what name did you do this?"

[8]Then Peter, filled with the Holy Spirit, said to them: "Rulers and elders of the people! [9]If we are being called to account today for an act of kindness shown to a man who was lame and are being asked how he was healed, [10]then know this, you and all the people of Israel: It is by the name of Jesus Christ of Nazareth, whom you crucified but whom God raised from the dead, that this man stands before you healed. [11]Jesus is

"'the stone you builders rejected,
    which has become the cornerstone.'[c]

[12]Salvation is found in no one else, for there is no other name under heaven given to mankind by which we must be saved."

[13]When they saw the courage of Peter and John and realized that they were unschooled, ordinary men, they were astonished and they took note that these men had been with Jesus. [14]But since they could see the man who had been healed standing there with them, there was nothing they could say. [15]So they ordered them to withdraw from the Sanhedrin and then conferred together. [16]"What are we going to do with these men?" they asked. "Everyone living in Jerusalem knows they have performed a notable sign, and we cannot deny it. [17]But to stop this thing from spreading any further among the people, we must warn them to speak no longer to anyone in this name."

[18]Then they called them in again and commanded them not to speak or teach at all in the name of Jesus. [19]But Peter and John replied, "Which is right in God's eyes: to listen to you, or to him? You be the judges! [20]As for us, we cannot help speaking about what we have seen and heard."

[21]After further threats they let them go. They could not decide how to punish them, because all the people were praising God for what had happened. [22]For the man who was miraculously healed was over forty years old.

The Believers Pray

[23]On their release, Peter and John went back to their own people and reported all that the chief priests and the elders had said to them. [24]When they heard this, they raised their voices together in prayer to God. "Sovereign Lord," they said, "you made the heavens and the earth and the sea, and everything in

---

[a] 23 Deut. 18:15,18,19   [b] 25 Gen. 22:18; 26:4   [c] 11 Psalm 118:22

them. [25]You spoke by the Holy Spirit through the mouth of your servant, our father David:

> "'Why do the nations rage
>   and the peoples plot in vain?
> [26]The kings of the earth rise up
>   and the rulers band together
> against the Lord
>   and against his anointed one.[a][b]

[27]Indeed Herod and Pontius Pilate met together with the Gentiles and the people of Israel in this city to conspire against your holy servant Jesus, whom you anointed. [28]They did what your power and will had decided beforehand should happen. [29]Now, Lord, consider their threats and enable your servants to speak your word with great boldness. [30]Stretch out your hand to heal and perform signs and wonders through the name of your holy servant Jesus."

[31]After they prayed, the place where they were meeting was shaken. And they were all filled with the Holy Spirit and spoke the word of God boldly.

The Believers Share Their Possessions

[32]All the believers were one in heart and mind. No one claimed that any of their possessions was their own, but they shared everything they had. [33]With great power the apostles continued to testify to the resurrection of the Lord Jesus. And God's grace was so powerfully at work in them all [34]that there were no needy persons among them. For from time to time those who owned land or houses sold them, brought the money from the sales [35]and put it at the apostles' feet, and it was distributed to anyone who had need.

[36]Joseph, a Levite from Cyprus, whom the apostles called Barnabas (which means "son of encouragement"), [37]sold a field he owned and brought the money and put it at the apostles' feet.

Ananias and Sapphira

5 Now a man named Ananias, together with his wife Sapphira, also sold a piece of property. [2]With his wife's full knowledge he kept back part of the money for himself, but brought the rest and put it at the apostles' feet.

[3]Then Peter said, "Ananias, how is it that Satan has so filled your heart that you have lied to the Holy Spirit and have kept for yourself some of the money you received for the land? [4]Didn't it belong to you before it was sold? And after it was sold, wasn't the money at your disposal? What made you think of doing such a thing? You have not lied just to human beings but to God."

[5]When Ananias heard this, he fell down and died. And great fear seized all who heard what had happened. [6]Then some young men came forward, wrapped up his body, and carried him out and buried him.

[7]About three hours later his wife came in, not knowing what had happened. [8]Peter asked her, "Tell me, is this the price you and Ananias got for the land?"

"Yes," she said, "that is the price."

[9]Peter said to her, "How could you conspire to test the Spirit of the Lord? Listen! The feet of the men who buried your husband are at the door, and they will carry you out also."

[10]At that moment she fell down at his feet and died. Then the young men came in and, finding her dead, carried her out and buried her beside her husband. [11]Great fear seized the whole church and all who heard about these events.

The Apostles Heal Many

[12]The apostles performed many signs and wonders among the people. And all the believers used to meet together in Solomon's Colonnade. [13]No one else dared join them, even though they were highly regarded by the people. [14]Nevertheless, more and more men and women believed in the Lord and were added to their number. [15]As a result, people brought the sick into the streets and laid them on beds and mats so that at least Peter's shadow might fall on some of them as he passed by. [16]Crowds gathered also from the towns around Jerusalem, bringing their sick and those tormented by impure spirits, and all of them were healed.

The Apostles Persecuted

[17]Then the high priest and all his associates, who were members of the party of the Sadducees, were filled with jealousy. [18]They arrested the apostles and put them in the public jail. [19]But during the night an angel of the Lord opened the doors of the jail and brought them out. [20]"Go, stand in the temple courts," he said, "and tell the people all about this new life."

[21]At daybreak they entered the temple courts, as they had been told, and began to teach the people.

When the high priest and his associates arrived, they called together the Sanhedrin—the full assembly of the elders of Israel—and sent to the jail for the apostles. [22]But on arriving at the jail, the officers did not find them there. So they went back and reported, [23]"We found the jail securely locked, with the guards standing at the doors; but when we opened them, we found no one inside." [24]On hearing this report, the captain of the temple guard and the chief priests were at a loss, wondering what this might lead to.

[25]Then someone came and said, "Look! The men you put in jail are standing in the temple courts teaching the people." [26]At that, the captain went with his officers and brought the apostles. They did not use force, because they feared that the people would stone them.

[27]The apostles were brought in and made to appear before the Sanhedrin to be questioned by the high priest. [28]"We gave you strict orders not to teach in this name," he said. "Yet you have filled Jerusalem with your teaching

---

[a] 26 That is, Messiah or Christ   [b] 26 Psalm 2:1,2

and are determined to make us guilty of this man's blood."

²⁹Peter and the other apostles replied: "We must obey God rather than human beings! ³⁰The God of our ancestors raised Jesus from the dead—whom you killed by hanging him on a cross. ³¹God exalted him to his own right hand as Prince and Savior that he might bring Israel to repentance and forgive their sins. ³²We are witnesses of these things, and so is the Holy Spirit, whom God has given to those who obey him."

³³When they heard this, they were furious and wanted to put them to death. ³⁴But a Pharisee named Gamaliel, a teacher of the law, who was honored by all the people, stood up in the Sanhedrin and ordered that the men be put outside for a little while. ³⁵Then he addressed the Sanhedrin: "Men of Israel, consider carefully what you intend to do to these men. ³⁶Some time ago Theudas appeared, claiming to be somebody, and about four hundred men rallied to him. He was killed, all his followers were dispersed, and it all came to nothing. ³⁷After him, Judas the Galilean appeared in the days of the census and led a band of people in revolt. He too was killed, and all his followers were scattered. ³⁸Therefore, in the present case I advise you: Leave these men alone! Let them go! For if their purpose or activity is of human origin, it will fail. ³⁹But if it is from God, you will not be able to stop these men; you will only find yourselves fighting against God."

⁴⁰His speech persuaded them. They called the apostles in and had them flogged. Then they ordered them not to speak in the name of Jesus, and let them go.

⁴¹The apostles left the Sanhedrin, rejoicing because they had been counted worthy of suffering disgrace for the Name. ⁴²Day after day, in the temple courts and from house to house, they never stopped teaching and proclaiming the good news that Jesus is the Messiah.

The Choosing of the Seven

6 In those days when the number of disciples was increasing, the Hellenistic Jews[a] among them complained against the Hebraic Jews because their widows were being overlooked in the daily distribution of food. ²So the Twelve gathered all the disciples together and said, "It would not be right for us to neglect the ministry of the word of God in order to wait on tables. ³Brothers and sisters, choose seven men from among you who are known to be full of the Spirit and wisdom. We will turn this responsibility over to them ⁴and will give our attention to prayer and the ministry of the word."

⁵This proposal pleased the whole group. They chose Stephen, a man full of faith and of the Holy Spirit; also Philip, Procorus, Nicanor, Timon, Parmenas, and Nicolas from Antioch, a convert to Judaism. ⁶They presented these men to the apostles, who prayed and laid their hands on them.

⁷So the word of God spread. The number of disciples in Jerusalem increased rapidly, and a large number of priests became obedient to the faith.

Stephen Seized

⁸Now Stephen, a man full of God's grace and power, performed great wonders and signs among the people. ⁹Opposition arose, however, from members of the Synagogue of the Freedmen (as it was called)—Jews of Cyrene and Alexandria as well as the provinces of Cilicia and Asia—who began to argue with Stephen. ¹⁰But they could not stand up against the wisdom the Spirit gave him as he spoke. ¹¹Then they secretly persuaded some men to say, "We have heard Stephen speak blasphemous words against Moses and against God."

¹²So they stirred up the people and the elders and the teachers of the law. They seized Stephen and brought him before the Sanhedrin. ¹³They produced false witnesses, who testified, "This fellow never stops speaking against this holy place and against the law. ¹⁴For we have heard him say that this Jesus of Nazareth will destroy this place and change the customs Moses handed down to us."

¹⁵All who were sitting in the Sanhedrin looked intently at Stephen, and they saw that his face was like the face of an angel.

Stephen's Speech to the Sanhedrin

7 Then the high priest asked Stephen, "Are these charges true?"

²To this he replied: "Brothers and fathers, listen to me! The God of glory appeared to our father Abraham while he was still in Mesopotamia, before he lived in Harran. ³'Leave your country and your people,' God said, 'and go to the land I will show you.'[b]

⁴"So he left the land of the Chaldeans and settled in Harran. After the death of his father, God sent him to this land where you are now living. ⁵He gave him no inheritance here, not even enough ground to set his foot on. But God promised him that he and his descendants after him would possess the land, even though at that time Abraham had no child. ⁶God spoke to him in this way: 'For four hundred years your descendants will be strangers in a country not their own, and they will be enslaved and mistreated. ⁷But I will punish the nation they serve as slaves,' God said, 'and afterward they will come out of that country and worship me in this place.'[c] ⁸Then he gave Abraham the covenant of circumcision. And Abraham became the father of Isaac and circumcised him eight days after his birth. Later Isaac became the father of Jacob, and Jacob became the father of the twelve patriarchs.

⁹"Because the patriarchs were jealous of Joseph, they sold him as a slave into Egypt. But God was with him ¹⁰and rescued him from all his troubles. He gave Joseph wisdom and enabled him to gain the goodwill of Pharaoh

---

[a] 1 That is, Jews who had adopted the Greek language and culture   [b] 3 Gen. 12:1   [c] 7 Gen. 15:13,14

king of Egypt. So Pharaoh made him ruler over Egypt and all his palace.

¹¹"Then a famine struck all Egypt and Canaan, bringing great suffering, and our ancestors could not find food. ¹²When Jacob heard that there was grain in Egypt, he sent our forefathers on their first visit. ¹³On their second visit, Joseph told his brothers who he was, and Pharaoh learned about Joseph's family. ¹⁴After this, Joseph sent for his father Jacob and his whole family, seventy-five in all. ¹⁵Then Jacob went down to Egypt, where he and our ancestors died. ¹⁶Their bodies were brought back to Shechem and placed in the tomb that Abraham had bought from the sons of Hamor at Shechem for a certain sum of money.

¹⁷"As the time drew near for God to fulfill his promise to Abraham, the number of our people in Egypt had greatly increased. ¹⁸Then 'a new king, to whom Joseph meant nothing, came to power in Egypt.'ᵃ ¹⁹He dealt treacherously with our people and oppressed our ancestors by forcing them to throw out their newborn babies so that they would die.

²⁰"At that time Moses was born, and he was no ordinary child.ᵇ For three months he was cared for by his family. ²¹When he was placed outside, Pharaoh's daughter took him and brought him up as her own son. ²²Moses was educated in all the wisdom of the Egyptians and was powerful in speech and action.

²³"When Moses was forty years old, he decided to visit his own people, the Israelites. ²⁴He saw one of them being mistreated by an Egyptian, so he went to his defense and avenged him by killing the Egyptian. ²⁵Moses thought that his own people would realize that God was using him to rescue them, but they did not. ²⁶The next day Moses came upon two Israelites who were fighting. He tried to reconcile them by saying, 'Men, you are brothers; why do you want to hurt each other?'

²⁷"But the man who was mistreating the other pushed Moses aside and said, 'Who made you ruler and judge over us? ²⁸Are you thinking of killing me as you killed the Egyptian yesterday?'ᶜ ²⁹When Moses heard this, he fled to Midian, where he settled as a foreigner and had two sons.

³⁰"After forty years had passed, an angel appeared to Moses in the flames of a burning bush in the desert near Mount Sinai. ³¹When he saw this, he was amazed at the sight. As he went over to get a closer look, he heard the Lord say: ³²'I am the God of your fathers, the God of Abraham, Isaac and Jacob.'ᵈ Moses trembled with fear and did not dare to look.

³³"Then the Lord said to him, 'Take off your sandals, for the place where you are standing is holy ground. ³⁴I have indeed seen the oppression of my people in Egypt. I have heard their groaning and have come down to set them free. Now come, I will send you back to Egypt.'ᵉ

³⁵"This is the same Moses they had reject-ed with the words, 'Who made you ruler and judge?' He was sent to be their ruler and deliverer by God himself, through the angel who appeared to him in the bush. ³⁶He led them out of Egypt and performed wonders and signs in Egypt, at the Red Sea and for forty years in the wilderness.

³⁷"This is the Moses who told the Israelites, 'God will raise up for you a prophet like me from your own people.'ᶠ ³⁸He was in the assembly in the wilderness, with the angel who spoke to him on Mount Sinai, and with our ancestors; and he received living words to pass on to us.

³⁹"But our ancestors refused to obey him. Instead, they rejected him and in their hearts turned back to Egypt. ⁴⁰They told Aaron, 'Make us gods who will go before us. As for this fellow Moses who led us out of Egypt—we don't know what has happened to him!'ᵍ ⁴¹That was the time they made an idol in the form of a calf. They brought sacrifices to it and reveled in what their own hands had made. ⁴²But God turned away from them and gave them over to the worship of the sun, moon and stars. This agrees with what is written in the book of the prophets:

"'Did you bring me sacrifices and offerings
    forty years in the wilderness, people of Israel?
⁴³You have taken up the tabernacle of Molek
    and the star of your god Rephan,
    the idols you made to worship.
Therefore I will send you into exile'ʰ
    beyond Babylon.

⁴⁴"Our ancestors had the tabernacle of the covenant law with them in the wilderness. It had been made as God directed Moses, according to the pattern he had seen. ⁴⁵After receiving the tabernacle, our ancestors under Joshua brought it with them when they took the land from the nations God drove out before them. It remained in the land until the time of David, ⁴⁶who enjoyed God's favor and asked that he might provide a dwelling place for the God of Jacob.ⁱ ⁴⁷But it was Solomon who built a house for him.

⁴⁸"However, the Most High does not live in houses made by human hands. As the prophet says:

⁴⁹"'Heaven is my throne,
    and the earth is my footstool.
What kind of house will you build for me?
        says the Lord.
    Or where will my resting place be?
⁵⁰Has not my hand made all these things?'ʲ

⁵¹"You stiff-necked people! Your hearts and ears are still uncircumcised. You are just like your ancestors: You always resist the Holy Spirit! ⁵²Was there ever a prophet your ancestors did not persecute? They even killed

---

ᵃ 18 Exodus 1:8   ᵇ 20 Or *was fair in the sight of God*   ᶜ 28 Exodus 2:14   ᵈ 32 Exodus 3:6
ᵉ 34 Exodus 3:5,7,8,10   ᶠ 37 Deut. 18:15   ᵍ 40 Exodus 32:1   ʰ 43 Amos 5:25-27 (see Septuagint)
ⁱ 46 Some early manuscripts *the house of Jacob*   ʲ 50 Isaiah 66:1,2

those who predicted the coming of the Righteous One. And now you have betrayed and murdered him— 53you who have received the law that was given through angels but have not obeyed it."

The Stoning of Stephen

54When the members of the Sanhedrin heard this, they were furious and gnashed their teeth at him. 55But Stephen, full of the Holy Spirit, looked up to heaven and saw the glory of God, and Jesus standing at the right hand of God. 56"Look," he said, "I see heaven open and the Son of Man standing at the right hand of God."

57At this they covered their ears and, yelling at the top of their voices, they all rushed at him, 58dragged him out of the city and began to stone him. Meanwhile, the witnesses laid their coats at the feet of a young man named Saul.

59While they were stoning him, Stephen prayed, "Lord Jesus, receive my spirit." 60Then he fell on his knees and cried out, "Lord, do not hold this sin against them." When he had said this, he fell asleep.

8 And Saul approved of their killing him.

The Church Persecuted and Scattered

On that day a great persecution broke out against the church in Jerusalem, and all except the apostles were scattered throughout Judea and Samaria. 2Godly men buried Stephen and mourned deeply for him. 3But Saul began to destroy the church. Going from house to house, he dragged off both men and women and put them in prison.

Philip in Samaria

4Those who had been scattered preached the word wherever they went. 5Philip went down to a city in Samaria and proclaimed the Messiah there. 6When the crowds heard Philip and saw the signs he performed, they all paid close attention to what he said. 7For with shrieks, impure spirits came out of many, and many who were paralyzed or lame were healed. 8So there was great joy in that city.

Simon the Sorcerer

9Now for some time a man named Simon had practiced sorcery in the city and amazed all the people of Samaria. He boasted that he was someone great, 10and all the people, both high and low, gave him their attention and exclaimed, "This man is rightly called the Great Power of God." 11They followed him because he had amazed them for a long time with his sorcery. 12But when they believed Philip as he proclaimed the good news of the kingdom of God and the name of Jesus Christ, they were baptized, both men and women. 13Simon himself believed and was baptized. And he followed Philip everywhere, astonished by the great signs and miracles he saw.

14When the apostles in Jerusalem heard that Samaria had accepted the word of God, they sent Peter and John to Samaria. 15When they arrived, they prayed for the new believers there that they might receive the Holy Spirit, 16because the Holy Spirit had not yet come on any of them; they had simply been baptized in the name of the Lord Jesus. 17Then Peter and John placed their hands on them, and they received the Holy Spirit.

18When Simon saw that the Spirit was given at the laying on of the apostles' hands, he offered them money 19and said, "Give me also this ability so that everyone on whom I lay my hands may receive the Holy Spirit."

20Peter answered: "May your money perish with you, because you thought you could buy the gift of God with money! 21You have no part or share in this ministry, because your heart is not right before God. 22Repent of this wickedness and pray to the Lord in the hope that he may forgive you for having such a thought in your heart. 23For I see that you are full of bitterness and captive to sin."

24Then Simon answered, "Pray to the Lord for me so that nothing you have said may happen to me."

25After they had further proclaimed the word of the Lord and testified about Jesus, Peter and John returned to Jerusalem, preaching the gospel in many Samaritan villages.

Philip and the Ethiopian

26Now an angel of the Lord said to Philip, "Go south to the road—the desert road—that goes down from Jerusalem to Gaza." 27So he started out, and on his way he met an Ethiopian^a eunuch, an important official in charge of all the treasury of the Kandake (which means "queen of the Ethiopians"). This man had gone to Jerusalem to worship, 28and on his way home was sitting in his chariot reading the Book of Isaiah the prophet. 29The Spirit told Philip, "Go to that chariot and stay near it."

30Then Philip ran up to the chariot and heard the man reading Isaiah the prophet. "Do you understand what you are reading?" Philip asked.

31"How can I," he said, "unless someone explains it to me?" So he invited Philip to come up and sit with him.

32This is the passage of Scripture the eunuch was reading:

"He was led like a sheep to the slaughter,
   and as a lamb before its shearer is
      silent,
   so he did not open his mouth.
33In his humiliation he was deprived of
      justice.
   Who can speak of his descendants?
   For his life was taken from the earth."^{b}

34The eunuch asked Philip, "Tell me, please, who is the prophet talking about, himself or someone else?" 35Then Philip began with that very passage of Scripture and told him the good news about Jesus.

36As they traveled along the road, they came to some water and the eunuch said, "Look,

---

^{a} 27 That is, from the southern Nile region ^{b} 33 Isaiah 53:7,8 (see Septuagint)

here is water. What can stand in the way of my being baptized?" [37][a] 38And he gave orders to stop the chariot. Then both Philip and the eunuch went down into the water and Philip baptized him. 39When they came up out of the water, the Spirit of the Lord suddenly took Philip away, and the eunuch did not see him again, but went on his way rejoicing. 40Philip, however, appeared at Azotus and traveled about, preaching the gospel in all the towns until he reached Caesarea.

Saul's Conversion

9 Meanwhile, Saul was still breathing out murderous threats against the Lord's disciples. He went to the high priest 2and asked him for letters to the synagogues in Damascus, so that if he found any there who belonged to the Way, whether men or women, he might take them as prisoners to Jerusalem. 3As he neared Damascus on his journey, suddenly a light from heaven flashed around him. 4He fell to the ground and heard a voice say to him, "Saul, Saul, why do you persecute me?"

5"Who are you, Lord?" Saul asked.

"I am Jesus, whom you are persecuting," he replied. 6"Now get up and go into the city, and you will be told what you must do."

7The men traveling with Saul stood there speechless; they heard the sound but did not see anyone. 8Saul got up from the ground, but when he opened his eyes he could see nothing. So they led him by the hand into Damascus. 9For three days he was blind, and did not eat or drink anything.

10In Damascus there was a disciple named Ananias. The Lord called to him in a vision, "Ananias!"

"Yes, Lord," he answered.

11The Lord told him, "Go to the house of Judas on Straight Street and ask for a man from Tarsus named Saul, for he is praying. 12In a vision he has seen a man named Ananias come and place his hands on him to restore his sight."

13"Lord," Ananias answered, "I have heard many reports about this man and all the harm he has done to your holy people in Jerusalem. 14And he has come here with authority from the chief priests to arrest all who call on your name."

15But the Lord said to Ananias, "Go! This man is my chosen instrument to proclaim my name to the Gentiles and their kings and to the people of Israel. 16I will show him how much he must suffer for my name."

17Then Ananias went to the house and entered it. Placing his hands on Saul, he said, "Brother Saul, the Lord—Jesus, who appeared to you on the road as you were coming here—has sent me so that you may see again and be filled with the Holy Spirit." 18Immediately, something like scales fell from Saul's eyes, and he could see again. He got up and

was baptized, 19and after taking some food, he regained his strength.

Saul in Damascus and Jerusalem

Saul spent several days with the disciples in Damascus. 20At once he began to preach in the synagogues that Jesus is the Son of God. 21All those who heard him were astonished and asked, "Isn't he the man who raised havoc in Jerusalem among those who call on this name? And hasn't he come here to take them as prisoners to the chief priests?" 22Yet Saul grew more and more powerful and baffled the Jews living in Damascus by proving that Jesus is the Messiah.

23After many days had gone by, there was a conspiracy among the Jews to kill him, 24but Saul learned of their plan. Day and night they kept close watch on the city gates in order to kill him. 25But his followers took him by night and lowered him in a basket through an opening in the wall.

26When he came to Jerusalem, he tried to join the disciples, but they were all afraid of him, not believing that he really was a disciple. 27But Barnabas took him and brought him to the apostles. He told them how Saul on his journey had seen the Lord and that the Lord had spoken to him, and how in Damascus he had preached fearlessly in the name of Jesus. 28So Saul stayed with them and moved about freely in Jerusalem, speaking boldly in the name of the Lord. 29He talked and debated with the Hellenistic Jews,[b] but they tried to kill him. 30When the believers learned of this, they took him down to Caesarea and sent him off to Tarsus.

31Then the church throughout Judea, Galilee and Samaria enjoyed a time of peace and was strengthened. Living in the fear of the Lord and encouraged by the Holy Spirit, it increased in numbers.

Aeneas and Dorcas

32As Peter traveled about the country, he went to visit the Lord's people who lived in Lydda. 33There he found a man named Aeneas, who was paralyzed and had been bedridden for eight years. 34"Aeneas," Peter said to him, "Jesus Christ heals you. Get up and roll up your mat." Immediately Aeneas got up. 35All those who lived in Lydda and Sharon saw him and turned to the Lord.

36In Joppa there was a disciple named Tabitha (in Greek her name is Dorcas); she was always doing good and helping the poor. 37About that time she became sick and died, and her body was washed and placed in an upstairs room. 38Lydda was near Joppa; so when the disciples heard that Peter was in Lydda, they sent two men to him and urged him, "Please come at once!"

39Peter went with them, and when he arrived he was taken upstairs to the room. All the widows stood around him, crying and

---

a 37 Some manuscripts include here Philip said, "If you believe with all your heart, you may." The eunuch answered, "I believe that Jesus Christ is the Son of God."   b 29 That is, Jews who had adopted the Greek language and culture

showing him the robes and other clothing that Dorcas had made while she was still with them.

⁴⁰Peter sent them all out of the room; then he got down on his knees and prayed. Turning toward the dead woman, he said, "Tabitha, get up." She opened her eyes, and seeing Peter she sat up. ⁴¹He took her by the hand and helped her to her feet. Then he called for the believers, especially the widows, and presented her to them alive. ⁴²This became known all over Joppa, and many people believed in the Lord. ⁴³Peter stayed in Joppa for some time with a tanner named Simon.

Cornelius Calls for Peter

10 At Caesarea there was a man named Cornelius, a centurion in what was known as the Italian Regiment. ²He and all his family were devout and God-fearing; he gave generously to those in need and prayed to God regularly. ³One day at about three in the afternoon he had a vision. He distinctly saw an angel of God, who came to him and said, "Cornelius!"

⁴Cornelius stared at him in fear. "What is it, Lord?" he asked.

The angel answered, "Your prayers and gifts to the poor have come up as a memorial offering before God. ⁵Now send men to Joppa to bring back a man named Simon who is called Peter. ⁶He is staying with Simon the tanner, whose house is by the sea."

⁷When the angel who spoke to him had gone, Cornelius called two of his servants and a devout soldier who was one of his attendants. ⁸He told them everything that had happened and sent them to Joppa.

Peter's Vision

⁹About noon the following day as they were on their journey and approaching the city, Peter went up on the roof to pray. ¹⁰He became hungry and wanted something to eat, and while the meal was being prepared, he fell into a trance. ¹¹He saw heaven opened and something like a large sheet being let down to earth by its four corners. ¹²It contained all kinds of four-footed animals, as well as reptiles and birds. ¹³Then a voice told him, "Get up, Peter. Kill and eat."

¹⁴"Surely not, Lord!" Peter replied. "I have never eaten anything impure or unclean."

¹⁵The voice spoke to him a second time, "Do not call anything impure that God has made clean."

¹⁶This happened three times, and immediately the sheet was taken back to heaven.

¹⁷While Peter was wondering about the meaning of the vision, the men sent by Cornelius found out where Simon's house was and stopped at the gate. ¹⁸They called out, asking if Simon who was known as Peter was staying there.

¹⁹While Peter was still thinking about the vision, the Spirit said to him, "Simon, three*a*

men are looking for you. ²⁰So get up and go downstairs. Do not hesitate to go with them, for I have sent them."

²¹Peter went down and said to the men, "I'm the one you're looking for. Why have you come?"

²²The men replied, "We have come from Cornelius the centurion. He is a righteous and God-fearing man, who is respected by all the Jewish people. A holy angel told him to ask you to come to his house so that he could hear what you have to say." ²³Then Peter invited the men into the house to be his guests.

Peter at Cornelius's House

The next day Peter started out with them, and some of the believers from Joppa went along. ²⁴The following day he arrived in Caesarea. Cornelius was expecting them and had called together his relatives and close friends. ²⁵As Peter entered the house, Cornelius met him and fell at his feet in reverence. ²⁶But Peter made him get up. "Stand up," he said, "I am only a man myself."

²⁷While talking with him, Peter went inside and found a large gathering of people. ²⁸He said to them: "You are well aware that it is against our law for a Jew to associate with or visit a Gentile. But God has shown me that I should not call anyone impure or unclean. ²⁹So when I was sent for, I came without raising any objection. May I ask why you sent for me?"

³⁰Cornelius answered: "Three days ago I was in my house praying at this hour, at three in the afternoon. Suddenly a man in shining clothes stood before me ³¹and said, 'Cornelius, God has heard your prayer and remembered your gifts to the poor. ³²Send to Joppa for Simon who is called Peter. He is a guest in the home of Simon the tanner, who lives by the sea.' ³³So I sent for you immediately, and it was good of you to come. Now we are all here in the presence of God to listen to everything the Lord has commanded you to tell us."

³⁴Then Peter began to speak: "I now realize how true it is that God does not show favoritism ³⁵but accepts from every nation the one who fears him and does what is right. ³⁶You know the message God sent to the people of Israel, announcing the good news of peace through Jesus Christ, who is Lord of all. ³⁷You know what has happened throughout the province of Judea, beginning in Galilee after the baptism that John preached— ³⁸how God anointed Jesus of Nazareth with the Holy Spirit and power, and how he went around doing good and healing all who were under the power of the devil, because God was with him. ³⁹"We are witnesses of everything he did in the country of the Jews and in Jerusalem. They killed him by hanging him on a cross, ⁴⁰but God raised him from the dead on the third day and caused him to be seen. ⁴¹He was not seen by all the people, but by witnesses whom God had already chosen—by us who ate and drank with him after he rose from the

---

a 19 One early manuscript *two*; other manuscripts do not have the number.

dead. ⁴²He commanded us to preach to the people and to testify that he is the one whom God appointed as judge of the living and the dead. ⁴³All the prophets testify about him that everyone who believes in him receives forgiveness of sins through his name."

⁴⁴While Peter was still speaking these words, the Holy Spirit came on all who heard the message. ⁴⁵The circumcised believers who had come with Peter were astonished that the gift of the Holy Spirit had been poured out even on Gentiles. ⁴⁶For they heard them speaking in tongues*a* and praising God.

Then Peter said, ⁴⁷"Surely no one can stand in the way of their being baptized with water. They have received the Holy Spirit just as we have." ⁴⁸So he ordered that they be baptized in the name of Jesus Christ. Then they asked Peter to stay with them for a few days.

Peter Explains His Actions

11 The apostles and the believers throughout Judea heard that the Gentiles also had received the word of God. ²So when Peter went up to Jerusalem, the circumcised believers criticized him ³and said, "You went into the house of uncircumcised men and ate with them."

⁴Starting from the beginning, Peter told them the whole story: ⁵"I was in the city of Joppa praying, and in a trance I saw a vision. I saw something like a large sheet being let down from heaven by its four corners, and it came down to where I was. ⁶I looked into it and saw four-footed animals of the earth, wild beasts, reptiles and birds. ⁷Then I heard a voice telling me, 'Get up, Peter. Kill and eat.'

⁸"I replied, 'Surely not, Lord! Nothing impure or unclean has ever entered my mouth.'

⁹"The voice spoke from heaven a second time, 'Do not call anything impure that God has made clean.' ¹⁰This happened three times, and then it was all pulled up to heaven again.

¹¹"Right then three men who had been sent to me from Caesarea stopped at the house where I was staying. ¹²The Spirit told me to have no hesitation about going with them. These six brothers also went with me, and we entered the man's house. ¹³He told us how he had seen an angel appear in his house and say, 'Send to Joppa for Simon who is called Peter. ¹⁴He will bring you a message through which you and all your household will be saved.'

¹⁵"As I began to speak, the Holy Spirit came on them as he had come on us at the beginning. ¹⁶Then I remembered what the Lord had said: 'John baptized with*b* water, but you will be baptized with*b* the Holy Spirit.' ¹⁷So if God gave them the same gift he gave us who believed in the Lord Jesus Christ, who was I to think that I could stand in God's way?"

¹⁸When they heard this, they had no further objections and praised God, saying, "So then, even to Gentiles God has granted repentance that leads to life."

The Church in Antioch

¹⁹Now those who had been scattered by the persecution that broke out when Stephen was killed traveled as far as Phoenicia, Cyprus and Antioch, spreading the word only among Jews. ²⁰Some of them, however, men from Cyprus and Cyrene, went to Antioch and began to speak to Greeks also, telling them the good news about the Lord Jesus. ²¹The Lord's hand was with them, and a great number of people believed and turned to the Lord.

²²News of this reached the church in Jerusalem, and they sent Barnabas to Antioch. ²³When he arrived and saw what the grace of God had done, he was glad and encouraged them all to remain true to the Lord with all their hearts. ²⁴He was a good man, full of the Holy Spirit and faith, and a great number of people were brought to the Lord.

²⁵Then Barnabas went to Tarsus to look for Saul, ²⁶and when he found him, he brought him to Antioch. So for a whole year Barnabas and Saul met with the church and taught great numbers of people. The disciples were called Christians first at Antioch.

²⁷During this time some prophets came down from Jerusalem to Antioch. ²⁸One of them, named Agabus, stood up and through the Spirit predicted that a severe famine would spread over the entire Roman world. (This happened during the reign of Claudius.) ²⁹The disciples, as each one was able, decided to provide help for the brothers and sisters living in Judea. ³⁰This they did, sending their gift to the elders by Barnabas and Saul.

Peter's Miraculous Escape From Prison

12 It was about this time that King Herod arrested some who belonged to the church, intending to persecute them. ²He had James, the brother of John, put to death with the sword. ³When he saw that this met with approval among the Jews, he proceeded to seize Peter also. This happened during the Festival of Unleavened Bread. ⁴After arresting him, he put him in prison, handing him over to be guarded by four squads of four soldiers each. Herod intended to bring him out for public trial after the Passover.

⁵So Peter was kept in prison, but the church was earnestly praying to God for him.

⁶The night before Herod was to bring him to trial, Peter was sleeping between two soldiers, bound with two chains, and sentries stood guard at the entrance. ⁷Suddenly an angel of the Lord appeared and a light shone in the cell. He struck Peter on the side and woke him up. "Quick, get up!" he said, and the chains fell off Peter's wrists.

⁸Then the angel said to him, "Put on your clothes and sandals." And Peter did so. "Wrap your cloak around you and follow me," the angel told him. ⁹Peter followed him out of the prison, but he had no idea that what the angel was doing was really happening; he thought he was seeing a vision. ¹⁰They passed the first

---

a 46 Or other languages   *b 16 Or in*

and second guards and came to the iron gate leading to the city. It opened for them by itself, and they went through it. When they had walked the length of one street, suddenly the angel left him.

[11]Then Peter came to himself and said, "Now I know without a doubt that the Lord has sent his angel and rescued me from Herod's clutches and from everything the Jewish people were hoping would happen."

[12]When this had dawned on him, he went to the house of Mary the mother of John, also called Mark, where many people had gathered and were praying. [13]Peter knocked at the outer entrance, and a servant named Rhoda came to answer the door. [14]When she recognized Peter's voice, she was so overjoyed she ran back without opening it and exclaimed, "Peter is at the door!"

[15]"You're out of your mind," they told her. When she kept insisting that it was so, they said, "It must be his angel."

[16]But Peter kept on knocking, and when they opened the door and saw him, they were astonished. [17]Peter motioned with his hand for them to be quiet and described how the Lord had brought him out of prison. "Tell James and the other brothers and sisters about this," he said, and then he left for another place.

[18]In the morning, there was no small commotion among the soldiers as to what had become of Peter. [19]After Herod had a thorough search made for him and did not find him, he cross-examined the guards and ordered that they be executed.

Herod's Death

Then Herod went from Judea to Caesarea and stayed there. [20]He had been quarreling with the people of Tyre and Sidon; they now joined together and sought an audience with him. After securing the support of Blastus, a trusted personal servant of the king, they asked for peace, because they depended on the king's country for their food supply.

[21]On the appointed day Herod, wearing his royal robes, sat on his throne and delivered a public address to the people. [22]They shouted, "This is the voice of a god, not of a man." [23]Immediately, because Herod did not give praise to God, an angel of the Lord struck him down, and he was eaten by worms and died.

[24]But the word of God continued to spread and flourish.

Barnabas and Saul Sent Off

[25]When Barnabas and Saul had finished their mission, they returned from[a] Jerusalem, taking with them John, also called Mark.

13 [1]Now in the church at Antioch there were prophets and teachers: Barnabas, Simeon called Niger, Lucius of Cyrene, Manaen (who had been brought up with Herod the tetrarch) and Saul. [2]While they were worshiping the Lord and fasting, the Holy Spirit said, "Set apart for me Barnabas and Saul for the

work to which I have called them." [3]So after they had fasted and prayed, they placed their hands on them and sent them off.

On Cyprus

[4]The two of them, sent on their way by the Holy Spirit, went down to Seleucia and sailed from there to Cyprus. [5]When they arrived at Salamis, they proclaimed the word of God in the Jewish synagogues. John was with them as their helper.

[6]They traveled through the whole island until they came to Paphos. There they met a Jewish sorcerer and false prophet named Bar-Jesus, [7]who was an attendant of the proconsul, Sergius Paulus. The proconsul, an intelligent man, sent for Barnabas and Saul because he wanted to hear the word of God. [8]But Elymas the sorcerer (for that is what his name means) opposed them and tried to turn the proconsul from the faith. [9]Then Saul, who was also called Paul, filled with the Holy Spirit, looked straight at Elymas and said, [10]"You are a child of the devil and an enemy of everything that is right! You are full of all kinds of deceit and trickery. Will you never stop perverting the right ways of the Lord? [11]Now the hand of the Lord is against you. You are going to be blind for a time, not even able to see the light of the sun."

Immediately mist and darkness came over him, and he groped about, seeking someone to lead him by the hand. [12]When the proconsul saw what had happened, he believed, for he was amazed at the teaching about the Lord.

In Pisidian Antioch

[13]From Paphos, Paul and his companions sailed to Perga in Pamphylia, where John left them to return to Jerusalem. [14]From Perga they went on to Pisidian Antioch. On the Sabbath they entered the synagogue and sat down. [15]After the reading from the Law and the Prophets, the leaders of the synagogue sent word to them, saying, "Brothers, if you have a word of exhortation for the people, please speak."

[16]Standing up, Paul motioned with his hand and said: "Fellow Israelites and you Gentiles who worship God, listen to me! [17]The God of the people of Israel chose our ancestors; he made the people prosper during their stay in Egypt; with mighty power he led them out of that country; [18]for about forty years he endured their conduct[b] in the wilderness; [19]and he overthrew seven nations in Canaan, giving their land to his people as their inheritance. [20]All this took about 450 years.

"After this, God gave them judges until the time of Samuel the prophet. [21]Then the people asked for a king, and he gave them Saul son of Kish, of the tribe of Benjamin, who ruled forty years. [22]After removing Saul, he made David their king. God testified concerning him: 'I have found David son of Jesse, a man after my own heart; he will do everything I want him to do.'

---

[a] 25 Some manuscripts *to*   [b] 18 Some manuscripts *he cared for them*

23"From this man's descendants God has brought to Israel the Savior Jesus, as he promised. 24Before the coming of Jesus, John preached repentance and baptism to all the people of Israel. 25As John was completing his work, he said: 'Who do you suppose I am? I am not the one you are looking for. But there is one coming after me whose sandals I am not worthy to untie.'

26"Fellow children of Abraham and you God-fearing Gentiles, it is to us that this message of salvation has been sent. 27The people of Jerusalem and their rulers did not recognize Jesus, yet in condemning him they fulfilled the words of the prophets that are read every Sabbath. 28Though they found no proper ground for a death sentence, they asked Pilate to have him executed. 29When they had carried out all that was written about him, they took him down from the cross and laid him in a tomb. 30But God raised him from the dead, 31and for many days he was seen by those who had traveled with him from Galilee to Jerusalem. They are now his witnesses to our people.

32"We tell you the good news: What God promised our ancestors 33he has fulfilled for us, their children, by raising up Jesus. As it is written in the second Psalm:

" 'You are my son;
today I have become your father.'ᵃ

34God raised him from the dead so that he will never be subject to decay. As God has said,

" 'I will give you the holy and sure blessings promised to David.'ᵇ

35So it is also stated elsewhere:

" 'You will not let your holy one see decay.'ᶜ

36"Now when David had served God's purpose in his own generation, he fell asleep; he was buried with his ancestors and his body decayed. 37But the one whom God raised from the dead did not see decay.

38"Therefore, my friends, I want you to know that through Jesus the forgiveness of sins is proclaimed to you. 39Through him everyone who believes is set free from every sin, a justification you were not able to obtain under the law of Moses. 40Take care that what the prophets have said does not happen to you:

41" 'Look, you scoffers,
wonder and perish,
for I am going to do something in your days
that you would never believe,
even if someone told you.'ᵈ"

42As Paul and Barnabas were leaving the synagogue, the people invited them to speak further about these things on the next Sabbath. 43When the congregation was dismissed, many of the Jews and devout converts to Judaism followed Paul and Barnabas, who talked with them and urged them to continue in the grace of God.

44On the next Sabbath almost the whole city gathered to hear the word of the Lord. 45When the Jews saw the crowds, they were filled with jealousy. They began to contradict what Paul was saying and heaped abuse on him.

46Then Paul and Barnabas answered them boldly: "We had to speak the word of God to you first. Since you reject it and do not consider yourselves worthy of eternal life, we now turn to the Gentiles. 47For this is what the Lord has commanded us:

" 'I have made youᵉ a light for the Gentiles,
that youᵉ may bring salvation to the ends of the earth.'ᶠ"

48When the Gentiles heard this, they were glad and honored the word of the Lord; and all who were appointed for eternal life believed.

49The word of the Lord spread through the whole region. 50But the Jewish leaders incited the God-fearing women of high standing and the leading men of the city. They stirred up persecution against Paul and Barnabas, and expelled them from their region. 51So they shook the dust off their feet as a warning to them and went to Iconium. 52And the disciples were filled with joy and with the Holy Spirit.

In Iconium

14 At Iconium Paul and Barnabas went as usual into the Jewish synagogue. There they spoke so effectively that a great number of Jews and Greeks believed. 2But the Jews who refused to believe stirred up the other Gentiles and poisoned their minds against the brothers. 3So Paul and Barnabas spent considerable time there, speaking boldly for the Lord, who confirmed the message of his grace by enabling them to perform signs and wonders. 4The people of the city were divided; some sided with the Jews, others with the apostles. 5There was a plot afoot among both Gentiles and Jews, together with their leaders, to mistreat them and stone them. 6But they found out about it and fled to the Lycaonian cities of Lystra and Derbe and to the surrounding country, 7where they continued to preach the gospel.

In Lystra and Derbe

8In Lystra there sat a man who was lame. He had been that way from birth and had never walked. 9He listened to Paul as he was speaking. Paul looked directly at him, saw that he had faith to be healed 10and called out, "Stand up on your feet!" At that, the man jumped up and began to walk.

11When the crowd saw what Paul had done, they shouted in the Lycaonian language, "The gods have come down to us in human form!" 12Barnabas they called Zeus, and Paul they called Hermes because he was the chief speaker. 13The priest of Zeus, whose temple

---

ᵃ 33 Psalm 2:7   ᵇ 34 Isaiah 55:3   ᶜ 35 Psalm 16:10 (see Septuagint)   ᵈ 41 Hab. 1:5
ᵉ 47 The Greek is singular.   ᶠ 47 Isaiah 49:6

was just outside the city, brought bulls and wreaths to the city gates because he and the crowd wanted to offer sacrifices to them. [14]But when the apostles Barnabas and Paul heard of this, they tore their clothes and rushed out into the crowd, shouting: [15]"Friends, why are you doing this? We too are only human, like you. We are bringing you good news, telling you to turn from these worthless things to the living God, who made the heavens and the earth and the sea and everything in them. [16]In the past, he let all nations go their own way. [17]Yet he has not left himself without testimony: He has shown kindness by giving you rain from heaven and crops in their seasons; he provides you with plenty of food and fills your hearts with joy." [18]Even with these words, they had difficulty keeping the crowd from sacrificing to them.

[19]Then some Jews came from Antioch and Iconium and won the crowd over. They stoned Paul and dragged him outside the city, thinking he was dead. [20]But after the disciples had gathered around him, he got up and went back into the city. The next day he and Barnabas left for Derbe.

The Return to Antioch in Syria

[21]They preached the gospel in that city and won a large number of disciples. Then they returned to Lystra, Iconium and Antioch, [22]strengthening the disciples and encouraging them to remain true to the faith. "We must go through many hardships to enter the kingdom of God," they said. [23]Paul and Barnabas appointed elders[a] for them in each church and, with prayer and fasting, committed them to the Lord, in whom they had put their trust. [24]After going through Pisidia, they came into Pamphylia, [25]and when they had preached the word in Perga, they went down to Attalia.

[26]From Attalia they sailed back to Antioch, where they had been committed to the grace of God for the work they had now completed. [27]On arriving there, they gathered the church together and reported all that God had done through them and how he had opened a door of faith to the Gentiles. [28]And they stayed there a long time with the disciples.

The Council at Jerusalem

15 Certain people came down from Judea to Antioch and were teaching the believers: "Unless you are circumcised, according to the custom taught by Moses, you cannot be saved." [2]This brought Paul and Barnabas into sharp dispute and debate with them. So Paul and Barnabas were appointed, along with some other believers, to go up to Jerusalem to see the apostles and elders about this question. [3]The church sent them on their way, and as they traveled through Phoenicia and Samaria, they told how the Gentiles had been converted. This news made all the believers very glad. [4]When they

came to Jerusalem, they were welcomed by the church and the apostles and elders, to whom they reported everything God had done through them.

[5]Then some of the believers who belonged to the party of the Pharisees stood up and said, "The Gentiles must be circumcised and required to keep the law of Moses."

[6]The apostles and elders met to consider this question. [7]After much discussion, Peter got up and addressed them: "Brothers, you know that some time ago God made a choice among you that the Gentiles might hear from my lips the message of the gospel and believe. [8]God, who knows the heart, showed that he accepted them by giving the Holy Spirit to them, just as he did to us. [9]He did not discriminate between us and them, for he purified their hearts by faith. [10]Now then, why do you try to test God by putting on the necks of Gentiles a yoke that neither we nor our ancestors have been able to bear? [11]No! We believe it is through the grace of our Lord Jesus that we are saved, just as they are."

[12]The whole assembly became silent as they listened to Barnabas and Paul telling about the signs and wonders God had done among the Gentiles through them. [13]When they finished, James spoke up. "Brothers," he said, "listen to me. [14]Simon[b] has described to us how God first intervened to choose a people for his name from the Gentiles. [15]The words of the prophets are in agreement with this, as it is written:

[16]"'After this I will return
  and rebuild David's fallen tent.
 Its ruins I will rebuild,
  and I will restore it,
[17]that the rest of mankind may seek the
  Lord,
  even all the Gentiles who bear my
  name,
 says the Lord, who does these
  things'[c]—
[18] things known from long ago.[d]

[19]"It is my judgment, therefore, that we should not make it difficult for the Gentiles who are turning to God. [20]Instead we should write to them, telling them to abstain from food polluted by idols, from sexual immorality, from the meat of strangled animals and from blood. [21]For the law of Moses has been preached in every city from the earliest times and is read in the synagogues on every Sabbath."

The Council's Letter to Gentile Believers

[22]Then the apostles and elders, with the whole church, decided to choose some of their own men and send them to Antioch with Paul and Barnabas. They chose Judas (called Barsabbas) and Silas, men who were leaders among the believers. [23]With them they sent the following letter:

---

[a] 23 Or *Barnabas ordained elders*; or *Barnabas had elders elected*   [b] 14 Greek *Simeon*, a variant of *Simon*; that is, Peter   [c] 17 Amos 9:11,12 (see Septuagint)   [d] 17,18 Some manuscripts *things'*— / [18]*the Lord's work is known to him from long ago*

The apostles and elders, your brothers,

To the Gentile believers in Antioch, Syria and Cilicia:

Greetings.

24We have heard that some went out from us without our authorization and disturbed you, troubling your minds by what they said. 25So we all agreed to choose some men and send them to you with our dear friends Barnabas and Paul— 26men who have risked their lives for the name of our Lord Jesus Christ. 27Therefore we are sending Judas and Silas to confirm by word of mouth what we are writing. 28It seemed good to the Holy Spirit and to us not to burden you with anything beyond the following requirements: 29You are to abstain from food sacrificed to idols, from blood, from the meat of strangled animals and from sexual immorality. You will do well to avoid these things.

Farewell.

30So the men were sent off and went down to Antioch, where they gathered the church together and delivered the letter. 31The people read it and were glad for its encouraging message. 32Judas and Silas, who themselves were prophets, said much to encourage and strengthen the believers. 33After spending some time there, they were sent off by the believers with the blessing of peace to return to those who had sent them. [34]a 35But Paul and Barnabas remained in Antioch, where they and many others taught and preached the word of the Lord.

Disagreement Between Paul and Barnabas

36Some time later Paul said to Barnabas, "Let us go back and visit the believers in all the towns where we preached the word of the Lord and see how they are doing." 37Barnabas wanted to take John, also called Mark, with them, 38but Paul did not think it wise to take him, because he had deserted them in Pamphylia and had not continued with them in the work. 39They had such a sharp disagreement that they parted company. Barnabas took Mark and sailed for Cyprus, 40but Paul chose Silas and left, commended by the believers to the grace of the Lord. 41He went through Syria and Cilicia, strengthening the churches.

Timothy Joins Paul and Silas

16 Paul came to Derbe and then to Lystra, where a disciple named Timothy lived, whose mother was Jewish and a believer but whose father was a Greek. 2The believers at Lystra and Iconium spoke well of him. 3Paul wanted to take him along on the journey, so he circumcised him because of the Jews who lived in that area, for they all knew that his father was a Greek. 4As they traveled from town to town, they delivered the decisions reached by the apostles and elders in Jerusalem for the people to obey. 5So the churches were strengthened in the faith and grew daily in numbers.

Paul's Vision of the Man of Macedonia

6Paul and his companions traveled throughout the region of Phrygia and Galatia, having been kept by the Holy Spirit from preaching the word in the province of Asia. 7When they came to the border of Mysia, they tried to enter Bithynia, but the Spirit of Jesus would not allow them to. 8So they passed by Mysia and went down to Troas. 9During the night Paul had a vision of a man of Macedonia standing and begging him, "Come over to Macedonia and help us." 10After Paul had seen the vision, we got ready at once to leave for Macedonia, concluding that God had called us to preach the gospel to them.

Lydia's Conversion in Philippi

11From Troas we put out to sea and sailed straight for Samothrace, and the next day we went on to Neapolis. 12From there we traveled to Philippi, a Roman colony and the leading city of that districtb of Macedonia. And we stayed there several days.

13On the Sabbath we went outside the city gate to the river, where we expected to find a place of prayer. We sat down and began to speak to the women who had gathered there. 14One of those listening was a woman from the city of Thyatira named Lydia, a dealer in purple cloth. She was a worshiper of God. The Lord opened her heart to respond to Paul's message. 15When she and the members of her household were baptized, she invited us to her home. "If you consider me a believer in the Lord," she said, "come and stay at my house." And she persuaded us.

Paul and Silas in Prison

16Once when we were going to the place of prayer, we were met by a female slave who had a spirit by which she predicted the future. She earned a great deal of money for her owners by fortune-telling. 17She followed Paul and the rest of us, shouting, "These men are servants of the Most High God, who are telling you the way to be saved." 18She kept this up for many days. Finally Paul became so annoyed that he turned around and said to the spirit, "In the name of Jesus Christ I command you to come out of her!" At that moment the spirit left her.

19When her owners realized that their hope of making money was gone, they seized Paul and Silas and dragged them into the marketplace to face the authorities. 20They brought them before the magistrates and said, "These men are Jews, and are throwing our city into an uproar 21by advocating customs unlawful for us Romans to accept or practice."

---

a 34 Some manuscripts include here *But Silas decided to remain there.*   b 12 The text and meaning of the Greek for *the leading city of that district* are uncertain.

22The crowd joined in the attack against Paul and Silas, and the magistrates ordered them to be stripped and beaten with rods. 23After they had been severely flogged, they were thrown into prison, and the jailer was commanded to guard them carefully. 24When he received these orders, he put them in the inner cell and fastened their feet in the stocks.

25About midnight Paul and Silas were praying and singing hymns to God, and the other prisoners were listening to them. 26Suddenly there was such a violent earthquake that the foundations of the prison were shaken. At once all the prison doors flew open, and everyone's chains came loose. 27The jailer woke up, and when he saw the prison doors open, he drew his sword and was about to kill himself because he thought the prisoners had escaped. 28But Paul shouted, "Don't harm yourself! We are all here!"

29The jailer called for lights, rushed in and fell trembling before Paul and Silas. 30He then brought them out and asked, "Sirs, what must I do to be saved?"

31They replied, "Believe in the Lord Jesus, and you will be saved—you and your household." 32Then they spoke the word of the Lord to him and to all the others in his house. 33At that hour of the night the jailer took them and washed their wounds; then immediately he and all his household were baptized. 34The jailer brought them into his house and set a meal before them; he was filled with joy because he had come to believe in God—he and his whole household.

35When it was daylight, the magistrates sent their officers to the jailer with the order: "Release those men." 36The jailer told Paul, "The magistrates have ordered that you and Silas be released. Now you can leave. Go in peace."

37But Paul said to the officers: "They beat us publicly without a trial, even though we are Roman citizens, and threw us into prison. And now do they want to get rid of us quietly? No! Let them come themselves and escort us out."

38The officers reported this to the magistrates, and when they heard that Paul and Silas were Roman citizens, they were alarmed. 39They came to appease them and escorted them from the prison, requesting them to leave the city. 40After Paul and Silas came out of the prison, they went to Lydia's house, where they met with the brothers and sisters and encouraged them. Then they left.

In Thessalonica

17 When Paul and his companions had passed through Amphipolis and Apollonia, they came to Thessalonica, where there was a Jewish synagogue. 2As was his custom, Paul went into the synagogue, and on three Sabbath days he reasoned with them from the Scriptures, 3explaining and proving that the Messiah had to suffer and rise from the dead. "This Jesus I am proclaiming to you is the Messiah," he said. 4Some of the Jews were persuaded and joined Paul and Silas, as did

a large number of God-fearing Greeks and quite a few prominent women.

5But other Jews were jealous; so they rounded up some bad characters from the marketplace, formed a mob and started a riot in the city. They rushed to Jason's house in search of Paul and Silas in order to bring them out to the crowd.ᵃ 6But when they did not find them, they dragged Jason and some other believers before the city officials, shouting: "These men who have caused trouble all over the world have now come here, 7and Jason has welcomed them into his house. They are all defying Caesar's decrees, saying that there is another king, one called Jesus." 8When they heard this, the crowd and the city officials were thrown into turmoil. 9Then they made Jason and the others post bond and let them go.

In Berea

10As soon as it was night, the believers sent Paul and Silas away to Berea. On arriving there, they went to the Jewish synagogue. 11Now the Berean Jews were of more noble character than those in Thessalonica, for they received the message with great eagerness and examined the Scriptures every day to see if what Paul said was true. 12As a result, many of them believed, as did also a number of prominent Greek women and many Greek men.

13But when the Jews in Thessalonica learned that Paul was preaching the word of God at Berea, some of them went there too, agitating the crowds and stirring them up. 14The believers immediately sent Paul to the coast, but Silas and Timothy stayed at Berea. 15Those who escorted Paul brought him to Athens and then left with instructions for Silas and Timothy to join him as soon as possible.

In Athens

16While Paul was waiting for them in Athens, he was greatly distressed to see that the city was full of idols. 17So he reasoned in the synagogue with both Jews and God-fearing Greeks, as well as in the marketplace day by day with those who happened to be there. 18A group of Epicurean and Stoic philosophers began to debate with him. Some of them asked, "What is this babbler trying to say?" Others remarked, "He seems to be advocating foreign gods." They said this because Paul was preaching the good news about Jesus and the resurrection. 19Then they took him and brought him to a meeting of the Areopagus, where they said to him, "May we know what this new teaching is that you are presenting? 20You are bringing some strange ideas to our ears, and we would like to know what they mean." 21(All the Athenians and the foreigners who lived there spent their time doing nothing but talking about and listening to the latest ideas.)

ᵃ 5 Or *the assembly of the people*

[22]Paul then stood up in the meeting of the Areopagus and said: "People of Athens! I see that in every way you are very religious. [23]For as I walked around and looked carefully at your objects of worship, I even found an altar with this inscription: TO AN UNKNOWN GOD. So you are ignorant of the very thing you worship—and this is what I am going to proclaim to you.

[24]"The God who made the world and everything in it is the Lord of heaven and earth and does not live in temples built by human hands. [25]And he is not served by human hands, as if he needed anything. Rather, he himself gives everyone life and breath and everything else. [26]From one man he made all the nations, that they should inhabit the whole earth; and he marked out their appointed times in history and the boundaries of their lands. [27]God did this so that they would seek him and perhaps reach out for him and find him, though he is not far from any one of us. [28]'For in him we live and move and have our being.' As some of your own poets have said, 'We are his offspring.'[b]

[29]"Therefore since we are God's offspring, we should not think that the divine being is like gold or silver or stone—an image made by human design and skill. [30]In the past God overlooked such ignorance, but now he commands all people everywhere to repent. [31]For he has set a day when he will judge the world with justice by the man he has appointed. He has given proof of this to everyone by raising him from the dead."

[32]When they heard about the resurrection of the dead, some of them sneered, but others said, "We want to hear you again on this subject." [33]At that, Paul left the Council. [34]Some of the people became followers of Paul and believed. Among them was Dionysius, a member of the Areopagus, also a woman named Damaris, and a number of others.

In Corinth

18 After this, Paul left Athens and went to Corinth. [2]There he met a Jew named Aquila, a native of Pontus, who had recently come from Italy with his wife Priscilla, because Claudius had ordered all Jews to leave Rome. Paul went to see them, [3]and because he was a tentmaker as they were, he stayed and worked with them. [4]Every Sabbath he reasoned in the synagogue, trying to persuade Jews and Greeks.

[5]When Silas and Timothy came from Macedonia, Paul devoted himself exclusively to preaching, testifying to the Jews that Jesus was the Messiah. [6]But when they opposed Paul and became abusive, he shook out his clothes in protest and said to them, "Your blood be on your own heads! I am innocent of it. From now on I will go to the Gentiles."

[7]Then Paul left the synagogue and went next door to the house of Titius Justus, a worshiper of God. [8]Crispus, the synagogue leader, and his entire household believed in the Lord; and many of the Corinthians who heard Paul believed and were baptized.

[9]One night the Lord spoke to Paul in a vision: "Do not be afraid; keep on speaking, do not be silent. [10]For I am with you, and no one is going to attack and harm you, because I have many people in this city." [11]So Paul stayed in Corinth for a year and a half, teaching them the word of God.

[12]While Gallio was proconsul of Achaia, the Jews of Corinth made a united attack on Paul and brought him to the place of judgment. [13]"This man," they charged, "is persuading the people to worship God in ways contrary to the law."

[14]Just as Paul was about to speak, Gallio said to them, "If you Jews were making a complaint about some misdemeanor or serious crime, it would be reasonable for me to listen to you. [15]But since it involves questions about words and names and your own law—settle the matter yourselves. I will not be a judge of such things." [16]So he drove them off. [17]Then the crowd there turned on Sosthenes the synagogue leader and beat him in front of the proconsul; and Gallio showed no concern whatever.

Priscilla, Aquila and Apollos

[18]Paul stayed on in Corinth for some time. Then he left the brothers and sisters and sailed for Syria, accompanied by Priscilla and Aquila. Before he sailed, he had his hair cut off at Cenchreae because of a vow he had taken. [19]They arrived at Ephesus, where Paul left Priscilla and Aquila. He himself went into the synagogue and reasoned with the Jews. [20]When they asked him to spend more time with them, he declined. [21]But as he left, he promised, "I will come back if it is God's will." Then he set sail from Ephesus. [22]When he landed at Caesarea, he went up to Jerusalem and greeted the church and then went down to Antioch.

[23]After spending some time in Antioch, Paul set out from there and traveled from place to place throughout the region of Galatia and Phrygia, strengthening all the disciples.

[24]Meanwhile a Jew named Apollos, a native of Alexandria, came to Ephesus. He was a learned man, with a thorough knowledge of the Scriptures. [25]He had been instructed in the way of the Lord, and he spoke with great fervor[c] and taught about Jesus accurately, though he knew only the baptism of John. [26]He began to speak boldly in the synagogue. When Priscilla and Aquila heard him, they invited him to their home and explained to him the way of God more adequately.

[27]When Apollos wanted to go to Achaia, the brothers and sisters encouraged him and wrote to the disciples there to welcome him. When he arrived, he was a great help to those who by grace had believed. [28]For he vigorously refuted his Jewish opponents in public

---

[a] 28 From the Cretan philosopher Epimenides [b] 28 From the Cilician Stoic philosopher Aratus
[c] 25 Or *with fervor in the Spirit*

debate, proving from the Scriptures that Jesus was the Messiah.

Paul in Ephesus

19 While Apollos was at Corinth, Paul took the road through the interior and arrived at Ephesus. There he found some disciples [2]and asked them, "Did you receive the Holy Spirit when[a] you believed?"

They answered, "No, we have not even heard that there is a Holy Spirit."

[3]So Paul asked, "Then what baptism did you receive?"

"John's baptism," they replied.

[4]Paul said, "John's baptism was a baptism of repentance. He told the people to believe in the one coming after him, that is, in Jesus." [5]On hearing this, they were baptized in the name of the Lord Jesus. [6]When Paul placed his hands on them, the Holy Spirit came on them, and they spoke in tongues[b] and prophesied. [7]There were about twelve men in all.

[8]Paul entered the synagogue and spoke boldly there for three months, arguing persuasively about the kingdom of God. [9]But some of them became obstinate; they refused to believe and publicly maligned the Way. So Paul left them. He took the disciples with him and had discussions daily in the lecture hall of Tyrannus. [10]This went on for two years, so that all the Jews and Greeks who lived in the province of Asia heard the word of the Lord.

[11]God did extraordinary miracles through Paul, [12]so that even handkerchiefs and aprons that had touched him were taken to the sick, and their illnesses were cured and the evil spirits left them.

[13]Some Jews who went around driving out evil spirits tried to invoke the name of the Lord Jesus over those who were demon-possessed. They would say, "In the name of the Jesus whom Paul preaches, I command you to come out." [14]Seven sons of Sceva, a Jewish chief priest, were doing this. [15]One day the evil spirit answered them, "Jesus I know, and Paul I know about, but who are you?" [16]Then the man who had the evil spirit jumped on them and overpowered them all. He gave them such a beating that they ran out of the house naked and bleeding.

[17]When this became known to the Jews and Greeks living in Ephesus, they were all seized with fear, and the name of the Lord Jesus was held in high honor. [18]Many of those who believed now came and openly confessed what they had done. [19]A number who had practiced sorcery brought their scrolls together and burned them publicly. When they calculated the value of the scrolls, the total came to fifty thousand drachmas.[c] [20]In this way the word of the Lord spread widely and grew in power.

[21]After all this had happened, Paul decided[d] to go to Jerusalem, passing through Macedonia and Achaia. "After I have been there," he said, "I must visit Rome also." [22]He sent two of his helpers, Timothy and Erastus, to Macedonia, while he stayed in the province of Asia a little longer.

The Riot in Ephesus

[23]About that time there arose a great disturbance about the Way. [24]A silversmith named Demetrius, who made silver shrines of Artemis, brought in a lot of business for the craftsmen there. [25]He called them together, along with the workers in related trades, and said: "You know, my friends, that we receive a good income from this business. [26]And you see and hear how this fellow Paul has convinced and led astray large numbers of people here in Ephesus and in practically the whole province of Asia. He says that gods made by human hands are no gods at all. [27]There is danger not only that our trade will lose its good name, but also that the temple of the great goddess Artemis will be discredited; and the goddess herself, who is worshiped throughout the province of Asia and the world, will be robbed of her divine majesty."

[28]When they heard this, they were furious and began shouting: "Great is Artemis of the Ephesians!" [29]Soon the whole city was in an uproar. The people seized Gaius and Aristarchus, Paul's traveling companions from Macedonia, and all of them rushed into the theater together. [30]Paul wanted to appear before the crowd, but the disciples would not let him. [31]Even some of the officials of the province, friends of Paul, sent him a message begging him not to venture into the theater.

[32]The assembly was in confusion: Some were shouting one thing, some another. Most of the people did not even know why they were there. [33]The Jews in the crowd pushed Alexander to the front, and they shouted instructions to him. He motioned for silence in order to make a defense before the people. [34]But when they realized he was a Jew, they all shouted in unison for about two hours: "Great is Artemis of the Ephesians!"

[35]The city clerk quieted the crowd and said: "Fellow Ephesians, doesn't all the world know that the city of Ephesus is the guardian of the temple of the great Artemis and of her image, which fell from heaven? [36]Therefore, since these facts are undeniable, you ought to calm down and not do anything rash. [37]You have brought these men here, though they have neither robbed temples nor blasphemed our goddess. [38]If, then, Demetrius and his fellow craftsmen have a grievance against anybody, the courts are open and there are proconsuls. They can press charges. [39]If there is anything further you want to bring up, it must be settled in a legal assembly. [40]As it is, we are in danger of being charged with rioting because of what happened today. In that case we would not be able to account for this commotion, since there is no reason for it." [41]After he had said this, he dismissed the assembly.

---

[a] 2 Or *after*   [b] 6 Or *other languages*   [c] 19 A drachma was a silver coin worth about a day's wages.
[d] 21 Or *decided in the Spirit*

Through Macedonia and Greece

20 When the uproar had ended, Paul sent for the disciples and, after encouraging them, said goodbye and set out for Macedonia. ²He traveled through that area, speaking many words of encouragement to the people, and finally arrived in Greece, ³where he stayed three months. Because some Jews had plotted against him just as he was about to sail for Syria, he decided to go back through Macedonia. ⁴He was accompanied by Sopater son of Pyrrhus from Berea, Aristarchus and Secundus from Thessalonica, Gaius from Derbe, Timothy also, and Tychicus and Trophimus from the province of Asia. ⁵These men went on ahead and waited for us at Troas. ⁶But we sailed from Philippi after the Festival of Unleavened Bread, and five days later joined the others at Troas, where we stayed seven days.

Eutychus Raised From the Dead at Troas

⁷On the first day of the week we came together to break bread. Paul spoke to the people and, because he intended to leave the next day, kept on talking until midnight. ⁸There were many lamps in the upstairs room where we were meeting. ⁹Seated in a window was a young man named Eutychus, who was sinking into a deep sleep as Paul talked on and on. When he was sound asleep, he fell to the ground from the third story and was picked up dead. ¹⁰Paul went down, threw himself on the young man and put his arms around him. "Don't be alarmed," he said. "He's alive!" ¹¹Then he went upstairs again and broke bread and ate. After talking until daylight, he left. ¹²The people took the young man home alive and were greatly comforted.

Paul's Farewell to the Ephesian Elders

¹³We went on ahead to the ship and sailed for Assos, where we were going to take Paul aboard. He had made this arrangement because he was going there on foot. ¹⁴When he met us at Assos, we took him aboard and went on to Mitylene. ¹⁵The next day we set sail from there and arrived off Chios. The day after that we crossed over to Samos, and on the following day arrived at Miletus. ¹⁶Paul had decided to sail past Ephesus to avoid spending time in the province of Asia, for he was in a hurry to reach Jerusalem, if possible, by the day of Pentecost.

¹⁷From Miletus, Paul sent to Ephesus for the elders of the church. ¹⁸When they arrived, he said to them: "You know how I lived the whole time I was with you, from the first day I came into the province of Asia. ¹⁹I served the Lord with great humility and with tears and in the midst of severe testing by the plots of my Jewish opponents. ²⁰You know that I have not hesitated to preach anything that would be helpful to you but have taught you publicly and from house to house. ²¹I have declared to both Jews and Greeks that they must turn to God in repentance and have faith in our Lord Jesus.

²²"And now, compelled by the Spirit, I am going to Jerusalem, not knowing what will happen to me there. ²³I only know that in every city the Holy Spirit warns me that prison and hardships are facing me. ²⁴However, I consider my life worth nothing to me; my only aim is to finish the race and complete the task the Lord Jesus has given me—the task of testifying to the good news of God's grace.

²⁵"Now I know that none of you among whom I have gone about preaching the kingdom will ever see me again. ²⁶Therefore, I declare to you today that I am innocent of the blood of any of you. ²⁷For I have not hesitated to proclaim to you the whole will of God. ²⁸Keep watch over yourselves and all the flock of which the Holy Spirit has made you overseers. Be shepherds of the church of God,ᵃ which he bought with his own blood.ᵇ ²⁹I know that after I leave, savage wolves will come in among you and will not spare the flock. ³⁰Even from your own number men will arise and distort the truth in order to draw away disciples after them. ³¹So be on your guard! Remember that for three years I never stopped warning each of you night and day with tears.

³²"Now I commit you to God and to the word of his grace, which can build you up and give you an inheritance among all those who are sanctified. ³³I have not coveted anyone's silver or gold or clothing. ³⁴You yourselves know that these hands of mine have supplied my own needs and the needs of my companions. ³⁵In everything I did, I showed you that by this kind of hard work we must help the weak, remembering the words the Lord Jesus himself said: 'It is more blessed to give than to receive.' "

³⁶When Paul had finished speaking, he knelt down with all of them and prayed. ³⁷They all wept as they embraced him and kissed him. ³⁸What grieved them most was his statement that they would never see his face again. Then they accompanied him to the ship.

On to Jerusalem

21 After we had torn ourselves away from them, we put out to sea and sailed straight to Kos. The next day we went to Rhodes and from there to Patara. ²We found a ship crossing over to Phoenicia, went on board and set sail. ³After sighting Cyprus and passing to the south of it, we sailed on to Syria. We landed at Tyre, where our ship was to unload its cargo. ⁴We sought out the disciples there and stayed with them seven days. Through the Spirit they urged Paul not to go on to Jerusalem. ⁵When it was time to leave, we left and continued on our way. All of them, including wives and children, accompanied us out of the city, and there on the beach we knelt to pray. ⁶After saying goodbye to each other, we went aboard the ship, and they returned home.

⁷We continued our voyage from Tyre and landed at Ptolemais, where we greeted the

---

ᵃ 28 Many manuscripts *of the Lord*   ᵇ 28 Or *with the blood of his own Son.*

brothers and sisters and stayed with them for a day. ⁸Leaving the next day, we reached Caesarea and stayed at the house of Philip the evangelist, one of the Seven. ⁹He had four unmarried daughters who prophesied.

¹⁰After we had been there a number of days, a prophet named Agabus came down from Judea. ¹¹Coming over to us, he took Paul's belt, tied his own hands and feet with it and said, "The Holy Spirit says, 'In this way the Jewish leaders in Jerusalem will bind the owner of this belt and will hand him over to the Gentiles.'"

¹²When we heard this, we and the people there pleaded with Paul not to go up to Jerusalem. ¹³Then Paul answered, "Why are you weeping and breaking my heart? I am ready not only to be bound, but also to die in Jerusalem for the name of the Lord Jesus." ¹⁴When he would not be dissuaded, we gave up and said, "The Lord's will be done."

¹⁵After this, we started on our way up to Jerusalem. ¹⁶Some of the disciples from Caesarea accompanied us and brought us to the home of Mnason, where we were to stay. He was a man from Cyprus and one of the early disciples.

Paul's Arrival at Jerusalem

¹⁷When we arrived at Jerusalem, the brothers and sisters received us warmly. ¹⁸The next day Paul and the rest of us went to see James, and all the elders were present. ¹⁹Paul greeted them and reported in detail what God had done among the Gentiles through his ministry.

²⁰When they heard this, they praised God. Then they said to Paul: "You see, brother, how many thousands of Jews have believed, and all of them are zealous for the law. ²¹They have been informed that you teach all the Jews who live among the Gentiles to turn away from Moses, telling them not to circumcise their children or live according to our customs. ²²What shall we do? They will certainly hear that you have come, ²³so do what we tell you. There are four men with us who have made a vow. ²⁴Take these men, join in their purification rites and pay their expenses, so that they can have their heads shaved. Then everyone will know there is no truth in these reports about you, but that you yourself are living in obedience to the law. ²⁵As for the Gentile believers, we have written to them our decision that they should abstain from food sacrificed to idols, from blood, from the meat of strangled animals and from sexual immorality."

²⁶The next day Paul took the men and purified himself along with them. Then he went to the temple to give notice of the date when the days of purification would end and the offering would be made for each of them.

Paul Arrested

²⁷When the seven days were nearly over, some Jews from the province of Asia saw Paul at the temple. They stirred up the whole crowd and seized him, ²⁸shouting, "Fellow Israelites, help us! This is the man who teaches everyone everywhere against our people and our law and this place. And besides, he has brought Greeks into the temple and defiled this holy place." ²⁹(They had previously seen Trophimus the Ephesian in the city with Paul and assumed that Paul had brought him into the temple.)

³⁰The whole city was aroused, and the people came running from all directions. Seizing Paul, they dragged him from the temple, and immediately the gates were shut. ³¹While they were trying to kill him, news reached the commander of the Roman troops that the whole city of Jerusalem was in an uproar. ³²He at once took some officers and soldiers and ran down to the crowd. When the rioters saw the commander and his soldiers, they stopped beating Paul.

³³The commander came up and arrested him and ordered him to be bound with two chains. Then he asked who he was and what he had done. ³⁴Some in the crowd shouted one thing and some another, and since the commander could not get at the truth because of the uproar, he ordered that Paul be taken into the barracks. ³⁵When Paul reached the steps, the violence of the mob was so great he had to be carried by the soldiers. ³⁶The crowd that followed kept shouting, "Get rid of him!"

Paul Speaks to the Crowd

³⁷As the soldiers were about to take Paul into the barracks, he asked the commander, "May I say something to you?"

"Do you speak Greek?" he replied. ³⁸"Aren't you the Egyptian who started a revolt and led four thousand terrorists out into the wilderness some time ago?"

³⁹Paul answered, "I am a Jew, from Tarsus in Cilicia, a citizen of no ordinary city. Please let me speak to the people."

⁴⁰After receiving the commander's permission, Paul stood on the steps and motioned to the crowd. When they were all silent, he said to them in Aramaic:ᵃ: ¹"Brothers and fathers, listen now to my defense."

22 ²When they heard him speak to them in Aramaic, they became very quiet.

Then Paul said: ³"I am a Jew, born in Tarsus of Cilicia, but brought up in this city. I studied under Gamaliel and was thoroughly trained in the law of our ancestors. I was just as zealous for God as any of you are today. ⁴I persecuted the followers of this Way to their death, arresting both men and women and throwing them into prison, ⁵as the high priest and all the Council can themselves testify. I even obtained letters from them to their associates in Damascus, and went there to bring these people as prisoners to Jerusalem to be punished.

⁶"About noon as I came near Damascus, suddenly a bright light from heaven flashed around me. ⁷I fell to the ground and heard

ᵃ 40 Or possibly *Hebrew*; also in 22:2

a voice say to me, 'Saul! Saul! Why do you persecute me?'

⁸"'Who are you, Lord?' I asked.

"'I am Jesus of Nazareth, whom you are persecuting,' he replied. ⁹My companions saw the light, but they did not understand the voice of him who was speaking to me.

¹⁰"'What shall I do, Lord?' I asked.

"'Get up,' the Lord said, 'and go into Damascus. There you will be told all that you have been assigned to do.' ¹¹My companions led me by the hand into Damascus, because the brilliance of the light had blinded me.

¹²"A man named Ananias came to see me. He was a devout observer of the law and highly respected by all the Jews living there. ¹³He stood beside me and said, 'Brother Saul, receive your sight!' And at that very moment I was able to see him.

¹⁴"Then he said: 'The God of our ancestors has chosen you to know his will and to see the Righteous One and to hear words from his mouth. ¹⁵You will be his witness to all people of what you have seen and heard. ¹⁶And now what are you waiting for? Get up, be baptized and wash your sins away, calling on his name.'

¹⁷"When I returned to Jerusalem and was praying at the temple, I fell into a trance ¹⁸and saw the Lord speaking to me. 'Quick!' he said. 'Leave Jerusalem immediately, because the people here will not accept your testimony about me.'

¹⁹"'Lord,' I replied, 'these people know that I went from one synagogue to another to imprison and beat those who believe in you. ²⁰And when the blood of your martyr^a Stephen was shed, I stood there giving my approval and guarding the clothes of those who were killing him.'

²¹"Then the Lord said to me, 'Go; I will send you far away to the Gentiles.' "

Paul the Roman Citizen

²²The crowd listened to Paul until he said this. Then they raised their voices and shouted, "Rid the earth of him! He's not fit to live!"

²³As they were shouting and throwing off their cloaks and flinging dust into the air, ²⁴the commander ordered that Paul be taken into the barracks. He directed that he be flogged and interrogated in order to find out why the people were shouting at him like this. ²⁵As they stretched him out to flog him, Paul said to the centurion standing there, "Is it legal for you to flog a Roman citizen who hasn't even been found guilty?"

²⁶When the centurion heard this, he went to the commander and reported it. "What are you going to do?" he asked. "This man is a Roman citizen."

²⁷The commander went to Paul and asked, "Tell me, are you a Roman citizen?"

"Yes, I am," he answered.

²⁸Then the commander said, "I had to pay a lot of money for my citizenship."

"But I was born a citizen," Paul replied.

²⁹Those who were about to interrogate him withdrew immediately. The commander himself was alarmed when he realized that he had put Paul, a Roman citizen, in chains.

Paul Before the Sanhedrin

³⁰The commander wanted to find out exactly why Paul was being accused by the Jews. So the next day he released him and ordered the chief priests and all the members of the Sanhedrin to assemble. Then he brought Paul and had him stand before them.

23 Paul looked straight at the Sanhedrin and said, "My brothers, I have fulfilled my duty to God in all good conscience to this day." ²At this the high priest Ananias ordered those standing near Paul to strike him on the mouth. ³Then Paul said to him, "God will strike you, you whitewashed wall! You sit there to judge me according to the law, yet you yourself violate the law by commanding that I be struck!"

⁴Those who were standing near Paul said, "How dare you insult God's high priest!"

⁵Paul replied, "Brothers, I did not realize that he was the high priest; for it is written: 'Do not speak evil about the ruler of your people.'^b"

⁶Then Paul, knowing that some of them were Sadducees and the others Pharisees, called out in the Sanhedrin, "My brothers, I am a Pharisee, descended from Pharisees. I stand on trial because of the hope of the resurrection of the dead." ⁷When he said this, a dispute broke out between the Pharisees and the Sadducees, and the assembly was divided. ⁸(The Sadducees say that there is no resurrection, and that there are neither angels nor spirits, but the Pharisees believe all these things.)

⁹There was a great uproar, and some of the teachers of the law who were Pharisees stood up and argued vigorously. "We find nothing wrong with this man," they said. "What if a spirit or an angel has spoken to him?" ¹⁰The dispute became so violent that the commander was afraid Paul would be torn to pieces by them. He ordered the troops to go down and take him away from them by force and bring him into the barracks.

¹¹The following night the Lord stood near Paul and said, "Take courage! As you have testified about me in Jerusalem, so you must also testify in Rome."

The Plot to Kill Paul

¹²The next morning some Jews formed a conspiracy and bound themselves with an oath not to eat or drink until they had killed Paul. ¹³More than forty men were involved in this plot. ¹⁴They went to the chief priests and the elders and said, "We have taken a solemn oath not to eat anything until we have killed Paul. ¹⁵Now then, you and the Sanhedrin petition the commander to bring him before you on the pretext of wanting more accurate in-

---

^a 20 Or witness   ^b 5 Exodus 22:28

formation about his case. We are ready to kill him before he gets here."

[16]But when the son of Paul's sister heard of this plot, he went into the barracks and told Paul.

[17]Then Paul called one of the centurions and said, "Take this young man to the commander; he has something to tell him." [18]So he took him to the commander.

The centurion said, "Paul, the prisoner, sent for me and asked me to bring this young man to you because he has something to tell you."

[19]The commander took the young man by the hand, drew him aside and asked, "What is it you want to tell me?"

[20]He said: "Some Jews have agreed to ask you to bring Paul before the Sanhedrin tomorrow on the pretext of wanting more accurate information about him. [21]Don't give in to them, because more than forty of them are waiting in ambush for him. They have taken an oath not to eat or drink until they have killed him. They are ready now, waiting for your consent to their request."

[22]The commander dismissed the young man with this warning: "Don't tell anyone that you have reported this to me."

Paul Transferred to Caesarea

[23]Then he called two of his centurions and ordered them, "Get ready a detachment of two hundred soldiers, seventy horsemen and two hundred spearmen[a] to go to Caesarea at nine tonight. [24]Provide horses for Paul so that he may be taken safely to Governor Felix."

[25]He wrote a letter as follows:

[26]Claudius Lysias,

To His Excellency, Governor Felix:

Greetings.

[27]This man was seized by the Jews and they were about to kill him, but I came with my troops and rescued him, for I had learned that he is a Roman citizen. [28]I wanted to know why they were accusing him, so I brought him to their Sanhedrin. [29]I found that the accusation had to do with questions about their law, but there was no charge against him that deserved death or imprisonment. [30]When I was informed of a plot to be carried out against the man, I sent him to you at once. I also ordered his accusers to present to you their case against him.

[31]So the soldiers, carrying out their orders, took Paul with them during the night and brought him as far as Antipatris. [32]The next day they let the cavalry go on with him, while they returned to the barracks. [33]When the cavalry arrived in Caesarea, they delivered the letter to the governor and handed Paul over to him. [34]The governor read the letter and asked

what province he was from. Learning that he was from Cilicia, [35]he said, "I will hear your case when your accusers get here." Then he ordered that Paul be kept under guard in Herod's palace.

Paul's Trial Before Felix

24 Five days later the high priest Ananias went down to Caesarea with some of the elders and a lawyer named Tertullus, and they brought their charges against Paul before the governor. [2]When Paul was called in, Tertullus presented his case before Felix: "We have enjoyed a long period of peace under you, and your foresight has brought about reforms in this nation. [3]Everywhere and in every way, most excellent Felix, we acknowledge this with profound gratitude. [4]But in order not to weary you further, I would request that you be kind enough to hear us briefly.

[5]"We have found this man to be a troublemaker, stirring up riots among the Jews all over the world. He is a ringleader of the Nazarene sect [6]and even tried to desecrate the temple; so we seized him. [7][b] [8]By examining him yourself you will be able to learn the truth about all these charges we are bringing against him."

[9]The other Jews joined in the accusation, asserting that these things were true.

[10]When the governor motioned for him to speak, Paul replied: "I know that for a number of years you have been a judge over this nation; so I gladly make my defense. [11]You can easily verify that no more than twelve days ago I went up to Jerusalem to worship. [12]My accusers did not find me arguing with anyone at the temple, or stirring up a crowd in the synagogues or anywhere else in the city. [13]And they cannot prove to you the charges they are now making against me. [14]However, I admit that I worship the God of our ancestors as a follower of the Way, which they call a sect. I believe everything that is in accordance with the Law and that is written in the Prophets, [15]and I have the same hope in God as these men themselves have, that there will be a resurrection of both the righteous and the wicked. [16]So I strive always to keep my conscience clear before God and man.

[17]"After an absence of several years, I came to Jerusalem to bring my people gifts for the poor and to present offerings. [18]I was ceremonially clean when they found me in the temple courts doing this. There was no crowd with me, nor was I involved in any disturbance. [19]But there are some Jews from the province of Asia, who ought to be here before you and bring charges if they have anything against me. [20]Or these who are here should state what crime they found in me when I stood before the Sanhedrin— [21]unless it was this one thing I shouted as I stood in their presence: 'It is concerning the resurrection of the dead that I am on trial before you today.'"

---

[a] 23 The meaning of the Greek for this word is uncertain.   [b] 6-8 Some manuscripts include here *him, and we would have judged him in accordance with our law.* [7]*But the commander Lysias came and took him from us with much violence,* [8]*ordering his accusers to come before you.*

²²Then Felix, who was well acquainted with the Way, adjourned the proceedings. "When Lysias the commander comes," he said, "I will decide your case." ²³He ordered the centurion to keep Paul under guard but to give him some freedom and permit his friends to take care of his needs.

²⁴Several days later Felix came with his wife Drusilla, who was Jewish. He sent for Paul and listened to him as he spoke about faith in Christ Jesus. ²⁵As Paul talked about righteousness, self-control and the judgment to come, Felix was afraid and said, "That's enough for now! You may leave. When I find it convenient, I will send for you." ²⁶At the same time he was hoping that Paul would offer him a bribe, so he sent for him frequently and talked with him.

²⁷When two years had passed, Felix was succeeded by Porcius Festus, but because Felix wanted to grant a favor to the Jews, he left Paul in prison.

Paul's Trial Before Festus

25 Three days after arriving in the province, Festus went up from Caesarea to Jerusalem, ²where the chief priests and the Jewish leaders appeared before him and presented the charges against Paul. ³They requested Festus, as a favor to them, to have Paul transferred to Jerusalem, for they were preparing an ambush to kill him along the way. ⁴Festus answered, "Paul is being held at Caesarea, and I myself am going there soon. ⁵Let some of your leaders come with me, and if the man has done anything wrong, they can press charges against him there."

⁶After spending eight or ten days with them, Festus went down to Caesarea. The next day he convened the court and ordered that Paul be brought before him. ⁷When Paul came in, the Jews who had come down from Jerusalem stood around him. They brought many serious charges against him, but they could not prove them.

⁸Then Paul made his defense: "I have done nothing wrong against the Jewish law or against the temple or against Caesar."

⁹Festus, wishing to do the Jews a favor, said to Paul, "Are you willing to go up to Jerusalem and stand trial before me there on these charges?"

¹⁰Paul answered: "I am now standing before Caesar's court, where I ought to be tried. I have not done any wrong to the Jews, as you yourself know very well. ¹¹If, however, I am guilty of doing anything deserving death, I do not refuse to die. But if the charges brought against me by these Jews are not true, no one has the right to hand me over to them. I appeal to Caesar!"

¹²After Festus had conferred with his council, he declared: "You have appealed to Caesar. To Caesar you will go!"

Festus Consults King Agrippa

¹³A few days later King Agrippa and Bernice arrived at Caesarea to pay their respects to Festus. ¹⁴Since they were spending many days there, Festus discussed Paul's case with the king. He said: "There is a man here whom Felix left as a prisoner. ¹⁵When I went to Jerusalem, the chief priests and the elders of the Jews brought charges against him and asked that he be condemned.

¹⁶"I told them that it is not the Roman custom to hand over anyone before they have faced their accusers and have had an opportunity to defend themselves against the charges. ¹⁷When they came here with me, I did not delay the case, but convened the court the next day and ordered the man to be brought in. ¹⁸When his accusers got up to speak, they did not charge him with any of the crimes I had expected. ¹⁹Instead, they had some points of dispute with him about their own religion and about a dead man named Jesus who Paul claimed was alive. ²⁰I was at a loss how to investigate such matters; so I asked if he would be willing to go to Jerusalem and stand trial there on these charges. ²¹But when Paul made his appeal to be held over for the Emperor's decision, I ordered him held until I could send him to Caesar."

²²Then Agrippa said to Festus, "I would like to hear this man myself."

He replied, "Tomorrow you will hear him."

Paul Before Agrippa

²³The next day Agrippa and Bernice came with great pomp and entered the audience room with the high-ranking military officers and the prominent men of the city. At the command of Festus, Paul was brought in. ²⁴Festus said: "King Agrippa, and all who are present with us, you see this man! The whole Jewish community has petitioned me about him in Jerusalem and here in Caesarea, shouting that he ought not to live any longer. ²⁵I found he had done nothing deserving of death, but because he made his appeal to the Emperor I decided to send him to Rome. ²⁶But I have nothing definite to write to His Majesty about him. Therefore I have brought him before all of you, and especially before you, King Agrippa, so that as a result of this investigation I may have something to write. ²⁷For I think it is unreasonable to send a prisoner on to Rome without specifying the charges against him."

26 Then Agrippa said to Paul, "You have permission to speak for yourself."

So Paul motioned with his hand and began his defense: ²"King Agrippa, I consider myself fortunate to stand before you today as I make my defense against all the accusations of the Jews, ³and especially so because you are well acquainted with all the Jewish customs and controversies. Therefore, I beg you to listen to me patiently.

⁴"The Jewish people all know the way I have lived ever since I was a child, from the beginning of my life in my own country, and also in Jerusalem. ⁵They have known me for a long time and can testify, if they are willing, that I conformed to the strictest sect of our religion, living as a Pharisee. ⁶And now it is because

of my hope in what God has promised our ancestors that I am on trial today. ⁷This is the promise our twelve tribes are hoping to see fulfilled as they earnestly serve God day and night. King Agrippa, it is because of this hope that these Jews are accusing me. ⁸Why should any of you consider it incredible that God raises the dead?

⁹"I too was convinced that I ought to do all that was possible to oppose the name of Jesus of Nazareth. ¹⁰And that is just what I did in Jerusalem. On the authority of the chief priests I put many of the Lord's people in prison, and when they were put to death, I cast my vote against them. ¹¹Many a time I went from one synagogue to another to have them punished, and I tried to force them to blaspheme. I was so obsessed with persecuting them that I even hunted them down in foreign cities.

¹²"On one of these journeys I was going to Damascus with the authority and commission of the chief priests. ¹³About noon, King Agrippa, as I was on the road, I saw a light from heaven, brighter than the sun, blazing around me and my companions. ¹⁴We all fell to the ground, and I heard a voice saying to me in Aramaic,ᵃ 'Saul, Saul, why do you persecute me? It is hard for you to kick against the goads.'

¹⁵"Then I asked, 'Who are you, Lord?'

" 'I am Jesus, whom you are persecuting,' the Lord replied. ¹⁶'Now get up and stand on your feet. I have appeared to you to appoint you as a servant and as a witness of what you have seen and will see of me. ¹⁷I will rescue you from your own people and from the Gentiles. I am sending you to them ¹⁸to open their eyes and turn them from darkness to light, and from the power of Satan to God, so that they may receive forgiveness of sins and a place among those who are sanctified by faith in me.'

¹⁹"So then, King Agrippa, I was not disobedient to the vision from heaven. ²⁰First to those in Damascus, then to those in Jerusalem and in all Judea, and then to the Gentiles, I preached that they should repent and turn to God and demonstrate their repentance by their deeds. ²¹That is why some Jews seized me in the temple courts and tried to kill me. ²²But God has helped me to this very day; so I stand here and testify to small and great alike. I am saying nothing beyond what the prophets and Moses said would happen— ²³that the Messiah would suffer and, as the first to rise from the dead, would bring the message of light to his own people and to the Gentiles."

²⁴At this point Festus interrupted Paul's defense. "You are out of your mind, Paul!" he shouted. "Your great learning is driving you insane."

²⁵"I am not insane, most excellent Festus," Paul replied. "What I am saying is true and reasonable. ²⁶The king is familiar with these things, and I can speak freely to him. I am convinced that none of this has escaped his notice, because it was not done in a corner.

²⁷King Agrippa, do you believe the prophets? I know you do."

²⁸Then Agrippa said to Paul, "Do you think that in such a short time you can persuade me to be a Christian?"

²⁹Paul replied, "Short time or long—I pray to God that not only you but all who are listening to me today may become what I am, except for these chains."

³⁰The king rose, and with him the governor and Bernice and those sitting with them. ³¹After they left the room, they began saying to one another, "This man is not doing anything that deserves death or imprisonment."

³²Agrippa said to Festus, "This man could have been set free if he had not appealed to Caesar."

Paul Sails for Rome

27 When it was decided that we would sail for Italy, Paul and some other prisoners were handed over to a centurion named Julius, who belonged to the Imperial Regiment. ²We boarded a ship from Adramyttium about to sail for ports along the coast of the province of Asia, and we put out to sea. Aristarchus, a Macedonian from Thessalonica, was with us.

³The next day we landed at Sidon; and Julius, in kindness to Paul, allowed him to go to his friends so they might provide for his needs. ⁴From there we put out to sea again and passed to the lee of Cyprus because the winds were against us. ⁵When we had sailed across the open sea off the coast of Cilicia and Pamphylia, we landed at Myra in Lycia. ⁶There the centurion found an Alexandrian ship sailing for Italy and put us on board. ⁷We made slow headway for many days and had difficulty arriving off Cnidus. When the wind did not allow us to hold our course, we sailed to the lee of Crete, opposite Salmone. ⁸We moved along the coast with difficulty and came to a place called Fair Havens, near the town of Lasea.

⁹Much time had been lost, and sailing had already become dangerous because by now it was after the Day of Atonement.ᵇ So Paul warned them, ¹⁰"Men, I can see that our voyage is going to be disastrous and bring great loss to ship and cargo, and to our own lives also." ¹¹But the centurion, instead of listening to what Paul said, followed the advice of the pilot and of the owner of the ship. ¹²Since the harbor was unsuitable to winter in, the majority decided that we should sail on, hoping to reach Phoenix and winter there. This was a harbor in Crete, facing both southwest and northwest.

The Storm

¹³When a gentle south wind began to blow, they saw their opportunity; so they weighed anchor and sailed along the shore of Crete. ¹⁴Before very long, a wind of hurricane force, called the Northeaster, swept down from the

ᵃ 14 Or Hebrew   ᵇ 9 That is, Yom Kippur

island. [15]The ship was caught by the storm and could not head into the wind; so we gave way to it and were driven along. [16]As we passed to the lee of a small island called Cauda, we were hardly able to make the lifeboat secure, [17]so the men hoisted it aboard. Then they passed ropes under the ship itself to hold it together. Because they were afraid they would run aground on the sandbars of Syrtis, they lowered the sea anchor[a] and let the ship be driven along. [18]We took such a violent battering from the storm that the next day they began to throw the cargo overboard. [19]On the third day, they threw the ship's tackle overboard with their own hands. [20]When neither sun nor stars appeared for many days and the storm continued raging, we finally gave up all hope of being saved.

[21]After they had gone a long time without food, Paul stood up before them and said: "Men, you should have taken my advice not to sail from Crete; then you would have spared yourselves this damage and loss. [22]But now I urge you to keep up your courage, because not one of you will be lost; only the ship will be destroyed. [23]Last night an angel of the God to whom I belong and whom I serve stood beside me [24]and said, 'Do not be afraid, Paul. You must stand trial before Caesar; and God has graciously given you the lives of all who sail with you.' [25]So keep up your courage, men, for I have faith in God that it will happen just as he told me. [26]Nevertheless, we must run aground on some island."

The Shipwreck

[27]On the fourteenth night we were still being driven across the Adriatic[b] Sea, when about midnight the sailors sensed they were approaching land. [28]They took soundings and found that the water was a hundred and twenty feet[c] deep. A short time later they took soundings again and found it was ninety feet[d] deep. [29]Fearing that we would be dashed against the rocks, they dropped four anchors from the stern and prayed for daylight. [30]In an attempt to escape from the ship, the sailors let the lifeboat down into the sea, pretending they were going to lower some anchors from the bow. [31]Then Paul said to the centurion and the soldiers, "Unless these men stay with the ship, you cannot be saved." [32]So the soldiers cut the ropes that held the lifeboat and let it drift away.

[33]Just before dawn Paul urged them all to eat. "For the last fourteen days," he said, "you have been in constant suspense and have gone without food—you haven't eaten anything. [34]Now I urge you to take some food. You need it to survive. Not one of you will lose a single hair from his head." [35]After he said this, he took some bread and gave thanks to God in front of them all. Then he broke it and began to eat. [36]They were all encouraged and ate some food themselves. [37]Altogether there were 276 of us on board. [38]When they had eaten as much as they wanted, they lightened the ship by throwing the grain into the sea.

[39]When daylight came, they did not recognize the land, but they saw a bay with a sandy beach, where they decided to run the ship aground if they could. [40]Cutting loose the anchors, they left them in the sea and at the same time untied the ropes that held the rudders. Then they hoisted the foresail to the wind and made for the beach. [41]But the ship struck a sandbar and ran aground. The bow stuck fast and would not move, and the stern was broken to pieces by the pounding of the surf.

[42]The soldiers planned to kill the prisoners to prevent any of them from swimming away and escaping. [43]But the centurion wanted to spare Paul's life and kept them from carrying out their plan. He ordered those who could swim to jump overboard first and get to land. [44]The rest were to get there on planks or on other pieces of the ship. In this way everyone reached land safely.

Paul Ashore on Malta

28 Once safely on shore, we found out that the island was called Malta. [2]The islanders showed us unusual kindness. They built a fire and welcomed us all because it was raining and cold. [3]Paul gathered a pile of brushwood and, as he put it on the fire, a viper, driven out by the heat, fastened itself on his hand. [4]When the islanders saw the snake hanging from his hand, they said to each other, "This man must be a murderer; for though he escaped from the sea, the goddess Justice has not allowed him to live." [5]But Paul shook the snake off into the fire and suffered no ill effects. [6]The people expected him to swell up or suddenly fall dead; but after waiting a long time and seeing nothing unusual happen to him, they changed their minds and said he was a god.

[7]There was an estate nearby that belonged to Publius, the chief official of the island. He welcomed us to his home and showed us generous hospitality for three days. [8]His father was sick in bed, suffering from fever and dysentery. Paul went in to see him and, after prayer, placed his hands on him and healed him. [9]When this had happened, the rest of the sick on the island came and were cured. [10]They honored us in many ways; and when we were ready to sail, they furnished us with the supplies we needed.

Paul's Arrival at Rome

[11]After three months we put out to sea in a ship that had wintered in the island—it was an Alexandrian ship with the figurehead of the twin gods Castor and Pollux. [12]We put in at Syracuse and stayed there three days. [13]From there we set sail and arrived at Rhegium. The next day the south wind came up, and on the following day we reached Puteoli. [14]There we found some brothers and sisters who invited

---

a 17 Or *the sails*   *b* 27 In ancient times the name referred to an area extending well south of Italy.
c 28 Or about 37 meters   *d* 28 Or about 27 meters

us to spend a week with them. And so we came to Rome. [15]The brothers and sisters there had heard that we were coming, and they traveled as far as the Forum of Appius and the Three Taverns to meet us. At the sight of these people Paul thanked God and was encouraged. [16]When we got to Rome, Paul was allowed to live by himself, with a soldier to guard him.

Paul Preaches at Rome Under Guard

[17]Three days later he called together the local Jewish leaders. When they had assembled, Paul said to them: "My brothers, although I have done nothing against our people or against the customs of our ancestors, I was arrested in Jerusalem and handed over to the Romans. [18]They examined me and wanted to release me, because I was not guilty of any crime deserving death. [19]The Jews objected, so I was compelled to make an appeal to Caesar. I certainly did not intend to bring any charge against my own people. [20]For this reason I have asked to see you and talk with you. It is because of the hope of Israel that I am bound with this chain."

[21]They replied, "We have not received any letters from Judea concerning you, and none of our people who have come from there has reported or said anything bad about you. [22]But we want to hear what your views are, for we know that people everywhere are talking against this sect."

[23]They arranged to meet Paul on a certain day, and came in even larger numbers to the place where he was staying. He witnessed to them from morning till evening, explaining about the kingdom of God, and from the Law of Moses and from the Prophets he tried to persuade them about Jesus. [24]Some were convinced by what he said, but others would not believe. [25]They disagreed among themselves and began to leave after Paul had made this final statement: "The Holy Spirit spoke the truth to your ancestors when he said through Isaiah the prophet:

[26]" 'Go to this people and say,
"You will be ever hearing but never
   understanding;
   you will be ever seeing but never
      perceiving."
[27]For this people's heart has become
   calloused;
   they hardly hear with their ears,
   and they have closed their eyes.
Otherwise they might see with their eyes,
   hear with their ears,
   understand with their hearts
and turn, and I would heal them.'[a]

[28]"Therefore I want you to know that God's salvation has been sent to the Gentiles, and they will listen!" [29][b]

[30]For two whole years Paul stayed there in his own rented house and welcomed all who came to see him. [31]He proclaimed the kingdom of God and taught about the Lord Jesus Christ—with all boldness and without hindrance!

Romans

1

Paul, a servant of Christ Jesus, called to be an apostle and set apart for the gospel of God— [2]the gospel he promised beforehand through his prophets in the Holy Scriptures [3]regarding his Son, who as to his earthly life[c] was a descendant of David, [4]and who through the Spirit of holiness was appointed the Son of God in power[d] by his resurrection from the dead: Jesus Christ our Lord. [5]Through him we received grace and apostleship to call all the Gentiles to the obedience that comes from[e] faith for his name's sake. [6]And you also are among those Gentiles who are called to belong to Jesus Christ.

[7]To all in Rome who are loved by God and called to be his holy people:

Grace and peace to you from God our Father and from the Lord Jesus Christ.

Paul's Longing to Visit Rome

[8]First, I thank my God through Jesus Christ for all of you, because your faith is being reported all over the world. [9]God, whom I serve in my spirit in preaching the gospel of his Son, is my witness how constantly I remember you [10]in my prayers at all times; and I pray that now at last by God's will the way may be opened for me to come to you.

[11]I long to see you so that I may impart to you some spiritual gift to make you strong— [12]that is, that you and I may be mutually encouraged by each other's faith. [13]I do not want you to be unaware, brothers and sisters,[f] that I planned many times to come to you (but have been prevented from doing so until now) in order that I might have a harvest among you, just as I have had among the other Gentiles.

---

[a] 27 Isaiah 6:9,10 (see Septuagint)   [b] 29 Some manuscripts include here *After he said this, the Jews left, arguing vigorously among themselves.*   [c] 3 Or *who according to the flesh*   [d] 4 Or *was declared with power to be the Son of God*   [e] 5 Or *that is*   [f] 13 The Greek word for *brothers and sisters (adelphoi)* refers here to believers, both men and women, as part of God's family; also in 7:1, 4; 8:12, 29; 10:1; 11:25; 12:1; 15:14, 30; 16:14, 17.

¹⁴I am obligated both to Greeks and non-Greeks, both to the wise and the foolish. ¹⁵That is why I am so eager to preach the gospel also to you who are in Rome.

¹⁶For I am not ashamed of the gospel, because it is the power of God that brings salvation to everyone who believes: first to the Jew, then to the Gentile. ¹⁷For in the gospel the righteousness of God is revealed—a righteousness that is by faith from first to last,[a] just as it is written: "The righteous will live by faith."[b]

God's Wrath Against Sinful Humanity

¹⁸The wrath of God is being revealed from heaven against all the godlessness and wickedness of people, who suppress the truth by their wickedness, ¹⁹since what may be known about God is plain to them, because God has made it plain to them. ²⁰For since the creation of the world God's invisible qualities—his eternal power and divine nature—have been clearly seen, being understood from what has been made, so that people are without excuse.

²¹For although they knew God, they neither glorified him as God nor gave thanks to him, but their thinking became futile and their foolish hearts were darkened. ²²Although they claimed to be wise, they became fools ²³and exchanged the glory of the immortal God for images made to look like a mortal human being and birds and animals and reptiles.

²⁴Therefore God gave them over in the sinful desires of their hearts to sexual impurity for the degrading of their bodies with one another. ²⁵They exchanged the truth about God for a lie, and worshiped and served created things rather than the Creator—who is forever praised. Amen.

²⁶Because of this, God gave them over to shameful lusts. Even their women exchanged natural sexual relations for unnatural ones. ²⁷In the same way the men also abandoned natural relations with women and were inflamed with lust for one another. Men committed shameful acts with other men, and received in themselves the due penalty for their error.

²⁸Furthermore, just as they did not think it worthwhile to retain the knowledge of God, so God gave them over to a depraved mind, so that they do what ought not to be done. ²⁹They have become filled with every kind of wickedness, evil, greed and depravity. They are full of envy, murder, strife, deceit and malice. They are gossips, ³⁰slanderers, God-haters, insolent, arrogant and boastful; they invent ways of doing evil; they disobey their parents; ³¹they have no understanding, no fidelity, no love, no mercy. ³²Although they know God's righteous decree that those who do such things deserve death, they not only continue to do these very things but also approve of those who practice them.

God's Righteous Judgment

2 You, therefore, have no excuse, you who pass judgment on someone else, for at whatever point you judge another, you are condemning yourself, because you who pass judgment do the same things. ²Now we know that God's judgment against those who do such things is based on truth. ³So when you, a mere human being, pass judgment on them and yet do the same things, do you think you will escape God's judgment? ⁴Or do you show contempt for the riches of his kindness, forbearance and patience, not realizing that God's kindness is intended to lead you to repentance?

⁵But because of your stubbornness and your unrepentant heart, you are storing up wrath against yourself for the day of God's wrath, when his righteous judgment will be revealed. ⁶God "will repay each person according to what they have done."[c] ⁷To those who by persistence in doing good seek glory, honor and immortality, he will give eternal life. ⁸But for those who are self-seeking and who reject the truth and follow evil, there will be wrath and anger. ⁹There will be trouble and distress for every human being who does evil: first for the Jew, then for the Gentile; ¹⁰but glory, honor and peace for everyone who does good: first for the Jew, then for the Gentile. ¹¹For God does not show favoritism.

¹²All who sin apart from the law will also perish apart from the law, and all who sin under the law will be judged by the law. ¹³For it is not those who hear the law who are righteous in God's sight, but it is those who obey the law who will be declared righteous. ¹⁴(Indeed, when Gentiles, who do not have the law, do by nature things required by the law, they are a law for themselves, even though they do not have the law. ¹⁵They show that the requirements of the law are written on their hearts, their consciences also bearing witness, and their thoughts sometimes accusing them and at other times even defending them.) ¹⁶This will take place on the day when God judges people's secrets through Jesus Christ, as my gospel declares.

The Jews and the Law

¹⁷Now you, if you call yourself a Jew; if you rely on the law and boast in God; ¹⁸if you know his will and approve of what is superior because you are instructed by the law; ¹⁹if you are convinced that you are a guide for the blind, a light for those who are in the dark, ²⁰an instructor of the foolish, a teacher of little children, because you have in the law the embodiment of knowledge and truth— ²¹you, then, who teach others, do you not teach yourself? You who preach against stealing, do you steal? ²²You who say that people should not commit adultery, do you commit adultery? You who abhor idols, do you rob temples? ²³You who boast in the law, do you dishonor God by breaking the law? ²⁴As it is written:

---

[a] 17 Or *is from faith to faith*   [b] 17 Hab. 2:4   [c] 6 Psalm 62:12; Prov. 24:12

"God's name is blasphemed among the Gentiles because of you."[a] [25]Circumcision has value if you observe the law, but if you break the law, you have become as though you had not been circumcised. [26]So then, if those who are not circumcised keep the law's requirements, will they not be regarded as though they were circumcised? [27]The one who is not circumcised physically and yet obeys the law will condemn you who, even though you have the[b] written code and circumcision, are a lawbreaker.

[28]A person is not a Jew who is one only outwardly, nor is circumcision merely outward and physical. [29]No, a person is a Jew who is one inwardly; and circumcision is circumcision of the heart, by the Spirit, not by the written code. Such a person's praise is not from other people, but from God.

God's Faithfulness

3 What advantage, then, is there in being a Jew, or what value is there in circumcision? [2]Much in every way! First of all, the Jews have been entrusted with the very words of God.

[3]What if some were unfaithful? Will their unfaithfulness nullify God's faithfulness? [4]Not at all! Let God be true, and every human being a liar. As it is written:

"So that you may be proved right when
    you speak
and prevail when you judge."[c]

[5]But if our unrighteousness brings out God's righteousness more clearly, what shall we say? That God is unjust in bringing his wrath on us? (I am using a human argument.) [6]Certainly not! If that were so, how could God judge the world? [7]Someone might argue, "If my falsehood enhances God's truthfulness and so increases his glory, why am I still condemned as a sinner?" [8]Why not say—as some slanderously claim that we say—"Let us do evil that good may result"? Their condemnation is just!

No One Is Righteous

[9]What shall we conclude then? Do we have any advantage? Not at all! For we have already made the charge that Jews and Gentiles alike are all under the power of sin. [10]As it is written:

"There is no one righteous, not even one;
[11]   there is no one who understands;
    there is no one who seeks God.
[12]All have turned away,
    they have together become worthless;
there is no one who does good,
    not even one."[d]
[13]"Their throats are open graves;
    their tongues practice deceit."[e]

"The poison of vipers is on their lips."[f]
[14]   "Their mouths are full of cursing and
        bitterness."[g]
[15]"Their feet are swift to shed blood;
[16]   ruin and misery mark their ways,
[17]and the way of peace they do not know."[h]
[18]   "There is no fear of God before their
        eyes."[i]

[19]Now we know that whatever the law says, it says to those who are under the law, so that every mouth may be silenced and the whole world held accountable to God. [20]Therefore no one will be declared righteous in God's sight by the works of the law; rather, through the law we become conscious of our sin.

Righteousness Through Faith

[21]But now apart from the law the righteousness of God has been made known, to which the Law and the Prophets testify. [22]This righteousness is given through faith in[j] Jesus Christ to all who believe. There is no difference between Jew and Gentile, [23]for all have sinned and fall short of the glory of God, [24]and all are justified freely by his grace through the redemption that came by Christ Jesus. [25]God presented Christ as a sacrifice of atonement,[k] through the shedding of his blood—to be received by faith. He did this to demonstrate his righteousness, because in his forbearance he had left the sins committed beforehand unpunished— [26]he did it to demonstrate his righteousness at the present time, so as to be just and the one who justifies those who have faith in Jesus.

[27]Where, then, is boasting? It is excluded. Because of what law? The law that requires works? No, because of the law that requires faith. [28]For we maintain that a person is justified by faith apart from the works of the law. [29]Or is God the God of Jews only? Is he not the God of Gentiles too? Yes, of Gentiles too, [30]since there is only one God, who will justify the circumcised by faith and the uncircumcised through that same faith. [31]Do we, then, nullify the law by this faith? Not at all! Rather, we uphold the law.

Abraham Justified by Faith

4 What then shall we say that Abraham, our forefather according to the flesh, discovered in this matter? [2]If, in fact, Abraham was justified by works, he had something to boast about—but not before God. [3]What does Scripture say? "Abraham believed God, and it was credited to him as righteousness."[l]

[4]Now to the one who works, wages are not credited as a gift but as an obligation. [5]However, to the one who does not work but trusts God who justifies the ungodly, their faith is credited as righteousness. [6]David says the same thing when he speaks of the blessedness

[a] 24 Isaiah 52:5 (see Septuagint); Ezek. 36:20,22   [b] 27 Or who, by means of a   [c] 4 Psalm 51:4
[d] 12 Psalms 14:1-3; 53:1-3; Eccles. 7:20   [e] 13 Psalm 5:9   [f] 13 Psalm 140:3   [g] 14 Psalm 10:7 (see Septuagint)   [h] 17 Isaiah 59:7,8   [i] 18 Psalm 36:1   [j] 22 Or through the faithfulness of   [k] 25 The Greek for sacrifice of atonement refers to the atonement cover on the ark of the covenant (see Lev. 16:15,16).   [l] 3 Gen. 15:6; also in verse 22

of the one to whom God credits righteousness apart from works:

⁷"Blessed are those
whose transgressions are forgiven,
whose sins are covered.
⁸Blessed is the one
whose sin the Lord will never count
against them."ᵃ

⁹Is this blessedness only for the circumcised, or also for the uncircumcised? We have been saying that Abraham's faith was credited to him as righteousness. ¹⁰Under what circumstances was it credited? Was it after he was circumcised, or before? It was not after, but before! ¹¹And he received circumcision as a sign, a seal of the righteousness that he had by faith while he was still uncircumcised. So then, he is the father of all who believe but have not been circumcised, in order that righteousness might be credited to them. ¹²And he is then also the father of the circumcised who not only are circumcised but who also follow in the footsteps of the faith that our father Abraham had before he was circumcised.

¹³It was not through the law that Abraham and his offspring received the promise that he would be heir of the world, but through the righteousness that comes by faith. ¹⁴For if those who depend on the law are heirs, faith means nothing and the promise is worthless, ¹⁵because the law brings wrath. And where there is no law there is no transgression.

¹⁶Therefore, the promise comes by faith, so that it may be by grace and may be guaranteed to all Abraham's offspring—not only to those who are of the law but also to those who have the faith of Abraham. He is the father of us all. ¹⁷As it is written: "I have made you a father of many nations."ᵇ He is our father in the sight of God, in whom he believed—the God who gives life to the dead and calls into being things that were not.

¹⁸Against all hope, Abraham in hope believed and so became the father of many nations, just as it had been said to him, "So shall your offspring be."ᶜ ¹⁹Without weakening in his faith, he faced the fact that his body was as good as dead—since he was about a hundred years old—and that Sarah's womb was also dead. ²⁰Yet he did not waver through unbelief regarding the promise of God, but was strengthened in his faith and gave glory to God, ²¹being fully persuaded that God had power to do what he had promised. ²²This is why "it was credited to him as righteousness." ²³The words "it was credited to him" were written not for him alone, ²⁴but also for us, to whom God will credit righteousness—for us who believe in him who raised Jesus our Lord from the dead. ²⁵He was delivered over to death for our sins and was raised to life for our justification.

Peace and Hope

5 Therefore, since we have been justified through faith, weᵈ have peace with God through our Lord Jesus Christ, ²through whom we have gained access by faith into this grace in which we now stand. And weᵉ boast in the hope of the glory of God. ³Not only so, but weᵉ also glory in our sufferings, because we know that suffering produces perseverance; ⁴perseverance, character; and character, hope. ⁵And hope does not put us to shame, because God's love has been poured out into our hearts through the Holy Spirit, who has been given to us.

⁶You see, at just the right time, when we were still powerless, Christ died for the ungodly. ⁷Very rarely will anyone die for a righteous person, though for a good person someone might possibly dare to die. ⁸But God demonstrates his own love for us in this: While we were still sinners, Christ died for us.

⁹Since we have now been justified by his blood, how much more shall we be saved from God's wrath through him! ¹⁰For if, while we were God's enemies, we were reconciled to him through the death of his Son, how much more, having been reconciled, shall we be saved through his life! ¹¹Not only is this so, but we also boast in God through our Lord Jesus Christ, through whom we have now received reconciliation.

Death Through Adam, Life Through Christ

¹²Therefore, just as sin entered the world through one man, and death through sin, and in this way death came to all people, because all sinned—

¹³To be sure, sin was in the world before the law was given, but sin is not charged against anyone's account where there is no law. ¹⁴Nevertheless, death reigned from the time of Adam to the time of Moses, even over those who did not sin by breaking a command, as did Adam, who is a pattern of the one to come.

¹⁵But the gift is not like the trespass. For if the many died by the trespass of the one man, how much more did God's grace and the gift that came by the grace of the one man, Jesus Christ, overflow to the many! ¹⁶Nor can the gift of God be compared with the result of one man's sin: The judgment followed one sin and brought condemnation, but the gift followed many trespasses and brought justification. ¹⁷For if, by the trespass of the one man, death reigned through that one man, how much more will those who receive God's abundant provision of grace and of the gift of righteousness reign in life through the one man, Jesus Christ!

¹⁸Consequently, just as one trespass resulted in condemnation for all people, so also one righteous act resulted in justification and life for all people. ¹⁹For just as through the disobedience of the one man the many were made sinners, so also through the obedience of the one man the many will be made righteous.

²⁰The law was brought in so that the trespass might increase. But where sin increased, grace increased all the more, ²¹so that, just as sin reigned in death, so also grace might

---

ᵃ 8 Psalm 32:1,2   ᵇ 17 Gen. 17:5   ᶜ 18 Gen. 15:5   ᵈ 1 Many manuscripts *let us*   ᵉ 2,3 Or *let us*

reign through righteousness to bring eternal life through Jesus Christ our Lord.

Dead to Sin, Alive in Christ

6 What shall we say, then? Shall we go on sinning so that grace may increase? [2]By no means! We are those who have died to sin; how can we live in it any longer? [3]Or don't you know that all of us who were baptized into Christ Jesus were baptized into his death? [4]We were therefore buried with him through baptism into death in order that, just as Christ was raised from the dead through the glory of the Father, we too may live a new life.

[5]For if we have been united with him in a death like his, we will certainly also be united with him in a resurrection like his. [6]For we know that our old self was crucified with him so that the body ruled by sin might be done away with,[a] that we should no longer be slaves to sin— [7]because anyone who has died has been set free from sin.

[8]Now if we died with Christ, we believe that we will also live with him. [9]For we know that since Christ was raised from the dead, he cannot die again; death no longer has mastery over him. [10]The death he died, he died to sin once for all; but the life he lives, he lives to God.

[11]In the same way, count yourselves dead to sin but alive to God in Christ Jesus. [12]Therefore do not let sin reign in your mortal body so that you obey its evil desires. [13]Do not offer any part of yourself to sin as an instrument of wickedness, but rather offer yourselves to God as those who have been brought from death to life; and offer every part of yourself to him as an instrument of righteousness. [14]For sin shall no longer be your master, because you are not under the law, but under grace.

Slaves to Righteousness

[15]What then? Shall we sin because we are not under the law but under grace? By no means! [16]Don't you know that when you offer yourselves to someone as obedient slaves, you are slaves of the one you obey—whether you are slaves to sin, which leads to death, or to obedience, which leads to righteousness? [17]But thanks be to God that, though you used to be slaves to sin, you have come to obey from your heart the pattern of teaching that has now claimed your allegiance. [18]You have been set free from sin and have become slaves to righteousness.

[19]I am using an example from everyday life because of your human limitations. Just as you used to offer yourselves as slaves to impurity and to ever-increasing wickedness, so now offer yourselves as slaves to righteousness leading to holiness. [20]When you were slaves to sin, you were free from the control of righteousness. [21]What benefit did you reap at that time from the things you are now ashamed of? Those things result in death! [22]But now that you have been set free from sin and have become slaves of God, the benefit you reap leads to holiness, and the result is eternal life. [23]For the wages of sin is death, but the gift of God is eternal life in[b] Christ Jesus our Lord.

Released From the Law, Bound to Christ

7 Do you not know, brothers and sisters— for I am speaking to those who know the law—that the law has authority over someone only as long as that person lives? [2]For example, by law a married woman is bound to her husband as long as he is alive, but if her husband dies, she is released from the law that binds her to him. [3]So then, if she has sexual relations with another man while her husband is still alive, she is called an adulteress. But if her husband dies, she is released from that law and is not an adulteress if she marries another man.

[4]So, my brothers and sisters, you also died to the law through the body of Christ, that you might belong to another, to him who was raised from the dead, in order that we might bear fruit for God. [5]For when we were in the realm of the flesh,[c] the sinful passions aroused by the law were at work in us, so that we bore fruit for death. [6]But now, by dying to what once bound us, we have been released from the law so that we serve in the new way of the Spirit, and not in the old way of the written code.

The Law and Sin

[7]What shall we say, then? Is the law sinful? Certainly not! Nevertheless, I would not have known what sin was had it not been for the law. For I would not have known what coveting really was if the law had not said, "You shall not covet."[d] [8]But sin, seizing the opportunity afforded by the commandment, produced in me every kind of coveting. For apart from the law, sin was dead. [9]Once I was alive apart from the law; but when the commandment came, sin sprang to life and I died. [10]I found that the very commandment that was intended to bring life actually brought death. [11]For sin, seizing the opportunity afforded by the commandment, deceived me, and through the commandment put me to death. [12]So then, the law is holy, and the commandment is holy, righteous and good.

[13]Did that which is good, then, become death to me? By no means! Nevertheless, in order that sin might be recognized as sin, it used what is good to bring about my death, so that through the commandment sin might become utterly sinful.

[14]We know that the law is spiritual; but I am unspiritual, sold as a slave to sin. [15]I do not understand what I do. For what I want to do I do not do, but what I hate I do. [16]And if I do what I do not want to do, I agree that the law is good. [17]As it is, it is no longer I myself who

[a] 6 Or be rendered powerless   [b] 23 Or through   [c] 5 In contexts like this, the Greek word for flesh (sarx) refers to the sinful state of human beings, often presented as a power in opposition to the Spirit.
[d] 7 Exodus 20:17; Deut. 5:21

do it, but it is sin living in me. [18]For I know that good itself does not dwell in me, that is, in my sinful nature.[a] For I have the desire to do what is good, but I cannot carry it out. [19]For I do not do the good I want to do, but the evil I do not want to do—this I keep on doing. [20]Now if I do what I do not want to do, it is no longer I who do it, but it is sin living in me that does it.

[21]So I find this law at work: Although I want to do good, evil is right there with me. [22]For in my inner being I delight in God's law; [23]but I see another law at work in me, waging war against the law of my mind and making me a prisoner of the law of sin at work within me. [24]What a wretched man I am! Who will rescue me from this body that is subject to death? [25]Thanks be to God, who delivers me through Jesus Christ our Lord!

So then, I myself in my mind am a slave to God's law, but in my sinful nature[b] a slave to the law of sin.

Life Through the Spirit

8 Therefore, there is now no condemnation for those who are in Christ Jesus, [2]because through Christ Jesus the law of the Spirit who gives life has set you[c] free from the law of sin and death. [3]For what the law was powerless to do because it was weakened by the flesh,[d] God did by sending his own Son in the likeness of sinful flesh to be a sin offering.[e] And so he condemned sin in the flesh, [4]in order that the righteous requirement of the law might be fully met in us, who do not live according to the flesh but according to the Spirit.

[5]Those who live according to the flesh have their minds set on what the flesh desires; but those who live in accordance with the Spirit have their minds set on what the Spirit desires. [6]The mind governed by the flesh is death, but the mind governed by the Spirit is life and peace. [7]The mind governed by the flesh is hostile to God; it does not submit to God's law, nor can it do so. [8]Those who are in the realm of the flesh cannot please God.

[9]You, however, are not in the realm of the flesh but are in the realm of the Spirit, if indeed the Spirit of God lives in you. And if anyone does not have the Spirit of Christ, they do not belong to Christ. [10]But if Christ is in you, then even though your body is subject to death because of sin, the Spirit gives life[f] because of righteousness. [11]And if the Spirit of him who raised Jesus from the dead is living in you, he who raised Christ from the dead will also give life to your mortal bodies because of[g] his Spirit who lives in you.

[12]Therefore, brothers and sisters, we have an obligation—but it is not to the flesh, to live according to it. [13]For if you live according to the flesh, you will die; but if by the Spirit you put to death the misdeeds of the body, you will live.

[14]For those who are led by the Spirit of God are the children of God. [15]The Spirit you received does not make you slaves, so that you live in fear again; rather, the Spirit you received brought about your adoption to sonship.[h] And by him we cry, "Abba,[i] Father." [16]The Spirit himself testifies with our spirit that we are God's children. [17]Now if we are children, then we are heirs—heirs of God and co-heirs with Christ, if indeed we share in his sufferings in order that we may also share in his glory.

Present Suffering and Future Glory

[18]I consider that our present sufferings are not worth comparing with the glory that will be revealed in us. [19]For the creation waits in eager expectation for the children of God to be revealed. [20]For the creation was subjected to frustration, not by its own choice, but by the will of the one who subjected it, in hope [21]that[j] the creation itself will be liberated from its bondage to decay and brought into the freedom and glory of the children of God.

[22]We know that the whole creation has been groaning as in the pains of childbirth right up to the present time. [23]Not only so, but we ourselves, who have the firstfruits of the Spirit, groan inwardly as we wait eagerly for our adoption to sonship, the redemption of our bodies. [24]For in this hope we were saved. But hope that is seen is no hope at all. Who hopes for what they already have? [25]But if we hope for what we do not yet have, we wait for it patiently.

[26]In the same way, the Spirit helps us in our weakness. We do not know what we ought to pray for, but the Spirit himself intercedes for us through wordless groans. [27]And he who searches our hearts knows the mind of the Spirit, because the Spirit intercedes for God's people in accordance with the will of God.

[28]And we know that in all things God works for the good of those who love him, who[k] have been called according to his purpose. [29]For those God foreknew he also predestined to be conformed to the image of his Son, that he might be the firstborn among many brothers and sisters. [30]And those he predestined, he also called; those he called, he also justified; those he justified, he also glorified.

More Than Conquerors

[31]What, then, shall we say in response to these things? If God is for us, who can be against us? [32]He who did not spare his own

---

[a] 18 Or my flesh   [b] 25 Or in the flesh   [c] 2 The Greek is singular; some manuscripts me   [d] 3 In contexts like this, the Greek word for flesh (sarx) refers to the sinful state of human beings, often presented as a power in opposition to the Spirit; also in verses 4-13.   [e] 3 Or flesh, for sin   [f] 10 Or you, your body is dead because of sin, yet your spirit is alive   [g] 11 Some manuscripts bodies through   [h] 15 The Greek word for adoption to sonship is a term referring to the full legal standing of an adopted male heir in Roman culture; also in verse 23.   [i] 15 Aramaic for father   [j] 20,21 Or subjected it in hope. 21For   [k] 28 Or that all things work together for good to those who love God, who; or that in all things God works together with those who love him to bring about what is good—with those who

Son, but gave him up for us all—how will he not also, along with him, graciously give us all things? ³³Who will bring any charge against those whom God has chosen? It is God who justifies. ³⁴Who then is the one who condemns? No one. Christ Jesus who died—more than that, who was raised to life—is at the right hand of God and is also interceding for us. ³⁵Who shall separate us from the love of Christ? Shall trouble or hardship or persecution or famine or nakedness or danger or sword? ³⁶As it is written:

"For your sake we face death all day
    long;
we are considered as sheep to be
    slaughtered."[a]

³⁷No, in all these things we are more than conquerors through him who loved us. ³⁸For I am convinced that neither death nor life, neither angels nor demons,[b] neither the present nor the future, nor any powers, ³⁹neither height nor depth, nor anything else in all creation, will be able to separate us from the love of God that is in Christ Jesus our Lord.

Paul's Anguish Over Israel

9 I speak the truth in Christ—I am not lying, my conscience confirms it through the Holy Spirit— ²I have great sorrow and unceasing anguish in my heart. ³For I could wish that I myself were cursed and cut off from Christ for the sake of my people, those of my own race, ⁴the people of Israel. Theirs is the adoption to sonship; theirs the divine glory, the covenants, the receiving of the law, the temple worship and the promises. ⁵Theirs are the patriarchs, and from them is traced the human ancestry of the Messiah, who is God over all, forever praised![c] Amen.

God's Sovereign Choice

⁶It is not as though God's word had failed. For not all who are descended from Israel are Israel. ⁷Nor because they are his descendants are they all Abraham's children. On the contrary, "It is through Isaac that your offspring will be reckoned."[d] ⁸In other words, it is not the children by physical descent who are God's children, but it is the children of the promise who are regarded as Abraham's offspring. ⁹For this was how the promise was stated: "At the appointed time I will return, and Sarah will have a son."[e]

¹⁰Not only that, but Rebekah's children were conceived at the same time by our father Isaac. ¹¹Yet, before the twins were born or had done anything good or bad—in order that God's purpose in election might stand: ¹²not by works but by him who calls—she was told, "The older will serve the younger."[f] ¹³Just as it is written: "Jacob I loved, but Esau I hated."[g]

¹⁴What then shall we say? Is God unjust? Not at all! ¹⁵For he says to Moses,

"I will have mercy on whom I have mercy,
    and I will have compassion on whom I
    have compassion."[h]

¹⁶It does not, therefore, depend on human desire or effort, but on God's mercy. ¹⁷For Scripture says to Pharaoh: "I raised you up for this very purpose, that I might display my power in you and that my name might be proclaimed in all the earth."[i] ¹⁸Therefore God has mercy on whom he wants to have mercy, and he hardens whom he wants to harden.

¹⁹One of you will say to me: "Then why does God still blame us? For who is able to resist his will?" ²⁰But who are you, a human being, to talk back to God? "Shall what is formed say to the one who formed it, 'Why did you make me like this?'"[j] ²¹Does not the potter have the right to make out of the same lump of clay some pottery for special purposes and some for common use?

²²What if God, although choosing to show his wrath and make his power known, bore with great patience the objects of his wrath—prepared for destruction? ²³What if he did this to make the riches of his glory known to the objects of his mercy, whom he prepared in advance for glory— ²⁴even us, whom he also called, not only from the Jews but also from the Gentiles? ²⁵As he says in Hosea:

"I will call them 'my people' who are not
    my people;
    and I will call her 'my loved one' who is
    not my loved one,"[k]

²⁶and,

"In the very place where it was said to
    them,
    'You are not my people,'
there they will be called 'children of the
    living God.'"[l]

²⁷Isaiah cries out concerning Israel:

"Though the number of the Israelites be
    like the sand by the sea,
    only the remnant will be saved.
²⁸For the Lord will carry out
    his sentence on earth with speed and
    finality."[m]

²⁹It is just as Isaiah said previously:

"Unless the Lord Almighty
    had left us descendants,
we would have become like Sodom,
    we would have been like Gomorrah."[n]

Israel's Unbelief

³⁰What then shall we say? That the Gentiles, who did not pursue righteousness, have obtained it, a righteousness that is by faith; ³¹but the people of Israel, who pursued the law as the way of righteousness, have not attained their goal. ³²Why not? Because they pursued it not by faith but as if it were by works. They

---

[a] 36 Psalm 44:22   [b] 38 Or *nor heavenly rulers*   [c] 5 Or *Messiah, who is over all. God be forever praised!* Or *Messiah. God who is over all be forever praised!*   [d] 7 Gen. 21:12   [e] 9 Gen. 18:10,14 [f] 12 Gen. 25:23   [g] 13 Mal. 1:2,3   [h] 15 Exodus 33:19   [i] 17 Exodus 9:16   [j] 20 Isaiah 29:16; 45:9 [k] 25 Hosea 2:23   [l] 26 Hosea 1:10   [m] 28 Isaiah 10:22,23 (see Septuagint)   [n] 29 Isaiah 1:9

stumbled over the stumbling stone. 33 As it is
written:

"See, I lay in Zion a stone that causes
people to stumble
and a rock that makes them fall,
and the one who believes in him will
never be put to shame."[a]

10 Brothers and sisters, my heart's desire
and prayer to God for the Israelites is
that they may be saved. 2 For I can testify about
them that they are zealous for God, but their
zeal is not based on knowledge. 3 Since they
did not know the righteousness of God and
sought to establish their own, they did not
submit to God's righteousness. 4 Christ is the
culmination of the law so that there may be
righteousness for everyone who believes.
5 Moses writes this about the righteousness
that is by the law: "The person who does these
things will live by them."[b] 6 But the righteousness that is by faith says: "Do not say in your
heart, 'Who will ascend into heaven?'"[c] (that is,
to bring Christ down) 7 "or 'Who will descend
into the deep?'"[d] (that is, to bring Christ up from
the dead). 8 But what does it say? "The word is
near you; it is in your mouth and in your heart,"[e]
that is, the message concerning faith that we
proclaim: 9 If you declare with your mouth,
"Jesus is Lord," and believe in your heart that
God raised him from the dead, you will be
saved. 10 For it is with your heart that you believe and are justified, and it is with your mouth
that you profess your faith and are saved. 11 As
Scripture says, "Anyone who believes in him
will never be put to shame."[f] 12 For there is no
difference between Jew and Gentile—the same
Lord is Lord of all and richly blesses all who
call on him, 13 for, "Everyone who calls on the
name of the Lord will be saved."[g]
14 How, then, can they call on the one they
have not believed in? And how can they believe in the one of whom they have not heard?
And how can they hear without someone
preaching to them? 15 And how can anyone
preach unless they are sent? As it is written:
"How beautiful are the feet of those who bring
good news!"[h]
16 But not all the Israelites accepted the good
news. For Isaiah says, "Lord, who has believed
our message?"[i] 17 Consequently, faith comes
from hearing the message, and the message
is heard through the word about Christ. 18 But
I ask: Did they not hear? Of course they did:

"Their voice has gone out into all the
earth,
their words to the ends of the world."[j]

19 Again I ask: Did Israel not understand? First,
Moses says,

"I will make you envious by those who
are not a nation;
I will make you angry by a nation that
has no understanding."[k]

20 And Isaiah boldly says,

"I was found by those who did not seek
me;
I revealed myself to those who did not
ask for me."[l]

21 But concerning Israel he says,

"All day long I have held out my hands
to a disobedient and obstinate
people."[m]

The Remnant of Israel

11 I ask then: Did God reject his people?
By no means! I am an Israelite myself,
a descendant of Abraham, from the tribe of
Benjamin. 2 God did not reject his people,
whom he foreknew. Don't you know what
Scripture says in the passage about Elijah—
how he appealed to God against Israel: 3 "Lord,
they have killed your prophets and torn down
your altars; I am the only one left, and they
are trying to kill me"[n]? 4 And what was God's
answer to him? "I have reserved for myself
seven thousand who have not bowed the knee
to Baal."[o] 5 So too, at the present time there is
a remnant chosen by grace. 6 And if by grace,
then it cannot be based on works; if it were,
grace would no longer be grace.
7 What then? What the people of Israel
sought so earnestly they did not obtain. The
elect among them did, but the others were
hardened, 8 as it is written:

"God gave them a spirit of stupor,
eyes that could not see
and ears that could not hear,
to this very day."[p]

9 And David says:

"May their table become a snare and a
trap,
a stumbling block and a retribution for
them.
10 May their eyes be darkened so they
cannot see,
and their backs be bent forever."[q]

Ingrafted Branches

11 Again I ask: Did they stumble so as to
fall beyond recovery? Not at all! Rather, because of their transgression, salvation has
come to the Gentiles to make Israel envious.
12 But if their transgression means riches for
the world, and their loss means riches for the
Gentiles, how much greater riches will their
full inclusion bring!
13 I am talking to you Gentiles. Inasmuch as
I am the apostle to the Gentiles, I take pride
in my ministry 14 in the hope that I may somehow arouse my own people to envy and save
some of them. 15 For if their rejection brought
reconciliation to the world, what will their
acceptance be but life from the dead? 16 If the
part of the dough offered as firstfruits is holy,

[a] *33* Isaiah 8:14; 28:16 [b] *5* Lev. 18:5 [c] *6* Deut. 30:12 [d] *7* Deut. 30:13 [e] *8* Deut. 30:14
[f] *11* Isaiah 28:16 (see Septuagint) [g] *13* Joel 2:32 [h] *15* Isaiah 52:7 [i] *16* Isaiah 53:1
[j] *18* Psalm 19:4 [k] *19* Deut. 32:21 [l] *20* Isaiah 65:1 [m] *21* Isaiah 65:2 [n] *3* 1 Kings 19:10,14
[o] *4* 1 Kings 19:18 [p] *8* Deut. 29:4; Isaiah 29:10 [q] *10* Psalm 69:22,23

then the whole batch is holy; if the root is holy, so are the branches.

[17]If some of the branches have been broken off, and you, though a wild olive shoot, have been grafted in among the others and now share in the nourishing sap from the olive root, [18]do not consider yourself to be superior to those other branches. If you do, consider this: You do not support the root, but the root supports you. [19]You will say then, "Branches were broken off so that I could be grafted in." [20]Granted. But they were broken off because of unbelief, and you stand by faith. Do not be arrogant, but tremble. [21]For if God did not spare the natural branches, he will not spare you either.

[22]Consider therefore the kindness and sternness of God: sternness to those who fell, but kindness to you, provided that you continue in his kindness. Otherwise, you also will be cut off. [23]And if they do not persist in unbelief, they will be grafted in, for God is able to graft them in again. [24]After all, if you were cut out of an olive tree that is wild by nature, and contrary to nature were grafted into a cultivated olive tree, how much more readily will these, the natural branches, be grafted into their own olive tree!

All Israel Will Be Saved

[25]I do not want you to be ignorant of this mystery, brothers and sisters, so that you may not be conceited: Israel has experienced a hardening in part until the full number of the Gentiles has come in, [26]and in this way[a] all Israel will be saved. As it is written:

"The deliverer will come from Zion;
    he will turn godlessness away from
        Jacob.
[27]And this is[b] my covenant with them
    when I take away their sins."[c]

[28]As far as the gospel is concerned, they are enemies for your sake; but as far as election is concerned, they are loved on account of the patriarchs, [29]for God's gifts and his call are irrevocable. [30]Just as you who were at one time disobedient to God have now received mercy as a result of their disobedience, [31]so they too have now become disobedient in order that they too may now[d] receive mercy as a result of God's mercy to you. [32]For God has bound everyone over to disobedience so that he may have mercy on them all.

Doxology

[33]Oh, the depth of the riches of the wisdom
    and[e] knowledge of God!
    How unsearchable his judgments,
        and his paths beyond tracing out!
[34]"Who has known the mind of the Lord?
    Or who has been his counselor?"[f]
[35]"Who has ever given to God,
    that God should repay them?"[g]

[36]For from him and through him and for
        him are all things.
    To him be the glory forever! Amen.

A Living Sacrifice

12 Therefore, I urge you, brothers and sisters, in view of God's mercy, to offer your bodies as a living sacrifice, holy and pleasing to God—this is your true and proper worship. [2]Do not conform to the pattern of this world, but be transformed by the renewing of your mind. Then you will be able to test and approve what God's will is—his good, pleasing and perfect will.

Humble Service in the Body of Christ

[3]For by the grace given me I say to every one of you: Do not think of yourself more highly than you ought, but rather think of yourself with sober judgment, in accordance with the faith God has distributed to each of you. [4]For just as each of us has one body with many members, and these members do not all have the same function, [5]so in Christ we, though many, form one body, and each member belongs to all the others. [6]We have different gifts, according to the grace given to each of us. If your gift is prophesying, then prophesy in accordance with your[h] faith; [7]if it is serving, then serve; if it is teaching, then teach; [8]if it is to encourage, then give encouragement; if it is giving, then give generously; if it is to lead,[i] do it diligently; if it is to show mercy, do it cheerfully.

Love in Action

[9]Love must be sincere. Hate what is evil; cling to what is good. [10]Be devoted to one another in love. Honor one another above yourselves. [11]Never be lacking in zeal, but keep your spiritual fervor, serving the Lord. [12]Be joyful in hope, patient in affliction, faithful in prayer. [13]Share with the Lord's people who are in need. Practice hospitality.

[14]Bless those who persecute you; bless and do not curse. [15]Rejoice with those who rejoice; mourn with those who mourn. [16]Live in harmony with one another. Do not be proud, but be willing to associate with people of low position.[j] Do not be conceited.

[17]Do not repay anyone evil for evil. Be careful to do what is right in the eyes of everyone. [18]If it is possible, as far as it depends on you, live at peace with everyone. [19]Do not take revenge, my dear friends, but leave room for God's wrath, for it is written: "It is mine to avenge; I will repay,"[k] says the Lord. [20]On the contrary:

"If your enemy is hungry, feed him;
    if he is thirsty, give him something to
        drink.
In doing this, you will heap burning coals
    on his head."[l]

---

[a] 26 Or *and so*   [b] 27 Or *will be*   [c] 27 Isaiah 59:20,21; 27:9 (see Septuagint); Jer. 31:33,34
[d] 31 Some manuscripts do not have *now*.   [e] 33 Or *riches and the wisdom and the*   [f] 34 Isaiah 40:13
[g] 35 Job 41:11   [h] 6 Or *the*   [i] 8 Or *to provide for others*   [j] 16 Or *willing to do menial work*
[k] 19 Deut. 32:35   [l] 20 Prov. 25:21,22

[21]Do not be overcome by evil, but overcome evil with good.

Submission to Governing Authorities

13 Let everyone be subject to the governing authorities, for there is no authority except that which God has established. The authorities that exist have been established by God. [2]Consequently, whoever rebels against the authority is rebelling against what God has instituted, and those who do so will bring judgment on themselves. [3]For rulers hold no terror for those who do right, but for those who do wrong. Do you want to be free from fear of the one in authority? Then do what is right and you will be commended. [4]For the one in authority is God's servant for your good. But if you do wrong, be afraid, for rulers do not bear the sword for no reason. They are God's servants, agents of wrath to bring punishment on the wrongdoer. [5]Therefore, it is necessary to submit to the authorities, not only because of possible punishment but also as a matter of conscience.

[6]This is also why you pay taxes, for the authorities are God's servants, who give their full time to governing. [7]Give to everyone what you owe them: If you owe taxes, pay taxes; if revenue, then revenue; if respect, then respect; if honor, then honor.

Love Fulfills the Law

[8]Let no debt remain outstanding, except the continuing debt to love one another, for whoever loves others has fulfilled the law. [9]The commandments, "You shall not commit adultery," "You shall not murder," "You shall not steal," "You shall not covet,"[a] and whatever other command there may be, are summed up in this one command: "Love your neighbor as yourself."[b] [10]Love does no harm to a neighbor. Therefore love is the fulfillment of the law.

The Day Is Near

[11]And do this, understanding the present time: The hour has already come for you to wake up from your slumber, because our salvation is nearer now than when we first believed. [12]The night is nearly over; the day is almost here. So let us put aside the deeds of darkness and put on the armor of light. [13]Let us behave decently, as in the daytime, not in carousing and drunkenness, not in sexual immorality and debauchery, not in dissension and jealousy. [14]Rather, clothe yourselves with the Lord Jesus Christ, and do not think about how to gratify the desires of the flesh.[c]

The Weak and the Strong

14 Accept the one whose faith is weak, without quarreling over disputable matters. [2]One person's faith allows them to eat anything, but another, whose faith is weak,

eats only vegetables. [3]The one who eats everything must not treat with contempt the one who does not, and the one who does not eat everything must not judge the one who does, for God has accepted them. [4]Who are you to judge someone else's servant? To their own master, servants stand or fall. And they will stand, for the Lord is able to make them stand.

[5]One person considers one day more sacred than another; another considers every day alike. Each of them should be fully convinced in their own mind. [6]Whoever regards one day as special does so to the Lord. Whoever eats meat does so to the Lord, for they give thanks to God; and whoever abstains does so to the Lord and gives thanks to God. [7]For none of us lives for ourselves alone, and none of us dies for ourselves alone. [8]If we live, we live for the Lord; and if we die, we die for the Lord. So, whether we live or die, we belong to the Lord. [9]For this very reason, Christ died and returned to life so that he might be the Lord of both the dead and the living.

[10]You, then, why do you judge your brother or sister[d]? Or why do you treat them with contempt? For we will all stand before God's judgment seat. [11]It is written:

"'As surely as I live,' says the Lord,
'every knee will bow before me;
    every tongue will acknowledge God.'"[e]

[12]So then, each of us will give an account of ourselves to God.

[13]Therefore let us stop passing judgment on one another. Instead, make up your mind not to put any stumbling block or obstacle in the way of a brother or sister. [14]I am convinced, being fully persuaded in the Lord Jesus, that nothing is unclean in itself. But if anyone regards something as unclean, then for that person it is unclean. [15]If your brother or sister is distressed because of what you eat, you are no longer acting in love. Do not by your eating destroy someone for whom Christ died. [16]Therefore do not let what you know is good be spoken of as evil. [17]For the kingdom of God is not a matter of eating and drinking, but of righteousness, peace and joy in the Holy Spirit, [18]because anyone who serves Christ in this way is pleasing to God and receives human approval.

[19]Let us therefore make every effort to do what leads to peace and to mutual edification. [20]Do not destroy the work of God for the sake of food. All food is clean, but it is wrong for a person to eat anything that causes someone else to stumble. [21]It is better not to eat meat or drink wine or to do anything else that will cause your brother or sister to fall.

[22]So whatever you believe about these things keep between yourself and God. Blessed is the one who does not condemn himself by what he approves. [23]But whoever has doubts is condemned if they eat, because

---

[a] 9 Exodus 20:13-15,17; Deut. 5:17-19,21   [b] 9 Lev. 19:18   [c] 14 In contexts like this, the Greek word for *flesh* (sarx) refers to the sinful state of human beings, often presented as a power in opposition to the Spirit.   [d] 10 The Greek word for *brother or sister* (adelphos) refers here to a believer, whether man or woman, as part of God's family; also in verses 13, 15 and 21.   [e] 11 Isaiah 45:23

their eating is not from faith; and everything that does not come from faith is sin.[a]

15 We who are strong ought to bear with the failings of the weak and not to please ourselves. [2]Each of us should please our neighbors for their good, to build them up. [3]For even Christ did not please himself but, as it is written: "The insults of those who insult you have fallen on me."[b] [4]For everything that was written in the past was written to teach us, so that through the endurance taught in the Scriptures and the encouragement they provide we might have hope.

[5]May the God who gives endurance and encouragement give you the same attitude of mind toward each other that Christ Jesus had, [6]so that with one mind and one voice you may glorify the God and Father of our Lord Jesus Christ.

[7]Accept one another, then, just as Christ accepted you, in order to bring praise to God. [8]For I tell you that Christ has become a servant of the Jews[c] on behalf of God's truth, so that the promises made to the patriarchs might be confirmed [9]and, moreover, that the Gentiles might glorify God for his mercy. As it is written:

"Therefore I will praise you among the
    Gentiles;
    I will sing the praises of your name."[d]

[10]Again, it says,

"Rejoice, you Gentiles, with his people."[e]

[11]And again,

"Praise the Lord, all you Gentiles;
    let all the peoples extol him."[f]

[12]And again, Isaiah says,

"The Root of Jesse will spring up,
    one who will arise to rule over the
        nations;
    in him the Gentiles will hope."[g]

[13]May the God of hope fill you with all joy and peace as you trust in him, so that you may overflow with hope by the power of the Holy Spirit.

Paul the Minister to the Gentiles

[14]I myself am convinced, my brothers and sisters, that you yourselves are full of goodness, filled with knowledge and competent to instruct one another. [15]Yet I have written you quite boldly on some points to remind you of them again, because of the grace God gave me [16]to be a minister of Christ Jesus to the Gentiles. He gave me the priestly duty of proclaiming the gospel of God, so that the Gentiles might become an offering acceptable to God, sanctified by the Holy Spirit.

[17]Therefore I glory in Christ Jesus in my service to God. [18]I will not venture to speak of anything except what Christ has accomplished through me in leading the Gentiles to obey God by what I have said and done— [19]by the power of signs and wonders, through the power of the Spirit of God. So from Jerusalem all the way around to Illyricum, I have fully proclaimed the gospel of Christ. [20]It has always been my ambition to preach the gospel where Christ was not known, so that I would not be building on someone else's foundation. [21]Rather, as it is written:

"Those who were not told about him will
    see,
    and those who have not heard will
        understand."[h]

[22]This is why I have often been hindered from coming to you.

Paul's Plan to Visit Rome

[23]But now that there is no more place for me to work in these regions, and since I have been longing for many years to visit you, [24]I plan to do so when I go to Spain. I hope to see you while passing through and to have you assist me on my journey there, after I have enjoyed your company for a while. [25]Now, however, I am on my way to Jerusalem in the service of the Lord's people there. [26]For Macedonia and Achaia were pleased to make a contribution for the poor among the Lord's people in Jerusalem. [27]They were pleased to do it, and indeed they owe it to them. For if the Gentiles have shared in the Jews' spiritual blessings, they owe it to the Jews to share with them their material blessings. [28]So after I have completed this task and have made sure that they have received this contribution, I will go to Spain and visit you on the way. [29]I know that when I come to you, I will come in the full measure of the blessing of Christ.

[30]I urge you, brothers and sisters, by our Lord Jesus Christ and by the love of the Spirit, to join me in my struggle by praying to God for me. [31]Pray that I may be kept safe from the unbelievers in Judea and that the contribution I take to Jerusalem may be favorably received by the Lord's people there, [32]so that I may come to you with joy, by God's will, and in your company be refreshed. [33]The God of peace be with you all. Amen.

Personal Greetings

16 I commend to you our sister Phoebe, a deacon[i,j] of the church in Cenchreae. [2]I ask you to receive her in the Lord in a way worthy of his people and to give her any help she may need from you, for she has been the benefactor of many people, including me.

[3]Greet Priscilla[k] and Aquila, my co-workers in Christ Jesus. [4]They risked their lives

---

[a] 23 Some manuscripts place 16:25-27 here; others after 15:33.   [b] 3 Psalm 69:9   [c] 8 Greek circumcision   [d] 9 2 Samuel 22:50; Psalm 18:49   [e] 10 Deut. 32:43   [f] 11 Psalm 117:1   [g] 12 Isaiah 11:10 (see Septuagint)   [h] 21 Isaiah 52:15 (see Septuagint)   [i] 1 Or servant   [j] 1 The word deacon refers here to a Christian designated to serve with the overseers/elders of the church in a variety of ways; similarly in Phil. 1:1 and 1 Tim. 3:8,12.   [k] 3 Greek Prisca, a variant of Priscilla

for me. Not only I but all the churches of the Gentiles are grateful to them.

⁵Greet also the church that meets at their house.

Greet my dear friend Epenetus, who was the first convert to Christ in the province of Asia.

⁶Greet Mary, who worked very hard for you.

⁷Greet Andronicus and Junia, my fellow Jews who have been in prison with me. They are outstanding among*a* the apostles, and they were in Christ before I was.

⁸Greet Ampliatus, my dear friend in the Lord.

⁹Greet Urbanus, our co-worker in Christ, and my dear friend Stachys.

¹⁰Greet Apelles, whose fidelity to Christ has stood the test.

Greet those who belong to the household of Aristobulus.

¹¹Greet Herodion, my fellow Jew.

Greet those in the household of Narcissus who are in the Lord.

¹²Greet Tryphena and Tryphosa, those women who work hard in the Lord.

Greet my dear friend Persis, another woman who has worked very hard in the Lord.

¹³Greet Rufus, chosen in the Lord, and his mother, who has been a mother to me, too.

¹⁴Greet Asyncritus, Phlegon, Hermes, Patrobas, Hermas and the other brothers and sisters with them.

¹⁵Greet Philologus, Julia, Nereus and his sister, and Olympas and all the Lord's people who are with them.

¹⁶Greet one another with a holy kiss.

All the churches of Christ send greetings.

¹⁷I urge you, brothers and sisters, to watch out for those who cause divisions and put obstacles in your way that are contrary to the teaching you have learned. Keep away from them. ¹⁸For such people are not serving our Lord Christ, but their own appetites. By smooth talk and flattery they deceive the minds of naive people. ¹⁹Everyone has heard about your obedience, so I rejoice because of you; but I want you to be wise about what is good, and innocent about what is evil.

²⁰The God of peace will soon crush Satan under your feet.

The grace of our Lord Jesus be with you.

²¹Timothy, my co-worker, sends his greetings to you, as do Lucius, Jason and Sosipater, my fellow Jews.

²²I, Tertius, who wrote down this letter, greet you in the Lord.

²³Gaius, whose hospitality I and the whole church here enjoy, sends you his greetings.

Erastus, who is the city's director of public works, and our brother Quartus send you their greetings. [24]*b*

²⁵Now to him who is able to establish you in accordance with my gospel, the message I proclaim about Jesus Christ, in keeping with the revelation of the mystery hidden for long ages past, ²⁶but now revealed and made known through the prophetic writings by the command of the eternal God, so that all the Gentiles might come to the obedience that comes from*c* faith— ²⁷to the only wise God be glory forever through Jesus Christ! Amen.

1 Corinthians

1 Paul, called to be an apostle of Christ Jesus by the will of God, and our brother Sosthenes,

²To the church of God in Corinth, to those sanctified in Christ Jesus and called to be his holy people, together with all those everywhere who call on the name of our Lord Jesus Christ—their Lord and ours:

³Grace and peace to you from God our Father and the Lord Jesus Christ.

Thanksgiving

⁴I always thank my God for you because of his grace given you in Christ Jesus. ⁵For in him you have been enriched in every way—

with all kinds of speech and with all knowledge— ⁶God thus confirming our testimony about Christ among you. ⁷Therefore you do not lack any spiritual gift as you eagerly wait for our Lord Jesus Christ to be revealed. ⁸He will also keep you firm to the end, so that you will be blameless on the day of our Lord Jesus Christ. ⁹God is faithful, who has called you into fellowship with his Son, Jesus Christ our Lord.

A Church Divided Over Leaders

¹⁰I appeal to you, brothers and sisters,*d* in the name of our Lord Jesus Christ, that all of you agree with one another in what you say and that there be no divisions among

---

a 7 Or *are esteemed by*   *b* 24 Some manuscripts include here *May the grace of our Lord Jesus Christ be with all of you. Amen.*   *c* 26 Or *that is*   *d* 10 The Greek word for *brothers and sisters (adelphoi)* refers here to believers, both men and women, as part of God's family; also in verses 11 and 26; and in 2:1; 3:1; 4:6; 6:8; 7:24, 29; 10:1; 11:33; 12:1; 14:6, 20, 26, 39; 15:1, 6, 50, 58; 16:15, 20.

you, but that you be perfectly united in mind and thought. [11]My brothers and sisters, some from Chloe's household have informed me that there are quarrels among you. [12]What I mean is this: One of you says, "I follow Paul"; another, "I follow Apollos"; another, "I follow Cephas[a]"; still another, "I follow Christ."

[13]Is Christ divided? Was Paul crucified for you? Were you baptized in the name of Paul? [14]I thank God that I did not baptize any of you except Crispus and Gaius, [15]so no one can say that you were baptized in my name. [16](Yes, I also baptized the household of Stephanas; beyond that, I don't remember if I baptized anyone else.) [17]For Christ did not send me to baptize, but to preach the gospel—not with wisdom and eloquence, lest the cross of Christ be emptied of its power.

Christ Crucified Is God's Power and Wisdom

[18]For the message of the cross is foolishness to those who are perishing, but to us who are being saved it is the power of God. [19]For it is written:

"I will destroy the wisdom of the wise;
    the intelligence of the intelligent I will
        frustrate."[b]

[20]Where is the wise person? Where is the teacher of the law? Where is the philosopher of this age? Has not God made foolish the wisdom of the world? [21]For since in the wisdom of God the world through its wisdom did not know him, God was pleased through the foolishness of what was preached to save those who believe. [22]Jews demand signs and Greeks look for wisdom, [23]but we preach Christ crucified: a stumbling block to Jews and foolishness to Gentiles, [24]but to those whom God has called, both Jews and Greeks, Christ the power of God and the wisdom of God. [25]For the foolishness of God is wiser than human wisdom, and the weakness of God is stronger than human strength.

[26]Brothers and sisters, think of what you were when you were called. Not many of you were wise by human standards; not many were influential; not many were of noble birth. [27]But God chose the foolish things of the world to shame the wise; God chose the weak things of the world to shame the strong. [28]God chose the lowly things of this world and the despised things—and the things that are not—to nullify the things that are, [29]so that no one may boast before him. [30]It is because of him that you are in Christ Jesus, who has become for us wisdom from God—that is, our righteousness, holiness and redemption. [31]Therefore, as it is written: "Let the one who boasts boast in the Lord."[c]

2 And so it was with me, brothers and sisters. When I came to you, I did not come with eloquence or human wisdom as I proclaimed to you the testimony about God.[d] [2]For I resolved to know nothing while I was with you

except Jesus Christ and him crucified. [3]I came to you in weakness with great fear and trembling. [4]My message and my preaching were not with wise and persuasive words, but with a demonstration of the Spirit's power, [5]so that your faith might not rest on human wisdom, but on God's power.

God's Wisdom Revealed by the Spirit

[6]We do, however, speak a message of wisdom among the mature, but not the wisdom of this age or of the rulers of this age, who are coming to nothing. [7]No, we declare God's wisdom, a mystery that has been hidden and that God destined for our glory before time began. [8]None of the rulers of this age understood it, for if they had, they would not have crucified the Lord of glory. [9]However, as it is written:

"What no eye has seen,
    what no ear has heard,
and what no human mind has
        conceived"[e]—
    the things God has prepared for those
        who love him—

[10]these are the things God has revealed to us by his Spirit.

The Spirit searches all things, even the deep things of God. [11]For who knows a person's thoughts except their own spirit within them? In the same way no one knows the thoughts of God except the Spirit of God. [12]What we have received is not the spirit of the world, but the Spirit who is from God, so that we may understand what God has freely given us. [13]This is what we speak, not in words taught us by human wisdom but in words taught by the Spirit, explaining spiritual realities with Spirit-taught words.[f] [14]The person without the Spirit does not accept the things that come from the Spirit of God but considers them foolishness, and cannot understand them because they are discerned only through the Spirit. [15]The person with the Spirit makes judgments about all things, but such a person is not subject to merely human judgments, [16]for,

"Who has known the mind of the Lord
    so as to instruct him?"[g]

But we have the mind of Christ.

The Church and Its Leaders

3 Brothers and sisters, I could not address you as people who live by the Spirit but as people who are still worldly—mere infants in Christ. [2]I gave you milk, not solid food, for you were not yet ready for it. Indeed, you are still not ready. [3]You are still worldly. For since there is jealousy and quarreling among you, are you not worldly? Are you not acting like mere humans? [4]For when one says, "I follow Paul," and another, "I follow Apollos," are you not mere human beings?

[5]What, after all, is Apollos? And what is Paul? Only servants, through whom you came

to believe—as the Lord has assigned to each his task. [6]I planted the seed, Apollos watered it, but God has been making it grow. [7]So neither the one who plants nor the one who waters is anything, but only God, who makes things grow. [8]The one who plants and the one who waters have one purpose, and they will each be rewarded according to their own labor. [9]For we are co-workers in God's service; you are God's field, God's building.

[10]By the grace God has given me, I laid a foundation as a wise builder, and someone else is building on it. But each one should build with care. [11]For no one can lay any foundation other than the one already laid, which is Jesus Christ. [12]If anyone builds on this foundation using gold, silver, costly stones, wood, hay or straw, [13]their work will be shown for what it is, because the Day will bring it to light. It will be revealed with fire, and the fire will test the quality of each person's work. [14]If what has been built survives, the builder will receive a reward. [15]If it is burned up, the builder will suffer loss but yet will be saved—even though only as one escaping through the flames.

[16]Don't you know that you yourselves are God's temple and that God's Spirit dwells in your midst? [17]If anyone destroys God's temple, God will destroy that person; for God's temple is sacred, and you together are that temple.

[18]Do not deceive yourselves. If any of you think you are wise by the standards of this age, you should become "fools" so that you may become wise. [19]For the wisdom of this world is foolishness in God's sight. As it is written: "He catches the wise in their craftiness"[a]; [20]and again, "The Lord knows that the thoughts of the wise are futile."[b] [21]So then, no more boasting about human leaders! All things are yours, [22]whether Paul or Apollos or Cephas[c] or the world or life or death or the present or the future—all are yours, [23]and you are of Christ, and Christ is of God.

The Nature of True Apostleship

4 This, then, is how you ought to regard us: as servants of Christ and as those entrusted with the mysteries God has revealed. [2]Now it is required that those who have been given a trust must prove faithful. [3]I care very little if I am judged by you or by any human court; indeed, I do not even judge myself. [4]My conscience is clear, but that does not make me innocent. It is the Lord who judges me. [5]Therefore judge nothing before the appointed time; wait until the Lord comes. He will bring to light what is hidden in darkness and will expose the motives of the heart. At that time each will receive their praise from God.

[6]Now, brothers and sisters, I have applied these things to myself and Apollos for your benefit, so that you may learn from us the meaning of the saying, "Do not go beyond what is written." Then you will not be puffed up in being a follower of one of us over against the other. [7]For who makes you different from anyone else? What do you have that you did not receive? And if you did receive it, why do you boast as though you did not?

[8]Already you have all you want! Already you have become rich! You have begun to reign—and that without us! How I wish that you really had begun to reign so that we also might reign with you! [9]For it seems to me that God has put us apostles on display at the end of the procession, like those condemned to die in the arena. We have been made a spectacle to the whole universe, to angels as well as to human beings. [10]We are fools for Christ, but you are so wise in Christ! We are weak, but you are strong! You are honored, we are dishonored! [11]To this very hour we go hungry and thirsty, we are in rags, we are brutally treated, we are homeless. [12]We work hard with our own hands. When we are cursed, we bless; when we are persecuted, we endure it; [13]when we are slandered, we answer kindly. We have become the scum of the earth, the garbage of the world—right up to this moment.

Paul's Appeal and Warning

[14]I am writing this not to shame you but to warn you as my dear children. [15]Even if you had ten thousand guardians in Christ, you do not have many fathers, for in Christ Jesus I became your father through the gospel. [16]Therefore I urge you to imitate me. [17]For this reason I have sent to you Timothy, my son whom I love, who is faithful in the Lord. He will remind you of my way of life in Christ Jesus, which agrees with what I teach everywhere in every church.

[18]Some of you have become arrogant, as if I were not coming to you. [19]But I will come to you very soon, if the Lord is willing, and then I will find out not only how these arrogant people are talking, but what power they have. [20]For the kingdom of God is not a matter of talk but of power. [21]What do you prefer? Shall I come to you with a rod of discipline, or shall I come in love and with a gentle spirit?

Dealing With a Case of Incest

5 It is actually reported that there is sexual immorality among you, and of a kind that even pagans do not tolerate: A man is sleeping with his father's wife. [2]And you are proud! Shouldn't you rather have gone into mourning and have put out of your fellowship the man who has been doing this? [3]For my part, even though I am not physically present, I am with you in spirit. As one who is present with you in this way, I have already passed judgment in the name of our Lord Jesus on the one who has been doing this. [4]So when you are assembled and I am with you in spirit, and the power of our Lord Jesus is present, [5]hand this man over to Satan for the destruction of the flesh,[d,e] so that his spirit may be saved on the day of the Lord.

---

[a] 19 Job 5:13   [b] 20 Psalm 94:11   [c] 22 That is, Peter   [d] 5 In contexts like this, the Greek word for flesh (sarx) refers to the sinful state of human beings, often presented as a power in opposition to the Spirit.   [e] 5 Or of his body

⁶Your boasting is not good. Don't you know that a little yeast leavens the whole batch of dough? ⁷Get rid of the old yeast, so that you may be a new unleavened batch—as you really are. For Christ, our Passover lamb, has been sacrificed. ⁸Therefore let us keep the Festival, not with the old bread leavened with malice and wickedness, but with the unleavened bread of sincerity and truth.

⁹I wrote to you in my letter not to associate with sexually immoral people— ¹⁰not at all meaning the people of this world who are immoral, or the greedy and swindlers, or idolaters. In that case you would have to leave this world. ¹¹But now I am writing to you that you must not associate with anyone who claims to be a brother or sister*a* but is sexually immoral or greedy, an idolater or slanderer, a drunkard or swindler. Do not even eat with such people.

¹²What business is it of mine to judge those outside the church? Are you not to judge those inside? ¹³God will judge those outside. "Expel the wicked person from among you."*b*

Lawsuits Among Believers

6 If any of you has a dispute with another, do you dare to take it before the ungodly for judgment instead of before the Lord's people? ²Or do you not know that the Lord's people will judge the world? And if you are to judge the world, are you not competent to judge trivial cases? ³Do you not know that we will judge angels? How much more the things of this life! ⁴Therefore, if you have disputes about such matters, do you ask for a ruling from those whose way of life is scorned in the church? ⁵I say this to shame you. Is it possible that there is nobody among you wise enough to judge a dispute between believers? ⁶But instead, one brother takes another to court—and this in front of unbelievers!

⁷The very fact that you have lawsuits among you means you have been completely defeated already. Why not rather be wronged? Why not rather be cheated? ⁸Instead, you yourselves cheat and do wrong, and you do this to your brothers and sisters. ⁹Or do you not know that wrongdoers will not inherit the kingdom of God? Do not be deceived: Neither the sexually immoral nor idolaters nor adulterers nor men who have sex with men*c* ¹⁰nor thieves nor the greedy nor drunkards nor slanderers nor swindlers will inherit the kingdom of God. ¹¹And that is what some of you were. But you were washed, you were sanctified, you were justified in the name of the Lord Jesus Christ and by the Spirit of our God.

Sexual Immorality

¹²"I have the right to do anything," you say—but not everything is beneficial. "I have the right to do anything"—but I will not be mastered by anything. ¹³You say, "Food for the stomach and the stomach for food, and God

will destroy them both." The body, however, is not meant for sexual immorality but for the Lord, and the Lord for the body. ¹⁴By his power God raised the Lord from the dead, and he will raise us also. ¹⁵Do you not know that your bodies are members of Christ himself? Shall I then take the members of Christ and unite them with a prostitute? Never! ¹⁶Do you not know that he who unites himself with a prostitute is one with her in body? For it is said, "The two will become one flesh."*d* ¹⁷But whoever is united with the Lord is one with him in spirit.*e*

¹⁸Flee from sexual immorality. All other sins a person commits are outside the body, but whoever sins sexually, sins against their own body. ¹⁹Do you not know that your bodies are temples of the Holy Spirit, who is in you, whom you have received from God? You are not your own; ²⁰you were bought at a price. Therefore honor God with your bodies.

Concerning Married Life

7 Now for the matters you wrote about: "It is good for a man not to have sexual relations with a woman." ²But since sexual immorality is occurring, each man should have sexual relations with his own wife, and each woman with her own husband. ³The husband should fulfill his marital duty to his wife, and likewise the wife to her husband. ⁴The wife does not have authority over her own body but yields it to her husband. In the same way, the husband does not have authority over his own body but yields it to his wife. ⁵Do not deprive each other except perhaps by mutual consent and for a time, so that you may devote yourselves to prayer. Then come together again so that Satan will not tempt you because of your lack of self-control. ⁶I say this as a concession, not as a command. ⁷I wish that all of you were as I am. But each of you has your own gift from God; one has this gift, another has that.

⁸Now to the unmarried*f* and the widows I say: It is good for them to stay unmarried, as I do. ⁹But if they cannot control themselves, they should marry, for it is better to marry than to burn with passion.

¹⁰To the married I give this command (not I, but the Lord): A wife must not separate from her husband. ¹¹But if she does, she must remain unmarried or else be reconciled to her husband. And a husband must not divorce his wife.

¹²To the rest I say this (I, not the Lord): If any brother has a wife who is not a believer and she is willing to live with him, he must not divorce her. ¹³And if a woman has a husband who is not a believer and he is willing to live with her, she must not divorce him. ¹⁴For the unbelieving husband has been sanctified through his wife, and the unbelieving wife has been sanctified through her believing

---

a 11 The Greek word for *brother or sister* (*adelphos*) refers here to a believer, whether man or woman, as part of God's family; also in 8:11, 13.   *b* 13 Deut. 13:5; 17:7; 19:19; 21:21; 22:21,24; 24:7   *c* 9 The words *men who have sex with men* translate two Greek words that refer to the passive and active participants in homosexual acts.   *d* 16 Gen. 2:24   *e* 17 Or *in the Spirit*   *f* 8 Or *widowers*

husband. Otherwise your children would be unclean, but as it is, they are holy.

15But if the unbeliever leaves, let it be so. The brother or the sister is not bound in such circumstances; God has called us to live in peace. 16How do you know, wife, whether you will save your husband? Or, how do you know, husband, whether you will save your wife?

Concerning Change of Status

17Nevertheless, each person should live as a believer in whatever situation the Lord has assigned to them, just as God has called them. This is the rule I lay down in all the churches. 18Was a man already circumcised when he was called? He should not become uncircumcised. Was a man uncircumcised when he was called? He should not be circumcised. 19Circumcision is nothing and uncircumcision is nothing. Keeping God's commands is what counts. 20Each person should remain in the situation they were in when God called them.

21Were you a slave when you were called? Don't let it trouble you—although if you can gain your freedom, do so. 22For the one who was a slave when called to faith in the Lord is the Lord's freed person; similarly, the one who was free when called is Christ's slave. 23You were bought at a price; do not become slaves of human beings. 24Brothers and sisters, each person, as responsible to God, should remain in the situation they were in when God called them.

Concerning the Unmarried

25Now about virgins: I have no command from the Lord, but I give a judgment as one who by the Lord's mercy is trustworthy. 26Because of the present crisis, I think that it is good for a man to remain as he is. 27Are you pledged to a woman? Do not seek to be released. Are you free from such a commitment? Do not look for a wife. 28But if you do marry, you have not sinned; and if a virgin marries, she has not sinned. But those who marry will face many troubles in this life, and I want to spare you this.

29What I mean, brothers and sisters, is that the time is short. From now on those who have wives should live as if they do not; 30those who mourn, as if they did not; those who are happy, as if they were not; those who buy something, as if it were not theirs to keep; 31those who use the things of the world, as if not engrossed in them. For this world in its present form is passing away.

32I would like you to be free from concern. An unmarried man is concerned about the Lord's affairs—how he can please the Lord. 33But a married man is concerned about the affairs of this world—how he can please his wife— 34and his interests are divided. An unmarried woman or virgin is concerned about the Lord's affairs: Her aim is to be devoted to the Lord in both body and spirit. But a married woman is concerned about the affairs of this world—how she can please her husband. 35I am saying this for your own good, not to restrict you, but that you may live in a right way in undivided devotion to the Lord.

36If anyone is worried that he might not be acting honorably toward the virgin he is engaged to, and if his passions are too strong[a] and he feels he ought to marry, he should do as he wants. He is not sinning. They should get married. 37But the man who has settled the matter in his own mind, who is under no compulsion but has control over his own will, and who has made up his mind not to marry the virgin—this man also does the right thing. 38So then, he who marries the virgin does right, but he who does not marry her does better.[b]

39A woman is bound to her husband as long as he lives. But if her husband dies, she is free to marry anyone she wishes, but he must belong to the Lord. 40In my judgment, she is happier if she stays as she is—and I think that I too have the Spirit of God.

Concerning Food Sacrificed to Idols

8 Now about food sacrificed to idols: We know that "We all possess knowledge." But knowledge puffs up while love builds up. 2Those who think they know something do not yet know as they ought to know. 3But whoever loves God is known by God.[c]

4So then, about eating food sacrificed to idols: We know that "An idol is nothing at all in the world" and that "There is no God but one." 5For even if there are so-called gods, whether in heaven or on earth (as indeed there are many "gods" and many "lords"), 6yet for us there is but one God, the Father, from whom all things came and for whom we live; and there is but one Lord, Jesus Christ, through whom all things came and through whom we live.

7But not everyone possesses this knowledge. Some people are still so accustomed to idols that when they eat sacrificial food they think of it as having been sacrificed to a god, and since their conscience is weak, it is defiled. 8But food does not bring us near to God; we are no worse if we do not eat, and no better if we do.

9Be careful, however, that the exercise of your rights does not become a stumbling block to the weak. 10For if someone with a weak conscience sees you, with all your

---

a 36 Or if she is getting beyond the usual age for marriage   b 36-38 Or 36If anyone thinks he is not treating his daughter properly, and if she is getting along in years (or if her passions are too strong), and he feels she ought to marry, he should do as he wants. He is not sinning. He should let her get married. 37But the man who has settled the matter in his own mind, who is under no compulsion but has control over his own will, and who has made up his mind to keep the virgin unmarried—this man also does the right thing. 38So then, he who gives his virgin in marriage does right, but he who does not give her in marriage does better.   c 2,3 An early manuscript and another ancient witness think they have knowledge do not yet know as they ought to know. 3But whoever loves truly knows.

knowledge, eating in an idol's temple, won't that person be emboldened to eat what is sacrificed to idols? [11]So this weak brother or sister, for whom Christ died, is destroyed by your knowledge. [12]When you sin against them in this way and wound their weak conscience, you sin against Christ. [13]Therefore, if what I eat causes my brother or sister to fall into sin, I will never eat meat again, so that I will not cause them to fall.

Paul's Rights as an Apostle

9 Am I not free? Am I not an apostle? Have I not seen Jesus our Lord? Are you not the result of my work in the Lord? [2]Even though I may not be an apostle to others, surely I am to you! For you are the seal of my apostleship in the Lord.

[3]This is my defense to those who sit in judgment on me. [4]Don't we have the right to food and drink? [5]Don't we have the right to take a believing wife along with us, as do the other apostles and the Lord's brothers and Cephas[a]? [6]Or is it only I and Barnabas who lack the right to not work for a living?

[7]Who serves as a soldier at his own expense? Who plants a vineyard and does not eat its grapes? Who tends a flock and does not drink the milk? [8]Do I say this merely on human authority? Doesn't the Law say the same thing? [9]For it is written in the Law of Moses: "Do not muzzle an ox while it is treading out the grain."[b] Is it about oxen that God is concerned? [10]Surely he says this for us, doesn't he? Yes, this was written for us, because whoever plows and threshes should be able to do so in the hope of sharing in the harvest. [11]If we have sown spiritual seed among you, is it too much if we reap a material harvest from you? [12]If others have this right of support from you, shouldn't we have it all the more?

But we did not use this right. On the contrary, we put up with anything rather than hinder the gospel of Christ.

[13]Don't you know that those who serve in the temple get their food from the temple, and that those who serve at the altar share in what is offered on the altar? [14]In the same way, the Lord has commanded that those who preach the gospel should receive their living from the gospel.

[15]But I have not used any of these rights. And I am not writing this in the hope that you will do such things for me, for I would rather die than allow anyone to deprive me of this boast. [16]For when I preach the gospel, I cannot boast, since I am compelled to preach. Woe to me if I do not preach the gospel! [17]If I preach voluntarily, I have a reward; if not voluntarily, I am simply discharging the trust committed to me. [18]What then is my reward? Just this: that in preaching the gospel I may offer it free of charge, and so not make full use of my rights as a preacher of the gospel.

Paul's Use of His Freedom

[19]Though I am free and belong to no one, I have made myself a slave to everyone, to win as many as possible. [20]To the Jews I became like a Jew, to win the Jews. To those under the law I became like one under the law (though I myself am not under the law), so as to win those under the law. [21]To those not having the law I became like one not having the law (though I am not free from God's law but am under Christ's law), so as to win those not having the law. [22]To the weak I became weak, to win the weak. I have become all things to all people so that by all possible means I might save some. [23]I do all this for the sake of the gospel, that I may share in its blessings.

The Need for Self-Discipline

[24]Do you not know that in a race all the runners run, but only one gets the prize? Run in such a way as to get the prize. [25]Everyone who competes in the games goes into strict training. They do it to get a crown that will not last, but we do it to get a crown that will last forever. [26]Therefore I do not run like someone running aimlessly; I do not fight like a boxer beating the air. [27]No, I strike a blow to my body and make it my slave so that after I have preached to others, I myself will not be disqualified for the prize.

Warnings From Israel's History

10 For I do not want you to be ignorant of the fact, brothers and sisters, that our ancestors were all under the cloud and that they all passed through the sea. [2]They were all baptized into Moses in the cloud and in the sea. [3]They all ate the same spiritual food [4]and drank the same spiritual drink; for they drank from the spiritual rock that accompanied them, and that rock was Christ. [5]Nevertheless, God was not pleased with most of them; their bodies were scattered in the wilderness.

[6]Now these things occurred as examples to keep us from setting our hearts on evil things as they did. [7]Do not be idolaters, as some of them were; as it is written: "The people sat down to eat and drink and got up to indulge in revelry."[c] [8]We should not commit sexual immorality, as some of them did—and in one day twenty-three thousand of them died. [9]We should not test Christ,[d] as some of them did—and were killed by snakes. [10]And do not grumble, as some of them did—and were killed by the destroying angel.

[11]These things happened to them as examples and were written down as warnings for us, on whom the culmination of the ages has come. [12]So, if you think you are standing firm, be careful that you don't fall! [13]No temptation[e] has overtaken you except what is common to mankind. And God is faithful; he will not let you be tempted[e] beyond what you can bear. But when you are tempted,[e] he will also provide a way out so that you can endure it.

[a] 5 That is, Peter   [b] 9 Deut. 25:4   [c] 7 Exodus 32:6   [d] 9 Some manuscripts *test the Lord*
[e] 13 The Greek for *temptation* and *tempted* can also mean *testing* and *tested*.

Idol Feasts and the Lord's Supper

[14]Therefore, my dear friends, flee from idolatry. [15]I speak to sensible people; judge for yourselves what I say. [16]Is not the cup of thanksgiving for which we give thanks a participation in the blood of Christ? And is not the bread that we break a participation in the body of Christ? [17]Because there is one loaf, we, who are many, are one body, for we all share the one loaf.

[18]Consider the people of Israel: Do not those who eat the sacrifices participate in the altar? [19]Do I mean then that food sacrificed to an idol is anything, or that an idol is anything? [20]No, but the sacrifices of pagans are offered to demons, not to God, and I do not want you to be participants with demons. [21]You cannot drink the cup of the Lord and the cup of demons too; you cannot have a part in both the Lord's table and the table of demons. [22]Are we trying to arouse the Lord's jealousy? Are we stronger than he?

The Believer's Freedom

[23]"I have the right to do anything," you say—but not everything is beneficial. "I have the right to do anything"—but not everything is constructive. [24]No one should seek their own good, but the good of others.

[25]Eat anything sold in the meat market without raising questions of conscience, [26]for, "The earth is the Lord's, and everything in it."[a]

[27]If an unbeliever invites you to a meal and you want to go, eat whatever is put before you without raising questions of conscience. [28]But if someone says to you, "This has been offered in sacrifice," then do not eat it, both for the sake of the one who told you and for the sake of conscience. [29]I am referring to the other person's conscience, not yours. For why is my freedom being judged by another's conscience? [30]If I take part in the meal with thankfulness, why am I denounced because of something I thank God for?

[31]So whether you eat or drink or whatever you do, do it all for the glory of God. [32]Do not cause anyone to stumble, whether Jews, Greeks or the church of God— [33]even as I try to please everyone in every way. For I am not seeking my own good but the good of many, **11** so that they may be saved. [1]Follow my example, as I follow the example of Christ.

On Covering the Head in Worship

[2]I praise you for remembering me in everything and for holding to the traditions just as I passed them on to you. [3]But I want you to realize that the head of every man is Christ, and the head of the woman is man,[b] and the head of Christ is God. [4]Every man who prays or prophesies with his head covered dishonors his head. [5]But every woman who prays or prophesies with her head uncovered dishonors her head—it is the same as having her head shaved. [6]For if a woman does not cover her head, she might as well have her hair cut off; but if it is a disgrace for a woman to have her hair cut off or her head shaved, then she should cover her head.

[7]A man ought not to cover his head,[c] since he is the image and glory of God; but woman is the glory of man. [8]For man did not come from woman, but woman from man; [9]neither was man created for woman, but woman for man. [10]It is for this reason that a woman ought to have authority over her own[d] head, because of the angels. [11]Nevertheless, in the Lord woman is not independent of man, nor is man independent of woman. [12]For as woman came from man, so also man is born of woman. But everything comes from God.

[13]Judge for yourselves: Is it proper for a woman to pray to God with her head uncovered? [14]Does not the very nature of things teach you that if a man has long hair, it is a disgrace to him, [15]but that if a woman has long hair, it is her glory? For long hair is given to her as a covering. [16]If anyone wants to be contentious about this, we have no other practice—nor do the churches of God.

Correcting an Abuse of the Lord's Supper

[17]In the following directives I have no praise for you, for your meetings do more harm than good. [18]In the first place, I hear that when you come together as a church, there are divisions among you, and to some extent I believe it. [19]No doubt there have to be differences among you to show which of you have God's approval. [20]So then, when you come together, it is not the Lord's Supper you eat, [21]for when you are eating, some of you go ahead with your own private suppers. As a result, one person remains hungry and another gets drunk. [22]Don't you have homes to eat and drink in? Or do you despise the church of God by humiliating those who have nothing? What shall I say to you? Shall I praise you? Certainly not in this matter!

[23]For I received from the Lord what I also passed on to you: The Lord Jesus, on the night he was betrayed, took bread, [24]and when he had given thanks, he broke it and said, "This is my body, which is for you; do this in remembrance of me." [25]In the same way, after supper he took the cup, saying, "This cup is the new covenant in my blood; do this, whenever you drink it, in remembrance of me." [26]For whenever you eat this bread and drink this cup, you proclaim the Lord's death until he comes.

[27]So then, whoever eats the bread or drinks the cup of the Lord in an unworthy manner will be guilty of sinning against the body and blood of the Lord. [28]Everyone ought to examine themselves before they eat of the

---

[a] 26 Psalm 24:1   [b] 3 Or of the wife is her husband   [c] 4-7 Or [4]Every man who prays or prophesies with long hair dishonors his head. [5]But every woman who prays or prophesies with no covering of hair dishonors her head—she is just like one of the "shorn women." [6]If a woman has no covering, let her for now with short hair; but since it is a disgrace for a woman to have her hair shorn or shaved, she should grow it again. [7]A man ought not to have long hair   [d] 10 Or have a sign of authority on her

bread and drink from the cup. ²⁹For those who eat and drink without discerning the body of Christ eat and drink judgment on themselves. ³⁰That is why many among you are weak and sick, and a number of you have fallen asleep. ³¹But if we were more discerning with regard to ourselves, we would not come under such judgment. ³²Nevertheless, when we are judged in this way by the Lord, we are being disciplined so that we will not be finally condemned with the world.

³³So then, my brothers and sisters, when you gather to eat, you should all eat together. ³⁴Anyone who is hungry should eat something at home, so that when you meet together it may not result in judgment.

And when I come I will give further directions.

Concerning Spiritual Gifts

12 Now about the gifts of the Spirit, brothers and sisters, I do not want you to be uninformed. ²You know that when you were pagans, somehow or other you were influenced and led astray to mute idols. ³Therefore I want you to know that no one who is speaking by the Spirit of God says, "Jesus is cursed," and no one can say, "Jesus is Lord," except by the Holy Spirit.

⁴There are different kinds of gifts, but the same Spirit distributes them. ⁵There are different kinds of service, but the same Lord. ⁶There are different kinds of working, but in all of them and in everyone it is the same God at work.

⁷Now to each one the manifestation of the Spirit is given for the common good. ⁸To one there is given through the Spirit a message of wisdom, to another a message of knowledge by means of the same Spirit, ⁹to another faith by the same Spirit, to another gifts of healing by that one Spirit, ¹⁰to another miraculous powers, to another prophecy, to another distinguishing between spirits, to another speaking in different kinds of tongues,ᵃ and to still another the interpretation of tongues.ᵃ ¹¹All these are the work of one and the same Spirit, and he distributes them to each one, just as he determines.

Unity and Diversity in the Body

¹²Just as a body, though one, has many parts, but all its many parts form one body, so it is with Christ. ¹³For we were all baptized byᵇ one Spirit so as to form one body—whether Jews or Gentiles, slave or free—and we were all given the one Spirit to drink. ¹⁴Even so the body is not made up of one part but of many.

¹⁵Now if the foot should say, "Because I am not a hand, I do not belong to the body," it would not for that reason stop being part of the body. ¹⁶And if the ear should say, "Because I am not an eye, I do not belong to the body," it would not for that reason stop being part of the body. ¹⁷If the whole body were an eye, where would the sense of hearing be? If the whole body were an ear, where would the sense of smell be? ¹⁸But in fact God has placed the parts in the body, every one of them, just as he wanted them to be. ¹⁹If they were all one part, where would the body be? ²⁰As it is, there are many parts, but one body.

²¹The eye cannot say to the hand, "I don't need you!" And the head cannot say to the feet, "I don't need you!" ²²On the contrary, those parts of the body that seem to be weaker are indispensable, ²³and the parts that we think are less honorable we treat with special honor. And the parts that are unpresentable are treated with special modesty, ²⁴while our presentable parts need no special treatment. But God has put the body together, giving greater honor to the parts that lacked it, ²⁵so that there should be no division in the body, but that its parts should have equal concern for each other. ²⁶If one part suffers, every part suffers with it; if one part is honored, every part rejoices with it.

²⁷Now you are the body of Christ, and each one of you is a part of it. ²⁸And God has placed in the church first of all apostles, second prophets, third teachers, then miracles, then gifts of healing, of helping, of guidance, and of different kinds of tongues. ²⁹Are all apostles? Are all prophets? Are all teachers? Do all work miracles? ³⁰Do all have gifts of healing? Do all speak in tonguesᶜ? Do all interpret? ³¹Now eagerly desire the greater gifts.

Love Is Indispensable

And yet I will show you the most excellent way.

13 If I speak in the tonguesᵈ of men or of angels, but do not have love, I am only a resounding gong or a clanging cymbal. ²If I have the gift of prophecy and can fathom all mysteries and all knowledge, and if I have a faith that can move mountains, but do not have love, I am nothing. ³If I give all I possess to the poor and give over my body to hardship that I may boast,ᵉ but do not have love, I gain nothing.

⁴Love is patient, loveᵉ is kind. It does not envy, it does not boast, it is not proud. ⁵It does not dishonor others, it is not self-seeking, it is not easily angered, it keeps no record of wrongs. ⁶Love does not delight in evil but rejoices with the truth. ⁷It always protects, always trusts, always hopes, always perseveres.

⁸Love never fails. But where there are prophecies, they will cease; where there are tongues, they will be stilled; where there is knowledge, it will pass away. ⁹For we know in part and we prophesy in part, ¹⁰but when completeness comes, what is in part disappears. ¹¹When I was a child, I talked like a child, I thought like a child, I reasoned like a child. When I became a man, I put the ways of childhood behind me. ¹²For now we see only a reflection as in a mirror; then we shall see face to face. Now I know in part; then I shall know fully, even as I am fully known.

ᵃ 10 Or *languages*; also in verse 28   ᵇ 13 Or *with*; or *in*   ᶜ 30 Or *other languages*
ᵈ 1 Or *languages*   ᵉ 3 Some manuscripts *body to the flames*

13And now these three remain: faith, hope and love. But the greatest of these is love.

Intelligibility in Worship

14 Follow the way of love and eagerly desire gifts of the Spirit, especially prophecy. 2For anyone who speaks in a tongue[a] does not speak to people but to God. Indeed, no one understands them; they utter mysteries by the Spirit. 3But the one who prophesies speaks to people for their strengthening, encouraging and comfort. 4Anyone who speaks in a tongue edifies themselves, but the one who prophesies edifies the church. 5I would like every one of you to speak in tongues,[b] but I would rather have you prophesy. The one who prophesies is greater than the one who speaks in tongues,[b] unless someone interprets, so that the church may be edified.

6Now, brothers and sisters, if I come to you and speak in tongues, what good will I be to you, unless I bring you some revelation or knowledge or prophecy or word of instruction? 7Even in the case of lifeless things that make sounds, such as the pipe or harp, how will anyone know what tune is being played unless there is a distinction in the notes? 8Again, if the trumpet does not sound a clear call, who will get ready for battle? 9So it is with you. Unless you speak intelligible words with your tongue, how will anyone know what you are saying? You will just be speaking into the air. 10Undoubtedly there are all sorts of languages in the world, yet none of them is without meaning. 11If then I do not grasp the meaning of what someone is saying, I am a foreigner to the speaker, and the speaker is a foreigner to me. 12So it is with you. Since you are eager for gifts of the Spirit, try to excel in those that build up the church.

13For this reason the one who speaks in a tongue should pray that they may interpret what they say. 14For if I pray in a tongue, my spirit prays, but my mind is unfruitful. 15So what shall I do? I will pray with my spirit, but I will also pray with my understanding; I will sing with my spirit, but I will also sing with my understanding. 16Otherwise when you are praising God in the Spirit, how can someone else, who is now put in the position of an inquirer,[c] say "Amen" to your thanksgiving, since they do not know what you are saying? 17You are giving thanks well enough, but no one else is edified.

18I thank God that I speak in tongues more than all of you. 19But in the church I would rather speak five intelligible words to instruct others than ten thousand words in a tongue.

20Brothers and sisters, stop thinking like children. In regard to evil be infants, but in your thinking be adults. 21In the Law it is written:

"With other tongues
 and through the lips of foreigners
I will speak to this people,
 but even then they will not listen to me,
 says the Lord."[d]

22Tongues, then, are a sign, not for believers but for unbelievers; prophecy, however, is not for unbelievers but for believers. 23So if the whole church comes together and everyone speaks in tongues, and inquirers or unbelievers come in, will they not say that you are out of your mind? 24But if an unbeliever or an inquirer comes in while everyone is prophesying, they are convicted of sin and are brought under judgment by all, 25as the secrets of their hearts are laid bare. So they will fall down and worship God, exclaiming, "God is really among you!"

Good Order in Worship

26What then shall we say, brothers and sisters? When you come together, each of you has a hymn, or a word of instruction, a revelation, a tongue or an interpretation. Everything must be done so that the church may be built up. 27If anyone speaks in a tongue, two—or at the most three—should speak, one at a time, and someone must interpret. 28If there is no interpreter, the speaker should keep quiet in the church and speak to himself and to God.

29Two or three prophets should speak, and the others should weigh carefully what is said. 30And if a revelation comes to someone who is sitting down, the first speaker should stop. 31For you can all prophesy in turn so that everyone may be instructed and encouraged. 32The spirits of prophets are subject to the control of prophets. 33For God is not a God of disorder but of peace—as in all the congregations of the Lord's people.

34Women[e] should remain silent in the churches. They are not allowed to speak, but must be in submission, as the law says. 35If they want to inquire about something, they should ask their own husbands at home; for it is disgraceful for a woman to speak in the church.[f]

36Or did the word of God originate with you? Or are you the only people it has reached? 37If anyone thinks they are a prophet or otherwise gifted by the Spirit, let them acknowledge that what I am writing to you is the Lord's command. 38But if anyone ignores this, they will themselves be ignored.[g]

39Therefore, my brothers and sisters, be eager to prophesy, and do not forbid speaking in tongues. 40But everything should be done in a fitting and orderly way.

The Resurrection of Christ

15 Now, brothers and sisters, I want to remind you of the gospel I preached to you, which you received and on which you have taken your stand. 2By this gospel you

---

a 2 Or *in another language*; also in verses 4, 13, 14, 19, 26 and 27   *b 5* Or *in other languages*; also in verses 6, 18, 22, 23 and 39   *c 16* The Greek word for *inquirer* is a technical term for someone not fully initiated into a religion; also in verses 23 and 24.   *d 21* Isaiah 28:11,12   *e 33,34* Or *peace. As in all the congregations of the Lord's people,* 34*women*   *f 34,35* In a few manuscripts these verses come after verse 40.   *g 38* Some manuscripts *But anyone who is ignorant of this will be ignorant*

are saved, if you hold firmly to the word I preached to you. Otherwise, you have believed in vain.

³For what I received I passed on to you as of first importance*a*: that Christ died for our sins according to the Scriptures, ⁴that he was buried, that he was raised on the third day according to the Scriptures, ⁵and that he appeared to Cephas,*b* and then to the Twelve. ⁶After that, he appeared to more than five hundred of the brothers and sisters at the same time, most of whom are still living, though some have fallen asleep. ⁷Then he appeared to James, then to all the apostles, ⁸and last of all he appeared to me also, as to one abnormally born.

⁹For I am the least of the apostles and do not even deserve to be called an apostle, because I persecuted the church of God. ¹⁰But by the grace of God I am what I am, and his grace to me was not without effect. No, I worked harder than all of them—yet not I, but the grace of God that was with me. ¹¹Whether, then, it is I or they, this is what we preach, and this is what you believed.

The Resurrection of the Dead

¹²But if it is preached that Christ has been raised from the dead, how can some of you say that there is no resurrection of the dead? ¹³If there is no resurrection of the dead, then not even Christ has been raised. ¹⁴And if Christ has not been raised, our preaching is useless and so is your faith. ¹⁵More than that, we are then found to be false witnesses about God, for we have testified about God that he raised Christ from the dead. But he did not raise him if in fact the dead are not raised. ¹⁶For if the dead are not raised, then Christ has not been raised either. ¹⁷And if Christ has not been raised, your faith is futile; you are still in your sins. ¹⁸Then those also who have fallen asleep in Christ are lost. ¹⁹If only for this life we have hope in Christ, we are of all people most to be pitied.

²⁰But Christ has indeed been raised from the dead, the firstfruits of those who have fallen asleep. ²¹For since death came through a man, the resurrection of the dead comes also through a man. ²²For as in Adam all die, so in Christ all will be made alive. ²³But each in turn: Christ, the firstfruits; then, when he comes, those who belong to him. ²⁴Then the end will come, when he hands over the kingdom to God the Father after he has destroyed all dominion, authority and power. ²⁵For he must reign until he has put all his enemies under his feet. ²⁶The last enemy to be destroyed is death. ²⁷For he "has put everything under his feet."*c* Now when it says that "everything" has been put under him, it is clear that this does not include God himself, who put everything under Christ. ²⁸When he has done this, then the Son himself will be made subject to him who put everything under him, so that God may be all in all.

²⁹Now if there is no resurrection, what will those who are baptized for the dead do? If the dead are not raised at all, why are people baptized for them? ³⁰And as for us, why do we endanger ourselves every hour? ³¹I face death every day—yes, just as surely as I boast about you in Christ Jesus our Lord. ³²If I fought wild beasts in Ephesus with no more than human hopes, what have I gained? If the dead are not raised,

"Let us eat and drink,
  for tomorrow we die."*d*

³³Do not be misled: "Bad company corrupts good character."*e* ³⁴Come back to your senses as you ought, and stop sinning; for there are some who are ignorant of God—I say this to your shame.

The Resurrection Body

³⁵But someone will ask, "How are the dead raised? With what kind of body will they come?" ³⁶How foolish! What you sow does not come to life unless it dies. ³⁷When you sow, you do not plant the body that will be, but just a seed, perhaps of wheat or of something else. ³⁸But God gives it a body as he has determined, and to each kind of seed he gives its own body. ³⁹Not all flesh is the same: People have one kind of flesh, animals have another, birds another and fish another. ⁴⁰There are also heavenly bodies and there are earthly bodies; but the splendor of the heavenly bodies is one kind, and the splendor of the earthly bodies is another. ⁴¹The sun has one kind of splendor, the moon another and the stars another; and star differs from star in splendor.

⁴²So will it be with the resurrection of the dead. The body that is sown is perishable, it is raised imperishable; ⁴³it is sown in dishonor, it is raised in glory; it is sown in weakness, it is raised in power; ⁴⁴it is sown a natural body, it is raised a spiritual body.

If there is a natural body, there is also a spiritual body. ⁴⁵So it is written: "The first man Adam became a living being"*f*; the last Adam, a life-giving spirit. ⁴⁶The spiritual did not come first, but the natural, and after that the spiritual. ⁴⁷The first man was of the dust of the earth; the second man is of heaven. ⁴⁸As was the earthly man, so are those who are of the earth; and as is the heavenly man, so also are those who are of heaven. ⁴⁹And just as we have borne the image of the earthly man, so shall we*g* bear the image of the heavenly man.

⁵⁰I declare to you, brothers and sisters, that flesh and blood cannot inherit the kingdom of God, nor does the perishable inherit the imperishable. ⁵¹Listen, I tell you a mystery: We will not all sleep, but we will all be changed— ⁵²in a flash, in the twinkling of an eye, at the last trumpet. For the trumpet will sound, the dead will be raised imperishable, and we will be changed. ⁵³For the perishable must clothe itself with the imperishable, and the mortal

---

a 3 Or *you at the first*   *b* 5 That is, Peter   *c* 27 Psalm 8:6   *d* 32 Isaiah 22:13   *e* 33 From the Greek poet Menander   *f* 45 Gen. 2:7   *g* 49 Some early manuscripts *so let us*

with immortality. [54]When the perishable has been clothed with the imperishable, and the mortal with immortality, then the saying that is written will come true: "Death has been swallowed up in victory."[a]

[55] "Where, O death, is your victory?
Where, O death, is your sting?"[b]

[56]The sting of death is sin, and the power of sin is the law. [57]But thanks be to God! He gives us the victory through our Lord Jesus Christ. [58]Therefore, my dear brothers and sisters, stand firm. Let nothing move you. Always give yourselves fully to the work of the Lord, because you know that your labor in the Lord is not in vain.

The Collection for the Lord's People

16 Now about the collection for the Lord's people: Do what I told the Galatian churches to do. [2]On the first day of every week, each one of you should set aside a sum of money in keeping with your income, saving it up, so that when I come no collections will have to be made. [3]Then, when I arrive, I will give letters of introduction to the men you approve and send them with your gift to Jerusalem. [4]If it seems advisable for me to go also, they will accompany me.

Personal Requests

[5]After I go through Macedonia, I will come to you—for I will be going through Macedonia. [6]Perhaps I will stay with you for a while, or even spend the winter, so that you can help me on my journey, wherever I go. [7]For I do not want to see you now and make only a passing visit; I hope to spend some time with you, if the Lord permits. [8]But I will stay on at Ephesus until Pentecost, [9]because a great door for effective work has opened to me, and there are many who oppose me.

[10]When Timothy comes, see to it that he has nothing to fear while he is with you, for he is carrying on the work of the Lord, just as I am. [11]No one, then, should treat him with contempt. Send him on his way in peace so that he may return to me. I am expecting him along with the brothers.

[12]Now about our brother Apollos: I strongly urged him to go to you with the brothers. He was quite unwilling to go now, but he will go when he has the opportunity.

[13]Be on your guard; stand firm in the faith; be courageous; be strong. [14]Do everything in love.

[15]You know that the household of Stephanas were the first converts in Achaia, and they have devoted themselves to the service of the Lord's people. I urge you, brothers and sisters, [16]to submit to such people and to everyone who joins in the work and labors at it. [17]I was glad when Stephanas, Fortunatus and Achaicus arrived, because they have supplied what was lacking from you. [18]For they refreshed my spirit and yours also. Such men deserve recognition.

Final Greetings

[19]The churches in the province of Asia send you greetings. Aquila and Priscilla[c] greet you warmly in the Lord, and so does the church that meets at their house. [20]All the brothers and sisters here send you greetings. Greet one another with a holy kiss.

[21]I, Paul, write this greeting in my own hand.

[22]If anyone does not love the Lord, let that person be cursed! Come, Lord[d]!

[23]The grace of the Lord Jesus be with you.

[24]My love to all of you in Christ Jesus. Amen.[e]

2 Corinthians

1 Paul, an apostle of Christ Jesus by the will of God, and Timothy our brother,

To the church of God in Corinth, together with all his holy people throughout Achaia:

[2]Grace and peace to you from God our Father and the Lord Jesus Christ.

Praise to the God of All Comfort

[3]Praise be to the God and Father of our Lord Jesus Christ, the Father of compassion and the God of all comfort, [4]who comforts us in all our troubles, so that we can comfort those in any trouble with the comfort we ourselves receive from God. [5]For just as we share abundantly in the sufferings of Christ, so also our comfort abounds through Christ. [6]If we are distressed, it is for your comfort and salvation; if we are comforted, it is for your comfort, which produces in you patient endurance of the same sufferings we suffer. [7]And our hope for you is firm, because we know that just as you share in our sufferings, so also you share in our comfort.

[8]We do not want you to be uninformed, brothers and sisters,[f] about the troubles we experi-

---

[a] 54 Isaiah 25:8   [b] 55 Hosea 13:14   [c] 19 Greek *Prisca*, a variant of *Priscilla*   [d] 22 The Greek for *Come, Lord* reproduces an Aramaic expression (*Marana tha*) used by early Christians.   [e] 24 Some manuscripts do not have *Amen*.   [f] 8 The Greek word for *brothers and sisters* (*adelphoi*) refers here to believers, both men and women, as part of God's family; also in 8:1; 13:11.

enced in the province of Asia. We were under great pressure, far beyond our ability to endure, so that we despaired of life itself. [9]Indeed, we felt we had received the sentence of death. But this happened that we might not rely on ourselves but on God, who raises the dead. [10]He has delivered us from such a deadly peril, and he will deliver us again. On him we have set our hope that he will continue to deliver us, [11]as you help us by your prayers. Then many will give thanks on our behalf for the gracious favor granted us in answer to the prayers of many.

Paul's Change of Plans

[12]Now this is our boast: Our conscience testifies that we have conducted ourselves in the world, and especially in our relations with you, with integrity[a] and godly sincerity. We have done so, relying not on worldly wisdom but on God's grace. [13]For we do not write you anything you cannot read or understand. And I hope that, [14]as you have understood us in part, you will come to understand fully that you can boast of us just as we will boast of you in the day of the Lord Jesus.

[15]Because I was confident of this, I wanted to visit you first so that you might benefit twice. [16]I wanted to visit you on my way to Macedonia and to come back to you from Macedonia, and then to have you send me on my way to Judea. [17]Was I fickle when I intended to do this? Or do I make my plans in a worldly manner so that in the same breath I say both "Yes, yes" and "No, no"?

[18]But as surely as God is faithful, our message to you is not "Yes" and "No." [19]For the Son of God, Jesus Christ, who was preached among you by us—by me and Silas[b] and Timothy—was not "Yes" and "No," but in him it has always been "Yes." [20]For no matter how many promises God has made, they are "Yes" in Christ. And so through him the "Amen" is spoken by us to the glory of God. [21]Now it is God who makes both us and you stand firm in Christ. He anointed us, [22]set his seal of ownership on us, and put his Spirit in our hearts as a deposit, guaranteeing what is to come.

[23]I call God as my witness—and I stake my life on it—that it was in order to spare you that I did not return to Corinth. [24]Not that we lord it over your faith, but we work with you for your joy, because it is by faith you stand firm.

2 [1]So I made up my mind that I would not make another painful visit to you. [2]For if I grieve you, who is left to make me glad but you whom I have grieved? [3]I wrote as I did, so that when I came I would not be distressed by those who should have made me rejoice. I had confidence in all of you, that you would all share my joy. [4]For I wrote you out of great distress and anguish of heart and with many tears, not to grieve you but to let you know the depth of my love for you.

Forgiveness for the Offender

[5]If anyone has caused grief, he has not so much grieved me as he has grieved all of you to some extent—not to put it too severely. [6]The punishment inflicted on him by the majority is sufficient. [7]Now instead, you ought to forgive and comfort him, so that he will not be overwhelmed by excessive sorrow. [8]I urge you, therefore, to reaffirm your love for him. [9]Another reason I wrote you was to see if you would stand the test and be obedient in everything. [10]Anyone you forgive, I also forgive. And what I have forgiven—if there was anything to forgive—I have forgiven in the sight of Christ for your sake, [11]in order that Satan might not outwit us. For we are not unaware of his schemes.

Ministers of the New Covenant

[12]Now when I went to Troas to preach the gospel of Christ and found that the Lord had opened a door for me, [13]I still had no peace of mind, because I did not find my brother Titus there. So I said goodbye to them and went on to Macedonia.

[14]But thanks be to God, who always leads us as captives in Christ's triumphal procession and uses us to spread the aroma of the knowledge of him everywhere. [15]For we are to God the pleasing aroma of Christ among those who are being saved and those who are perishing. [16]To the one we are an aroma that brings death; to the other, an aroma that brings life. And who is equal to such a task? [17]Unlike so many, we do not peddle the word of God for profit. On the contrary, in Christ we speak before God with sincerity, as those sent from God.

3 [1]Are we beginning to commend ourselves again? Or do we need, like some people, letters of recommendation to you or from you? [2]You yourselves are our letter, written on our hearts, known and read by everyone. [3]You show that you are a letter from Christ, the result of our ministry, written not with ink but with the Spirit of the living God, not on tablets of stone but on tablets of human hearts.

[4]Such confidence we have through Christ before God. [5]Not that we are competent in ourselves to claim anything for ourselves, but our competence comes from God. [6]He has made us competent as ministers of a new covenant—not of the letter but of the Spirit; for the letter kills, but the Spirit gives life.

The Greater Glory of the New Covenant

[7]Now if the ministry that brought death, which was engraved in letters on stone, came with glory, so that the Israelites could not look steadily at the face of Moses because of its glory, transitory though it was, [8]will not the ministry of the Spirit be even more glorious? [9]If the ministry that brought condemnation was glorious, how much more glorious is the ministry that brings righteousness! [10]For what was glorious has no glory now in comparison with the surpassing glory. [11]And if what was transitory came with glory, how much greater is the glory of that which lasts!

---

[a] 12 Many manuscripts *holiness*   [b] 19 Greek *Silvanus*, a variant of *Silas*

[12]Therefore, since we have such a hope, we are very bold. [13]We are not like Moses, who would put a veil over his face to prevent the Israelites from seeing the end of what was passing away. [14]But their minds were made dull, for to this day the same veil remains when the old covenant is read. It has not been removed, because only in Christ is it taken away. [15]Even to this day when Moses is read, a veil covers their hearts. [16]But whenever anyone turns to the Lord, the veil is taken away. [17]Now the Lord is the Spirit, and where the Spirit of the Lord is, there is freedom. [18]And we all, who with unveiled faces contemplate[a] the Lord's glory, are being transformed into his image with ever-increasing glory, which comes from the Lord, who is the Spirit.

Present Weakness and Resurrection Life

4 Therefore, since through God's mercy we have this ministry, we do not lose heart. [2]Rather, we have renounced secret and shameful ways; we do not use deception, nor do we distort the word of God. On the contrary, by setting forth the truth plainly we commend ourselves to everyone's conscience in the sight of God. [3]And even if our gospel is veiled, it is veiled to those who are perishing. [4]The god of this age has blinded the minds of unbelievers, so that they cannot see the light of the gospel that displays the glory of Christ, who is the image of God. [5]For what we preach is not ourselves, but Jesus Christ as Lord, and ourselves as your servants for Jesus' sake. [6]For God, who said, "Let light shine out of darkness,"[b] made his light shine in our hearts to give us the light of the knowledge of God's glory displayed in the face of Christ.

[7]But we have this treasure in jars of clay to show that this all-surpassing power is from God and not from us. [8]We are hard pressed on every side, but not crushed; perplexed, but not in despair; [9]persecuted, but not abandoned; struck down, but not destroyed. [10]We always carry around in our body the death of Jesus, so that the life of Jesus may also be revealed in our body. [11]For we who are alive are always being given over to death for Jesus' sake, so that his life may also be revealed in our mortal body. [12]So then, death is at work in us, but life is at work in you.

[13]It is written: "I believed; therefore I have spoken."[c] Since we have that same spirit of[d] faith, we also believe and therefore speak, [14]because we know that the one who raised the Lord Jesus from the dead will also raise us with Jesus and present us with you to himself. [15]All this is for your benefit, so that the grace that is reaching more and more people may cause thanksgiving to overflow to the glory of God.

[16]Therefore we do not lose heart. Though outwardly we are wasting away, yet inwardly we are being renewed day by day. [17]For our light and momentary troubles are achieving for us an eternal glory that far outweighs them all. [18]So we fix our eyes not on what is seen, but on what is unseen, since what is seen is temporary, but what is unseen is eternal.

Awaiting the New Body

5 For we know that if the earthly tent we live in is destroyed, we have a building from God, an eternal house in heaven, not built by human hands. [2]Meanwhile we groan, longing to be clothed instead with our heavenly dwelling, [3]because when we are clothed, we will not be found naked. [4]For while we are in this tent, we groan and are burdened, because we do not wish to be unclothed but to be clothed instead with our heavenly dwelling, so that what is mortal may be swallowed up by life. [5]Now the one who has fashioned us for this very purpose is God, who has given us the Spirit as a deposit, guaranteeing what is to come.

[6]Therefore we are always confident and know that as long as we are at home in the body we are away from the Lord. [7]For we live by faith, not by sight. [8]We are confident, I say, and would prefer to be away from the body and at home with the Lord. [9]So we make it our goal to please him, whether we are at home in the body or away from it. [10]For we must all appear before the judgment seat of Christ, so that each of us may receive what is due us for the things done while in the body, whether good or bad.

The Ministry of Reconciliation

[11]Since, then, we know what it is to fear the Lord, we try to persuade others. What we are is plain to God, and I hope it is also plain to your conscience. [12]We are not trying to commend ourselves to you again, but are giving you an opportunity to take pride in us, so that you can answer those who take pride in what is seen rather than in what is in the heart. [13]If we are "out of our mind," as some say, it is for God; if we are in our right mind, it is for you. [14]For Christ's love compels us, because we are convinced that one died for all, and therefore all died. [15]And he died for all, that those who live should no longer live for themselves but for him who died for them and was raised again.

[16]So from now on we regard no one from a worldly point of view. Though we once regarded Christ in this way, we do so no longer. [17]Therefore, if anyone is in Christ, the new creation has come:[e] The old has gone, the new is here! [18]All this is from God, who reconciled us to himself through Christ and gave us the ministry of reconciliation: [19]that God was reconciling the world to himself in Christ, not counting people's sins against them. And he has committed to us the message of reconciliation. [20]We are therefore Christ's ambassadors, as though God were making his appeal through us. We implore you on Christ's behalf: Be reconciled to God. [21]God made him who had no sin to be sin[f] for us, so that in him we might become the righteousness of God.

---

[a] 18 Or reflect   [b] 6 Gen. 1:3   [c] 13 Psalm 116:10 (see Septuagint)   [d] 13 Or Spirit-given
[e] 17 Or Christ, that person is a new creation.   [f] 21 Or be a sin offering

6 As God's co-workers we urge you not to receive God's grace in vain. [2]For he says,

"In the time of my favor I heard you,
and in the day of salvation I helped you."[a]

I tell you, now is the time of God's favor, now is the day of salvation.

Paul's Hardships

[3]We put no stumbling block in anyone's path, so that our ministry will not be discredited. [4]Rather, as servants of God we commend ourselves in every way: in great endurance; in troubles, hardships and distresses; [5]in beatings, imprisonments and riots; in hard work, sleepless nights and hunger; [6]in purity, understanding, patience and kindness; in the Holy Spirit and in sincere love; [7]in truthful speech and in the power of God; with weapons of righteousness in the right hand and in the left; [8]through glory and dishonor, bad report and good report; genuine, yet regarded as impostors; [9]known, yet regarded as unknown; dying, and yet we live on; beaten, and yet not killed; [10]sorrowful, yet always rejoicing; poor, yet making many rich; having nothing, and yet possessing everything.

[11]We have spoken freely to you, Corinthians, and opened wide our hearts to you. [12]We are not withholding our affection from you, but you are withholding yours from us. [13]As a fair exchange—I speak as to my children—open wide your hearts also.

Warning Against Idolatry

[14]Do not be yoked together with unbelievers. For what do righteousness and wickedness have in common? Or what fellowship can light have with darkness? [15]What harmony is there between Christ and Belial[b]? Or what does a believer have in common with an unbeliever? [16]What agreement is there between the temple of God and idols? For we are the temple of the living God. As God has said:

"I will live with them
and walk among them,
and I will be their God,
and they will be my people."[c]

[17]Therefore,

"Come out from them
and be separate,

says the Lord.

Touch no unclean thing,
and I will receive you."[d]

[18]And,

"I will be a Father to you,
and you will be my sons and daughters,
says the Lord Almighty."[e]

7 Therefore, since we have these promises, dear friends, let us purify ourselves from everything that contaminates body and spirit, perfecting holiness out of reverence for God.

Paul's Joy Over the Church's Repentance

[2]Make room for us in your hearts. We have wronged no one, we have corrupted no one, we have exploited no one. [3]I do not say this to condemn you; I have said before that you have such a place in our hearts that we would live or die with you. [4]I have spoken to you with great frankness; I take great pride in you. I am greatly encouraged; in all our troubles my joy knows no bounds.

[5]For when we came into Macedonia, we had no rest, but we were harassed at every turn—conflicts on the outside, fears within. [6]But God, who comforts the downcast, comforted us by the coming of Titus, [7]and not only by his coming but also by the comfort you had given him. He told us about your longing for me, your deep sorrow, your ardent concern for me, so that my joy was greater than ever.

[8]Even if I caused you sorrow by my letter, I do not regret it. Though I did regret it—I see that my letter hurt you, but only for a little while— [9]yet now I am happy, not because you were made sorry, but because your sorrow led you to repentance. For you became sorrowful as God intended and so were not harmed in any way by us. [10]Godly sorrow brings repentance that leads to salvation and leaves no regret, but worldly sorrow brings death. [11]See what this godly sorrow has produced in you: what earnestness, what eagerness to clear yourselves, what indignation, what alarm, what longing, what concern, what readiness to see justice done. At every point you have proved yourselves to be innocent in this matter. [12]So even though I wrote to you, it was neither on account of the one who did the wrong nor on account of the injured party, but rather that before God you could see for yourselves how devoted to us you are. [13]By all this we are encouraged.

In addition to our own encouragement, we were especially delighted to see how happy Titus was, because his spirit has been refreshed by all of you. [14]I had boasted to him about you, and you have not embarrassed me. But just as everything we said to you was true, so our boasting about you to Titus has proved to be true as well. [15]And his affection for you is all the greater when he remembers that you were all obedient, receiving him with fear and trembling. [16]I am glad I can have complete confidence in you.

The Collection for the Lord's People

8 And now, brothers and sisters, we want you to know about the grace that God has given the Macedonian churches. [2]In the midst of a very severe trial, their overflowing joy and their extreme poverty welled up in rich generosity. [3]For I testify that they gave as much as they were able, and even beyond their ability. Entirely on their own, [4]they urgently pleaded with us for the privilege of sharing in this service to the Lord's people. [5]And they exceeded our expectations: They

---

[a] 2 Isaiah 49:8   [b] 15 Greek *Beliar*, a variant of *Belial*   [c] 16 Lev. 26:12; Jer. 32:38; Ezek. 37:27
[d] 17 Isaiah 52:11; Ezek. 20:34,41   [e] 18 2 Samuel 7:14; 7:8

gave themselves first of all to the Lord, and then by the will of God also to us. ⁶So we urged Titus, just as he had earlier made a beginning, to bring also to completion this act of grace on your part. ⁷But since you excel in everything—in faith, in speech, in knowledge, in complete earnestness and in the love we have kindled in youᵃ—see that you also excel in this grace of giving.

⁸I am not commanding you, but I want to test the sincerity of your love by comparing it with the earnestness of others. ⁹For you know the grace of our Lord Jesus Christ, that though he was rich, yet for your sake he became poor, so that you through his poverty might become rich.

¹⁰And here is my judgment about what is best for you in this matter. Last year you were the first not only to give but also to have the desire to do so. ¹¹Now finish the work, so that your eager willingness to do it may be matched by your completion of it, according to your means. ¹²For if the willingness is there, the gift is acceptable according to what one has, not according to what one does not have.

¹³Our desire is not that others might be relieved while you are hard pressed, but that there might be equality. ¹⁴At the present time your plenty will supply what they need, so that in turn their plenty will supply what you need. The goal is equality, ¹⁵as it is written: "The one who gathered much did not have too much, and the one who gathered little did not have too little."ᵇ

Titus Sent to Receive the Collection

¹⁶Thanks be to God, who put into the heart of Titus the same concern I have for you. ¹⁷For Titus not only welcomed our appeal, but he is coming to you with much enthusiasm and on his own initiative. ¹⁸And we are sending along with him the brother who is praised by all the churches for his service to the gospel. ¹⁹What is more, he was chosen by the churches to accompany us as we carry the offering, which we administer in order to honor the Lord himself and to show our eagerness to help. ²⁰We want to avoid any criticism of the way we administer this liberal gift. ²¹For we are taking pains to do what is right, not only in the eyes of the Lord but also in the eyes of man.

²²In addition, we are sending with them our brother who has often proved to us in many ways that he is zealous, and now even more so because of his great confidence in you. ²³As for Titus, he is my partner and co-worker among you; as for our brothers, they are representatives of the churches and an honor to Christ. ²⁴Therefore show these men the proof of your love and the reason for our pride in you, so that the churches can see it.

9 There is no need for me to write to you about this service to the Lord's people. ²For I know your eagerness to help, and I have been boasting about it to the Macedonians, telling them that since last year you in Achaia were ready to give; and your enthusiasm has stirred most of them to action. ³But I am sending the brothers in order that our boasting about you in this matter should not prove hollow, but that you may be ready, as I said you would be. ⁴For if any Macedonians come with me and find you unprepared, we—not to say anything about you—would be ashamed of having been so confident. ⁵So I thought it necessary to urge the brothers to visit you in advance and finish the arrangements for the generous gift you had promised. Then it will be ready as a generous gift, not as one grudgingly given.

Generosity Encouraged

⁶Remember this: Whoever sows sparingly will also reap sparingly, and whoever sows generously will also reap generously. ⁷Each of you should give what you have decided in your heart to give, not reluctantly or under compulsion, for God loves a cheerful giver. ⁸And God is able to bless you abundantly, so that in all things at all times, having all that you need, you will abound in every good work. ⁹As it is written:

"They have freely scattered their gifts to
the poor;
their righteousness endures forever."ᶜ

¹⁰Now he who supplies seed to the sower and bread for food will also supply and increase your store of seed and will enlarge the harvest of your righteousness. ¹¹You will be enriched in every way so that you can be generous on every occasion, and through us your generosity will result in thanksgiving to God.

¹²This service that you perform is not only supplying the needs of the Lord's people but is also overflowing in many expressions of thanks to God. ¹³Because of the service by which you have proved yourselves, others will praise God for the obedience that accompanies your confession of the gospel of Christ, and for your generosity in sharing with them and with everyone else. ¹⁴And in their prayers for you their hearts will go out to you, because of the surpassing grace God has given you. ¹⁵Thanks be to God for his indescribable gift!

Paul's Defense of His Ministry

10 By the humility and gentleness of Christ, I appeal to you—I, Paul, who am "timid" when face to face with you, but "bold" toward you when away! ²I beg you that when I come I may not have to be as bold as I expect to be toward some people who think that we live by the standards of this world. ³For though we live in the world, we do not wage war as the world does. ⁴The weapons we fight with are not the weapons of the world. On the contrary, they have divine power to demolish strongholds. ⁵We demolish arguments and every pretension that sets itself up against the knowledge of God, and we take captive every thought to make it obedient to Christ. ⁶And we will be ready to punish every act of disobedience, once your obedience is complete.

ᵃ 7 Some manuscripts *and in your love for us*   ᵇ 15 Exodus 16:18   ᶜ 9 Psalm 112:9

[7]You are judging by appearances.[a] If anyone is confident that they belong to Christ, they should consider again that we belong to Christ just as much as they do. [8]So even if I boast somewhat freely about the authority the Lord gave us for building you up rather than tearing you down, I will not be ashamed of it. [9]I do not want to seem to be trying to frighten you with my letters. [10]For some say, "His letters are weighty and forceful, but in person he is unimpressive and his speaking amounts to nothing." [11]Such people should realize that what we are in our letters when we are absent, we will be in our actions when we are present.

[12]We do not dare to classify or compare ourselves with some who commend themselves. When they measure themselves by themselves and compare themselves with themselves, they are not wise. [13]We, however, will not boast beyond proper limits, but will confine our boasting to the sphere of service God himself has assigned to us, a sphere that also includes you. [14]We are not going too far in our boasting, as would be the case if we had not come to you, for we did get as far as you with the gospel of Christ. [15]Neither do we go beyond our limits by boasting of work done by others. Our hope is that, as your faith continues to grow, our sphere of activity among you will greatly expand, [16]so that we can preach the gospel in the regions beyond you. For we do not want to boast about work already done in someone else's territory. [17]But, "Let the one who boasts boast in the Lord."[b] [18]For it is not the one who commends himself who is approved, but the one whom the Lord commends.

Paul and the False Apostles

11 I hope you will put up with me in a little foolishness. Yes, please put up with me! [2]I am jealous for you with a godly jealousy. I promised you to one husband, to Christ, so that I might present you as a pure virgin to him. [3]But I am afraid that just as Eve was deceived by the serpent's cunning, your minds may somehow be led astray from your sincere and pure devotion to Christ. [4]For if someone comes to you and preaches a Jesus other than the Jesus we preached, or if you receive a different spirit from the Spirit you received, or a different gospel from the one you accepted, you put up with it easily enough.

[5]I do not think I am in the least inferior to those "super-apostles."[c] [6]I may indeed be untrained as a speaker, but I do have knowledge. We have made this perfectly clear to you in every way. [7]Was it a sin for me to lower myself in order to elevate you by preaching the gospel of God to you free of charge? [8]I robbed other churches by receiving support from them so as to serve you. [9]And when I was with you and needed something, I was not a burden to anyone, for the brothers who came from Macedonia supplied what I needed.

I have kept myself from being a burden to you in any way, and will continue to do so. [10]As surely as the truth of Christ is in me, nobody in the regions of Achaia will stop this boasting of mine. [11]Why? Because I do not love you? God knows I do!

[12]And I will keep on doing what I am doing in order to cut the ground from under those who want an opportunity to be considered equal with us in the things they boast about. [13]For such people are false apostles, deceitful workers, masquerading as apostles of Christ. [14]And no wonder, for Satan himself masquerades as an angel of light. [15]It is not surprising, then, if his servants also masquerade as servants of righteousness. Their end will be what their actions deserve.

Paul Boasts About His Sufferings

[16]I repeat: Let no one take me for a fool. But if you do, then tolerate me just as you would a fool, so that I may do a little boasting. [17]In this self-confident boasting I am not talking as the Lord would, but as a fool. [18]Since many are boasting in the way the world does, I too will boast. [19]You gladly put up with fools since you are so wise! [20]In fact, you even put up with anyone who enslaves you or exploits you or takes advantage of you or puts on airs or slaps you in the face. [21]To my shame I admit that we were too weak for that!

Whatever anyone else dares to boast about—I am speaking as a fool—I also dare to boast about. [22]Are they Hebrews? So am I. Are they Israelites? So am I. Are they Abraham's descendants? So am I. [23]Are they servants of Christ? (I am out of my mind to talk like this.) I am more. I have worked much harder, been in prison more frequently, been flogged more severely, and been exposed to death again and again. [24]Five times I received from the Jews the forty lashes minus one. [25]Three times I was beaten with rods, once I was pelted with stones, three times I was shipwrecked, I spent a night and a day in the open sea, [26]I have been constantly on the move. I have been in danger from rivers, in danger from bandits, in danger from my fellow Jews, in danger from Gentiles; in danger in the city, in danger in the country, in danger at sea; and in danger from false believers. [27]I have labored and toiled and have often gone without sleep; I have known hunger and thirst and have often gone without food; I have been cold and naked. [28]Besides everything else, I face daily the pressure of my concern for all the churches. [29]Who is weak, and I do not feel weak? Who is led into sin, and I do not inwardly burn?

[30]If I must boast, I will boast of the things that show my weakness. [31]The God and Father of the Lord Jesus, who is to be praised forever, knows that I am not lying. [32]In Damascus the governor under King Aretas had the city of the Damascenes guarded in order to arrest me. [33]But I was lowered in a basket from a window in the wall and slipped through his hands.

---

[a] 7 Or *Look at the obvious facts*   [b] 17 Jer. 9:24   [c] 5 Or *to the most eminent apostles*

Paul's Vision and His Thorn

12 I must go on boasting. Although there is nothing to be gained, I will go on to visions and revelations from the Lord. [2]I know a man in Christ who fourteen years ago was caught up to the third heaven. Whether it was in the body or out of the body I do not know—God knows. [3]And I know that this man—whether in the body or apart from the body I do not know, but God knows— [4]was caught up to paradise and heard inexpressible things, things that no one is permitted to tell. [5]I will boast about a man like that, but I will not boast about myself, except about my weaknesses. [6]Even if I should choose to boast, I would not be a fool, because I would be speaking the truth. But I refrain, so no one will think more of me than is warranted by what I do or say, [7]or because of these surpassingly great revelations. Therefore, in order to keep me from becoming conceited, I was given a thorn in my flesh, a messenger of Satan, to torment me. [8]Three times I pleaded with the Lord to take it away from me. [9]But he said to me, "My grace is sufficient for you, for my power is made perfect in weakness." Therefore I will boast all the more gladly about my weaknesses, so that Christ's power may rest on me. [10]That is why, for Christ's sake, I delight in weaknesses, in insults, in hardships, in persecutions, in difficulties. For when I am weak, then I am strong.

Paul's Concern for the Corinthians

[11]I have made a fool of myself, but you drove me to it. I ought to have been commended by you, for I am not in the least inferior to the "super-apostles,"[a] even though I am nothing. [12]I persevered in demonstrating among you the marks of a true apostle, including signs, wonders and miracles. [13]How were you inferior to the other churches, except that I was never a burden to you? Forgive me this wrong!

[14]Now I am ready to visit you for the third time, and I will not be a burden to you, because what I want is not your possessions but you. After all, children should not have to save up for their parents, but parents for their children. [15]So I will very gladly spend for you everything I have and expend myself as well. If I love you more, will you love me less? [16]Be that as it may, I have not been a burden to you. Yet, crafty fellow that I am, I caught you by trickery! [17]Did I exploit you through any of the men I sent to you? [18]I urged Titus to go to you and I sent our brother with him. Titus did not exploit you, did he? Did we not walk in the same footsteps by the same Spirit?

[19]Have you been thinking all along that we have been defending ourselves to you? We have been speaking in the sight of God as those in Christ; and everything we do, dear friends, is for your strengthening. [20]For I am afraid that when I come I may not find you as I want you to be, and you may not find me as you want me to be. I fear that there may be discord, jealousy, fits of rage, selfish ambition, slander, gossip, arrogance and disorder. [21]I am afraid that when I come again my God will humble me before you, and I will be grieved over many who have sinned earlier and have not repented of the impurity, sexual sin and debauchery in which they have indulged.

Final Warnings

13 This will be my third visit to you. "Every matter must be established by the testimony of two or three witnesses."[b] [2]I already gave you a warning when I was with you the second time. I now repeat it while absent: On my return I will not spare those who sinned earlier or any of the others, [3]since you are demanding proof that Christ is speaking through me. He is not weak in dealing with you, but is powerful among you. [4]For to be sure, he was crucified in weakness, yet he lives by God's power. Likewise, we are weak in him, yet by God's power we will live with him in our dealing with you.

[5]Examine yourselves to see whether you are in the faith; test yourselves. Do you not realize that Christ Jesus is in you—unless, of course, you fail the test? [6]And I trust that you will discover that we have not failed the test. [7]Now we pray to God that you will not do anything wrong—not so that people will see that we have stood the test but so that you will do what is right even though we may seem to have failed. [8]For we cannot do anything against the truth, but only for the truth. [9]We are glad whenever we are weak but you are strong; and our prayer is that you may be fully restored. [10]This is why I write these things when I am absent, that when I come I may not have to be harsh in my use of authority—the authority the Lord gave me for building you up, not for tearing you down.

Final Greetings

[11]Finally, brothers and sisters, rejoice! Strive for full restoration, encourage one another, be of one mind, live in peace. And the God of love and peace will be with you.

[12]Greet one another with a holy kiss. [13]All God's people here send their greetings.

[14]May the grace of the Lord Jesus Christ, and the love of God, and the fellowship of the Holy Spirit be with you all.

---

[a] 11 Or *the most eminent apostles*   [b] 1 Deut. 19:15

Galatians

1 Paul, an apostle—sent not from men nor by a man, but by Jesus Christ and God the Father, who raised him from the dead— ²and all the brothers and sisters[a] with me,

To the churches in Galatia:

³Grace and peace to you from God our Father and the Lord Jesus Christ, ⁴who gave himself for our sins to rescue us from the present evil age, according to the will of our God and Father, ⁵to whom be glory for ever and ever. Amen.

No Other Gospel

⁶I am astonished that you are so quickly deserting the one who called you to live in the grace of Christ and are turning to a different gospel— ⁷which is really no gospel at all. Evidently some people are throwing you into confusion and are trying to pervert the gospel of Christ. ⁸But even if we or an angel from heaven should preach a gospel other than the one we preached to you, let them be under God's curse! ⁹As we have already said, so now I say again: If anybody is preaching to you a gospel other than what you accepted, let them be under God's curse!

¹⁰Am I now trying to win the approval of human beings, or of God? Or am I trying to please people? If I were still trying to please people, I would not be a servant of Christ.

Paul Called by God

¹¹I want you to know, brothers and sisters, that the gospel I preached is not of human origin. ¹²I did not receive it from any man, nor was I taught it; rather, I received it by revelation from Jesus Christ.

¹³For you have heard of my previous way of life in Judaism, how intensely I persecuted the church of God and tried to destroy it. ¹⁴I was advancing in Judaism beyond many of my own age among my people and was extremely zealous for the traditions of my fathers. ¹⁵But when God, who set me apart from my mother's womb and called me by his grace, was pleased ¹⁶to reveal his Son in me so that I might preach him among the Gentiles, my immediate response was not to consult any human being. ¹⁷I did not go up to Jerusalem to see those who were apostles before I was, but I went into Arabia. Later I returned to Damascus.

¹⁸Then after three years, I went up to Jerusalem to get acquainted with Cephas[b] and stayed with him fifteen days. ¹⁹I saw none of the other apostles—only James, the Lord's brother. ²⁰I assure you before God that what I am writing you is no lie.

²¹Then I went to Syria and Cilicia. ²²I was personally unknown to the churches of Judea that are in Christ. ²³They only heard the report: "The man who formerly persecuted us is now preaching the faith he once tried to destroy." ²⁴And they praised God because of me.

Paul Accepted by the Apostles

2 Then after fourteen years, I went up again to Jerusalem, this time with Barnabas. I took Titus along also. ²I went in response to a revelation and, meeting privately with those esteemed as leaders, I presented to them the gospel that I preach among the Gentiles. I wanted to be sure I was not running and had not been running my race in vain. ³Yet not even Titus, who was with me, was compelled to be circumcised, even though he was a Greek. ⁴This matter arose because some false believers had infiltrated our ranks to spy on the freedom we have in Christ Jesus and to make us slaves. ⁵We did not give in to them for a moment, so that the truth of the gospel might be preserved for you.

⁶As for those who were held in high esteem—whatever they were makes no difference to me; God does not show favoritism—they added nothing to my message. ⁷On the contrary, they recognized that I had been entrusted with the task of preaching the gospel to the uncircumcised,[c] just as Peter had been to the circumcised.[d] ⁸For God, who was at work in Peter as an apostle to the circumcised, was also at work in me as an apostle to the Gentiles. ⁹James, Cephas[e] and John, those esteemed as pillars, gave me and Barnabas the right hand of fellowship when they recognized the grace given to me. They agreed that we should go to the Gentiles, and they to the circumcised. ¹⁰All they asked was that we should continue to remember the poor, the very thing I had been eager to do all along.

Paul Opposes Cephas

¹¹When Cephas came to Antioch, I opposed him to his face, because he stood condemned. ¹²For before certain men came from James, he used to eat with the Gentiles. But when they arrived, he began to draw back and separate himself from the Gentiles because he was afraid of those who belonged to the circumcision group. ¹³The other Jews joined him in his hypocrisy, so that by their hypocrisy even Barnabas was led astray.

¹⁴When I saw that they were not acting in line with the truth of the gospel, I said to Cephas in front of them all, "You are a Jew, yet you live like a Gentile and not like a Jew. How

---

a 2 The Greek word for *brothers and sisters* (*adelphoi*) refers here to believers, both men and women, as part of God's family; also in verse 11; and in 3:15; 4:12, 28, 31; 5:11, 13; 6:1, 18.   *b 18* That is, Peter   *c 7* That is, Gentiles   *d 7* That is, Jews; also in verses 8 and 9   *e 9* That is, Peter; also in verses 11 and 14

is it, then, that you force Gentiles to follow Jewish customs?

[15]"We who are Jews by birth and not sinful Gentiles [16]know that a person is not justified by the works of the law, but by faith in Jesus Christ. So we, too, have put our faith in Christ Jesus that we may be justified by faith in[a] Christ and not by the works of the law, because by the works of the law no one will be justified.

[17]"But if, in seeking to be justified in Christ, we Jews find ourselves also among the sinners, doesn't that mean that Christ promotes sin? Absolutely not! [18]If I rebuild what I destroyed, then I really would be a lawbreaker. [19]"For through the law I died to the law so that I might live for God. [20]I have been crucified with Christ and I no longer live, but Christ lives in me. The life I now live in the body, I live by faith in the Son of God, who loved me and gave himself for me. [21]I do not set aside the grace of God, for if righteousness could be gained through the law, Christ died for nothing!"[b]

Faith or Works of the Law

3 You foolish Galatians! Who has bewitched you? Before your very eyes Jesus Christ was clearly portrayed as crucified. [2]I would like to learn just one thing from you: Did you receive the Spirit by the works of the law, or by believing what you heard? [3]Are you so foolish? After beginning by means of the Spirit, are you now trying to finish by means of the flesh?[c] [4]Have you experienced[d] so much in vain—if it really was in vain? [5]So again I ask, does God give you his Spirit and work miracles among you by the works of the law, or by your believing what you heard? [6]So also Abraham "believed God, and it was credited to him as righteousness."[e]

[7]Understand, then, that those who have faith are children of Abraham. [8]Scripture foresaw that God would justify the Gentiles by faith, and announced the gospel in advance to Abraham: "All nations will be blessed through you."[f] [9]So those who rely on faith are blessed along with Abraham, the man of faith.

[10]For all who rely on the works of the law are under a curse, as it is written: "Cursed is everyone who does not continue to do everything written in the Book of the Law."[g] [11]Clearly no one who relies on the law is justified before God, because "the righteous will live by faith."[h] [12]The law is not based on faith; on the contrary, it says, "The person who does these things will live by them."[i] [13]Christ redeemed us from the curse of the law by becoming a curse for us, for it is written: "Cursed is everyone who is hung on a pole."[j] [14]He redeemed us in order that the blessing given to Abraham might come to the Gentiles through Christ

Jesus, so that by faith we might receive the promise of the Spirit.

The Law and the Promise

[15]Brothers and sisters, let me take an example from everyday life. Just as no one can set aside or add to a human covenant that has been duly established, so it is in this case. [16]The promises were spoken to Abraham and to his seed. Scripture does not say "and to seeds," meaning many people, but "and to your seed,"[k] meaning one person, who is Christ. [17]What I mean is this: The law, introduced 430 years later, does not set aside the covenant previously established by God and thus do away with the promise. [18]For if the inheritance depends on the law, then it no longer depends on the promise; but God in his grace gave it to Abraham through a promise.

[19]Why, then, was the law given at all? It was added because of transgressions until the Seed to whom the promise referred had come. The law was given through angels and entrusted to a mediator. [20]A mediator, however, implies more than one party; but God is one. [21]Is the law, therefore, opposed to the promises of God? Absolutely not! For if a law had been given that could impart life, then righteousness would certainly have come by the law. [22]But Scripture has locked up everything under the control of sin, so that what was promised, being given through faith in Jesus Christ, might be given to those who believe.

Children of God

[23]Before the coming of this faith,[l] we were held in custody under the law, locked up until the faith that was to come would be revealed. [24]So the law was our guardian until Christ came that we might be justified by faith. [25]Now that this faith has come, we are no longer under a guardian.

[26]So in Christ Jesus you are all children of God through faith, [27]for all of you who were baptized into Christ have clothed yourselves with Christ. [28]There is neither Jew nor Gentile, neither slave nor free, nor is there male and female, for you are all one in Christ Jesus. [29]If you belong to Christ, then you are Abraham's seed, and heirs according to the promise.

4 What I am saying is that as long as an heir is underage, he is no different from a slave, although he owns the whole estate. [2]The heir is subject to guardians and trustees until the time set by his father. [3]So also, when we were underage, we were in slavery under the elemental spiritual forces[m] of the world. [4]But when the set time had fully come, God sent his Son, born of a woman, born under the law, [5]to redeem those under the law, that we might receive adoption to sonship.[n] [6]Be-

---

[a] 16 Or *but through the faithfulness of . . . justified on the basis of the faithfulness of*   [b] 21 Some interpreters end the quotation after verse 14.   [c] 3 In contexts like this, the Greek word for *flesh (sarx)* refers to the sinful state of human beings, often presented as a power in opposition to the Spirit.
[d] 4 Or *suffered*   [e] 6 Gen. 15:6   [f] 8 Gen. 12:3; 18:18; 22:18   [g] 10 Deut. 27:26   [h] 11 Hab. 2:4
[i] 12 Lev. 18:5   [j] 13 Deut. 21:23   [k] 16 Gen. 12:7; 13:15; 24:7   [l] 22,23 Or *through the faithfulness of Jesus . . . 23Before faith came*   [m] 3 Or *under the basic principles*   [n] 5 The Greek word for *adoption to sonship* is a legal term referring to the full legal standing of an adopted male heir in Roman culture.

cause you are his sons, God sent the Spirit of his Son into our hearts, the Spirit who calls out, "*Abba*,[a] Father." [7]So you are no longer a slave, but God's child; and since you are his child, God has made you also an heir.

Paul's Concern for the Galatians

[8]Formerly, when you did not know God, you were slaves to those who by nature are not gods. [9]But now that you know God—or rather are known by God—how is it that you are turning back to those weak and miserable forces[b]? Do you wish to be enslaved by them all over again? [10]You are observing special days and months and seasons and years! [11]I fear for you, that somehow I have wasted my efforts on you.

[12]I plead with you, brothers and sisters, become like me, for I became like you. You did me no wrong. [13]As you know, it was because of an illness that I first preached the gospel to you, [14]and even though my illness was a trial to you, you did not treat me with contempt or scorn. Instead, you welcomed me as if I were an angel of God, as if I were Christ Jesus himself. [15]Where, then, is your blessing of me now? I can testify that, if you could have done so, you would have torn out your eyes and given them to me. [16]Have I now become your enemy by telling you the truth?

[17]Those people are zealous to win you over, but for no good. What they want is to alienate you from us, so that you may have zeal for them. [18]It is fine to be zealous, provided the purpose is good, and to be so always, not just when I am with you. [19]My dear children, for whom I am again in the pains of childbirth until Christ is formed in you, [20]how I wish I could be with you now and change my tone, because I am perplexed about you!

Hagar and Sarah

[21]Tell me, you who want to be under the law, are you not aware of what the law says? [22]For it is written that Abraham had two sons, one by the slave woman and the other by the free woman. [23]His son by the slave woman was born according to the flesh, but his son by the free woman was born as the result of a divine promise.

[24]These things are being taken figuratively: The women represent two covenants. One covenant is from Mount Sinai and bears children who are to be slaves: This is Hagar. [25]Now Hagar stands for Mount Sinai in Arabia and corresponds to the present city of Jerusalem, because she is in slavery with her children. [26]But the Jerusalem that is above is free, and she is our mother. [27]For it is written:

"Be glad, barren woman,
　you who never bore a child;
shout for joy and cry aloud,
　you who were never in labor;

because more are the children of the
　desolate woman
　　than of her who has a husband."[c]

[28]Now you, brothers and sisters, like Isaac, are children of promise. [29]At that time the son born according to the flesh persecuted the son born by the power of the Spirit. It is the same now. [30]But what does Scripture say? "Get rid of the slave woman and her son, for the slave woman's son will never share in the inheritance with the free woman's son."[d] [31]Therefore, brothers and sisters, we are not children of the slave woman, but of the free woman.

Freedom in Christ

5 It is for freedom that Christ has set us free. Stand firm, then, and do not let yourselves be burdened again by a yoke of slavery.

[2]Mark my words! I, Paul, tell you that if you let yourselves be circumcised, Christ will be of no value to you at all. [3]Again I declare to every man who lets himself be circumcised that he is obligated to obey the whole law. [4]You who are trying to be justified by the law have been alienated from Christ; you have fallen away from grace. [5]For through the Spirit we eagerly await by faith the righteousness for which we hope. [6]For in Christ Jesus neither circumcision nor uncircumcision has any value. The only thing that counts is faith expressing itself through love.

[7]You were running a good race. Who cut in on you to keep you from obeying the truth? [8]That kind of persuasion does not come from the one who calls you. [9]"A little yeast works through the whole batch of dough." [10]I am confident in the Lord that you will take no other view. The one who is throwing you into confusion, whoever that may be, will have to pay the penalty. [11]Brothers and sisters, if I am still preaching circumcision, why am I still being persecuted? In that case the offense of the cross has been abolished. [12]As for those agitators, I wish they would go the whole way and emasculate themselves!

Life by the Spirit

[13]You, my brothers and sisters, were called to be free. But do not use your freedom to indulge the flesh[e]; rather, serve one another humbly in love. [14]For the entire law is fulfilled in keeping this one command: "Love your neighbor as yourself."[f] [15]If you bite and devour each other, watch out or you will be destroyed by each other.

[16]So I say, walk by the Spirit, and you will not gratify the desires of the flesh. [17]For the flesh desires what is contrary to the Spirit, and the Spirit what is contrary to the flesh. They are in conflict with each other, so that you are not to do whatever[g] you want. [18]But if you are led by the Spirit, you are not under the law.

---

[a] 6 Aramaic for *Father*　　[b] 9 Or *principles*　　[c] 27 Isaiah 54:1　　[d] 30 Gen. 21:10　　[e] 13 In contexts like this, the Greek word for *flesh* (*sarx*) refers to the sinful state of human beings, often presented as a power in opposition to the Spirit; also in verses 16, 17, 19 and 24; and in 6:8.　　[f] 14 Lev. 19:18　　[g] 17 Or *you do not do what*

¹⁹The acts of the flesh are obvious: sexual immorality, impurity and debauchery; ²⁰idolatry and witchcraft; hatred, discord, jealousy, fits of rage, selfish ambition, dissensions, factions ²¹and envy; drunkenness, orgies, and the like. I warn you, as I did before, that those who live like this will not inherit the kingdom of God.

²²But the fruit of the Spirit is love, joy, peace, forbearance, kindness, goodness, faithfulness, ²³gentleness and self-control. Against such things there is no law. ²⁴Those who belong to Christ Jesus have crucified the flesh with its passions and desires. ²⁵Since we live by the Spirit, let us keep in step with the Spirit. ²⁶Let us not become conceited, provoking and envying each other.

Doing Good to All

6 Brothers and sisters, if someone is caught in a sin, you who live by the Spirit should restore that person gently. But watch yourselves, or you also may be tempted. ²Carry each other's burdens, and in this way you will fulfill the law of Christ. ³If anyone thinks they are something when they are not, they deceive themselves. ⁴Each one should test their own actions. Then they can take pride in themselves alone, without comparing themselves to someone else, ⁵for each one should carry their own load. ⁶Nevertheless, the one who receives instruction in the word should share all good things with their instructor.

⁷Do not be deceived: God cannot be mocked. A man reaps what he sows. ⁸Whoever sows to please their flesh, from the flesh will reap destruction; whoever sows to please the Spirit, from the Spirit will reap eternal life. ⁹Let us not become weary in doing good, for at the proper time we will reap a harvest if we do not give up. ¹⁰Therefore, as we have opportunity, let us do good to all people, especially to those who belong to the family of believers.

Not Circumcision but the New Creation

¹¹See what large letters I use as I write to you with my own hand!

¹²Those who want to impress people by means of the flesh are trying to compel you to be circumcised. The only reason they do this is to avoid being persecuted for the cross of Christ. ¹³Not even those who are circumcised keep the law, yet they want you to be circumcised that they may boast about your circumcision in the flesh. ¹⁴May I never boast except in the cross of our Lord Jesus Christ, through which*ᵃ* the world has been crucified to me, and I to the world. ¹⁵Neither circumcision nor uncircumcision means anything; what counts is the new creation. ¹⁶Peace and mercy to all who follow this rule—to*ᵇ* the Israel of God.

¹⁷From now on, let no one cause me trouble, for I bear on my body the marks of Jesus.

¹⁸The grace of our Lord Jesus Christ be with your spirit, brothers and sisters. Amen.

Ephesians

1 Paul, an apostle of Christ Jesus by the will of God,

To God's holy people in Ephesus,*ᶜ* the faithful in Christ Jesus:

²Grace and peace to you from God our Father and the Lord Jesus Christ.

Praise for Spiritual Blessings in Christ

³Praise be to the God and Father of our Lord Jesus Christ, who has blessed us in the heavenly realms with every spiritual blessing in Christ. ⁴For he chose us in him before the creation of the world to be holy and blameless in his sight. In love ⁵he*ᵈ* predestined us for adoption to sonship*ᵉ* through Jesus Christ, in accordance with his pleasure and will— ⁶to the praise of his glorious grace, which he has freely given us in the One he loves. ⁷In him we have redemption through his blood,

the forgiveness of sins, in accordance with the riches of God's grace ⁸that he lavished on us. With all wisdom and understanding, ⁹he*ᶠ* made known to us the mystery of his will according to his good pleasure, which he purposed in Christ, ¹⁰to be put into effect when the times reach their fulfillment—to bring unity to all things in heaven and on earth under Christ.

¹¹In him we were also chosen,*ᵍ* having been predestined according to the plan of him who works out everything in conformity with the purpose of his will, ¹²in order that we, who were the first to put our hope in Christ, might be for the praise of his glory. ¹³And you also were included in Christ when you heard the message of truth, the gospel of your salvation. When you believed, you were marked in him with a seal, the promised Holy Spirit, ¹⁴who is a deposit guaranteeing our inheritance until

ᵃ 14 Or *whom*   *ᵇ 16* Or *rule and to*   *ᶜ 1* Some early manuscripts do not have *in Ephesus.*
ᵈ 4,5 Or *sight in love.* ⁵*He*   *ᵉ 5* The Greek word for *adoption to sonship* is a legal term referring to the full legal standing of an adopted male heir in Roman culture.   *ᶠ 8,9* Or *us with all wisdom and understanding.* ⁹*And he*   *ᵍ 11* Or *were made heirs*

the redemption of those who are God's possession—to the praise of his glory.

Thanksgiving and Prayer

[15]For this reason, ever since I heard about your faith in the Lord Jesus and your love for all God's people, [16]I have not stopped giving thanks for you, remembering you in my prayers. [17]I keep asking that the God of our Lord Jesus Christ, the glorious Father, may give you the Spirit[a] of wisdom and revelation, so that you may know him better. [18]I pray that the eyes of your heart may be enlightened in order that you may know the hope to which he has called you, the riches of his glorious inheritance in his holy people, [19]and his incomparably great power for us who believe. That power is the same as the mighty strength [20]he exerted when he raised Christ from the dead and seated him at his right hand in the heavenly realms, [21]far above all rule and authority, power and dominion, and every name that is invoked, not only in the present age but also in the one to come. [22]And God placed all things under his feet and appointed him to be head over everything for the church, [23]which is his body, the fullness of him who fills everything in every way.

Made Alive in Christ

2 As for you, you were dead in your transgressions and sins, [2]in which you used to live when you followed the ways of this world and of the ruler of the kingdom of the air, the spirit who is now at work in those who are disobedient. [3]All of us also lived among them at one time, gratifying the cravings of our flesh[b] and following its desires and thoughts. Like the rest, we were by nature deserving of wrath. [4]But because of his great love for us, God, who is rich in mercy, [5]made us alive with Christ even when we were dead in transgressions—it is by grace you have been saved. [6]And God raised us up with Christ and seated us with him in the heavenly realms in Christ Jesus, [7]in order that in the coming ages he might show the incomparable riches of his grace, expressed in his kindness to us in Christ Jesus. [8]For it is by grace you have been saved, through faith—and this is not from yourselves, it is the gift of God— [9]not by works, so that no one can boast. [10]For we are God's handiwork, created in Christ Jesus to do good works, which God prepared in advance for us to do.

Jew and Gentile Reconciled Through Christ

[11]Therefore, remember that formerly you who are Gentiles by birth and called "uncircumcised" by those who call themselves "the circumcision" (which is done in the body by human hands)— [12]remember that at that time you were separate from Christ, excluded from citizenship in Israel and foreigners to the covenants of the promise, without hope and without God in the world. [13]But now in Christ Jesus you who once were far away have been brought near by the blood of Christ.

[14]For he himself is our peace, who has made the two groups one and has destroyed the barrier, the dividing wall of hostility, [15]by setting aside in his flesh the law with its commands and regulations. His purpose was to create in himself one new humanity out of the two, thus making peace, [16]and in one body to reconcile both of them to God through the cross, by which he put to death their hostility. [17]He came and preached peace to you who were far away and peace to those who were near. [18]For through him we both have access to the Father by one Spirit.

[19]Consequently, you are no longer foreigners and strangers, but fellow citizens with God's people and also members of his household, [20]built on the foundation of the apostles and prophets, with Christ Jesus himself as the chief cornerstone. [21]In him the whole building is joined together and rises to become a holy temple in the Lord. [22]And in him you too are being built together to become a dwelling in which God lives by his Spirit.

God's Marvelous Plan for the Gentiles

3 For this reason I, Paul, the prisoner of Christ Jesus for the sake of you Gentiles— [2]Surely you have heard about the administration of God's grace that was given to me for you, [3]that is, the mystery made known to me by revelation, as I have already written briefly. [4]In reading this, then, you will be able to understand my insight into the mystery of Christ, [5]which was not made known to people in other generations as it has now been revealed by the Spirit to God's holy apostles and prophets. [6]This mystery is that through the gospel the Gentiles are heirs together with Israel, members together of one body, and sharers together in the promise in Christ Jesus.

[7]I became a servant of this gospel by the gift of God's grace given me through the working of his power. [8]Although I am less than the least of all the Lord's people, this grace was given me: to preach to the Gentiles the boundless riches of Christ, [9]and to make plain to everyone the administration of this mystery, which for ages past was kept hidden in God, who created all things. [10]His intent was that now, through the church, the manifold wisdom of God should be made known to the rulers and authorities in the heavenly realms, [11]according to his eternal purpose that he accomplished in Christ Jesus our Lord. [12]In him and through faith in him we may approach God with freedom and confidence. [13]I ask you, therefore, not to be discouraged because of my sufferings for you, which are your glory.

A Prayer for the Ephesians

[14]For this reason I kneel before the Father, [15]from whom every family[c] in heaven and on

---

[a] 17 Or *a spirit*   [b] 3 In contexts like this, the Greek word for *flesh* (*sarx*) refers to the sinful state of human beings, often presented as a power in opposition to the Spirit.   [c] 15 The Greek for *family* (*patria*) is derived from the Greek for *father* (*pater*).

earth derives its name. [16]I pray that out of his glorious riches he may strengthen you with power through his Spirit in your inner being, [17]so that Christ may dwell in your hearts through faith. And I pray that you, being rooted and established in love, [18]may have power, together with all the Lord's holy people, to grasp how wide and long and high and deep is the love of Christ, [19]and to know this love that surpasses knowledge—that you may be filled to the measure of all the fullness of God.

[20]Now to him who is able to do immeasurably more than all we ask or imagine, according to his power that is at work within us, [21]to him be glory in the church and in Christ Jesus throughout all generations, for ever and ever! Amen.

Unity and Maturity in the Body of Christ

4 As a prisoner for the Lord, then, I urge you to live a life worthy of the calling you have received. [2]Be completely humble and gentle; be patient, bearing with one another in love. [3]Make every effort to keep the unity of the Spirit through the bond of peace. [4]There is one body and one Spirit, just as you were called to one hope when you were called; [5]one Lord, one faith, one baptism; [6]one God and Father of all, who is over all and through all and in all.

[7]But to each one of us grace has been given as Christ apportioned it. [8]This is why it[a] says:

"When he ascended on high,
    he took many captives
    and gave gifts to his people."[b]

[9](What does "he ascended" mean except that he also descended to the lower, earthly regions[c]? [10]He who descended is the very one who ascended higher than all the heavens, in order to fill the whole universe.) [11]So Christ himself gave the apostles, the prophets, the evangelists, the pastors and teachers, [12]to equip his people for works of service, so that the body of Christ may be built up [13]until we all reach unity in the faith and in the knowledge of the Son of God and become mature, attaining to the whole measure of the fullness of Christ.

[14]Then we will no longer be infants, tossed back and forth by the waves, and blown here and there by every wind of teaching and by the cunning and craftiness of people in their deceitful scheming. [15]Instead, speaking the truth in love, we will grow to become in every respect the mature body of him who is the head, that is, Christ. [16]From him the whole body, joined and held together by every supporting ligament, grows and builds itself up in love, as each part does its work.

Instructions for Christian Living

[17]So I tell you this, and insist on it in the Lord, that you must no longer live as the Gentiles do, in the futility of their thinking. [18]They are darkened in their understanding and separated from the life of God because of the ignorance that is in them due to the hardening of their hearts. [19]Having lost all sensitivity, they have given themselves over to sensuality so as to indulge in every kind of impurity, and they are full of greed.

[20]That, however, is not the way of life you learned [21]when you heard about Christ and were taught in him in accordance with the truth that is in Jesus. [22]You were taught, with regard to your former way of life, to put off your old self, which is being corrupted by its deceitful desires; [23]to be made new in the attitude of your minds; [24]and to put on the new self, created to be like God in true righteousness and holiness.

[25]Therefore each of you must put off falsehood and speak truthfully to your neighbor, for we are all members of one body. [26]"In your anger do not sin"[d]: Do not let the sun go down while you are still angry, [27]and do not give the devil a foothold. [28]Anyone who has been stealing must steal no longer, but must work, doing something useful with their own hands, that they may have something to share with those in need.

[29]Do not let any unwholesome talk come out of your mouths, but only what is helpful for building others up according to their needs, that it may benefit those who listen. [30]And do not grieve the Holy Spirit of God, with whom you were sealed for the day of redemption. [31]Get rid of all bitterness, rage and anger, brawling and slander, along with every form of malice. [32]Be kind and compassionate to one another, forgiving each other, just as in Christ God forgave you.

5 Follow God's example, therefore, as dearly loved children [2]and walk in the way of love, just as Christ loved us and gave himself up for us as a fragrant offering and sacrifice to God.

[3]But among you there must not be even a hint of sexual immorality, or of any kind of impurity, or of greed, because these are improper for God's holy people. [4]Nor should there be obscenity, foolish talk or coarse joking, which are out of place, but rather thanksgiving. [5]For of this you can be sure: No immoral, impure or greedy person—such a person is an idolater—has any inheritance in the kingdom of Christ and of God.[e] [6]Let no one deceive you with empty words, for because of such things God's wrath comes on those who are disobedient. [7]Therefore do not be partners with them.

[8]For you were once darkness, but now you are light in the Lord. Live as children of light [9](for the fruit of the light consists in all goodness, righteousness and truth) [10]and find out what pleases the Lord. [11]Have nothing to do with the fruitless deeds of darkness, but rather expose them. [12]It is shameful even to mention what the disobedient do in secret. [13]But everything exposed by the light becomes visible—and everything that is illuminated becomes a light. [14]This is why it is said:

"Wake up, sleeper,
    rise from the dead,
    and Christ will shine on you."

---

[a] 8 Or God   [b] 8 Psalm 68:18   [c] 9 Or the depths of the earth   [d] 26 Psalm 4:4 (see Septuagint)
[e] 5 Or kingdom of the Messiah and God

[15]Be very careful, then, how you live—not as unwise but as wise, [16]making the most of every opportunity, because the days are evil. [17]Therefore do not be foolish, but understand what the Lord's will is. [18]Do not get drunk on wine, which leads to debauchery. Instead, be filled with the Spirit, [19]speaking to one another with psalms, hymns, and songs from the Spirit. Sing and make music from your heart to the Lord, [20]always giving thanks to God the Father for everything, in the name of our Lord Jesus Christ.

Instructions for Christian Households

[21]Submit to one another out of reverence for Christ.

[22]Wives, submit yourselves to your own husbands as you do to the Lord. [23]For the husband is the head of the wife as Christ is the head of the church, his body, of which he is the Savior. [24]Now as the church submits to Christ, so also wives should submit to their husbands in everything.

[25]Husbands, love your wives, just as Christ loved the church and gave himself up for her [26]to make her holy, cleansing[a] her by the washing with water through the word, [27]and to present her to himself as a radiant church, without stain or wrinkle or any other blemish, but holy and blameless. [28]In this same way, husbands ought to love their wives as their own bodies. He who loves his wife loves himself. [29]After all, no one ever hated their own body, but they feed and care for their body, just as Christ does the church— [30]for we are members of his body. [31]"For this reason a man will leave his father and mother and be united to his wife, and the two will become one flesh."[b] [32]This is a profound mystery—but I am talking about Christ and the church. [33]However, each one of you also must love his wife as he loves himself, and the wife must respect her husband.

6 Children, obey your parents in the Lord, for this is right. [2]"Honor your father and mother"—which is the first commandment with a promise— [3]"so that it may go well with you and that you may enjoy long life on the earth."[c]

[4]Fathers,[d] do not exasperate your children; instead, bring them up in the training and instruction of the Lord.

[5]Slaves, obey your earthly masters with respect and fear, and with sincerity of heart, just as you would obey Christ. [6]Obey them not only to win their favor when their eye is on you, but as slaves of Christ, doing the will of God from your heart. [7]Serve wholeheartedly, as if you were serving the Lord, not people, [8]because you know that the Lord will reward each one for whatever good they do, whether they are slave or free.

[9]And masters, treat your slaves in the same way. Do not threaten them, since you know that he who is both their Master and yours is in heaven, and there is no favoritism with him.

The Armor of God

[10]Finally, be strong in the Lord and in his mighty power. [11]Put on the full armor of God, so that you can take your stand against the devil's schemes. [12]For our struggle is not against flesh and blood, but against the rulers, against the authorities, against the powers of this dark world and against the spiritual forces of evil in the heavenly realms. [13]Therefore put on the full armor of God, so that when the day of evil comes, you may be able to stand your ground, and after you have done everything, to stand. [14]Stand firm then, with the belt of truth buckled around your waist, with the breastplate of righteousness in place, [15]and with your feet fitted with the readiness that comes from the gospel of peace. [16]In addition to all this, take up the shield of faith, with which you can extinguish all the flaming arrows of the evil one. [17]Take the helmet of salvation and the sword of the Spirit, which is the word of God.

[18]And pray in the Spirit on all occasions with all kinds of prayers and requests. With this in mind, be alert and always keep on praying for all the Lord's people. [19]Pray also for me, that whenever I speak, words may be given me so that I will fearlessly make known the mystery of the gospel, [20]for which I am an ambassador in chains. Pray that I may declare it fearlessly, as I should.

Final Greetings

[21]Tychicus, the dear brother and faithful servant in the Lord, will tell you everything, so that you also may know how I am and what I am doing. [22]I am sending him to you for this very purpose, that you may know how we are, and that he may encourage you.

[23]Peace to the brothers and sisters,[e] and love with faith from God the Father and the Lord Jesus Christ. [24]Grace to all who love our Lord Jesus Christ with an undying love.[f]

---

[a] 26 Or *having cleansed*   [b] 31 Gen. 2:24   [c] 3 Deut. 5:16   [d] 4 Or *Parents*   [e] 23 The Greek word for *brothers and sisters* (*adelphoi*) refers here to believers, both men and women, as part of God's family.   [f] 24 Or *Grace and immortality to all who love our Lord Jesus Christ.*

Philippians

1 Paul and Timothy, servants of Christ Jesus,

To all God's holy people in Christ Jesus at Philippi, together with the overseers and deacons[a]:

²Grace and peace to you from God our Father and the Lord Jesus Christ.

Thanksgiving and Prayer

³I thank my God every time I remember you. ⁴In all my prayers for all of you, I always pray with joy ⁵because of your partnership in the gospel from the first day until now, ⁶being confident of this, that he who began a good work in you will carry it on to completion until the day of Christ Jesus.

⁷It is right for me to feel this way about all of you, since I have you in my heart and, whether I am in chains or defending and confirming the gospel, all of you share in God's grace with me. ⁸God can testify how I long for all of you with the affection of Christ Jesus.

⁹And this is my prayer: that your love may abound more and more in knowledge and depth of insight, ¹⁰so that you may be able to discern what is best and may be pure and blameless for the day of Christ, ¹¹filled with the fruit of righteousness that comes through Jesus Christ—to the glory and praise of God.

Paul's Chains Advance the Gospel

¹²Now I want you to know, brothers and sisters,[b] that what has happened to me has actually served to advance the gospel. ¹³As a result, it has become clear throughout the whole palace guard[c] and to everyone else that I am in chains for Christ. ¹⁴And because of my chains, most of the brothers and sisters have become confident in the Lord and dare all the more to proclaim the gospel without fear.

¹⁵It is true that some preach Christ out of envy and rivalry, but others out of goodwill. ¹⁶The latter do so out of love, knowing that I am put here for the defense of the gospel. ¹⁷The former preach Christ out of selfish ambition, not sincerely, supposing that they can stir up trouble for me while I am in chains. ¹⁸But what does it matter? The important thing is that in every way, whether from false motives or true, Christ is preached. And because of this I rejoice.

Yes, and I will continue to rejoice, ¹⁹for I know that through your prayers and God's provision of the Spirit of Jesus Christ what has happened to me will turn out for my deliverance.[d] ²⁰I eagerly expect and hope that I will in no way be ashamed, but will have sufficient courage so that now as always Christ will be exalted in my body, whether by life or by death. ²¹For to me, to live is Christ and to die is gain. ²²If I am to go on living in the body, this will mean fruitful labor for me. Yet what shall I choose? I do not know! ²³I am torn between the two: I desire to depart and be with Christ, which is better by far; ²⁴but it is more necessary for you that I remain in the body. ²⁵Convinced of this, I know that I will remain, and I will continue with all of you for your progress and joy in the faith, ²⁶so that through my being with you again your boasting in Christ Jesus will abound on account of me.

Life Worthy of the Gospel

²⁷Whatever happens, conduct yourselves in a manner worthy of the gospel of Christ. Then, whether I come and see you or only hear about you in my absence, I will know that you stand firm in the one Spirit,[e] striving together as one for the faith of the gospel ²⁸without being frightened in any way by those who oppose you. This is a sign to them that they will be destroyed, but that you will be saved—and that by God. ²⁹For it has been granted to you on behalf of Christ not only to believe in him, but also to suffer for him, ³⁰since you are going through the same struggle you saw I had, and now hear that I still have.

Imitating Christ's Humility

2 Therefore if you have any encouragement from being united with Christ, if any comfort from his love, if any common sharing in the Spirit, if any tenderness and compassion, ²then make my joy complete by being likeminded, having the same love, being one in spirit and of one mind. ³Do nothing out of selfish ambition or vain conceit. Rather, in humility value others above yourselves, ⁴not looking to your own interests but each of you to the interests of the others.

⁵In your relationships with one another, have the same mindset as Christ Jesus:

⁶Who, being in very nature[f] God,
  did not consider equality with God
    something to be used to his own
      advantage;
⁷rather, he made himself nothing
  by taking the very nature[g] of a servant,
    being made in human likeness.
⁸And being found in appearance as a man,
  he humbled himself
    by becoming obedient to death—
      even death on a cross!

---

a 1 The word *deacons* refers here to Christians designated to serve with the overseers/elders of the church in a variety of ways; similarly in Romans 16:1 and 1 Tim. 3:8,12.   *b 12* The Greek word for *brothers and sisters (adelphoi)* refers here to believers, both men and women, as part of God's family; also in verse 14; and in 3:1, 13, 17; 4:1, 8, 21.   *c 13* Or *whole palace*   *d 19* Or *vindication*; or *salvation*   *e 27* Or *in one spirit*   *f 6* Or *in the form of*   *g 7* Or *the form*

[9] Therefore God exalted him to the highest place
and gave him the name that is above every name,
[10] that at the name of Jesus every knee should bow,
in heaven and on earth and under the earth,
[11] and every tongue acknowledge that Jesus Christ is Lord,
to the glory of God the Father.

Do Everything Without Grumbling

[12] Therefore, my dear friends, as you have always obeyed—not only in my presence, but now much more in my absence—continue to work out your salvation with fear and trembling, [13] for it is God who works in you to will and to act in order to fulfill his good purpose.

[14] Do everything without grumbling or arguing, [15] so that you may become blameless and pure, "children of God without fault in a warped and crooked generation."[a] Then you will shine among them like stars in the sky [16] as you hold firmly to the word of life. And then I will be able to boast on the day of Christ that I did not run or labor in vain. [17] But even if I am being poured out like a drink offering on the sacrifice and service coming from your faith, I am glad and rejoice with all of you. [18] So you too should be glad and rejoice with me.

Timothy and Epaphroditus

[19] I hope in the Lord Jesus to send Timothy to you soon, that I also may be cheered when I receive news about you. [20] I have no one else like him, who will show genuine concern for your welfare. [21] For everyone looks out for their own interests, not those of Jesus Christ. [22] But you know that Timothy has proved himself, because as a son with his father he has served with me in the work of the gospel. [23] I hope, therefore, to send him as soon as I see how things go with me. [24] And I am confident in the Lord that I myself will come soon.

[25] But I think it is necessary to send back to you Epaphroditus, my brother, co-worker and fellow soldier, who is also your messenger, whom you sent to take care of my needs. [26] For he longs for all of you and is distressed because you heard he was ill. [27] Indeed he was ill, and almost died. But God had mercy on him, and not on him only but also on me, to spare me sorrow upon sorrow. [28] Therefore I am all the more eager to send him, so that when you see him again you may be glad and I may have less anxiety. [29] So then, welcome him in the Lord with great joy, and honor people like him, [30] because he almost died for the work of Christ. He risked his life to make up for the help you yourselves could not give me.

No Confidence in the Flesh

3 Further, my brothers and sisters, rejoice in the Lord! It is no trouble for me to write the same things to you again, and it is a safeguard for you. [2] Watch out for those dogs, those evildoers, those mutilators of the flesh. [3] For it is we who are the circumcision, we who serve God by his Spirit, who boast in Christ Jesus, and who put no confidence in the flesh— [4] though I myself have reasons for such confidence.

If someone else thinks they have reasons to put confidence in the flesh, I have more: [5] circumcised on the eighth day, of the people of Israel, of the tribe of Benjamin, a Hebrew of Hebrews; in regard to the law, a Pharisee; [6] as for zeal, persecuting the church; as for righteousness based on the law, faultless.

[7] But whatever were gains to me I now consider loss for the sake of Christ. [8] What is more, I consider everything a loss because of the surpassing worth of knowing Christ Jesus my Lord, for whose sake I have lost all things. I consider them garbage, that I may gain Christ [9] and be found in him, not having a righteousness of my own that comes from the law, but that which is through faith in[b] Christ—the righteousness that comes from God on the basis of faith. [10] I want to know Christ—yes, to know the power of his resurrection and participation in his sufferings, becoming like him in his death, [11] and so, somehow, attaining to the resurrection from the dead.

[12] Not that I have already obtained all this, or have already arrived at my goal, but I press on to take hold of that for which Christ Jesus took hold of me. [13] Brothers and sisters, I do not consider myself yet to have taken hold of it. But one thing I do: Forgetting what is behind and straining toward what is ahead, [14] I press on toward the goal to win the prize for which God has called me heavenward in Christ Jesus.

Following Paul's Example

[15] All of us, then, who are mature should take such a view of things. And if on some point you think differently, that too God will make clear to you. [16] Only let us live up to what we have already attained.

[17] Join together in following my example, brothers and sisters, and just as you have us as a model, keep your eyes on those who live as we do. [18] For, as I have often told you before and now tell you again even with tears, many live as enemies of the cross of Christ. [19] Their destiny is destruction, their god is their stomach, and their glory is in their shame. Their mind is set on earthly things. [20] But our citizenship is in heaven. And we eagerly await a Savior from there, the Lord Jesus Christ, [21] who, by the power that enables him to bring everything under his control, will transform our lowly bodies so that they will be like his glorious body.

Closing Appeal for Steadfastness and Unity

4 Therefore, my brothers and sisters, you whom I love and long for, my joy and crown, stand firm in the Lord in this way, dear friends!

---

[a] 15 Deut. 32:5   [b] 9 Or *through the faithfulness of*

[2]I plead with Euodia and I plead with Syntyche to be of the same mind in the Lord. [3]Yes, and I ask you, my true companion, help these women since they have contended at my side in the cause of the gospel, along with Clement and the rest of my co-workers, whose names are in the book of life.

Final Exhortations

[4]Rejoice in the Lord always. I will say it again: Rejoice! [5]Let your gentleness be evident to all. The Lord is near. [6]Do not be anxious about anything, but in every situation, by prayer and petition, with thanksgiving, present your requests to God. [7]And the peace of God, which transcends all understanding, will guard your hearts and your minds in Christ Jesus.

[8]Finally, brothers and sisters, whatever is true, whatever is noble, whatever is right, whatever is pure, whatever is lovely, whatever is admirable—if anything is excellent or praiseworthy—think about such things. [9]Whatever you have learned or received or heard from me, or seen in me—put it into practice. And the God of peace will be with you.

Thanks for Their Gifts

[10]I rejoiced greatly in the Lord that at last you renewed your concern for me. Indeed, you were concerned, but you had no opportunity to show it. [11]I am not saying this because I am in need, for I have learned to be content whatever the circumstances. [12]I know what it is to be in need, and I know what it is to have plenty. I have learned the secret of being content in any and every situation, whether well fed or hungry, whether living in plenty or in want. [13]I can do all this through him who gives me strength.

[14]Yet it was good of you to share in my troubles. [15]Moreover, as you Philippians know, in the early days of your acquaintance with the gospel, when I set out from Macedonia, not one church shared with me in the matter of giving and receiving, except you only; [16]for even when I was in Thessalonica, you sent me aid more than once when I was in need. [17]Not that I desire your gifts; what I desire is that more be credited to your account. [18]I have received full payment and have more than enough. I am amply supplied, now that I have received from Epaphroditus the gifts you sent. They are a fragrant offering, an acceptable sacrifice, pleasing to God. [19]And my God will meet all your needs according to the riches of his glory in Christ Jesus.

[20]To our God and Father be glory for ever and ever. Amen.

Final Greetings

[21]Greet all God's people in Christ Jesus. The brothers and sisters who are with me send greetings. [22]All God's people here send you greetings, especially those who belong to Caesar's household.

[23]The grace of the Lord Jesus Christ be with your spirit. Amen.[a]

Colossians

1 Paul, an apostle of Christ Jesus by the will of God, and Timothy our brother,

[2]To God's holy people in Colossae, the faithful brothers and sisters[b] in Christ:

Grace and peace to you from God our Father.[c]

Thanksgiving and Prayer

[3]We always thank God, the Father of our Lord Jesus Christ, when we pray for you, [4]because we have heard of your faith in Christ Jesus and of the love you have for all God's people— [5]the faith and love that spring from the hope stored up for you in heaven and about which you have already heard in the true message of the gospel [6]that has come to you. In the same way, the gospel is bearing fruit and growing throughout the whole world—just as it has been doing among you since the day you heard it and truly understood God's grace. [7]You learned it from Epaphras, our dear fellow servant,[d] who is a faithful minister of Christ on our[e] behalf, [8]and who also told us of your love in the Spirit.

[9]For this reason, since the day we heard about you, we have not stopped praying for you. We continually ask God to fill you with the knowledge of his will through all the wisdom and understanding that the Spirit gives,[f] [10]so that you may live a life worthy of the Lord and please him in every way: bearing fruit in every good work, growing in the knowledge of God, [11]being strengthened with all power according to his glorious might so that you may have great endurance and patience, [12]and giving joyful thanks to the Father, who has qualified you[g] to share in the inheritance of

---

[a] 23 Some manuscripts do not have Amen.   [b] 2 The Greek word for brothers and sisters (adelphoi) refers here to believers, both men and women, as part of God's family; also in 4:15.   [c] 2 Some manuscripts Father and the Lord Jesus Christ   [d] 7 Or slave   [e] 7 Some manuscripts your   [f] 9 Or all spiritual wisdom and understanding   [g] 12 Some manuscripts us

his holy people in the kingdom of light. ¹³For he has rescued us from the dominion of darkness and brought us into the kingdom of the Son he loves, ¹⁴in whom we have redemption, the forgiveness of sins.

The Supremacy of the Son of God

¹⁵The Son is the image of the invisible God, the firstborn over all creation. ¹⁶For in him all things were created: things in heaven and on earth, visible and invisible, whether thrones or powers or rulers or authorities; all things have been created through him and for him. ¹⁷He is before all things, and in him all things hold together. ¹⁸And he is the head of the body, the church; he is the beginning and the firstborn from among the dead, so that in everything he might have the supremacy. ¹⁹For God was pleased to have all his fullness dwell in him, ²⁰and through him to reconcile to himself all things, whether things on earth or things in heaven, by making peace through his blood, shed on the cross.

²¹Once you were alienated from God and were enemies in your minds because of*ᵃ* your evil behavior. ²²But now he has reconciled you by Christ's physical body through death to present you holy in his sight, without blemish and free from accusation— ²³if you continue in your faith, established and firm, and do not move from the hope held out in the gospel. This is the gospel that you heard and that has been proclaimed to every creature under heaven, and of which I, Paul, have become a servant.

Paul's Labor for the Church

²⁴Now I rejoice in what I am suffering for you, and I fill up in my flesh what is still lacking in regard to Christ's afflictions, for the sake of his body, which is the church. ²⁵I have become its servant by the commission God gave me to present to you the word of God in its fullness— ²⁶the mystery that has been kept hidden for ages and generations, but is now disclosed to the Lord's people. ²⁷To them God has chosen to make known among the Gentiles the glorious riches of this mystery, which is Christ in you, the hope of glory.

²⁸He is the one we proclaim, admonishing and teaching everyone with all wisdom, so that we may present everyone fully mature in Christ. ²⁹To this end I strenuously contend with all the energy Christ so powerfully works in me.

2 I want you to know how hard I am contending for you and for those at Laodicea, and for all who have not met me personally. ²My goal is that they may be encouraged in heart and united in love, so that they may have the full riches of complete understanding, in order that they may know the mystery of God, namely, Christ, ³in whom are hidden all the treasures of wisdom and knowledge. ⁴I tell you this so that no one may deceive you by fine-sounding arguments. ⁵For though I am absent from you in body, I am present with you in spirit and delight to see how disciplined you are and how firm your faith in Christ is.

Spiritual Fullness in Christ

⁶So then, just as you received Christ Jesus as Lord, continue to live your lives in him, ⁷rooted and built up in him, strengthened in the faith as you were taught, and overflowing with thankfulness.

⁸See to it that no one takes you captive through hollow and deceptive philosophy, which depends on human tradition and the elemental spiritual forcesᵇ of this world rather than on Christ.

⁹For in Christ all the fullness of the Deity lives in bodily form, ¹⁰and in Christ you have been brought to fullness. He is the head over every power and authority. ¹¹In him you were also circumcised with a circumcision not performed by human hands. Your whole self ruled by the fleshᶜ was put off when you were circumcised byᵈ Christ, ¹²having been buried with him in baptism, in which you were also raised with him through your faith in the working of God, who raised him from the dead.

¹³When you were dead in your sins and in the uncircumcision of your flesh, God made youᵉ alive with Christ. He forgave us all our sins, ¹⁴having canceled the charge of our legal indebtedness, which stood against us and condemned us; he has taken it away, nailing it to the cross. ¹⁵And having disarmed the powers and authorities, he made a public spectacle of them, triumphing over them by the cross.ᶠ

Freedom From Human Rules

¹⁶Therefore do not let anyone judge you by what you eat or drink, or with regard to a religious festival, a New Moon celebration or a Sabbath day. ¹⁷These are a shadow of the things that were to come; the reality, however, is found in Christ. ¹⁸Do not let anyone who delights in false humility and the worship of angels disqualify you. Such a person also goes into great detail about what they have seen; they are puffed up with idle notions by their unspiritual mind. ¹⁹They have lost connection with the head, from whom the whole body, supported and held together by its ligaments and sinews, grows as God causes it to grow.

²⁰Since you died with Christ to the elemental spiritual forces of this world, why, as though you still belonged to the world, do you submit to its rules: ²¹"Do not handle! Do not taste! Do not touch!"? ²²These rules, which have to do with things that are all destined to perish with use, are based on merely human commands and teachings. ²³Such regulations indeed have an appearance of wisdom, with their self-imposed worship, their false

ᵃ 21 Or minds, as shown by   ᵇ 8 Or the basic principles; also in verse 20   ᶜ 11 In contexts like this, the Greek word for flesh (sarx) refers to the sinful state of human beings, often presented as a power in opposition to the Spirit; also in verse 13.   ᵈ 11 Or put off in the circumcision of   ᵉ 13 Some manuscripts us   ᶠ 15 Or them in him

humility and their harsh treatment of the body, but they lack any value in restraining sensual indulgence.

Living as Those Made Alive in Christ

3 Since, then, you have been raised with Christ, set your hearts on things above, where Christ is, seated at the right hand of God. ²Set your minds on things above, not on earthly things. ³For you died, and your life is now hidden with Christ in God. ⁴When Christ, who is your*a* life, appears, then you also will appear with him in glory.

⁵Put to death, therefore, whatever belongs to your earthly nature: sexual immorality, impurity, lust, evil desires and greed, which is idolatry. ⁶Because of these, the wrath of God is coming.*b* ⁷You used to walk in these ways, in the life you once lived. ⁸But now you must also rid yourselves of all such things as these: anger, rage, malice, slander, and filthy language from your lips. ⁹Do not lie to each other, since you have taken off your old self with its practices ¹⁰and have put on the new self, which is being renewed in knowledge in the image of its Creator. ¹¹Here there is no Gentile or Jew, circumcised or uncircumcised, barbarian, Scythian, slave or free, but Christ is all, and is in all.

¹²Therefore, as God's chosen people, holy and dearly loved, clothe yourselves with compassion, kindness, humility, gentleness and patience. ¹³Bear with each other and forgive one another if any of you has a grievance against someone. Forgive as the Lord forgave you. ¹⁴And over all these virtues put on love, which binds them all together in perfect unity.

¹⁵Let the peace of Christ rule in your hearts, since as members of one body you were called to peace. And be thankful. ¹⁶Let the message of Christ dwell among you richly as you teach and admonish one another with all wisdom through psalms, hymns, and songs from the Spirit, singing to God with gratitude in your hearts. ¹⁷And whatever you do, whether in word or deed, do it all in the name of the Lord Jesus, giving thanks to God the Father through him.

Instructions for Christian Households

¹⁸Wives, submit yourselves to your husbands, as is fitting in the Lord.

¹⁹Husbands, love your wives and do not be harsh with them.

²⁰Children, obey your parents in everything, for this pleases the Lord.

²¹Fathers,*c* do not embitter your children, or they will become discouraged.

²²Slaves, obey your earthly masters in everything; and do it, not only when their eye is on you and to curry their favor, but with sincerity of heart and reverence for the Lord.

²³Whatever you do, work at it with all your heart, as working for the Lord, not for human masters, ²⁴since you know that you will receive an inheritance from the Lord as a reward. It is the Lord Christ you are serving. ²⁵Anyone who does wrong will be repaid for their wrongs, and there is no favoritism.

4 Masters, provide your slaves with what is right and fair, because you know that you also have a Master in heaven.

Further Instructions

²Devote yourselves to prayer, being watchful and thankful. ³And pray for us, too, that God may open a door for our message, so that we may proclaim the mystery of Christ, for which I am in chains. ⁴Pray that I may proclaim it clearly, as I should. ⁵Be wise in the way you act toward outsiders; make the most of every opportunity. ⁶Let your conversation be always full of grace, seasoned with salt, so that you may know how to answer everyone.

Final Greetings

⁷Tychicus will tell you all the news about me. He is a dear brother, a faithful minister and fellow servant*d* in the Lord. ⁸I am sending him to you for the express purpose that you may know about our*e* circumstances and that he may encourage your hearts. ⁹He is coming with Onesimus, our faithful and dear brother, who is one of you. They will tell you everything that is happening here.

¹⁰My fellow prisoner Aristarchus sends you his greetings, as does Mark, the cousin of Barnabas. (You have received instructions about him; if he comes to you, welcome him.) ¹¹Jesus, who is called Justus, also sends greetings. These are the only Jews*f* among my co-workers for the kingdom of God, and they have proved a comfort to me. ¹²Epaphras, who is one of you and a servant of Christ Jesus, sends greetings. He is always wrestling in prayer for you, that you may stand firm in all the will of God, mature and fully assured. ¹³I vouch for him that he is working hard for you and for those at Laodicea and Hierapolis. ¹⁴Our dear friend Luke, the doctor, and Demas send greetings. ¹⁵Give my greetings to the brothers and sisters at Laodicea, and to Nympha and the church in her house.

¹⁶After this letter has been read to you, see that it is also read in the church of the Laodiceans and that you in turn read the letter from Laodicea.

¹⁷Tell Archippus: "See to it that you complete the ministry you have received in the Lord."

¹⁸I, Paul, write this greeting in my own hand. Remember my chains. Grace be with you.

---

a 4 Some manuscripts *our*   *b* 6 Some early manuscripts *coming on those who are disobedient*   *c* 21 Or *Parents*   *d* 7 Or *slave*; also in verse 12   *e* 8 Some manuscripts *that he may know about your*   *f* 11 Greek *only ones of the circumcision group*

1 Thessalonians

1 Paul, Silas[a] and Timothy,

To the church of the Thessalonians in God the Father and the Lord Jesus Christ:

Grace and peace to you.

Thanksgiving for the Thessalonians' Faith

[2]We always thank God for all of you and continually mention you in our prayers. [3]We remember before our God and Father your work produced by faith, your labor prompted by love, and your endurance inspired by hope in our Lord Jesus Christ.

[4]For we know, brothers and sisters[b] loved by God, that he has chosen you, [5]because our gospel came to you not simply with words but also with power, with the Holy Spirit and deep conviction. You know how we lived among you for your sake. [6]You became imitators of us and of the Lord, for you welcomed the message in the midst of severe suffering with the joy given by the Holy Spirit. [7]And so you became a model to all the believers in Macedonia and Achaia. [8]The Lord's message rang out from you not only in Macedonia and Achaia—your faith in God has become known everywhere. Therefore we do not need to say anything about it, [9]for they themselves report what kind of reception you gave us. They tell how you turned to God from idols to serve the living and true God, [10]and to wait for his Son from heaven, whom he raised from the dead—Jesus, who rescues us from the coming wrath.

Paul's Ministry in Thessalonica

2 You know, brothers and sisters, that our visit to you was not without results. [2]We had previously suffered and been treated outrageously in Philippi, as you know, but with the help of our God we dared to tell you his gospel in the face of strong opposition. [3]For the appeal we make does not spring from error or impure motives, nor are we trying to trick you. [4]On the contrary, we speak as those approved by God to be entrusted with the gospel. We are not trying to please people but God, who tests our hearts. [5]You know we never used flattery, nor did we put on a mask to cover up greed—God is our witness. [6]We were not looking for praise from people, not from you or anyone else, even though as apostles of Christ we could have asserted our authority. [7]Instead, we were like young children[c] among you.

Just as a nursing mother cares for her children, [8]so we cared for you. Because we loved you so much, we were delighted to share with you not only the gospel of God but our lives as well. [9]Surely you remember, brothers and sisters, our toil and hardship; we worked night and day in order not to be a burden to anyone while we preached the gospel of God to you. [10]You are witnesses, and so is God, of how holy, righteous and blameless we were among you who believed. [11]For you know that we dealt with each of you as a father deals with his own children, [12]encouraging, comforting and urging you to live lives worthy of God, who calls you into his kingdom and glory.

[13]And we also thank God continually because, when you received the word of God, which you heard from us, you accepted it not as a human word, but as it actually is, the word of God, which is indeed at work in you who believe. [14]For you, brothers and sisters, became imitators of God's churches in Judea, which are in Christ Jesus: You suffered from your own people the same things those churches suffered from the Jews [15]who killed the Lord Jesus and the prophets and also drove us out. They displease God and are hostile to everyone [16]in their effort to keep us from speaking to the Gentiles so that they may be saved. In this way they always heap up their sins to the limit. The wrath of God has come upon them at last.[d]

Paul's Longing to See the Thessalonians

[17]But, brothers and sisters, when we were orphaned by being separated from you for a short time (in person, not in thought), out of our intense longing we made every effort to see you. [18]For we wanted to come to you—certainly I, Paul, did, again and again—but Satan blocked our way. [19]For what is our hope, our joy, or the crown in which we will glory in the presence of our Lord Jesus when he comes? Is it not you? [20]Indeed, you are our glory and joy.

3 So when we could stand it no longer, we thought it best to be left by ourselves in Athens. [2]We sent Timothy, who is our brother and co-worker in God's service in spreading the gospel of Christ, to strengthen and encourage you in your faith, [3]so that no one would be unsettled by these trials. For you know quite well that we are destined for them. [4]In fact, when we were with you, we kept telling you that we would be persecuted. And it turned out that way, as you well know. [5]For this reason, when I could stand it no longer, I sent to find out about your faith. I was afraid that in some way the tempter had tempted you and that our labors might have been in vain.

---

[a] 1 Greek *Silvanus*, a variant of *Silas*   [b] 4 The Greek word for *brothers and sisters (adelphoi)* refers here to believers, both men and women, as part of God's family; also in 2:1, 9, 14, 17; 3:7; 4:1, 10, 13; 5:1, 4, 12, 14, 25, 27.   [c] 7 Some manuscripts *were gentle*   [d] 16 Or *them fully*

Timothy's Encouraging Report

⁶But Timothy has just now come to us from you and has brought good news about your faith and love. He has told us that you always have pleasant memories of us and that you long to see us, just as we also long to see you. ⁷Therefore, brothers and sisters, in all our distress and persecution we were encouraged about you because of your faith. ⁸For now we really live, since you are standing firm in the Lord. ⁹How can we thank God enough for you in return for all the joy we have in the presence of our God because of you? ¹⁰Night and day we pray most earnestly that we may see you again and supply what is lacking in your faith.

¹¹Now may our God and Father himself and our Lord Jesus clear the way for us to come to you. ¹²May the Lord make your love increase and overflow for each other and for everyone else, just as ours does for you. ¹³May he strengthen your hearts so that you will be blameless and holy in the presence of our God and Father when our Lord Jesus comes with all his holy ones.

Living to Please God

4 As for other matters, brothers and sisters, we instructed you how to live in order to please God, as in fact you are living. Now we ask you and urge you in the Lord Jesus to do this more and more. ²For you know what instructions we gave you by the authority of the Lord Jesus.

³It is God's will that you should be sanctified: that you should avoid sexual immorality; ⁴that each of you should learn to control your own body*a* in a way that is holy and honorable, ⁵not in passionate lust like the pagans, who do not know God; ⁶and that in this matter no one should wrong or take advantage of a brother or sister.*b* The Lord will punish all those who commit such sins, as we told you and warned you before. ⁷For God did not call us to be impure, but to live a holy life. ⁸Therefore, anyone who rejects this instruction does not reject a human being but God, the very God who gives you his Holy Spirit.

⁹Now about your love for one another we do not need to write to you, for you yourselves have been taught by God to love each other. ¹⁰And in fact, you do love all of God's family throughout Macedonia. Yet we urge you, brothers and sisters, to do so more and more, ¹¹and to make it your ambition to lead a quiet life: You should mind your own business and work with your hands, just as we told you, ¹²so that your daily life may win the respect of outsiders and so that you will not be dependent on anybody.

Believers Who Have Died

¹³Brothers and sisters, we do not want you to be uninformed about those who sleep in death, so that you do not grieve like the rest of mankind, who have no hope. ¹⁴For we believe that Jesus died and rose again, and so we believe that God will bring with Jesus those who have fallen asleep in him. ¹⁵According to the Lord's word, we tell you that we who are still alive, who are left until the coming of the Lord, will certainly not precede those who have fallen asleep. ¹⁶For the Lord himself will come down from heaven, with a loud command, with the voice of the archangel and with the trumpet call of God, and the dead in Christ will rise first. ¹⁷After that, we who are still alive and are left will be caught up together with them in the clouds to meet the Lord in the air. And so we will be with the Lord forever. ¹⁸Therefore encourage one another with these words.

The Day of the Lord

5 Now, brothers and sisters, about times and dates we do not need to write to you, ²for you know very well that the day of the Lord will come like a thief in the night. ³While people are saying, "Peace and safety," destruction will come on them suddenly, as labor pains on a pregnant woman, and they will not escape.

⁴But you, brothers and sisters, are not in darkness so that this day should surprise you like a thief. ⁵You are all children of the light and children of the day. We do not belong to the night or to the darkness. ⁶So then, let us not be like others, who are asleep, but let us be awake and sober. ⁷For those who sleep, sleep at night, and those who get drunk, get drunk at night. ⁸But since we belong to the day, let us be sober, putting on faith and love as a breastplate, and the hope of salvation as a helmet. ⁹For God did not appoint us to suffer wrath but to receive salvation through our Lord Jesus Christ. ¹⁰He died for us so that, whether we are awake or asleep, we may live together with him. ¹¹Therefore encourage one another and build each other up, just as in fact you are doing.

Final Instructions

¹²Now we ask you, brothers and sisters, to acknowledge those who work hard among you, who care for you in the Lord and who admonish you. ¹³Hold them in the highest regard in love because of their work. Live in peace with each other. ¹⁴And we urge you, brothers and sisters, warn those who are idle and disruptive, encourage the disheartened, help the weak, be patient with everyone. ¹⁵Make sure that nobody pays back wrong for wrong, but always strive to do what is good for each other and for everyone else.

¹⁶Rejoice always, ¹⁷pray continually, ¹⁸give thanks in all circumstances; for this is God's will for you in Christ Jesus.

¹⁹Do not quench the Spirit. ²⁰Do not treat prophecies with contempt ²¹but test them all; hold on to what is good, ²²reject every kind of evil.

---

a 4 Or *learn to live with your own wife*; or *learn to acquire a wife*   *b* 6 The Greek word for *brother or sister (adelphos)* refers here to a believer, whether man or woman, as part of God's family.

²³May God himself, the God of peace, sanctify you through and through. May your whole spirit, soul and body be kept blameless at the coming of our Lord Jesus Christ. ²⁴The one who calls you is faithful, and he will do it.

²⁵Brothers and sisters, pray for us. ²⁶Greet all God's people with a holy kiss. ²⁷I charge you before the Lord to have this letter read to all the brothers and sisters.

²⁸The grace of our Lord Jesus Christ be with you.

2 Thessalonians

1 Paul, Silas*ᵃ* and Timothy,

To the church of the Thessalonians in God our Father and the Lord Jesus Christ:

²Grace and peace to you from God the Father and the Lord Jesus Christ.

Thanksgiving and Prayer

³We ought always to thank God for you, brothers and sisters,*ᵇ* and rightly so, because your faith is growing more and more, and the love all of you have for one another is increasing. ⁴Therefore, among God's churches we boast about your perseverance and faith in all the persecutions and trials you are enduring.

⁵All this is evidence that God's judgment is right, and as a result you will be counted worthy of the kingdom of God, for which you are suffering. ⁶God is just: He will pay back trouble to those who trouble you ⁷and give relief to you who are troubled, and to us as well. This will happen when the Lord Jesus is revealed from heaven in blazing fire with his powerful angels. ⁸He will punish those who do not know God and do not obey the gospel of our Lord Jesus. ⁹They will be punished with everlasting destruction and shut out from the presence of the Lord and from the glory of his might ¹⁰on the day he comes to be glorified in his holy people and to be marveled at among all those who have believed. This includes you, because you believed our testimony to you.

¹¹With this in mind, we constantly pray for you, that our God may make you worthy of his calling, and that by his power he may bring to fruition your every desire for goodness and your every deed prompted by faith. ¹²We pray this so that the name of our Lord Jesus may be glorified in you, and you in him, according to the grace of our God and the Lord Jesus Christ.*ᶜ*

The Man of Lawlessness

2 Concerning the coming of our Lord Jesus Christ and our being gathered to him, we ask you, brothers and sisters, ²not to become easily unsettled or alarmed by the teaching allegedly from us—whether by a prophecy or by word of mouth or by letter—asserting that the day of the Lord has already come. ³Don't let anyone deceive you in any way, for that day will not come until the rebellion occurs and the man of lawlessness*ᵈ* is revealed, the man doomed to destruction. ⁴He will oppose and will exalt himself over everything that is called God or is worshiped, so that he sets himself up in God's temple, proclaiming himself to be God.

⁵Don't you remember that when I was with you I used to tell you these things? ⁶And now you know what is holding him back, so that he may be revealed at the proper time. ⁷For the secret power of lawlessness is already at work; but the one who now holds it back will continue to do so till he is taken out of the way. ⁸And then the lawless one will be revealed, whom the Lord Jesus will overthrow with the breath of his mouth and destroy by the splendor of his coming. ⁹The coming of the lawless one will be in accordance with how Satan works. He will use all sorts of displays of power through signs and wonders that serve the lie, ¹⁰and all the ways that wickedness deceives those who are perishing. They perish because they refused to love the truth and so be saved. ¹¹For this reason God sends them a powerful delusion so that they will believe the lie ¹²and so that all will be condemned who have not believed the truth but have delighted in wickedness.

Stand Firm

¹³But we ought always to thank God for you, brothers and sisters loved by the Lord, because God chose you as firstfruits*ᵉ* to be saved through the sanctifying work of the Spirit and through belief in the truth. ¹⁴He called you to this through our gospel, that you might share in the glory of our Lord Jesus Christ.

¹⁵So then, brothers and sisters, stand firm and hold fast to the teachings*ᶠ* we passed on to you, whether by word of mouth or by letter.

¹⁶May our Lord Jesus Christ himself and

ᵃ 1 Greek *Silvanus*, a variant of *Silas*   *ᵇ* 3 The Greek word for *brothers and sisters* (*adelphoi*) refers here to believers, both men and women, as part of God's family; also in 2:1, 13, 15; 3:1, 6, 13.   *ᶜ* 12 Or *God and Lord, Jesus Christ*   *ᵈ* 3 Some manuscripts *sin*   *ᵉ* 13 Some manuscripts *because from the beginning God chose you*   *ᶠ* 15 Or *traditions*

God our Father, who loved us and by his grace gave us eternal encouragement and good hope, [17]encourage your hearts and strengthen you in every good deed and word.

Request for Prayer

3 As for other matters, brothers and sisters, pray for us that the message of the Lord may spread rapidly and be honored, just as it was with you. [2]And pray that we may be delivered from wicked and evil people, for not everyone has faith. [3]But the Lord is faithful, and he will strengthen you and protect you from the evil one. [4]We have confidence in the Lord that you are doing and will continue to do the things we command. [5]May the Lord direct your hearts into God's love and Christ's perseverance.

Warning Against Idleness

[6]In the name of the Lord Jesus Christ, we command you, brothers and sisters, to keep away from every believer who is idle and disruptive and does not live according to the teaching[a] you received from us. [7]For you yourselves know how you ought to follow our example. We were not idle when we were with you, [8]nor did we eat anyone's food without paying for it. On the contrary, we worked night and day, laboring and toiling so that we would not be a burden to any of you. [9]We did this, not because we do not have the right to such help, but in order to offer ourselves as a model for you to imitate. [10]For even when we were with you, we gave you this rule: "The one who is unwilling to work shall not eat."

[11]We hear that some among you are idle and disruptive. They are not busy; they are busybodies. [12]Such people we command and urge in the Lord Jesus Christ to settle down and earn the food they eat. [13]And as for you, brothers and sisters, never tire of doing what is good.

[14]Take special note of anyone who does not obey our instruction in this letter. Do not associate with them, in order that they may feel ashamed. [15]Yet do not regard them as an enemy, but warn them as you would a fellow believer.

Final Greetings

[16]Now may the Lord of peace himself give you peace at all times and in every way. The Lord be with all of you.

[17]I, Paul, write this greeting in my own hand, which is the distinguishing mark in all my letters. This is how I write.

[18]The grace of our Lord Jesus Christ be with you all.

1 Timothy

1 Paul, an apostle of Christ Jesus by the command of God our Savior and of Christ Jesus our hope,

[2]To Timothy my true son in the faith:

Grace, mercy and peace from God the Father and Christ Jesus our Lord.

Timothy Charged to Oppose False Teachers

[3]As I urged you when I went into Macedonia, stay there in Ephesus so that you may command certain people not to teach false doctrines any longer [4]or to devote themselves to myths and endless genealogies. Such things promote controversial speculations rather than advancing God's work—which is by faith. [5]The goal of this command is love, which comes from a pure heart and a good conscience and a sincere faith. [6]Some have departed from these and have turned to meaningless talk. [7]They want to be teachers of the law, but they do not know what they are talking about or what they so confidently affirm.

[8]We know that the law is good if one uses it properly. [9]We also know that the law is made not for the righteous but for lawbreakers and rebels, the ungodly and sinful, the unholy and irreligious, for those who kill their fathers or mothers, for murderers, [10]for the sexually immoral, for those practicing homosexuality, for slave traders and liars and perjurers—and for whatever else is contrary to the sound doctrine [11]that conforms to the gospel concerning the glory of the blessed God, which he entrusted to me.

The Lord's Grace to Paul

[12]I thank Christ Jesus our Lord, who has given me strength, that he considered me trustworthy, appointing me to his service. [13]Even though I was once a blasphemer and a persecutor and a violent man, I was shown mercy because I acted in ignorance and unbelief. [14]The grace of our Lord was poured out on me abundantly, along with the faith and love that are in Christ Jesus.

[15]Here is a trustworthy saying that deserves full acceptance: Christ Jesus came into the world to save sinners—of whom I am the worst. [16]But for that very reason I was shown mercy so that in me, the worst of sinners, Christ Jesus might display his immense

---

[a] 6 Or tradition

patience as an example for those who would believe in him and receive eternal life. [17]Now to the King eternal, immortal, invisible, the only God, be honor and glory for ever and ever. Amen.

The Charge to Timothy Renewed

[18]Timothy, my son, I am giving you this command in keeping with the prophecies once made about you, so that by recalling them you may fight the battle well, [19]holding on to faith and a good conscience, which some have rejected and so have suffered shipwreck with regard to the faith. [20]Among them are Hymenaeus and Alexander, whom I have handed over to Satan to be taught not to blaspheme.

Instructions on Worship

2 I urge, then, first of all, that petitions, prayers, intercession and thanksgiving be made for all people— [2]for kings and all those in authority, that we may live peaceful and quiet lives in all godliness and holiness. [3]This is good, and pleases God our Savior, [4]who wants all people to be saved and to come to a knowledge of the truth. [5]For there is one God and one mediator between God and mankind, the man Christ Jesus, [6]who gave himself as a ransom for all people. This has now been witnessed to at the proper time. [7]And for this purpose I was appointed a herald and an apostle—I am telling the truth, I am not lying—and a true and faithful teacher of the Gentiles.

[8]Therefore I want the men everywhere to pray, lifting up holy hands without anger or disputing. [9]I also want the women to dress modestly, with decency and propriety, adorning themselves, not with elaborate hairstyles or gold or pearls or expensive clothes, [10]but with good deeds, appropriate for women who profess to worship God.

[11]A woman[a] should learn in quietness and full submission. [12]I do not permit a woman to teach or to assume authority over a man;[b] she must be quiet. [13]For Adam was formed first, then Eve. [14]And Adam was not the one deceived; it was the woman who was deceived and became a sinner. [15]But women[c] will be saved through childbearing—if they continue in faith, love and holiness with propriety.

Qualifications for Overseers and Deacons

3 Here is a trustworthy saying: Whoever aspires to be an overseer desires a noble task. [2]Now the overseer is to be above reproach, faithful to his wife, temperate, self-controlled, respectable, hospitable, able to teach, [3]not given to drunkenness, not violent but gentle, not quarrelsome, not a lover of money. [4]He must manage his own family well and see that his children obey him, and he must do so in a manner worthy of full[d] respect. [5](If anyone does not know how to manage his own family, how can he take care of God's church?) [6]He must not be a recent convert, or he may become conceited and fall under the same judgment as the devil. [7]He must also have a good reputation with outsiders, so that he will not fall into disgrace and into the devil's trap.

[8]In the same way, deacons[e] are to be worthy of respect, sincere, not indulging in much wine, and not pursuing dishonest gain. [9]They must keep hold of the deep truths of the faith with a clear conscience. [10]They must first be tested; and then if there is nothing against them, let them serve as deacons.

[11]In the same way, the women[f] are to be worthy of respect, not malicious talkers but temperate and trustworthy in everything.

[12]A deacon must be faithful to his wife and must manage his children and his household well. [13]Those who have served well gain an excellent standing and great assurance in their faith in Christ Jesus.

Reasons for Paul's Instructions

[14]Although I hope to come to you soon, I am writing you these instructions so that, [15]if I am delayed, you will know how people ought to conduct themselves in God's household, which is the church of the living God, the pillar and foundation of the truth. [16]Beyond all question, the mystery from which true godliness springs is great:

He appeared in the flesh,
was vindicated by the Spirit,[g]
was seen by angels,
was preached among the nations,
was believed on in the world,
was taken up in glory.

4 The Spirit clearly says that in later times some will abandon the faith and follow deceiving spirits and things taught by demons. [2]Such teachings come through hypocritical liars, whose consciences have been seared as with a hot iron. [3]They forbid people to marry and order them to abstain from certain foods, which God created to be received with thanksgiving by those who believe and who know the truth. [4]For everything God created is good, and nothing is to be rejected if it is received with thanksgiving, [5]because it is consecrated by the word of God and prayer.

[6]If you point these things out to the brothers and sisters,[h] you will be a good minister of Christ Jesus, nourished on the truths of the faith and of the good teaching that you have followed. [7]Have nothing to do with godless myths and old wives' tales; rather, train yourself to be godly. [8]For physical training is of some value, but godliness has value for all things, holding promise for both the present life and the life to come. [9]This is a trustworthy

---

[a] 11 Or *wife*; also in verse 12   [b] 12 Or *over her husband*   [c] 15 Greek *she*   [d] 4 Or *him with proper*
[e] 8 The word *deacons* refers here to Christians designated to serve with the overseers/elders of the church in a variety of ways; similarly in verse 12; and in Romans 16:1 and Phil. 1:1.   [f] 11 Possibly
deacons' wives or women who are deacons   [g] 16 Or *vindicated in spirit*   [h] 6 The Greek word for *brothers and sisters* (*adelphoi*) refers here to believers, both men and women, as part of God's family.

saying that deserves full acceptance. ¹⁰That is why we labor and strive, because we have put our hope in the living God, who is the Savior of all people, and especially of those who believe.

¹¹Command and teach these things. ¹²Don't let anyone look down on you because you are young, but set an example for the believers in speech, in conduct, in love, in faith and in purity. ¹³Until I come, devote yourself to the public reading of Scripture, to preaching and to teaching. ¹⁴Do not neglect your gift, which was given you through prophecy when the body of elders laid their hands on you.

¹⁵Be diligent in these matters; give yourself wholly to them, so that everyone may see your progress. ¹⁶Watch your life and doctrine closely. Persevere in them, because if you do, you will save both yourself and your hearers.

Widows, Elders and Slaves

5 Do not rebuke an older man harshly, but exhort him as if he were your father. Treat younger men as brothers, ²older women as mothers, and younger women as sisters, with absolute purity.

³Give proper recognition to those widows who are really in need. ⁴But if a widow has children or grandchildren, these should learn first of all to put their religion into practice by caring for their own family and so repaying their parents and grandparents, for this is pleasing to God. ⁵The widow who is really in need and left all alone puts her hope in God and continues night and day to pray and to ask God for help. ⁶But the widow who lives for pleasure is dead even while she lives. ⁷Give the people these instructions, so that no one may be open to blame. ⁸Anyone who does not provide for their relatives, and especially for their own household, has denied the faith and is worse than an unbeliever.

⁹No widow may be put on the list of widows unless she is over sixty, has been faithful to her husband, ¹⁰and is well known for her good deeds, such as bringing up children, showing hospitality, washing the feet of the Lord's people, helping those in trouble and devoting herself to all kinds of good deeds.

¹¹As for younger widows, do not put them on such a list. For when their sensual desires overcome their dedication to Christ, they want to marry. ¹²Thus they bring judgment on themselves, because they have broken their first pledge. ¹³Besides, they get into the habit of being idle and going about from house to house. And not only do they become idlers, but also busybodies who talk nonsense, saying things they ought not to. ¹⁴So I counsel younger widows to marry, to have children, to manage their homes and to give the enemy no opportunity for slander. ¹⁵Some have in fact already turned away to follow Satan.

¹⁶If any woman who is a believer has widows in her care, she should continue to help them and not let the church be burdened with them, so that the church can help those widows who are really in need.

¹⁷The elders who direct the affairs of the church well are worthy of double honor, especially those whose work is preaching and teaching. ¹⁸For Scripture says, "Do not muzzle an ox while it is treading out the grain,"ᵃ and "The worker deserves his wages."ᵇ ¹⁹Do not entertain an accusation against an elder unless it is brought by two or three witnesses. ²⁰But those elders who are sinning you are to reprove before everyone, so that the others may take warning. ²¹I charge you, in the sight of God and Christ Jesus and the elect angels, to keep these instructions without partiality, and to do nothing out of favoritism.

²²Do not be hasty in the laying on of hands, and do not share in the sins of others. Keep yourself pure.

²³Stop drinking only water, and use a little wine because of your stomach and your frequent illnesses.

²⁴The sins of some are obvious, reaching the place of judgment ahead of them; the sins of others trail behind them. ²⁵In the same way, good deeds are obvious, and even those that are not obvious cannot remain hidden forever.

6 All who are under the yoke of slavery should consider their masters worthy of full respect, so that God's name and our teaching may not be slandered. ²Those who have believing masters should not show them disrespect just because they are fellow believers. Instead, they should serve them even better because their masters are dear to them as fellow believers and are devoted to the welfareᶜ of their slaves.

False Teachers and the Love of Money

These are the things you are to teach and insist on. ³If anyone teaches otherwise and does not agree to the sound instruction of our Lord Jesus Christ and to godly teaching, ⁴they are conceited and understand nothing. They have an unhealthy interest in controversies and quarrels about words that result in envy, strife, malicious talk, evil suspicions ⁵and constant friction between people of corrupt mind, who have been robbed of the truth and who think that godliness is a means to financial gain.

⁶But godliness with contentment is great gain. ⁷For we brought nothing into the world, and we can take nothing out of it. ⁸But if we have food and clothing, we will be content with that. ⁹Those who want to get rich fall into temptation and a trap and into many foolish and harmful desires that plunge people into ruin and destruction. ¹⁰For the love of money is a root of all kinds of evil. Some people, eager for money, have wandered from the faith and pierced themselves with many griefs.

Final Charge to Timothy

¹¹But you, man of God, flee from all this, and pursue righteousness, godliness, faith,

---

ᵃ 18 Deut. 25:4   ᵇ 18 Luke 10:7   ᶜ 2 Or *and benefit from the service* love, endurance and gentleness. [12]Fight the good fight of the faith. Take hold of the eternal life to which you were called when you made your good confession in the presence of many witnesses. [13]In the sight of God, who gives life to everything, and of Christ Jesus, who while testifying before Pontius Pilate made the good confession, I charge you [14]to keep this command without spot or blame until the appearing of our Lord Jesus Christ, [15]which God will bring about in his own time—God, the blessed and only Ruler, the King of kings and Lord of lords, [16]who alone is immortal and who lives in unapproachable light, whom no one has seen or can see. To him be honor and might forever. Amen.

[17]Command those who are rich in this present world not to be arrogant nor to put their hope in wealth, which is so uncertain, but to put their hope in God, who richly provides us with everything for our enjoyment. [18]Command them to do good, to be rich in good deeds, and to be generous and willing to share. [19]In this way they will lay up treasure for themselves as a firm foundation for the coming age, so that they may take hold of the life that is truly life.

[20]Timothy, guard what has been entrusted to your care. Turn away from godless chatter and the opposing ideas of what is falsely called knowledge, [21]which some have professed and in so doing have departed from the faith.

Grace be with you all.

2 Timothy

1 Paul, an apostle of Christ Jesus by the will of God, in keeping with the promise of life that is in Christ Jesus,

[2]To Timothy, my dear son:

Grace, mercy and peace from God the Father and Christ Jesus our Lord.

Thanksgiving

[3]I thank God, whom I serve, as my ancestors did, with a clear conscience, as night and day I constantly remember you in my prayers. [4]Recalling your tears, I long to see you, so that I may be filled with joy. [5]I am reminded of your sincere faith, which first lived in your grandmother Lois and in your mother Eunice and, I am persuaded, now lives in you also.

Appeal for Loyalty to Paul and the Gospel

[6]For this reason I remind you to fan into flame the gift of God, which is in you through the laying on of my hands. [7]For the Spirit God gave us does not make us timid, but gives us power, love and self-discipline. [8]So do not be ashamed of the testimony about our Lord or of me his prisoner. Rather, join with me in suffering for the gospel, by the power of God. [9]He has saved us and called us to a holy life—not because of anything we have done but because of his own purpose and grace. This grace was given us in Christ Jesus before the beginning of time, [10]but it has now been revealed through the appearing of our Savior, Christ Jesus, who has destroyed death and has brought life and immortality to light through the gospel. [11]And of this gospel I was appointed a herald and an apostle and a teacher. [12]That is why I am suffering as I am. Yet this is no cause for shame, because I know whom I have believed, and am convinced that he is able to guard what I have entrusted to him until that day.

[13]What you heard from me, keep as the pattern of sound teaching, with faith and love in Christ Jesus. [14]Guard the good deposit that was entrusted to you—guard it with the help of the Holy Spirit who lives in us.

Examples of Disloyalty and Loyalty

[15]You know that everyone in the province of Asia has deserted me, including Phygelus and Hermogenes.

[16]May the Lord show mercy to the household of Onesiphorus, because he often refreshed me and was not ashamed of my chains. [17]On the contrary, when he was in Rome, he searched hard for me until he found me. [18]May the Lord grant that he will find mercy from the Lord on that day! You know very well in how many ways he helped me in Ephesus.

The Appeal Renewed

2 You then, my son, be strong in the grace that is in Christ Jesus. [2]And the things you have heard me say in the presence of many witnesses entrust to reliable people who will also be qualified to teach others. [3]Join with me in suffering, like a good soldier of Christ Jesus. [4]No one serving as a soldier gets entangled in civilian affairs, but rather tries to please his commanding officer. [5]Similarly, anyone who competes as an athlete does not receive the victor's crown except by competing according to the rules. [6]The hardworking farmer should be the first to receive a share of the crops. [7]Reflect on what I am saying, for the Lord will give you insight into all this.

[8]Remember Jesus Christ, raised from the dead, descended from David. This is my gospel, [9]for which I am suffering even to the point of being chained like a criminal. But God's word is not chained. [10]Therefore I endure everything for the sake of the elect, that they

too may obtain the salvation that is in Christ Jesus, with eternal glory. [11]Here is a trustworthy saying:

If we died with him,
we will also live with him;
[12]if we endure,
we will also reign with him.
If we disown him,
he will also disown us;
[13]if we are faithless,
he remains faithful,
for he cannot disown himself.

Dealing With False Teachers

[14]Keep reminding God's people of these things. Warn them before God against quarreling about words; it is of no value, and only ruins those who listen. [15]Do your best to present yourself to God as one approved, a worker who does not need to be ashamed and who correctly handles the word of truth. [16]Avoid godless chatter, because those who indulge in it will become more and more ungodly. [17]Their teaching will spread like gangrene. Among them are Hymenaeus and Philetus, [18]who have departed from the truth. They say that the resurrection has already taken place, and they destroy the faith of some. [19]Nevertheless, God's solid foundation stands firm, sealed with this inscription: "The Lord knows those who are his," and, "Everyone who confesses the name of the Lord must turn away from wickedness."

[20]In a large house there are articles not only of gold and silver, but also of wood and clay; some are for special purposes and some for common use. [21]Those who cleanse themselves from the latter will be instruments for special purposes, made holy, useful to the Master and prepared to do any good work.

[22]Flee the evil desires of youth and pursue righteousness, faith, love and peace, along with those who call on the Lord out of a pure heart. [23]Don't have anything to do with foolish and stupid arguments, because you know they produce quarrels. [24]And the Lord's servant must not be quarrelsome but must be kind to everyone, able to teach, not resentful. [25]Opponents must be gently instructed, in the hope that God will grant them repentance leading them to a knowledge of the truth, [26]and that they will come to their senses and escape from the trap of the devil, who has taken them captive to do his will.

3 But mark this: There will be terrible times in the last days. [2]People will be lovers of themselves, lovers of money, boastful, proud, abusive, disobedient to their parents, ungrateful, unholy, [3]without love, unforgiving, slanderous, without self-control, brutal, not lovers of the good, [4]treacherous, rash, conceited, lovers of pleasure rather than lovers of God— [5]having a form of godliness but denying its power. Have nothing to do with such people.

[6]They are the kind who worm their way into homes and gain control over gullible women, who are loaded down with sins and are swayed by all kinds of evil desires, [7]always learning but never able to come to a knowledge of the truth. [8]Just as Jannes and Jambres opposed Moses, so also these teachers oppose the truth. They are men of depraved minds, who, as far as the faith is concerned, are rejected. [9]But they will not get very far because, as in the case of those men, their folly will be clear to everyone.

A Final Charge to Timothy

[10]You, however, know all about my teaching, my way of life, my purpose, faith, patience, love, endurance, [11]persecutions, sufferings—what kinds of things happened to me in Antioch, Iconium and Lystra, the persecutions I endured. Yet the Lord rescued me from all of them. [12]In fact, everyone who wants to live a godly life in Christ Jesus will be persecuted, [13]while evildoers and impostors will go from bad to worse, deceiving and being deceived. [14]But as for you, continue in what you have learned and have become convinced of, because you know those from whom you learned it, [15]and how from infancy you have known the Holy Scriptures, which are able to make you wise for salvation through faith in Christ Jesus. [16]All Scripture is God-breathed and is useful for teaching, rebuking, correcting and training in righteousness, [17]so that the servant of God[a] may be thoroughly equipped for every good work.

4 In the presence of God and of Christ Jesus, who will judge the living and the dead, and in view of his appearing and his kingdom, I give you this charge: [2]Preach the word; be prepared in season and out of season; correct, rebuke and encourage—with great patience and careful instruction. [3]For the time will come when people will not put up with sound doctrine. Instead, to suit their own desires, they will gather around them a great number of teachers to say what their itching ears want to hear. [4]They will turn their ears away from the truth and turn aside to myths. [5]But you, keep your head in all situations, endure hardship, do the work of an evangelist, discharge all the duties of your ministry.

[6]For I am already being poured out like a drink offering, and the time for my departure is near. [7]I have fought the good fight, I have finished the race, I have kept the faith. [8]Now there is in store for me the crown of righteousness, which the Lord, the righteous Judge, will award to me on that day—and not only to me, but also to all who have longed for his appearing.

Personal Remarks

[9]Do your best to come to me quickly, [10]for Demas, because he loved this world, has deserted me and has gone to Thessalonica. Crescens has gone to Galatia, and Titus to Dalmatia. [11]Only Luke is with me. Get Mark and bring him with you, because he is helpful

---

[a] 17 Or that you, a man of God,

to me in my ministry. [12]I sent Tychicus to Ephesus. [13]When you come, bring the cloak that I left with Carpus at Troas, and my scrolls, especially the parchments.

[14]Alexander the metalworker did me a great deal of harm. The Lord will repay him for what he has done. [15]You too should be on your guard against him, because he strongly opposed our message.

[16]At my first defense, no one came to my support, but everyone deserted me. May it not be held against them. [17]But the Lord stood at my side and gave me strength, so that through me the message might be fully proclaimed and all the Gentiles might hear it. And I was delivered from the lion's mouth. [18]The Lord will rescue me from every evil attack and will bring me safely to his heavenly kingdom. To him be glory for ever and ever. Amen.

Final Greetings

[19]Greet Priscilla[a] and Aquila and the household of Onesiphorus. [20]Erastus stayed in Corinth, and I left Trophimus sick in Miletus. [21]Do your best to get here before winter. Eubulus greets you, and so do Pudens, Linus, Claudia and all the brothers and sisters.[b]

[22]The Lord be with your spirit. Grace be with you all.

Titus

1 Paul, a servant of God and an apostle of Jesus Christ to further the faith of God's elect and their knowledge of the truth that leads to godliness— [2]in the hope of eternal life, which God, who does not lie, promised before the beginning of time, [3]and which now at his appointed season he has brought to light through the preaching entrusted to me by the command of God our Savior,

[4]To Titus, my true son in our common faith:

Grace and peace from God the Father and Christ Jesus our Savior.

Appointing Elders Who Love What Is Good

[5]The reason I left you in Crete was that you might put in order what was left unfinished and appoint[c] elders in every town, as I directed you. [6]An elder must be blameless, faithful to his wife, a man whose children believe[d] and are not open to the charge of being wild and disobedient. [7]Since an overseer manages God's household, he must be blameless—not overbearing, not quick-tempered, not given to drunkenness, not violent, not pursuing dishonest gain. [8]Rather, he must be hospitable, one who loves what is good, who is self-controlled, upright, holy and disciplined. [9]He must hold firmly to the trustworthy message as it has been taught, so that he can encourage others by sound doctrine and refute those who oppose it.

Rebuking Those Who Fail to Do Good

[10]For there are many rebellious people, full of meaningless talk and deception, especially those of the circumcision group. [11]They must be silenced, because they are disrupting whole households by teaching things they ought not to teach—and that for the sake of dishonest gain. [12]One of Crete's own prophets has said it: "Cretans are always liars, evil brutes, lazy gluttons."[e] [13]This saying is true. Therefore rebuke them sharply, so that they will be sound in the faith [14]and will pay no attention to Jewish myths or to the merely human commands of those who reject the truth. [15]To the pure, all things are pure, but to those who are corrupted and do not believe, nothing is pure. In fact, both their minds and consciences are corrupted. [16]They claim to know God, but by their actions they deny him. They are detestable, disobedient and unfit for doing anything good.

Doing Good for the Sake of the Gospel

2 You, however, must teach what is appropriate to sound doctrine. [2]Teach the older men to be temperate, worthy of respect, self-controlled, and sound in faith, in love and in endurance.

[3]Likewise, teach the older women to be reverent in the way they live, not to be slanderers or addicted to much wine, but to teach what is good. [4]Then they can urge the younger women to love their husbands and children, [5]to be self-controlled and pure, to be busy at home, to be kind, and to be subject to their husbands, so that no one will malign the word of God.

[6]Similarly, encourage the young men to be self-controlled. [7]In everything set them an example by doing what is good. In your teaching show integrity, seriousness [8]and soundness of speech that cannot be condemned, so that those who oppose you may be ashamed because they have nothing bad to say about us.

[9]Teach slaves to be subject to their masters

---

[a] 19 Greek *Prisca*, a variant of *Priscilla*   [b] 21 The Greek word for *brothers and sisters* (*adelphoi*) refers here to believers, both men and women, as part of God's family.   [c] 5 Or *ordain*   [d] 6 Or *children are trustworthy*   [e] 12 From the Cretan philosopher Epimenides

in everything, to try to please them, not to talk back to them, ¹⁰and not to steal from them, but to show that they can be fully trusted, so that in every way they will make the teaching about God our Savior attractive.

¹¹For the grace of God has appeared that offers salvation to all people. ¹²It teaches us to say "No" to ungodliness and worldly passions, and to live self-controlled, upright and godly lives in this present age, ¹³while we wait for the blessed hope—the appearing of the glory of our great God and Savior, Jesus Christ, ¹⁴who gave himself for us to redeem us from all wickedness and to purify for himself a people that are his very own, eager to do what is good.

¹⁵These, then, are the things you should teach. Encourage and rebuke with all authority. Do not let anyone despise you.

Saved in Order to Do Good

3 Remind the people to be subject to rulers and authorities, to be obedient, to be ready to do whatever is good, ²to slander no one, to be peaceable and considerate, and always to be gentle toward everyone.

³At one time we too were foolish, disobedient, deceived and enslaved by all kinds of passions and pleasures. We lived in malice and envy, being hated and hating one another. ⁴But when the kindness and love of God our Savior appeared, ⁵he saved us, not because of righteous things we had done, but because of his mercy. He saved us through the washing of rebirth and renewal by the Holy Spirit, ⁶whom he poured out on us generously through Jesus Christ our Savior, ⁷so that, having been justified by his grace, we might become heirs having the hope of eternal life. ⁸This is a trustworthy saying. And I want you to stress these things, so that those who have trusted in God may be careful to devote themselves to doing what is good. These things are excellent and profitable for everyone.

⁹But avoid foolish controversies and genealogies and arguments and quarrels about the law, because these are unprofitable and useless. ¹⁰Warn a divisive person once, and then warn them a second time. After that, have nothing to do with them. ¹¹You may be sure that such people are warped and sinful; they are self-condemned.

Final Remarks

¹²As soon as I send Artemas or Tychicus to you, do your best to come to me at Nicopolis, because I have decided to winter there. ¹³Do everything you can to help Zenas the lawyer and Apollos on their way and see that they have everything they need. ¹⁴Our people must learn to devote themselves to doing what is good, in order to provide for urgent needs and not live unproductive lives.

¹⁵Everyone with me sends you greetings. Greet those who love us in the faith.

Grace be with you all.

Philemon

¹Paul, a prisoner of Christ Jesus, and Timothy our brother,

To Philemon our dear friend and fellow worker— ²also to Apphia our sister and Archippus our fellow soldier—and to the church that meets in your home:

³Grace and peace to youᵃ from God our Father and the Lord Jesus Christ.

Thanksgiving and Prayer

⁴I always thank my God as I remember you in my prayers, ⁵because I hear about your love for all his holy people and your faith in the Lord Jesus. ⁶I pray that your partnership with us in the faith may be effective in deepening your understanding of every good thing we share for the sake of Christ. ⁷Your love has given me great joy and encouragement, because you, brother, have refreshed the hearts of the Lord's people.

Paul's Plea for Onesimus

⁸Therefore, although in Christ I could be bold and order you to do what you ought to do, ⁹yet I prefer to appeal to you on the basis of love. It is as none other than Paul—an old man and now also a prisoner of Christ Jesus— ¹⁰that I appeal to you for my son Onesimus,ᵇ who became my son while I was in chains. ¹¹Formerly he was useless to you, but now he has become useful both to you and to me.

¹²I am sending him—who is my very heart—back to you. ¹³I would have liked to keep him with me so that he could take your place in helping me while I am in chains for the gospel. ¹⁴But I did not want to do anything without your consent, so that any favor you do would not seem forced but would be voluntary. ¹⁵Perhaps the reason he was separated from you for a little while was that you might have him back forever— ¹⁶no longer as a slave, but better than a slave, as a dear

---

ᵃ 3 The Greek is plural; also in verses 22 and 25; elsewhere in this letter "you" is singular.
ᵇ 10 Onesimus means useful.

brother. He is very dear to me but even dearer to you, both as a fellow man and as a brother in the Lord.

¹⁷So if you consider me a partner, welcome him as you would welcome me. ¹⁸If he has done you any wrong or owes you anything, charge it to me. ¹⁹I, Paul, am writing this with my own hand. I will pay it back—not to mention that you owe me your very self. ²⁰I do wish, brother, that I may have some benefit from you in the Lord; refresh my heart in Christ. ²¹Confident of your obedience, I write to you, knowing that you will do even more than I ask.

²²And one thing more: Prepare a guest room for me, because I hope to be restored to you in answer to your prayers.

²³Epaphras, my fellow prisoner in Christ Jesus, sends you greetings. ²⁴And so do Mark, Aristarchus, Demas and Luke, my fellow workers.

²⁵The grace of the Lord Jesus Christ be with your spirit.

Hebrews

God's Final Word: His Son

1 In the past God spoke to our ancestors through the prophets at many times and in various ways, ²but in these last days he has spoken to us by his Son, whom he appointed heir of all things, and through whom also he made the universe. ³The Son is the radiance of God's glory and the exact representation of his being, sustaining all things by his powerful word. After he had provided purification for sins, he sat down at the right hand of the Majesty in heaven. ⁴So he became as much superior to the angels as the name he has inherited is superior to theirs.

The Son Superior to Angels

⁵For to which of the angels did God ever say,

"You are my Son;
today I have become your Father"ᵃ?

Or again,

"I will be his Father,
and he will be my Son"ᵇ?

⁶And again, when God brings his firstborn into the world, he says,

"Let all God's angels worship him."ᶜ

⁷In speaking of the angels he says,

"He makes his angels spirits,
and his servants flames of fire."ᵈ

⁸But about the Son he says,

"Your throne, O God, will last for ever
and ever;
a scepter of justice will be the scepter of
your kingdom.
⁹You have loved righteousness and hated
wickedness;
therefore God, your God, has set you
above your companions
by anointing you with the oil of joy."ᵉ

¹⁰He also says,

"In the beginning, Lord, you laid the
foundations of the earth,
and the heavens are the work of your
hands.
¹¹They will perish, but you remain;
they will all wear out like a garment.
¹²You will roll them up like a robe;
like a garment they will be changed.
But you remain the same,
and your years will never end."ᶠ

¹³To which of the angels did God ever say,

"Sit at my right hand
until I make your enemies
a footstool for your feet"ᵍ?

¹⁴Are not all angels ministering spirits sent to serve those who will inherit salvation?

Warning to Pay Attention

2 We must pay the most careful attention, therefore, to what we have heard, so that we do not drift away. ²For since the message spoken through angels was binding, and every violation and disobedience received its just punishment, ³how shall we escape if we ignore so great a salvation? This salvation, which was first announced by the Lord, was confirmed to us by those who heard him. ⁴God also testified to it by signs, wonders and various miracles, and by gifts of the Holy Spirit distributed according to his will.

Jesus Made Fully Human

⁵It is not to angels that he has subjected the world to come, about which we are speaking. ⁶But there is a place where someone has testified:

"What is mankind that you are mindful
of them,
a son of man that you care for him?

ᵃ 5 Psalm 2:7   ᵇ 5 2 Samuel 7:14; 1 Chron. 17:13   ᶜ 6 Deut. 32:43 (see Dead Sea Scrolls and Septuagint)   ᵈ 7 Psalm 104:4   ᵉ 9 Psalm 45:6,7   ᶠ 12 Psalm 102:25-27   ᵍ 13 Psalm 110:1

[7] You made them a little[a] lower than the angels;
you crowned them with glory and honor
[8] and put everything under their feet."[b,c]

In putting everything under them,[d] God left nothing that is not subject to them.[d] Yet at present we do not see everything subject to them.[d] [9] But we do see Jesus, who was made lower than the angels for a little while, now crowned with glory and honor because he suffered death, so that by the grace of God he might taste death for everyone.

[10] In bringing many sons and daughters to glory, it was fitting that God, for whom and through whom everything exists, should make the pioneer of their salvation perfect through what he suffered. [11] Both the one who makes people holy and those who are made holy are of the same family. So Jesus is not ashamed to call them brothers and sisters.[e] [12] He says,

"I will declare your name to my brothers and sisters;
in the assembly I will sing your praises."[f]

[13] And again,

"I will put my trust in him."[g]

And again he says,

"Here am I, and the children God has given me."[h]

[14] Since the children have flesh and blood, he too shared in their humanity so that by his death he might break the power of him who holds the power of death—that is, the devil— [15] and free those who all their lives were held in slavery by their fear of death. [16] For surely it is not angels he helps, but Abraham's descendants. [17] For this reason he had to be made like them,[i] fully human in every way, in order that he might become a merciful and faithful high priest in service to God, and that he might make atonement for the sins of the people. [18] Because he himself suffered when he was tempted, he is able to help those who are being tempted.

Jesus Greater Than Moses

3 Therefore, holy brothers and sisters, who share in the heavenly calling, fix your thoughts on Jesus, whom we acknowledge as our apostle and high priest. [2] He was faithful to the one who appointed him, just as Moses was faithful in all God's house. [3] Jesus has been found worthy of greater honor than Moses, just as the builder of a house has greater honor than the house itself. [4] For every house is built by someone, but God is the builder of everything. [5] "Moses was faithful as a servant in all God's house,"[j] bearing witness to what would be spoken by God in the future. [6] But Christ is faithful as the Son over God's house. And we are his house, if indeed we hold firmly to our confidence and the hope in which we glory.

Warning Against Unbelief

[7] So, as the Holy Spirit says:

"Today, if you hear his voice,
[8] do not harden your hearts
as you did in the rebellion,
during the time of testing in the wilderness,
[9] where your ancestors tested and tried me,
though for forty years they saw what I did.
[10] That is why I was angry with that generation;
I said, 'Their hearts are always going astray,
and they have not known my ways.'
[11] So I declared on oath in my anger,
'They shall never enter my rest.'"[k]

[12] See to it, brothers and sisters, that none of you has a sinful, unbelieving heart that turns away from the living God. [13] But encourage one another daily, as long as it is called "Today," so that none of you may be hardened by sin's deceitfulness. [14] We have come to share in Christ, if indeed we hold our original conviction firmly to the very end. [15] As has just been said:

"Today, if you hear his voice,
do not harden your hearts
as you did in the rebellion."[l]

[16] Who were they who heard and rebelled? Were they not all those Moses led out of Egypt? [17] And with whom was he angry for forty years? Was it not with those who sinned, whose bodies perished in the wilderness? [18] And to whom did God swear that they would never enter his rest if not to those who disobeyed? [19] So we see that they were not able to enter, because of their unbelief.

A Sabbath-Rest for the People of God

4 Therefore, since the promise of entering his rest still stands, let us be careful that none of you be found to have fallen short of it. [2] For we also have had the good news proclaimed to us, just as they did; but the message they heard was of no value to them, because they did not share the faith of those who obeyed.[m] [3] Now we who have believed enter that rest, just as God has said,

"So I declared on oath in my anger,
'They shall never enter my rest.'"[n]

[a] 7 Or *them for a little while*   [b] 6-8 Psalm 8:4-6   [c] 7,8 Or *[7]You made him a little lower than the angels;[/] you crowned him with glory and honor/ [8]and put everything under his feet.*   [d] 8 Or *him*   [e] 11 The Greek word for *brothers and sisters (adelphoi)* refers here to believers, both men and women, as part of God's family; also in verse 12; and in 3:1, 12; 10:19; 13:22.   [f] 12 Psalm 22:22   [g] 13 Isaiah 8:17   [h] 13 Isaiah 8:18   [i] 17 Or *like his brothers*   [j] 5 Num. 12:7   [k] 11 Psalm 95:7-11   [l] 15 Psalm 95:7,8   [m] 2 Some manuscripts *because those who heard did not combine it with faith*   [n] 3 Psalm 95:11; also in verse 5

And yet his works have been finished since the creation of the world. [4]For somewhere he has spoken about the seventh day in these words: "On the seventh day God rested from all his works."[a] [5]And again in the passage above he says, "They shall never enter my rest."

[6]Therefore since it still remains for some to enter that rest, and since those who formerly had the good news proclaimed to them did not go in because of their disobedience, [7]God again set a certain day, calling it "Today." This he did when a long time later he spoke through David, as in the passage already quoted:

"Today, if you hear his voice,
    do not harden your hearts."[b]

[8]For if Joshua had given them rest, God would not have spoken later about another day. [9]There remains, then, a Sabbath-rest for the people of God; [10]for anyone who enters God's rest also rests from their works,[c] just as God did from his. [11]Let us, therefore, make every effort to enter that rest, so that no one will perish by following their example of disobedience.

[12]For the word of God is alive and active. Sharper than any double-edged sword, it penetrates even to dividing soul and spirit, joints and marrow; it judges the thoughts and attitudes of the heart. [13]Nothing in all creation is hidden from God's sight. Everything is uncovered and laid bare before the eyes of him to whom we must give account.

Jesus the Great High Priest

[14]Therefore, since we have a great high priest who has ascended into heaven,[d] Jesus the Son of God, let us hold firmly to the faith we profess. [15]For we do not have a high priest who is unable to empathize with our weaknesses, but we have one who has been tempted in every way, just as we are—yet he did not sin. [16]Let us then approach God's throne of grace with confidence, so that we may receive mercy and find grace to help us in our time of need.

5 Every high priest is selected from among the people and is appointed to represent the people in matters related to God, to offer gifts and sacrifices for sins. [2]He is able to deal gently with those who are ignorant and are going astray, since he himself is subject to weakness. [3]This is why he has to offer sacrifices for his own sins, as well as for the sins of the people. [4]And no one takes this honor on himself, but he receives it when called by God, just as Aaron was.

[5]In the same way, Christ did not take on himself the glory of becoming a high priest. But God said to him,

"You are my Son;
    today I have become your Father."[e]

[6]And he says in another place,

"You are a priest forever,
    in the order of Melchizedek."[f]

[7]During the days of Jesus' life on earth, he offered up prayers and petitions with fervent cries and tears to the one who could save him from death, and he was heard because of his reverent submission. [8]Son though he was, he learned obedience from what he suffered [9]and, once made perfect, he became the source of eternal salvation for all who obey him [10]and was designated by God to be high priest in the order of Melchizedek.

Warning Against Falling Away

[11]We have much to say about this, but it is hard to make it clear to you because you no longer try to understand. [12]In fact, though by this time you ought to be teachers, you need someone to teach you the elementary truths of God's word all over again. You need milk, not solid food! [13]Anyone who lives on milk, being still an infant, is not acquainted with the teaching about righteousness. [14]But solid food is for the mature, who by constant use have trained themselves to distinguish good from evil.

6 Therefore let us move beyond the elementary teachings about Christ and be taken forward to maturity, not laying again the foundation of repentance from acts that lead to death,[g] and of faith in God, [2]instruction about cleansing rites,[h] the laying on of hands, the resurrection of the dead, and eternal judgment. [3]And God permitting, we will do so.

[4]It is impossible for those who have once been enlightened, who have tasted the heavenly gift, who have shared in the Holy Spirit, [5]who have tasted the goodness of the word of God and the powers of the coming age [6]and who have fallen[i] away, to be brought back to repentance. To their loss they are crucifying the Son of God all over again and subjecting him to public disgrace. [7]Land that drinks in the rain often falling on it and that produces a crop useful to those for whom it is farmed receives the blessing of God. [8]But land that produces thorns and thistles is worthless and is in danger of being cursed. In the end it will be burned.

[9]Even though we speak like this, dear friends, we are convinced of better things in your case—the things that have to do with salvation. [10]God is not unjust; he will not forget your work and the love you have shown him as you have helped his people and continue to help them. [11]We want each of you to show this same diligence to the very end, so that what you hope for may be fully realized. [12]We do not want you to become lazy, but to imitate those who through faith and patience inherit what has been promised.

The Certainty of God's Promise

[13]When God made his promise to Abraham, since there was no one greater for him

---

[a] 4 Gen. 2:2   [b] 7 Psalm 95:7,8   [c] 10 Or labor   [d] 14 Greek has gone through the heavens
[e] 5 Psalm 2:7   [f] 6 Psalm 110:4   [g] 1 Or from useless rituals · [h] 2 Or about baptisms   [i] 6 Or age,
[6]if they fall

to swear by, he swore by himself, [14]saying, "I will surely bless you and give you many descendants."[a] [15]And so after waiting patiently, Abraham received what was promised.

[16]People swear by someone greater than themselves, and the oath confirms what is said and puts an end to all argument. [17]Because God wanted to make the unchanging nature of his purpose very clear to the heirs of what was promised, he confirmed it with an oath. [18]God did this so that, by two unchangeable things in which it is impossible for God to lie, we who have fled to take hold of the hope set before us may be greatly encouraged. [19]We have this hope as an anchor for the soul, firm and secure. It enters the inner sanctuary behind the curtain, [20]where our forerunner, Jesus, has entered on our behalf. He has become a high priest forever, in the order of Melchizedek.

Melchizedek the Priest

7 This Melchizedek was king of Salem and priest of God Most High. He met Abraham returning from the defeat of the kings and blessed him, [2]and Abraham gave him a tenth of everything. First, the name Melchizedek means "king of righteousness"; then also, "king of Salem" means "king of peace." [3]Without father or mother, without genealogy, without beginning of days or end of life, resembling the Son of God, he remains a priest forever.

[4]Just think how great he was: Even the patriarch Abraham gave him a tenth of the plunder! [5]Now the law requires the descendants of Levi who become priests to collect a tenth from the people—that is, from their fellow Israelites—even though they also are descended from Abraham. [6]This man, however, did not trace his descent from Levi, yet he collected a tenth from Abraham and blessed him who had the promises. [7]And without doubt the lesser is blessed by the greater. [8]In the one case, the tenth is collected by people who die; but in the other case, by him who is declared to be living. [9]One might even say that Levi, who collects the tenth, paid the tenth through Abraham, [10]because when Melchizedek met Abraham, Levi was still in the body of his ancestor.

Jesus Like Melchizedek

[11]If perfection could have been attained through the Levitical priesthood—and indeed the law given to the people established that priesthood—why was there still need for another priest to come, one in the order of Melchizedek, not in the order of Aaron? [12]For when the priesthood is changed, the law must be changed also. [13]He of whom these things are said belonged to a different tribe, and no one from that tribe has ever served at the altar. [14]For it is clear that our Lord descended from Judah, and in regard to that tribe Moses said nothing about priests. [15]And what we

have said is even more clear if another priest like Melchizedek appears, [16]one who has become a priest not on the basis of a regulation as to his ancestry but on the basis of the power of an indestructible life. [17]For it is declared:

"You are a priest forever,
in the order of Melchizedek."[b]

[18]The former regulation is set aside because it was weak and useless [19](for the law made nothing perfect), and a better hope is introduced, by which we draw near to God.

[20]And it was not without an oath! Others became priests without any oath, [21]but he became a priest with an oath when God said to him:

"The Lord has sworn
and will not change his mind:
'You are a priest forever.'"[b]

[22]Because of this oath, Jesus has become the guarantor of a better covenant.

[23]Now there have been many of those priests, since death prevented them from continuing in office; [24]but because Jesus lives forever, he has a permanent priesthood. [25]Therefore he is able to save completely[c] those who come to God through him, because he always lives to intercede for them.

[26]Such a high priest truly meets our need—one who is holy, blameless, pure, set apart from sinners, exalted above the heavens. [27]Unlike the other high priests, he does not need to offer sacrifices day after day, first for his own sins, and then for the sins of the people. He sacrificed for their sins once for all when he offered himself. [28]For the law appoints as high priests men in all their weakness; but the oath, which came after the law, appointed the Son, who has been made perfect forever.

The High Priest of a New Covenant

8 Now the main point of what we are saying is this: We do have such a high priest, who sat down at the right hand of the throne of the Majesty in heaven, [2]and who serves in the sanctuary, the true tabernacle set up by the Lord, not by a mere human being.

[3]Every high priest is appointed to offer both gifts and sacrifices, and so it was necessary for this one also to have something to offer. [4]If he were on earth, he would not be a priest, for there are already priests who offer the gifts prescribed by the law. [5]They serve at a sanctuary that is a copy and shadow of what is in heaven. This is why Moses was warned when he was about to build the tabernacle: "See to it that you make everything according to the pattern shown you on the mountain."[d] [6]But in fact the ministry Jesus has received is as superior to theirs as the covenant of which he is mediator is superior to the old one, since the new covenant is established on better promises.

[7]For if there had been nothing wrong with that first covenant, no place would have been

---

[a] 14 Gen. 22:17   [b] 17,21 Psalm 110:4   [c] 25 Or *forever*   [d] 5 Exodus 25:40

sought for another. [8]But God found fault with the people and said[a]:

"The days are coming, declares the
　　　Lord,
　when I will make a new covenant
with the people of Israel
　and with the people of Judah.
[9]It will not be like the covenant
　I made with their ancestors
when I took them by the hand
　to lead them out of Egypt,
because they did not remain faithful to
　　　my covenant,
　and I turned away from them,
　　　　　　declares the Lord.
[10]This is the covenant I will establish with
　　　the people of Israel
　after that time, declares the Lord.
I will put my laws in their minds
　and write them on their hearts.
I will be their God,
　and they will be my people.
[11]No longer will they teach their neighbor,
　or say to one another, 'Know the
　　　Lord,'
because they will all know me,
　from the least of them to the greatest.
[12]For I will forgive their wickedness
　and will remember their sins no
　　　more."[b]

[13]By calling this covenant "new," he has made the first one obsolete; and what is obsolete and outdated will soon disappear.

Worship in the Earthly Tabernacle

9 Now the first covenant had regulations for worship and also an earthly sanctuary. [2]A tabernacle was set up. In its first room were the lampstand and the table with its consecrated bread; this was called the Holy Place. [3]Behind the second curtain was a room called the Most Holy Place, [4]which had the golden altar of incense and the gold-covered ark of the covenant. This ark contained the gold jar of manna, Aaron's staff that had budded, and the stone tablets of the covenant. [5]Above the ark were the cherubim of the Glory, overshadowing the atonement cover. But we cannot discuss these things in detail now.

[6]When everything had been arranged like this, the priests entered regularly into the outer room to carry on their ministry. [7]But only the high priest entered the inner room, and that only once a year, and never without blood, which he offered for himself and for the sins the people had committed in ignorance. [8]The Holy Spirit was showing by this that the way into the Most Holy Place had not yet been disclosed as long as the first tabernacle was still functioning. [9]This is an illustration for the present time, indicating that the gifts and sacrifices being offered were not able to clear the conscience of the worshiper. [10]They are only a matter of food and drink and various ceremonial washings—external regulations applying until the time of the new order.

The Blood of Christ

[11]But when Christ came as high priest of the good things that are now already here,[c] he went through the greater and more perfect tabernacle that is not made with human hands, that is to say, is not a part of this creation. [12]He did not enter by means of the blood of goats and calves; but he entered the Most Holy Place once for all by his own blood, thus obtaining[d] eternal redemption. [13]The blood of goats and bulls and the ashes of a heifer sprinkled on those who are ceremonially unclean sanctify them so that they are outwardly clean. [14]How much more, then, will the blood of Christ, who through the eternal Spirit offered himself unblemished to God, cleanse our consciences from acts that lead to death,[e] so that we may serve the living God!

[15]For this reason Christ is the mediator of a new covenant, that those who are called may receive the promised eternal inheritance— now that he has died as a ransom to set them free from the sins committed under the first covenant.

[16]In the case of a will,[f] it is necessary to prove the death of the one who made it, [17]because a will is in force only when somebody has died; it never takes effect while the one who made it is living. [18]This is why even the first covenant was not put into effect without blood. [19]When Moses had proclaimed every command of the law to all the people, he took the blood of calves, together with water, scarlet wool and branches of hyssop, and sprinkled the scroll and all the people. [20]He said, "This is the blood of the covenant, which God has commanded you to keep."[g] [21]In the same way, he sprinkled with the blood both the tabernacle and everything used in its ceremonies. [22]In fact, the law requires that nearly everything be cleansed with blood, and without the shedding of blood there is no forgiveness.

[23]It was necessary, then, for the copies of the heavenly things to be purified with these sacrifices, but the heavenly things themselves with better sacrifices than these. [24]For Christ did not enter a sanctuary made with human hands that was only a copy of the true one; he entered heaven itself, now to appear for us in God's presence. [25]Nor did he enter heaven to offer himself again and again, the way the high priest enters the Most Holy Place every year with blood that is not his own. [26]Otherwise Christ would have had to suffer many times since the creation of the world. But he has appeared once for all at the culmination of the ages to do away with sin by the sacrifice of himself. [27]Just as people are destined to die once, and after that to face judgment, [28]so Christ was sacrificed once to take away the sins of many; and he will appear a second

---

[a] 8 Some manuscripts may be translated *fault and said to the people.*　　[b] 12 Jer. 31:31-34　　[c] 11 Some early manuscripts *are to come*　　[d] 12 Or *blood, having obtained*　　[e] 14 Or *from useless rituals*
[f] 16 Same Greek word as *covenant*; also in verse 17　　[g] 20 Exodus 24:8

time, not to bear sin, but to bring salvation to those who are waiting for him.

Christ's Sacrifice Once for All

10 The law is only a shadow of the good things that are coming—not the realities themselves. For this reason it can never, by the same sacrifices repeated endlessly year after year, make perfect those who draw near to worship. ²Otherwise, would they not have stopped being offered? For the worshipers would have been cleansed once for all, and would no longer have felt guilty for their sins. ³But those sacrifices are an annual reminder of sins. ⁴It is impossible for the blood of bulls and goats to take away sins.

⁵Therefore, when Christ came into the world, he said:

"Sacrifice and offering you did not desire,
    but a body you prepared for me;
⁶with burnt offerings and sin offerings
    you were not pleased.
⁷Then I said, 'Here I am—it is written
    about me in the scroll—
I have come to do your will, my God.' "ᵃ

⁸First he said, "Sacrifices and offerings, burnt offerings and sin offerings you did not desire, nor were you pleased with them"—though they were offered in accordance with the law. ⁹Then he said, "Here I am, I have come to do your will." He sets aside the first to establish the second. ¹⁰And by that will, we have been made holy through the sacrifice of the body of Jesus Christ once for all.

¹¹Day after day every priest stands and performs his religious duties; again and again he offers the same sacrifices, which can never take away sins. ¹²But when this priest had offered for all time one sacrifice for sins, he sat down at the right hand of God, ¹³and since that time he waits for his enemies to be made his footstool. ¹⁴For by one sacrifice he has made perfect forever those who are being made holy.

¹⁵The Holy Spirit also testifies to us about this. First he says:

¹⁶ "This is the covenant I will make with them
        after that time, says the Lord.
I will put my laws in their hearts,
    and I will write them on their minds."ᵇ

¹⁷Then he adds:

"Their sins and lawless acts
    I will remember no more."ᶜ

¹⁸And where these have been forgiven, sacrifice for sin is no longer necessary.

A Call to Persevere in Faith

¹⁹Therefore, brothers and sisters, since we have confidence to enter the Most Holy Place by the blood of Jesus, ²⁰by a new and living way opened for us through the curtain, that is, his body, ²¹and since we have a great priest over the house of God, ²²let us draw near to God with a sincere heart and with the full assurance that faith brings, having our hearts sprinkled to cleanse us from a guilty conscience and having our bodies washed with pure water. ²³Let us hold unswervingly to the hope we profess, for he who promised is faithful. ²⁴And let us consider how we may spur one another on toward love and good deeds, ²⁵not giving up meeting together, as some are in the habit of doing, but encouraging one another—and all the more as you see the Day approaching.

²⁶If we deliberately keep on sinning after we have received the knowledge of the truth, no sacrifice for sins is left, ²⁷but only a fearful expectation of judgment and of raging fire that will consume the enemies of God. ²⁸Anyone who rejected the law of Moses died without mercy on the testimony of two or three witnesses. ²⁹How much more severely do you think someone deserves to be punished who has trampled the Son of God underfoot, who has treated as an unholy thing the blood of the covenant that sanctified them, and who has insulted the Spirit of grace? ³⁰For we know him who said, "It is mine to avenge; I will repay,"ᵈ and again, "The Lord will judge his people."ᵉ ³¹It is a dreadful thing to fall into the hands of the living God.

³²Remember those earlier days after you had received the light, when you endured in a great conflict full of suffering. ³³Sometimes you were publicly exposed to insult and persecution; at other times you stood side by side with those who were so treated. ³⁴You suffered along with those in prison and joyfully accepted the confiscation of your property, because you knew that you yourselves had better and lasting possessions. ³⁵So do not throw away your confidence; it will be richly rewarded.

³⁶You need to persevere so that when you have done the will of God, you will receive what he has promised. ³⁷For,

"In just a little while,
    he who is coming will come
    and will not delay."ᶠ

³⁸And,

"But my righteousᵍ one will live by faith.
    And I take no pleasure
    in the one who shrinks back."ʰ

³⁹But we do not belong to those who shrink back and are destroyed, but to those who have faith and are saved.

Faith in Action

11 Now faith is confidence in what we hope for and assurance about what we do not see. ²This is what the ancients were commended for.

³By faith we understand that the universe was formed at God's command, so that what is seen was not made out of what was visible.

ᵃ 7 Psalm 40:6-8 (see Septuagint)   ᵇ 16 Jer. 31:33   ᶜ 17 Jer. 31:34   ᵈ 30 Deut. 32:35
ᵉ 30 Deut. 32:36; Psalm 135:14   ᶠ 37 Isaiah 26:20; Hab. 2:3   ᵍ 38 Some early manuscripts *But the righteous*   ʰ 38 Hab. 2:4 (see Septuagint)

[4]By faith Abel brought God a better offering than Cain did. By faith he was commended as righteous, when God spoke well of his offerings. And by faith Abel still speaks, even though he is dead.

[5]By faith Enoch was taken from this life, so that he did not experience death: "He could not be found, because God had taken him away."[a] For before he was taken, he was commended as one who pleased God. [6]And without faith it is impossible to please God, because anyone who comes to him must believe that he exists and that he rewards those who earnestly seek him.

[7]By faith Noah, when warned about things not yet seen, in holy fear built an ark to save his family. By his faith he condemned the world and became heir of the righteousness that is in keeping with faith.

[8]By faith Abraham, when called to go to a place he would later receive as his inheritance, obeyed and went, even though he did not know where he was going. [9]By faith he made his home in the promised land like a stranger in a foreign country; he lived in tents, as did Isaac and Jacob, who were heirs with him of the same promise. [10]For he was looking forward to the city with foundations, whose architect and builder is God. [11]And by faith even Sarah, who was past childbearing age, was enabled to bear children because she[b] considered him faithful who had made the promise. [12]And so from this one man, and he as good as dead, came descendants as numerous as the stars in the sky and as countless as the sand on the seashore.

[13]All these people were still living by faith when they died. They did not receive the things promised; they only saw them and welcomed them from a distance, admitting that they were foreigners and strangers on earth. [14]People who say such things show that they are looking for a country of their own. [15]If they had been thinking of the country they had left, they would have had opportunity to return. [16]Instead, they were longing for a better country—a heavenly one. Therefore God is not ashamed to be called their God, for he has prepared a city for them.

[17]By faith Abraham, when God tested him, offered Isaac as a sacrifice. He who had embraced the promises was about to sacrifice his one and only son, [18]even though God had said to him, "It is through Isaac that your offspring will be reckoned."[c] [19]Abraham reasoned that God could even raise the dead, and so in a manner of speaking he did receive Isaac back from death.

[20]By faith Isaac blessed Jacob and Esau in regard to their future.

[21]By faith Jacob, when he was dying, blessed each of Joseph's sons, and worshiped as he leaned on the top of his staff.

[22]By faith Joseph, when his end was near, spoke about the exodus of the Israelites from Egypt and gave instructions concerning the burial of his bones.

[23]By faith Moses' parents hid him for three months after he was born, because they saw he was no ordinary child, and they were not afraid of the king's edict.

[24]By faith Moses, when he had grown up, refused to be known as the son of Pharaoh's daughter. [25]He chose to be mistreated along with the people of God rather than to enjoy the fleeting pleasures of sin. [26]He regarded disgrace for the sake of Christ as of greater value than the treasures of Egypt, because he was looking ahead to his reward. [27]By faith he left Egypt, not fearing the king's anger; he persevered because he saw him who is invisible. [28]By faith he kept the Passover and the application of blood, so that the destroyer of the firstborn would not touch the firstborn of Israel.

[29]By faith the people passed through the Red Sea as on dry land; but when the Egyptians tried to do so, they were drowned.

[30]By faith the walls of Jericho fell, after the army had marched around them for seven days.

[31]By faith the prostitute Rahab, because she welcomed the spies, was not killed with those who were disobedient.[d]

[32]And what more shall I say? I do not have time to tell about Gideon, Barak, Samson and Jephthah, about David and Samuel and the prophets, [33]who through faith conquered kingdoms, administered justice, and gained what was promised; who shut the mouths of lions, [34]quenched the fury of the flames, and escaped the edge of the sword; whose weakness was turned to strength; and who became powerful in battle and routed foreign armies. [35]Women received back their dead, raised to life again. There were others who were tortured, refusing to be released so that they might gain an even better resurrection. [36]Some faced jeers and flogging, and even chains and imprisonment. [37]They were put to death by stoning;[e] they were sawed in two; they were killed by the sword. They went about in sheepskins and goatskins, destitute, persecuted and mistreated— [38]the world was not worthy of them. They wandered in deserts and mountains, living in caves and in holes in the ground.

[39]These were all commended for their faith, yet none of them received what had been promised, [40]since God had planned something better for us so that only together with us would they be made perfect.

12 Therefore, since we are surrounded by such a great cloud of witnesses, let us throw off everything that hinders and the sin that so easily entangles. And let us run with perseverance the race marked out for us, [2]fixing our eyes on Jesus, the pioneer and perfecter of faith. For the joy set before him he endured the cross, scorning its shame, and sat

---

[a] 5 Gen. 5:24   [b] 11 Or By faith Abraham, even though he was too old to have children—and Sarah herself was not able to conceive—was enabled to become a father because he   [c] 18 Gen. 21:12
[d] 31 Or unbelieving   [e] 37 Some early manuscripts stoning; they were put to the test;

down at the right hand of the throne of God. [3]Consider him who endured such opposition from sinners, so that you will not grow weary and lose heart.

God Disciplines His Children

[4]In your struggle against sin, you have not yet resisted to the point of shedding your blood. [5]And have you completely forgotten this word of encouragement that addresses you as a father addresses his son? It says,

"My son, do not make light of the Lord's discipline,
    and do not lose heart when he rebukes you,
[6]because the Lord disciplines the one he loves,
    and he chastens everyone he accepts as his son."[a]

[7]Endure hardship as discipline; God is treating you as his children. For what children are not disciplined by their father? [8]If you are not disciplined—and everyone undergoes discipline—then you are not legitimate, not true sons and daughters at all. [9]Moreover, we have all had human fathers who disciplined us and we respected them for it. How much more should we submit to the Father of spirits and live! [10]They disciplined us for a little while as they thought best; but God disciplines us for our good, in order that we may share in his holiness. [11]No discipline seems pleasant at the time, but painful. Later on, however, it produces a harvest of righteousness and peace for those who have been trained by it.

[12]Therefore, strengthen your feeble arms and weak knees. [13]"Make level paths for your feet,"[b] so that the lame may not be disabled, but rather healed.

Warning and Encouragement

[14]Make every effort to live in peace with everyone and to be holy; without holiness no one will see the Lord. [15]See to it that no one falls short of the grace of God and that no bitter root grows up to cause trouble and defile many. [16]See that no one is sexually immoral, or is godless like Esau, who for a single meal sold his inheritance rights as the oldest son. [17]Afterward, as you know, when he wanted to inherit this blessing, he was rejected. Even though he sought the blessing with tears, he could not change what he had done.

The Mountain of Fear and the Mountain of Joy

[18]You have not come to a mountain that can be touched and that is burning with fire; to darkness, gloom and storm; [19]to a trumpet blast or to such a voice speaking words that those who heard it begged that no further word be spoken to them, [20]because they could not bear what was commanded: "If even an animal touches the mountain, it must be stoned to death."[c] [21]The sight was so terrifying that Moses said, "I am trembling with fear."[d]

[22]But you have come to Mount Zion, to the city of the living God, the heavenly Jerusalem. You have come to thousands upon thousands of angels in joyful assembly, [23]to the church of the firstborn, whose names are written in heaven. You have come to God, the Judge of all, to the spirits of the righteous made perfect, [24]to Jesus the mediator of a new covenant, and to the sprinkled blood that speaks a better word than the blood of Abel.

[25]See to it that you do not refuse him who speaks. If they did not escape when they refused him who warned them on earth, how much less will we, if we turn away from him who warns us from heaven? [26]At that time his voice shook the earth, but now he has promised, "Once more I will shake not only the earth but also the heavens."[e] [27]The words "once more" indicate the removing of what can be shaken—that is, created things—so that what cannot be shaken may remain.

[28]Therefore, since we are receiving a kingdom that cannot be shaken, let us be thankful, and so worship God acceptably with reverence and awe, [29]for our "God is a consuming fire."[f]

Concluding Exhortations

13 Keep on loving one another as brothers and sisters. [2]Do not forget to show hospitality to strangers, for by so doing some people have shown hospitality to angels without knowing it. [3]Continue to remember those in prison as if you were together with them in prison, and those who are mistreated as if you yourselves were suffering.

[4]Marriage should be honored by all, and the marriage bed kept pure, for God will judge the adulterer and all the sexually immoral. [5]Keep your lives free from the love of money and be content with what you have, because God has said,

"Never will I leave you;
    never will I forsake you."[g]

[6]So we say with confidence,

"The Lord is my helper; I will not be afraid.
    What can mere mortals do to me?"[h]

[7]Remember your leaders, who spoke the word of God to you. Consider the outcome of their way of life and imitate their faith. [8]Jesus Christ is the same yesterday and today and forever.

[9]Do not be carried away by all kinds of strange teachings. It is good for our hearts to be strengthened by grace, not by eating ceremonial foods, which is of no benefit to those who do so. [10]We have an altar from which those who minister at the tabernacle have no right to eat.

[11]The high priest carries the blood of an-

a 5,6 Prov. 3:11,12 (see Septuagint)   b 13 Prov. 4:26   c 20 Exodus 19:12,13   d 21 See Deut. 9:19.
e 26 Haggai 2:6   f 29 Deut. 4:24   g 5 Deut. 31:6   h 6 Psalm 118:6,7

imals into the Most Holy Place as a sin offering, but the bodies are burned outside the camp. [12]And so Jesus also suffered outside the city gate to make the people holy through his own blood. [13]Let us, then, go to him outside the camp, bearing the disgrace he bore. [14]For here we do not have an enduring city, but we are looking for the city that is to come.

[15]Through Jesus, therefore, let us continually offer to God a sacrifice of praise—the fruit of lips that openly profess his name. [16]And do not forget to do good and to share with others, for with such sacrifices God is pleased.

[17]Have confidence in your leaders and submit to their authority, because they keep watch over you as those who must give an account. Do this so that their work will be a joy, not a burden, for that would be of no benefit to you.

[18]Pray for us. We are sure that we have a clear conscience and desire to live honorably in every way. [19]I particularly urge you to pray so that I may be restored to you soon.

Benediction and Final Greetings

[20]Now may the God of peace, who through the blood of the eternal covenant brought back from the dead our Lord Jesus, that great Shepherd of the sheep, [21]equip you with everything good for doing his will, and may he work in us what is pleasing to him, through Jesus Christ, to whom be glory for ever and ever. Amen.

[22]Brothers and sisters, I urge you to bear with my word of exhortation, for in fact I have written to you quite briefly.

[23]I want you to know that our brother Timothy has been released. If he arrives soon, I will come with him to see you.

[24]Greet all your leaders and all the Lord's people. Those from Italy send you their greetings. [25]Grace be with you all.

James

1 James, a servant of God and of the Lord Jesus Christ,

To the twelve tribes scattered among the nations:

Greetings.

Trials and Temptations

[2]Consider it pure joy, my brothers and sisters,[a] whenever you face trials of many kinds, [3]because you know that the testing of your faith produces perseverance. [4]Let perseverance finish its work so that you may be mature and complete, not lacking anything. [5]If any of you lacks wisdom, you should ask God, who gives generously to all without finding fault, and it will be given to you. [6]But when you ask, you must believe and not doubt, because the one who doubts is like a wave of the sea, blown and tossed by the wind. [7]That person should not expect to receive anything from the Lord. [8]Such a person is double-minded and unstable in all they do.

[9]Believers in humble circumstances ought to take pride in their high position. [10]But the rich should take pride in their humiliation—since they will pass away like a wild flower. [11]For the sun rises with scorching heat and withers the plant; its blossom falls and its beauty is destroyed. In the same way, the rich will fade away even while they go about their business.

[12]Blessed is the one who perseveres under trial because, having stood the test, that person will receive the crown of life that the Lord has promised to those who love him.

[13]When tempted, no one should say, "God is tempting me." For God cannot be tempted by evil, nor does he tempt anyone; [14]but each person is tempted when they are dragged away by their own evil desire and enticed. [15]Then, after desire has conceived, it gives birth to sin; and sin, when it is full-grown, gives birth to death.

[16]Don't be deceived, my dear brothers and sisters. [17]Every good and perfect gift is from above, coming down from the Father of the heavenly lights, who does not change like shifting shadows. [18]He chose to give us birth through the word of truth, that we might be a kind of firstfruits of all he created.

Listening and Doing

[19]My dear brothers and sisters, take note of this: Everyone should be quick to listen, slow to speak and slow to become angry, [20]because human anger does not produce the righteousness that God desires. [21]Therefore, get rid of all moral filth and the evil that is so prevalent and humbly accept the word planted in you, which can save you.

[22]Do not merely listen to the word, and so deceive yourselves. Do what it says. [23]Anyone who listens to the word but does not do what it says is like someone who looks at his face in a mirror [24]and, after looking at himself, goes away and immediately forgets what he looks like. [25]But whoever looks intently into the perfect law that gives freedom, and continues in

[a] 2 The Greek word for *brothers and sisters* (*adelphoi*) refers here to believers, both men and women, as part of God's family; also in verses 16 and 19; and in 2:1, 5, 14; 3:10, 12; 4:11; 5:7, 9, 10, 12, 19.

it—not forgetting what they have heard, but doing it—they will be blessed in what they do.

²⁶Those who consider themselves religious and yet do not keep a tight rein on their tongues deceive themselves, and their religion is worthless. ²⁷Religion that God our Father accepts as pure and faultless is this: to look after orphans and widows in their distress and to keep oneself from being polluted by the world.

Favoritism Forbidden

2 My brothers and sisters, believers in our glorious Lord Jesus Christ must not show favoritism. ²Suppose a man comes into your meeting wearing a gold ring and fine clothes, and a poor man in filthy old clothes also comes in. ³If you show special attention to the man wearing fine clothes and say, "Here's a good seat for you," but say to the poor man, "You stand there" or "Sit on the floor by my feet," ⁴have you not discriminated among yourselves and become judges with evil thoughts?

⁵Listen, my dear brothers and sisters: Has not God chosen those who are poor in the eyes of the world to be rich in faith and to inherit the kingdom he promised those who love him? ⁶But you have dishonored the poor. Is it not the rich who are exploiting you? Are they not the ones who are dragging you into court? ⁷Are they not the ones who are blaspheming the noble name of him to whom you belong?

⁸If you really keep the royal law found in Scripture, "Love your neighbor as yourself,"ᵃ you are doing right. ⁹But if you show favoritism, you sin and are convicted by the law as lawbreakers. ¹⁰For whoever keeps the whole law and yet stumbles at just one point is guilty of breaking all of it. ¹¹For he who said, "You shall not commit adultery,"ᵇ also said, "You shall not murder."ᶜ If you do not commit adultery but do commit murder, you have become a lawbreaker.

¹²Speak and act as those who are going to be judged by the law that gives freedom, ¹³because judgment without mercy will be shown to anyone who has not been merciful. Mercy triumphs over judgment.

Faith and Deeds

¹⁴What good is it, my brothers and sisters, if someone claims to have faith but has no deeds? Can such faith save them? ¹⁵Suppose a brother or a sister is without clothes and daily food. ¹⁶If one of you says to them, "Go in peace; keep warm and well fed," but does nothing about their physical needs, what good is it? ¹⁷In the same way, faith by itself, if it is not accompanied by action, is dead.

¹⁸But someone will say, "You have faith; I have deeds."

Show me your faith without deeds, and I will show you my faith by my deeds. ¹⁹You believe that there is one God. Good! Even the demons believe that—and shudder.

²⁰You foolish person, do you want evidence that faith without deeds is uselessᵈ? ²¹Was not our father Abraham considered righteous for what he did when he offered his son Isaac on the altar? ²²You see that his faith and his actions were working together, and his faith was made complete by what he did. ²³And the scripture was fulfilled that says, "Abraham believed God, and it was credited to him as righteousness,"ᵉ and he was called God's friend. ²⁴You see that a person is considered righteous by what they do and not by faith alone.

²⁵In the same way, was not even Rahab the prostitute considered righteous for what she did when she gave lodging to the spies and sent them off in a different direction? ²⁶As the body without the spirit is dead, so faith without deeds is dead.

Taming the Tongue

3 Not many of you should become teachers, my fellow believers, because you know that we who teach will be judged more strictly. ²We all stumble in many ways. Anyone who is never at fault in what they say is perfect, able to keep their whole body in check.

³When we put bits into the mouths of horses to make them obey us, we can turn the whole animal. ⁴Or take ships as an example. Although they are so large and are driven by strong winds, they are steered by a very small rudder wherever the pilot wants to go. ⁵Likewise, the tongue is a small part of the body, but it makes great boasts. Consider what a great forest is set on fire by a small spark. ⁶The tongue also is a fire, a world of evil among the parts of the body. It corrupts the whole body, sets the whole course of one's life on fire, and is itself set on fire by hell.

⁷All kinds of animals, birds, reptiles and sea creatures are being tamed and have been tamed by mankind, ⁸but no human being can tame the tongue. It is a restless evil, full of deadly poison.

⁹With the tongue we praise our Lord and Father, and with it we curse human beings, who have been made in God's likeness. ¹⁰Out of the same mouth come praise and cursing. My brothers and sisters, this should not be. ¹¹Can both fresh water and salt water flow from the same spring? ¹²My brothers and sisters, can a fig tree bear olives, or a grapevine bear figs? Neither can a salt spring produce fresh water.

Two Kinds of Wisdom

¹³Who is wise and understanding among you? Let them show it by their good life, by deeds done in the humility that comes from wisdom. ¹⁴But if you harbor bitter envy and selfish ambition in your hearts, do not boast about it or deny the truth. ¹⁵Such "wisdom" does not come down from heaven but is earthly, unspiritual, demonic. ¹⁶For where you have envy and selfish ambition, there you find disorder and every evil practice.

ᵃ 8 Lev. 19:18   ᵇ 11 Exodus 20:14; Deut. 5:18   ᶜ 11 Exodus 20:13; Deut. 5:17   ᵈ 20 Some early manuscripts dead   ᵉ 23 Gen. 15:6

[17]But the wisdom that comes from heaven is first of all pure; then peace-loving, considerate, submissive, full of mercy and good fruit, impartial and sincere. [18]Peacemakers who sow in peace reap a harvest of righteousness.

Submit Yourselves to God

4 What causes fights and quarrels among you? Don't they come from your desires that battle within you? [2]You desire but do not have, so you kill. You covet but you cannot get what you want, so you quarrel and fight. You do not have because you do not ask God. [3]When you ask, you do not receive, because you ask with wrong motives, that you may spend what you get on your pleasures.

[4]You adulterous people,[a] don't you know that friendship with the world means enmity against God? Therefore, anyone who chooses to be a friend of the world becomes an enemy of God. [5]Or do you think Scripture says without reason that he jealously longs for the spirit he has caused to dwell in us[b]? [6]But he gives us more grace. That is why Scripture says:

"God opposes the proud
  but shows favor to the humble."[c]

[7]Submit yourselves, then, to God. Resist the devil, and he will flee from you. [8]Come near to God and he will come near to you. Wash your hands, you sinners, and purify your hearts, you double-minded. [9]Grieve, mourn and wail. Change your laughter to mourning and your joy to gloom. [10]Humble yourselves before the Lord, and he will lift you up.

[11]Brothers and sisters, do not slander one another. Anyone who speaks against a brother or sister[d] or judges them speaks against the law and judges it. When you judge the law, you are not keeping it, but sitting in judgment on it. [12]There is only one Lawgiver and Judge, the one who is able to save and destroy. But you—who are you to judge your neighbor?

Boasting About Tomorrow

[13]Now listen, you who say, "Today or tomorrow we will go to this or that city, spend a year there, carry on business and make money." [14]Why, you do not even know what will happen tomorrow. What is your life? You are a mist that appears for a little while and then vanishes. [15]Instead, you ought to say, "If it is the Lord's will, we will live and do this or that." [16]As it is, you boast in your arrogant schemes. All such boasting is evil. [17]If anyone, then, knows the good they ought to do and doesn't do it, it is sin for them.

Warning to Rich Oppressors

5 Now listen, you rich people, weep and wail because of the misery that is coming on you. [2]Your wealth has rotted, and moths have eaten your clothes. [3]Your gold and silver are corroded. Their corrosion will testify against you and eat your flesh like fire. You have hoarded wealth in the last days. [4]Look! The wages you failed to pay the workers who mowed your fields are crying out against you. The cries of the harvesters have reached the ears of the Lord Almighty. [5]You have lived on earth in luxury and self-indulgence. You have fattened yourselves in the day of slaughter.[e] [6]You have condemned and murdered the innocent one, who was not opposing you.

Patience in Suffering

[7]Be patient, then, brothers and sisters, until the Lord's coming. See how the farmer waits for the land to yield its valuable crop, patiently waiting for the autumn and spring rains. [8]You too, be patient and stand firm, because the Lord's coming is near. [9]Don't grumble against one another, brothers and sisters, or you will be judged. The Judge is standing at the door!

[10]Brothers and sisters, as an example of patience in the face of suffering, take the prophets who spoke in the name of the Lord. [11]As you know, we count as blessed those who have persevered. You have heard of Job's perseverance and have seen what the Lord finally brought about. The Lord is full of compassion and mercy.

[12]Above all, my brothers and sisters, do not swear—not by heaven or by earth or by anything else. All you need to say is a simple "Yes" or "No." Otherwise you will be condemned.

The Prayer of Faith

[13]Is anyone among you in trouble? Let them pray. Is anyone happy? Let them sing songs of praise. [14]Is anyone among you sick? Let them call the elders of the church to pray over them and anoint them with oil in the name of the Lord. [15]And the prayer offered in faith will make the sick person well; the Lord will raise them up. If they have sinned, they will be forgiven. [16]Therefore confess your sins to each other and pray for each other so that you may be healed. The prayer of a righteous person is powerful and effective.

[17]Elijah was a human being, even as we are. He prayed earnestly that it would not rain, and it did not rain on the land for three and a half years. [18]Again he prayed, and the heavens gave rain, and the earth produced its crops.

[19]My brothers and sisters, if one of you should wander from the truth and someone should bring that person back, [20]remember this: Whoever turns a sinner from the error of their way will save them from death and cover over a multitude of sins.

---

[a] 4 An allusion to covenant unfaithfulness; see Hosea 3:1.   [b] 5 Or *that the spirit he caused to dwell in us envies intensely;* or *that the Spirit he caused to dwell in us longs jealously*   [c] 6 Prov. 3:34
[d] 11 The Greek word for *brother or sister (adelphos)* refers here to a believer, whether man or woman, as part of God's family.   [e] 5 Or *yourselves as in a day of feasting*

1 Peter

1 Peter, an apostle of Jesus Christ,

To God's elect, exiles scattered throughout the provinces of Pontus, Galatia, Cappadocia, Asia and Bithynia, [2]who have been chosen according to the foreknowledge of God the Father, through the sanctifying work of the Spirit, to be obedient to Jesus Christ and sprinkled with his blood:

Grace and peace be yours in abundance.

Praise to God for a Living Hope

[3]Praise be to the God and Father of our Lord Jesus Christ! In his great mercy he has given us new birth into a living hope through the resurrection of Jesus Christ from the dead, [4]and into an inheritance that can never perish, spoil or fade. This inheritance is kept in heaven for you, [5]who through faith are shielded by God's power until the coming of the salvation that is ready to be revealed in the last time. [6]In all this you greatly rejoice, though now for a little while you may have had to suffer grief in all kinds of trials. [7]These have come so that the proven genuineness of your faith—of greater worth than gold, which perishes even though refined by fire—may result in praise, glory and honor when Jesus Christ is revealed. [8]Though you have not seen him, you love him; and even though you do not see him now, you believe in him and are filled with an inexpressible and glorious joy, [9]for you are receiving the end result of your faith, the salvation of your souls.

[10]Concerning this salvation, the prophets, who spoke of the grace that was to come to you, searched intently and with the greatest care, [11]trying to find out the time and circumstances to which the Spirit of Christ in them was pointing when he predicted the sufferings of the Messiah and the glories that would follow. [12]It was revealed to them that they were not serving themselves but you, when they spoke of the things that have now been told you by those who have preached the gospel to you by the Holy Spirit sent from heaven. Even angels long to look into these things.

Be Holy

[13]Therefore, with minds that are alert and fully sober, set your hope on the grace to be brought to you when Jesus Christ is revealed at his coming. [14]As obedient children, do not conform to the evil desires you had when you lived in ignorance. [15]But just as he who called you is holy, so be holy in all you do; [16]for it is written: "Be holy, because I am holy."[a]

[17]Since you call on a Father who judges each person's work impartially, live out your time as foreigners here in reverent fear. [18]For you know that it was not with perishable things such as silver or gold that you were redeemed from the empty way of life handed down to you from your ancestors, [19]but with the precious blood of Christ, a lamb without blemish or defect. [20]He was chosen before the creation of the world, but was revealed in these last times for your sake. [21]Through him you believe in God, who raised him from the dead and glorified him, and so your faith and hope are in God.

[22]Now that you have purified yourselves by obeying the truth so that you have sincere love for each other, love one another deeply, from the heart.[b] [23]For you have been born again, not of perishable seed, but of imperishable, through the living and enduring word of God. [24]For,

"All people are like grass,
   and all their glory is like the flowers of
      the field;
the grass withers and the flowers fall,
25   but the word of the Lord endures forever."[c]

And this is the word that was preached to you.

2 Therefore, rid yourselves of all malice and all deceit, hypocrisy, envy, and slander of every kind. [2]Like newborn babies, crave pure spiritual milk, so that by it you may grow up in your salvation, [3]now that you have tasted that the Lord is good.

The Living Stone and a Chosen People

[4]As you come to him, the living Stone—rejected by humans but chosen by God and precious to him— [5]you also, like living stones, are being built into a spiritual house[d] to be a holy priesthood, offering spiritual sacrifices acceptable to God through Jesus Christ. [6]For in Scripture it says:

"See, I lay a stone in Zion,
   a chosen and precious cornerstone,
and the one who trusts in him
   will never be put to shame."[e]

[7]Now to you who believe, this stone is precious. But to those who do not believe,

"The stone the builders rejected
   has become the cornerstone,"[f]

[8]and,

"A stone that causes people to stumble
   and a rock that makes them fall."[g]

They stumble because they disobey the message—which is also what they were destined for.

[9]But you are a chosen people, a royal priesthood, a holy nation, God's special possession, that you may declare the praises of him who called you out of darkness into his wonderful light. [10]Once you were not a people, but now

---

a 16 Lev. 11:44,45; 19:2   *b 22* Some early manuscripts *from a pure heart*   *c 25* Isaiah 40:6-8 (see Septuagint)   *d 5* Or *into a temple of the Spirit*   *e 6* Isaiah 28:16   *f 7* Psalm 118:22   *g 8* Isaiah 8:14

you are the people of God; once you had not received mercy, but now you have received mercy.

Living Godly Lives in a Pagan Society

[11]Dear friends, I urge you, as foreigners and exiles, to abstain from sinful desires, which wage war against your soul. [12]Live such good lives among the pagans that, though they accuse you of doing wrong, they may see your good deeds and glorify God on the day he visits us.

[13]Submit yourselves for the Lord's sake to every human authority: whether to the emperor, as the supreme authority, [14]or to governors, who are sent by him to punish those who do wrong and to commend those who do right. [15]For it is God's will that by doing good you should silence the ignorant talk of foolish people. [16]Live as free people, but do not use your freedom as a cover-up for evil; live as God's slaves. [17]Show proper respect to everyone, love the family of believers, fear God, honor the emperor.

[18]Slaves, in reverent fear of God submit yourselves to your masters, not only to those who are good and considerate, but also to those who are harsh. [19]For it is commendable if someone bears up under the pain of unjust suffering because they are conscious of God. [20]But how is it to your credit if you receive a beating for doing wrong and endure it? But if you suffer for doing good and you endure it, this is commendable before God. [21]To this you were called, because Christ suffered for you, leaving you an example, that you should follow in his steps.

[22]"He committed no sin,
  and no deceit was found in his mouth."[a]

[23]When they hurled their insults at him, he did not retaliate; when he suffered, he made no threats. Instead, he entrusted himself to him who judges justly. [24]"He himself bore our sins" in his body on the cross, so that we might die to sins and live for righteousness; "by his wounds you have been healed." [25]For "you were like sheep going astray,"[b] but now you have returned to the Shepherd and Overseer of your souls.

3 Wives, in the same way submit yourselves to your own husbands so that, if any of them do not believe the word, they may be won over without words by the behavior of their wives, [2]when they see the purity and reverence of your lives. [3]Your beauty should not come from outward adornment, such as elaborate hairstyles and the wearing of gold jewelry or fine clothes. [4]Rather, it should be that of your inner self, the unfading beauty of a gentle and quiet spirit, which is of great worth in God's sight. [5]For this is the way the holy women of the past who put their hope in God used to adorn themselves. They submitted themselves to their own husbands, [6]like Sarah, who obeyed Abraham and called him her lord. You are her daughters if you do what is right and do not give way to fear.

[7]Husbands, in the same way be considerate as you live with your wives, and treat them with respect as the weaker partner and as heirs with you of the gracious gift of life, so that nothing will hinder your prayers.

Suffering for Doing Good

[8]Finally, all of you, be like-minded, be sympathetic, love one another, be compassionate and humble. [9]Do not repay evil with evil or insult with insult. On the contrary, repay evil with blessing, because to this you were called so that you may inherit a blessing. [10]For,

"Whoever would love life
  and see good days
must keep their tongue from evil
  and their lips from deceitful speech.
[11]They must turn from evil and do good;
  they must seek peace and pursue it.
[12]For the eyes of the Lord are on the
    righteous
  and his ears are attentive to their prayer,
but the face of the Lord is against those
    who do evil."[c]

[13]Who is going to harm you if you are eager to do good? [14]But even if you should suffer for what is right, you are blessed. "Do not fear their threats[d]; do not be frightened."[e] [15]But in your hearts revere Christ as Lord. Always be prepared to give an answer to everyone who asks you to give the reason for the hope that you have. But do this with gentleness and respect, [16]keeping a clear conscience, so that those who speak maliciously against your good behavior in Christ may be ashamed of their slander. [17]For it is better, if it is God's will, to suffer for doing good than for doing evil. [18]For Christ also suffered once for sins, the righteous for the unrighteous, to bring you to God. He was put to death in the body but made alive in the Spirit. [19]After being made alive,[f] he went and made proclamation to the imprisoned spirits— [20]to those who were disobedient long ago when God waited patiently in the days of Noah while the ark was being built. In it only a few people, eight in all, were saved through water, [21]and this water symbolizes baptism that now saves you also—not the removal of dirt from the body but the pledge of a clear conscience toward God.[g] It saves you by the resurrection of Jesus Christ, [22]who has gone into heaven and is at God's right hand—with angels, authorities and powers in submission to him.

Living for God

4 Therefore, since Christ suffered in his body, arm yourselves also with the same attitude, because whoever suffers in the body is done with sin. [2]As a result, they do not live the rest of their earthly lives for evil human desires, but rather for the will of God. [3]For you have spent enough time in the past doing what pagans choose to do—living in debauchery, lust, drunkenness, orgies, carousing and detestable

---

[a] 22 Isaiah 53:9   [b] 24,25 Isaiah 53:4,5,6 (see Septuagint)   [c] 12 Psalm 34:12-16   [d] 14 Or fear what they fear   [e] 14 Isaiah 8:12   [f] 18,19 Or but made alive in the spirit, [19]in which also   [g] 21 Or but an appeal to God for a clear conscience

idolatry. [4]They are surprised that you do not join them in their reckless, wild living, and they heap abuse on you. [5]But they will have to give account to him who is ready to judge the living and the dead. [6]For this is the reason the gospel was preached even to those who are now dead, so that they might be judged according to human standards in regard to the body, but live according to God in regard to the spirit.

[7]The end of all things is near. Therefore be alert and of sober mind so that you may pray. [8]Above all, love each other deeply, because love covers over a multitude of sins. [9]Offer hospitality to one another without grumbling. [10]Each of you should use whatever gift you have received to serve others, as faithful stewards of God's grace in its various forms. [11]If anyone speaks, they should do so as one who speaks the very words of God. If anyone serves, they should do so with the strength God provides, so that in all things God may be praised through Jesus Christ. To him be the glory and the power for ever and ever. Amen.

Suffering for Being a Christian

[12]Dear friends, do not be surprised at the fiery ordeal that has come on you to test you, as though something strange were happening to you. [13]But rejoice inasmuch as you participate in the sufferings of Christ, so that you may be overjoyed when his glory is revealed. [14]If you are insulted because of the name of Christ, you are blessed, for the Spirit of glory and of God rests on you. [15]If you suffer, it should not be as a murderer or thief or any other kind of criminal, or even as a meddler. [16]However, if you suffer as a Christian, do not be ashamed, but praise God that you bear that name. [17]For it is time for judgment to begin with God's household; and if it begins with us, what will the outcome be for those who do not obey the gospel of God? [18]And,

"If it is hard for the righteous to be saved,
    what will become of the ungodly and
        the sinner?"[a]

[19]So then, those who suffer according to God's will should commit themselves to their faithful Creator and continue to do good.

To the Elders and the Flock

5 To the elders among you, I appeal as a fellow elder and a witness of Christ's sufferings who also will share in the glory to be revealed: [2]Be shepherds of God's flock that is under your care, watching over them—not because you must, but because you are willing, as God wants you to be; not pursuing dishonest gain, but eager to serve; [3]not lording it over those entrusted to you, but being examples to the flock. [4]And when the Chief Shepherd appears, you will receive the crown of glory that will never fade away.

[5]In the same way, you who are younger, submit yourselves to your elders. All of you, clothe yourselves with humility toward one another, because,

"God opposes the proud
    but shows favor to the humble."[b]

[6]Humble yourselves, therefore, under God's mighty hand, that he may lift you up in due time. [7]Cast all your anxiety on him because he cares for you.

[8]Be alert and of sober mind. Your enemy the devil prowls around like a roaring lion looking for someone to devour. [9]Resist him, standing firm in the faith, because you know that the family of believers throughout the world is undergoing the same kind of sufferings.

[10]And the God of all grace, who called you to his eternal glory in Christ, after you have suffered a little while, will himself restore you and make you strong, firm and steadfast. [11]To him be the power for ever and ever. Amen.

Final Greetings

[12]With the help of Silas,[c] whom I regard as a faithful brother, I have written to you briefly, encouraging you and testifying that this is the true grace of God. Stand fast in it.

[13]She who is in Babylon, chosen together with you, sends you her greetings, and so does my son Mark. [14]Greet one another with a kiss of love.

Peace to all of you who are in Christ.

2 Peter

1 Simon Peter, a servant and apostle of Jesus Christ,

To those who through the righteousness of our God and Savior Jesus Christ have received a faith as precious as ours:

[2]Grace and peace be yours in abundance through the knowledge of God and of Jesus our Lord.

Confirming One's Calling and Election

[3]His divine power has given us everything we need for a godly life through our knowledge of him who called us by his own glory and goodness. [4]Through these he has given us his very great and precious promises, so that through them you may participate in the divine nature, having escaped the corruption in the world caused by evil desires.

---

[a] 18 Prov. 11:31 (see Septuagint)   [b] 5 Prov. 3:34   [c] 12 Greek *Silvanus*, a variant of *Silas*

⁵For this very reason, make every effort to add to your faith goodness; and to goodness, knowledge; ⁶and to knowledge, self-control; and to self-control, perseverance; and to perseverance, godliness; ⁷and to godliness, mutual affection; and to mutual affection, love. ⁸For if you possess these qualities in increasing measure, they will keep you from being ineffective and unproductive in your knowledge of our Lord Jesus Christ. ⁹But whoever does not have them is nearsighted and blind, forgetting that they have been cleansed from their past sins.

¹⁰Therefore, my brothers and sisters,ᵃ make every effort to confirm your calling and election. For if you do these things, you will never stumble, ¹¹and you will receive a rich welcome into the eternal kingdom of our Lord and Savior Jesus Christ.

Prophecy of Scripture

¹²So I will always remind you of these things, even though you know them and are firmly established in the truth you now have. ¹³I think it is right to refresh your memory as long as I live in the tent of this body, ¹⁴because I know that I will soon put it aside, as our Lord Jesus Christ has made clear to me. ¹⁵And I will make every effort to see that after my departure you will always be able to remember these things.

¹⁶For we did not follow cleverly devised stories when we told you about the coming of our Lord Jesus Christ in power, but we were eyewitnesses of his majesty. ¹⁷He received honor and glory from God the Father when the voice came to him from the Majestic Glory, saying, "This is my Son, whom I love; with him I am well pleased."ᵇ ¹⁸We ourselves heard this voice that came from heaven when we were with him on the sacred mountain.

¹⁹We also have the prophetic message as something completely reliable, and you will do well to pay attention to it, as to a light shining in a dark place, until the day dawns and the morning star rises in your hearts. ²⁰Above all, you must understand that no prophecy of Scripture came about by the prophet's own interpretation of things. ²¹For prophecy never had its origin in the human will, but prophets, though human, spoke from God as they were carried along by the Holy Spirit.

False Teachers and Their Destruction

2 But there were also false prophets among the people, just as there will be false teachers among you. They will secretly introduce destructive heresies, even denying the sovereign Lord who bought them—bringing swift destruction on themselves. ²Many will follow their depraved conduct and will bring the way of truth into disrepute. ³In their greed these teachers will exploit you with fabricated stories. Their condemnation has long been hanging over them, and their destruction has not been sleeping.

⁴For if God did not spare angels when they sinned, but sent them to hell,ᶜ putting them in chains of darknessᵈ to be held for judgment; ⁵if he did not spare the ancient world when he brought the flood on its ungodly people, but protected Noah, a preacher of righteousness, and seven others; ⁶if he condemned the cities of Sodom and Gomorrah by burning them to ashes, and made them an example of what is going to happen to the ungodly; ⁷and if he rescued Lot, a righteous man, who was distressed by the depraved conduct of the lawless ⁸(for that righteous man, living among them day after day, was tormented in his righteous soul by the lawless deeds he saw and heard)— ⁹if this is so, then the Lord knows how to rescue the godly from trials and to hold the unrighteous for punishment on the day of judgment. ¹⁰This is especially true of those who follow the corrupt desire of the fleshᵉ and despise authority.

Bold and arrogant, they are not afraid to heap abuse on celestial beings; ¹¹yet even angels, although they are stronger and more powerful, do not heap abuse on such beings when bringing judgment on them fromᶠ the Lord. ¹²But these people blaspheme in matters they do not understand. They are like unreasoning animals, creatures of instinct, born only to be caught and destroyed, and like animals they too will perish.

¹³They will be paid back with harm for the harm they have done. Their idea of pleasure is to carouse in broad daylight. They are blots and blemishes, reveling in their pleasures while they feast with you.ᵍ ¹⁴With eyes full of adultery, they never stop sinning; they seduce the unstable; they are experts in greed—an accursed brood! ¹⁵They have left the straight way and wandered off to follow the way of Balaam son of Bezer,ʰ who loved the wages of wickedness. ¹⁶But he was rebuked for his wrongdoing by a donkey—an animal without speech—who spoke with a human voice and restrained the prophet's madness.

¹⁷These people are springs without water and mists driven by a storm. Blackest darkness is reserved for them. ¹⁸For they mouth empty, boastful words and, by appealing to the lustful desires of the flesh, they entice people who are just escaping from those who live in error. ¹⁹They promise them freedom, while they themselves are slaves of depravity—for "people are slaves to whatever has mastered them." ²⁰If they have escaped the corruption of the world by knowing our Lord and Savior Jesus Christ and are again entangled in it and are overcome, they are worse off at the end than they were at the beginning. ²¹It would

---

ᵃ 10 The Greek word for *brothers and sisters* (*adelphoi*) refers here to believers, both men and women, as part of God's family.   ᵇ 17 Matt. 17:5; Mark 9:7; Luke 9:35   ᶜ 4 Greek *Tartarus*   ᵈ 4 Some manuscripts *in gloomy dungeons*   ᵉ 10 In contexts like this, the Greek word for *flesh* (*sarx*) refers to the sinful state of human beings, often presented as a power in opposition to the Spirit; also in verse 18.   ᶠ 11 Many manuscripts *beings in the presence of*   ᵍ 13 Some manuscripts *in their love feasts*   ʰ 15 Greek *Bosor*

have been better for them not to have known the way of righteousness, than to have known it and then to turn their backs on the sacred command that was passed on to them. ²²Of them the proverbs are true: "A dog returns to its vomit,"ᵃ and, "A sow that is washed returns to her wallowing in the mud."

The Day of the Lord

3 Dear friends, this is now my second letter to you. I have written both of them as reminders to stimulate you to wholesome thinking. ²I want you to recall the words spoken in the past by the holy prophets and the command given by our Lord and Savior through your apostles.

³Above all, you must understand that in the last days scoffers will come, scoffing and following their own evil desires. ⁴They will say, "Where is this 'coming' he promised? Ever since our ancestors died, everything goes on as it has since the beginning of creation." ⁵But they deliberately forget that long ago by God's word the heavens came into being and the earth was formed out of water and by water. ⁶By these waters also the world of that time was deluged and destroyed. ⁷By the same word the present heavens and earth are reserved for fire, being kept for the day of judgment and destruction of the ungodly.

⁸But do not forget this one thing, dear friends: With the Lord a day is like a thousand years, and a thousand years are like a day. ⁹The Lord is not slow in keeping his promise, as some understand slowness. Instead he is patient with you, not wanting anyone to perish, but everyone to come to repentance.

¹⁰But the day of the Lord will come like a thief. The heavens will disappear with a roar; the elements will be destroyed by fire, and the earth and everything done in it will be laid bare.ᵇ

¹¹Since everything will be destroyed in this way, what kind of people ought you to be? You ought to live holy and godly lives ¹²as you look forward to the day of God and speed its coming.ᶜ That day will bring about the destruction of the heavens by fire, and the elements will melt in the heat. ¹³But in keeping with his promise we are looking forward to a new heaven and a new earth, where righteousness dwells.

¹⁴So then, dear friends, since you are looking forward to this, make every effort to be found spotless, blameless and at peace with him. ¹⁵Bear in mind that our Lord's patience means salvation, just as our dear brother Paul also wrote you with the wisdom that God gave him. ¹⁶He writes the same way in all his letters, speaking in them of these matters. His letters contain some things that are hard to understand, which ignorant and unstable people distort, as they do the other Scriptures, to their own destruction.

¹⁷Therefore, dear friends, since you have been forewarned, be on your guard so that you may not be carried away by the error of the lawless and fall from your secure position. ¹⁸But grow in the grace and knowledge of our Lord and Savior Jesus Christ. To him be glory both now and forever! Amen.

1 John

The Incarnation of the Word of Life

1 That which was from the beginning, which we have heard, which we have seen with our eyes, which we have looked at and our hands have touched—this we proclaim concerning the Word of life. ²The life appeared; we have seen it and testify to it, and we proclaim to you the eternal life, which was with the Father and has appeared to us. ³We proclaim to you what we have seen and heard, so that you also may have fellowship with us. And our fellowship is with the Father and with his Son, Jesus Christ. ⁴We write this to make ourᵈ joy complete.

Light and Darkness, Sin and Forgiveness

⁵This is the message we have heard from him and declare to you: God is light; in him there is no darkness at all. ⁶If we claim to have fellowship with him and yet walk in the darkness, we lie and do not live out the truth. ⁷But if we walk in the light, as he is in the light, we have fellowship with one another, and the blood of Jesus, his Son, purifies us from allᵉ sin.

⁸If we claim to be without sin, we deceive ourselves and the truth is not in us. ⁹If we confess our sins, he is faithful and just and will forgive us our sins and purify us from all unrighteousness. ¹⁰If we claim we have not sinned, we make him out to be a liar and his word is not in us.

2 My dear children, I write this to you so that you will not sin. But if anybody does sin, we have an advocate with the Father—Jesus Christ, the Righteous One. ²He is the atoning sacrifice for our sins, and not only for ours but also for the sins of the whole world.

ᵃ 22 Prov. 26:11   ᵇ 10 Some manuscripts *be burned up*   ᶜ 12 Or *as you wait eagerly for the day of God to come*   ᵈ 4 Some manuscripts *your*   ᵉ 7 Or *every*

Love and Hatred for Fellow Believers

³We know that we have come to know him if we keep his commands. ⁴Whoever says, "I know him," but does not do what he commands is a liar, and the truth is not in that person. ⁵But if anyone obeys his word, love for God*ᵃ* is truly made complete in them. This is how we know we are in him: ⁶Whoever claims to live in him must live as Jesus did.

⁷Dear friends, I am not writing you a new command but an old one, which you have had since the beginning. This old command is the message you have heard. ⁸Yet I am writing you a new command; its truth is seen in him and in you, because the darkness is passing and the true light is already shining.

⁹Anyone who claims to be in the light but hates a brother or sister*ᵇ* is still in the darkness. ¹⁰Anyone who loves their brother and sister*ᶜ* lives in the light, and there is nothing in them to make them stumble. ¹¹But anyone who hates a brother or sister is in the darkness and walks around in the darkness. They do not know where they are going, because the darkness has blinded them.

Reasons for Writing

¹²I am writing to you, dear children,
   because your sins have been forgiven
      on account of his name.
¹³I am writing to you, fathers,
   because you know him who is from the
      beginning.
I am writing to you, young men,
   because you have overcome the evil
      one.
¹⁴I write to you, dear children,
   because you know the Father.
I write to you, fathers,
   because you know him who is from the
      beginning.
I write to you, young men,
   because you are strong,
   and the word of God lives in you,
   and you have overcome the evil one.

On Not Loving the World

¹⁵Do not love the world or anything in the world. If anyone loves the world, love for the Father*ᵈ* is not in them. ¹⁶For everything in the world—the lust of the flesh, the lust of the eyes, and the pride of life—comes not from the Father but from the world. ¹⁷The world and its desires pass away, but whoever does the will of God lives forever.

Warnings Against Denying the Son

¹⁸Dear children, this is the last hour; and as you have heard that the antichrist is coming, even now many antichrists have come. This is how we know it is the last hour. ¹⁹They went out from us, but they did not really belong to us. For if they had belonged to us, they would have remained with us; but their going showed that none of them belonged to us. ²⁰But you have an anointing from the Holy One, and all of you know the truth.*ᵉ* ²¹I do not write to you because you do not know the truth, but because you do know it and because no lie comes from the truth. ²²Who is the liar? It is whoever denies that Jesus is the Christ. Such a person is the antichrist—denying the Father and the Son. ²³No one who denies the Son has the Father; whoever acknowledges the Son has the Father also.

²⁴As for you, see that what you have heard from the beginning remains in you. If it does, you also will remain in the Son and in the Father. ²⁵And this is what he promised us—eternal life.

²⁶I am writing these things to you about those who are trying to lead you astray. ²⁷As for you, the anointing you received from him remains in you, and you do not need anyone to teach you. But as his anointing teaches you about all things and as that anointing is real, not counterfeit—just as it has taught you, remain in him.

God's Children and Sin

²⁸And now, dear children, continue in him, so that when he appears we may be confident and unashamed before him at his coming. ²⁹If you know that he is righteous, you know that everyone who does what is right has been born of him.

3 See what great love the Father has lavished on us, that we should be called children of God! And that is what we are! The reason the world does not know us is that it did not know him. ²Dear friends, now we are children of God, and what we will be has not yet been made known. But we know that when Christ appears,*ᶠ* we shall be like him, for we shall see him as he is. ³All who have this hope in him purify themselves, just as he is pure.

⁴Everyone who sins breaks the law; in fact, sin is lawlessness. ⁵But you know that he appeared so that he might take away our sins. And in him is no sin. ⁶No one who lives in him keeps on sinning. No one who continues to sin has either seen him or known him.

⁷Dear children, do not let anyone lead you astray. The one who does what is right is righteous, just as he is righteous. ⁸The one who does what is sinful is of the devil, because the devil has been sinning from the beginning. The reason the Son of God appeared was to destroy the devil's work. ⁹No one who is born of God will continue to sin, because God's seed remains in them; they cannot go on sinning, because they have been born of God. ¹⁰This is how we know who the children of God are and who the children of the devil are: Anyone who does not do what is right is

---

ᵃ 5 Or *word, God's love*   *ᵇ* 9 The Greek word for *brother or sister* (*adelphos*) refers here to a believer, whether man or woman, as part of God's family; also in verse 11; and in 3:15, 17; 4:20; 5:16.   *ᶜ* 10 The Greek word for *brother and sister* (*adelphos*) refers here to a believer, whether man or woman, as part of God's family; also in 3:10; 4:20, 21.   *ᵈ* 15 Or *world, the Father's love*   *ᵉ* 20 Some manuscripts *and you know all things*   *ᶠ* 2 Or *when it is made known*

not God's child, nor is anyone who does not love their brother and sister.

More on Love and Hatred

[11]For this is the message you heard from the beginning: We should love one another. [12]Do not be like Cain, who belonged to the evil one and murdered his brother. And why did he murder him? Because his own actions were evil and his brother's were righteous. [13]Do not be surprised, my brothers and sisters,[a] if the world hates you. [14]We know that we have passed from death to life, because we love each other. Anyone who does not love remains in death. [15]Anyone who hates a brother or sister is a murderer, and you know that no murderer has eternal life residing in him.

[16]This is how we know what love is: Jesus Christ laid down his life for us. And we ought to lay down our lives for our brothers and sisters. [17]If anyone has material possessions and sees a brother or sister in need but has no pity on them, how can the love of God be in that person? [18]Dear children, let us not love with words or speech but with actions and in truth.

[19]This is how we know that we belong to the truth and how we set our hearts at rest in his presence: [20]If our hearts condemn us, we know that God is greater than our hearts, and he knows everything. [21]Dear friends, if our hearts do not condemn us, we have confidence before God [22]and receive from him anything we ask, because we keep his commands and do what pleases him. [23]And this is his command: to believe in the name of his Son, Jesus Christ, and to love one another as he commanded us. [24]The one who keeps God's commands lives in him, and he in them. And this is how we know that he lives in us: We know it by the Spirit he gave us.

On Denying the Incarnation

4 Dear friends, do not believe every spirit, but test the spirits to see whether they are from God, because many false prophets have gone out into the world. [2]This is how you can recognize the Spirit of God: Every spirit that acknowledges that Jesus Christ has come in the flesh is from God, [3]but every spirit that does not acknowledge Jesus is not from God. This is the spirit of the antichrist, which you have heard is coming and even now is already in the world.

[4]You, dear children, are from God and have overcome them, because the one who is in you is greater than the one who is in the world. [5]They are from the world and therefore speak from the viewpoint of the world, and the world listens to them. [6]We are from God, and whoever knows God listens to us; but whoever is not from God does not listen to us. This is how we recognize the Spirit[b] of truth and the spirit of falsehood.

God's Love and Ours

[7]Dear friends, let us love one another, for love comes from God. Everyone who loves has been born of God and knows God. [8]Whoever does not love does not know God, because God is love. [9]This is how God showed his love among us: He sent his one and only Son into the world that we might live through him. [10]This is love: not that we loved God, but that he loved us and sent his Son as an atoning sacrifice for our sins. [11]Dear friends, since God so loved us, we also ought to love one another. [12]No one has ever seen God; but if we love one another, God lives in us and his love is made complete in us.

[13]This is how we know that we live in him and he in us: He has given us of his Spirit. [14]And we have seen and testify that the Father has sent his Son to be the Savior of the world. [15]If anyone acknowledges that Jesus is the Son of God, God lives in them and they in God. [16]And so we know and rely on the love God has for us.

God is love. Whoever lives in love lives in God, and God in them. [17]This is how love is made complete among us so that we will have confidence on the day of judgment: In this world we are like Jesus. [18]There is no fear in love. But perfect love drives out fear, because fear has to do with punishment. The one who fears is not made perfect in love.

[19]We love because he first loved us. [20]Whoever claims to love God yet hates a brother or sister is a liar. For whoever does not love their brother and sister, whom they have seen, cannot love God, whom they have not seen. [21]And he has given us this command: Anyone who loves God must also love their brother and sister.

Faith in the Incarnate Son of God

5 Everyone who believes that Jesus is the Christ is born of God, and everyone who loves the father loves his child as well. [2]This is how we know that we love the children of God: by loving God and carrying out his commands. [3]In fact, this is love for God: to keep his commands. And his commands are not burdensome, [4]for everyone born of God overcomes the world. This is the victory that has overcome the world, even our faith. [5]Who is it that overcomes the world? Only the one who believes that Jesus is the Son of God.

[6]This is the one who came by water and blood—Jesus Christ. He did not come by water only, but by water and blood. And it is the Spirit who testifies, because the Spirit is the truth. [7]For there are three that testify: [8]the[c] Spirit, the water and the blood; and the three are in agreement. [9]We accept human testimony, but God's testimony is greater because it is the testimony of God, which he has given about his Son. [10]Whoever believes in the Son of God accepts this testimony. Whoever does

---

[a] 13 The Greek word for *brothers and sisters* (*adelphoi*) refers here to believers, both men and women, as part of God's family; also in verse 16.   [b] 6 Or *spirit*   [c] 7,8 Late manuscripts of the Vulgate *testify in heaven: the Father, the Word and the Holy Spirit, and these three are one.* [8]*And there are three that testify on earth: the* (not found in any Greek manuscript before the fourteenth century)

not believe God has made him out to be a liar, because they have not believed the testimony God has given about his Son. ¹¹And this is the testimony: God has given us eternal life, and this life is in his Son. ¹²Whoever has the Son has life; whoever does not have the Son of God does not have life.

Concluding Affirmations

¹³I write these things to you who believe in the name of the Son of God so that you may know that you have eternal life. ¹⁴This is the confidence we have in approaching God: that if we ask anything according to his will, he hears us. ¹⁵And if we know that he hears us—whatever we ask—we know that we have what we asked of him.

¹⁶If you see any brother or sister commit a sin that does not lead to death, you should pray and God will give them life. I refer to those whose sin does not lead to death. There is a sin that leads to death. I am not saying that you should pray about that. ¹⁷All wrongdoing is sin, and there is sin that does not lead to death.

¹⁸We know that anyone born of God does not continue to sin; the One who was born of God keeps them safe, and the evil one cannot harm them. ¹⁹We know that we are children of God, and that the whole world is under the control of the evil one. ²⁰We know also that the Son of God has come and has given us understanding, so that we may know him who is true. And we are in him who is true by being in his Son Jesus Christ. He is the true God and eternal life.

²¹Dear children, keep yourselves from idols.

2 John

¹The elder,

To the lady chosen by God and to her children, whom I love in the truth—and not I only, but also all who know the truth— ²because of the truth, which lives in us and will be with us forever:

³Grace, mercy and peace from God the Father and from Jesus Christ, the Father's Son, will be with us in truth and love.

⁴It has given me great joy to find some of your children walking in the truth, just as the Father commanded us. ⁵And now, dear lady, I am not writing you a new command but one we have had from the beginning. I ask that we love one another. ⁶And this is love: that we walk in obedience to his commands. As you have heard from the beginning, his command is that you walk in love.

⁷I say this because many deceivers, who do not acknowledge Jesus Christ as coming in the flesh, have gone out into the world. Any such person is the deceiver and the antichrist. ⁸Watch out that you do not lose what weᵃ have worked for, but that you may be rewarded fully. ⁹Anyone who runs ahead and does not continue in the teaching of Christ does not have God; whoever continues in the teaching has both the Father and the Son. ¹⁰If anyone comes to you and does not bring this teaching, do not take them into your house or welcome them. ¹¹Anyone who welcomes them shares in their wicked work.

¹²I have much to write to you, but I do not want to use paper and ink. Instead, I hope to visit you and talk with you face to face, so that our joy may be complete.

¹³The children of your sister, who is chosen by God, send their greetings.

3 John

¹The elder,

To my dear friend Gaius, whom I love in the truth.

²Dear friend, I pray that you may enjoy good health and that all may go well with you, even as your soul is getting along well. ³It gave me great joy when some believers came and testified about your faithfulness to the truth, telling how you continue to walk in it. ⁴I have no greater joy than to hear that my children are walking in the truth.

⁵Dear friend, you are faithful in what you

ᵃ 8 Some manuscripts *you*

are doing for the brothers and sisters,*a* even though they are strangers to you. 6They have told the church about your love. Please send them on their way in a manner that honors God. 7It was for the sake of the Name that they went out, receiving no help from the pagans. 8We ought therefore to show hospitality to such people so that we may work together for the truth.

9I wrote to the church, but Diotrephes, who loves to be first, will not welcome us. 10So when I come, I will call attention to what he is doing, spreading malicious nonsense about us. Not satisfied with that, he even refuses to welcome other believers. He also stops those who want to do so and puts them out of the church.

11Dear friend, do not imitate what is evil but what is good. Anyone who does what is good is from God. Anyone who does what is evil has not seen God. 12Demetrius is well spoken of by everyone—and even by the truth itself. We also speak well of him, and you know that our testimony is true.

13I have much to write you, but I do not want to do so with pen and ink. 14I hope to see you soon, and we will talk face to face.

Peace to you. The friends here send their greetings. Greet the friends there by name.

Jude

1Jude, a servant of Jesus Christ and a brother of James,

To those who have been called, who are loved in God the Father and kept for*b* Jesus Christ:

2Mercy, peace and love be yours in abundance.

The Sin and Doom of Ungodly People

3Dear friends, although I was very eager to write to you about the salvation we share, I felt compelled to write and urge you to contend for the faith that was once for all entrusted to God's holy people. 4For certain individuals whose condemnation was written about*c* long ago have secretly slipped in among you. They are ungodly people, who pervert the grace of our God into a license for immorality and deny Jesus Christ our only Sovereign and Lord.

5Though you already know all this, I want to remind you that the Lord*d* at one time delivered his people out of Egypt, but later destroyed those who did not believe. 6And the angels who did not keep their positions of authority but abandoned their proper dwelling— these he has kept in darkness, bound with everlasting chains for judgment on the great Day. 7In a similar way, Sodom and Gomorrah and the surrounding towns gave themselves up to sexual immorality and perversion. They serve as an example of those who suffer the punishment of eternal fire.

8In the very same way, on the strength of their dreams these ungodly people pollute their own bodies, reject authority and heap abuse on celestial beings. 9But even the archangel Michael, when he was disputing with the devil about the body of Moses, did not himself dare to condemn him for slander but said, "The Lord rebuke you!"*e* 10Yet these people slander whatever they do not understand, and the very things they do understand by instinct—as irrational animals do—will destroy them.

11Woe to them! They have taken the way of Cain; they have rushed for profit into Balaam's error; they have been destroyed in Korah's rebellion.

12These people are blemishes at your love feasts, eating with you without the slightest qualm—shepherds who feed only themselves. They are clouds without rain, blown along by the wind; autumn trees, without fruit and uprooted—twice dead. 13They are wild waves of the sea, foaming up their shame; wandering stars, for whom blackest darkness has been reserved forever.

14Enoch, the seventh from Adam, prophesied about them: "See, the Lord is coming with thousands upon thousands of his holy ones 15to judge everyone, and to convict all of them of all the ungodly acts they have committed in their ungodliness, and of all the defiant words ungodly sinners have spoken against him."*f* 16These people are grumblers and faultfinders; they follow their own evil desires; they boast about themselves and flatter others for their own advantage.

A Call to Persevere

17But, dear friends, remember what the apostles of our Lord Jesus Christ foretold.

---

a 5 The Greek word for *brothers and sisters (adelphoi)* refers here to believers, both men and women, as part of God's family.   *b 1* Or *by;* or *in*   *c 4* Or *individuals who were marked out for condemnation*   *d 5* Some early manuscripts *Jesus*   *e 9* Jude is alluding to the Jewish *Testament of Moses* (approximately the first century A.D.).   *f 14,15* From the Jewish *First Book of Enoch* (approximately the first century B.C.)

[18]They said to you, "In the last times there will be scoffers who will follow their own ungodly desires." [19]These are the people who divide you, who follow mere natural instincts and do not have the Spirit.

[20]But you, dear friends, by building yourselves up in your most holy faith and praying in the Holy Spirit, [21]keep yourselves in God's love as you wait for the mercy of our Lord Jesus Christ to bring you to eternal life.

[22]Be merciful to those who doubt; [23]save others by snatching them from the fire; to others show mercy, mixed with fear—hating even the clothing stained by corrupted flesh.[a]

Doxology

[24]To him who is able to keep you from stumbling and to present you before his glorious presence without fault and with great joy— [25]to the only God our Savior be glory, majesty, power and authority, through Jesus Christ our Lord, before all ages, now and forevermore! Amen.

Revelation

Prologue

1 The revelation from Jesus Christ, which God gave him to show his servants what must soon take place. He made it known by sending his angel to his servant John, [2]who testifies to everything he saw—that is, the word of God and the testimony of Jesus Christ. [3]Blessed is the one who reads aloud the words of this prophecy, and blessed are those who hear it and take to heart what is written in it, because the time is near.

Greetings and Doxology

[4]John,

To the seven churches in the province of Asia:

Grace and peace to you from him who is, and who was, and who is to come, and from the seven spirits[b] before his throne, [5]and from Jesus Christ, who is the faithful witness, the firstborn from the dead, and the ruler of the kings of the earth.

To him who loves us and has freed us from our sins by his blood, [6]and has made us to be a kingdom and priests to serve his God and Father—to him be glory and power for ever and ever! Amen.

[7]"Look, he is coming with the clouds,"[c]
    and "every eye will see him,
even those who pierced him";
    and all peoples on earth "will mourn
        because of him."[d]
            So shall it be! Amen.

[8]"I am the Alpha and the Omega," says the Lord God, "who is, and who was, and who is to come, the Almighty."

John's Vision of Christ

[9]I, John, your brother and companion in the suffering and kingdom and patient endurance that are ours in Jesus, was on the island of Patmos because of the word of God and the testimony of Jesus. [10]On the Lord's Day I was in the Spirit, and I heard behind me a loud voice like a trumpet, [11]which said: "Write on a scroll what you see and send it to the seven churches: to Ephesus, Smyrna, Pergamum, Thyatira, Sardis, Philadelphia and Laodicea."

[12]I turned around to see the voice that was speaking to me. And when I turned I saw seven golden lampstands, [13]and among the lampstands was someone like a son of man,[e] dressed in a robe reaching down to his feet and with a golden sash around his chest. [14]The hair on his head was white like wool, as white as snow, and his eyes were like blazing fire. [15]His feet were like bronze glowing in a furnace, and his voice was like the sound of rushing waters. [16]In his right hand he held seven stars, and coming out of his mouth was a sharp, double-edged sword. His face was like the sun shining in all its brilliance.

[17]When I saw him, I fell at his feet as though dead. Then he placed his right hand on me and said: "Do not be afraid. I am the First and the Last. [18]I am the Living One; I was dead, and now look, I am alive for ever and ever! And I hold the keys of death and Hades.

[19]"Write, therefore, what you have seen, what is now and what will take place later. [20]The mystery of the seven stars that you saw in my right hand and of the seven golden lampstands is this: The seven stars are the angels[f] of the seven churches, and the seven lampstands are the seven churches.

To the Church in Ephesus

2 "To the angel[g] of the church in Ephesus write:

These are the words of him who holds the seven stars in his right hand and walks among the seven golden lampstands.

---

[a] 22,23 The Greek manuscripts of these verses vary at several points.   [b] 4 That is, the sevenfold Spirit   [c] 7 Daniel 7:13   [d] 7 Zech. 12:10   [e] 13 See Daniel 7:13.   [f] 20 Or messengers
[g] 1 Or messenger; also in verses 8, 12 and 18

²I know your deeds, your hard work and your perseverance. I know that you cannot tolerate wicked people, that you have tested those who claim to be apostles but are not, and have found them false. ³You have persevered and have endured hardships for my name, and have not grown weary.

⁴Yet I hold this against you: You have forsaken the love you had at first. ⁵Consider how far you have fallen! Repent and do the things you did at first. If you do not repent, I will come to you and remove your lampstand from its place. ⁶But you have this in your favor: You hate the practices of the Nicolaitans, which I also hate.

⁷Whoever has ears, let them hear what the Spirit says to the churches. To the one who is victorious, I will give the right to eat from the tree of life, which is in the paradise of God.

To the Church in Smyrna

⁸"To the angel of the church in Smyrna write:

These are the words of him who is the First and the Last, who died and came to life again. ⁹I know your afflictions and your poverty—yet you are rich! I know about the slander of those who say they are Jews and are not, but are a synagogue of Satan. ¹⁰Do not be afraid of what you are about to suffer. I tell you, the devil will put some of you in prison to test you, and you will suffer persecution for ten days. Be faithful, even to the point of death, and I will give you life as your victor's crown.

¹¹Whoever has ears, let them hear what the Spirit says to the churches. The one who is victorious will not be hurt at all by the second death.

To the Church in Pergamum

¹²"To the angel of the church in Pergamum write:

These are the words of him who has the sharp, double-edged sword. ¹³I know where you live—where Satan has his throne. Yet you remain true to my name. You did not renounce your faith in me, not even in the days of Antipas, my faithful witness, who was put to death in your city—where Satan lives.

¹⁴Nevertheless, I have a few things against you: There are some among you who hold to the teaching of Balaam, who taught Balak to entice the Israelites to sin so that they ate food sacrificed to idols and committed sexual immorality. ¹⁵Likewise, you also have those who hold to the teaching of the Nicolaitans. ¹⁶Repent therefore! Otherwise, I will soon come to you and will fight against them with the sword of my mouth.

¹⁷Whoever has ears, let them hear what the Spirit says to the churches. To the one who is victorious, I will give some of the hidden manna. I will also give that person a white stone with a new name written on it, known only to the one who receives it.

To the Church in Thyatira

¹⁸"To the angel of the church in Thyatira write:

These are the words of the Son of God, whose eyes are like blazing fire and whose feet are like burnished bronze. ¹⁹I know your deeds, your love and faith, your service and perseverance, and that you are now doing more than you did at first.

²⁰Nevertheless, I have this against you: You tolerate that woman Jezebel, who calls herself a prophet. By her teaching she misleads my servants into sexual immorality and the eating of food sacrificed to idols. ²¹I have given her time to repent of her immorality, but she is unwilling. ²²So I will cast her on a bed of suffering, and I will make those who commit adultery with her suffer intensely, unless they repent of her ways. ²³I will strike her children dead. Then all the churches will know that I am he who searches hearts and minds, and I will repay each of you according to your deeds.

²⁴Now I say to the rest of you in Thyatira, to you who do not hold to her teaching and have not learned Satan's so-called deep secrets, 'I will not impose any other burden on you, ²⁵except to hold on to what you have until I come.'

²⁶To the one who is victorious and does my will to the end, I will give authority over the nations— ²⁷that one 'will rule them with an iron scepter and will dash them to pieces like pottery'ᵃ—just as I have received authority from my Father. ²⁸I will also give that one the morning star. ²⁹Whoever has ears, let them hear what the Spirit says to the churches.

To the Church in Sardis

3 "To the angelᵇ of the church in Sardis write:

These are the words of him who holds the seven spiritsᶜ of God and the seven stars. I know your deeds; you have a reputation of being alive, but you are dead. ²Wake up! Strengthen what remains and is about to die, for I have found your deeds unfinished in the sight of my God. ³Remember, therefore, what you have received and heard; hold it fast, and repent. But if you do not wake up, I will come like a thief, and you will not know at what time I will come to you.

⁴Yet you have a few people in Sardis who have not soiled their clothes. They will walk with me, dressed in white, for they are worthy. ⁵The one who is victorious will, like them, be dressed in white. I

ᵃ 27 Psalm 2:9   ᵇ 1 Or *messenger*; also in verses 7 and 14   ᶜ 1 That is, the sevenfold Spirit

will never blot out the name of that person from the book of life, but will acknowledge that name before my Father and his angels. ⁶Whoever has ears, let them hear what the Spirit says to the churches.

To the Church in Philadelphia

⁷"To the angel of the church in Philadelphia write:

These are the words of him who is holy and true, who holds the key of David. What he opens no one can shut, and what he shuts no one can open. ⁸I know your deeds. See, I have placed before you an open door that no one can shut. I know that you have little strength, yet you have kept my word and have not denied my name. ⁹I will make those who are of the synagogue of Satan, who claim to be Jews though they are not, but are liars—I will make them come and fall down at your feet and acknowledge that I have loved you. ¹⁰Since you have kept my command to endure patiently, I will also keep you from the hour of trial that is going to come on the whole world to test the inhabitants of the earth.

¹¹I am coming soon. Hold on to what you have, so that no one will take your crown. ¹²The one who is victorious I will make a pillar in the temple of my God. Never again will they leave it. I will write on them the name of my God and the name of the city of my God, the new Jerusalem, which is coming down out of heaven from my God; and I will also write on them my new name. ¹³Whoever has ears, let them hear what the Spirit says to the churches.

To the Church in Laodicea

¹⁴"To the angel of the church in Laodicea write:

These are the words of the Amen, the faithful and true witness, the ruler of God's creation. ¹⁵I know your deeds, that you are neither cold nor hot. I wish you were either one or the other! ¹⁶So, because you are lukewarm—neither hot nor cold—I am about to spit you out of my mouth. ¹⁷You say, 'I am rich; I have acquired wealth and do not need a thing.' But you do not realize that you are wretched, pitiful, poor, blind and naked. ¹⁸I counsel you to buy from me gold refined in the fire, so you can become rich; and white clothes to wear, so you can cover your shameful nakedness; and salve to put on your eyes, so you can see. ¹⁹Those whom I love I rebuke and discipline. So be earnest and repent. ²⁰Here I am! I stand at the door and knock. If anyone hears my voice and opens the door, I will come in and eat with that person, and they with me.

²¹To the one who is victorious, I will give the right to sit with me on my throne, just as I was victorious and sat down with my Father on his throne. ²²Whoever has ears, let them hear what the Spirit says to the churches."

The Throne in Heaven

4 After this I looked, and there before me was a door standing open in heaven. And the voice I had first heard speaking to me like a trumpet said, "Come up here, and I will show you what must take place after this." ²At once I was in the Spirit, and there before me was a throne in heaven with someone sitting on it. ³And the one who sat there had the appearance of jasper and ruby. A rainbow that shone like an emerald encircled the throne. ⁴Surrounding the throne were twenty-four other thrones, and seated on them were twenty-four elders. They were dressed in white and had crowns of gold on their heads. ⁵From the throne came flashes of lightning, rumblings and peals of thunder. In front of the throne, seven lamps were blazing. These are the seven spirits ᵃ of God. ⁶Also in front of the throne there was what looked like a sea of glass, clear as crystal.

In the center, around the throne, were four living creatures, and they were covered with eyes, in front and in back. ⁷The first living creature was like a lion, the second was like an ox, the third had a face like a man, the fourth was like a flying eagle. ⁸Each of the four living creatures had six wings and was covered with eyes all around, even under its wings. Day and night they never stop saying:

" 'Holy, holy, holy
is the Lord God Almighty,' ᵇ
who was, and is, and is to come."

⁹Whenever the living creatures give glory, honor and thanks to him who sits on the throne and who lives for ever and ever, ¹⁰the twenty-four elders fall down before him who sits on the throne and worship him who lives for ever and ever. They lay their crowns before the throne and say:

¹¹ "You are worthy, our Lord and God,
to receive glory and honor and power,
for you created all things,
and by your will they were created
and have their being."

The Scroll and the Lamb

5 Then I saw in the right hand of him who sat on the throne a scroll with writing on both sides and sealed with seven seals. ²And I saw a mighty angel proclaiming in a loud voice, "Who is worthy to break the seals and open the scroll?" ³But no one in heaven or on earth or under the earth could open the scroll or even look inside it. ⁴I wept and wept because no one was found who was worthy to open the scroll or look inside. ⁵Then one of the elders said to me, "Do not weep! See, the

ᵃ 5 That is, the sevenfold Spirit   ᵇ 8 Isaiah 6:3

Lion of the tribe of Judah, the Root of David, has triumphed. He is able to open the scroll and its seven seals."

⁶Then I saw a Lamb, looking as if it had been slain, standing at the center of the throne, encircled by the four living creatures and the elders. The Lamb had seven horns and seven eyes, which are the seven spirits*ᵃ* of God sent out into all the earth. ⁷He went and took the scroll from the right hand of him who sat on the throne. ⁸And when he had taken it, the four living creatures and the twenty-four elders fell down before the Lamb. Each one had a harp and they were holding golden bowls full of incense, which are the prayers of God's people. ⁹And they sang a new song, saying:

> "You are worthy to take the scroll
>   and to open its seals,
> because you were slain,
>   and with your blood you purchased for
>   God
>   persons from every tribe and language
>   and people and nation.
> ¹⁰You have made them to be a kingdom and
>   priests to serve our God,
>   and they will reign*ᵇ* on the earth."

¹¹Then I looked and heard the voice of many angels, numbering thousands upon thousands, and ten thousand times ten thousand. They encircled the throne and the living creatures and the elders. ¹²In a loud voice they were saying:

> "Worthy is the Lamb, who was slain,
>   to receive power and wealth and
>   wisdom and strength
>   and honor and glory and praise!"

¹³Then I heard every creature in heaven and on earth and under the earth and on the sea, and all that is in them, saying:

> "To him who sits on the throne and to the
>   Lamb
> be praise and honor and glory and
>   power,
>   for ever and ever!"

¹⁴The four living creatures said, "Amen," and the elders fell down and worshiped.

The Seals

6 I watched as the Lamb opened the first of the seven seals. Then I heard one of the four living creatures say in a voice like thunder, "Come!" ²I looked, and there before me was a white horse! Its rider held a bow, and he was given a crown, and he rode out as a conqueror bent on conquest.

³When the Lamb opened the second seal, I heard the second living creature say, "Come!" ⁴Then another horse came out, a fiery red one. Its rider was given power to take peace from the earth and to make people kill each other. To him was given a large sword.

⁵When the Lamb opened the third seal, I heard the third living creature say, "Come!" I looked, and there before me was a black horse! Its rider was holding a pair of scales in his hand. ⁶Then I heard what sounded like a voice among the four living creatures, saying, "Two pounds*ᶜ* of wheat for a day's wages,*ᵈ* and six pounds*ᵉ* of barley for a day's wages,*ᵈ* and do not damage the oil and the wine!"

⁷When the Lamb opened the fourth seal, I heard the voice of the fourth living creature say, "Come!" ⁸I looked, and there before me was a pale horse! Its rider was named Death, and Hades was following close behind him. They were given power over a fourth of the earth to kill by sword, famine and plague, and by the wild beasts of the earth.

⁹When he opened the fifth seal, I saw under the altar the souls of those who had been slain because of the word of God and the testimony they had maintained. ¹⁰They called out in a loud voice, "How long, Sovereign Lord, holy and true, until you judge the inhabitants of the earth and avenge our blood?" ¹¹Then each of them was given a white robe, and they were told to wait a little longer, until the full number of their fellow servants, their brothers and sisters,*ᶠ* were killed just as they had been.

¹²I watched as he opened the sixth seal. There was a great earthquake. The sun turned black like sackcloth made of goat hair, the whole moon turned blood red, ¹³and the stars in the sky fell to earth, as figs drop from a fig tree when shaken by a strong wind. ¹⁴The heavens receded like a scroll being rolled up, and every mountain and island was removed from its place.

¹⁵Then the kings of the earth, the princes, the generals, the rich, the mighty, and everyone else, both slave and free, hid in caves and among the rocks of the mountains. ¹⁶They called to the mountains and the rocks, "Fall on us and hide us*ᵍ* from the face of him who sits on the throne and from the wrath of the Lamb! ¹⁷For the great day of their*ʰ* wrath has come, and who can withstand it?"

144,000 Sealed

7 After this I saw four angels standing at the four corners of the earth, holding back the four winds of the earth to prevent any wind from blowing on the land or on the sea or on any tree. ²Then I saw another angel coming up from the east, having the seal of the living God. He called out in a loud voice to the four angels who had been given power to harm the land and the sea: ³"Do not harm the land or the sea or the trees until we put a seal on the foreheads of the servants of our God." ⁴Then I heard the number of those who were sealed: 144,000 from all the tribes of Israel.

> ⁵From the tribe of Judah 12,000 were
>   sealed,
>   from the tribe of Reuben 12,000,

ᵃ 6 That is, the sevenfold Spirit   *ᵇ 10* Some manuscripts *they reign*   *ᶜ 6* Or about 1 kilogram   *ᵈ 6* Greek *a denarius*   *ᵉ 6* Or about 3 kilograms   *ᶠ 11* The Greek word for *brothers and sisters* (*adelphoi*) refers here to believers, both men and women, as part of God's family; also in 12:10; 19:10.   *ᵍ 16* See Hosea 10:8.   *ʰ 17* Some manuscripts *his*

from the tribe of Gad 12,000,
[6]from the tribe of Asher 12,000,
from the tribe of Naphtali 12,000,
from the tribe of Manasseh 12,000,
[7]from the tribe of Simeon 12,000,
from the tribe of Levi 12,000,
from the tribe of Issachar 12,000,
[8]from the tribe of Zebulun 12,000,
from the tribe of Joseph 12,000,
from the tribe of Benjamin 12,000.

The Great Multitude in White Robes

[9]After this I looked, and there before me was a great multitude that no one could count, from every nation, tribe, people and language, standing before the throne and before the Lamb. They were wearing white robes and were holding palm branches in their hands. [10]And they cried out in a loud voice:

"Salvation belongs to our God,
who sits on the throne,
and to the Lamb."

[11]All the angels were standing around the throne and around the elders and the four living creatures. They fell down on their faces before the throne and worshiped God, [12]saying:

"Amen!
Praise and glory
and wisdom and thanks and honor
and power and strength
be to our God for ever and ever.
Amen!"

[13]Then one of the elders asked me, "These in white robes—who are they, and where did they come from?"

[14]I answered, "Sir, you know."

And he said, "These are they who have come out of the great tribulation; they have washed their robes and made them white in the blood of the Lamb. [15]Therefore,

"they are before the throne of God
and serve him day and night in his
temple;
and he who sits on the throne
will shelter them with his presence.
[16]'Never again will they hunger;
never again will they thirst.
The sun will not beat down on them,'[a]
nor any scorching heat.
[17]For the Lamb at the center of the throne
will be their shepherd;
'he will lead them to springs of living
water.'[a]
'And God will wipe away every tear
from their eyes.'[b]"

The Seventh Seal and the Golden Censer

8 When he opened the seventh seal, there was silence in heaven for about half an hour.

[2]And I saw the seven angels who stand before God, and seven trumpets were given to them.

[3]Another angel, who had a golden censer, came and stood at the altar. He was given much incense to offer, with the prayers of all God's people, on the golden altar in front of the throne. [4]The smoke of the incense, together with the prayers of God's people, went up before God from the angel's hand. [5]Then the angel took the censer, filled it with fire from the altar, and hurled it on the earth; and there came peals of thunder, rumblings, flashes of lightning and an earthquake.

The Trumpets

[6]Then the seven angels who had the seven trumpets prepared to sound them.

[7]The first angel sounded his trumpet, and there came hail and fire mixed with blood, and it was hurled down on the earth. A third of the earth was burned up, a third of the trees were burned up, and all the green grass was burned up.

[8]The second angel sounded his trumpet, and something like a huge mountain, all ablaze, was thrown into the sea. A third of the sea turned into blood, [9]a third of the living creatures in the sea died, and a third of the ships were destroyed.

[10]The third angel sounded his trumpet, and a great star, blazing like a torch, fell from the sky on a third of the rivers and on the springs of water— [11]the name of the star is Wormwood.[c] A third of the waters turned bitter, and many people died from the waters that had become bitter.

[12]The fourth angel sounded his trumpet, and a third of the sun was struck, a third of the moon, and a third of the stars, so that a third of them turned dark. A third of the day was without light, and also a third of the night.

[13]As I watched, I heard an eagle that was flying in midair call out in a loud voice: "Woe! Woe! Woe to the inhabitants of the earth, because of the trumpet blasts about to be sounded by the other three angels!"

9 The fifth angel sounded his trumpet, and I saw a star that had fallen from the sky to the earth. The star was given the key to the shaft of the Abyss. [2]When he opened the Abyss, smoke rose from it like the smoke from a gigantic furnace. The sun and sky were darkened by the smoke from the Abyss. [3]And out of the smoke locusts came down on the earth and were given power like that of scorpions of the earth. [4]They were told not to harm the grass of the earth or any plant or tree, but only those people who did not have the seal of God on their foreheads. [5]They were not allowed to kill them but only to torture them for five months. And the agony they suffered was like that of the sting of a scorpion when it strikes. [6]During those days people will seek death but will not find it; they will long to die, but death will elude them.

[7]The locusts looked like horses prepared for battle. On their heads they wore something like crowns of gold, and their faces resembled human faces. [8]Their hair was like

---

a 16,17 Isaiah 49:10   *b 17* Isaiah 25:8   *c 11* Wormwood is a bitter substance.

women's hair, and their teeth were like lions' teeth. [9]They had breastplates like breastplates of iron, and the sound of their wings was like the thundering of many horses and chariots rushing into battle. [10]They had tails with stingers, like scorpions, and in their tails they had power to torment people for five months. [11]They had as king over them the angel of the Abyss, whose name in Hebrew is Abaddon and in Greek is Apollyon (that is, Destroyer).

[12]The first woe is past; two other woes are yet to come.

[13]The sixth angel sounded his trumpet, and I heard a voice coming from the four horns of the golden altar that is before God. [14]It said to the sixth angel who had the trumpet, "Release the four angels who are bound at the great river Euphrates." [15]And the four angels who had been kept ready for this very hour and day and month and year were released to kill a third of mankind. [16]The number of the mounted troops was twice ten thousand times ten thousand. I heard their number.

[17]The horses and riders I saw in my vision looked like this: Their breastplates were fiery red, dark blue, and yellow as sulfur. The heads of the horses resembled the heads of lions, and out of their mouths came fire, smoke and sulfur. [18]A third of mankind was killed by the three plagues of fire, smoke and sulfur that came out of their mouths. [19]The power of the horses was in their mouths and in their tails; for their tails were like snakes, having heads with which they inflict injury.

[20]The rest of mankind who were not killed by these plagues still did not repent of the work of their hands; they did not stop worshiping demons, and idols of gold, silver, bronze, stone and wood—idols that cannot see or hear or walk. [21]Nor did they repent of their murders, their magic arts, their sexual immorality or their thefts.

The Angel and the Little Scroll

10 Then I saw another mighty angel coming down from heaven. He was robed in a cloud, with a rainbow above his head; his face was like the sun, and his legs were like fiery pillars. [2]He was holding a little scroll, which lay open in his hand. He planted his right foot on the sea and his left foot on the land, [3]and he gave a loud shout like the roar of a lion. When he shouted, the voices of the seven thunders spoke. [4]And when the seven thunders spoke, I was about to write; but I heard a voice from heaven say, "Seal up what the seven thunders have said and do not write it down."

[5]Then the angel I had seen standing on the sea and on the land raised his right hand to heaven. [6]And he swore by him who lives for ever and ever, who created the heavens and all that is in them, the earth and all that is in it, and the sea and all that is in it, and said, "There will be no more delay! [7]But in the days when the seventh angel is about to sound his

trumpet, the mystery of God will be accomplished, just as he announced to his servants the prophets."

[8]Then the voice that I had heard from heaven spoke to me once more: "Go, take the scroll that lies open in the hand of the angel who is standing on the sea and on the land."

[9]So I went to the angel and asked him to give me the little scroll. He said to me, "Take it and eat it. It will turn your stomach sour, but 'in your mouth it will be as sweet as honey.'[a]" [10]I took the little scroll from the angel's hand and ate it. It tasted as sweet as honey in my mouth, but when I had eaten it, my stomach turned sour. [11]Then I was told, "You must prophesy again about many peoples, nations, languages and kings."

The Two Witnesses

11 I was given a reed like a measuring rod and was told, "Go and measure the temple of God and the altar, with its worshipers. [2]But exclude the outer court; do not measure it, because it has been given to the Gentiles. They will trample on the holy city for 42 months. [3]And I will appoint my two witnesses, and they will prophesy for 1,260 days, clothed in sackcloth." [4]They are "the two olive trees" and the two lampstands, and "they stand before the Lord of the earth."[b] [5]If anyone tries to harm them, fire comes from their mouths and devours their enemies. This is how anyone who wants to harm them must die. [6]They have power to shut up the heavens so that it will not rain during the time they are prophesying; and they have power to turn the waters into blood and to strike the earth with every kind of plague as often as they want.

[7]Now when they have finished their testimony, the beast that comes up from the Abyss will attack them, and overpower and kill them. [8]Their bodies will lie in the public square of the great city—which is figuratively called Sodom and Egypt—where also their Lord was crucified. [9]For three and a half days some from every people, tribe, language and nation will gaze on their bodies and refuse them burial. [10]The inhabitants of the earth will gloat over them and will celebrate by sending each other gifts, because these two prophets had tormented those who live on the earth.

[11]But after the three and a half days the breath[c] of life from God entered them, and they stood on their feet, and terror struck those who saw them. [12]Then they heard a loud voice from heaven saying to them, "Come up here." And they went up to heaven in a cloud, while their enemies looked on.

[13]At that very hour there was a severe earthquake and a tenth of the city collapsed. Seven thousand people were killed in the earthquake, and the survivors were terrified and gave glory to the God of heaven.

[14]The second woe has passed; the third woe is coming soon.

---

[a] 9 Ezek. 3:3   [b] 4 See Zech. 4:3,11,14.   [c] 11 Or *Spirit* (see Ezek. 37:5,14)

The Seventh Trumpet

¹⁵The seventh angel sounded his trumpet, and there were loud voices in heaven, which said:

"The kingdom of the world has become
the kingdom of our Lord and of his
Messiah,
and he will reign for ever and ever."

¹⁶And the twenty-four elders, who were seated on their thrones before God, fell on their faces and worshiped God, ¹⁷saying:

"We give thanks to you, Lord God
Almighty,
the One who is and who was,
because you have taken your great
power
and have begun to reign.
¹⁸The nations were angry,
and your wrath has come.
The time has come for judging the dead,
and for rewarding your servants the
prophets
and your people who revere your name,
both great and small—
and for destroying those who destroy the
earth."

¹⁹Then God's temple in heaven was opened, and within his temple was seen the ark of his covenant. And there came flashes of lightning, rumblings, peals of thunder, an earthquake and a severe hailstorm.

The Woman and the Dragon

12 A great sign appeared in heaven: a woman clothed with the sun, with the moon under her feet and a crown of twelve stars on her head. ²She was pregnant and cried out in pain as she was about to give birth. ³Then another sign appeared in heaven: an enormous red dragon with seven heads and ten horns and seven crowns on its heads. ⁴Its tail swept a third of the stars out of the sky and flung them to the earth. The dragon stood in front of the woman who was about to give birth, so that it might devour her child the moment he was born. ⁵She gave birth to a son, a male child, who "will rule all the nations with an iron scepter."ᵃ And her child was snatched up to God and to his throne. ⁶The woman fled into the wilderness to a place prepared for her by God, where she might be taken care of for 1,260 days.

⁷Then war broke out in heaven. Michael and his angels fought against the dragon, and the dragon and his angels fought back. ⁸But he was not strong enough, and they lost their place in heaven. ⁹The great dragon was hurled down—that ancient serpent called the devil, or Satan, who leads the whole world astray. He was hurled to the earth, and his angels with him.

¹⁰Then I heard a loud voice in heaven say:

"Now have come the salvation and the
power

and the kingdom of our God,
and the authority of his Messiah.
For the accuser of our brothers and
sisters,
who accuses them before our God day
and night,
has been hurled down.
¹¹They triumphed over him
by the blood of the Lamb
and by the word of their testimony;
they did not love their lives so much
as to shrink from death.
¹²Therefore rejoice, you heavens
and you who dwell in them!
But woe to the earth and the sea,
because the devil has gone down to
you!
He is filled with fury,
because he knows that his time is
short."

¹³When the dragon saw that he had been hurled to the earth, he pursued the woman who had given birth to the male child. ¹⁴The woman was given the two wings of a great eagle, so that she might fly to the place prepared for her in the wilderness, where she would be taken care of for a time, times and half a time, out of the serpent's reach. ¹⁵Then from his mouth the serpent spewed water like a river, to overtake the woman and sweep her away with the torrent. ¹⁶But the earth helped the woman by opening its mouth and swallowing the river that the dragon had spewed out of his mouth. ¹⁷Then the dragon was enraged at the woman and went off to wage war against the rest of her offspring—those who keep God's commands and hold fast their testimony about Jesus.

The Beast out of the Sea

13 The dragonᵇ stood on the shore of the sea. And I saw a beast coming out of the sea. It had ten horns and seven heads, with ten crowns on its horns, and on each head a blasphemous name. ²The beast I saw resembled a leopard, but had feet like those of a bear and a mouth like that of a lion. The dragon gave the beast his power and his throne and great authority. ³One of the heads of the beast seemed to have had a fatal wound, but the fatal wound had been healed. The whole world was filled with wonder and followed the beast. ⁴People worshiped the dragon because he had given authority to the beast, and they also worshiped the beast and asked, "Who is like the beast? Who can wage war against it?"

⁵The beast was given a mouth to utter proud words and blasphemies and to exercise its authority for forty-two months. ⁶It opened its mouth to blaspheme God, and to slander his name and his dwelling place and those who live in heaven. ⁷It was given power to wage war against God's holy people and to conquer them. And it was given authority over every tribe, people, language and nation. ⁸All inhabitants of the earth will worship the beast—all

---

ᵃ 5 Psalm 2:9   ᵇ 1 Some manuscripts *And I*

whose names have not been written in the Lamb's book of life, the Lamb who was slain from the creation of the world.*a*

[9]Whoever has ears, let them hear.

[10]"If anyone is to go into captivity,
  into captivity they will go.
If anyone is to be killed*b* with the sword,
  with the sword they will be killed."*c*

This calls for patient endurance and faithfulness on the part of God's people.

The Beast out of the Earth

[11]Then I saw a second beast, coming out of the earth. It had two horns like a lamb, but it spoke like a dragon. [12]It exercised all the authority of the first beast on its behalf, and made the earth and its inhabitants worship the first beast, whose fatal wound had been healed. [13]And it performed great signs, even causing fire to come down from heaven to the earth in full view of the people. [14]Because of the signs it was given power to perform on behalf of the first beast, it deceived the inhabitants of the earth. It ordered them to set up an image in honor of the beast who was wounded by the sword and yet lived. [15]The second beast was given power to give breath to the image of the first beast, so that the image could speak and cause all who refused to worship the image to be killed. [16]It also forced all people, great and small, rich and poor, free and slave, to receive a mark on their right hands or on their foreheads, [17]so that they could not buy or sell unless they had the mark, which is the name of the beast or the number of its name.

[18]This calls for wisdom. Let the person who has insight calculate the number of the beast, for it is the number of a man.*d* That number is 666.

The Lamb and the 144,000

14 Then I looked, and there before me was the Lamb, standing on Mount Zion, and with him 144,000 who had his name and his Father's name written on their foreheads. [2]And I heard a sound from heaven like the roar of rushing waters and like a loud peal of thunder. The sound I heard was like that of harpists playing their harps. [3]And they sang a new song before the throne and before the four living creatures and the elders. No one could learn the song except the 144,000 who had been redeemed from the earth. [4]These are those who did not defile themselves with women, for they remained virgins. They follow the Lamb wherever he goes. They were purchased from among mankind and offered as firstfruits to God and the Lamb. [5]No lie was found in their mouths; they are blameless.

The Three Angels

[6]Then I saw another angel flying in midair, and he had the eternal gospel to proclaim to those who live on the earth—to every nation, tribe, language and people. [7]He said in a loud voice, "Fear God and give him glory, because the hour of his judgment has come. Worship him who made the heavens, the earth, the sea and the springs of water."

[8]A second angel followed and said, "'Fallen! Fallen is Babylon the Great,'*e* which made all the nations drink the maddening wine of her adulteries."

[9]A third angel followed them and said in a loud voice: "If anyone worships the beast and its image and receives its mark on their forehead or on their hand, [10]they, too, will drink the wine of God's fury, which has been poured full strength into the cup of his wrath. They will be tormented with burning sulfur in the presence of the holy angels and of the Lamb. [11]And the smoke of their torment will rise for ever and ever. There will be no rest day or night for those who worship the beast and its image, or for anyone who receives the mark of its name." [12]This calls for patient endurance on the part of the people of God who keep his commands and remain faithful to Jesus.

[13]Then I heard a voice from heaven say, "Write this: Blessed are the dead who die in the Lord from now on."

"Yes," says the Spirit, "they will rest from their labor, for their deeds will follow them."

Harvesting the Earth and Trampling the Winepress

[14]I looked, and there before me was a white cloud, and seated on the cloud was one like a son of man*f* with a crown of gold on his head and a sharp sickle in his hand. [15]Then another angel came out of the temple and called in a loud voice to him who was sitting on the cloud, "Take your sickle and reap, because the time to reap has come, for the harvest of the earth is ripe." [16]So he who was seated on the cloud swung his sickle over the earth, and the earth was harvested.

[17]Another angel came out of the temple in heaven, and he too had a sharp sickle. [18]Still another angel, who had charge of the fire, came from the altar and called in a loud voice to him who had the sharp sickle, "Take your sharp sickle and gather the clusters of grapes from the earth's vine, because its grapes are ripe." [19]The angel swung his sickle on the earth, gathered its grapes and threw them into the great winepress of God's wrath. [20]They were trampled in the winepress outside the city, and blood flowed out of the press, rising as high as the horses' bridles for a distance of 1,600 stadia.*g*

Seven Angels With Seven Plagues

15 I saw in heaven another great and marvelous sign: seven angels with the seven last plagues—last, because with them God's wrath is completed. [2]And I saw what

---

a 8 Or *written from the creation of the world in the book of life belonging to the Lamb who was slain*
b 10 Some manuscripts *anyone kills*   *c* 10 Jer. 15:2   *d* 18 Or *is humanity's number*   *e* 8 Isaiah 21:9
f 14 See Daniel 7:13.   *g* 20 That is, about 180 miles or about 300 kilometers

looked like a sea of glass glowing with fire and, standing beside the sea, those who had been victorious over the beast and its image and over the number of its name. They held harps given them by God [3]and sang the song of God's servant Moses and of the Lamb:

"Great and marvelous are your deeds,
 Lord God Almighty.
Just and true are your ways,
 King of the nations.[a]
[4]Who will not fear you, Lord,
 and bring glory to your name?
For you alone are holy.
All nations will come
 and worship before you,
for your righteous acts have been
 revealed."[b]

[5]After this I looked, and I saw in heaven the temple—that is, the tabernacle of the covenant law—and it was opened. [6]Out of the temple came the seven angels with the seven plagues. They were dressed in clean, shining linen and wore golden sashes around their chests. [7]Then one of the four living creatures gave to the seven angels seven golden bowls filled with the wrath of God, who lives for ever and ever. [8]And the temple was filled with smoke from the glory of God and from his power, and no one could enter the temple until the seven plagues of the seven angels were completed.

The Seven Bowls of God's Wrath

16 Then I heard a loud voice from the temple saying to the seven angels, "Go, pour out the seven bowls of God's wrath on the earth."

[2]The first angel went and poured out his bowl on the land, and ugly, festering sores broke out on the people who had the mark of the beast and worshiped its image.

[3]The second angel poured out his bowl on the sea, and it turned into blood like that of a dead person, and every living thing in the sea died.

[4]The third angel poured out his bowl on the rivers and springs of water, and they became blood. [5]Then I heard the angel in charge of the waters say:

"You are just in these judgments, O Holy
 One,
 you who are and who were;
[6]for they have shed the blood of your holy
 people and your prophets,
 and you have given them blood to drink
 as they deserve."

[7]And I heard the altar respond:

"Yes, Lord God Almighty,
 true and just are your judgments."

[8]The fourth angel poured out his bowl on the sun, and the sun was allowed to scorch people with fire. [9]They were seared by the intense heat and they cursed the name of God,

who had control over these plagues, but they refused to repent and glorify him.

[10]The fifth angel poured out his bowl on the throne of the beast, and its kingdom was plunged into darkness. People gnawed their tongues in agony [11]and cursed the God of heaven because of their pains and their sores, but they refused to repent of what they had done.

[12]The sixth angel poured out his bowl on the great river Euphrates, and its water was dried up to prepare the way for the kings from the East. [13]Then I saw three impure spirits that looked like frogs; they came out of the mouth of the dragon, out of the mouth of the beast and out of the mouth of the false prophet. [14]They are demonic spirits that perform signs, and they go out to the kings of the whole world, to gather them for the battle on the great day of God Almighty.

[15]"Look, I come like a thief! Blessed is the one who stays awake and remains clothed, so as not to go naked and be shamefully exposed."

[16]Then they gathered the kings together to the place that in Hebrew is called Armageddon.

[17]The seventh angel poured out his bowl into the air, and out of the temple came a loud voice from the throne, saying, "It is done!" [18]Then there came flashes of lightning, rumblings, peals of thunder and a severe earthquake. No earthquake like it has ever occurred since mankind has been on earth, so tremendous was the quake. [19]The great city split into three parts, and the cities of the nations collapsed. God remembered Babylon the Great and gave her the cup filled with the wine of the fury of his wrath. [20]Every island fled away and the mountains could not be found. [21]From the sky huge hailstones, each weighing about a hundred pounds,[c] fell on people. And they cursed God on account of the plague of hail, because the plague was so terrible.

Babylon, the Prostitute on the Beast

17 One of the seven angels who had the seven bowls came and said to me, "Come, I will show you the punishment of the great prostitute, who sits by many waters. [2]With her the kings of the earth committed adultery, and the inhabitants of the earth were intoxicated with the wine of her adulteries."

[3]Then the angel carried me away in the Spirit into a wilderness. There I saw a woman sitting on a scarlet beast that was covered with blasphemous names and had seven heads and ten horns. [4]The woman was dressed in purple and scarlet, and was glittering with gold, precious stones and pearls. She held a golden cup in her hand, filled with abominable things and the filth of her adulteries. [5]The name written on her forehead was a mystery:

BABYLON THE GREAT
THE MOTHER OF PROSTITUTES
AND OF THE ABOMINATIONS OF THE EARTH.

---

[a] 3 Some manuscripts *ages*   [b] 3,4 Phrases in this song are drawn from Psalm 111:2,3; Deut. 32:4; Jer. 10:7; Psalms 86:9; 98:2.   [c] 21 Or about 45 kilograms

[6]I saw that the woman was drunk with the blood of God's holy people, the blood of those who bore testimony to Jesus.

When I saw her, I was greatly astonished. [7]Then the angel said to me: "Why are you astonished? I will explain to you the mystery of the woman and of the beast she rides, which has the seven heads and ten horns. [8]The beast, which you saw, once was, now is not, and yet will come up out of the Abyss and go to its destruction. The inhabitants of the earth whose names have not been written in the book of life from the creation of the world will be astonished when they see the beast, because it once was, now is not, and yet will come.

[9]"This calls for a mind with wisdom. The seven heads are seven hills on which the woman sits. [10]They are also seven kings. Five have fallen, one is, the other has not yet come; but when he does come, he must remain for only a little while. [11]The beast who once was, and now is not, is an eighth king. He belongs to the seven and is going to his destruction.

[12]"The ten horns you saw are ten kings who have not yet received a kingdom, but who for one hour will receive authority as kings along with the beast. [13]They have one purpose and will give their power and authority to the beast. [14]They will wage war against the Lamb, but the Lamb will triumph over them because he is Lord of lords and King of kings—and with him will be his called, chosen and faithful followers."

[15]Then the angel said to me, "The waters you saw, where the prostitute sits, are peoples, multitudes, nations and languages. [16]The beast and the ten horns you saw will hate the prostitute. They will bring her to ruin and leave her naked; they will eat her flesh and burn her with fire. [17]For God has put it into their hearts to accomplish his purpose by agreeing to hand over to the beast their royal authority, until God's words are fulfilled. [18]The woman you saw is the great city that rules over the kings of the earth."

Lament Over Fallen Babylon

18 After this I saw another angel coming down from heaven. He had great authority, and the earth was illuminated by his splendor. [2]With a mighty voice he shouted:

"'Fallen! Fallen is Babylon the Great!'[a]
She has become a dwelling for demons
and a haunt for every impure spirit,
a haunt for every unclean bird,
a haunt for every unclean and
detestable animal.
[3]For all the nations have drunk
the maddening wine of her adulteries.
The kings of the earth committed
adultery with her,
and the merchants of the earth grew
rich from her excessive luxuries."

Warning to Escape Babylon's Judgment

[4]Then I heard another voice from heaven say:

"'Come out of her, my people,'[b]
so that you will not share in her sins,
so that you will not receive any of her
plagues;
[5]for her sins are piled up to heaven,
and God has remembered her crimes.
[6]Give back to her as she has given;
pay her back double for what she has
done.
Pour her a double portion from her own
cup.
[7]Give her as much torment and grief
as the glory and luxury she gave
herself.
In her heart she boasts,
'I sit enthroned as queen.
I am not a widow;[c]
I will never mourn.'
[8]Therefore in one day her plagues will
overtake her:
death, mourning and famine.
She will be consumed by fire,
for mighty is the Lord God who judges
her.

Threefold Woe Over Babylon's Fall

[9]"When the kings of the earth who committed adultery with her and shared her luxury see the smoke of her burning, they will weep and mourn over her. [10]Terrified at her torment, they will stand far off and cry:

"'Woe! Woe to you, great city,
you mighty city of Babylon!
In one hour your doom has come!'

[11]"The merchants of the earth will weep and mourn over her because no one buys their cargoes anymore— [12]cargoes of gold, silver, precious stones and pearls; fine linen, purple, silk and scarlet cloth; every sort of citron wood, and articles of every kind made of ivory, costly wood, bronze, iron and marble; [13]cargoes of cinnamon and spice, of incense, myrrh and frankincense, of wine and olive oil, of fine flour and wheat; cattle and sheep; horses and carriages; and human beings sold as slaves.

[14]"They will say, 'The fruit you longed for is gone from you. All your luxury and splendor have vanished, never to be recovered.' [15]The merchants who sold these things and gained their wealth from her will stand far off, terrified at her torment. They will weep and mourn [16]and cry out:

"'Woe! Woe to you, great city,
dressed in fine linen, purple and
scarlet,
and glittering with gold, precious
stones and pearls!
[17]In one hour such great wealth has been
brought to ruin!'

"Every sea captain, and all who travel by ship, the sailors, and all who earn their living from the sea, will stand far off. [18]When they see the smoke of her burning, they will exclaim, 'Was there ever a city like this great

a 2 Isaiah 21:9   b 4 Jer. 51:45   c 7 See Isaiah 47:7,8.

city?' ¹⁹They will throw dust on their heads, and with weeping and mourning cry out:

"'Woe! Woe to you, great city,
    where all who had ships on the sea
    became rich through her wealth!
In one hour she has been brought to ruin!'

²⁰"Rejoice over her, you heavens!
    Rejoice, you people of God!
    Rejoice, apostles and prophets!
For God has judged her
    with the judgment she imposed on
        you."

The Finality of Babylon's Doom

²¹Then a mighty angel picked up a boulder the size of a large millstone and threw it into the sea, and said:

"With such violence
    the great city of Babylon will be thrown
        down,
    never to be found again.
²²The music of harpists and musicians,
        pipers and trumpeters,
    will never be heard in you again.
No worker of any trade
    will ever be found in you again.
The sound of a millstone
    will never be heard in you again.
²³The light of a lamp
    will never shine in you again.
The voice of bridegroom and bride
    will never be heard in you again.
Your merchants were the world's
        important people.
    By your magic spell all the nations
        were led astray.
²⁴In her was found the blood of prophets
        and of God's holy people,
    of all who have been slaughtered on the
        earth."

Threefold Hallelujah Over Babylon's Fall

19 After this I heard what sounded like the roar of a great multitude in heaven shouting:

"Hallelujah!
Salvation and glory and power belong to
    our God,
²   for true and just are his judgments.
He has condemned the great prostitute
    who corrupted the earth by her
        adulteries.
He has avenged on her the blood of his
    servants."

³And again they shouted:

"Hallelujah!
The smoke from her goes up for ever and
    ever."

⁴The twenty-four elders and the four living creatures fell down and worshiped God, who was seated on the throne. And they cried:

"Amen, Hallelujah!"

⁵Then a voice came from the throne, saying:

"Praise our God,
    all you his servants,
you who fear him,
    both great and small!"

⁶Then I heard what sounded like a great multitude, like the roar of rushing waters and like loud peals of thunder, shouting:

"Hallelujah!
    For our Lord God Almighty reigns.
⁷Let us rejoice and be glad
    and give him glory!
For the wedding of the Lamb has come,
    and his bride has made herself ready.
⁸Fine linen, bright and clean,
    was given her to wear."
(Fine linen stands for the righteous acts of God's holy people.)

⁹Then the angel said to me, "Write this: Blessed are those who are invited to the wedding supper of the Lamb!" And he added, "These are the true words of God."
¹⁰At this I fell at his feet to worship him. But he said to me, "Don't do that! I am a fellow servant with you and with your brothers and sisters who hold to the testimony of Jesus. Worship God! For it is the Spirit of prophecy who bears testimony to Jesus."

The Heavenly Warrior Defeats the Beast

¹¹I saw heaven standing open and there before me was a white horse, whose rider is called Faithful and True. With justice he judges and wages war. ¹²His eyes are like blazing fire, and on his head are many crowns. He has a name written on him that no one knows but he himself. ¹³He is dressed in a robe dipped in blood, and his name is the Word of God. ¹⁴The armies of heaven were following him, riding on white horses and dressed in fine linen, white and clean. ¹⁵Coming out of his mouth is a sharp sword with which to strike down the nations. "He will rule them with an iron scepter."ᵃ He treads the winepress of the fury of the wrath of God Almighty. ¹⁶On his robe and on his thigh he has this name written:

KING OF KINGS AND LORD OF LORDS.

¹⁷And I saw an angel standing in the sun, who cried in a loud voice to all the birds flying in midair, "Come, gather together for the great supper of God, ¹⁸so that you may eat the flesh of kings, generals, and the mighty, of horses and their riders, and the flesh of all people, free and slave, great and small."
¹⁹Then I saw the beast and the kings of the earth and their armies gathered together to wage war against the rider on the horse and his army. ²⁰But the beast was captured, and with it the false prophet who had performed the signs on its behalf. With these signs he had deluded those who had received the mark of the beast and worshiped its image. The two of them were thrown alive into the fiery lake

ᵃ 15 Psalm 2:9

of burning sulfur. ²¹The rest were killed with the sword coming out of the mouth of the rider on the horse, and all the birds gorged themselves on their flesh.

The Thousand Years

20 And I saw an angel coming down out of heaven, having the key to the Abyss and holding in his hand a great chain. ²He seized the dragon, that ancient serpent, who is the devil, or Satan, and bound him for a thousand years. ³He threw him into the Abyss, and locked and sealed it over him, to keep him from deceiving the nations anymore until the thousand years were ended. After that, he must be set free for a short time.

⁴I saw thrones on which were seated those who had been given authority to judge. And I saw the souls of those who had been beheaded because of their testimony about Jesus and because of the word of God. They*ᵃ* had not worshiped the beast or its image and had not received its mark on their foreheads or their hands. They came to life and reigned with Christ a thousand years. ⁵(The rest of the dead did not come to life until the thousand years were ended.) This is the first resurrection. ⁶Blessed and holy are those who share in the first resurrection. The second death has no power over them, but they will be priests of God and of Christ and will reign with him for a thousand years.

The Judgment of Satan

⁷When the thousand years are over, Satan will be released from his prison ⁸and will go out to deceive the nations in the four corners of the earth—Gog and Magog—and to gather them for battle. In number they are like the sand on the seashore. ⁹They marched across the breadth of the earth and surrounded the camp of God's people, the city he loves. But fire came down from heaven and devoured them. ¹⁰And the devil, who deceived them, was thrown into the lake of burning sulfur, where the beast and the false prophet had been thrown. They will be tormented day and night for ever and ever.

The Judgment of the Dead

¹¹Then I saw a great white throne and him who was seated on it. The earth and the heavens fled from his presence, and there was no place for them. ¹²And I saw the dead, great and small, standing before the throne, and books were opened. Another book was opened, which is the book of life. The dead were judged according to what they had done as recorded in the books. ¹³The sea gave up the dead that were in it, and death and Hades gave up the dead that were in them, and each person was judged according to what they had done. ¹⁴Then death and Hades were thrown into the lake of fire. The lake of fire is the second death. ¹⁵Anyone whose name was not found written in the book of life was thrown into the lake of fire.

A New Heaven and a New Earth

21 Then I saw "a new heaven and a new earth,"ᵇ for the first heaven and the first earth had passed away, and there was no longer any sea. ²I saw the Holy City, the new Jerusalem, coming down out of heaven from God, prepared as a bride beautifully dressed for her husband. ³And I heard a loud voice from the throne saying, "Look! God's dwelling place is now among the people, and he will dwell with them. They will be his people, and God himself will be with them and be their God. ⁴'He will wipe every tear from their eyes. There will be no more death'ᶜ or mourning or crying or pain, for the old order of things has passed away."

⁵He who was seated on the throne said, "I am making everything new!" Then he said, "Write this down, for these words are trustworthy and true."

⁶He said to me: "It is done. I am the Alpha and the Omega, the Beginning and the End. To the thirsty I will give water without cost from the spring of the water of life. ⁷Those who are victorious will inherit all this, and I will be their God and they will be my children. ⁸But the cowardly, the unbelieving, the vile, the murderers, the sexually immoral, those who practice magic arts, the idolaters and all liars—they will be consigned to the fiery lake of burning sulfur. This is the second death."

The New Jerusalem, the Bride of the Lamb

⁹One of the seven angels who had the seven bowls full of the seven last plagues came and said to me, "Come, I will show you the bride, the wife of the Lamb." ¹⁰And he carried me away in the Spirit to a mountain great and high, and showed me the Holy City, Jerusalem, coming down out of heaven from God. ¹¹It shone with the glory of God, and its brilliance was like that of a very precious jewel, like a jasper, clear as crystal. ¹²It had a great, high wall with twelve gates, and with twelve angels at the gates. On the gates were written the names of the twelve tribes of Israel. ¹³There were three gates on the east, three on the north, three on the south and three on the west. ¹⁴The wall of the city had twelve foundations, and on them were the names of the twelve apostles of the Lamb.

¹⁵The angel who talked with me had a measuring rod of gold to measure the city, its gates and its walls. ¹⁶The city was laid out like a square, as long as it was wide. He measured the city with the rod and found it to be 12,000 stadiaᵈ in length, and as wide and high as it is long. ¹⁷The angel measured the wall using human measurement, and it was 144 cubitsᵉ thick.ᶠ ¹⁸The wall was made of jasper, and the city of pure gold, as pure as glass. ¹⁹The foundations of the city walls were decorated with every kind of precious stone. The first

---

foundation was jasper, the second sapphire, the third agate, the fourth emerald, [20]the fifth onyx, the sixth ruby, the seventh chrysolite, the eighth beryl, the ninth topaz, the tenth turquoise, the eleventh jacinth, and the twelfth amethyst.[a] [21]The twelve gates were twelve pearls, each gate made of a single pearl. The great street of the city was of gold, as pure as transparent glass.

[22]I did not see a temple in the city, because the Lord God Almighty and the Lamb are its temple. [23]The city does not need the sun or the moon to shine on it, for the glory of God gives it light, and the Lamb is its lamp. [24]The nations will walk by its light, and the kings of the earth will bring their splendor into it. [25]On no day will its gates ever be shut, for there will be no night there. [26]The glory and honor of the nations will be brought into it. [27]Nothing impure will ever enter it, nor will anyone who does what is shameful or deceitful, but only those whose names are written in the Lamb's book of life.

Eden Restored

22 Then the angel showed me the river of the water of life, as clear as crystal, flowing from the throne of God and of the Lamb [2]down the middle of the great street of the city. On each side of the river stood the tree of life, bearing twelve crops of fruit, yielding its fruit every month. And the leaves of the tree are for the healing of the nations. [3]No longer will there be any curse. The throne of God and of the Lamb will be in the city, and his servants will serve him. [4]They will see his face, and his name will be on their foreheads. [5]There will be no more night. They will not need the light of a lamp or the light of the sun, for the Lord God will give them light. And they will reign for ever and ever.

John and the Angel

[6]The angel said to me, "These words are trustworthy and true. The Lord, the God who inspires the prophets, sent his angel to show his servants the things that must soon take place."

[7]"Look, I am coming soon! Blessed is the one who keeps the words of the prophecy written in this scroll."

[8]I, John, am the one who heard and saw these things. And when I had heard and seen them, I fell down to worship at the feet of the angel who had been showing them to me. [9]But he said to me, "Don't do that! I am a fellow servant with you and with your fellow prophets and with all who keep the words of this scroll. Worship God!"

[10]Then he told me, "Do not seal up the words of the prophecy of this scroll, because the time is near. [11]Let the one who does wrong continue to do wrong; let the vile person continue to be vile; let the one who does right continue to do right; and let the holy person continue to be holy."

Epilogue: Invitation and Warning

[12]"Look, I am coming soon! My reward is with me, and I will give to each person according to what they have done. [13]I am the Alpha and the Omega, the First and the Last, the Beginning and the End.

[14]"Blessed are those who wash their robes, that they may have the right to the tree of life and may go through the gates into the city. [15]Outside are the dogs, those who practice magic arts, the sexually immoral, the murderers, the idolaters and everyone who loves and practices falsehood.

[16]"I, Jesus, have sent my angel to give you[b] this testimony for the churches. I am the Root and the Offspring of David, and the bright Morning Star."

[17]The Spirit and the bride say, "Come!" And let the one who hears say, "Come!" Let the one who is thirsty come; and let the one who wishes take the free gift of the water of life.

[18]I warn everyone who hears the words of the prophecy of this scroll: If anyone adds anything to them, God will add to that person the plagues described in this scroll. [19]And if anyone takes words away from this scroll of prophecy, God will take away from that person any share in the tree of life and in the Holy City, which are described in this scroll.

[20]He who testifies to these things says, "Yes, I am coming soon."

Amen. Come, Lord Jesus.

[21]The grace of the Lord Jesus be with God's people. Amen.

---

[a] 20 The precise identification of some of these precious stones is uncertain.   [b] 16 The Greek is plural.

Table of Weights and Measures

	Biblical Unit	Approximate American Equivalent	Approximate Metric Equivalent
Weights	talent (60 minas)	75 pounds	34 kilograms
	mina (50 shekels)	1 1/4 pounds	560 grams
	shekel (2 bekas)	2/5 ounce	11.5 grams
	pim (2/3 shekel)	1/4 ounce	7.8 grams
	beka (10 gerahs)	1/5 ounce	5.7 grams
	gerah	1/50 ounce	0.6 gram
	daric	1/3 ounce	8.4 grams
Length	cubit	18 inches	45 centimeters
	span	9 inches	23 centimeters
	handbreadth	3 inches	7.5 centimeters
	stadion (pl. stadia)	600 feet	183 meters
Capacity *Dry Measure*	cor [homer] (10 ephahs)	6 bushels	220 liters
	lethek (5 ephahs)	3 bushels	110 liters
	ephah (10 omers)	3/5 bushel	22 liters
	seah (1/3 ephah)	7 quarts	7.5 liters
	omer (1/10 ephah)	2 quarts	2 liters
	cab (1/18 ephah)	1 quart	1 liter
Liquid Measure	bath (1 ephah)	6 gallons	22 liters
	hin (1/6 bath)	1 gallon	3.8 liters
	log (1/72 bath)	1/3 quart	0.3 liter

The figures of the table are calculated on the basis of a shekel equaling 11.5 grams, a cubit equaling 18 inches and an ephah equaling 22 liters. The quart referred to is either a dry quart (slightly larger than a liter) or a liquid quart (slightly smaller than a liter), whichever is applicable. The ton referred to in the footnotes is the American ton of 2,000 pounds. These weights are calculated relative to the particular commodity involved. Accordingly, the same measure of capacity in the text may be converted into different weights in the footnotes.

This table is based upon the best available information, but it is not intended to be mathematically precise; like the measurement equivalents in the footnotes, it merely gives approximate amounts and distances. Weights and measures differed somewhat at various times and places in the ancient world. There is uncertainty particularly about the ephah and the bath; further discoveries may shed more light on these units of capacity.

Study Resources

Getting to Know God

God created you because he wants a relationship with you. He loves you. He wants you to know him personally and intimately, not just know about him. Through God's written Word (the Bible), and through his only Son (Jesus), God reveals that he wants you to enjoy a life that's in line with his purpose and destiny for you. He wants to be a nurturing and powerful presence in your life, not just an idea in your head. Knowing him means receiving his love. Following him means following his leadership. And let's tell it like it is: Accepting that leadership will affect your lifestyle. As you come to know God, he no longer is a concept simply to be believed or disbelieved; he is a living reality who is known and followed along a pathway that leads to freedom.

According to the Bible, until you come to terms with Jesus, you haven't dealt with the issue that's most important in getting to know God. In John 14:6, Jesus said, "I am the way and the truth and the life. No one comes to the Father except through me." Through him, countless millions have come to know the Father, transforming their lives as well as the entire course of human history.

And Jesus continues to change history—one person at a time. He wants to change your life too. But he will not do so unless you ask him. It's not enough simply to agree intellectually with Jesus' claims. You must believe in him—believe that he is the Son of God sent to earth to pay the penalty for all sin, once for all, through his death on the cross—and ask him to come into your life.

Receiving this free gift of salvation is as simple as saying, "Jesus, I acknowledge my sin and your payment for it on the cross. I now ask you to forgive me, and I willingly give my life to you." At that moment, he will come into your innermost being and start you on a wonderful journey toward intimacy with God.

Another way to explain this is through a step-by-step "path of salvation." Many people find this sort of process helpful as they consider the important decision to give their life to Jesus. Here is a brief four-step system explaining why we all need the Lord and how we can go about making that decision. It includes key Scripture passages supporting each statement. You can look up these verses in the Bible if you'd like to read more of the context.

First:

Realize that everyone needs to be saved. No one is righteous. We are all guilty of breaking God's law in some way and therefore already condemned and sentenced.

> **Romans 3:19–20** "Now we know that whatever the law says, it says to those who are under the law, so that every mouth may be silenced and the whole world held accountable to God. Therefore no one will be declared righteous in God's sight by the works of the law; rather, through the law we become conscious of our sin."

Second:

Understand that there is hope in Christ. Salvation does not come by keeping laws or being good or doing good works, but only through faith in Christ. All have sinned, but anyone who receives Christ can be forgiven and accepted by God as righteous.

> **Romans 3:21–25** "But now apart from the law the righteousness of God has been made known, to which the Law and the Prophets testify. This righteousness is given through faith in Jesus Christ to all who believe. There is no difference between Jew and Gentile, for all have sinned and fall short of the glory of God, and all are justified freely by his grace through the redemption that came by Christ Jesus. God presented Christ as a sacrifice of atonement, through the shedding of his blood—to be received by faith. He did this to demonstrate his righteousness, because in his forbearance he had left the sins committed beforehand unpunished."

> **Romans 5:8** "But God demonstrates his own love for us in this: While we were still sinners, Christ died for us."

> **Romans 6:23** "For the wages of sin is death, but the gift of God is eternal life in Christ Jesus our Lord."

Third:
Know that God forgives and accepts unconditionally anyone who believes in Christ.

Romans 8:1-2 "Therefore, there is now no condemnation for those who are in Christ Jesus, because through Christ Jesus the law of the Spirit who gives life has set you free from the law of sin and death."

Finally:
Trust Christ in your heart and confess him as Lord with your mouth.

Romans 10:9-10 "If you declare with your mouth, 'Jesus is Lord,' and believe in your heart that God raised him from the dead, you will be saved. For it is with your heart that you believe and are justified, and it is with your mouth that you profess your faith and are saved."

Repeat aloud this prayer (or something similar—what you mean is what matters, not the exact words you use):

I thank you, heavenly Father, for sending your own Son, Jesus Christ, to die on the cross and pay the penalty for sin. I now believe in him and accept him as my Lord. Thank you that I am saved in him.

In Jesus' name, Amen.

Some other helpful passages relating to the topic of salvation:

Luke 18:9-14 "To some who were confident of their own righteousness and looked down on everyone else, Jesus told this parable: 'Two men went up to the temple to pray, one a Pharisee and the other a tax collector. The Pharisee stood by himself and prayed: "God, I thank you that I am not like other people—robbers, evildoers, adulterers—or even like this tax collector. I fast twice a week and give a tenth of all I get."

"'But the tax collector stood at a distance. He would not even look up to heaven, but beat his breast and said, "God, have mercy on me, a sinner."

"'I tell you that this man, rather than the other, went home justified before God. For all those who exalt themselves will be humbled, and those who humble themselves will be exalted.'"

John 1:12 "Yet to all who did receive him, to those who believed in his name, he gave the right to become children of God."

John 3:16-18 "For God so loved the world that he gave his one and only Son, that whoever believes in him shall not perish but have eternal life. For God did not send his Son into the world to condemn the world, but to save the world through him. Whoever believes in him is not condemned, but whoever does not believe stands condemned already because they have not believed in the name of God's one and only Son."

John 5:24 "Very truly I tell you, whoever hears my word and believes him who sent me has eternal life and will not be judged but has crossed over from death to life."

John 20:31 "But these are written that you may believe that Jesus is the Messiah, the Son of God, and that by believing you may have life in his name."

Acts 10:43 "All the prophets testify about him that everyone who believes in him receives forgiveness of sins through his name."

2 Corinthians 6:2 "For he says, 'In the time of my favor I heard you, and in the day of salvation I helped you.' I tell you, now is the time of God's favor, now is the day of salvation."

Hebrews 11:6 "And without faith it is impossible to please God, because anyone who comes to him must believe that he exists and that he rewards those who earnestly seek him."

1 John 1:9 "If we confess our sins, he is faithful and just and will forgive us our sins and purify us from all unrighteousness."

1 John 5:13 "I write these things to you who believe in the name of the Son of God so that you may know that you have eternal life."

Revelation 3:20 "'Here I am! I stand at the door and knock. If anyone hears my voice and opens the door, I will come in and eat with that person, and they with me.'"

You may be wondering what kinds of practical steps you might take to guide you as you discover your personal path toward knowing God. Consider some of these ideas:

- Ask God to reveal himself to you if you're not sure he's there.
- Talk to people who display a genuine relationship with God—those who obviously love him and who live by a different set of principles.
- Spend time enjoying God's creation.
- Listen to the stories of older people who have walked with God for a long time.
- Be a lover of truth, and don't hesitate to raise questions about things many others seem to take for granted.
- Follow the leading of the Holy Spirit. You can trust God's "gentle whisper" to give you direction. If you lack understanding, ask him for it.
- Read what other believers have said about Christianity. Ask your Christian friends for a list of authors who have inspired them in their walk with God.
- Write down your questions, including those that occur to you as you read the Bible, and take them to a believer who will respect your search for the truth.
- Be aware that moments of doubts and questions are normal and legitimate as you discover your personal path of faith.
- Be alert to your presuppositions—the things you already believe—and your personal roadblocks, and try not to let them stand in the way of your discovery process.
- Keep a journal of your thoughts and feelings during your search.
- Determine to spend a specified time each day walking the pathway toward faith, and keep evaluating your progress.
- Act on what you decide.

The ABCs of Salvation

A—**All** people are sinners.

All have sinned and fall short of the glory of God. —Romans 3:23

B—The **Bible** is God's word of love and salvation.

But these are written that you may believe that Jesus is the Messiah, the Son of God, and that by believing you may have life in his name. —John 20:31

C—The **condition** of sinners is serious.

All will be condemned who have not believed the truth but have delighted in wickedness. —2 Thessalonians 2:12

D—Christ **died** to save sinners.

While we were still sinners, Christ died for us. —Romans 5:8

E—**Everyone** who believes will have **eternal** life.

Whoever believes in [Jesus] shall not perish but have eternal life. —John 3:16

F—We are saved through **faith**.

For in the gospel the righteousness of God is revealed—a righteousness that is by faith from first to last, just as it is written: "The righteous will live by faith." —Romans 1:17

G—**Good works** will not save you.

For it is by grace you have been saved, through faith—and this is not from yourselves, it is the gift of God—not by works, so that no one can boast. —Ephesians 2:8–9

H—**Hell** and punishment await unbelievers.

He will punish those who do not know God and do not obey the gospel of our Lord Jesus. They will be punished with everlasting destruction and shut out from the presence of the Lord and from the glory of his might. —2 Thessalonians 1:8–9

I—Nothing is **impossible** for God.

For no word from God will ever fail. —Luke 1:37

J—There is **joy** in heaven over one sinner who repents.

"There is rejoicing in the presence of the angels of God over one sinner who repents." —Luke 15:10

K—If we trust God, he will **keep** us from sin.

[Give praise] to him who is able to keep you from stumbling and to present you before his glorious presence without fault and with great joy. —Jude 24

L—God **loves** sinners and wants to save them.

For God so loved the world that he gave his one and only Son, that whoever believes in him shall not perish but have eternal life. —John 3:16

M—God has **mercy** on unbelievers.

For God has bound everyone over to disobedience so that he may have mercy on them all. —Romans 11:32

N—Jesus is the only **name** by which we can be saved.

Salvation is found in no one else, for there is no other name under heaven given to mankind by which we must be saved. —Acts 4:12

O—We show God we love him by **obeying** his commandments.

This is love for God: to keep his commands. And his commands are not burdensome. —1 John 5:3

P—God is **patient** with unbelievers.

The Lord is not slow in keeping his promise, as some understand slowness. Instead he is patient with you, not wanting anyone to perish, but everyone to come to repentance. —2 Peter 3:9

Q—Those who don't believe should **quickly** decide to follow Jesus.

I tell you, now is the time of God's favor, now is the day of salvation. —2 Corinthians 6:2

R—Christians have a reason to **rejoice**.

"Rejoice that your names are written in heaven." —Luke 10:20

S—The Bible, the **Scriptures,** can teach us how to be saved.

From infancy you have known the Holy Scriptures, which are able to make you wise for salvation through faith in Christ Jesus. —2 Timothy 3:15

T—We should give **thanks** to God for the wonderful gift of salvation.

Thanks be to God for his indescribable gift! —2 Corinthians 9:15

U—The Holy Spirit helps us **understand** God's Word.

What we have received is not the spirit of the world, but the Spirit who is from God, so that we may understand what God has freely given us. —1 Corinthians 2:12

V—Jesus has gained **victory** over death for us.

When the perishable has been clothed with the imperishable, and the mortal with immortality, then the saying that is written will come true: "Death has been swallowed up in victory." —1 Corinthians 15:54

W—**Whoever** calls on Jesus will be saved.

"Everyone who calls on the name of the Lord will be saved." —Acts 2:21

Y—God loves **you** so much he calls you his child.

See what great love the Father has lavished on us, that we should be called children of God! And that is what we are! —1 John 3:1

Life in New Testament Times

Many years ago there were trails that came into the land of Israel. They came from the east and from the north. Other trails led from Egypt in the south. Traders used these trails to travel from one place to another. They traveled mostly by camel. They bought and sold goods along the way. The trails went through Israel. But they also met in Israel. It was almost as if Israel was the center of the world.

In a way, Israel was the center of the world. Jesus was born there. All of the things that happened in Bible times seemed to say, "Israel is a special land."

Places of Worship

The beautiful temple stood in the city of Jerusalem. It was the center of worship for the Jews. Herod rebuilt the temple not long before Jesus was born. The temple was on a hill. Its white marble walls could be seen all over the city. Large stone gates opened on all four sides. Jesus called this temple his Father's house (John 2:16).

Each Jewish town also had a smaller meeting place. These were called "synagogues." The leader of the synagogue studied the Old Testament and the Jewish laws. He then could teach the people.

On the inside, synagogues looked much like some of our churches. The people sat on benches, and the leader stood on a stage. A special box held the scrolls of the books of the Bible.

On the Sabbath day, the people came to the synagogue to worship. The leader read a verse to call the people to worship. Then there were readings of thanksgiving and praise. Someone would lead in prayer. After that, the leader might ask someone to read from the Bible. Any member who was able to teach could give the sermon. The service was closed with a blessing.

The Laws of God

God gave the Jews the Ten Commandments and many other laws at Mount Sinai. These laws taught the people how to worship God and live holy lives.

Jesus later told the Jews that following rules was important, but loving God and others was most important.

The Sabbath Day

God gave the people of Israel the Sabbath as a day of rest (Exodus 20:8–11). On the seventh day of every week they rested from their work and offered special sacrifices to God.

The scribes and Pharisees later added hundreds of laws about how people should keep the Sabbath day holy. Then the people forgot that God gave the Sabbath day to be a special day. Instead they just worried about obeying all the rules.

On the Sabbath day, people could not travel very far. They could not carry anything from one place to another. They were not supposed to spit on the ground. If they did, they might be plowing a little row in the dirt. And that would be work! If a hen laid an egg on the Sabbath, they were not supposed to eat that egg. The hen had worked on the Sabbath to lay it.

When Jesus and his disciples picked some grain and ate it on the Sabbath, the Pharisees said they were working. When Jesus healed sick people on the Sabbath, the Pharisees said he was breaking the law. They got angry and wanted to kill him.

Religious Groups

Two religious groups in New Testament times were the Pharisees and the Sadducees. The Sadducees were rich and powerful men. The high priest, the chief priests and rich businessmen were all Sadducees. The Sadducees were against any new group that tried to change Jewish life. That's why they were against Jesus and his disciples. The Sadducees also turned away from many of the teachings of the Pharisees. They did not believe that people would rise from the dead. They did not believe in angels or demons. They did not keep all the laws of the Pharisees. They only kept the Law of Moses.

The Pharisees added hundreds of laws to the law God gave Moses. They were mostly interested in keeping all these laws. But many of the Pharisees forgot some of God's other laws. They were proud of how good they were, and they did not love other people. However, there were also Pharisees who truly loved God and tried to do what was right.

Seventy of the most important Pharisees and Sadducees made up the Jewish high court. This court was called the Sanhedrin. The high priest was the leader of the court. The Romans let this court decide what to do when someone had broken a Jewish law. But this court did not have the power to put anyone to death. If the Sanhedrin thought someone should die, they had to bring the person to the Roman courts.

The Roman Empire

Rome had begun to grow larger and stronger before Christ was born. Wars were fought, and many new lands were added to the Roman Empire. This empire was very large. It included Spain and Germany, North Africa, Asia Minor, Syria and Israel.

Many good things happened because of Roman rule. There was peace among all the different countries in the empire. The Romans also set up good government everywhere. They built roads for safe and easy travel. Many of the people were able to speak and understand the same language—Greek.

The Romans did not know that all these things would make it easier for the gospel to spread to many lands. They did not know that God had prepared the way for Jesus and the spread of the Good News. Later Jesus' disciples traveled more easily to faraway lands because there was peace and because there were good roads. They could take the gospel in the Greek language to many people in many areas.

Tax Collectors

The Jews hated the Romans. They believed the Romans had no right to rule over them. They believed the Romans had no right to take their money for taxes. They didn't like the soldiers who lived in their country. The Jews also hated the Romans because they tried to change the Jewish way of life. The Romans wanted everyone to act like Romans. The Jews were looking for the Messiah. They thought he would become their king and would free them from the Romans.

The Jews hated tax collectors even more than they hated Romans. Many tax collectors were Jews who were working for Rome. Many tax collectors were not honest. They took more money than they were supposed to take. They cheated their own people to help the enemy.

Jesus often talked and ate with tax collectors. Matthew was a tax collector. So was Zacchaeus. Both men became followers of Jesus.

Everyday Life

Life in New Testament times was much different from life today. It was a simple life. Most people did not have any extras. In fact, they often had just enough to live. The people worked hard, and children had to share in the work.

The people built their houses of mud bricks that were hardened by laying them out in the sun. Sometimes the front part of the house had no roof over it. This part was like a small yard. Behind it was a living room with small bedrooms at the back. The floor of the house was of hard and smooth clay. Builders made the roof of heavy wooden beams with boards laid across them. They covered the boards with a mixture of mud and straw. This flat roof was a good place to work or to sit. Sometimes people slept on the roof on hot nights. Usually a ladder or sometimes steps led up to the roof.

Most people had very little furniture—just some wooden stools, a low wooden table and some sleeping mats. There was a place for a fire and sometimes a small clay oven for baking bread. There was no chimney, so the smoke had to find its way out of the small, high window openings. Some houses had wooden doors. Others had doorways covered with grass mats or cloth.

Food

The people ate foods like milk and cheese, grapes, figs, olives, honey and barley cakes, eggs, chicken, fish, goat meat, beans, cucumbers and onions.

The first meal of the day was usually bread and cheese. Sometimes a family would eat a light meal at noon. Again, bread was the main part. The people had their large meal of the day in the evening. They usually ate bread and fish, fruit and vegetables. The common people often ate meat only on very special days.

Clothing

The clothing of New Testament times was simple. Besides underclothing, the people wore robes with a belt tied around the waist. Over the robe they often wore a cape. Children usually had shorter knee-length clothing. They sometimes wore a kind of pullover shirt. Women decorated their clothing with brightly colored weaving and sewing.

The people wore sandals without socks. Their feet were often dusty from walking on the dirt streets and roads. They washed their feet often.

Work

The people did many different kinds of work. Some were farmers, builders or makers of pottery. Others were bakers, doctors or teachers. There were watchmen who guarded the cities. There were scribes who wrote letters and copied the laws and the books of the Bible. There were people who made things out of leather and people who made things out of metal. Jesus' father was a carpenter. Jesus also knew about herding sheep. Peter, James and John were fishermen. Matthew was a tax collector.

Women had to work hard in their homes. The first thing they would do in the morning was to make bread for the day. They would grind the grain into flour, then make the dough and shape it into loaves of bread and bake them. The women also had to carry water from the well and get wood for the fire. They made all the clothes for the family, spinning and weaving their own cloth out of flax and wool.

Parents expected their children to help with the work. Girls helped their mothers with all the household work. Boys helped their fathers in their work and every boy was expected to follow the same trade as his father.

Schools

Parents taught their children Scripture when they were still very young. They learned verses from the law and stories from the Old Testament.

When boys were five or six years old, they went to school. The leader of the synagogue taught them. For the first four years, they studied mostly the first five books of the Bible. By then they knew the laws of God. They also learned how to read and write Hebrew. For the next several years they studied other books of the Bible and other Jewish writings.

When a Jewish boy reached the age of twelve or thirteen, he was considered to be a man. The boy and his family and friends celebrated with a special ceremony and often a party. Most boys left school at this age.

Girls were taught at home to be wives and mothers. Most girls did not go to school or learn to read or write. By early adolescence, many girls were married.

Conclusion

The time of the New Testament was the best possible time for Jesus to come. The people were looking and waiting for him. The safe roads made it much easier for early Christians to travel to spread the Good News of the Savior. The common language made it much easier for them to tell others about Jesus. People were eager to hear about him. God had everything planned and ready.

30 Days With Jesus

Ministry of Jesus

Event	Place	Matthew	Mark	Luke	John
Jesus baptized	Jordan River	3:13–17	1:9–11	3:21–22	1:29–34
Jesus tempted by Satan	Desert	4:1–11	1:12–13	4:1–13	
Jesus' first miracle	Cana				2:1–11
Jesus and Nicodemus	Judea				3:1–21
Jesus talks to a Samaritan woman	Samaria				4:5–42
Jesus heals an official's son	Cana				4:46–54
People of Nazareth try to kill Jesus	Nazareth			4:16–30	
Jesus calls four fishermen	Sea of Galilee	4:18–22	1:16–20	5:1–11	
Jesus heals Peter's mother-in-law	Capernaum	8:14–15	1:29–31	4:38–39	
Jesus begins preaching in Galilee	Galilee	4:23–25	1:35–39	4:42–44	
Matthew decides to follow Jesus	Capernaum	9:9–13	2:13–17	5:27–32	
Jesus chooses twelve disciples	Galilee	10:2–4	3:13–19	6:12–15	
Jesus preaches Sermon on the Mount	Galilee	5:1—7:29		6:20–49	
A sinful woman anoints Jesus	Capernaum			7:36–50	
Jesus travels again through Galilee	Galilee			8:1–3	
Jesus tells kingdom parables	Galilee	13:1–52	4:1–34	8:4–18	
Jesus quiets the storm	Sea of Galilee	8:23–27	4:35–41	8:22–25	
Jairus's daughter raised to life	Capernaum	9:18–26	5:21–43	8:40–56	
Jesus sends out the Twelve	Galilee	9:35—11:1	6:6–13	9:1–6	
John the Baptist killed by Herod	Machaerus in Judea	14:1–12	6:14–29	9:7–9	
Jesus feeds the 5,000	Bethsaida	14:13–21	6:30–44	9:10–17	6:1–14
Jesus walks on water	Sea of Galilee	14:22–32	6:47–52		6:16–21
Jesus feeds the 4,000	Sea of Galilee	15:32–39	8:1–10		
Peter confesses Jesus as the Son of God	Caesarea Philippi	16:13–20	8:27–30	9:18–21	
Jesus predicts his death	Caesarea Philippi	16:21–26	8:31–37	9:22–25	
Jesus is transfigured	Mount Hermon	17:1–13	9:2–13	9:28–36	
Jesus pays his temple taxes	Capernaum	17:24–27			
Jesus attends Feast of Tabernacles	Jerusalem				7:10–52
Jesus heals a man born blind	Jerusalem				9:1–41
Jesus visits Mary and Martha	Bethany			10:38–42	

Event	Place	Matthew	Mark	Luke	John
Jesus raises Lazarus from the dead	Bethany				11:1–44
Jesus begins his last trip to Jerusalem	Border road			17:11	
Jesus blesses the little children	Transjordan	19:13–15	10:13–16	18:15–17	
Jesus talks to the rich young man	Transjordan	19:16–30	10:17–31	18:18–30	
Jesus again predicts his death	Near the Jordan	20:17–19	10:32–34	18:31–34	
Jesus heals blind Bartimaeus	Jericho	20:29–34	10:46–52	18:35–43	
Jesus talks to Zacchaeus	Jericho			19:1–10	
Jesus visits Mary and Martha again	Bethany				12:1–11

Parables of Jesus

Parable	Matthew	Mark	Luke
Lamp under a bowl	5:14–15	4:21–22	8:16; 11:33
Wise and foolish builders	7:24–27		6:47–49
New cloth on an old coat	9:16	2:21	5:36
New wine in old wineskins	9:17	2:22	5:37–38
Sower and the soils	13:3–8,18–23	4:3–8,14–20	8:5–8,11–15
Weeds	13:24–30,36–43		
Mustard seed	13:31–32	4:30–32	13:18–19
Yeast	13:33		13:20–21
Hidden treasure	13:44		
Valuable pearl	13:45–46		
Net	13:47–50		
Owner of a house	13:52		
Lost sheep	18:12–14		15:4–7
Unmerciful servant	18:23–34		
Workers in the vineyard	20:1–16		
Two sons	21:28–32		
Tenants	21:33–44	12:1–11	2:9–18
Wedding banquet	22:2–14		
Fig tree	24:32–35	13:28–29	21:29–31
Faithful and wise servant	24:45–51		12:42–48
Ten virgins	25:1–13		
Talents (minas)	25:14–30		19:12–27
Sheep and goats	25:31–46		
Growing seed		4:26–29	
Watchful servants		13:35–37	12:35–40
Moneylender			7:41–43
Good Samaritan			10:30–37
Friend in need			11:5–8
Rich fool			12:16–21
Unfruitful fig tree			13:6–9
Lowest seat at the feast			14:7–14
Great banquet			14:16–24
Cost of discipleship			14:28–33
Lost coin			15:8–10
Lost (prodigal) son			15:11–32
Shrewd manager			16:1–8
Rich man and Lazarus			16:19–31
Master and his servant			17:7–10
Persistent widow			18:2–8
Pharisee and tax collector			18:10–14

Miracles of Jesus

HEALING MIRACLES

	Matthew	Mark	Luke	John
Man with leprosy	8:2–4	1:40–42	5:12–13	
Roman centurion's servant	8:5–13		7:1–10	
Peter's mother-in-law	8:14–15	1:30–31	4:38–39	
Two men from Gadara	8:28–34	5:1–15	8:27–35	
Paralyzed man	9:2–7	2:3–12	5:18–25	
Woman with bleeding	9:20–22	5:25–29	8:43–48	
Two blind men	9:27–31			
Mute, demon-possessed man	9:32–33			
Man with a shriveled hand	12:10–13	3:1–5	6:6–10	
Blind, mute, demon-possessed man	12:22		11:14	
Canaanite woman's daughter	15:21–28	7:24–30		
Boy with a demon	17:14–18	9:17–29	9:38–43	
Two blind men (including Bartimaeus)	20:29–34	10:46–52	18:35–43	
Deaf and mute man		7:31–37		
Possessed man in synagogue		1:23–26	4:33–35	
Blind man at Bethsaida		8:22–26		
Crippled woman			13:11–13	
Man with abnormal swelling			14:1–4	
Ten men with leprosy			17:11–19	
The high priest's servant			22:50–51	
Official's son at Capernaum				4:46–54
Sick man at pool of Bethesda				5:1–9
Man born blind				9:1–7

MIRACLES SHOWING POWER OVER NATURE

	Matthew	Mark	Luke	John
Calming the storm	8:23–27	4:37–41	8:22–25	
Walking on water	14:25	6:48–51		6:19–21
Feeding of the 5,000	14:15–21	6:35–44	9:12–17	6:6–13
Feeding of the 4,000	15:32–38	8:1–9		
Coin in fish	17:24–27			

	Matthew	Mark	Luke	John
Fig tree withered	21:18–22	11:12–14, 20–25		
Large catch of fish			5:4–11	
Water turned into wine				2:1–11
Another large catch of fish				21:1–11

MIRACLES OF RAISING THE DEAD				
	Matthew	Mark	Luke	John
Jairus's daughter	9:18–19, 23–25	5:22–24, 38–42	8:41–42, 49–56	
Widow's son at Nain			7:11–15	
Lazarus				11:1–44

Miracles of the Apostles

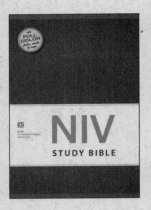
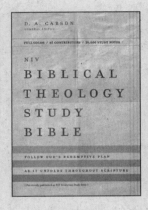

NEW INTERNATIONAL
VERSION

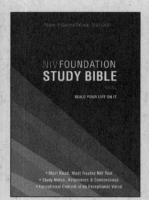

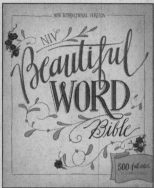

NIV Foundation Study Bible

An approachable and affordable study Bible featuring an easy-to-use layout with engaging and informative notes from respected Evangelical scholars.

ISBN: 9780310441861

NIV Beautiful Word Bible

A full-color Bible filled with 500 illustrated verses that offers a one-of-kind visual treatment of Scripture, encouraging you to understand and experience God's Word in a fresh way.

ISBN: 9780310444268

NIV Journal the Word Bible

This Bible allows you to creatively express yourself every day with plenty of room for journaling or creating Bible art next to your treasured verses.

ISBN: 9780310445548